AMERICAN TEACHERS

AMERICAN TEACHERS

HISTORIES OF A PROFESSION AT WORK

DONALD WARREN
Editor

A Publication of the American Educational Research Association

MACMILLAN PUBLISHING COMPANY
NEW YORK

Collier Macmillan Publishers
LONDON

Macmillan Publishing Company
866 Third Avenue, New York, N.Y. 10022

Collier Macmillan Canada, Inc.

Library of Congress Catalog Card Number: 88-36783

Printed in the United States of America

printing number
1 2 3 4 5 6 7 8 9 10

Library of Congress Cataloging-in-Publication Data

American teachers : histories of a profession at work / Donald Warren, editor.
p. cm.
"A Publication of the American Educational Research Association."
Bibliography: p.
Includes index.
ISBN 0-02-900963-4
1. Teachers—United States. 2. Teaching. I. Warren, Donald R.
LB2832.2.A45 1989
371.1′00973—dc19

88-36783
CIP

For
Oma Chastain Warren
and
Loren H. Warren
Who filled a family with possibilities

Contents

SECTION THREE
Teacher Education and Certification

SECTION FOUR
Issues and Questions

Contributors

Barbara Beatty is assistant professor of education at Wellesley College.

Susan B. Carter is associate professor of economics at Smith College.

Geraldine Jonçich Clifford is professor of education in the Graduate School of Education, and also teaches in the Women's Studies and Social Science Field Major Programs in the College of Letters and Science, University of California, Berkeley.

David K. Cohen is John A. Hannah Professor of Education and Social Policy at Michigan State University.

Larry Cuban is professor of education at Stanford University.

James W. Fraser is assistant professor in the College of Public and Community Service at the University of Massachusetts—Boston.

Wayne E. Fuller is professor emeritus of history at the University of Texas at El Paso.

Jurgen Herbst is professor of educational policy studies and history at the University of Wisconsin—Madison.

William R. Johnson is associate professor of education at the University of Maryland, Baltimore County.

David F. Labaree is associate professor of education at Michigan State University.

Linda M. Perkins is Senior Educational Equity Specialist at the Southwest Regional Educational Laboratory.

John L. Rury is associate professor in the School for New Learning, an alternative liberal arts college for adults at DePaul University.

Michael W. Sedlak is associate professor of educational history and senior researcher with the Institute for Research on Teaching at Michigan State University.

David Tyack is Vida Jacks Professor of Education and professor of history at Stanford University.

Wayne J. Urban is professor of education and of history at Georgia State University.

Donald Warren is professor and department chair of education policy, planning, and administration at the University of Maryland, College Park.

Acknowledgments

This book was William J. Reese's idea. Recalling the critical and (at least modest) financial success of the collection edited by John Best in 1983, others of us in the American Educational Research Association thought that the time had come for AERA to sponsor another volume of historical research.[1] More to the point, we agreed that the current educational reform movement in the United States would benefit from historical perspective. Except in obligatory background statements, it was not much in evidence in the national debate. Several policy issues came to mind as likely topics, but from the outset Bill Reese insisted that the focus should be on teachers. He wrote the initial rationale for the project, outlined a proposed book, and gave it a title: "A Most Maligned Profession: Teachers, Their Lives, and Their Work." Thereafter, his offspring acquired a life of its own.

The Publications Committee of AERA's Division F (History and Historiography) approved the proposal and sent it forward through the Association's various levels of review. David Angus chaired this committee, joined by Virginia Brereton, Jeffrey Mirel, Michael Sedlak, and Maris Vinovskis. Carl Kaestle, vice president of AERA for Division F, monitored the process and lent intellectual and moral support. Once the proposal won approval, however, the most qualified candidates for editor seemed to disappear. At a meeting I must have missed, a consensus was reached, and AERA President Lauren Resnick subsequently asked me to take the assignment. Still dubious about the choice of an editor whose specialty is not the history of teachers, I am nonetheless grateful for both her invitation and her commitment to the project.

The first task was to formulate a detailed plan, and in this effort the Editorial Board demonstrated how intellectual collaboration ought to work. Geraldine Jonçich Clifford, Linda M. Perkins, William J. Reese, and David Tyack, all of whom have made substantive and methodological contributions to the history of teachers, joined me in identifying topics and outlining proposed chapters. At the end of a full day and the better part of an evening spent hashing over such matters in Geraldine's living room, we realized that we were about to launch an exciting and potentially important venture. That meeting occurred in December 1986. The conversation continued for two years. The Board's imprint is evident throughout the book.

Finding a publisher proved to be unexpectedly easy, thanks to the immediate enthusiasm of Lloyd Chilton, executive editor at Macmillan. He saw the significance of the proposed book, provided encouragement throughout the writing stages, and inserted some gentle bullying when deadlines seemed in danger of slipping away. I am grateful to John Best for introducing me to this gifted and uncommonly effective editor. AERA Executive Officer William J. Russell probably breathed a sigh of relief over the selection of a publisher, given Macmillan's role in producing several highly successful Association publications, including the most recent edition of the *Encyclopedia of Educational Research*. He was not a distant observer, however. He supported this project with sound advice, technical assistance, and steadying optimism—although I suspect that he harbors a vague feeling that most historians are a little crazy.

No editor could complete a project of this magnitude and complexity without considerable institutional support. The University of Maryland, College Park, provided it at every turn and in several forms. A sabbatical leave allowed me to begin work on the book in relative freedom from administrative and teaching responsibilities. Robert F. Carbone, vice chair of my department, continued to fend off intrusions after I returned, despite his own heavy research commitments. Vicki Brewer, department secretary of Education Policy, Planning, and Administration, lengthened the hours of her work days, and devoted weekends as well, typing manuscripts, maintaining contact with chapter authors, and corresponding with the Editorial Board and the editorial staff at Macmillan. Quite literally, this book is a product of her labors. Mary K. Gillot assisted with the typing.

John Ventre, who received his Ph.D. last year from my department, chased fugitive and incomplete references, and constructed the comprehensive bibliography. His attention to detail prevented numerous citation errors. My colleague and friend Barbara Finkelstein, a pioneer in the history of teachers, cast her critical eye on various outlines and drafts at crucial stages and helped me to negotiate needed midcourse corrections.

Dale Scannell, Dean of the College of Education and a leader in the reform of teacher education, provided both intellectual and material support. He is a patient listener and perceptive critic. A grant from his office helped meet prepublication costs. Richard Arends, professor and past chair of the Department of Curriculum and Instruction, offered the insight of a committed teacher-education researcher, principally through the vehicle of a doctoral seminar on teacher education which he jointly taught with Dale Scannell and me.

Thanks to an invitation from Dean John Dolly to join the Education faculty at the University of Hawaii at Manoa as a visiting professor, I completed much of the organizational work on this book at his institution. Faculty in the Department of Educational Foundations joined discussions on initial plans, and department secretary Irene Oka took charge of a growing correspondence with quiet efficiency and good humor. Barry Bull was particularly helpful. His work in bringing conceptual clarity to the analysis of various education policy issues led him to take an interest in this project.[2] He listened to a lot of long-winded chatter, offered critiques of chapter outlines, and suggested sources and directions that should be pursued.

As readers will see, the significant work on this book has been contributed by the chapter authors. They read and commented on each other's initial drafts, sought and maintained a sense of partnership, and kept their composure even when the editor did not. This has been a collaborative venture, and even though some of us never met, we journeyed well together.

Donald Warren
UNIVERSITY OF MARYLAND, COLLEGE PARK

Notes

1. John Hardin Best (ed)., *Historical Inquiry in Education: A Reserach Agenda* (Washington, DC: American Educational Research Association, 1983).
2. See, e.g., Barry L. Bull, ''Professionalism and the Nature of Teacher Autonomy,'' paper presented at the annual meeting of the American Educational Research Association, New Orleans, April 1988.

AMERICAN TEACHERS

INTRODUCTION

Teachers, Reformers, and Historians

Donald Warren

If a single premise could be stated for this book, it would be that teachers, reformers, and historians need each other in pursuing their respective aims. Some qualifiers, however, are probably necessary. For one, the term "effective," which seems to crop up frequently in optimistic discussions about schools, could be inserted in several places. Also, as we admit in the title, the book has limited territorial aspirations; it is about American teachers, primarily those who have worked in public institutions.

Our premise is our argument. The evidence suggests that educational reformers, including policy makers, improve their chances of success when they devise goals and plans in concert with teachers and when they have the experience of history at their disposal. Teachers need reformers and historians to help them both define publicly the significance of teaching as a civic function, and expand their sense of context and mission beyond the pressures of immediate responsibilities. For their part, historians rely on reformers to generate the kinds of debate and controversy that enable them to look afresh at the educational past. And they need the insiders' perspectives of teachers to keep them honest. In the following chapters there are additional arguments for encouraging collaboration among this trio, but perhaps these brief observations will suffice initially. The relationship we have in mind includes an alliance of resources. Historians who work on educational topics, for example, typically do not observe teaching, but rather expect to look back on it, using written records and interviews. As readers will soon discover, however, the proposition that historians of education ought to consult teachers at all—past or present—has been revived only recently.

This development, combined with the contemporary debate over educational reform, has served to define the book and the audience we hope to reach. Increased activity concerning the history of teachers has brought substantive and methodological contributions which are only now beginning to be felt in the larger community of historians. The critique of present educational conditions has also interested us greatly. Conflict over public schools may be as American as apple pie, but the current debate has subjected teachers to almost unprecedented scrutiny. Two critically important arguments have emerged, one within a scholarly discipline and the other in a more public arena. We want to connect them by addressing a broader audience, not historians alone. While the book draws its organization and principal themes from recent historical research on teachers, we interpret this literature as insightful not only on the educational past but also on projects striving to reform the profession. In a manner of speaking we have tried to occupy that band of thought shared by the overlapping spheres of history and public policy.

As many historians are acutely aware, educational reform in the United States has tended to follow a pattern. When debate breaks out periodically over educational reform, attention eventually settles on teachers. The pattern is consistent, even if the version of it that we experienced in the 1980s focused on teachers with unusual intensity. In debates over school reform, especially, teachers represent highly visible targets. The following are among the most familiar criticisms of teachers: Their front-line roles in the formal education and socialization of the young suggest a unique capacity to advance or impede plans for improvement; compared with those entering other professions, teachers tend not to have strong academic backgrounds; their training lacks rigor and substance; their interactions with students smack of insecure pedantry; and worst of all, too many of their students fail to acquire basic skills and knowledge. Reformers solicit teachers' help, but they also routinely cite them as deficient. As both objects and instruments of reform, American teachers have thus enjoyed an uncertain status in strategies to strengthen public education. No plan calculated for success can ignore them completely, for however grand or mundane, aspirations for better schools must ultimately prove their worth in classrooms and other places where teachers preside. Yet in public discussions of educational goals and practices, teachers tend not to be thought of as authors of reform. More likely, they find themselves listed as part of the problem.

History can help us understand this oddly discordant attitude toward teachers. It places them and their critics in social, cultural, and institutional settings, thus permitting us to revisit the cycles of educational reform. By expanding and deepening the context of reform intentions beyond concerns of the moment, it also lays foundations for tough-minded, substantive questions about educational processes and institutions, and about the policy environment in which they proceed. It is a strange state of affairs, however, that educational reform in the United States has typically lacked a memory. With regard to reforms for teachers, historians of late have only recently rediscovered the plight of teachers for themselves.

The latest general history of teachers in this country was Willard Elsbree's *The American Teacher: Evolution of a Profession in a Democracy*. It was published 50 years ago. Elsbree intended to correct the failure of historians of education, like Ellwood P. Cubberley, to stress "the role of classroom teachers in the development of public education in the United States."[1] He saw a gap in the history rather than a need to reorder it, and the book's organization and descriptive content reflected this initial perception. Adapted from a structure followed in standard histories of schooling, it offered a chronological narrative, beginning with the colonial period and ending with a section titled "The Emergence of the Professional Teacher." It was a progressive, hopeful account of education, yet it was resentful of the low regard for teachers that had been passed along from generation to generation. Comprehensive in scope, it included discussions of professional preparation, certification, and teachers' working conditions. Throughout, Elsbree paid close attention to teachers' salaries, social status, and the growing proportion of women in the profession. In addition to correcting omissions in familiar survey accounts, he intended to write a book that would encourage teachers to study their own history.

Anticipating its use in the curricula of teacher-training programs, he meant to challenge teacher educators and their students to ever higher standards of professionalism. His message was addressed primarily to this audience in its particular institutional setting.

The title of our book reflects a debt to Elsbree, even as it establishes critical distance. We have followed his general scheme, which linked the histories of teachers, teaching, and teacher education. In like fashion, we have explored the policy environment within which teachers work. But like the recent historical research on teachers, our treatments of these matters take the form of case studies. As a result, our organization is more topical than chronological, and emphasis falls on the variety of stories to be told rather than on a unified narrative. To be fair, Elsbree appreciated this diversity and provided ample evidence of it, despite what one might infer from the title of his book. But he was even more interested in charting the emergence of a profession from lowly beginnings. Admittedly, his optimism functioned within bounds, for he had little expectation that people from the ''higher economic classes'' could be drawn into teaching, or that teachers' salaries relative to those of other professionals could be raised.[2] Rather, he rested teachers' hopes for a brighter future on teacher-education institutions, which he saw assuming ''the major responsibility'' for surrounding prospective teachers with rich cultural opportunities and experiences. ''Through such a process of osmosis,'' Elsbree concluded, ''American teachers may achieve a professional and cultural level beyond the dreams of present-day educators.''[3] We read the evidence differently. Although teachers' working conditions have improved dramatically over the past two centuries, we detect recurring conflicts and problems that have required attention in each generation rather than inexorable movement toward an ideal state. And we trace these difficulties to persistent economic, political, and cultural conditions, rather than limit our inquiry to perceived deficiencies of teachers, schools, or teacher-training programs.

We also place greater emphasis than Elsbree did on analyzing teachers' concerns. Teachers occupied the center of his narrative, but its perspective remained that of an outsider. It was a story of what happened to teachers and of what ought to be done for them. Our aim has not been to *give* teachers a voice but rather to heed their voices. For indeed, over the years an amazing number of them left written records of their views in diaries, correspondence, lesson plans, and published memoirs. From such sources we learn, for example, that teachers have played a number of social and institutional roles. They functioned as instructors, to be sure, but also as curriculum planners, community leaders, and political activists. We hear that although a teaching job meant independence to a young woman, she nonetheless resented the limited professional opportunities open to her, and that she often harbored less than charitable views of the mostly male school administration.

In addition, we catch glimpses of what might be labeled teachers' ''secret calisthenics,'' those exercises in which they negotiated the internal contradictions of their jobs. They spent considerable time in the company of children, and yet even those who were barely beyond childhood themselves were expected to avoid becoming child-like. They worked intimately with students and parents and yet needed to remain objective about both. In its daily practice, teaching required levels of skill and energy comparable to those of acknowledged professionals, but unlike these higher-status groups, teachers knew in advance that their plans and goals had to conform to a relatively fixed schedule. The professional "magic" that they performed occurred according to the school calendar, or it lost momentum. Finally, among their duties was the preparation of future citizens, but those who were women taught such lessons while being denied formally or tacitly the full privileges of citizenship. (It is a fact worth noting that women have constituted the majority of American teachers since the 1860s.) Teachers of black students, most of whom were black themselves, confronted even harsher political realities.

These materials, representing insiders' perspectives, enable us to understand (at least partially) the work of teaching. They also take us inside schools and communities, refracting light at a different angle on a wide range of educational issues. They give us access to the culture of schools, the workings of educational organizations, and the covert realm of tacit policy. They help uncover distributions of status and power that not only defined teachers' formal roles but also shaped the ways they viewed themselves.

None of our chapters, however, relies solely on personal histories for its sources. In fact, several authors rely primarily on nineteenth- and early twentieth-century public documents, periodicals, and statistical reports. Thus, in addition to hearing from teachers about their roles, expectations, and activities, we have approached various education policy questions with the concerns and experiences of teachers, past and present, in mind. We examine the demography of teaching and try to understand the incentives that have drawn some people into the occupation and pushed others away from it. We explore why women have tended to teach, while men more often have served in leadership roles. We document the opposition of rural teachers to "progressive" educational reforms and the reasons teachers in all regions resisted the bureaucratization of schools and school systems. And we try to explain the seemingly endless conflict over the purposes and content of teacher education. In sum, we have intended to expose teachers' voices and to understand the contexts in which those voices spoke. Much of this content, and the conceptual and analytical tools that we have found most useful, were not available to Elsbree. They have been derived from historical investigations conducted in the years after he wrote *The American Teacher*.

One glaring omission in Elsbree's book requires special mention. He made no reference to black teacher-training institutions, the status of black teachers, or the distorted policy environment in which they worked. His silence is notable, given his extended discussion of the differing treatments accorded male and female teachers, particularly with regard to salary. In any discourse on historical salary data of teachers, the wages of black teachers stand out like angry warnings. We now know a great deal about such matters, thanks to recent historical research on the education of black people. But relevant sources were not lacking in the 1930s. In addition to the path-breaking histories of black Americans by W. E. B. DuBois, whose writings frequently returned to educational topics, Horace Mann Bond published a major work on the history of black education in the United States five years before *The American Teacher* appeared.[4] More prominent (at least for Elsbree) was the monumental study of teachers and teacher education directed in the 1930s by Edward S. Evenden, Elsbree's colleague at Teachers College in New York City.

One of the six volumes of this *National Survey of the Education of Teachers* dealt exclusively with black teachers.[5]

With the additional sources now available, we address issues about the history and education of black people in two ways. First, analyses have been used that incorporate recent historical research on black teachers, their professional preparation, and their working conditions. Second, a separate chapter focuses specifically on the experiences of black people with regard to teacher education, recruitment, and retention. The authors have attempted to contribute to the conceptual foundation needed for more complete and, in that sense, more accurate general histories of the profession. Elsbree intended to write a comprehensive account of teaching but seemed unaware that he left it with a glaring omission.

I have used Elsbree's book, I hope not smugly or unfairly, as a foil to help explain the intentions of our work. We have relied heavily on recent historical research. This literature has recovered a growing body of primary and secondary sources, including old statistical reports and documents written by teachers themselves. Its findings bring an intriguing mix of fresh contributions to knowledge, appraisals of often forgotten works, and newly unearthed primary materials. The authors of this volume have been among the key contributors of this research. We have emphasized the variety of stories that emerge in this literature. To this end, disagreements among the contributors have not been resolved. Some are significant, others less so, but readers can easily detect them. In our view, this diversity—which speaks of *histories* of teachers—well serves the interests of teachers themselves, as well as those of historians and reformers, including education policy makers. All benefit from an understanding of the various meanings that have been attached to the work of teachers and from knowledge of the multiple arenas in which they have been active. Finally, in a hopeful vein, we have meant to demonstrate some of the uses of history. We have said, in effect, that history is too important to be left to historians alone. Included among its contributions to society has been its use as a powerful tool for the education of the public. In the spirit of that tradition, we offer *American Teachers: Histories of a Profession at Work.*

Notes

1. Willard S. Elsbree, *The American Teacher: Evolution of a Profession in a Democracy* (New York: American Book Company, 1939), p. v.
2. Ibid., p. 555.
3. Ibid.
4. W. E. B. DuBois, *Black Reconstruction in America: An Essay Toward a History of the Part Which Black Folk Played in the Attempt to Reconstruct Democracy in America, 1860–1880* (Cleveland: The World Publishing Company, 1964). First published by Harcourt, Brace and Company in 1935. Also, Horace Mann Bond, *The Education of the Negro in the American Social Order* (New York: Octagon Books, 1966). Reprint of the 1934 edition by Prentice–Hall.
5. Ambrose Caliver, *Education of Negro Teachers* (Westport, CT: Greenwood Press, 1970). Originally published as Vol. 4 of the *National Survey of the Education of Teachers,* U.S. Office of Education, *Bulletin* 1933, No. 10 (Washington, DC: Government Printing Office, 1933).

SECTION ONE

Those Who Taught —and Why

To the extent permitted by available sources and recent research, the authors of this volume have tended to consult teachers in the writing of their own history. That may seem a common-sensical thing to do, but it is a relatively new approach to the history of teachers. Class records, diaries, autobiographies, correspondence, and other personal history documents left by teachers give us intimate glimpses of schools and teaching. They suggest the variety of roles that teachers saw themselves playing, and permit access to educational institutions and processes via the slant of insiders' perspectives. Without such sources, historians have trouble getting past the schoolhouse door.

The two chapters in Section One identify common themes in these multiple stories. By analyzing both demographic characteristics of the teaching force over time and longitudinal salary data, John Rury and Susan Carter help frame and link the histories empirically. They also shed light on the reasons why teaching has not been considered a profession, and why teachers have found this judgment frustrating and demeaning.

Teachers have from the start been expected to promote learning, good citizenships, and morality—to be models of educational attainment and cultural refinement. Their contributions to the distribution of knowledge have produced both individual and societal benefits; their work has had economic and political value. Yet their reward has for the most part been small indeed. Increasingly over the nineteenth century the overwhelming majority of them were young women who could not vote, working for wages that would not support investments in their own training. True, various changes in circumstances have occurred in this century, but teachers still are said to be unworthy of professional status. They are as yet mostly women, their salaries are low, their social backgrounds are "wrong." They spend too much time in the company of children. They lack specialized knowledge, a judgment which Susan Carter observes might be challenged on economic grounds if none other. Not unexpectedly, contradictions between educational ideals and realities have been greatest for black teachers. A troubling conclusion emerges: The growth of American public education over the past two centuries owes much to the philanthropy of teachers, effort above and beyond what could be reasonably purchased either by their salaries or by any intangible benefits that came their way. The democraphic characteristics of the teaching force, and the incentives that have pushed and pulled people into it, have reflected both social conditions and the effects of individual aspiration and personal belief. But, divorced from adequate salary, none of the other inducements has retained much influence over time—at least for teachers who have had other career choices. As Rury reports, many have felt called to teach, but large numbers have exited in rather short order. Carter suggests why this has been the case.

1

Who Became Teachers?

The Social Characteristics of Teachers in American History

John L. Rury

"Who became teachers?" may be among the most essential questions asked in this study of the history of teachers and teacher education in America. The fact is that the social characteristics of teachers (personal attributes which help to identify where a given person or group stands in the social structure) can tell us a great deal about the status of teaching from one period to the next. Unlike law or medicine, teaching has not been acknowledged as a profession historically. But important changes have marked the evolution of the nation's teaching force, as the social characteristics of teachers have shifted dramatically over the past two centuries. In this Chapter I will examine the social characteristics of American teachers at five points in history: the late colonial period, the mid-nineteenth century, the start of the twentieth century, the mid-twentieth century, and the present (the late 1980s). In this fashion I hope to identify both lines of continuity and patterns of change in the social composition of the teaching population.

Examining the past often helps us to comprehend forces at work in the present which may have a bearing on what is to come. In the case of teaching, the past several decades have witnessed a series of changes with important implications for the future of the profession. Scrutinizing the social characteristics of teachers in the past, and identifying important related patterns of development in the nation's teaching force, can help both to underscore the significance of these shifts and to anticipate their impact on the decades ahead.

Defining Social Characteristics

The study of social characteristics begins with the values which a particular social system places on various background characteristics. In the United States, social status historically has been identified with wealth and income, race and ethnicity, and/or gender.[1] It is necessary to start any consideration of the social origins of teachers by examining characteristics such as these.

Throughout American history, teachers have generally come from what can be described as middle-class backgrounds. After all, teaching often has required a comparatively high level of education, and at least the appearance of respectability, attributes generally beyond the grasp of people in the working class. But, as with other professions, which were much smaller numerically, the largest groups of teachers appear to have come from *lower* middle-class families. They typically possessed more education than their parents, and often attained a higher level of social status. (At least those who remained in the teaching profession did.) Perhaps more than any other professional group in American life, teachers have been identified with the great mass of middling farmers, shopkeepers, artisans, and low-level managers who have occupied the rough edge between manual and intellectual labor. For individuals from backgrounds such as these, teaching may have appeared to represent a step up into the educated professions. But the very fact that so many teachers hailed from such relatively modest means helped to ensure that teaching would never achieve the same level of status typically accorded the more selective professions.[2]

It is impossible to discuss the social background characteristics of American teachers, of course, without dealing with the issue of gender. Since the mid-nineteenth century (and perhaps before), teaching has been largely a female occupation, though the extent of feminization has varied from one part of the country to another. The reasons for this are complex (and will be dealt with in detail below), but the association of teaching with women at a time when virtually every other profession in American life was dominated by men also helped to assure that teaching would not be recognized as a profession in the same terms, say, as law or medicine. By the third decade of the twentieth century, when nearly 80 percent of all teachers in the country were female, teaching had become firmly identified in the popular consciousness as "women's work." In a society which was permeated with sexist conventions about success, the identification of teaching with women often meant that teachers were held in low esteem.[3]

The vast majority of American teachers have been white and of national origin. In proportional terms, black Americans, immigrants, and other ethnic minorities have been under-represented in the nation's teaching population. This is a sad commentary on the discriminatory character of American education. However (though it is not a fact one finds pleasant to report), black Americans have been better represented among teachers than in any other professional group! In this regard the teaching profession has provided an important avenue for the development of an educated cadre of leaders in the African-American community. Likewise, large numbers of immigrants and their children became teachers in the United States. Indeed, by the turn of the century the children of immigrants were better represented among the nation's teachers than any other group. Of course, the fact that teaching was associated with blacks and immigrants also served to undermine the social status of teachers as professionals in the United States, simply because of racist and ethnocentric attitudes endemic to American culture. Because teaching was a relatively accessible profession, and therefore attracted educated members of social groups generally denied access to the high-status professions, it often was viewed as second-rate.

Age was yet another factor which helped to define the teaching profession in the public mind. Through most of American history, teachers have been quite young. Until recently it probably was not accurate to speak of teaching as a career in the conventional sense of the term. Rather, teaching was a pursuit undertaken in one's youth, before starting the serious business of life—whether it was a career in a learned profession or business for men, or marriage and a family for women. The identification of teaching with youth, and with a generally transient work force, further distinguished teachers from lawyers, doctors, and other more highly esteemed professionals in popular thinking. Despite the commonplace association of teachers with formal education, they have often been held in low regard simply because wisdom and knowledge have been widely regarded in American culture as attributes of experience and age. As long as teaching was largely conducted by young people, it suffered from a persistent image of immaturity and incompetence which perpetuated the notion that teaching was a mere way station for men and women intent on bigger and better things in life.[4]

So the social characteristics of American teachers did indeed have an impact on the public perception of teaching, which clearly was not a highly regarded activity throughout much of American history. In fact, throughout that history, teachers have been relegated to the very edge of professional respectability. And yet Americans have almost always acknowledged the critical role played by teachers in transmitting essential values, skills, and knowledge to the nation's children. How then did this so poorly viewed yet vital task come to be relegated to relatively low-status groups in American life? How did it, important as it was, come to provide a critical outlet for social groups generally denied access to other occupations requiring education?

It is here that the matter of teachers' social characteristics becomes ever more subject to inquiry. How, for instance, did women move into teaching at a time when virtually all other professions were closed to them? Under what circumstances did black and immigrant teachers appear in large numbers? How did the age structure of teaching change over time, and in what settings does it appear to have changed? Answers to these and related questions are essential to understanding how the social characteristics of American teachers evolve. And to seeing how the changing social profile of the teaching population is a barometer of the status of teaching as a profession in the United States.

Teachers in Colonial America

Because of the poor condition of historical records, and the scarcity of relevant statistical data, it is difficult to identify the very first teachers in English-speaking North America with great certainty. Clearly, however, teachers as a group in colonial America were overwhelmingly white and male, largely middle-class and young, and often (though not always) well-educated—at least by seventeenth- and eighteenth-century standards. As Bernard Bailyn, Edmund Morgan, and other historians have pointed out, most education in colonial North America was probably conducted informally in homes and businesses, either by children's parents or within the context of apprenticeships of other work-related experiences. In most colonies the clergy operated schools for the indigent, partly as a service to charity and partly to inculcate traditional moral standards and Christian principles. Formal education for the largest portion of the population—the middling classes—was a rather haphazard affair, generally conducted by tutors or masters who operated their schools for a fee. Public education, as the term is understood today, did not exist in colonial America (except perhaps in parts of New England).[5]

In order to work in circumstances such as these, a prospective teacher needed to command the appropriate status and legal rights to conduct his own business. Under the traditional English regime that governed most colonies, women and blacks often faced discriminatory legal and social restrictions which limited their ability to do this. Perhaps the most important of these limitations was a widespread antipathy to providing these groups with access to higher education in any form. Teaching was thus largely the province of men. Furthermore, since schooling was relatively expensive in many of the colonies, formal education generally was limited to the middling and upper classes. These groups undoubtedly expected teachers to represent a social background and value system similar to their own. This meant that most teachers were probably themselves from middle- or upper-class backgrounds, or at least maintained the appearance of middle-class origins. Colonial society was very traditional in orientation, and its schools were conservative institutions. In an age when the egalitarian ethic of modern public education had not yet been articulated, it is little wonder that representatives of the most privileged social group—white middle- and upper-class males—appear to have constituted the vast majority of the period's teachers.[6]

It is difficult to make general statements about any group in colonial America, of course, because there were important differences which distinguished the social organization of the various colonies. In the Southern colonies, for instance, a highly commercialized plantation system of agriculture—organized initially around tobacco and later around cotton—dominated the region's economic and social life. From the very start, Southern society was divided between large landholders and landless indentured servants and slaves. The middle class (in colonial society skilled tradesmen and middling farmers made up the largest part of the "middle class") was relatively small and politically impotent.

There was virtually no urban development in the South throughout the colonial period. The rural quality of Southern life, aggravated by the relatively large sizes of farms, slowed the development of educational institutions. Since most of the economic and political power in the region rested in the hands of the large landowners, it was they who dictated prevailing patterns of formal education. Instead of sending their children to school, many Southern plantation owners simply hired a tutor to instruct the children for a portion of the year. Masters would travel from one area to another on a schedule, teaching children from various plantation families at different times of the year.

While teaching in this fashion was a job suitable generally only for men (simply because it was not acceptable for upper-class women to move around so), it was best suited to *young* men, those without families and other obligations. Teaching in the colonial south, then, was not a stable career to which educated men could devote their lives. Rather, it drew principally from the ranks of educated men who were preparing for yet another career, perhaps the law or (particularly) the ministry. A poorly developed school system and a widely dispersed population (conditions which themselves were related) helped to account for a peculiar pattern of employing relatively young—or otherwise unsettled—men as teachers.[7]

Little is known about colonial education in other rural areas of the country, with the possible exception of New England, and it is likely that the pattern of teacher employment observed in the South existed elsewhere in this period as well. Other colonies, however, had rapidly growing urban areas and highly developed pockets of commercial agriculture organized around major towns and cities. It was in these settings that a relatively high degree of population density and affluence made it possible for private schools to serve the needs of middling and upper-class families for education. In his study of education in New York City, Carl Kaestle has argued that such schools served nearly half of the city's school-age population and were within the means of most skilled tradesmen. Every one of the masters Kaestle identified was male, and several had apparently conducted their schools for a number of years.

If Kaestle's findings are at all representative, it is possible that school teaching offered career opportunities to a small cadre of entrepreneurial men serving a largely urban clientele. Little is known about the backgrounds of these teachers. Yet they probably differed little from the groups they served. Kaestle characterized these school masters as being similar in status to the skilled tradesmen who formed the bulk of the city's work force at that time. If he is correct, they were solidly in the middle of the social structure of their day, through probably lower in status than other "educated" occupational groups (such as lawyers or ministers). In New York—and by inference in other large colonial cities and towns—where school teaching did offer men a stable career opportunity, teaching appears to have been more a trade than a profession, and teachers probably were recruited from the ranks of middling (and not wealthy or highly esteemed) families. Thus, from its earliest stages of development as a distinct occupational alternative for men, teaching appears to have been firmly middle-class in orientation.[8]

Another model of school organization in colonial America, excluding charity schools run by the clergy in virtually every colony, was found in New England. Massachusetts was the first English colony on the continent to establish publicly supported schools, and by the eighteenth century most towns in New England provided some form of publicly supported education. The principal reason for this was to guarantee that each new generation would be properly acquainted with the Bible and would be able to participate fully in the life of religious community which New England had been established to sustain. Irrespective of whether they accomplished this, however, the early public schools of New England also offered yet another field of employment for prospective teachers.[9] As was the case in other colonies in this period, the overwhelming majority of teachers in New England's schools were men. For much of the colonial period women were excluded from the public schools altogether, making education virtually an exclusively male prerogative.

Since towns were required by law to maintain these schools with local taxes, the committees that administered them generally sought to keep expenses to a minimum. School terms were quite short by today's standards, often lasting as little as four to six weeks. Conducted in this fashion, schooling was intended as a supplement to a more complete program of studies in the home. This meant that school teaching constituted a variety of part-time work, occupying a relatively small portion of each teacher's time over the course of a year. Teaching was often combined with one or more other jobs, in order to complement the income of teachers. In her study of teaching in New England, Jo Anne Preston found that in the seventeenth century it was commonplace for men to hold other jobs, ranging from surveying to innkeeping, while teaching. But this pattern of employment also accounted for a good deal of instability in the teaching force. Looking at the period between 1653 and 1703, Preston found that half of the schoolmasters in Dedham, Massachusetts taught for no longer than a year, and that none stayed for more than five years.[10]

Other studies have noted similar patterns of teacher tenure in colonial New England. Many young men appear to have used teaching as a way to support themselves while preparing for other careers, particularly the ministry. The majority of teachers in colonial New England seem to have been young, many of them recent college graduates. James Axtell has estimated that 40 percent of Harvard's graduates over the entire colonial period became teachers, and 20 percent of Yale's, and that the vast majority of both groups of alumni eventually became ministers. Thus, even though the existence of tax-supported schools provided men with opportunities for a fairly stable career in teaching (supplemented with other forms of work), turnover among teachers was high. Teachers in colonial New England may have been relatively well educated, but few of them looked upon teaching as their principal calling. Rather, school keeping often was a step on the road to higher-status occupations in colonial society. Even in Calvinist New England, education was not important enough an enterprise to warrant the development of a cadre of teachers with professional standing.[11]

The experience of teachers in British North America probably changed little over the course of the colonial period. As cities and towns grew, the number of teachers like those Carl Kaestle identified in New York doubtlessly increased. The purview of clerically administered charity schools grew as well in the cities and large towns in the middle colonies, particularly in Pennsylvania, New Jersey, and New York. By the end of the seventeenth century the first "Dame" schools had appeared—small elementary schools for girls, usually run by women. These schools increased in number too, especially in the towns and cities along the coast, and opened up the first teaching opportunites for women.

Just the same, teaching remained a predominantly male occupation through the end of the eighteenth century. With the possible exception of masters in the independent-pay schools in New York and other big cities, men do not seem to have thought of teaching as a legitimate career option. Rather, teaching appears to have been a way to sustain oneself in the absence of other opportunities, or a stepping stone to other more lucrative or higher-status careers, such as law or medicine. Because it consisted of men with relatively high levels of education, however, teaching probably drew men from middle- and upper-class backgrounds in colonial America. Its inability to hold many of these individuals, however, was testimony to the low esteem given education in British North America, and to the contradictory quality of teaching as an educated profession in American life.

American Teachers in 1850

In America the first half of the nineteenth century was a period of frenetic economic growth and westward expansion, of rapid urbanization and industrialization in some parts of the country, and of sweeping institutional reforms, many of which dealt with schools and education. These changes in the economy (particularly those in the labor market) and in the educational system helped to bring about a correspondingly dramatic shift in the social composition of the teaching force. While teaching remained overwhelmingly white and middle-class, it also became increasingly female. The mid-nineteenth century witnessed the early but irresistible stages of the feminization of teaching in the United States.[12]

As was the case in discussing teachers in colonial America, it is difficult to quote comprehensive data on the social backgrounds of American teachers in 1850. Apart from state and federal census enumerations, surveys of virtually any element of the population were unheard of at that time. Of course, it is possible to construct a sample of American teachers by examining manuscripts of federal census returns from communities across the country in 1850. But a task of that magnitude is beyond the scope of a study such as this. The published federal census returns are only slightly more helpful. While it is possible to derive estimates of the numbers of men and women employed as teachers in each state, it is impossible to identify other characteristics of teachers' social backgrounds, such as ethnicity and social class.[13] It is not even possible to get consistent information on race, though it is clear that very few black men and women worked as teachers in the mid-nineteenth century. Part of the reason that feminization stands out as such an important theme in the history of American teachers in this period, accordingly, may be that little else is known about their background characteristics. These problems aside, it remains possible to identify a *limited* range of teacher characteristics in this period, and in this fashion to begin to compose the barest outline of who became teachers in 1850.

The Feminization of Teaching

Historians, economists, and other social scientists have devoted a great deal of attention in recent years to the issue of feminization in teaching. By-and-large, they agree that feminization occurred first and most rapidly in those parts of the country where modern school systems appeared in the nineteenth century. The most recent studies suggest that feminization was due to a combination of labor market forces, changing demands for teachers in the wake of educational reforms, and underlying shifts in popular perceptions of female roles.

Myra Strober and other scholars have observed that the feminization of teaching in the latter nineteenth century was associated with urbanization and with what Strober and Audry Langford have described as the ''formalization of schooling''—improved standards of certification and instruction associated with nineteenth-century school reform. This has led them to speculate that women were hired in large numbers as teachers in cities because of the inability of urban school systems to attract and hold men teachers (mainly because city school systems discouraged teachers from pursuing other careers while teaching). Teaching paid poorly compared with other jobs that men could get in urban areas, and the demands of teaching in big-city school systems—with eight months or more of school each year—precluded men teaching as a part-time job. Simultaneously, the nineteenth-century ideology of ''domestic feminism'' limited the range of occupations to which young middle-class women could aspire. Teaching therefore became popularly recognized as a variety of work which was acceptable for young women to undertake.

Strober's research suggests that while school committees may have had an incentive to hire women teachers simply because they were cheaper, the movement of women into the profession was less a matter of conscious policy on the part of penurious school committees than it was a function of the labor market. Men moved out of teaching because of changes in both schools and the urban labor market, and women moved in to fulfill a new set of roles defined for them.

The transition from employing male teachers to hiring women was by no means abrupt, however. Rather than turning men away in order to hire less-expensive women, school committees often searched in vain for men teachers before finally hiring women. One major concern was discipline, particularly for older boys. Male teachers often were valued for their ability to manage unruly rural schoolhouses which typically mixed older and younger children. In more highly developed school systems they were seen as potential role models for adolescent males. In many urban school systems, on the other hand, where age grading made classroom discipline less problematic and teachers could be assigned whole classes of younger children, there was greater openness to hiring women teachers. The very fact that feminization occurred gradually suggests that economy was not the only issue at play here. Indeed, the fact of saving money by hiring women as teachers may have been more of a consequence of feminization than a cause.[14]

As I have already said, the biggest problem in identifying forces at play in the development of the teaching force in the mid-nineteenth century is missing detailed recorded information. It is possible, however, to identify certain trends with the use of aggregate data taken from the published census returns, looking at trends in state- and regional-level statistics. In 1850 the United States was an overwhelmingly rural country with a distinctive regional division of labor. Less than a quarter of the population lived in cities, and the vast majority of those urbanites were located in the Northeast. The social structure in the South remained much as it had in the eighteenth century, although the plantation economy revolved more decisively around cotton and the institution of slavery than it had earlier. Most of the country's manufacturing activity was located in the Northeast, particularly in New England.

The western states (generally corresponding to today's Midwest) exported agricultural produce and raw materials. This national division of labor meant that there were important differences from one region to the next regarding the demand for certain kinds of labor *and* the types of school systems which developed in each part of the country. Regional differences in economic function also helped account for important cultural differences which distinguished each part of the country, though cultural traditions were also shaped by religious, ethnic, and political forces as well. In many respects the United States at mid-century comprised three or more smaller nations, each marked by a distinctive way of life (and thus often by a strong local identity). Given this, it is little wonder that there was a good deal of variation in the social characteristics of teachers from one part of the country to another.

Indeed, given the diversity of settings in which teachers worked in this period, it is difficult to generalize about their experiences. Introducing the concept of region (see Table 1.1) offers a means of identifying clear patterns of variation in teacher characteristics.[15]

Table 1.1 presents various social and economic characteristics of major American regions in 1850. In general, these characteristics correspond to the description of each region cited above. The North was urbanized and commercial, the South was agricultural, and the West (today's Midwest) was largely agricultural as well. The pattern of regional variation in the numbers of women teachers, however, was somewhat different. The feminization of teaching had clearly taken hold in the urban Northeast by the mid-nineteenth century, where school enrollments were quite high.[16] This finding corresponds to the argument made by Myra Strober and others that the feminization of teaching was associated with the development of modern, urban school systems. It is also compatible with the view that women were most likely to be hired in settings where there was considerable demand for teachers and where pressures may have existed to hold school costs down.

The nation's least urbanized region was the South; and it was in the Southern states that women teachers were least evident in this period. A very large number of Southern schools were in rural areas, where communities often preferred to have male teachers. In the midwestern states, on the other hand, the teaching force was highly feminized, despite the region's relatively low level of urbanization and commercial development. School enrollment levels were high in the Midwest, but

Table 1.1 Regional Characteristics in 1850
Regional means (standard deviations in parentheses)
State-level data (population size not controlled) (N = 30)

Factor (Percent)	*U.S. Total*	*Northeast*	*South*	*Midwest*
Teachers Female	60% (25)	80% (12)	35% (17)	82% (07)
School-aged population enrolled	52 (17)	71 (12)	37 (06)	58 (09)
Population urban	13 (14)	25 (18)	5 (07)	8 (03)
Male labor force in commerce	25 (11)	36 (10)	19 (08)	21 (04)
Male labor force in agriculture	49 (17)	35 (13)	58 (14)	60 (07)
Male labor force in manufacturing*	17 (06)	21 (05)	14 (05)	14 (03)
Male labor force professional	1.96 (.5)	1.56 (.2)	2.45 (.5)	1.8 (.9)

* Includes men employed in mining and other extractive enterprises.

not as high as in the northeastern states. Clearly, something apart from urbanization and enrollment levels accounted for the feminization of teaching in this part of the country. Just what it might be, though, is not immediately evident from the information presented in Table 1.1.

Table 1.2 presents a correlation matrix with several of the factors listed in Table 1.1 and a number of others. The variables in the analysis include urbanization; the average number of teachers per public school (a measure of the ''formalization'' of school systems); overall enrollment rate (ages 5 to 19); male employment levels in commerce and agriculture; percent of the male labor force employed as lawyers, doctors, and ministers; and dummy variables for the South and Northeast. The high level of regional identification in these variables makes it hazardous to perform multivariate analysis with this data set. Even so, it is possible to identify a number of key relationships with the correlation coefficients provided in this matrix.

Variables of interest are those which have figured prominently in the research on feminization. Urbanization is straightforward: It is both a generally recognized index of social and economic development, and a factor which earlier studies have associated decisively with the feminization of teaching. The number of teachers per school can be interpreted as representing the general level of development in a state's school system, at least insofar as systems with larger schools tended to be more ''formalized'' than others. Overall enrollment levels may indicate the severity of demand for teachers, and consequently the interests of local school leaders in holding down costs as well. Having more children to teach, after all, presented many schoolmen with the dilemma of rising expenses while taxpayers demanded fiscal restraint. The low costs of women teachers were no doubt attractive in all circumstances. The percent of all working men employed as learned professionals (doctors, laywers, and ministers) is intended to represent the quantity of men who

Table 1.2 Correlation Matrix: Education and Socio-Economic Development in 1850
State-level data (N = 30)

	(1)	*(2)*	*(3)*	*(4)*	*(5)*	*(6)*	*(7)*
Feminization of teaching (1)	—						
Urbanization (2)	.29	—					
Total enrollment rate (3)	.88	.34	—				
Teachers per school (4)	.58	.35	.75	—			
Percent men professional (5)	−.74	−.51	−.62	−.32	—		
Percent men commerce (6)	.31	.92	.37	.35	−.32	—	
Percent men agriculture (7)	−.21	−.84	−.28	−.37	.50	−.93	—
Northeast	.53	.56	.75	.64	−.51	.63	−.59
South	−.77	−.44	−.70	−.42	.72	−.46	.41

would be available to teach, if indeed teaching opportunities existed on a part-time (or less than full-time) basis. The other variables (employment in commerce and agriculture) are intended to represent the overall level of economic development in each state. The dummy variables show the association of two major regions with each of these factors.

Given these variables, the results of the analysis reported in Table 1.2 are remarkable in a number of respects. The variable most clearly associated with feminization was overall enrollment rates. This can be taken as support for the argument that feminization of teaching was firmly associated with high levels of school participation. It is not clear, however, just how high enrollment rates may have *caused* feminization—whether by generating greater demand for teachers or by exerting pressure on cost-conscious school committees. It is also possible that high enrollment rates were associated with school reform movements in this period, and particularly with longer school terms, which may have made it more difficult for men to teach on a part-time basis.

As indicated in Table 1.2, enrollment rates were positively associated with the number of teachers per school, an important dimension of the modernization of school systems at this time. Feminization was also associated with the number of teachers per school, supporting Strober's view that the movement of women into teaching was related to the development of formalized school systems. But the number of teachers was not as strongly related to feminization as were overall enrollment rates. Urbanization turned out to be a relatively unimportant variable in explaining feminization, at least in 1850. This casts doubt on the proposition that feminization was primarily due to the development of the modern, bureaucratic school systems historically associated with cities. In 1850, it appears, enrollments were high and modern school systems existed outside of the nation's highly urbanized areas. As a consequence, many women worked as teachers in nonurban settings.

Perhaps the most remarkable feature of the analysis in Table 1.2, however, was the performance of the "men employed as professionals" variable. This factor was negatively associated with feminization, indicating that men were most likely to work as teachers in those states where they also were employed in the learned professions in greatest proportions. This relationship simply may indicate that male teachers often were drawn from the ranks of the other learned professions, as they had been during the colonial period. Disproportionally large numbers of men pursuing these careers may simply have served as a willing cadre of part-time teachers. Interestingly, this factor is negatively related to enrollment levels and teachers per school, and positively associated with the South.

The feminization of teaching, it appears, was also associated with the availability of men with commensurate credentials who were able to combine teaching with another career in the professions. States with large numbers of men working in (or aspiring to) professional careers experienced less feminization of teaching, all other things being equal, than states where the learned professions constituted a smaller portion of the male labor force. A glance back at Table 1.1 indicates that it was the Southern states where men worked in these careers in greatest proportions, and where feminization was least evident in teaching. Of course, the Southern states also had the shortest school terms in this period, so that men employed as ministers, lawyers, or doctors might also work for short stretches as teachers.

Even in parts of the country where school terms were longer, the availability of relatively large numbers of educated men appears to have inhibited the process of feminization in teaching. In connection with this variable, Strober's analysis of the feminization process appears to make sense. Women moved into teaching most decisively in those parts of the country where there were relatively few educated men who might be willing to take a job as a teacher.

This discussion leaves many questions unanswered. For instance, it is not clear how labor market forces and educational reform interacted to produce the regional patterns of feminization evident in Table 1.1. Unfortunately, the high level of multicolinearity among the variables used in this analysis makes it impossible to perform a more sophisticated analysis of this issue. Given this limitation, only a few general patterns can be identified with certainty from Tables 1.1 and 1.2. In those parts of the country where enrollments were high, such as the Northeast, teaching was highly feminized. In those parts of the country where there were relatively large numbers of men pursuing careers in the learned professions, such as in the South—where enrollments were also low—there were more men than women employed as teachers.

The Social Origins of Teachers

Apart from the issue of feminization, who became teachers in the mid-nineteenth century? Unfortunately, this is a difficult question to answer, largely because systematic records on the origins of teachers were not kept in most nineteenth-century communities. The statistical analysis performed above provides clues about which social and economic groups supplied some teachers. But it is necessary to use altogether different types of evidence to piece together a more detailed social profile of American teachers at about mid-century. Once again, the matter of regional differences makes it difficult to generalize about the social origins of teachers, simply because of the important differences in cultural disposition, labor market forces, and educational systems which existed from one part of the country to another. Ideally, a study of American teachers in the nineteenth century would examine evidence from a number of communities selected to represent the nation's various regions. A research project of that scale, however, is beyond the scope of this chapter. Rather, I will use information derived from a number of disparate sources to identify characteristics of teachers in a limited number of contexts. While this will not provide a comprehensive picture of American teachers and their characteristics in the middle of the nineteenth century, it can be used to sketch the general contours of a social portrait.

Whatever else can be said about the social characteristics of American teachers in this period, the overwhelming majority were white. Most black Americans lived in a legal condition of slavery in 1850, and free blacks were largely excluded from teaching roles in the Southern states. In the North it was possible for free blacks to hold positions as teachers, though almost exclusively as teachers of black children.

Even these opportunities materialized haphazardly, as white school leaders often resisted hiring blacks as teachers until they were compelled to. In New York, for instance, the all-white Manumission Society did not hire black teachers for its African Free Schools until 1832, more than forty years after they were established, and then only after a successful boycott of the schools organized by black community leaders.

A decade later, however, the Public School Society in New York turned all of its black schools over to an all-black community organization—largely because white school visitors shunned assignments to black schools. Blacks in other cities had similar experiences. As black communities in large Northern cities began to devote their attention to the issue of education, and as racist attitudes caused whites to eschew service in black schools, job opportunities for black teachers materialized. Yet in 1850 these positions still were few in number. In small towns and rural areas, where most Americans lived in this period, teaching was virtually an all-white occupation. While black teachers may have been important members of local black communities, serving both as respected community leaders and as important role models for black youth, they were too few in number to seriously affect the overall social profile of American teachers.[17]

Beyond issues of race and gender, it is difficult to identify the social background characteristics of American teachers in the mid-nineteenth century. To paint the barest outline of who became teachers at this time it is necessary to use evidence froma limited range of sources, even if this sheds light on but a small fraction of the nation's teaching force. Given the previously cited wide regional differences in the characteristics of teachers, the results of this sort of treatment must be interpreted cautiously. But it does provide us with a modicum of evidence which can be used to construct a profile of *some* of the teachers we are trying to focus on.

Apart from the manuscript census schedules, which pose their own peculiar set of problems, perhaps the richest source of information about the social origins of American teachers is the records of normal schools. In 1850 the normal school, a permanent-type institution dedicated solely to training teachers, was still something of a novel idea in the United States. Although the nation's first normal school was established in Massachusetts in 1839, by mid-century only a handful of such institutions had been founded, most of them in the northeastern part of the country.[18] Richard M. Bernard and Maris A. Vinovskis have conducted an especially revealing study of the social origins of American teachers in the mid-nineteenth century, using records from Massachusetts normal schools.

Examining occupational data provided by these schools, Bernard and Vinovskis identified distinctive patterns in the social origins of Massachusetts teachers, or at least those who attended the normal schools. Restricting their analysis only to records from 1859 on (because of problems with data in earlier years), they found that some 43 percent of normal school students came from farm family backgrounds, and that another 28.5 percent came from artisan backgrounds. Only 1.7 percent of the state's normal school students were the daughters or sons of unskilled laborers, while nearly 12 percent had fathers who worked as professionals or merchants and managers.

If the characteristics of normal school students offer a fair indication, there appears to have been a slight middle- and upper-class bias in the process determining which social and economic groups would supply most of the state's teachers. Leaving aside the question of farmers, laborers—totaling nearly a quarter of the state's population—appear to have supplied a small fraction of its teachers. Artisans and professionals/merchant–managers, on the other hand, seem to have supplied teachers at about the same level, or a slightly higher one, than their share of the total population. What is especially striking in the results of Bernard and Vinovskis' study, however, is the disproportionately large number of normal school students who hailed from farm families in Massachusetts. As indicated in Table 1.1, only slightly more than a third of the population in the Northeast lived on farms, and the proportion was considerably less in Massachusetts. Yet almost half of all the normal school students came from farm backgrounds (if there was an urban bias in normal school enrollment, the proportion of teachers from farm families could have been even higher). This is an important finding, and one which sheds considerable light on the rural character of much of American education in the nineteenth century.[19]

Bernard and Vinovskis also noted differences in the occupational backgrounds of the students enrolled in coed and all-female normal schools. While nearly 60 percent of the students in the coed schools (n = 132) were from farm families, only 22.4 percent of the students in the all-female schools were (n = 107). Because male students constituted a minority in the coed schools, these differences probably cannot be attributed totally to differences in the backgrounds of men and women entering teaching. But, as a number of scholars have pointed out, the feminization of teaching occurred first—and most rapidly—in the cities. It is possible that much of the difference in social backgrounds distinguishing students from these two types of schools was associated with the relatively large proportion of men in rural teaching. Even so, the large number of prospective teachers from farm backgrounds in mid-nineteenth-century Massachusetts is striking. As Bernard and Vinovskis note, it may simply have reflected the attractiveness of teaching to a group of young people interested in leaving their rural communities and the restrictive confines of a family-centered culture.

For many young people growing up on farms—men and women alike—teaching must have seemed an alluring prospect indeed. It promised young men an opportunity to begin a career in the educated professions at a time when the state's agricultural economy was in decline; and it offered women a respectable avenue to a considerably larger world of social contacts and new responsibilities outside the narrow rural routine they had known as children. Given this, it is little wonder that such a large number of rural youth appear to have been attracted to the normal schools in Massachusetts. To them, teaching was one of the few occupational choices they knew first-hand which offered them the prospect of further opportunities in the years ahead.[20]

It is important to bear in mind several limitations of the Bernard and Vinovskis study. The authors analyzed only a single year of normal school enrollments. Even assuming that a high proportion of normal school students eventually went into teaching, they estimated that only about one in six Massachusetts teachers attended a normal school. And Massachusetts itself was representative of only a limited portion of the United States at that time. Just the same, their finding that the largest portion of teachers hailed from rural backgrounds probably was true of much of the country then.

If Massachusetts—a highly urbanized and industrialized state in 1850—had large numbers of teachers with farm backgrounds, other states probably had more. Other studies, based admittedly on less systematic evidence, appear to support such a supposition. For rural youth in all parts of the country, teaching seems to have been an especially attractive career alternative. The United States was a distinctively agricultural nation in the mid-nineteenth century, and it appears to have had a characteristically rural teaching force.[21] Eventually the pastoral quality of American life would change, but well into the following century teachers would continue to come from the countryside in large numbers.

American Teachers in 1900

The period between 1850 and 1900 was one of continued growth in the United States. It was a time of westward expansion, rapid industrialization, unprecedented urbanization, and large-scale immigration. It was also one of continued growth and development for the nation's school systems. City school districts grew especially rapidly in these years, as they struggled to keep pace with the demands of a booming urban population. State and federal agencies for monitoring and regulating schools were established and strengthened, and educators devoted more attention to extending school reforms (such as a longer school year) to parts of the country where education had long been neglected—such as the South. All of these changes (population growth, urbanization, continuing school reform) created a growing demand for teachers.[22]

Between 1870 and 1900, when this process of expansion was most pronounced, the number of teachers in the United States more than tripled, from 126,822 to nearly 450,000. At the same time the ratio of teachers to school-age children (5–19) in the country rose from less than one to a hundred to about one to fifty. This was a remarkable achievement, particularly at a time when the school-age population nearly doubled. There was an enormous demand for teachers, and it was in this period that the process of feminization proceeded most rapidly in the teaching population. In 1870 about two-thirds of American teachers were women, only slightly more than the proportion given in Table 1.1 for 1850. By 1900, however, nearly three-quarters of all teachers were female, as were more than 82 percent in cities with populations over 25,000. Given this, it is little wonder that most studies of the feminization process have focused on this period. By the turn of the century teaching was virtually an all-female occupation in some parts of the country. Examining the social backgrounds of American teachers in this period is essential to understanding how the teaching force changed during a time of enormous growth and rapid change.[23]

It is somewhat easier to locate evidence about teachers at the turn of the century than it is for teachers in 1850, largely because by the latter time educators themselves were concerned about growth and change in the teaching population. In addition to improved statistical evidence on school enrollment, attendance rates, and a variety of other general social and economic indices in the federal census (a consequence of general improvements in the census over the late nineteenth century), there were efforts on the part of educators and other social scientists to identify the background characteristics of teachers in this period. The result is a considerably larger body of data from which to make inferences about teachers' backgrounds than is available for earlier periods. Of course, any analysis of teachers' social characteristics in 1900 must be cast in terms of questions similar to those which informed the previous analysis of teacher backgrounds in 1850. Feminization in this period, which has drawn attention from scholars quite recently, was an issue of considerable interest to contemporaries as well. The availability of survey data on teachers' social origins makes it possible to answer questions posed by normal school data in the 1850s more definitively and to draw a somewhat better profile of American teachers for 1900 than it was for 1850.

Feminization in 1900

It appears that by 1900 feminization proceeded in much the same fashion in which it started earlier in the nineteenth century. The most highly developed and urbanized regions of the country experienced the highest levels of feminization in teaching. As in 1850, feminization was positively associated with urbanization and commercial development, and negatively associated with employment in agriculture. Because of changes in the federal census, however, it is also possible to measure the extent to which average school terms varied in length from one state to another in 1900. This is significant because longer school terms could have made it more difficult for men to undertake teaching as a part-time job, and/or to combine it with other careers. The lengthening of school terms was a major thrust of common school reform throughout the latter nineteenth century. The availability of this information makes it possible to determine whether it was the advance of reforms such as this, or simply the rising pressure of enrollments and associated costs, which most directly accounted for the feminization process in this period.[24]

A glance at Table 1.3 reveals the extent to which the feminization process was evident from one part of the country to another in this period. As was the case in 1850, the region with the highest proportion of women working as teachers was the Northeast, and the area with the lowest number was the South. The West (the Pacific states in Table 1.3, rather than the Midwest, as in Table 1.1) had a higher proportion of women teachers than the South, but a lower proportion than in the Northeast (the proportion in the Midwest ws generally the same as in the West). The level of urbanization was higher in all three regions than it had been in 1850, but the relative positions of the regions on this score had not changed. By-and-large the Northeast was the most economically developed region in the country and the South the least, with the West (and Midwest) somewhere in between. Overall enrollment levels were not very different from what they had been some 50 years earlier, and actually appear to have dropped in the Northeast. This may have been due to the rapid pace of urbanization in that part of the country, as enrollment levels generally were lower in large cities than elsewhere in this period.[25]

Table 1.3 Regional Characteristics in 1900
Regional means (standard deviations in parentheses)
State-level data (population size not controlled) (N = 48)

Factor (Percent)	*U.S. Total*	*Northeast*	*South*	*West*
Teachers female	74% (09)	85% (05)	67% (07)	75% (07)
School-aged population enrolled	53 (09)	57 (03)	40 (07)	58 (05)
School population attending 6 months	70 (25)	93 (04)	36 (11)	80 (10)
Population urban	32 (21)	59 (23)	14 (06)	31 (15)
Labor force agricultural	40 (19)	16 (11)	62 (10)	30 (07)
Labor force manufacturing	22 (12)	40 (08)	10 (04)	26 (04)
Male employment in professions*	1.4 (.3)	1.4 (.2)	1.3 (.3)	1.5 (.4)

* Employment in law, medicine and ministry.

Perhaps the most striking regional difference recorded in Table 1.3, however, is the variable measuring school *attendance*. This factor reflects the proportion of all students enrolled in school who attended for at least six months in the previous year. As I have indicated elsewhere, most of the variation in this factor was associated with state-to-state differences in the length of school terms. In regard to this aspect of school system development, the Northeast was clearly the most advanced region in the country, with more than nine out of ten children attending school for six months or more. The South had the shortest school terms in the country, on average, in this period, with barely a third of the children attending for six months or more. Once again the western states fell in between these two extremes but were much closer to the level of attendance observed in the Northeast than they were to the South.

These variations in the length of school terms, particularly the wide difference between North and South, undoubtedly reflected the impact of educational reform in these parts of the country. But differences in the length of school terms may also have had important consequences regarding the composition of the teaching force. If so, it is possible that feminization was a direct consequence of the advance of reform in this period and less a matter of conscious policy on the part of school leaders seeking to save money.[26]

Table 1.4 presents the elements of a regression equation analyzing state-level feminization rates in 1900. The variables in this regression are generally the same as were used in the analysis of 1850 data in Table 1.2. The principal difference is the inclusion of the school attendance variables listed in Table 1.3. The only other differences are the substitution of a regional dummy variable for the Northeast instead of an urbanization variable, and the exclusion of the North Central dummy. In this analysis the attendance variable is intended to represent the effect of school reform on feminization. With progressively longer school terms as a consequence of reform, it should have become more difficult for men to remain in teaching and

Table 1.4 Regression Analysis: The Feminization of Teaching in 1900
Dependent variable: percent teachers female
State-level data (N = 48)

Variable	*b*	*Standard Error*	*Probability*	*Partial R^2*
School population attending 6 months	.2087	.0542	.0004	.2561
Male professional employment	−10.9732	4.1726	.0118	.1386
Enrollment rate	.1783	.1398	.2091	.0364
Northeast	.0535	.0265	.0499	.0865

Constant = .6467
Standard error of estimate = .0623 Adjusted R^2 = .557

to hold other jobs at the same time. This means that the enrollment rate variable can be interpreted strictly in terms of the gross demand for teachers. Presumably, the higher the level of enrollment, the greater the demand for teachers and the greater the associated costs of instruction.

If the principal cause of feminization was concern over reducing costs, enrollments should be closely associated with the proportion of female teachers. The Male Professional Employment variable is the same in this analysis as in the earlier analysis. It is designed to capture the effect, on the supply of male teachers, of men being employed in other learned professions. Finally, the Northeast dummy is intended to control for the effect of urbanization. The Northeast was far and away the most urbanized region of the country at this time, and together with the Great Lakes states included nearly two-thirds of the nation's urban population. Additional factors were not included because of the high level of multicolinearity which typically exists in data defined at the state level. Together, these variables can help to distinguish between the two major explanations of feminization and to clarify the debate over why women moved so decisively into teaching in this period.

The results of the regression analysis of feminization in 1900 are presented in Table 1.4. As indicated in the "Partial R^2" column, the strongest factor in the equation is the attendance variable. The only other factor to achieve significance at the .01 level was Male Professional Employment. In both cases the signs on these variables were in the proper direction. Attendance for six months or longer in school—a function of the length of school terms—was positively associated with feminization, indicating that women were more likely to work as teachers in those states which featured longer school terms. Male Professional Employment, on the other hand, was negatively associated with feminization, as it was in the 1850 analysis. This suggests that a large supply of men describing themselves as members of the learned professions continued to be associated with male employment in teaching thrrough the latter half of the nineteenth century and into the twentieth.

Both of these factors were associated with conditions which may have affected the ability and the willingness of men to work as teachers. The length of school terms restricted options for additional employment for male teachers in the North and West, while a relatively large supply of men in the learned professions in the

South may have provided a willing cadre of male teachers to fill the region's classrooms. Whatever else can be said about the feminization process in teaching, it appears to have been firmly linked to state-to-state differences in the conditions under which men worked in this period. Indeed, viewed from this perspective, the feminization process appears to have been less a matter of women moving into teaching than men moving out.

Feminization, it is important to note, was an uneven process even within individual school systems. Some sectors of the educational system were more affected than others. The overwhelming majority of women teachers in this period worked in the elementary schools, where they constituted more than 70 percent of all public school teachers. In public high schools, on the other hand, women constituted barely 50 percent of the teaching force. Nearly the same ratios applied to private schools at this time.

In public school administration the picture was largely the same. While women constituted nearly 62 percent of elementary school principals in 1905, men occupied almost 95 percent of all high school principalships, and nearly all of the district superintendencies in the United States. Thus, while feminization clearly opened a wide field of opportunity for women in education, a clear-cut division of labor distinguished male and female roles in school systems around the country.

It is not clear whether this pattern was substantially different from the prevailing distribution of men and women in various educational roles in 1850: State-level data on the numbers of men and women in elementary, high school, and administrative positions simply are not available for comparison. Even a cursory reading of state and local school reports indicates, however, that female school administrators were relatively rare throughout the nineteenth century. As Myra Strober and David Tyack have pointed out, in the field of education women teach and men manage. The rapid transition of teaching from a male-dominated to an overwhelmingly female occupation in less than a century did not change the hierarchical quality of gender relations in education. Despite feminization, the positions with the greatest prestige and authority (and the best salaries) as a rule went to men.[27]

The feminization of teaching was a complex process of social transformation which appears to have involved men as much as women. The foregoing analysis does not prove, by any means, that women were not hired as teachers because they cost less than men. On the contrary, another way of interpreting the results presented in Table 1.4 would be to argue that feminization occurred because school districts were unwilling or unable to pay the rising costs of retaining male teachers as school terms became longer and teaching became less attractive to men. Nineteenth-century school leaders often commented on the substantial savings which hiring women teachers represented, even though experience appears to have been a more important determinant of teachers' salaries in this period than gender.

In any case, the variables in Table 1.4 represent only a little more than half of the total variation in state-to-state levels of feminization, and there were doubtless a range of other factors which helped account for the movement of women into teaching. One may have been the rapid growth of women's secondary and higher education in the latter nineteenth century. Economics historian Susan Carter has argued that wage levels for women teachers were partly determined by the availability of educated women in the latter nineteenth century. Had there not been a ready supply of educated women with few job opportunities in this period, feminization of the teaching force might have proceeded somewhat more slowly. As indicated in the analysis above, however, changes in the administration of schools—and particularly the extension of school terms to six months or more—was an especially important factor in making teaching a less attractive job prospect for men.

The feminization of teaching was an important development both in the history of American education and in the shaping of a distinctive pattern of labor-force participation for educated women in the United States. The battery of factors that accounted for the movement of women into teaching was complex, but it appears that feminization was largely a consequence of labor market forces affecting *both* men *and* women.

The Age Question

The overwhelming majority of American teachers at the turn of the century were quite young. The median age for teachers across the nation was only 27, and it was not uncommon for young women and men to begin their teaching careers as early as age 15 or 16 in rural and small-town schools. Teachers in urban areas appear to have been older than those teaching in the countryside. Turnover rates among teachers were extremely high. Most taught for only a few years before moving on to other interests. This appears to have been especially true of women. According to surveys conducted at the time, more than 80 percent of women teachers had less than ten years of teaching experience in 1910. The corresponding figure for men was about 65 percent. According to a representative sample of teachers drawn from the 1900 federal census, the mean age of male teachers (32) was nearly five years older than that of women (27).

If teaching functioned as a revolving door for young men and women ultimately interested in other careers, the door revolved especially fast for women. As I have argued elsewhere, it must have been quite difficult indeed for teachers working in circumstances such as these to maintain a high level of professional identity.[28]

The age structure of the teaching population reflects the development of a clear sexual divison of labor in teaching at this time. Men generally remained in teaching—or in education generally—longer than women. This meant that they took positions in school administration, at both the school and district levels, in disproportionately large numbers. Feminization meant the development of school systems in which large numbers of relatively young women teachers were supervised by older men.

This pattern of male management and female instruction was perpetuated by rules (formal in many cases, informal in others) restricting employment in teaching to unmarried women. Taking advantage of the relatively large numbers of educated young women available to teach at this time, school administrators argued that a married woman would have difficulty caring for both her own children and those in class. This reasoning was closely tied to the nineteenth-century ideology of domesticity, which defined female roles in narrow terms. But the resulting process of turning the teaching force over in relatively short periods helped to guarantee a generally compliant corps of teachers.

Feminization in teaching did not mean more power or prestige for most women who became teachers. Instead, it contributed ot the development of a two-tiered system of employment in education, one in which women did the bulk of the teaching under the supervision of an increasingly authoritative cadre of male administrators.[29]

The Social Origins of Teachers in 1900

It is considerably easier to discuss the origins of American teachers back in 1900 than it is of those from 1850. A variety of sources is available to identify who became these latter-day teachers and where they came from, including several contemporary surveys of working teachers. By-and-large, it appears that teachers in 1900 were rather similar to their counterparts from 50 years earlier, at least insofar as teachers in 1850 can be identified precisely. The 1900 generation were overwhelmingly white; they appear to have hailed largely from middling backgrounds; and many seem to have come from the country's rural areas. There undoubtedly were important differences in the distribution of these characteristics from one region to the next—and between men and women, elementary and high school teachers, and teachers and administrators—but the overall profile of the American teaching population appears to have generally remained the same throughout the latter half of the nineteenth century.

In 1900 the federal census provided information on the numbers of black teachers and white teachers in the country. About 5 percent of the nation's teachers at that time (one in 20) were black. Since blacks constituted about 11 percent of the nation's population, this means that they were seriously underrepresented among the nation's teachers. Put another way, while there were about 96 white teachers for every 10,000 whites over age 15 in the U.S. In 1900, there were only 40 black teachers for the same number of black people. This difference in the numbers of black teachers and white teachers was partly a reflection of the relatively poor quality of education provided black children in most parts of the country, and particularly in the South—where nine out of ten blacks lived at this time.

Since black teachers almost exclusively taught black children, and black class sizes were larger and enrollment rates lower than those for whites, fewer black teachers were hired. Additionally, the ratio of black to white teachers undoubtedly reflects discrimination in employment as well. In many school districts around the country, whites were employed rather than blacks to teach black children. Since the opposite was virtually never permitted, the result was substantially fewer black teachers nationally than whites. The right of black children to have black teachers was achieved in many parts of the country only as a consequence of hard-fought campaigns. The racial imbalance among American teachers offered further testimony to the continuing effects of racism on American education and American culture in general.[30]

Blacks were just one ethnic group among many in turn-of-the-century America, of course. In the decades following 1850, millions of immigrants had poured into the United States in search of freedom and fortune. Unlike earlier enumerations, which did not provide information about the ethnic distribution of occupational groups, the 1900 federal census sorted white teachers by nativity into three general groups: native-born of native parents, native-born of foreign parents, and foreign-born. Even though the resulting categories were very broad, and did not identify the particular ethnic groups teachers were identified with, they are useful for painting a general profile of teachers' social origins in this period.

Given the rural character of American teachers in the nineteenth century, it is not surprising that the majority of teachers in 1900 were of native parentage. But by the turn of the century immigrant communities—and particularly the children of immigrants—had made substantial inroads into the teaching profession. For the most part, the number of teachers from immigrant backgrounds outnumbered blacks and were more representative of the number of immigrant children in the schools than black teachers were of black children.

In 1900 immigrant teachers, including those born in this country of immigrant parents, numbered more than one of four teachers nationally, and nearly one of three white teachers. The vast majority of these teachers (about 75 percent) were second-generation immigrants, the daughters and sons of those who had come to this country from abroad. In fact, second-generation teachers were better represented in the nation's schools at this time than were teachers of native parentage.

As regards teachers born elsewhere, some 27,000 foreign-born teachers worked in American schools in 1900, more than 6 percent of the nation's teaching population, bringing at least a small measure of the period's cultural diversity to the schools. It is not known whether these teachers taught in the public schools or in the expanding parochial school systems then largely serving immigrant children. One reason why such large numbers of immigrant teachers were employed may have been the existence of a sizeable network of schools established and administered by immigrant religious orders. In any case, the fact of immigrant teachers constituting such a substantial block of the national teaching population represented a dramatic change in American education. The schools, so often called upon to preserve native values, were staffed increasingly by teachers intimately conversant with a foreign culture.[31]

Interestingly, there were important gender differences among immigrant teachers at this time. About 28 percent of white women teachers were second-generation immigrants, while only little more than 14 percent of white male teachers were. All told, immigrants (first and second generations combined) constituted about a third of the nation's women teachers at the turn of the century, but a little less than a quarter of the male teachers. The reasons for this may have been associated with the high proportion of women teaching in cities, and in the Northeast and Midwest generally (where most immigrants lived). The greatest concentration of male teachers, on the other hand, existed in the South, the region with the smallest number of immigrants. The largest group of immigrant teachers was the women, who must have constituted a substantial block of the teaching population in the nation's major cities in this period. With the advent of industrialization and the attendant growth of cities, the United States was fast becoming an urban nation; and it appears that its teaching population was changing in a like fashion.[32]

In light of the changes discussed above (particularly the great increase in the number of immigrant teachers at work in this period), it is natural to expect that the occupational backgrounds of American teachers changed in the decades following 1850 as well. Evidence on this question is a little harder to find than it was for the issues of race and nativity. The published federal census returns do not provide information on the occupational backgrounds of people in this period, just as they did not in 1850. Fortunately, there were social scientists interested in the social origins of American teachers, and organizations—the National Education Association in particular—interested in the changing composition of the teaching population.

The studies that resulted from these interests can help to address the issue of whether teachers' occupational background characteristics changed as dramatically as did patterns of teacher nativity in the latter nineteenth century. As was the case with earlier census data, even in manuscript form, the 1900 federal census did not provide information on the occupational backgrounds of persons not living with their parents. This is why it is especially fortuitous that survey data on teachers' social origins are available from this period. Consequently, there are considerably more resources with which to address the question of teachers' *class* origins than was the case in 1850. And yet, as will be seen below, even these data must be employed cautiously.[33]

The most useful source of information on the social origins of American teachers at the turn of the century is a survey which was conducted by Lotus Delta Coffman in 1910. Although the raw data used in this study are no longer available, the book that resulted from Coffman's effort (*The Social Composition of the Teaching Population*) is a veritable gold mine of information about teachers at that time. As a doctoral student at Teachers College, Columbia University, Coffman distributed thousands of questionnaires to teachers as they assembled for conventions, institutes, and other professional meetings. He also distributed them to teachers at schools in various cities. Some 5,215 of these questionnaires were judged complete enough to be used for Coffman's dissertation.

The sample was perhaps the most comprehensive of its day, covering seventeen states in virtually every part of the country. Despite the size of this sample, however, and the fact that he claimed that "every effort was made to have the selection entirely at random," Coffman's survey was not drawn scientifically. As I have demonstrated elsewhere, his sample was skewed away from the big-city school districts, where about a quarter of all teachers worked. About 88 percent of Coffman's teachers were from rural or "town" school districts, as opposed to only about 75 percent of the national teaching force. This means that Coffman's data contain a strong bias toward teachers working in nonurban contexts. Even so, the magnitude of his sample, and the detailed information he collected on a variety of issues, make his study an invaluable aid in assessing the social status of American teachers at the turn of the century.[34]

The occupational backgrounds of Coffman's teachers are summarized in Table 1.5. Given the rural bias in his sample, it is not surprising to see that a rather large

Table 1.5 Father's Occupation, Teachers in Coffman's Sample, 1910
(teachers from farm backgrounds excluded)

Father's Occupation	*Men Teachers*	*Women Teachers*
*Professionals**	*25%*	*17%*
Businessmen	21	28
Artisans	27	30
Laborers	23	21

* Includes public officials.

Source: Data from Lotus Delta Coffman, *The Social Composition of the Teaching Population* (New York: Teachers College Press, 1911), p. 73.

share of the teachers he surveyed came from farm families. Indeed, the figures in this table correspond rather closely with the occupational background statistics for Massachusetts normal school students provided by Bernard and Vinovskis for a period some five decades earlier. The United States had undergone a good deal of urban development in the interim, and Coffman's findings probably do not accurately reflect the real origins of American teachers at the turn of the century. Yet even if the rural bias of Coffman's study is taken into account, a great many American teachers hailed from farm backgrounds at the start of the twentieth century. If the proportion of teachers with farm backgrounds in both columns were reduced some 15 percent, and the difference distributed proportionally across the remaining categories, over half of the men and nearly 40 percent of the women teachers would still be from farm families, and the sons and daughters of farmers would still constitute the largest categories.

As indicated in Table 1.3, about 40 percent of the nation's labor force was in farming of one variety or another in 1900. Given this, Coffman's findings would indicate that the children of farmers went into teaching in numbers generally representative of their share of the population. Coffman also noted that wealth was a factor in determining the likelihood of farmers' children becoming teachers. In general, he found that teachers were drawn disproportionately from wealthier farm families than from those with fewer resources and less income. Teachers from farm backgrounds were generally middle-class, through perhaps somewhat less cosmopolitan than their more urban counterparts. If the results of Coffman's survey are in any way representative, many American teachers continued to come from rural backgrounds in the early twentieth century.[35]

Of course the United States had undergone rapid urbanization in the latter nineteenth century, and by 1900 many—perhaps most—teachers came from nonrural backgrounds. Even in Coffman's rurally biased sample, nearly half of all teachers came from nonfarm families. Interestingly, a considerably larger proportion of men teachers came from farm backgrounds than women, indicating that teaching may have continued to exert a particularly strong appeal to the sons of farmers in the early twentieth century. Among the women in Coffman's sample, on the other hand, fewer than 45 percent had fathers who were farmers. This undoubtedly reflects the large number of women who worked in urban school systems, most of whom probably came from urban backgrounds.

As Table 1.5 shows, a larger proportion of women than men teachers had fathers who worked as businessmen, artisans, and laborers. If just the teachers from nonfarm backgrounds are considered, however, the proportions of men and women in these categories are quite similar. The male teachers were about evenly divided among those with fathers in the professions, business, skilled labor, and unskilled labor. For nonfarm women the distribution was only a little different, with those from professional backgrounds somewhat more poorly represented than those in the other categories. The largest group of both men and women was those with artisan fathers, representing about 27 percent of the men and 30 percent of the women who did not have farmer fathers. Artisans represented a somewhat smaller portion of the nonfarm labor force, constituting only about a fifth of the nation's urban labor force in 1900. Businessmen and professionals as well were overrepresented among Coffman's teachers.

To the extent that this sample is representative of nonfarm teachers, it appears that American teachers were indeed quite middle-class in origin in the first decade of the twentieth century. Teachers from unskilled working-class backgrounds were in the only group which was substantially underrepresented in Table 1.5.[36] Even though teaching was hardly an elite profession at the turn of the century, it seems to have been a solidly middle-class one, at least judging from the backgrounds of the teachers who participate in Coffman's survey. In this regard it seems to have changed little in the decades since 1850.

American Teachers in 1950

The first half of the twentieth century was a time of rapid change in American life. In 1920 the number of Americans living in cities surpassed the number living on farms, and the following decade witnessed the emergence of a modern, consumer-oriented economy. The thirties and forties were a time of economic difficulty and global conflict, but by 1950 the United States had emerged as the leading nation in the Western world during a new period of prosperity and international stability.

The movement from the countryside to the city accelerated in the thirties and forties, as both depression and war exerted new pressures on the nation's farm economy. Advancing agricultural technology made it possible to attain higher levels of production with less labor, and the expansion of industry during the war years lured men and women from the countryside to the city. As a consequence, in the space of half a century the agricultural sector was reduced from about half of all workers in the country to less than a quarter.

In 1950, new jobs were opening in both the cities and the newly developing suburban communities that surrounded them. Many of these positions were in manufacturing, but even more were in the rapidly growing fields of white-collar work associated with the development of large corporate entities: clerical services, management and marketing, and specialized technical analysis. The appearance of this new configuration of employment marked the first signs of what is today called the postindustrial economy.[37]

There were other important developments that marked the beginning of a new era in American life, some of which held great significance for the nation's school systems. The year 1950 also witnessed the early stages of what has now become popularly known as the Postwar Baby Boom, a dramatic jump in fertility rates which extended from the late forties to the late 1950s. As a result, schools were hit with a flood of children which strained educational resources to new limits. These changes had direct policy consequences. Educators complained about a shortage of teachers throughout the following decade, and school districts began to alter rules regarding age limits for teachers, and the permissibility of married women to teach. At the same time, enrollment rates continued to climb in all parts of the country—perhaps because of changes in the economy—and the curricula of schools everywhere changed to meet the needs and interests of a new clientele.

Regional differences in enrollment, the length of school terms, and other dimensions of educational development diminshed in this period, as the nation's school systems became more uniform (at least in terms of delivering basic educational services). Schooling became an even larger aspect of American life in the wake of changes in both education and the economy. As will be seen below, the nation's teaching population underwent considerable change as well.[38]

Race and Gender in the Teaching Population, 1950

By the middle of the twentieth century, major regional differences in the feminization of teaching had disappeared. In the wake of the teacher shortage in the 1950s, educators no longer complained about the fact that there were three times as many women as men in teaching. On the other hand, important regional differences continued to mark other characteristics of the teaching population, particularly race. The vast majority of the nation's black teachers worked in the South, where most of the black population lived. There was a growing awareness of the importance of race as a factor in American society generally, and in education in particular. When the Supreme Court issued the *Brown* v. *Board of Education* decision in 1954, it was predictable that the issue of racial equality would become a fundamental question for educators throughout the country. Feminization generally had come to be an accepted feature of teaching in the United States, but the plight of black teachers was only beginning to find the attention of policy makers and the public.

No one has adequately studied the disappearance of the sharp regional distinctions in the feminization of teaching that occurred during the first half of the twentieth century. The process may have been associated with longer school terms and improved standards for teacher training and certification in the Southern states. In the generally buoyant postwar economy of 1950, men were unlikely to pursue a career in teaching when it could not be easily combined with other career interests. Feminization may also have resulted partly from the association of teaching with women's work, itself a consequence of the long process of feminization which occurred elsewhere in the nineteenth century.

Whatever the reasons, according to the 1950 federal census the American teaching population was almost universally three-quarters female in the middle of the twentieth century. This suggests that the important urban–rural differences in the feminization of teaching noted earlier had disappeared—or faded substantially—in the decades following Coffman's study. The South remained the least urban and industrial (and the most agricultural and poorest) region in the country, and yet its teaching force was feminized almost exactly to the same extent as were those of the other major regions.

The appearance of a uniform national rate of feminization in teaching at this time is yet more evidence of the manner in which the feminization process was associated with changes in education policy. As the terms of employment for teachers made it difficult or impossible for men to teach as a part-time job, and as teaching required a larger investment in training and certification, teaching everywhere was dominated (at least numerically) by women. The extent of feminization among teachers in 1950 is compelling evidence that American education was indeed becoming uniform. At least with regard to this one important dimension of social origin, the teaching profession shared the same general set of characteristics everywhere.[39]

If teaching was continuing to become a women's profession in the first half of the twentieth century, it also remained a largely white profession. According to the federal census, blacks constituted only about 7 percent of the nation's teachers in 1950, despite the fact that they were slightly more than 10 percent of the general population. Only a slight improvement over the number of black teachers in 1900, this underrepresentation undoubtedly reflected the relatively low number of blacks who could afford the rising costs of teacher training and certification. But it was also a consequence of discriminatory school-system policies—written as well as unwritten.

Not surprisingly, the vast majority of black teachers lived in the South, which still held the nation's largest concentration of blacks. As indicated in Table 1.6, blacks made up more than a fifth of the teaching force in the south, at a time when they constituted about a quarter of the region's population. The existence of this sizeable cadre of black teachers is largely attributable to the growth of segregated school systems in Southern states. Although these schools were markedly inferior in many respects to those provided white children, they did offer an important source of employment to black teachers.

The development of Jim Crow segregation in Southern education, along with a national teacher shortage which undoubtedly permitted white teachers so inclined to eschew service in black schools, help explain a rise in employment for black teachers in the south. In the North and West, where *de jure* segregation was practiced much less frequently and where blacks more often were forced to compete with whites for teaching jobs, black employment in teaching remained deplorably low. As may be seen in Table 1.6, blacks represented less than 2 percent of all teachers in regions outside the South in 1950. Studies of individual cities, moreover indicate that even in the North, where Jim Crow was not an explicit part of the legal structure governing school policies, most black teachers taught in schools which were predominantly black.

Despite signs of a new spirit of equity in public education, a powerful tradition of discrimination hindered the movement of blacks into teaching positions. It would take a massive grassroots civil rights movement, and more than a decade of social turmoil, to begin the process of reversing racial discrimination in teaching.[40]

Black women outnumbered black men in teaching by nearly four to one in 1950,

Table 1.6 American Teachers in 1950: By Principal Regions, Gender, and Race

Region	*Total Male*	*White*	*Black*	*Total Female*	*White*	*Black*
Northeast	73,762	99%	1%	209,806	98.5%	1.5%
North Central	82,139	98	2	247,161	97.9	2.1
South	88,735	81.9	18.1	270,272	78.4	21.6
Pacific	40,973	99.5	.5	107,757	99.1	.9

Source: Figures taken from United States Census, 1950, Vol. 2, *Characteristics of the Population* (Washington, D.C., 1953), Table 158. Teachers classified as "Other Races" have been left out of this analysis, though in no single region did they constitute as much as half of 1 percent of all teachers.

even though their numbers had been much closer at the turn of the century. Indeed, in virtually every region of the country the degree of feminization among black teachers was even greater than it was among whites.[41] This is difficult to explain without further study. Perhaps it was a function of the overall feminization of teaching—in the South particularly. As teaching became identified as a female occupation, it may have become less appealing to black men. On the other hand, school administrators may have preferred working with black women to working with black men, perhaps because they saw them as less threatening or more tractable. Since an even larger proportion of black teaching jobs were at the elementary level than was the case with white teachers, the high degree of feminization also may reflect the preferences of school administrators for women in elementary schools. In any case, the process of feminization among black teachers in the first half of the twentieth century is a historical conundrum which awaits a definitive answer.

Thus, by 1950 teaching had become a predominantly female occupation in all parts of the country, and among both blacks and whites. As had been the case at the turn of the century, women were a considerably larger proportion of elementary teachers than they were of secondary teachers. The overwhelming majority of school administrators were male. Teaching, particularly at the elementary level, had become sex-typed as women's work, and few contemporaries appear to have objected. Given the explosive growth of schools in the years following World War II, school and community leaders seem to have been happy to have women willing to work as teachers. It was in this context that the age structure of the teaching population began to change.

Age Structure of the Teaching Population in 1950

At the turn of the century the overwhelming majority of American teachers were quite young. Fifty years later the age structure of the teaching profession appeared to have changed dramatically. Figure 1.1 depicts the variation in teacher ages across eight age groups for men and women. Perhaps the most remarkable feature of the resulting distributions is the curious bimodal shape of women teachers' age profile. Women apparently entered teaching until they reached their mid-twenties, when they began to leave faster than they entered. This appears to have continued until

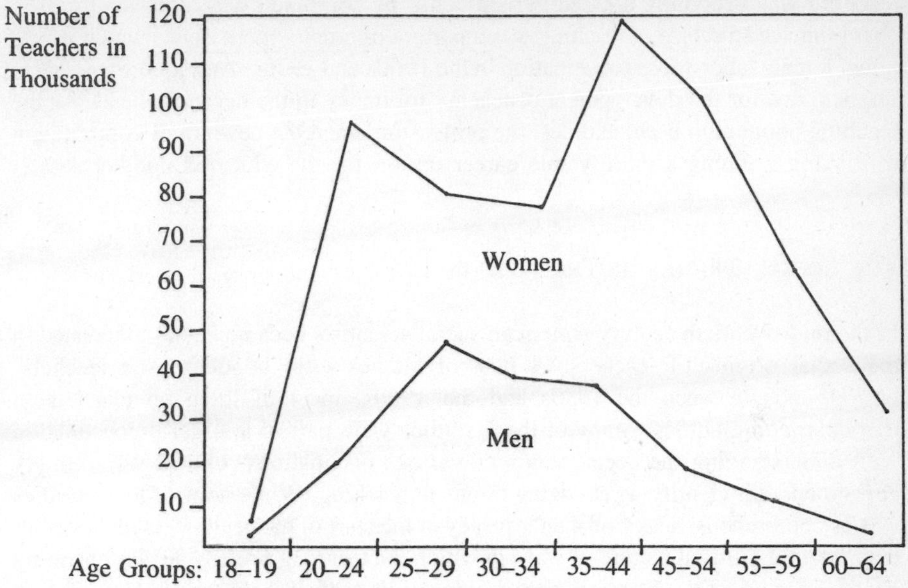

FIGURE 1.1. The Distribution of Teachers' Ages in 1950.

they reached their late thirties, when they began to enter faster than they left. The distribution for men, on the other hand, was quite normal, peaking in the 25-to-29 age bracket, and then declining as they got older and left teaching. The median ages for these groups probably were quite similar, but it was the movement of older women into teaching which accounted for the new maturity in the female teaching population.

In 1950 women still accounted for a large majority of the teachers in the United States, but were quite different from their counterparts some fifty years earlier. By the mid-twentieth century, women in teaching were more mature, less tractable, and increasingly interested in having a career outside of their families.[42]

The most obvious explanation for the bimodal distribution of women teachers' ages is the return of married women to teaching after their own children had entered school or left home. The Depression and World War II combined to end the malingering nineteenth-century taboo against married women working, and by the start of the 1950s a growing proportion of the women teachers in the United States were former domestic housewives. This was a development with enormous implications for the future of teaching. It meant that school administrators no longer dealt with a teaching corps which looking upon teaching as a middle passage between adolescence and marriage. Rather, they now contended with a growing number of women teachers concerned with teaching as a long-term career. This, coupled with the teacher shortage, gave teachers new power to improve working conditions and to raise salaries. Teacher unions, once restricted to a few large cities, became larger and extended their reach to smaller districts across the country.

While teacher turnover remained an important problem in public education, fewer teachers were leaving education altogether. Now, for women as well as men, teaching was becoming a career which could be combined with domesticity. The changing age structure of teaching was a portent of employment trends which would affect female labor-force participation in the 1960s and 1970s. And it bore important implications for the development of teacher militancy in the decades ahead. As the teaching population became older, the profession entered a new era of commitment to making teaching a more viable career option for the educated middle class.[43]

The Social Origins of Teachers in 1950

In the mid-twentieth century American social scientists became keenly interested in the social origins of teachers. A host of studies were conducted on teachers' backgrounds between the 1930s and the 1960s, most of them on teachers in particular communities. Many of these studies were part of a larger preoccupation with understanding the social status of various occupations. Others were simply concerned with identifying changing trends in teaching. While none of these studies was as comprehensive as Coffman's survey at the start of the century, taken together they do offer a useful picture of ways in which the teaching profession was changing in this period. Documenting the social origins of American teachers in the mid-twentieth century thus becomes easier than it was in earlier periods. The difficult part is interpreting the significance of disparate studies, each of which is rather narrowly focused on teachers in a particular locale. With a little effort, however, it is possible to construct a reasonably representative profile of American teachers in the 1950s.

Table 1.7 presents the results of three separate studies of the social origins of American teachers in the decade following 1950.[44] The categories employed in this table are purposefully vague. Although they represent distinct levels of social status (defined by occupation, wealth, education, residential area, and a number of other

Table 1.7 Social Origins of American Teachers in the 1950s: The Results of Three Studies

Social Origins	*Wattenberg, et al. (1957) Michigan (N = 240)*	*McGuire & White (1957) Texas (N = 150)*	*Carlson (1960) Bay Area (N = 304)*	*Pop. Est.*
Upper class	>23%	2%	4.4%	2
Upper middle class		35	16.7	10
Lower middle class	23	45	47.3	31
Working class	37	19	32.7	57

Social class categories and general population estimates for each category are adapted from Richard O. Carlson, "Variation and Myth in the Social Status of Teachers," *Journal of Educational Sociology* 35 (November 1961), pp. 11–113. Carlson took these categories and figures from Robert J. Havighurst and Bernice L. Neugarten, *Society and Education* (Boston: Allyn & Bacon, 1957), p. 18. They were meant to be representative of "communities with population from 5,000 to 100,000" at that time.

factors), they also correspond to popular perceptions of ranks in the modern status hierarchy. In two of the three studies these groupings have been defined in generally similar terms. In the third, which examines the social origin of teachers in Michigan, only occupational background information was provided. For purposes of consistency I have adapted these occupational rankings to the general status groups used in the other studies. Table 1.7 also includes estimates of the sizes of these different status categories for the general population, based on studies conducted in American communities during the fifties. While this mixing of classification schemes may not be methodologically pure, it does permit general comparisons of the results of studies conducted in communities in different parts of the country in this period. On the basis of Table 1.7, it appears that the findings of all three studies reveal a number of underlying consistencies.

Perhaps the most important finding revealed in Table 1.7 is the manner in which teachers from working-class backgrounds were underrepresented in all three samples. On the other hand, teachers from upper-class (including upper middle-class) backgrounds were overrepresented. There were marked differences in the sizes of these categories form one sample to another, some of which can be attributed to differences in the occupational structures of the communities being studied. These differences also may be due to inconsistencies in the definition of these categories for each sample. Even so, the general structure of the teaching force in all three communities was strikingly similar.

In general, teachers appear to have been drawn largely from the ranks of middle-class Americans in the 1950s. While the two middle-class categories in Table 1.7 constituted roughly 40 percent of the nation's population in the 1950s, they accounted for about 60 percent of the teachers in all three samples. A sizeable but much smaller fraction came from working-class backgrounds. Teaching was a solidly middle-class profession by the middle of the twentieth century, one which permitted a degree of status maintenance for many in the middle class and a small degree of social mobility for a number of others in the working class.

The backgrounds of teachers varied from one context to another. As noted above, a good deal of the variation in teacher backgrounds from one sample to another in Table 1.7 was probably due to differences in the occupational structures of the communities they were drawn from. Wattenberg's survey of teachers in Michigan, for instance, was taken primarily from Detroit, a large manufacturing center with proportionally fewer middle-class jobs than other cities. If Wattenberg had defined his background variable in residential terms (as Carlson did) or with a composite of characteristics (as McGuire and White did), instead of simply by occupation, the results of his analysis might have looked somewhat different. But it probably is also true that a larger proportion of teachers in communities such as Detroit, where most of the labor force holds blue-collar jobs, will have working-class backgrounds. The social background of teachers, after all, is partly a function of the peculiar mix of possibilities in each setting. When Wattenberg compared the backgrounds of teachers in Detroit with those working in rural schools, he found that a much higher proportion of the Detroit teachers hailed from blue-collar backgrounds than those in the country, where more came from farm families (classified as lower middle-class in Table 1.7). This is why it is critical to examine the results of a number of surveys, in order to construct a reasonably representative portrait of American teachers and their social origins at a given time.

Community differences aside, it also appears that there were important gender differences in the social background characteristics of American teachers. At the turn of the century, women teachers appear to have come from urban backgrounds, while a greater proportion of the men were from farm families. This may have been the case in the 1950s as well, although it is impossible to tell with the data on hand.

Two of the surveys cited in Table 1.7, however, provide information on the social background of men and women teachers in terms of the broad status categories discussed above. In general, they found that women teachers came from higher social status groups than did men teachers. In Carlson's study of teachers in the greater San Francisco area, women elementary teachers were four times as likely to come from upper middle or upper-class backgrounds as were men in secondary schools, even though they outnumbered them by almost two to one. The men, on the other hand, were more than twice as likely as the women to have come from working-class backgrounds. As Carlson notes, these differences would be a little less pronounced if male elementary teachers and female secondary teachers were included in the comparisons, but important gender differences in background remained independent of the level of schools involved.

McGuire and White found a similar pattern in their survey of teachers in Texas, although the differences probably were not quite as pronounced. There, some 35 percent of female elementary school teachers were from upper middle or upper-class backgrounds. The number of men teachers from similar backgrounds is difficult to determine because McGuire and White included administrators in their sample, but it may have been as low as a quarter. Other studies from this period report similar findings. In most parts of the country women teachers, it appears, came from generally higher social backgrounds than did their male colleagues.[46]

Perhaps the best explanation of this gender-determined distinction in the social origins of teachers at the time under consideration is associated with the different job prospects for middle- and upper-class men and women then. Since the fifties was a period of growth in the economy, educated men from middle- and upper-class families generally enjoyed an expanding range of opportunities in high-status occupations. Educated women from similar backgrounds, on the other hand, faced much more restricted professional employment opportunities. Teaching was one of only a few occupational choices available to women at that time which carried a degree of professional status. It is also possible, of course, that many young women from high-status backgrounds had *mothers* who had been teachers at one point in their lives, and that they had grown up with teaching as a preferred occupational choice. A number of studies have noted the relatively large number of women teachers who reported having former teachers as mothers. Thus it is of little surprise to see a higher proportion of middle- and upper-class women than men in teaching.

For working-class men, teaching offered a modest opportunity for social mobility, and the benefits of a higher level of income and employment security than most blue-collar jobs. And with the availability of government-subsidized higher education through the GI Bill, many young men from working-class backgrounds were able to think of teaching as a realistic career alternative. As a consequence, a subtle class distinction separated male and female teachers in the mid-twentieth century. For many women, teaching was a means of status maintenance, while for men it more often served as an avenue of social mobility. As in earlier periods in American history, the fact that women were restricted to a narrow range of professional career options meant that teaching attracted a disproportionately large number of well-educated and talented women from relatively high-status backgrounds. For men, on the other hand, teaching appears to have functioned as an important means of entering the educated professions. The realities of sex-differentiated labor markets continued to shape the social profile of American teachers through the first half of the twentieth century.[47]

Epilogue: Teachers in the 1980s

The three decades following 1950 were a time of continued change in American life. The civil rights movement and the rediscovery of urban poverty in the 1960s helped to make education an important national priority. At the same time, teachers succeeded in organizing powerful national unions to represent their interests, and as a consequence salaries and working conditions improved in many schools.

Attracted to teaching by the enhanced attention given education, a new generation of teachers dedicated themselves to making a career therein. Accordingly, the social composition of the teaching population began to change once again, this time reflecting a somewhat higher level of recognition of the teaching profession's importance in the life of the nation. This pattern of change continued until the 1980s, when trends in female employment began to open new doors to educated women. Slowly the ratio of women to men in teaching began to shift away from greater feminization. Recessions in the 1970s and 1980s, coupled with enrollment declines due to lowering birth rates, led to cuts in staffing which eliminated the jobs of many younger teachers. As a consequence, the mean age of teachers rose nearly everywhere.

Now, as a new generation of young children is beginning to enter the schools in large numbers, and as older teachers approach retirement, many areas of the country are facing the prospect of teacher shortages. Given the changing character of female labor-force participation in the past two decades, and the still relatively low salaries paid to teachers, school administrators may be hard-pressed to find capable teachers in the years ahead.

The reforms of the 1960s and 1970s in education had important consequences for the social composition of teaching in the United States. The civil rights movement opened higher education to blacks and other minorities on a scale unprecedented in American history. By the mid-seventies, blacks were represented among the nation's college students at about the same level as they were in the population at large.[48] This, coupled with public pressure on school districts in many parts of the country to hire minority teachers, led to a rise in the number of black teachers nationally. By 1980 nearly 10 percent of the nation's teachers were black, a higher proportion than at any earlier point in history. This also reflected the continuing appeal of teaching as a career choice among black Americans, and perhaps continuing problems with educated blacks' gaining access to other professions.

Even with increased representation in the teaching force, however, black teachers continued to lag far behind the size of the black student population in proportional terms. Because of somewhat higher fertility rates among black families, the number of black students grew faster than the student population of other groups. And the proportion of black students in *public* schools grew even faster, as large numbers of white parents sent their children to private schools in the 1970s and 1980s. As a consequence, school administrators in some parts of the country face a situation where a third or more of their students are from minority backgrounds, while a much smaller proportion of their teachers are.

Although the number of black teachers reached a relatively high level in the 1980s, an even larger number of blacks must be recruited to teaching in the future if the need for a proportionally representative body of minority teachers is to be met. Because of declining black college enrollments in the eighties, and new challenges to minority teachers posed by revised certification standards and competence testing for teachers, this goal may be difficult to reach.[49]

As education became a national issue in the 1960s and 1970s, and as teacher unions gradually pushed salary levels up, the number of men in teaching began to rise slowly. In 1980, men constituted nearly 30 percent of all the teachers in the country, up some 20 percent (in proportional terms) from three decades earlier. At the same time, female labor-force participation increased substantially, especially in the professions. It is not clear whether the movement of women into other professional fields and into business has seriously affected the supply of women interested in teaching, particularly since female enrollments in colleges have increased as well. But given the movement of women into other fields, and the greater interest exhibited by men in teaching, it is unlikely that feminization will occur again at the level seen in earlier periods.[50]

As regards the social origins of teachers in the eighties, most appear to have come from backgrounds quite similar to those in earlier decades. Although there have been only a few studies of teachers' social origins since 1970, all have shown generally the same patterns evident in 1950. By-and-large, women teachers still come from somewhat higher socioeconomic backgrounds than their male counterparts, and a higher proportion of men than women come into teaching from working-class backgrounds. Overall, however, teaching remains a disproportionately middle-class occupation into the closing decade of the twentieth century. There appears to be little reason to expect this to change in the foreseeable future.[51]

Perhaps the most important change in the social characteristics of American teachers is age. In 1980 the mean age of male teachers was slightly over 36; for women teachers it was about 35. In this regard the social profile of teachers in the 1980s was similar to that of the 1950s, but quite different from what it had been at the turn of the century. Teachers may have been older in 1980 partly because of shifting employment patterns in some districts where fewer younger teachers were hired due to cutbacks or enrollment declines. But, just as in 1950, the overall age structure reflected a commitment to teaching as a career which was *not* generally evident in earlier periods of American history, particularly among women.[52]

Even though turnover among teachers remained greater than in other professions, a considerably higher proportion of teachers remained in the profession than before World War II. While this trend may have created new problems, such as "teacher burnout" and cynicism in some older teachers, it moved teaching closer to becoming a commonplace career for more teachers than ever before. Teaching, though still not an established profession in the sense that law or medicine were, clearly stood on a better footing that it had through most of American history.

Conclusion

What points can we make about the social characteristics of American teachers through their history? First, teaching appears to have always been a generally middle-class profession, though perhaps somewhat less so than other educated professions in the United States. While teaching has been an important avenue for mobility for individuals (mainly men) from working-class backgrounds, the middle and upper middle classes have been disproportionally represented among the nation's teachers.

Second, since the mid-nineteenth century, teaching has been predominantly a female profession. While the proportion of teachers who were women reached 80 percent in the early twentieth century, it has recently declined slightly to about 70 percent. Feminization appears to have been due largely to the movement of men out of the profession as it became more difficult to combine teaching with other careers, and to growing demand for teachers, particularly in the nation's urban–industrial areas. Now, improved working conditions and salaries for teachers appear to have drawn men back into the profession, at a time when educated women are finding a variety of new career options available to them. It appears that feminization either may remain stable or decline in the future.

Finally, while teachers have historically been quite young, most of them teaching for only a short time before moving on to some other career, since World War II large numbers of teachers appear to have remained in the profession for a substantial length of time. Perhaps the most important dimension of this change has concerned women, most of whom left teaching for marriage at the turn of the century. From 1950 onward, women teachers have either remained in the profession after marriage, or returned to teaching after a short absence to care for their young children.

The arrival of large numbers of older women teachers in the 1950s and 1960s undoubtedly had an important impact on the evolution of the teaching profession in the United States. The precise effect of this change in the social composition of the nation's teaching population has not been assessed by historians. It is hoped that the chapters in this volume will mark the beginning of a new effort to identify the implications of changes now occurring in the teaching population.

Notes

AUTHOR'S NOTE: The author gratefully acknowledges the helpful comments of Les Goodchild, William Reese, David Tyack, Donald Warren, and Richard Yanikoski on earlier drafts of this essay. Any remaining inaccuracies or other shortcomings are my responsibility alone.

1. See Albert Szymanski, *Class Structure: A Critical Perspective* (New York: Praeger Publishers, 1983), *passim,* for a useful discussion of these issues.
2. Dan Lortie, *Schoolteacher: A Sociological Study* (Chicago: University of Chicago Press, 1975), pp. 6–13.
3. For discussion of this question, see Myra H. Strober and David B. Tyack, "Why Do Women Teach and Men Manage? A Report of Research on Schools," in *Signs: Journal of Women In Culture and Society* 5:3 (Spring 1980), pp. 494–503.
4. David Tyack, "An American Tradition: The Changing Role of Schooling and Teaching," in *Harvard Educational Review* 57:2 (May 1987), pp. 171–174.
5. Lawrence Cremin, *American Education: The Colonial Experience, 1607–1783* (New York: Harper & Row, 1970), Part II, "Institutions."
6. Ibid., pp. 184–192.
7. On the Southern colonies, see Jackson Turner Main, *The Social Structure of Revolutionary America* (Princeton, NJ: Princeton University Press, 1965), Ch. 2. On education in the South at this time, see Cremin, American Education: The Colonial Experience, Part VI.
8. Carl F. Kaestle, *The Evolution of an Urban School System: New York City, 1750–1850* (Cambridge, MA: Harvard University Press, 1973), pp. 5–7, 37–55.
9. James Axtell, *The School upon a Hill: Education and Society in Colonial New England* (New Haven, CN: Yale University Press, 1974), pp. 187–190.
10. Jo Anne Preston, "Feminization of an Occupation: Teaching Becomes Women's Work in Nineteenth Century New England" (unpublished Ph.D. Dissertation, Brandeis University, 1982), Ch. 2.
11. Cremin, *American Education,* Part VI; Axtel, *The School upon a Hill,* Ch. 5.
12. Carl F. Kaestle, *Pillars of the Republic: Common Schools and American Society, 1780–1860* (New York: Hill & Wang, 1983), *passim;* and Alice Felt Tyler, *Freedom's Ferment: Phases of American Social History from the Colonial Period to the Outbreak of the Civil War* (Minneapolis: University of Minnesota Press, 1944), *passim.*
13. There are serious limitations in the use of manuscript census data to study the social characterizations of teachers as well. The biggest problem concerns the study of teachers' social origins. Since the census does not provide information on the parents of individuals unless they happen to live together, it is impossible to determine the background characteristics of teachers living away from home. For this reason one must have survey data which directly represent family backgrounds of teachers in order to study adequately their social origins. For an account of the enumeration techniques used in the 1850 census, see U.S. Bureau of the Census, *The Seventh Census of the United States, 1850* (Washington, DC: Government Printing Office, 1853), pp. v–xiv.
14. John L. Rury, "Gender, Salaries and Career: American Teachers, 1900–1910," in *Issues in Education* 4:3 (Winter 1986), pp. 216–218; Myra H. Strober and Audri Gordon Lanford, "The Feminization of Public School Teaching: Cross Sectional Analysis, 1850–1880," in *Signs: Journal of Women in Culture and Society* 11:2 (Winter 1986), pp. 212–235; and Thomas Morain, "The Departure of Males from the Teaching Profession in Nineteenth Century Iowa," in *Civil War History* 26:2 (Summer 1980), pp. 161–170.
15. For a discussion of the regional diversity of American culture at this time, see Merril Jensen (ed.), *Regionalism in*

American History (Madison, WI: University of Wisconsin Press, 1951), *passim*. On the question of social and economic development, see Harvey Perloff, Edgar S. Dunn Jr., Erik E. Lampard, and Richard F. Muth, *Regions, Resources and Economic Growth* (Baltimore: Johns Hopkins University Press, 1960), *passim*. On regional diversity as it related to education, see Lawrence Cremin, *American Education: The National Experience* (New York: Harper & Row, 1979), Ch. 12. Also see Kaestle, *Pillars of the Republic*, Ch. 8.

16. The number of women teachers in each state is not directly provided by the 1950 federal census. The figures used in this study have been derived by subtracting the number of men (listed as teachers under the enumeration of males employed in various occupations) from the total number of teachers in each state (listed with the education statistics). For an example of these figures in one state, see U.S. Bureau of the Census, *The Seventh Census of the United States*, pp. 9–11.

17. John Rury, "The New York African Free School, 1825–1835: Conflict over Community Control," *Phylon* 45:3 (September 1983), pp. 187–198; *Idem.*, "Race and Common School Reform: The Strange Career of the NYSPECC, 1847–1860," *Urban Education* 20:4 (October 1986), pp. 473–492; and Stanley K. Schultz, *The Culture Factory: Public Schooling in Boston, 1790–1860* (New York: Oxford University Press, 1973), Chs. 5, 7, and 8.

18. Normal-school records, though an important source of information, are limited in scope because they probably are characteristic of only one region. Furthermore, only a small fraction of the teachers in this period ever attended a normal school. Until the twentieth century, when improved standards of teacher certification began to be enforced, most teachers barely possessed the equivalent of a high-school education and generally had little, if any, training in teaching methods. Because of this, the use of normal-school records as a source of information about teachers in this period must be approached cautiously. Because many prospective teachers simply could not afford to attend school for any length of time, normal-school students may have come disproportionately from the middle and upper classes. Still, looking at normal-school students can be a revealing way of determining which social and economic groups supplied teachers in the mid-nineteenth century. Perhaps the best introduction to the history of normal schools can be found in Willard Elsbree, *The American Teacher: Evolution of a Profession in a Democracy* (New York: American Book Co., 1939), Ch. 12. Also see Paul H. Mattingly, *The Classless Profession: American Schoolmen in The Nineteenth Century* (New York: New York University Press, 1975), Ch. 7.

19. Richard Bernard and Maris A. Vinovskis, "The Female School Teacher in Ante Bellum Massachusetts," in *Journal of Social History* 10 (Spring 1977), pp. 332–345.

20. Ibid., pp. 333–334.

21. Mattingly, *The Classless Profession*, pp. 135–142.

22. For an overview of social and economic development during this period, see Robert Higgs, *The Transformation of American Society, 1870–1914* (Englewood Cliffs, NJ: Prentice–Hall, 1974), *passim*. On the educational system, see David B. Tyack, *The One Best System* (Cambridge, MA: Harvard University Press, 1974), *passim*.

23. For an overview of the feminization process, see Strober and Lanford, "The Feminization of Public School Teaching," *passim;* Redding S. Sugg, Jr., *Motherteacher: The Feminization of American Education* (Charlottesville, VA: University of Virginia Press, 1978), *passim;* and Morain, "The Departure of Males from the Teaching Profession in Nineteenth Century Iowa," *passim*.

24. John L. Rury, "The Variable School Year: Measuring American School Terms in 1900," in *Journal of Research and Development in Education* 21:3 (Spring 1988), pp. 29–36.

25. John L. Rury, "American School Enrollment in the Progressive Era: An Interpretive Inquiry," in *History of Education (UK)* 13:1 (March 1985), pp. 49–67.
26. Rury, "Gender, Salaries and Career," pp. 216–232.
27. David Tyack and Elisabeth Hansot, *Managers of Virtue: Public School Leadership in America, 1820–1980* (New York: Basic Books, 1982), *passim.*
28. Rury, "Gender, Salaries and Career," pp. 219–223; and Susan B. Carter, "Occupational Segregation, Teacher Wages and American Economic Growth," in *Journal of Economic History* 56:2 (June 1986), pp. 373–383.
29. Rury, "Gender, Salaries and Career," pp. 216–231.
30. On the question of black education in the early twentieth century, see Horace Mann Bond, *Education of the Negro in the American Social Order* (New York: Prentice–Hall, 1934), Part II; on educational inequality in the South, see Louis Harlan, *Separate and Unequal: Public Schools and Racism in the Southern Seaboard States, 1901–1915* (New York: Antheneum, 1968), *passim.* Statistics are from U.S. Bureau of the Census, *Population, 1900,* Vol. I (Washington, DC: Government Printing Office, 1902), "Special Reports: Teachers," p. 482.
31. U.S. Bureau of the Census, *Population, 1900,* "Teachers," p. 484. On religious orders in the schools of one city, see James Sanders, *The Education of an Urban Minority, Catholics in Chicago, 1833–1965* (New York: Oxford University Press, 1977), pp. 144–147.
32. U.S. Bureau of the Census, *Population, 1900,* "Teachers," p. 489. Also see the discussion of immigrant women teaching in Nancy Hoffman, *Women's "True" Profession: Voices from the History of Teaching* (New York: Feminist Press, 1979), Part III; and Maxine Seller, *Immigrant Women* (Philadelphia: Temple University Press, 1982), Part VI.
33. Lotus Delta Coffman, *The Social Composition of the Teaching Population* (New York: Teachers College Press, 1911), *passim;* National Education Association, *Report of the Committee on Salaries, Tenure, and Pensions of Public School Teachers of the United States* (Winona, MN: National Education Association, 1905), *passim;* and National Education Association, *Report of the Committee on Teachers' Salaries and the Cost of Living* (Ann Arbor, MI: National Education Association, 1913), *passim.*
34. On Coffman's sampling technique, see *The Social Composition of the Teaching Population,* Ch. 1.
35. Ibid., pp. 72–73.
36. Interestingly, an examination of manuscript census data from 1900 reveals much the same result. Some 258 women teachers drawn from the 1900 *Public Use Sample,* a 1/750 sample of the entire U.S. population at the turn of the century, indicates that nearly two-thirds had fathers, or other relatives with whom they lived, working as businessmen or professionals. Barely a quarter, on the other hand, had relatives from working-class backgrounds. Of course, this sample is limited to those teachers who lived at home or with a relative, and may exclude many working-class women for whom such options did not exist. This, again, is a critical limitation of census data for determining background characteristics. Even so, the degree to which the background characteristics in this group reveal a solidly middle-class background for women teachers at this time is striking. For more information about the *Public Use Sample,* see Center for Studies in Demography and Ecology, University of Washington, *U.S. Census Data, 1900: Public Use Sample* (Ann Arbor: ICPSR, 1981), *passim.*
37. Godfrey Hodgson, *America in Our Time: From World War II to Nixon* (New York: Vintage Books, 1976), Chs. 1–4.
38. Diane Ravitch, *The Troubled Crusade: American Education Since 1945* (New York: Basic Books, 1964), Chs. 1 and 2.

39. U.S. Bureau of the Census, *Characteristics of the Population, 1950*, Summary Volume II (Washington, DC: U.S. Government Printing Office, 1951), Table 1–19.
40. Ibid. Also see Ravitch, *The Troubled Crusade*, Ch. 4; and Richard Kluger, *Simple Justice* (New York: Vintage Books, 1975), Part I.
41. U.S. Bureau of the Census, *Characteristics of the Population, 1950* (Washington, DC: Government Printing Office, 19—), Table 1–19. In 1900 there was less feminization among black teachers than whites, even outside the South, perhaps because so few other professional career options existed for black men. See U.S. Bureau of the Census, *Population, 1900,* Teachers,'' p. 482.
42. U.S. Bureau of the Centus, *Characteristics of the Population, 1950*, pp. 1–274.
43. David B. Tyack and Myra H. Strober, ''Jobs and Gender: A History of the Structuring of Educational Employment by Sex,'' in Patricia Schmuck, W. W. Charters Jr., and Richard O. Carlson (eds.), *Educational Policy and Management: Sex Differentials* (New York: Academic Press, 1981), pp. 146–147.
44. Chronologically, the first two of these studies both appeared in the same volume, Lindley J. Stiles, *The Teacher's Role in American Society* (New York: Harper & Bros., 1957): William Wattenberg et al., ''Social Origins of Teachers—a Northern Industrial City,'' pp. 13–22; and Carson McGuire and George D. White, ''The Social Origins of Teachers—in Texas,'' pp. 23–41. The third study was Richard O. Carlson, ''Variation and Myth in the Social Status of Teachers,'' in *Journal of Educational Sociology* 35 (November 1961), pp. 104–118.
45. Wattenberg and his associates did not use the general background characteristics employed in Table 7. Rather, they grouped teachers by their fathers' occupational backgrounds. For the sake of consistency, I have rearranged these groups in the following fashion: ''Professional'' and ''Business, etc.,'' have been defined as ''Upper and Upper Middle Class''; ''Other White Collar'' has been defined as ''Lower Middle Class''; ''Skilled Labor'' and ''Other Labor'' have been defined as ''Working Class.'' This may bring some distortion to the analysis associated with Table 7, but I believe these categories to be generally interchangeable. Nearly a fifth of the teachers in the Wattenberg study reported their fathers ''Unemployed, retired or dead.'' This group has been eliminated for purposes of this discussion. See Wattenberg et al., ''Social Origins of Teachers,'' p. 16.
46. For a useful discussion of this issue and a good summary of disparate studies, see Michael Sedlack and Steven Schlossman, ''Who Will Teach: Historical Perspectives on the Changing Appeal of Teaching as a Profession,'' in Ernst Z. Rothkopf (ed.), *Review of Research in Education* 14 (Washington: AERA, 1987), pp. 93–132.
47. For a general discussion of factors which have prevented women from working in the professions, see Shirley Dex, *The Sexual Division of Labor: Conceptual Revolutions in the Social Sciences* (New York: St. Martin's Press, 1985), Chs. 4 and 5. For a historical overview of women in the United States, see Lynn Y. Weiner, *From Working Girl to Working Mother: The Female Labor Force in the United States, 1820–1980* (Chapel Hill, NC: University of North Carolina Press, 1985), Part II.
48. See the discussion of these issues in Ravitch, *The Troubled Crusade*, Chs. 4 and 5. On the problems of minority teachers in the eighties, see Harvey Pressman and Alan Gartner, ''The New Racism in Education,'' in *Social Policy* 17:1 (September 1986), pp. 11–15.
49. Ravitch, *The Troubled Crusade*, Ch. 8; U.S. Bureau of the Census, *Characteristics of the Population, 1980: U.S. Summary*, Vol. I (Washington, DC: Government Printing Office, 1982), pp. 1–197.
50. U.S. Census, *Characteristics of the Population, 1980: U.S. Summary*, Vol. I, pp. 1–233 to 1–235. See the discussion of women moving into new areas of

employment in Julie A. Matthaei, ''The Breakdown of the Sex-Typing of Jobs,'' in *An Economic History of Women in America: Women's Work, the Sexual Division of Labor, and the Development of Capitalism* (New York: Schocken Books, 1982), Ch. 12.

51. For recent analyses of the social characteristics of teachers, see Ronald M. Pavalko, ''Recruitment to Teaching: Patterns of Selection and Retention,'' in *Sociology of Education* 43 (Summer 1970), pp. 340–353; Lortie, *Schoolteacher,* Ch. 2; and Anthony Gary Dworkin, ''The Changing Demography of Public School Teachers: Some Implications for Faculty Turnover in Urban Areas,'' in *Sociology of Education* 53 (April 1980), pp. 65–73.

52. U.S. Bureau of the Census, *Characteristics of the Population, 1980: U.S. Summary,* Vol. I, pp. 1–233 to 1–235.

2

Incentives and Rewards to Teaching

Susan B. Carter

Teachers have always been poorly paid relative to the skills their positions require. In the antebellum era, male teachers in urban areas earned only 80 percent of the salaries of fledgling civil engineers, and only a fifth of those of civil engineers with experience.[1] Salaries of rural teachers were lower still, about 85 percent of the earnings of unskilled male laborers.[2] In 1900 the average annual earnings of public school teachers were only 75 percent of those of manufacturing workers, and about a third those of postal and federal employees.[3] Male graduates of the land-grant colleges and universities who were high school teachers in 1930 earned 60 percent of the salaries garnered by civil engineers, and 32 percent of what physicians were earning.[4]

Teachers' salaries continue to be low today. Starting salary offers to bachelor's degree recipients going into public school teaching in 1985 were 82 percent of those of liberal arts majors, 77 percent of those of business administration graduates, and 57 percent of those of engineering majors.[5] Perhaps because of the small financial rewards, the phrase "incentives and rewards to teaching" often is taken to mean the challenges and personal satisfactions associated with the education of the young.[6] No one, it would seem, teaches for the money.

This chapter, however, focuses exclusively on the monetary incentives and rewards to teaching. The rationale for this approach is an assumption that the educational system is too large to be staffed entirely by "born teachers," those who would be in the classroom no matter how bad the pay and working conditions. If this assumption is correct, then an understanding of changes in the supply of teachers requires an understanding of the decision-making process of those with many talents and interests who consider a variety of careers in addition to teaching. For these, the likelihood of becoming a teacher has been shown to depend upon the rewards to teaching relative to rewards in other available occupations. Among the rewards which are easily measured, salary has been shown to have a large effect on supply.[7]

The first section of this chapter addresses the question of how the schools have managed to recruit good teachers for so long, given the low salaries they pay. The answer, I argue, is that teaching accepts many who suffer employment discrimination in other sectors. To them, teachers' wages may not seem so low.[8]

Who May Choose to Teach?

Until recently, employment in many of the professions and in almost all of the skilled trades was limited to white males. Access to the skilled trades was largely controlled by unionized white male craftsmen who organized and administered apprenticeship and training programs. Blacks, the foreign-born, and women were routinely denied entry into these programs and, by extension, the trade.[9] In fields such as medicine and law, professional schools' discriminatory admissions policies limited enrollments, and therefore employment, to white men.[10] Not until the 1960s and 1970s were many of the restrictions on the admission of women and minorities overturned.[11] By contrast, the teaching profession has been extraordinarily accessible. Blacks and whites, women and men have had teacher training and employment opportunities from a comparatively early date.

White women's access to teaching opportunities followed closely upon their entry into the schools as students. By 1850 in Massachusetts, girls' attendance rates were nearly equal to those of boys.[12] By 1870, women constituted 87 percent of all Massachusetts teachers.[13] Nor was white women's access to teaching opportunities diminished with the extension of schooling to the higher grades, or by the spread of credentialling requirements. Girls outnumbered boys in the high schools at the turn of the century, and accounted for over a third of all college students.[14] Their qualifications increased in equal measure with the educational requirements of the teaching profession.

Teacher training opportunities for black men and women actually preceded the appearance of mass educational opportunities for the black population. A handful of blacks received teacher training in the antebellum era at a time when those who were enslaved were denied instruction in even the rudiments of reading and writing.[15] After Emancipation, literally hundreds of normal schools, colleges, and universities for blacks were founded by Northern missionary and church groups, many with the express purpose of training black teachers.[16] At the same time, black leaders struggled in vain to establish more broad-based educational opportunities. Racism and poverty so thwarted these ambitions that in 1869 only 7 percent of the black school-age popoulation in the "Cotton South" were enrolled.[17]

The establishment of state school systems in the South in the 1870s and 1880s produced a rise in black enrollments, although the segregation embodied in them meant that the quality and quantity of black educational options were inferior to those of whites.[18] Robert Margo estimates that blacks born between 1886 and 1890 attended only 44 percent as many months of school as the average white. The 22 months of schooling indicated by this estimate led to literacy as defined by the census, but probably not much more (in Margo's view).[19] Segregated schools did create jobs for black teachers, however.[20] As late as 1950, nearly half of all black professionals were teachers, as compared with less than a quarter of white professionals.[21]

The enormous racial differential in educational attainment began to diminish in the 1940s, first with the large-scale migration of blacks out of the rural South, and then with the success of political and legal efforts to end the segregation of schools. The ratio of median years of schooling for blacks rose to 72 percent of the level of whites by 1950. By 1970 the ratio was 96 percent.[22] Although the end of legal racial segregation also did away with *de jure* black schools, the major employer of black teachers, these teachers' employment opportunities were buoyed by an increase in black voting power. Richard Freeman finds that:

> In the South, where segregation had created an especially favorable market for black teachers, some teachers and many principals were displaced, but the potentially disastrous effects of desegregation on teacher employment did not occur. In the North, demand increased greatly.[23]

In short, teaching has been accessible to white women as well as to white men from the mid-nineteenth century onward. Since educational opportunities for blacks have been far inferior to those of whites, blacks' access to all occupations requiring formal education—teaching included—has been more limited than has access for whites. Among occupations requiring formal education, however, teaching has imposed few *additional* barriers. Thus, among the skilled occupations it has been one of the most accessible to educated black men and women.

The Attractions of Teaching for White Men

In the early nineteenth century, when school terms were short and formal qualifications minimal, white men took teaching positions despite the low wages. Because teaching could be combined with other pursuits, it served as a means of earning income while getting established, much like digging the Erie Canal or doing farm labor. Lewis Stillman describes Vermont men who early in the nineteenth century financed their westward migration by brief stints teaching in schools along their route: "[T]eaching served as one of the easiest means of getting out of Vermont for any boy with more than a smattering of book learning."[24] Men planning to enter legal or religious careers often financed their education by teaching. The short teaching terms also meant that teaching could be carried out by farmers and artisans during the off season. Those aspiring to the ministry, politics, and the law could also use teaching as a means of gaining visibility within their communities.[25]

As the school term was lengthened and credentialling requirements were established, opportunities to combine teaching with other pursuits were reduced. Figure 2.1 presents evidence which indicates that teachers' wages did rise relative to those in other occupations as more was required of teachers. It shows the ratio of the weekly wage of urban male teachers to that of artisans and of laborers, annually between 1841 and 1920. Male teachers in urban areas were earning about 140 percent of the wage of urban artisans (such as carpenters and mechanics) in 1841, and roughly 250 percent of the average earnings of unskilled laborers. By the mid-1870s, teachers' salaries were over 200 percent those of artisans and 400 percent those of laborers.

After a drop in the late 1870s, the ratios remained at 200 and 375 percent respectively, to the eve of World War I. During World War I, teachers lost ground relative to artisans and laborers, although they were able to regain their position in

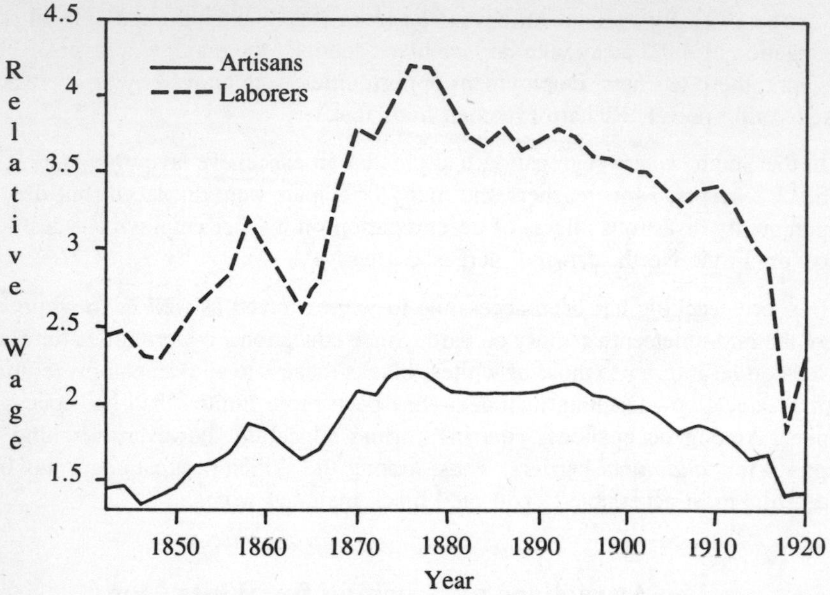

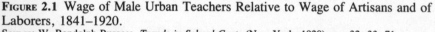

FIGURE 2.1 Wage of Male Urban Teachers Relative to Wage of Artisans and of Laborers, 1841–1920.
SOURCE: W. Randolph Burgess, *Trends in School Costs* (New York, 1920), pp. 32, 33, 71.

the wage structures in the 1920s. W. Randolph Burgess acknowledges the relative wage increases, but nonetheless interprets the evidence as indicative of a reduction in the relative return to teachers' skills:

> [Between 1841 and 1920] the requirements in terms of training and administrative ability have increased greatly. Then [in 1841] the typical man teacher was a grade teacher in elementary school. Today the typical city man teacher is a high school teacher or an executive. . . . The requirements of training for the artisan have increased hardly at all in 75 years; the requirements for the man city teacher have been increased many fold. The reward of the teacher has advanced, however, at about the same rate as the reward of the artisan. Relatively the position of the teacher is much less desirable.[26]

Figure 2.2 focuses on a later period and provides a comparison of teachers' salaries with those of manufacturing and postal employees, farm laborers, and ministers. The resulting graph needs to be interpreted with care, since the teacher salary series which underlies it is an average of the salaries of male and female, rural and urban public school teachers.

Because rural teachers' salaries were especially low, the ratio of teachers' salaries to those in other occupations is lower in Figure 2.2 than in Figure 2.1, where salaries for urban male teachers only serve as the basis of comparison. More importantly, since the proportion of teachers in rural areas was shrinking during this period, a smaller fraction of teachers were employed in the low-pay rural schools in 1926 than was the case in 1890. Because of this, teachers' average salary rises more

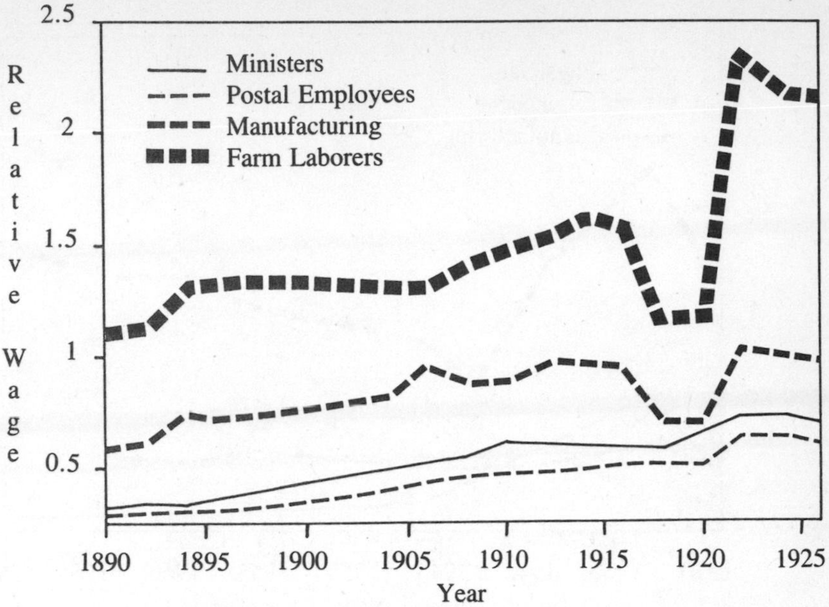

FIGURE 2.2 Wage of Public School Teachers Relative to Ministers, Postal Employees, Manufacturing Employees and Farm Laborers, 1890–1926.
SOURCE: United States Bureau of the Census, *Historical Statistics of the United States, Colonial Times to 1970*, Bicentennial Edition (Washington, D.C., 1975), Series D792, D793, D790, D781, and D789.

rapidly relative to salaries in other occupations than would be the case if salaries for either rural or urban teachers had been available separately.

With these qualifications in mind, we see that the patterns in Figure 2.2 indicate that, over the period 1890 to 1926, teachers' salaries were low relative to salaries in white-collar occupations and in manufacturing. In addition, the ratios indicate that, except for the drastic reduction in the relative earnings of teachers during and immediately following World War I, teachers maintained a roughly stable place in the wage hierarchy over this period. The only exception involves farm laborers. Compared with salaries available to farm laborers, teaching salaries were high, especially after 1920. This fact may explain the attraction of teaching for white males from farm backgrounds.[27]

For the period after 1929 it is possible to compare long-term trends in the wages of teachers with those in many more occupations. Figure 2.3 shows teachers' wages relative to those of physicians and engineers, as well as manufacturing wage earners, for the years 1929 through 1970. While teachers' relative earnings improved relative to those of physicians, engineers, and manufacturing wage earners in the early years of the Depression, the years 1933 through 1943 witnessed a radical reduction in teaching's relative rewards. Some of the losses relative to manufacturing workers were recovered in the post–World War II era, but teachers' gains lagged far behind those of other professionals. For white males with access to other professional employment, teaching must have seemed increasingly less attractive over this period.

Figure 2.4 recapitulates the long-term relationship between the wages of teachers

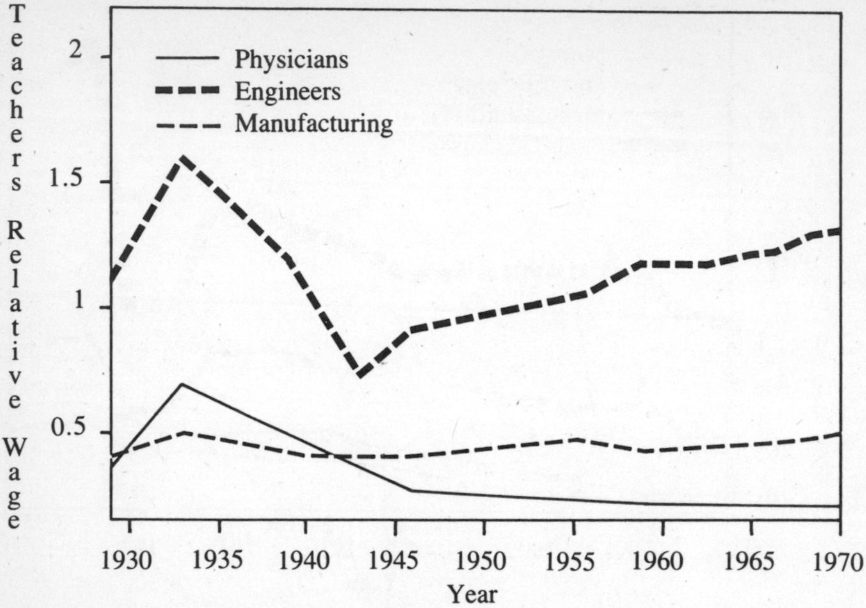

Figure 2.3 Average Annual Salary of Teachers Relative to Physicians, Engineers, and Manufacturing Employees, 1929–1970.
Source: United States Bureau of the Census, *Historical Statistics of the United States, Colonial Times to 1970*, Bicentennial Edition (Washington, D.C.,1975), Series H524, D918, D920, and D804.

and those of manufacturing workers, using wage series developed by economists Jeffrey Williamson and Peter Lindert for the period 1840 through 1970.[28] Apart from a number of sharp and relatively short-lived fluctuations, what stands out is a marked downward shift in the relative wage of teachers, in the middle of the Depression, from which recovery has been slow. The low point, reached in 1944, had been touched at only one prior point in the twentieth century, and then but briefly in the aftermath of World War I.

The realignment of teachers' relative wages during the Depression returned them to their relative earnings status prior to 1870, when most taught brief terms in rural schools. Even the post–World War II height of 134 percent of manufacturing wages, achieved in 1968, was substantially below the average of 147 for the period 1900 to 1935. This marked drop in teachers' earnings relative to earnings in the manufacturing sector is indicative of a major drop in teachers' position in the wage hierarchy. The reasons for this drop have not yet been analyzed.

Figures 2.5 and 2.6 present more recent data. Figure 2.5 compares teachers' salaries with those in the manufacturing sector between 1970 and 1985. It shows that in the 1970s, teachers' salaries continued to fall relative to those of manufacturing workers, but that in the first half of the 1980s there was a restoration of teachers' relative earnings to the 1970 level. Since the 1970 level was low by historical standards, however, this recovery would not be expected to result in any marked improvement in the attractiveness, to white men, of teaching.

Figure 2.6 compares the starting salary of teachers relative to that of engineering,

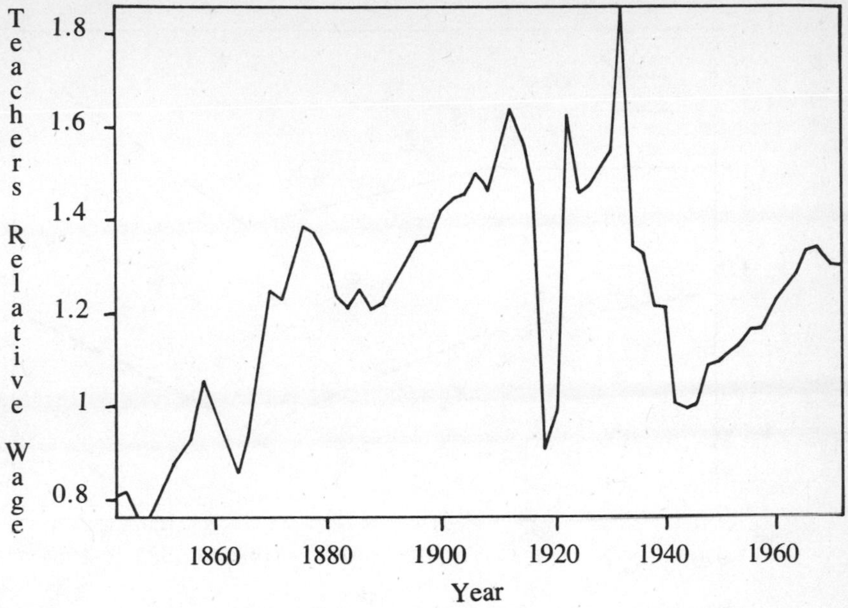

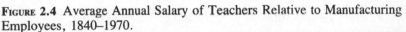

FIGURE 2.4 Average Annual Salary of Teachers Relative to Manufacturing Employees, 1840–1970.
SOURCE: Jeffrey Williamson and Peter Lindert, *American Inequality: A Macroeconomic History* (New York, 1980), Appendix D (8), p. 308.

business, and liberal-arts majors for the period 1975 through 1985. It shows a marked reduction in the starting salary of teachers relative to starting salaries in each of the other fields between 1975 and about 1983. Since 1983 there have been some improvements, although as of 1985 they had not been large enough to restore teachers' salaries to their relative position as of 1975.

Thus, over the past 140 years, teachers' wages, never high, have fallen relative to requirements, and relative to wages in manufacturing, managerial, and other professional occupations. For white men with access to alternative employments, these wage patterns made teaching an increasingly less attractive career.

The Attractions of Teaching for White Women

Wages paid to women teachers have been even lower than those paid to men.[29] But because women's alternative employment opportunities have been so much more limited, teaching has been considerably more attractive.

In the antebellum era, women's employment options were severely limited. Many women did domestic work despite the low pay, long hours, and limited privacy that the job entailed.[30] Others manufactured products such as straw hats, brooms, shirts, and shoes in their homes.[31] Factories also offered employment to young women. Richard Bernard and Maris Vinovskis note:

> School committees often lamented that many women were leaving the teaching profession in order to obtain higher wages in the textile mills. Although

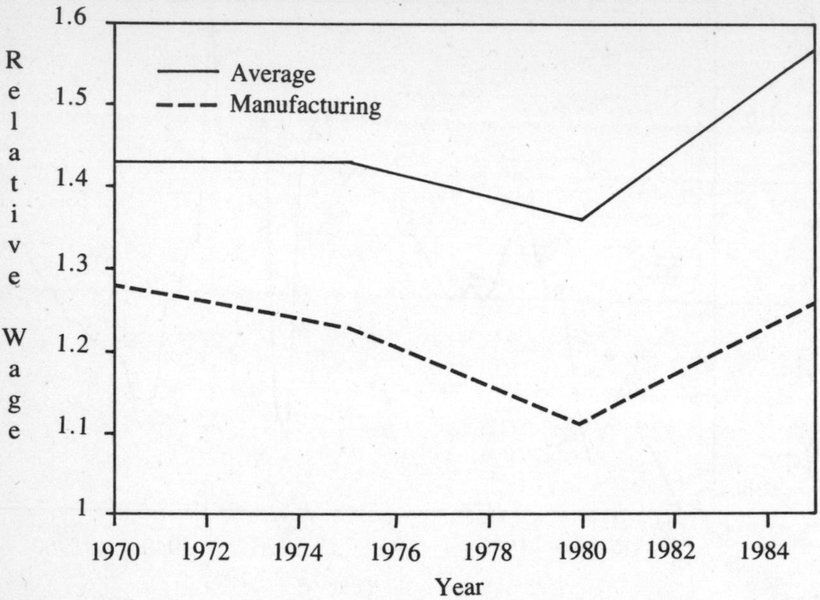

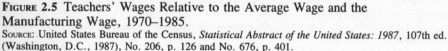

FIGURE 2.5 Teachers' Wages Relative to the Average Wage and the Manufacturing Wage, 1970–1985.
SOURCE: United States Bureau of the Census, *Statistical Abstract of the United States: 1987*, 107th ed. (Washington, D.C., 1987), No. 206, p. 126 and No. 676, p. 401.

> on the average women's wages in the mills were about the same as those in the schools, women teachers who went into the factories usually gained better positions and higher pay than other women because manufacturers felt that they made more productive and more disciplined workers. . . . As a result, there was a tendency for many teachers to leave for the milltown even though they were giving up a white-collar position for a blue-collar one.[32]

But in the 1840s a reduction in wages offered at the mill, and an influx of foreign-born workers anxious for employment, coincided with the withdrawal of native-born white women from the factory work force. Whether the women were involuntarily replaced, voluntarily withdrew because emerging notions of femininity were inconsistent with factory work, or left because more lucrative employment opportunities in teaching became available, is still subject to debate.[33] What is known is that by 1920 teaching was the second most important occupation among native-born white women of native parentage, accounting for 12 percent of total employment for this group.[34] Among college-educated white women, teaching was even more important. Thirty-eight percent of Smith College graduates from the classes of 1879 through 1888 became primary and secondary school teachers, while only 11 percent became doctors, professors, college deans, and architects *combined*.[35] Mary Cookingham reports:

> Survey data collected by the Association of Collegiate Alumnae in 1914 indicate that 64 percent of the women who graduated between 1865 and 1880

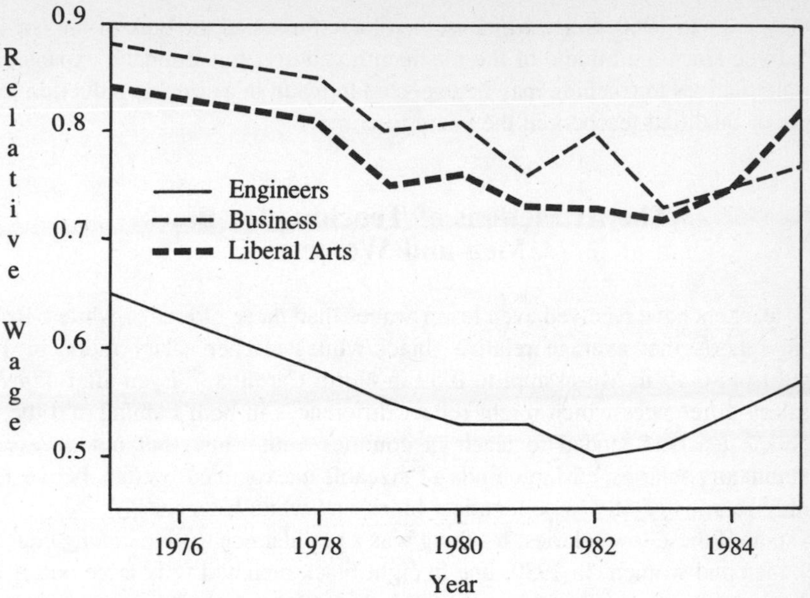

FIGURE 2.6 Starting Salary of Teachers Relative to Engineering, Business, and Liberal Arts Majors, 1975–1985.
SOURCE: United States Bureau of the Census, *Statistical Abstract of the United States: 1987*, 107th ed. (Washington, D.C., 1987), No. 208, p. 126.

worked for gain at some point in their lives; of these working women, a minimum of 67 percent taught.[36]

Alternatives to teaching began to appear in the late nineteenth century as the fields of social work, clerical work, and medicine began to employ women. After World War I, library science and home economics offered additional employment opportunities. Nonetheless, teaching remained the primary employer of educated women. As late as 1970, 53 percent of female college graduates who were working for wages taught in the elementary and secondary schools.[37]

But in the 1960s and 1970s a marked expansion in employment opportunities for educated white women occurred. Title IX of the Educational Amendments Act of 1972 led to a striking increase in women's share of enrollments in preprofessional and professional educational programs. Antidiscrimination legislation prompted employers to hire women in previously male-dominated fields like management, accounting, and engineering. The expansion of the service sector meant the creation of new jobs, without sex-typing, in the fields of medicine and law. Many of these went to women.[38]

As noted by Val Burris and Amy Wharton, the Duncan index, which gives the proportion of women who would have to change jobs in order for the distribution of women across occupations to match the distribution of men, fell from 65.6 in 1960 to 52.2 in 1979.[39] Although the index indicates that a substantial amount of gender-based occupational segregation still exists in the professions, the decline observed for the period 1960 to 1979 is in marked contrast to over half a century of stability prior to 1960. Since white women have furnished the bulk of the teaching work force since the middle of the nineteenth century, this dramatic expansion of their alternatives to teaching may be expected to result in a sizeable reduction in the supply of qualified teachers in the years to come.

The Attractions of Teaching for Black Men and Women

Black teachers have received even lower wages than those offered to whites. Robert Margo reports that average relative (black/white) teacher salary ratios in 1910 ranged from 0.49 in Mississippi to 0.59 in North Carolina.[40] Even after adjusting for salary differences which might reflect differences in both training and the fact that black teachers tended to teach in counties with "low, but not necessarily discriminatory salaries," Margo finds a "sizeable unexplained 'wedge' between the monthly salaries of otherwise identical black and white teachers."[41]

In spite of these low salaries, teaching was a popular occupation among educated black men and women. In 1930, one in eight black men and fully three out of four black women in the professions were teachers.[42] The popularity of teaching in the face of low wages was explained by Horace Mann Bond, who wrote:

> A much larger number of Negroes will seek employment as teachers, even when as graduates . . . they are offered greatly inferior wages, than would be the case among white candidates. . . . The white college graduate . . . [has] numerous choices—among clerical work, salesmanship in stores, banks, and securities houses, while the Negro . . . graduate is restricted to a few narrow lines of endeavor most promising of which is the teaching profession.[43]

This situation did not change very much until the 1960s, when there occurred an expansion in employment opportunities unrivaled by any previous decade.[44] As a result of these decreases in discrimination in other professional occupations, beginning in the 1960s, white women and black men and women who had been a sort of captive audience for the teaching profession have had a chance to look elsewhere. Thus the supply of teachers would be expected to have fallen, even in the absence of any fall in the relative earnings of teachers.

Variations in Teaching Salaries over the Business Cycle

As Figure 2.6 shows, however, teachers' salaries *did* fall relative to salaries in other professions during the 1970s and early 1980s. Some of this drop undoubtedly reflects a drop in demand for teachers in the wake of smaller cohorts of school-age children in these years. But the timing of the decline is also consistent with a long-run tendency for the relative wage of teachers to fall during inflations and rise in depressions. This pattern can be seen in Figure 2.4, which plots the ratio of the annual salary of teachers to unskilled industrial workers (as estimated by Jeffrey

Williamson and Peter Lindert) for the 130-year period between 1840 and 1970.[45]

During the Civil War, World War I, and World War II inflations, teachers' relative wages fell dramatically. During the deflationary episodes in the late nineteenth century and during the early years of the Great Depression, teachers' wages improved relative to the earnings of industrial workers.[46] This pattern is evident after 1970 as well. As Figures 2.5 and 2.6 indicate, the relative wage of teachers fell as the inflation rate climbed during the 1970s.

The abatement of inflation in the 1980s was associated with a rise in the relative earnings of teachers. Williamson and Lindert comment on the connection between the World War I inflation and the fall in teachers' relative wages, suggesting that the effect may be related to the relatively long-term contracts which govern teachers' salaries:

> The war effort made unskilled labor especially scarce, and its wage rates jumped. The wages of skilled and professional groups, by contrast, were bid up much less, partly because contracts in these occupations are always longer-term and slower to adjust to unanticipated inflation. The net result was an unprecedented contraction of pay scales between 1916 and 1920.[47]

It is also possible that these changes in the relative earnings may be responses to changes in the fund from which teachers' salaries are paid—local property-tax revenues. These revenues respond to price changes with a lag. At the onset of an unanticipated inflation, assessed valuation of taxable property does not increase as fast as other prices. Unless there is an immediate increase in the tax rate, the real value of property-tax collections will fall. Conversely, during deflations or depressed economic conditions, the assessed valuation of taxable property, and therefore the real value of tax revenues, does not fall as quickly as other prices. Unless taxes are immediately cut, local tax revenues will rise. Since property-tax revenues form the pool from which teachers' wages are paid, their tendency to fall in inflations and rise in depressions would be expected to impart a similar tendency to teachers' wages. During periods of economic instability, such as that in the United States since about 1970, these forces add to the difficulties of recruiting and retaining a well-qualified teaching force.

Conclusions

The thesis of this chapter is that until very recently the schools generally were able to attract qualified teachers despite the low salaries offered because they made use of the services of educated white women and educated black men and women whose alternative employment opportunities were quite limited. The political and legal movements of the 1960s and 1970s, by expanding alternative employment opportunities for these groups, eliminated the probability of this strategy's continuing to work in the future.

The implications of the fundamental shift in the supply of teachers described in this chapter have until very recently been masked by a reduction in the size of the school-age population. Thus demand was reduced as much as, or more than, supply in the 1970s and early 1980s.[48] But since the mid-1980s the school-age population has begun to increase, many older teachers are retiring, and the size of the college-age population from which new teachers have historically been drawn is declining. These facts suggest that a sizeable increase in teacher salaries will be needed to attract and keep well-qualified teachers.

Notes

AUTHOR'S NOTE: Extensive and detailed comments from John Rury and Donald Warren improved this chapter immensely. Remaining omissions and errors are my responsibility.

1. Ratios are for 1841. Teachers' salaries are from W. Randolph Burgess, *Trends in School Costs* (New York: Russell Sage, 1920). Salaries of engineers are from Mark Aldrich, "Earnings of American Civil Engineers, 1820–1859," in *Journal of Economic History* 31 (1971), pp. 407–419.
2. Ratios are for 1841. Computed from Burgess, *Trends in School Costs,* pp. 32 and 71. These teacher-salary estimates include an imputation for the value of food and shelter provided while "boarding around." Thus the relative monetary earnings of teachers was even lower than these numbers suggest.
3. U.S. Bureau of the Census, *Historical Statistics of the United States, Colonial Times to 1970, Bicentennial Edition,* Series D (Washington, DC: Government Printing Office, 1975), p. 168: columns 781, 790, 791, 792, and 793.
4. U.S. Department of the Interior, Office of Education, *Bulletin,* 1930, No. 9, "Survey of Land Grant Colleges and Universities" (Washington, DC: Government Printing Office, 1930), p. 382.
5. U.S. Bureau of the Census, *Statistical Abstract of the United States, 1987,* No. 208 (Washington, DC: Government Printing Office, 1987), p. 126.
6. See Dan C. Lortie, *Schoolteacher: A Sociological Study* (Chicago: University of Chicago Press, 1975); Philip W. Jackson, *Life in Classrooms* (New York: Holt, Rinehart & Winston, 1968); and Linda Darling-Hammond, *Beyond the Commission Reports: The Coming Crisis in Teaching* (Santa Monica: Rand Corporation, 1984).
7. C. Emily Feistritzer, *Profiles of Teachers in the United States* (Washington, DC: National Association for Educational Information, 1986).
8. This argument is made by Darling-Hammond, *Beyond the Commission Reports;* Susan B. Carter, "Occupational Segregation, Teachers' Wages, and American Economic Growth," in *Journal of Economic History* 46:2 (June 1986), pp. 373–383; and Michael Sedlak and Steven Schlossman, *Who Will Teach?* (Santa Monica: Rand Corporation, 1986).
9. Alice Kessler-Harris, *Out to Work* (New York: Oxford University Press, 1982), pp. 171–172.
10. Cynthia Fuchs Epstein, *Women's Place: Options and Limits in Professional Careers* (Berkeley: University of California Press, 1970); and Mary Roth Walsh, *"Doctors Wanted, No Women Need Apply": Sexual Barriers in the Medical Profession, 1835–1975* (New Haven: Yale University Press, 1977).
11. Michael J. Carter and Susan B. Carter, "Women's Recent Progress in the Professions, or Women Get a Ticket to Ride After the Gravy Train Has Left the Station" in *Feminist Studies* 7:3 (Fall 1981), pp. 477–504.
12. Myra H. Strober and Audri Gordon Lanford, "The Feminization of Public School Teaching: Cross-sectional Analysis, 1850–1880," in *Signs* 11:2 (Winter 1986), pp. 212–235.
13. See ibid.; Myra H. Strober and David Tyack, "Why Do Women Teach and Men Manage? A Report on Research on Schools," in *Signs* 5:3 (Spring 1980),

pp. 494–503; Tyack and Strober, "Jobs and Gender: A History of the Structuring of Educational Employment by Sex," in Patricia A. Schmuck, W. W. Charters, and Richard O. Carlson (eds.), *Educational Policy and Management: Sex Differentials* (New York: Academic Press, 1981), pp. 131–151; and John Rury, "Who Became Teachers? The Social Characteristics of Teachers in American History," Ch. 1 in this volume.

14. Susan B. Carter and Mark Prus, "The Labor Market and the American High School Girl: 1890–1928," in *Journal of Economic History* 42:1 (March 1982), p. 164; Rury, "Who Became Teachers?"; and Mabel Newcomer, *A Century of Higher Education for American Women* (New York: Harper, 1959), pp. 37 and 46.
15. Frank Bowles and Frank A. DeCosta, *Between Two Worlds: A Profile of Negro Higher Education* (New York: McGraw–Hill, 1971), p. 117.
16. Ibid., p. 33.
17. Roger L. Ransom and Richard Sutch, *One Kind of Freedom: The Economic Consequences of Emancipation* (New York: Cambridge University Press, 1977), p. 25.
18. Ibid., pp. 26–28; and Robert Margo, "Race, Educational Attainment, and the 1940 Census," in *Journal of Economic History* 46:1 (March 1986), pp. 189–198.
19. Ibid., p. 194.
20. H. Rabinowitz, "Half-a-Loaf: The Shift from White to Black Teachers in the Negro Schools in the Urban South, 1865–1890," in *Journal of Southern History* 40 (1974), pp. 565–594.
21. Richard B. Freeman, *Black Elite: The New Market for Highly Educated Black Americans* (New York: McGraw–Hill, 1976), p. 175.
22. U.S. Bureau of the Census, *Statistical Abstract of the United States: 1987*, No. 197, p. 121.
23. Freeman, *Black Elite*, p. 176.
24. Lewis D. Stillman, "Migration from Vermont (1776–1860)," in *Proceedings of the Vermont Historical Society*, New Series Vol. V, No. 1 (1937), p. 149.
25. Tyack and Strober, "Jobs and Gender," pp. 131–151.
26. Burgess, *Trends of School Costs*, pp. 80–81.
27. Lotus D. Coffman, *The Social Composition of the Teaching Population* (New York: Teachers College, 1911); William S. Learned and Ben D. Wood, *The Student and His Knowledge* (New York: Carnegie Foundation for the Advancement of Teaching, 1938); and Rury, "Who Became Teachers?"
28. Jeffrey G. Williamson and Peter Lindert, *American Inequality: A Macroeconomic History* (New York: Academic Press, 1980).
29. Myra H. Strober and Laura Best, "The Female/Male Salary Differential in the Public Schools: Some Lessons from San Francisco, 1879," in *Economic Inquiry* 17 (April 1979), pp. 218–236.
30. Geraldine Jonçich Clifford, " 'Marry, Stitch, Die, or Do Worse': Educating Women for Work," in Harvey Kantor and David B. Tyack (eds.), *Youth, Work, and Schooling: Historical Perspectives on Vocationalism in American Education* (Stanford: Stanford University Press, 1982), pp. 223–268.
31. Thomas Dublin, "Women and Outwork in a Nineteenth-Century New England Town: Fitzwilliam, New Hampshire, 1830–1850," in Steven Hahn and Jonathan Prude (eds.), *The Countryside in the Age of Capitalist Transformation* (Chapel Hill: University of North Carolina Press, 1985), pp. 51–70; and Ava Baron and Susan E. Klepp, " 'If I Didn't Have My Sewing Machine' . . . Women and Sewing Machine Technology," in Joan M. Jensen and Sue Davidson (eds.), *A Needle, a Bobbin, a Strike: Women Needleworkers in America* (Philadelphia: Temple University Press, 1984), pp. 20–59.
32. Richard M. Bernard and Maris A. Vinovskis, "The Female School Teacher in Antebellum America," in *Journal of Social History* 3 (1977), p. 338.
33. Thomas Dublin, *Women at Work: The Transformation of Work and Community*

in Lowell, Massachusetts, 1826–1860 (New York: Columbia University Press, 1979); Lynn Y. Weiner, *From Working Girl to Working Mother: The Female Labor Force in the United States, 1820–1980* (Chapel Hill: University of North Carolina Press, 1985); and Edith Abbott, *Women in Industry* (New York: D. Appleton, 1909).

34. Joseph A. Hill, *Women in Gainful Occupations 1870 to 1920,* Census Monographs IX (Washington, DC: Government Printing Office, 1929), p. 88.
35. Sarah H. Gordon, "Smith College Students: The First Ten Classes, 1879–1888," in *History of Education Quarterly* 15 (Summer 1975), pp. 147–167; and Barbara Miller Solomon, *In the Company of Educated Women* (New Haven: Yale University Press, 1985), pp. 31–34.
36. Mary E. Cookingham, "Bluestockings, Spinsters and Pedagogues: Women College Graduates, 1865–1910," in *Population Studies,* 38 (1984), pp. 349–364.
37. Freeman, *Black Elite,* p. 19.
38. Carter and Carter, "Gravy Train," pp. 477–478.
39. Val Burris and Amy Wharton, "Sex Segregation in the U.S. Labor Force," *Review of Radical Political Economy* 14:3 (Fall 1982), pp. 43–56.
40. Robert Margo, " 'Teacher Salaries in Black and White': The South in 1910," in *Explorations in Economic History* 21:3 (July 1984), p. 309.
41. Ibid., p. 316. On racial differences in teachers' salaries see also Horace Mann Bond, *The Education of the Negro in the American Social Order* (New York: Prentice–Hall, 1934); and George Stigler, "Employment and Compensation in Education," in *Occasional Paper No. 33* (New York: National Bureau of Economic Research, 1950).
42. U.S. Bureau of the Census, *Negro Population in the United States, 1790–1915* (Washington, DC: Government Printing Office, 1918).
43. Bond, *The Education of the Negro,* p. 271.
44. Freeman, *Black Elite,* Ch. 1; and Randy Albelda, "Occupational Segregation by Race and Gender, 1958–1981," in *Industrial and Labor Relations Review* 39:3 (April 1986), pp. 404–411.
45. Williamson and Lindert, *American Inequality* 8, Appendix D, p. 308.
46. David Tyack, Robert Lowe, and Elisabeth Hansot, *Public Schools in Hard Times: The Great Depression and Recent Years* (Cambridge: Harvard University Press, 1984), note the rise in the relative salaries of teachers in the early years of the Depression.
47. Williamson and Lindert, *American Inequality,* p. 81.
48. Darling-Hammond, *Beyond the Commission Reports,* makes this point.

SECTION

TWO

Teacher Workplaces

Recent historical research, most of it in the form of case studies, has contributed substantively and methodologically to our understanding of teachers' lives and work. It has also enabled us to explore conditions and practices within schools and classrooms of earlier periods. Many contributions to the history of teachers have been by-products of research on women, black people, or rural institutions and traditions. Scholars in the field of women's studies have often been as interested in teachers' lives as in their work. Much of the conceptual and empirical toughness of the new historical literature on teachers can be traced to current scholarship in women's studies. Methodologically, these otherwise disparate studies have approached their subjects at least in part through the eyes and sensibilities of teachers.

To the public, teachers have performed their most visible tasks in classrooms. But teachers themselves have tended to view their spheres more broadly. Their notions of "work" have carried them into reform movements, professional organizations, unions, churches, and political parties. They have joined the faculties of teacher-training institutions, lobbied aggressively for improved working conditions, and challenged overt and subtle forms of discrimination. With palpable disapproval of trends toward school bureaucratization, they have advocated decentralized forms of organization and greater autonomy for teachers with regard to matters such as curriculum development and evaluation of their own performance. Their sense of profession has embraced transactions with students as well as with school administrators, parents, community leaders, and each other. The history of teachers thus not only introduces us to schools as workplaces, it also expands the workplace concept well beyond schools and classrooms.

The chapters in Section Two organize the exmination of teacher workplaces by types of institution: kindergartens, elementary schools, high schools, and teacher organizations. Of the two chapters on elementary schools, one focuses on those in rural settings and the other on urban schools. Several themes are stressed throughout this section. Of particular interest are the unique experiences of women teachers and of black teachers (most of whom were women), the variety of roles performed by teachers, and their notions of profession. As the authors demonstrate, teachers were obviously influenced by the settings in which they worked, yet they shared basic values and objectives. And they pursued these commitments with a fierce and, under the circumstances, surprising determination.

Teacher Knowledge

3

Child Gardening

The Teaching of Young Children in American Schools

Barbara Beatty

In the second half of the nineteenth century, a small group of women and men began advocating a new type of teaching that challenged "the one best system" of American public education. "Child gardening," as its proponents sometimes called this special kind of teaching designed for young children, developed as a reaction against schooling. In the first kindergarten manual published in America, Elizabeth Peabody defined this new form of education largely by what it was not: It was neither a school ("not the old-fashioned infant-school") nor a "primary public school," but a very different kind of natural community for the very young, "a garden of children."[1]

Nineteenth-century child gardeners were highly critical of the traditional school curriculum. They thought that schools stifled children's true, spontaneous nature and failed to educate them in the universal, humane way that would help them to become happy, productive adults. "Kindergartners" (what the teachers, *not* the pupils, were called) professed to be more interested in preparing children for life than in teaching the preliminary skills necessary to do well in school. Their hope was that a few years in a kindergarten might innoculate children against the overly rigid discipline and deadening didacticism that, in their view, characterized the upper grades. And that it might also provide children with a grounding in the moral, social, and mental habits that kindergartners felt were more basic and important than the formal knowledge supplied by more advanced schools.

Because of the young age and needs of their pupils, kindergarten teachers, unlike most grade-school teachers, actively assumed some of the responsibilities of parents. They also considered their job to include the teaching of mothers as well as children. The kindergarten was intended to provide a bridge between the home and the school and to communicate teaching techniques and educational values to parents. In addition, kindergarten teachers saw their role as educators extending beyond the school to the community. They viewed the kindergarten as a means of social as well as educational reform, and focused on children and their families rather than on academic subjects.

The institution of this special kind of education for young children not only affirmed their value in society but also reflected a growing awareness of children's age as a determinant of school organization and curricula. The advent of public kindergartens marked Americans' acceptance of the preschool period (from about three to seven years of age) as a stage of life sufficiently important to warrant protection in a special institution. Prior to the existence of formal early childhood education programs, young children had been educated in private "dame schools" where, until they had mastered the basic skills necessary to attend grammar school, they were taught to read and write by women in a home setting.

With the institution of public primary schools in the early nineteenth century, children as young as four began receiving formal academic instruction outside the home. Entrance age varied, however, and was not strictly enforced; and younger children frequently accompanied older siblings to school as a form of child care. As urban public schools became increasingly specialized, however, teachers became more sensitive to age-appropriate behavior and achievement—to what younger and older children could or should do and not do—and were less willing to deal with the instructional difficulties of nongraded, undifferentiated classes. Kindergartens thus filled the double need of a new educational program that could meet the needs of young children and at the same time keep them out of regular school classrooms.[2]

Another important factor responsible for the relatively rapid spread of kindergartens in the late nineteenth century was the link between kindergartens and urban social reform. Kindergartens were one of many Progressive Era reforms directed at solving the problems of cities. Primarily an urban phenomenon, public kindergartens were instituted first in large cities; they were adopted less readily and developed more slowly in rural areas, where some districts did not sponsor kindergartens until well into the twentieth century. Kindergartens were promoted as an antidote to the harm that city life was supposedly doing to young children.

Urban kindergartners created country conditions in urban classrooms and, when possible, took children on outings to the country. They tried to turn back the clock and recreate the experiences of childhood on the farm for children who were growing up in cities. This rural nostalgia and glorification of an idealized lost American childhood became a powerful and unifying curricular motif, accounting for much of early childhood education's enduring popular appeal.[3]

Initially, child gardeners practiced their special style of teaching in private programs for the children of the middle and upper classes, and in charity kindergartens for the poor. But the cost of providing kindergartens for the growing numbers of poor and immigrant children in American cities was prohibitive. Private sources of funds proved unequal to the task. The shift to public funds, however, generated considerable controversy primarily because of limited tax monies for education. The transition from private to public funding occurred gradually through a series of fits and starts. By the turn of the century, public kindergartens had been established in most large, urban school systems, and in many smaller cities and towns throughout the country.

What happened to the practice of child gardening when kindergartens were no longer independent but were part of the institutions that kindergartners had so vocally condemned? Did kindergartners retain the reformist characteristics of their child-centered approach to teaching and change the schools, or did child gardening become more like school teaching?

Historians' answers to these questions have varied, ranging from older, Cubberleyesque accounts depicting the kindergarten as one of the major forces of liberalization in American education, to revisionist views of the kindergarten as an agency of social control which, after institutionalization into the public schools, became "simply an adjunct of first grade." Historial interpretations of early-childhood education, and the writings and work of kindergartners themselves, have been dominated by the issue of balance between freedom and control. But though child gardeners struggled continually with the idea and the reality of educating and training children, seeking to strike a balance between play and teaching, spontaneity and discipline, they did not recognize this balance as a trade-off. It is this tension between independence and constraint, between the expression of individuality and the need for group socialization, and the concomitant denial that such a tension exists, that is so characteristic of American early childhood education.[4]

The purpose of this chapter is to provide a context for understanding how the practice of child gardening evolved as the populations with whom and places in which child gardeners worked changed in the years from 1860 to 1930. Examination of primary sources such as kindergarten training manuals, United States Bureau of Education surveys, and empirical studies of teaching methods suggests that teachers of young children defined and did their jobs differently from teachers of older students. Educated in special training programs, with a separate professional literature and organizations, kindergarten teachers maintained a sense of identity distinct from that of other teachers. Even after kindergartens were institutionalized into the public schools, kindergartners were not fully part of the "one best system." They developed their own system, and the classrooms in which they taught, and methods they used, continued to differ in important ways from those of other teachers.

Although this chapter deals with the teaching of young children in American schools, it does not deal with the history of day nurseries, orphanages, or other programs wherein young children were cared for and taught, sometimes in a manner quite similar to kindergartning. Though this may seem an arbitrary distinction, it reflects a long-standing, deep division between education and child care. Institutionalized child care, which originated as a charity for the poor and lower classes, was perceived as a means of protection for children who were thought to be better off in institutions than in their own homes, on the street, or in factories. Preschool education, on the other hand, which generally consisted of about three hours a day in kindergarten or nursery school, was perceived as a positive good, something middle- and upper-class parents supported to enrich their children's lives and enhance their development.

Though these historical differences in how programs for young children were perceived did not necessarily alter the actual daily activities and experiences of teachers and children, perceptions of what young children from differing class backgrounds needed did affect the curriculum in some ways. When kindergartens entered the public schools and children from lower-class backgrounds began receiving formal early childhood education, the curriculum became more academic and oriented toward school readiness, as this kind of didactic teaching was thought to be what these children needed. Private preschools and public kindergartens which catered to middle- and upper-class children, however, continued to focus more on socialization, and were in fact antiacademic. This was because advantaged children were thought not to need early education beyond what they received from their well-educated parents at home, and, it was feared, might actually be harmed by excessive, forced didacticism. Child gardeners insisted vehemently that kindergartens were not schools. But at the same time, they did not want kindergartens to be thought of as day nurseries. Kindergartners thus claimed the mantle of education, in part to disassociate themselves from the custodial connotations of lower-class child care, yet distanced themselves from other teachers.[5]

The following presentation first briefly reviews the origins of the kindergarten and describes the teaching methods that prevailed in private and charity kindergartens in the latter part of the nineteenth century, and the training of kindergarten teachers. The organization and administration of public kindergartens is then discussed from the perspective of how they affected teachers, as are changes in child-gardening methods after 1900. Finally, some of the differences between kindergartens and other classrooms as workplaces for teachers and environments for children are analyzed in the light of debates over whether public schools should provide programs for three- and four-year-olds. The relevance of these differences to recent proposals for changing the content and structure of teacher education and certification, and upgrading the status of teaching as a profession, also is examined.

Origins of the Kindergarten

An outgrowth of the Rousseauan, Romantic critique of modernity, the kindergarten originated as a reaction against industrialized, urban life and its effects on young children. Johann Heinrich Pestalozzi, who was much influenced by Rousseau, was the first educator to develop and put into practice a pedagogy designed explicitly for young children. Born in Switzerland in 1747, Pestalozzi founded the ''infant school,'' an experimental educational institution copied after a model peasant home, in which teachers used methods based on informal child-rearing practices rather than academic instruction.[6]

Infant schools were intended to compensate for the damage that industrialization was doing to the children of the poor. Lower-class parents, however, were not as supportive of Pestalozzi's methods as were upper-class parents and social reformers. Though Pestalozzian pedagogy was meant to be less rigid than school teaching methods, in the hands of later proponents infant-school curricula came to consist primarily of didactic object teaching lessons, marching, clapping, and other routinized physical exercises.

Frequently sponsored by evangelical women's groups (female counterparts of the Sunday School societies started by men), infant schools in the early nineteenth century enjoyed a brief period of popularity among child-savers and the liberal intelligentsia in major Eastern cities in the United States. In the early 1830s, for instance, the Boston School Committee considered a proposal to incorporate infant schools into the public schools, but rejected the idea when primary school teachers complained that infant-school graduates were unruly and difficult to teach. Upper-class parents rejected infant schools as well when new child-rearing literature suggested that early schooling might be harmful to the development of young children. Though Pestalozzian teaching methods continued to be employed in some public schools, by the end of the 1830s most American infant schools had closed.[7]

The success of the kindergarten, the next form of early childhood education to be introduced to America, was due in part to the fact it was not called, or perceived of, as a school. Friedrich Froebel, the German educator who founded the first kindergarten in 1837, was influenced by Pestalozzi, at whose model school he had studied and lived. Froebel's pedagogy was an idiosyncratic blend of German pietism, idealism, and naturalistic philosophy. His central metaphor, that of the child as a plant and the school as a garden, was organic, and he envisioned education as a process of growth based on natural laws of development.

Froebel's educational methods were intentionally nonacademic. He invented a set of sequenced materials and activities called "gifts" and "occupations," through which he theorized young children would gain a symbolic understanding of universal forms, part–whole relationships, and the unity of the cosmos. His methods also involved patterned finger plays, games, and songs derived from traditional German folk life and the nursery play of mothers and children.[8]

Like the Pestalozzian infant school, the kindergarten was associated with social reform. Politically liberal German émigrés fleeing from the failure of the revolution of 1848 carried Froebel's pedagogical ideas to England and the United States, where Margarethe Meyer Schurz, the wife of abolitionist and civil-service reform leader Carl Schurz, began a small kindergarten in Watertown, Wisconsin in 1856. Other German kindergartens were established in the Midwest and elsewhere in the 1850s and 1860s, and articles about the kindergarten began appearing in liberal newspapers in Eastern cities. At an abolition meeting in 1859, Margarethe Schurz mentioned Froebel's ideas to Elizabeth Peabody, who opened the first English-speaking kindergarten in the United States in Boston, in 1860.[9]

Elizabeth Peabody and other mostly female educational and social reformers were primarily responsible for the spread of child gardening in America. Unlike infant-school teachers, kindergarten teachers were women, as were most kindergarten directors, trainers, and supporters—though there were important male kindergarten leaders and advocates, such as Henry Barnard and William Torrey Harris. Peabody used the ideology of domesticity and "woman's sphere" to promote child gardening as an occupation for American women. Drawing from earlier prescriptive literature on the importance of the mother's role in the education of young children, she proclaimed child gardening to be the ideal solution to the problem of what increasing numbers of educated women who sought meaningful, ladylike work should do with their lives. It was Froebel's genius, Peabody stated, to have discovered a means whereby women might again assume a socially useful, natural role in society. Becoming a child gardener, she argued, was the noblest vocation to which a woman could aspire, "the perfect development of womanliness—a working with God at the highest fountain of artistic and moral character."[10]

American women heeded the call to become child gardeners. Numerous private kindergartens were established in cities and towns in the East and Midwest in the 1860s and 1870s. Soon the success of the kindergarten movement sparked a demand for more teachers. German Froebelians came to this country as kindergarten trainers, and many small, proprietary training programs sprang up in Boston, New York, and elsewhere.

Elizabeth Peabody wrote a kindergarten manual which appeared in 1863; in 1873 she began publishing a kindergarten journal, *The Kindergarten Messenger;* and in 1877 she founded a kindergarten organization, the American Froebel Society. Numerous other kindergarten guides and manuals were published; a kindergarten department was started within the National Education Association; and an independent kindergarten organization, the International Kindergarten Union, grew rapidly to become for a while one of the largest educational associations in the country.

Froebelian Child-Gardening Methods

Friedrich Froebel's educational philosophy and methods dominated the practice and training of child gardeners from the introduction of the kindergarten until the turn of the century. Froebel designed a complete curriculum with detailed, explicit directions for teachers. His works, however, were not available in English translation until the mid-1890s. American kindergartners who could not read German thus relied on manuals which described Froebel's ideas and methods. Early kindergarten advocates such as Elizabeth Peabody insisted that "genuine" kindergarten teachers follow Froebel's instructions to the letter. Because of this emphasis on strict adherence to Froebel, a review of exemplary manuals and guides provides a sense of what it was like to teach in a nineteenth-century kindergarten.

Elizabeth Peabody's kindergarten guide, which was published in Boston in 1863, began by stressing the differences between a kindergarten and a school, the most salient of which, she felt, had to do with order. Peabody told future kindergartners to think of a kindergarten as "children in society . . . a commonwealth or republic of children," as "contrasted, in every particular, with the old-fashioned school, which is an absolute monarchy." But a kindergarten, she emphasized, was not without order. In the kindergarten it was "a serious purpose to organize *romping*."[11]

In a revised edition, Peabody made further comparisons between the relative freedom of the kindergarten and what she saw as the constraining atmosphere of the school. Unlike primary school teaching, which "consisted in keeping children still, and preventing them from playing," child gardening, Peabody posited, was based on play—on accepting, not opposing, children's "spontaneous" and "natural" activity and "genially directing it to a more certainly beautiful effect than it can attain when left to itself."[12]

Peabody used Froebel's horticultural imagery to stress the importance of kindergarten children being permitted to express their individuality. The gardener, she stated, studied the "individual natures" of his plants, treating each according to its needs but not letting them "grow wild." A kindergarten teacher has "as little power to override the characteristic individuality of a child, or to predetermine this characteristic, as the gardener of plants to say that a lily shall be a rose."[13]

In her revised guide, however, Peabody tempered her views on individuality, which she felt she had mistakenly overemphasized, and said that it was the universal in human nature which was to be cultivated. "Every process of Froebel's Kindergarten," she argued, was "good for all children, and, interfering with nothing original, leaves their individualities free to express themselves *sufficiently*." Though the reason she gave for this shift in focus was that children's "individual varieties" if "pampered" became "deformities," Peabody's newfound stress on the universality of Froebelianism was indicative of the uniformitarianism that was to be at the same time child gardening's greatest strength and weakness.[14]

The emotional climate of a kindergarten, according to Peabody, was less coercive than that of a regular school classroom. Kindergartners were to gently and lovingly lead children through the Froebelian play activities. Of course the result—the understanding that the child was to acquire from the play—the type of play, and the methods of play all were predetermined. But the attitude of kindergarten teachers toward their pupils was supposed to be different from that of other teachers, as the child's "own cooperation—or at least willingness—" was "to be conciliated and made instrumental to the end in view."[15]

The physical environment of a kindergarten was also intended to be different from that of a school. Two well-lighted and well-ventilated rooms were "indispensable," one for "quiet employments" and one for music, singing, physical activities and play, and there was to be a piano (or at least a hand organ or guitar) for the kindergarten teacher to use in leading songs and games. As these requirements suggest, a kindergarten could be an active, noisy place. That loudness and physical movement were permitted and even encouraged, albeit in a controlled fashion, was a radical departure from the strictly enforced quiet of most school classrooms.[16]

The furniture, arrangement, and supplies of a kindergarten, as Peabody described them, were to be different from those of a school classroom, too. Instead of desks bolted to the floor, there were moveable tables and chairs which were set up in various ways, depending upon the activity. In addition to paper, pencils, chalk, and slates, there were Froebelian materials: blocks, sticks and peas, beads, colored papers, threads, and so on. This profusion of materials, and the nature of some of the Froebelian activities (such as paper-cutting, weaving, and modeling with clay) could be messy at times, though of course there was great emphasis on orderliness and carefully putting things away. But in comparison to the relative bareness of many grade-level classrooms, a kindergarten was colorful and cluttered.

Kindergarten children were also to have a special outdoor play area, preferably a grassy one rather than cement, and a real garden as well. The teacher was to organize and participate in outdoor games with the children, not simply treat time spent out of the classroom as a break or recess. And gardening was to be done jointly too, which meant that kindergarten teachers and children must have gotten dirty together while digging and planting. Froebel provided exact specifications for the kindergarten garden, which was to include individual and group plots. If it was not possible to have a real garden, the teacher was supposed to bring nature indoors by giving each child a pot in which to plant flowers.

These outdoor activities, and the emphasis on nature, were such a departure from traditional school work that Peabody felt called upon to explain that the kindergarten was not entirely an open-air program, as its name implied. But the association of the kindergarten with the out-of-doors may have been what led her to suggest that, if possible, special glass-walled kindergartens should be constructed, "on the plan of the crystal palace," with storage areas, bathrooms, and wraparound chalkboards, all at child height and scale—though no such models of educational architecture for young children appear to have been built. In fact, kindergartens and other programs for young children often were housed in basements or other substandard locations, though some private kindergartens had adequate, commodious space.[17]

Unlike the grade-school curriculum, which consisted primarily of recitations, reading, written work, and drill, the kindergarten curriculum as Peabody described it included music, plays, gymnastics, and various other art, manual, and physical activities. Peabody gave directions for traditional Froebelian games such as "The Pigeon-House," "Hare in the Hollow," "The Weathercock," "The Pheasant," and others, which, she noted, the kindergarten teacher "should always play with the children." Though the kindergartner remained in charge, the fact that she was physically doing the activity with the children, joining in their play as if a child herself, contrasted with the relative noninvolvement of the typical schoolteacher positioned at the front of the room, separated from the students by an elevated desk.[18]

Peabody also emphasized differences in how kindergarten teachers and grade-school teachers disciplined children. In a section on moral and religious exercises, she argued that modeling habits of good moral behavior was the most effective form of discipline. She gave examples of how teachers should explain the symbolic meaning of hymns and prayers and should read parables and other religious stories to young children, and stressed in particular that teachers should be positive and not judgmental, so that children would not become defensive. In addition, she exhorted, there should be no punishments in a kindergarten, and suggested that children who misbehaved be sent home rather than disciplined physically or by other means.[19]

Peabody's first guide also included sections on advanced academic studies such as geometry, geography, and the teaching of reading, subjects she had taught herself which were not part of the Froebelian curriculum. In the revised edition, however, she added footnotes and new introductory sections to explain that she had been mistaken in combining primary subjects and methods such as these with kindergarten activities. Geometry, she noted, was "rather for the direction of children in the last than the first years of the kindergarten," and reading "[should] not come till children [were] hard upon seven years old, [after] the kindergarten exercises on blocks, sticks, peas, &c. [were] entirely exhausted."[20]

Other American kindergarten guides published in the 1860s and 1870s provided more detailed instructions to Froebel's gifts, occupations, songs, and play activities, plus illustrations of how to use Froebelian materials. Edward Wiebe's extremely popular *The Paradise of Childhood* (published in 1869 by Milton Bradley, one of the first producers of kindergarten equipment) included directions telling kindergarten teachers exactly what to say and do. Wiebe instructed kindergartners to always use the same terms to avoid producing "any ambiguity in the mind of the child," and stated that everything must be done "with a great deal of precision [as] order and regularity in all the performances [were] of utmost importance."[21]

William N. Hailmann's *Kindergarten Culture,* published in 1873, stressed the importance of wholeness, harmony, and continuity, and other of the more philosophical aspects of Froebel's pedagogy, along with the necessity of following the Froebelian curriculum. Like Peabody, Hailmann emphasized that the kindergarten "[was] not and should not be a school." He warned teachers of the dangers of schools where "precocity [was] encouraged at the expense of sound development"; where "the unreasonable parent [was] gratified and the outsider dazzled by the wonderful attainments of the unconscious little sufferers"; and he recommended the putting-off of later types of teaching appropriate for older children.[22]

Maria Kraus-Boelte's and John Kraus's much-used *Kindergarten Guide,* published in 1877 by Ernst Steiger, the other main supplier of kindergarten materials, followed the pattern and specificity of earlier guides and provided even more minutely detailed instructions for teachers. The directions for the seventh gift, for instance, a set of square and triangular flat parquetry blocks known as "tablets," ran to 92 pages and included 554 specific steps.[23] (See Figure 3.1.)

Despite the efforts of Elizabeth Peabody, William Hailmann, Maria Kraus-Boelte, and others to train a generation of child gardeners in the canon of Froebelian activities, the kindergarten gradually became Americanized. Louise Pollock, a German kindergartner who had come to the United States in 1864 to teach a private kindergarten at Nathaniel Allen's school in West Newton, Massachusetts, and then moved to Washington, D.C., where she ran what she called the National Kindergarten, was one of the first Froebelians to begin adapting kindergarten pedagogy to American children. Pollock recommended that kindergartners plan a theme for each day of the week, and gave examples from her own kindergarten. On Mondays the children were told a parable and did plays symbolizing the trades, such as food production, the railroad, and so on. Tuesdays were devoted to nature. On Wednesdays, the children looked at new pictures, finished up work or repeated it with different materials, and did weaving. The theme for Thursday was the human body, and on Friday, which was devoted to spherical objects, the children made balls of clay and did other Froebelian activities related to roundness.

Pollock also developed model lessons based on short stories or "conversations" about Froebelian gifts, and occupations which included American references. Though she included a script with questions for child gardeners to use with each activity, Pollock's directions were more open-ended and less detailed than those of earlier guides. In comparison to Kraus-Boelte, for instance, she described children playing with the tablets and making forms of their own choice which the teacher then asked them about, instead of having them construct hundreds of prescribed patterns.[24]

By the 1880s, some American kindergarten teachers were beginning to use their own judgment about improving Froebelian methods to better meet the needs of children in their classes, rather than relying slavishly on directions in manuals. Lucy Wheelock, a young kindergarten teacher at the Chauncy Hall School in Boston, stopped using Froebel's first and second gifts and having children do pinpricking and drawing on paper marked with small squares, for instance, because she thought the former activities were too simple for four-year-olds, and the latter too advanced. The changes that Wheelock made were influenced in part by the ideas of psychologist G. Stanley Hall, whose research with kindergarten-age children had

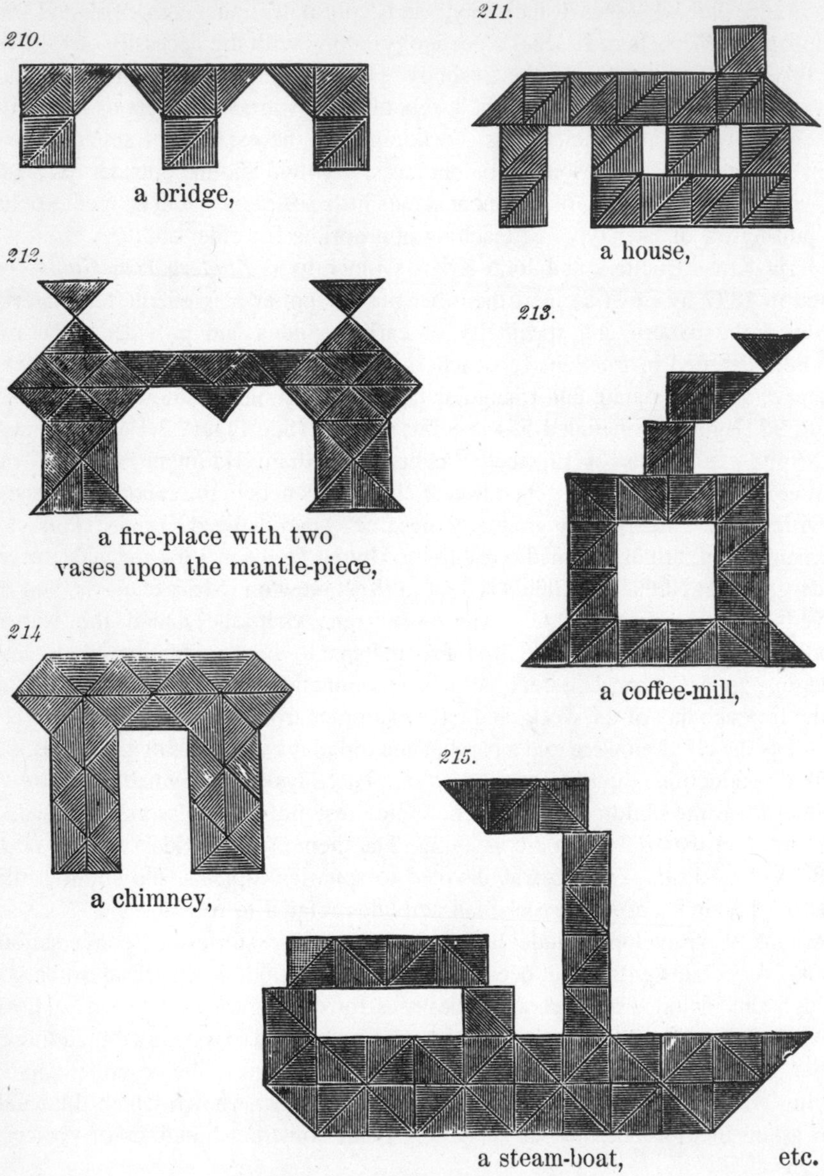

FIGURE 3.1. "The Seventh Gift."
Illustration from Maria Kraus-Boelte and John Kraus, *The Kindergarten Guide, an Illustrated Hand-book, designed for the Self-Instruction of Kindergartners, Mothers, and Nurses* (New York: E. Steiger, 1877), p. 175.

convinced him that the concentration and stress on fine-muscle work required for some Froebelian activities might induce eyestrain and fatigue. Wheelock looked to Hall and the new science of psychology for information about children, but like other younger advocates of kindergartens, she had confidence in her own ability as a teacher to define appropriate activities for young children.[25]

This growing independence attracted criticism. Wheelock was branded a heretic by some conservatives for her deviance from the so-called "Uniform Program," and reported overhearing another teacher ask, "How does Miss Wheelock know when to introduce the fifth gift? I wouldn't know, but Miss Blow does." Wheelock's critic was referring to the director of public kindergartens in St. Louis, Susan Blow, leader of the faction of older kindergartners who insisted upon adherence to orthodox Froebelianism.[26]

The Training of Child Gardeners

The first generation of American child gardeners were educated in private training programs and in the few public normal schools that offered courses in Froebelian philosophy and methods. Some of the private programs run by German and American kindergartners were relatively short-lived, but others, such as Maria Kraus-Boelte's training program in New York, Elizabeth Harrison's Chicago Kindergarten College, and Lucy Wheelock's school in Boston, were very successful, training numerous kindergarten teachers.

Operated by Froebelians and generally organized along similar lines, privately run kindergarten training programs existed in most American cities. The majority admitted young women who were high school graduates. The number of years required to receive a certificate or diploma varied considerably, however (ranging from six weeks to two years), and was the source of disagreement among kindergarten trainers. Though two years increasingly became the norm, kindergarten training usually was shorter than the normal-school course required for most elementary teachers.

Admissions requirements and tuitions varied as well. At Lucy Wheelock's kindergarten training class in Boston, for instance, admissions requirements were "an ability to sing, good health, a love of children, and a high-school education or its equivalent, and broad general culture." Applicants were to "furnish testimonials as to scholarship and moral character from the principal of the school last attended, or from some clergyman of their town and must be at least eighteen years of age." And the tuition in 1894 was $100 for the first year and $75 for the second, not including room and board or books and materials.[27]

Unlike female seminaries which emphasized the classics and religious education, or normal schools which prepared teachers in school subjects, kindergartners-in-training studied Froebel intensively and did Froebelian activities as if they themselves were children. Lecture courses were complemented by handwork. Students at Lucy Wheelock's training school in the 1890s took a "Survey of History of Pedagogy," "Applications of Pedagogic Principles," and "Psychology in Teaching," and studied science, music, and storytelling, along with courses on Froebelian philosophy, gifts and occupations, and games. In addition to works on Froebel and kindergarten guides, Miss Wheelock's students read such books as J. P. Richter's *Levana,* Lange's *Apperception,* and Ruskin's *The Ethics of Dust* and *The Stones of Venice*. They also observed and student-taught in real kindergartens where they served as teacher assistants and helpers.[28]

Most early kindergarten training programs were small, one-woman operations, the success of which depended on the personality and energy of the director. The women who ran the programs often developed a following and were greatly admired by their loyal students. Special rituals (such as the celebration of Froebel's birthday) and other events reinforced students' sense of purpose and dedication to the Froebelian cause. From the few accounts available, future kindergarten teachers seemed to enjoy their training. But the enormous amount of handwork required, laborious filling of notebook after notebook with intricate paper weavings, minute pin-prickings, and so on, must have been tedious and tiring. Nor could the strictness with which some German-trained Froebelians treated their students have been appealing to many young women.[29]

By the mid-1890s, when more public normal schools and some private colleges and universities offered kindergarten courses, more eclectic kinds of training replaced the rigidity of the Froebelian program. Younger kindergartners, such as Lucy Wheelock, Anna Bryan, Alice Putnam, and Patty Smith Hill, who had studied with G. Stanley Hall, incorporated child study, psychology, and other subjects into the curriculum of their training courses, and exercised increasing independence in determining how children and child gardeners should be educated.

Child Gardening with Children of the Poor

Though the first kindergartens catered primarily to middle- and upper-class white children, in the late 1870s, 1880s, and 1890s child gardening was taken up as a form of urban social reform and racial "uplifting." Charity or "free" kindergarten associations, often supported by the wives of wealthy industrialists, were formed in Boston, New York, Cincinnati, Chicago, St. Louis, San Francisco, and other cities, and kindergarten teaching became a part of settlement work. Churches sponsored kindergartens, as did reform groups such as the Ethical Culture Society in New York, and the National Association of Colored Women, which made the establishment of kindergartens for black children in the South one of its main priorities.

Though charity-kindergarten advocates' rationales often reflected their social class, and were replete with horrifying descriptions of the immoral, unhealthy conditions in which poor children were being raised, the remedy they prescribed—the Froebelian kindergarten—was universal. As free-kindergartner Patty Smith Hill put it, "Though the thought may be humiliating to some, psychology reveals the fact that the Creator has seen fit to develop the mind in all classes of society by the same laws." It was "wonderful," Hill thought, "to see the extremes of society . . . unfold and blossom, not only under the same laws and principles, but even in some cases under the same methods."[30]

In applying Froebelianism to the problems of the city, however, charity kindergartners were faced with the reality of children who needed physical care as well as education. Thus, in addition to the usual Froebelian activities, urban kindergartners supplied breakfast, washed children, and did home visiting in the afternoon. They led mothers' meetings at which they taught Froebelian techniques, and also dealt with health, housing, and other welfare problems.

Charity-kindergarten teachers thought of themselves as missionaries. They prided themselves on their ability to establish relationships with poor families and to perform socially beneficial tasks. Descriptions of settlement-house activities and records of free kindergarten associations document the good works of charity kindergartners outside of the kindergarten. But other urban teachers were involved in the lives of their students outside of school, too, particularly if they were of the same ethnicity and lived in the same community as their pupils—as was often not the case with kindergarten teachers. Though the number of lower-class, non-native-born kindergartners increased when kindergartens entered the public schools and public normal schools began providing kindergarten training, charity kindergartners generally came from higher social-class backgrounds than the children and mothers they taught. In Boston, for instance, the network of charity kindergartens sponsored by Pauline Agassiz Shaw, the daughter of Harvard's noted naturalist Louis Agassiz and wife of wealthy industrialist Quincy Adams Shaw, was directed and staffed by women educated in private kindergarten training schools such as those run by Mary Garland and Lucy Wheelock, which catered primarily to daughters of the non-immigrant, middle- and upper-managerial, merchant, and professional classes.[31]

Charity kindergartning was in some ways a continuation of the genteel voluntarism of earlier female reform efforts. Though more-scientific, politically liberal approaches toward child gardening developed during the Progressive Era, vestiges of this older benevolent mode remained. The differences between charity kindergartning and more radical forms of urban social reform were particularly apparent in settlement house work. Kindergartens were a central component of the settlement movement. There were even kindergarten settlements, such as the Elizabeth Peabody House in Boston, where kindergartning was the main focus of activity. Jane Addams supported Froebelian educational philosophy, and a kindergarten was the first organized program at Hull House. She acknowledged, however, a distinction between the kindergarten teacher at Hull House, who came just to teach and then returned home to an affluent Chicago suburb, and other members of the settlement, who lived in the urban community in which they worked.[32]

The differences between charity kindergartners and settlement workers in places like Hull House may have had as much to do with interests as with political orientation and how and where they lived. Most kindergartners saw themselves primarily as teachers rather than social workers. Their main contributions were to education, not social reform. That kindergarten teachers chose to concentrate their energies on educational concerns rather than on other forms of social welfare, and gradually withdrew from urban-reform efforts as kindergartens became part of public schools, need not be viewed as a wholly negative, conservative trend, as one historian has implied, but can be seen instead as a lesson in the more limited, but still valuable, goals that kindergartens and kindergartners could achieve.[33]

In fact, some kindergartners at the turn of the century were aware that the association between kindergarten teaching and social reform could have both positive and negative consequences. Nina Vandewalker, author of the first history of the kindergarten movement (published in 1908), was concerned that social-reform goals obscured the kindergarten's "educational significance." She worried that the emphasis on social welfare rather than on education lowered standards for training, since the goal of charity kindergartning was to provide as extensive service as rapidly as possible, rather than perfecting teaching techniques. Another difficulty was that charity-kindergarten teachers established the precedent of working for free or at a rate that did not reflect "the true valuation" of their work "in the educational labor market," and public kindergartens were thus slow in adjusting kindergarten teachers' pay to that of other teachers. But, Vandewalker felt, these problems were offset by the beneficial effects of the association between the kindergarten and social-reform efforts, which speeded the process of awareness and acceptance and provided the rationale for the institution of public kindergartens. Without the influence of settlements, churches, and other organizations, Vandewalker concluded, the kindergarten "would have lacked . . . the many-sided interpretation that has made it a significant influence in American life."[34]

Inside urban kindergartens, child gardeners modified the curriculum to emphasize the naturalistic aspects of Froebelianism that they felt city children needed most. Kindergartners transformed their classrooms into veritable greenhouses filled with plants and other natural objects. In contrast to reports of the lifelessness of most schoolrooms, Lucy Wheelock's description of her kindergarten in downtown Boston in the 1880s was typical of the colorful array of flora and fauna that urban kindergartners brought into their classrooms. Geraniums bloomed in the windows while children watched a caterpillar emerge from its cocoon. There was sand to play with; a shelf was filled with treasures such as a lump of coal, a piece of coral, and "pine cones, a branch of an oak tree with a cluster of green acorns, sea shells, chestnuts and other nuts"; and a large wasps' nest decorated one of the cabinets.[35]

Though the lengths to which urban kindergartners such as Lucy Wheelock went to create an artificially natural environment in their classrooms were criticized by some educators, this was common in other urban child-saving efforts as well. Many Progressive Era educators like Wheelock had grown up in small country towns and saw cities as unnatural, unhealthy environments. Kindergartners' belief in the efficacy of naturalism as a cure for urban problems was also bolstered by supposedly scientific research. G. Stanley Hall's observations in charity kindergartens in Boston in the 1880s, for instance, where he found that city children lacked knowledge of common natural objects, such as beehives and types of trees, exemplified this pervasive antiurban ideology and lent support to the naturalism inherent in Froebelian pedagogy.[36]

Though urban kindergartners changed the curriculum in some ways to meet the needs of their students, Froebelian pedagogy was still their guide. Charity kindergartners compensated for urban children's lack of exposure to Victorian ideals of nature and spent time dealing with physical needs and helping families, but in more kindergartens in the late nineteenth century the Froebelian educational program was implemented in a relatively uniform fashion, regardless of the social-class background of the children. Poor children played with the gifts and did the occupations in the same prescribed manner as upper-class children.

Because the kindergarten curriculum consisted primarily of manual exercises, singing, and games, all of which required little cultural knowledge, Froebelian activities were probably about equally manageable for children from different social-class backgrounds. There is no evidence of kindergarten teachers voicing worries over whether poor children could do the work, or that the quality of their work was inferior. In fact, one charity kindergartner suggested that rich children needed the kindergarten as much as poor children because of their more limited "dramatic expression and creative power" and difficulty with "symbolic games and original handwork."[37]

But though urban child gardeners may have been impartial and egalitarian in their implementation of kindergarten curricula, Froebelianism was not the universal method of early childhood education they believed it to be. Like all pedagogy, it reflected the class and cultural background of its originator and proponents. Charity kindergartners could not help imposing the white, Protestant, middle-class norms of Froebelianism and their own backgrounds of the poor, immigrant, and black children and mothers they taught. These biases were particularly obvious in some of the descriptions of the meetings that kindergartners conducted for mothers. Some kindergartners, however, such as Elizabeth Harrison, whose enormously popular classes for mothers were a forerunner of the National Congress of Mothers and (later) the Parent–Teacher Association, viewed mothers' meetings as an opportunity for women from different social class backgrounds to meet and learn from one another. "The mothers themselves will teach [the kindergarten teacher] many things and give her flashes of insight far deeper than they realize," Harrison said in a 1903 report on mothers' classes.[38]

But other kindergartners were more condescending. And while many mothers may have enjoyed kindergarten meetings and found them helpful, regardless of their class background, it is hard to know how women struggling to raise children in the environment of an urban slum felt about being schooled in Froebelian child-rearing techniques by zealous (and usually unmarried) women, some of whom may not have understood much about the conditions of their charges' lives. Harrison was aware of this problem, but insisted that it could be overcome because of the universality of women's concern for children's welfare: "Every mother enjoys seeing her child made happy, and the sight brings her a step nearer to the woman who has given this joy to her child," she wrote. This was the bond that linked kindergartners to the mothers of the children they taught, Harrison argued, despite differences in their circumstances.[39]

Exceptions to the relative uniformity of kindergarten curricula could be found in programs for black children wherein racial stereotypes sometimes superseded Froebelianism. Rationales for providing kindergartens for black children were frequently biased both by the background of the children and that of educational reformers. Some whites argued that black children needed the kindergarten more than white children because of the manual training it provided, and some blacks concurred. Other blacks, however, like Anna J. Murray, who organized kindergartens for black children in Washington, D. C., argued that black children too would benefit from the play experiences and "communion with nature" of the Froebelian kindergarten.[40]

In some kindergartens for black children, however, vocationalism seems to have won out over Froebelianism. An account of a week-long visit to a kindergarten at the Hampton Institute in 1907 illustrates this fact. The curriculum at the Hampton

Institute kindergarten was based on the "kitchen garden," an adaptation of the kindergarten to domestic training, developed in New York in the late 1870s by Emily Huntington. On Monday morning, children in the Hampton Institute kindergarten began by dusting the room of "invisible dust," and then washed clothes with hot water and real soap, while some children played with Froebelian gifts. In the afternoon they worked in the garden, hoeing and raking. On Tuesday morning the girls ironed, did some paper cutting and folding, and took care of their baby dolls, while on Wednesday they made doll furniture. On Thursday the class visited an orchard to watch a farmer planting, and then made farm tools out of clay. On Friday they did house cleaning. Though the kitchen garden curriculum was not designed specifically for black children, nor did all kindergartens for black children use these methods, there were clearly racial overtones in kindergarten programs such as the one at Hampton Institute, where black children were being trained for vocations in domestic service and agricultural work as much as, or more than, being educated in a generic Froebelian fashion.[41] (See Figure 3.2.)

Some black kindergartners, however, balanced the stereotype of manual training with black children's need for a general education. Josephine Yates, president of the National Association of Colored Women and author of a widely read column on education in the *Colored American Magazine,* actively promoted Froebelianism among black parents and advocated the universality of the kindergarten, rather than its supposed specific advantages for black children. In a 1906 article on "Education

FIGURE 3.2. Kindergarten at the Hampton Institute.
From *Southern Workman* 36 (1907): 544, © Hampton Institute, Hampton, VA. Reprinted by permission.

and Genetic Psychology,'' she stressed the importance of providing opportunities for play and an educational environment ''adjusted'' to harmonize with children's organic development.[42]

In another article, Yates described in detail the work of the Kindergarten Department of the National Association of Colored Women, which was headed by Haydee Campbell, a Froebelian kindergarten supervisor in the St. Louis public schools. An Oberlin graduate, Campbell won out over white competitors to supervise kindergartens for black children in St. Louis, the first city to adopt public kindergartens. Campbell, who trained a number of black kindergarten teachers, was probably trained herself by Susan Blow, the staunch Froebelian who had convinced Superintendent William Torrey Harris to initiate kindergartens in 1873. Louisville, Kentucky was another center for kindergarten training in the South. In 1899, the Louisville Free Kindergarten Association, headed by Patty Smith Hill, opened a normal class for black kindergartners, and by 1905 had trained 17 black kindergarten teachers.[43]

Yates's article also described the spread of mothers' clubs and private kindergartens, and the progress of public kindergarten education for black children. Black children, according to Yates, were most likely to attend kindergarten in public systems that did not operate separate schools for whites and blacks, though black children were sometimes denied admission to kindergarten even when they were permitted to attend upper grades. Southern school systems, particularly those in rural areas, were the least likely to provide kindergartens for black children. In fact, when Yates conducted a survey in 1901, she was unable to locate *any* public kindergartens for black children in the South. Black women's clubs, churches, and institutes such as Hampton and Tuskegee, and Howard University and Atlanta University, sponsored kindergartens, however. In the North, white charity groups and churches also provided kindergartens for black children. Lucy Wheelock, for instance, was instrumental in organizing a free kindergarten in 1895 in Hope Chapel of Old South Church, in what was then a black section of Boston, and similar programs were started in other major cities.[44]

Child Gardening in the Public Schools

Some child gardeners were ambivalent about the idea of public kindergartens, hoping instead that charity programs might be sufficient to meet the needs of the poor and immigrant children who filled America's cities. In the 1870s, Elizabeth Peabody, who had initially promoted public kindergartens in St. Louis and Boston, where a public kindergarten class had opened in 1870 and then closed a year later for financial reasons, began speaking out against institutionalization because what she saw as the increasingly bureaucratic nature of schools was inimical to kindergartning. Citing the difficulty of ''keeping the heart'' in an institution and the ''business character of superintendents,'' which, she felt, ''had fallen below the philanthropic spirit which should always preside over education,'' Peabody wanted to keep the kindergarten in private, loving, *female* hands.[45]

By the late 1880s, however, it was apparent that private philanthropy would be unable to serve the rapidly expanding urban population. Charity-kindergarten associations began to seek support from public schools. In Boston, for instance, where Pauline Agassiz Shaw spent more than $200,000 between 1882 and 1889 on a network of 31 charity kindergartens, some located in public school buildings, the School Committee agreed to assume permanent responsibility for Mrs. Shaw's kindergartens in 1888. In Washington, D.C., Louisa Mann, daughter-in-law of Horace and Mary Peabody Mann and founder of the Columbian Kindergarten Association, and Anna Murray, of the National Association of Colored Women, succeeded in convincing Congress to appropriate $8,000 for white kindergartens and $4,000 for black kindergartens in the public schools in 1898. Free-kindergartners in Philadelphia, Chicago, and New York also mounted successful campaigns to incorporate child gardening into the public schools. Though restrictive state laws and costs posed stumbling blocks, by the end of the 1890s kindergartens had been adopted by most large public school systems and in many suburbs and smaller cities.[46]

During the period from 1900 to 1930, the number of children enrolled in public kindergartens grew steadily. In 1912 over 350,000 children were enrolled in public kindergartens, a 133 percent increase from 1902. By 1930 enrollments in public kindergartens approached 780,000. Naturally, the demand for teachers rose accordingly. The number of public normal schools offering kindergarten training grew rapidly, from 33 in 1903 to 76 in 1916, and many private liberal-arts colleges and universities added kindergarten courses as well.[47]

The kindergarten as a workplace changed as charity kindergartens were incorporated into school systems. But there was continuity as well, as kindergartners maintained many of the hallmarks of their distinctive approach to teaching within the environment of the public school. Charity-kindergarten associations frequently were subsumed into urban school systems intact. Often the same staff and staffing pattern of assistant, teacher, director, trainer, and supervisor of preexisting private kindergarten organizations was kept in place. For instance, Laura Fisher, the director of Pauline Agassiz Shaw's charity kindergartens in Boston, became the director of kindergartens in the public system, and similar arrangements developed in New York, Philadelphia, and other cities.

Most large public school systems had separate kindergarten departments administered by a female supervisor. Though job descriptions varied from system to system, and often depended on the personalities and relative power of the supervisor and the superintendent, the kindergarten supervisor, like a private-kindergarten director, was generally responsible for most aspects of the public-kindergarten program. As a 1918 U.S. Bureau of Education study documented, in most cities supervisors made decisions about class size and promotion of children, ordered supplies and materials, ensured that there would be opportunities for outdoor and gardening activities, planned the kindergarten curriculum, provided for what today would be called in-service education, and supervised teachers. The architectural planning of new kindergarten rooms, however, was not usually within the purview of the supervisor, nor was the determination of the number of sessions a day or their length—possibly because the expense involved required that such decisions be made higher up in the system, and because these matters were controlled by state and school board regulations.[48]

An aspect of supervisors' responsibilities which affected individual teachers very directly was supervision and evaluation. It is interesting to note which characteristics kindergarten supervisors looked for in teachers. The qualities mentioned most frequently by supervisors surveyed were "sympathy, understanding, seeing from the child's standpoint," and "play-spirit," not what one would expect on evaluations of grade-level teachers where the teaching of basic skills would be highly ranked. In fact, as the author of the Bureau of Education survey (who was a kindergartner herself) noted, this was the main difference between kindergarten teachers and "grade teachers," the latter of whom were "trained to consider and deal with the child as a *learning* being, and not primarily as a feeling, doing individual."[49]

Most public kindergarten supervisors viewed their job as communicating "essential principles" rather than developing the daily program of activities, which was the responsibility of individual teachers. Some supervisors provided a curriculum outline or handbook, and a few required teachers to submit weekly or monthly lesson plans. In general, however, individual teachers were free to make decisions about their pupils' programmatic needs.

Despite this purported freedom, there were tensions between supervisors and teachers over control of the curriculum. Though most supervisors surveyed said they allowed "much freedom," permitted the teacher's "personality . . . to show itself," and kept the program "flexible," some public-kindergarten teachers felt they did not need a supervisor. Superintendents, who may have had their own axes to grind, criticized kindergarten supervisors for being too rigid and dogmatic, especially with younger teachers whose progressive ideas and methods sometimes conflicted with those of supervisors.

There also was concern that kindergarten teachers felt the need to "cater to the supervisor's whims for the sake of good standing," and that supervisors imposed too much uniformity. These criticisms notwithstanding, kindergartners were freer to design and implement their own curriculum in public schools than they had been in private kindergartens, where they worked under the constant, direct, daily supervision of a senior kindergarten director and trainer.[50]

The tensions between kindergarten supervisors, principals, and superintendents also affected teachers. Some superintendents sought to curtail the power and independence of kindergarten supervisors, or do away with them altogether and bring kindergartens under the administration of principals. But superintendents and principals were hampered in this effort by their lack of knowledge of kindergartning.

As the twentieth century progressed, battles between female kindergarten supervisors and male school administrators increased. Though the 1918 Bureau of Education survey on kindergarten supervision reported "a good spirit of cooperation" and "democratic" relationships between kindergarten supervisors, teachers, principals, and superintendents, the power of kindergarten supervisors gradually lessened. As a result, individual kindergarten teachers gained even more autonomy in their classrooms.[51]

Other important organizational changes affected the practice of child gardening when kindergartens entered the public schools. Class size increased and double sessions became common. In the years after 1900, superintendents, who were under growing pressure to accommodate larger numbers of children, became concerned about the cost of kindergartens, which, because of their smaller size and special materials, were more expensive than primary classes. The solution to this problem was to have kindergartners teach two sessions. A 1915 Bureau of Education survey reported that by the 1911–1912 school year, 546 of 867 school systems had instituted morning and afternoon kindergartens. Though there was considerable variety in schedule, size, and length of session, and rationales for assignment of children, most sessions were from two to two-and-a-half hours long, with older children generally attending in the morning.[52]

The change in sessions severely limited kindergartners' social welfare activities. Public-kindergarten teachers continued to make home visits and hold mothers' meetings, the mainstays of the charity-kindergarten program, but with double sessions they no longer had as much time for this community work. Kindergartners were loathe to give up their afternoons, as they felt their contacts with mothers were critical to the success of the kindergarten program. As one public-school kindergarten teacher described, she used mothers' meetings to teach about Froebel, explain kindergarten activities, and ensure that mothers promoted regular, punctual attendance, and dressed their children warmly. But there was a larger purpose, too, she explained, because the kindergarten was "the link that unites the school and the family," and children needed to "feel the bond of sympathy which exists" between mother and teacher.[53]

Most kindergarten teachers surveyed objected to double sessions because these weakened the relationship between the home and the kindergarten. As the director of kindergartens in the New York public schools stated, the kindergartner had a dual role: She was "not only a teacher, but a social worker," and there was a clear trade-off between her teaching and social welfare activities. "If it is more important to accommodate large numbers of children, then the double session may be introduced; but if the kindergartner is to take her rightful place in the community as an influence in the home as well as in the school, . . . then she must have some afternoon hours free."[54]

Another rationale for public kindergartners conducting mothers' meetings that became prominent in the first decades of the twentieth century was Americanization. In fact, the adoption of kindergartens by public schools was propelled in large part by concerns about the need to socialize the rapidly growing immigrant population. During World War I in particular, kindergarten teachers, like other teachers, were instructed to teach patriotism and American political values. The importance of this socializing function of schools was emphasized for kindergartners, who were in direct contact with foreign-born families.

A 1919 U.S. Bureau of Education pamphlet told kindergartners to "visit the immigrant mother oftener than American mothers," to teach English and civics in mothers' meetings because of the "danger" of the "new electoral power" that these women's husbands wielded, and to help immigrant women find substitutes for their native foods. A 1920 pamphlet, however, questioned whether it was in the American spirit to "rob the immigrants of all they hold dear—language, customs, racial traditions, religious beliefs." The pamphlet also suggested that kindergarten teachers use mothers' meetings for "reviving . . . foreign customs of dress, food, music," so that the meetings could be an "exchange of ideas . . . as well as the opening wedge for the tactful introduction of approved American customs."[55]

Despite these rationales for leaving kindergartners' afternoons free for home visits and community work, kindergarten teachers at most public school systems were assigned two sessions, primarily as an economy measure. The institution of double sessions also reflected a new concern for parity in the job descriptions of kindergarten and primary-grade teachers. In cities with only one session of kindergarten, kindergartners were sometimes asked to help other teachers and to engage in other within-school activities in the afternoon. A National Education Association report documented that by 1923 most kindergartners were paid about the same as primary teachers, with kindergartners in smaller towns (which frequently did not have special kindergarten supervisors) being paid somewhat more than primary teachers, and those in larger cities (where there tended to be supervisors) being paid somewhat less than primary teachers.[56]

Though kindergarten teachers' hours of in-class time were usually somewhat shorter than those of primary grade teachers, even with double sessions, kindergartners were convinced that they worked as hard, if not harder, than other teachers, and wanted this understood. "Kindergarten work is not more difficult, but takes more time," one kindergartner reported. And teaching young children was hard because, as another kindergartner surveyed responded, "it is more of a strain on the nerves and requires more patience." And a kindergarten teacher who taught double sessions "has two sets of children the same size as the primary teacher, and so has to respond to many differing personalities."[57]

Despite these feelings, and objections to the curtailing of their role as home visitors and family educators, public school kindergarten teachers gradually accepted the need for double sessions. They viewed the change as the price to be paid for acceptance of the kindergarten. As one child gardener put it, "The double session promotes a general feeling on the part of the community, the teaching body, and the teacher that the kindergarten is a vital, integral part of the school system and not a luxury, exceptional in its organization and privileges."[58]

There were differences, however, in how kindergartners reacted to being part of the public schools. Some adapted readily, others resisted. From the perspective of Patty Smith Hill, who supported institutionalization, there could be two equally unfortunate results: Some kindergartners reponded to the tendency of schools to reward teachers who were didactic disciplinarians, while other kindergartners, who clung to Froebelianism, saw schools as "always in the wrong," and rejected any form of compromise.[59]

In fact, many public kindergartens still functioned like separate programs, with an environment, philosophy, and methods so different from those of schools that kindergartners and school personnel worried increasingly that the gap between kindergarten and first grade might cause difficulties for young children. As one kindergartner stated, "the home and the kindergarten are sometimes felt to be more closely united than the kindergarten and the next grade of the school." This discontinuity led to a movement to "adjust" the kindergarten and first grade. Not surprisingly, however, a 1915 Bureau of Education survey found considerable disagreement over what and how adjustments between kindergarten and first grade should be made. Superintendents, principals, and primary teachers thought kindergarten children were too dependent during handwork periods, needed "constant help and supervision," evidenced "unnecessary communication and ill-timed play," and recommended that kindergartners provide less assistance and enforce more quietness. They also suggested that first-grade teachers introduce more handwork, permit greater freedom, discipline less strictly, use moveable furniture, have smaller classes, and assign more creative seatwork.[60]

When kindergartners were surveyed by a fellow kindergartner, they were asked how kindergarten prepared children for first grade and how first grade should be adjusted, not how kindergartens should be changed. In answer to the first question, kindergarten teachers ranked ability to read and write last, and described instead the preparation in color and shape discrimination which kindergarten activities provided. When asked how closer contacts should be formed between kindergarten and first grade, they mentioned requiring training courses in primary methods, observation, attending joint conferences, and other means, but nowhere suggested altering the kindergarten program. Kindergartners made the same suggestions for changing first grade as had superintendents, principals, and primary teachers, reiterating the importance of the "play-spirit" to young children.[61]

The institution of kindergartens in public schools had an impact on primary education, and vice versa. Observational studies of kindergarten and primary teaching methods in the late 1920s and early 1930s documented evidence of the infiltration of child-gardening methods into the primary grades. And primary methods came into use in kindergartens as well, as worksheets appeared; and "reading readiness" and other skill-oriented assignments were added to kindergarten curricula, cutting into the amount of time allotted for play and other nonacademic activities. Though kindergarten and first grade teaching methods continued to be quite different, as more and more teachers were trained in both kindergarten and primary pedagogy the notion of a "gap" or "chasm" between the two grades was replaced by terms like "correlation" and "coordination."[62]

Changes in Child-Gardening Methods After the Turn of the Century

In the decades after the turn of the century many different methods competed to fill the vacuum left by the decline of orthodox Froebelianism. While the views of progressives prevailed in academia, where kindergarten methods became a topic of scholarly debate, no single model replaced Froebelianism in the classroom. The concentric program, which tied activities to daily and weekly themes such as the home, commmunity helpers, transportation, food production, and other topics, became popular, as did other approaches—such as John Dewey's progressive industrial curriculum, in which children made useful objects rather than symbolic designs; Kilpatrick's project method; nature study; literature, music, and art; and seasonal programs.

Writing in 1920 in a pamphlet published by the Bureau of Education, Julia Wade Abbot documented this burgeoning variety of kindergarten subjects. As Abbot described, ''paper borders of pumpkins and grapes at Thanksgiving time, pictures of Christmas trees and holly at Christmas, flags and soldiers at Washington's Birthday, and flowers and rabbits at Easter'' all could be linked to handwork which expressed thought, and there were numerous other educationally valuable experiences for young children. ''Life in the kindergarten,'' Abbot exclaimed, provided ''an inexhaustible supply of things to be talked about.''[63]

The most radically open-ended approach to child gardening was the free-play curriculum, in which children were allowed time periods to play with materials and participate in activities of their own choice. In a year-long study conducted in public kindergartens in Santa Barbara, California in 1898, Superintendent of Schools Frederic Burk (a student of G. Stanley Hall) and Caroline Frear Burk found that, when given the choice, young children did not play with Froebelian materials but preferred dolls, swings, bean bags, and other toys. The problem with the kindergarten, the Burks declared, was that the child had not been ''particularly consulted either in the choice of material, or in the use to be made of it.'' The ''natural reaction toward these materials'' of the ''docile little puppets who furnish the background in the drama of the gifts and occupations'' was thus ''hard to determine.'' The Burks gave children two free-play periods, labeled ''recesses,'' which in later free-play kindergartens became the focus of the day, and encouraged teachers to become more aware of children's intrinsic interests.[64]

Changes in kindergarten teaching methods resulted both from pressures within school systems and from academic research. University psychologists and teacher trainers were sensitive to the demands of parents, teachers, and school administrators concerning useful information about children's education. New, academically based curricula such as those developed by Patty Smith Hill and Alice Temple reflected this awareness. In the 1920s Hill, who had replaced Susan Blow as a lecturer on kindergarten methods at Teachers College at Columbia University, began applying Edward Thorndike's psychological theories to kindergartning. The result was a behavioristic approach to kindergarten teaching, *A Conduct Curriculum,* which focused on habit formation.

Working with a group of teachers and other kindergarten trainers, Hill developed a ''Habit Inventory,'' a lengthy and specific list of kindergarten activities with the behavioral outcomes they were expected to produce. Under ''paperwork,'' for example, there were three groups of 15 activities with the learning outcomes for each, such as ''cutting paper,'' next to which were listed ''pleasure in activity'' and ''learning how to use scissors.'' The specificity of the ''Habit Inventory'' was attractive to teachers, who were used to such detailed instructions. The curriculum became very influential both as a guide to kindergarten evaluation and as a report form for individual children.[65]

A different, more comprehensive approach to kindergarten teaching evolved in the 1920s at the University of Chicago, the other main center for curriculum development, where Alice Temple was in charge of the kindergarten department. Much influenced by John Dewey, who had experimented with and modified Froebelian methods at the University of Chicago laboratory school in the late 1890s,

Temple had been director of the Chicago Free Kindergarten Association before coming to the university. At the school, she collaborated with elementary-curriculum specialist Samuel Chester Parker in the development of a textbook on combined kindergarten and first-grade teaching methods.

Temple and Parker's curriculum, *Unified Kindergarten and First-Grade Teaching,* published in 1925, showed the influence of Thorndike and the measurement movement, but was closer to Dewey in its emphasis on community life and social experience. More an explication of underlying principles than a how-to manual or directive guide, Temple and Parker's book tried to unify kindergarten and first-grade curricula in a way the authors stated would be "continuous and delightful." Though they sympathized with the desire of kindergartners to bring "more enjoyment" into children's lives, they saw "no necessary conflict" between Froebelian idealism and the teaching of basic skills, which they argued could be done in a gradual, developmentally appropriate manner.

Temple and Parker's broad curriculum linked social and cognitive skillls, such as "good will" and reading, with recreational activities, study of community life, health activities, and "civic and moral habits." They included examples of model lessons on topics such as the post office and the farm; a yearly calendar of seasonal themes; a list of habits, such as getting to school on time, and the importance of saying "please" and "thank you;" and concluded with a section on the "general spirit" of "happiness, freedom, orderly habits, obedience, courtesy, independence in thinking and acting, and confidence in and affection for the teacher," which should pervade the kindergarten and first grade.[66]

In the 1920s, other new forms of child gardening also became popular which shifted the attention of kindergartners to younger children. Nursery-school leaders such as Rachel and Margaret McMillan, Harriet Johnson, Lucy Sprague Mitchell, and Abigail Eliot, and such other advocates of education for young children as Maria Montessori, adapted psychological theories and developed new classroom methods for teachers. Nursery-school teaching methods in particular, which were less patterned and more focused on nurturance and physical and emotional development, began influencing kindergarten and primary teaching. And kindergarten and nursery-school teachers themselves continued to experiment with the curriculum. As the psychologist Arnold Gesell described in 1926, the issue of kindergarten–primary adjustment receded in the larger context of early childhood education from birth through the primary grades:

> For the moment the question of the adjustment of the kindergarten to the primary school has become overshadowed by the question "What shall the kindergarten do about younger children of nursery age?" In principle the older question of kindergarten–primary readjustment may be counted as solved—a primary school no longer considers itself modern unless it is imbued with the spirit of the progressive kindergarten. . . . The whole period from birth to the first molars is basically an educational period quite as consequential for social welfare as the years of public school attendance. . . . The great goal ought to be the unification of policy for the whole sphere of early elementary education from the lower primary to the nethermost level.[67]

Conclusions

The institutionalization of kindergartens in the public schools hastened the breakdown of the rigid Froebelian curriculum that had determined the practice of child gardening in the nineteenth century. Controversies over curricula, and changes in kindergarten organization after the turn of the century, resulted in more autonomy for teachers and increased diversity in kindergarten programs. Froebelian curriculum guides no longer supplied the only script for what to do. Nor did supposedly infallible private-kindergarten directors provide daily instructions on how to teach. Child gardeners had been given license to invent curricula themselves, and almost any topic, it seemed, could be a source for kindergarten discussions and activities. Even more radical was the idea that the children should create the curriculum. The uniform Froebelian program was gone. In its place, individual teachers and kindergarten and nursery-school directors and supervisors assumed responsibility for making decisions about what the practice of child gardening was to be like in kindergartens and nursery schools around the country.

But through there was more diversity than in the nineteenth century, when Froebelian manuals and kindergarten trainers directed teachers' and children's every move, in fact twentieth-century kindergartens were quite uniform. Most teachers used a version of what was sometimes called thc "reconstructed program," a combination of free play and teacher-directed activities, such as counting, color and form discrimination, and letter recognition exercises; the now standard seasonal motifs of the making of turkeys, snowmen, and so on; and curriculum units on the home, community, nature, and other topics considered to be of interest or relevance to young children. Child-gardening methods were different from school teaching, but kindergartners created their own orthodoxy, a "one best system" for young children, which became the dominant pedagogical model for children in preschools and kindergartens.

The characteristics of this educational system for young children changed considerably between 1860 and 1930, but there was underlying continuity in the relationship of child gardening to the larger culture and to schools. The Froebelian gifts and occupations, songs, and games, which supposedly corresponded to universal forms and laws of development and replicated nature and traditional German family life, were replaced by rather similar (though less rigidly patterned) sensory discrimination exercises based on modern, scientific concepts of children's development, reading readiness activities, and thematic units on the seasons and on middle-class American life. Character training through the inculcation of morals and models was replaced by habit formation and an equally pervasive emphasis on correct social attitudes and good behavior. These changes, though important in terms of what went on inside the classroom, did not alter the basic socialization process which was the main societal effect of child gardening. In this larger sense child gardening was, and continued to be, normative (and class-, ethnically-, and racially biased—as other historians have pointed out).

But there were aspects of kindergarten teaching methods which made the practice of child gardening—and, arguably, its effects—different from other forms of teaching. Kindergartens often were noisy, messy places where children were intended to play freely and enjoy themselves. In addition to such qualities as obedience and neatness, kindergarten guides and texts also prescribed happiness, freedom, and independence, characteristics unlikely to appear in training manuals for the upper grades. Child gardeners do not appear to have been aware of the contradictions of rewarding such divergent behaviors as orderliness and spontaneity, however. They hoped to somehow strike a balance, and remained optimistic that kindergartens and preschools could accomplish this ambitious task. Kindergartners' belief in the possibility of achieving harmony between the needs of the individual and the community prevented them from acknowledging the tensions underlying such an accommodation. It is this naive but appealing unwillingness to see the difficulties inherent in controlling children's behavior, yet wanting them to be "free," that most characterizes this approach to teaching.

From the evidence of twentieth-century curriculum guides, U.S. Bureau of Education surveys, and other descriptive and prescriptive literature of kindergarten teaching, this tension between freedom and order did not (as has been suggested) diminish when kindergartens entered the public schools. Preparation for first grade gradually replaced the goal of social reform, in part because it was thought that the lower-class children whom many public kindergartens served needed to be readied for school in order to succeed; but kindergartners continued to value nurturance.

Primary teaching methods were leavened by the progressive education movement generally, but kindergartners too were responsible for introducing some of the "play spirit" into the environment of the primary grades. And, though some female kindergarten supervisors were overshadowed by male school administrators, individual kindergarten teachers gained autonomy over their classrooms (more so than other teachers), and kindergarten departments remained onc of the last strongholds of female power within school systems.

The price of this relative autonomy, however, was marginality. Kindergartners, left more or less alone to develop and implement their own pedagogy, were ignored and undervalued. Though principals tended not to interfere with kindergarten teachers' work, this may have been more because male school administrators felt uncomfortable in the feminine atmosphere of the kindergarten, and with young children who required physical care and nurturance as much as instruction, than because they understood or respected the purposes or value of kindergartning. Isolated and lacking tangible evidence of the worth of the kindergarten, kindergartners did not supply the kind of evaluation results required to rationalize funding decisions in American public education. School administrators complained about the costs of kindergartens, and some school systems and states were slow in instituting kindergartens because of their expense.

Though the areas of conflict between kindergarten and upper-grade teachers diminished as kindergartners' hours and responsibilities came to approximate those of the upper grades, disagreements remain. These differences of opinion over children's needs and the nature of teaching are central to *current* debates over whether public schools should begin providing programs for three- and four-year-olds. There are parallels in the reactions of kindergartners to the institutionalization of the kindergarten historically, and early childhood education advocates today, who express concerns that young children's needs for flexibility, intimacy, security, and nurturance may be difficult to meet in the environment of a large public school system. Modern early childhood education advocates worry about loss of parent involvement and teacher–parent communication, for reasons very similar to concerns raised about double sessions at the turn of the century. Teachers of young children today also are fearful that the institution of preschools within the public schools may strengthen the trend toward academics for three- and four-year-olds, just as public kindergartens became more focused on reading readiness and other aspects of school preparation. And standardization is a concern, as proponents of early childhood education fear that the cultural pluralism and programmatic diversity of privately operated preschools may be lost if three- and four-year-olds are educated in the "one best system."[68]

As in the past, however, the benefits to children and their families must be weighed against concerns about program quality. Early childhood education advocates are aware of the trade-offs between quality and the delivery of services, and of the potential advantages of programs sponsored by the public schools. Preschool education in the public schools would be more equitable and less economically segregated than the current dual system, in which children from lower-income families attend state- and federally-funded programs and children from middle- and upper-class families attend private preschools. Readily accessible preschool programs in public schools, like kindergartens, would bring preschools out of the basements where they have frequently been housed, hopefully into specially designed spaces something like the one Elizabeth Peabody futuristically described. Finally, public-school-sponsored programs for three- and four-year-olds might help resolve the historical division of child care and early childhood education, by providing developmentally appropriate, flexibly scheduled, comprehensive services which meet the needs of young children and their families. The problems to which early childhood educators point are serious, however, and providing programs of sufficient quality would be expensive.

Recent proposals for changes in teacher preparation and certification present similar policy dilemmas. Requiring teachers of young children to major in one of the disciplines of the arts and sciences, as opposed to education, will provide them with a broader educational background and may counteract the isolation and marginality that have historically characterized child gardening, and help upgrade the professional status of teaching young children. It may also, however, diminish the child-centered orientation of teacher-training programs in early childhood education, and the attention that such programs pay to details of child life and classroom practice. It would be useful to apply early childhood educators' knowledge of children and teaching to developing a "knowledge base" for educational practice and redesigning teacher training at all levels.

For more than a century a relatively small but determined group of female (and a few male) educators have devoted their professional lives to the development of a special form of teaching characterized by qualities our society identifies with women—qualities that kindergartners felt were in short supply in schools. As the author of a Bureau of Education report on kindergartens wrote in 1914:

> Those who are watching the trend of school practice cannot yet decide whether the kindergarten teacher stands in peril of losing just that quality which has been so potent a factor in modifying school theory and practice. That quality, not easily described, grows out of the motherly, nurturing character of the kindergartner's work. It is not "an artificial pose of motherhood," but a genuine necessary element of the teaching relationship, lacking which all teaching becomes flat, dull, inert. Scientific it may be, but it fails to be humanized.

Hopefully the legacy of the history of child gardening, the fine-grained focus on and valuing of children's daily experiences and the nuances of the interactions among children, teachers, and parents, can be preserved as teachers of children young and old are educated in a more academically rigorous, clinically sophisticated fashion.[69]

Notes

1. David B. Tyack, *The One Best System: A History of American Urban Education* (Cambridge, Ma: Harvard University Press, 1974); and Elizabeth Peabody, "Kindergarten Guide," in Elizabeth Peabody and Mary Mann, *Moral Culture of Infancy and Kindergarten Guide* (Boston: T.O.H.P. Burham, 1863), p. 9.
2. For a discussion of the transition from dame schools to primary schools, and the attendance of younger children, see Carl F. Kaestle and Maris A. Vinovskis, "From Apronstrings to ABCs: School Entry in Nineteenth-Century Massachusetts," in *Education and Social Change in Nineteenth-Century Massachusetts* (New York: Cambridge University Press, 1980), pp. 46–71; and Maris Vinovskis, "Trends in Massachusetts Education, 1826–1860," in *History of Education Quarterly* 12 (Winter 1972), pp. 501–529.
3. On the spread of kindergartens, see Nina C. Vandewalker, "Kindergarten Progress from 1919–20 to 1921–22," in U.S. Bureau of Education, *Kindergarten Circular* (May 1924), No. 16 (Washington, DC: Government Printing Office, 1924), pp. 1–4.
4. Marvin Lazerson, "Urban Reform and the Schools: Kindergartens in Massachusetts, 1870–1915, in *History of Education Quarterly* 11 (Summer 1971), p. 132.
5. On the history of child care and the divisions between child care and education, see Virginia Kerr, "One Step Forward—Two Steps Back: Child Care's Long American History," in Pamela Roby (ed.), *Child Care—Who Cares?* (New York: Basic Books, 1973), pp. 85–99; Margaret Steinfels, *Who's Minding the Children? The History and Politics of Day Care in America* (New York: Simon and Schuster, 1973); Greta Fein and Alison Clarke-Stewart, *Day Care in Context* (New York: John Wiley & Sons, 1973); and Sonya Michel, "Children's Interests/Mothers' Rights: Women, Professionals, and the American Family, 1920–1945," doctoral dissertation, Brown University, 1986.
6. Joseph Featherstone, "Rousseau and Modernity," in *Daedalus* 107 (March 1978), pp. 167–192; and "Childhood, Modernity, and the Religion of Life," unpublished manuscript, 1978. For discussions of Pestalozzi and infant schools see Kate Silber, *Pestalozzi: the Man and His Work* (London: Routledge and Kegan Paul, 1960); and Gerald Lee Gutek, *Pestalozzi and Education* (New York: Random House, 1968).
7. Will S. Monroe, *History of the Pesta-*

lozzian Movement in the United States (Syracuse, NY: C. W. Bardeen, 1907). For accounts of infant schools in Boston, see Dean May and Maris Vinovskis, "A Ray of Millennial Light: Early Education and Social Reform in the Infant School Movement in Massachusetts, 1826–1840," in Tamara Hareven (ed.), *Family and Kin in Urban Communities, 1700–1930* (New York: New Viewpoints, 1977), pp. 62–99; and Barbara R. Beatty, "Infant Schools and the Early Kindergarten Movement: Early Childhood Education in Boston, 1828–1835, 1860–1888," qualifying paper, Harvard Graduate School of Education, 1979, Gutman Library, Cambridge, MA.

8. On Froebel, his educational philosophy, and his methods, see Friedrich Froebel, *Autobiography of Friedrich Froebel*, trans. and ed. Emilie Michaelis and H. Keatley Moore (Syracuse, NY: C. W. Bardeen, 1908); Froebel, *The Education of Man*, trans. William N. Hailmann (New York: D. Appleton and Co., 1889); and Froebel, *Pedagogics of the Kindergarten*, trans. Josephine Jarvis (New York: D. Appleton and Co., 1895). See also Denton J. Snider, *The Life of Friedrich Froebel: Founder of the Kindergarden* (Chicago: Sigma Publishing Co., 1900); Henry Barnard (ed.), *Kindergarten and Child Culture Papers* (Hartford: [Office of Barnard's] *American Journal of Education*, 1884); and Susan Blow, *Educational Issues in the Kindergarten* (New York: D. Appleton and Co., 1908).

9. On the history of kindergartens in the United States see Nina C. Vandewalker, *The Kindergarten in American Education* (New York: Macmillan, 1908); Evelyn Weber, *The Kindergarten: Its Encounter with Educational Thought in America* (New York: Teachers College Press, 1969); Marvin Lazerson, *The Origins of the Urban School* (Cambridge: Harvard University Press, 1971); Selwyn Troen, *The Public and the Schools: Shaping the St. Louis System 1838–1920* (Columbus, MO: University of Missouri Press, 1975); Elizabeth Dale Ross, *The Kindergarten Crusade* (Athens, OH: Ohio University Press, 1976); Robert L. Church and Michael W. Sedlack, *Education in the United States: An Interpretative History* (New York: Free Press, 1976); Dominick Cavallo, "From Perfection to Habit: Moral Training in the American Kindergarten, 1860–1920," in *History of Education Quarterly* 16 (Summer 1976), pp. 147–161; Cavallo, "The Politics of Latency: Kindergarten Pedagogy, 1860–1930," in Barbara Finkelstein (ed.), *Regulated Children/Liberated Children: Education in Psychological Perspective* (New York: Psychohistory Press, Publishers, 1979), pp. 158–183; Michael Steven Shapiro, *Child's Garden: The Kindergarten Movement from Froebel to Dewey* (University Park, PA: Pennsylvania State University Press, 1983); and Ann Taylor Allen, " 'Let Us Live with Our Children': Kindergarten Movements in Germany and the United States, 1840–1914," in *History of Education Quarterly* 28 (Spring 1988), pp. 23–48.

10. Elizabeth Peabody, "Child-Gardening as a Profession," in *Kindergarten Messenger* 1 (July 1873), p. 2; and Elizabeth Peabody, *Lectures in the Training Schools for Kindergartners* (Boston: D. C. Heath and Company, 1893), p. 13. For sources on Peabody, see Ruth M. Baylor, *Elizabeth Palmer Peabody: Kindergarten Pioneer* (Philadelphia: Temple University Press, 1965); Susan P. Conrad, *Perish the Thought: Intellectual Women in Romantic America, 1830–1860* (New York: Oxford University Press, 1976); Hersha S. Fisher, "The Education of Elizabeth Peabody," doctoral dissertation, Harvard University, 1980; and Bruce A. Ronda (ed.), *Letters of Elizabeth Palmer Peabody, American Renaissance Woman* (Middletown, CT: Wesleyan University, 1984). On women and the kindergarten, and kindergarten teaching as a woman's occupation, see Karen Wolk Feinstein, "Kindergartens, Feminism, and the Professionalization of Motherhood," in *International Journal of Women's Studies* 3 (January–February 1980), pp. 28–38; Barbara Beatty, " 'A Vocation from on High':

Preschool Teaching and Advocacy as a Career for Women in Nineteenth-Century Boston,'' doctoral dissertation, Harvard University, 1981; Ann Taylor Allen, ''Spiritual Motherhood: German Feminists and the Kindergarten Movement, 1848–1911,'' in *History of Education Quarterly* 22 (Fall 1982), pp. 319–340; and Barbara Finkelstein, ''The Revolt Against Selfishness: Women and the Dilemmas of Professionalism in Early Childhood Education,'' in Bernard Spodek, Olivia N. Saracho, and Donald L. Peters (eds.), *Professionalism and the Early Childhood Practitioner* (New York: Teachers College Press, 1988), pp. 10–28.

11. Peabody, *Kindergarten Guide,* pp. 14 and 15.
12. Elizabeth Peabody, *Guide to the Kindergarten and Intermediate Class* (New York: E. Steiger, 1877), p. 35.
13. Peabody, *Kindergarten Guide,* pp. 10 and 11.
14. Peabody, *Guide to the Kindergarten and Intermediate Class,* pp. iv–v.
15. Ibid., p. 36.
16. Ibid., p. 18.
17. Ibid., pp. 19, 20, and 21. A few kindergartens and nursery schools, notably college laboratory preschools, were located in buildings specifically designed for young children.
18. Ibid., p. 28.
19. Ibid., pp. 52–57.
20. Ibid., pp. 64 and 71.
21. Edward Wiebe, *The Paradise of Childhood: A Practical Guide to the Kindergarten* (Springfield, MA: Milton Bradley Co., 1906), p. 95.
22. William N. Hailmann, *Kindergarten Culture in the Family and Kindergarten* (New York: Van Antwerp, Bragg & Co., 1873), pp. 102 and 118–119.
23. Maria Kraus-Boelte and John Kraus, *The Kindergarten* (New York: E. Steiger, 1877). See Shapiro, *Child's Garden,* pp. 32–44, for a description of Maria Kraus-Boelte's influence on the early kindergarten movement.
24. Louise Pollock, *National Kindergarten Manual* (Boston: DeWolfe, Fiske and Company, 1889), pp. 8–10, 14, 16, and 33–35.
25. Lucy Wheelock, ''My Life Story,'' unpublished autobiography, Lucy Wheelock Collection, Archives, Wheelock College, p. 13.
26. Ibid.
27. Shapiro, *Child's Garden,* p. 147; also, ''Kindergarten Training Class at Chauncy-Hall School,'' a brochure dated 1894, Lucy Wheelock Collection, Archives, Wheelock College.
28. Barbara Beatty, '' 'The Kind of Knowledge of Most Worth to Young Women': Post-Secondary Vocational Training for Teaching and Motherhood at the Wheelock School, 1888–1914,'' in *History of Higher Education Annual* 6 (1986), pp. 29–50.
29. For accounts of kindergartners' reactions to training, see Wheelock, ''My Life Story,'' p. 76; Ross, *The Kindergarten Crusade,* pp. 52–66; Shapiro, *Child's Garden,* pp. 38–40; and Nina C. Vandewalker, ''Kindergarten Training Schools,'' in U.S. Bureau of Education, *Bulletin,* 1916, No. 5 (Washington, DC: Government Printing Office, 1916).
30. Patty Smith Hill, ''The Free Kindergarten as the Basis of Education,'' in Louisville Free Kindergarten Association, *Report for 1894–95* (Gutman Library, Harvard Graduate School of Education), p. 8.
31. On Shaw, see Biography File, Schlesinger Library, Radcliffe College. Data on backgrounds of charity kindergartners are from alumnae registers of the Garland School, held in the Archives at Simmons College, and in alumnae files and registers, Alumnae Office and Archives, Wheelock College.
32. Jane Addams, *Twenty Years at Hull-House, with Autobiographical Notes* (New York: New American Library, 1960), p. 83; and Shapiro, *Child's Garden,* pp. 103–104.
33. For a different view, see Lazerson, ''Urban Reform and the Schools: Kindergartens in Massachusetts, 1870–1915.''
34. Vandewalker, *The Kindergarten in American Education,* pp. 124, 125, 126, 127, and 128.

35. Lucy Wheelock, "My Life Story," pp. 12 and 14.

36. William Torrey Harris, Emily Talbot, and Henry Barnard, "Kindergarten System," in *Journal of Social Science* 12 (September 1880), pp. 8–10 (quoted in Shapiro, *Child's Garden*, p. 99); and G. Stanley Hall, "The Contents of Children's Minds," *Princeton Review* 11 (May 1883), pp. 249–272. On Hall, his research, the child-study movement, and the kindergarten, see Dorothy Ross, *G. Stanley Hall: The Psychologist as Prophet* (Chicago: University of Chicago Press, 1972); and Alexander W. Seigel and Sheldon H. White, "The Child Study Movement: Early Growth and Development of the Symbolized Child," in Hayne Waring Reese (ed.), *Advances in Child Development and Behavior* (New York: Academic Press, 1982), pp. 233–285.

37. Marion B. B. Langzettel, "Discussion," in National Education Association, *Addresses and Proceedings* (1903), p. 405.

38. Elizabeth Harrison, "The Scope and Result of Mothers' Classes," in National Education Association, *Addresses and Proceedings* (1903), p. 401.

39. Ibid.

40. Passie Fenton Ottley, "Kindergartens for Colored Children," in *Southern Workman* 30 (February 1901), pp. 103–104; Alice Dugged Cary, "Kindergartens for Negro Children," in *Southern Workman* 29 (August 1900), p. 492; and Anna J. Murray, "A New Key to the Situation," in *Southern Workman* 29 (September 1900), pp. 503 and 504. For an overview see Charles E. Cunningham and D. Keith Osborn, "A Historical Examination of Blacks in Early Childhood Education," in *Young Children* 34 (March 1979), pp. 20–29.

41. "A Week in the Hampton Kindergarten," *Southern Workman* 36 (October 1907), pp. 537–544.

42. Josephine Silone Yates, "Education and Genetic Psychology," in *Colored American Magazine* 10 (1906); pp. 293–297.

43. Josephine Silone Yates, "Kindergartens and Mothers' Clubs," in *Colored American Magazine* 8 (1905); pp. 304–311. On Haydee Campbell, see the biographical essay in Monroe A. Majors, *Noted Negro Women* (Chicago: Donohue & Henneberry, 1893), p. 329; and Cunningham and Osborn, p. 24. On kindergartens for black people, see Patty Smith Hill, "The Free Kindergarten as an Educational Need of the South," and Finie Murfree Burton, "The Louisville Free Kindergarten Association: Its History, Origin, and Work," in Louisville Free Kindergarten Association, *Seventeenth Annual Report, 1904–05*, (Gutman Library, Harvard Graduate School of Education), pp. 17–18.

44. Yates, "Kindergartens and Mothers' Clubs," p. 309. See also Andrew Billingsley and Jeanne M. Giovannoni, *Children of the Storm: Black Children and American Child Welfare* (New York: Harcourt Brace Jovanovich, 1972), pp. 55–56; and Cunningham and Osborn, p. 24. For statistics on the spread of public kindergartens in the South see Vandewalker, "Kindergarten Progress from 1919–20 to 1921–22," pp. 3–4.

45. On this first public kindergarten in Boston, see Douglas E. Lawson, "Corrective Note on the Early History of the American Kindergarten," in *Educational Administration and Supervision* 25 (1939), pp. 699–703. See also Elizabeth Peabody, "Report of the Sixth Meeting of the American Froebel Union," in *Kindergarten Messenger and the New Education* 3 (January 1879), p. 2.

46. Lazerson, "Urban Reform and the Schools," p. 124; and Ross, *The Kindergarten Crusade*, p. 80. For a first-person account of the establishment of public kindergartens for black children in Washington, DC, see Murray, "A New Key to the Situation."

47. "Kindergartens in the United States: Statistics and Present Problems," in U.S. Bureau of Education, *Bulletin*, 1914, No. 6 (Washington, DC: Government Printing Office, 1914), p. 7; "Statistical Summary of Education," in *Biennial Survey of Education in the United States, 1956–58*, quoted in Neith Headley, *The*

Kindergarten: Its Place in the Program of Education (New York: Center for Applied Research in Education, Inc., 1959), p. 11; and Nina C. Vandewalker, "Kindergarten Training Schools," in U.S. Bureau of Education, *Bulletin,* 1916, No. 5 (Washington, DC: Government Printing Office, 1916), p. 7.

48. Almira M. Winchester, "Kindergarten Supervision in City Schools," in U.S. Bureau of Education, *Bulletin,* 1918, No. 38 (Washington, DC: Government Printing Office, 1918), pp. 9–21, and 24–30.

49. Ibid., pp. 37 and 38.

50. Ibid., pp. 30, 31, and 46.

51. Ibid., p. 23.

52. Luella A. Palmer, "Adjustment Between Kindergarten and First Grade, Including a Study of Double Sessions in the Kindergarten," in U.S. Bureau of Education, *Bulletin,* 1915, No. 24 (Washington, DC: Government Printing Office, 1915), pp. 21, and 22–24. See also Lazerson, "Urban Reform and the Schools," pp. 130–135, for documentation of superintendents' concerns about the cost of kindergartens.

53. Helen S. Duncklee, "The Kindergartner and Her Mothers' Meeting," in *Kindergarten Review* 9 (September 1899), p. 14.

54. Palmer, "Adjustment Between Kindergarten and First Grade," p. 2.

55. "The Kindergartner and Americanization," in U.S. Bureau of Education, *Kindergarten Circular* (November 1918), No. 3 (Washington, DC: Government Printing Office, 1918), p. 3; and S. E. Weber, "The Kindergarten as an Americanizer," in U.S. Bureau of Education, *Kindergarten Circular,* (December 1919), No. 5 (Washington, DC: Government Printing Office, 1919), pp. 2 and 4.

56. National Education Association report on teachers' salaries and salary trends, July, 1923, p. 13, quoted in "Organizing Kindergartens in City School Systems," U.S. Bureau of Education, *Kindergarten Circular* (November 1923), No. 2 (Washington, DC: Government Printing Office, 1923), p. 3. See also James C. Boykin and Roberta King, "The Tangible Rewards of Teaching: A Detailed Statement of Salaries Paid to the Several Classes of Teachers and School Officers, in U.S. Bureau of Education, *Bulletin,* 1914, No. 16 (Washington, DC: Government Printing Office, 1914).

57. Palmer, "Adjustment Between Kindergarten and First Grade," p. 23.

58. Ibid., p. 25.

59. Patty Smith Hill, "The Future of the Kindergarten," in *Teachers College Record* 10 (November 1909), pp. 48–49.

60. Palmer, "Adjustment Between Kindergarten and First Grade," pp. 5, 6, 7, and 9.

61. Ibid., pp. 14, 17, and 18.

62. See Winifred E. Bain, *An Analytical Study of Teaching in Nursery School, Kindergarten, and First Grade* (New York: Bureau of Publications, Teachers College, Columbia University, 1928); and Grace Langdon, *Similarities and Differences in Teaching in Nursery School, Kindergarten, and First Grade* (New York: The John Day Company, 1933).

63. Julia Wade Abbot, "The Child and the Kindergarten," in U.S. Bureau of Education, *Kindergarten Circular* (February 1920), No. 6 (Washington, DC: Government Printing Office, 1920), p. 23.

64. Frederick Burk and Caroline Frear Burk, *A Study of the Kindergarten Problem* (San Francisco: The Whitaker & Ray Co., 1899), p. 81.

65. Agnes Burke et al., *A Conduct Curriculum for the Kindergarten and First Grade* (New York: Charles Scribner's Sons, 1923), pp. 44–45, quoted in Weber, *The Kindergarten,* p. 131.

66. Samuel Chester Parker and Alice Temple, *Unified Kindergarten and First-Grade Teaching* (Boston: Ginn and Company, 1925), pp. 1, 2, 23–24, and 569.

67. Arnold Gesell, "The Downward Extension of the Kindergarten," in *Childhood Education* 2 (November 1926), p. 53, quoted in Langdon, *Similarities and Differences in Teaching in Nursery School,*

Kindergarten, and First Grade, p. 17. For sources on nursery schools see, among others, Margaret McMillan, *The Nursery School* (London: J. M. Dent & Sons, 1923); Harriet Johnson, *Children in the Nursery School* (New York: Agathon Press, 1972 [1st ed. 1928]); *School Begins at Two* (New York: New Republic, Inc., 1936); and Joyce Antler, *Lucy Sprague Mitchell: The Making of a Modern Woman* (New Haven: Yale University Press, 1987).

68. Sharon L. Kagan and Edward F. Zigler, "Early Schooling: A National Opportunity?" in Sharon L. Kagan and Edward F. Zigler (eds.), *Early Schooling: The National Debate* (New Haven: Yale University Press, 1987), pp. 215–229. For an analysis of some of the parallels between the institutionalization of kindergartens and the provision of public preschools in California, see W. Norton Grubb and Marvin Lazerson, "Child Care, Government Financing and the Public Schools: Lessons from the California Children's Centers," in *School Review* 86 (November 1977), pp. 5–37.

69. "Kindergartens in the United States," in U.S. Bureau of Education, *Bulletin*, 1914, No. 6 (Washington, DC: Government Printing Office, 1914), pp. 11–12.

4

The Teacher in the Country School

Wayne E. Fuller

Richard Hofstadter's observations in his *Age of Reform* that "the United States was born in the country and has moved to the city," though obvious, makes a point that has had important consequences for the development of American education.[1] For the nation's schools, like most other American institutions, were shaped in a rural environment for a rural people. Even as late as 1910, rural children still composed 58 percent of the school population, and the effects upon the nation's school system of that prolonged period of education in a rural environment are still visible.[2]

The American attachment to the small neighborhood school, the idea of the self-contained classroom, and long summer vacations, owe much to the rural past. So, too, do the contemporary emphasis upon a practical, nontheoretical basic curriculum, and the faded notion that education should be controlled locally by the people who pay the bills and whose children attend the schools. Indeed, it was this latter principle that made possible the establishment of the nation's free public education system before the Civil War. It is worth noting that the expectations Americans had of their teachers' duties, responsibilities, and behavior for so long a time were also shaped in rural schools directly dominated by the people of the local community in whose schools they taught.

In the long era before the small one-room schools were absorbed into large centralized schools, teachers taught in a small world in which local control of the schools was exercised through school district systems that were themselves products of the rural environment. The most common of these was the small, independent district located primarily in the West and Midwest. Usually encompassing an area no larger than five or six sections, its affairs were almost completely controlled by the farmers who lived within its boundaries. They set the amount of school taxes they would pay; determined the length of their school terms; planned, built, repaired, and maintained their schoolhouses; elected their school directors; and often instructed those directors in the employment of their teachers.[3]

Because the small districts gave control of school affairs so completely to rural people with no training in administering school affairs, professional educators thought the locals inefficient, and even before the Civil War launched a crusade to enlarge the school districts in order to diminish the farmers' control. Where these educators were successful, townships, counties, and even magisterial units occupying about one-sixth of a county, became the school districts. Township districts that eliminated hundreds of school directors who had once governed the small schools throughout the township were established in New England, Pennsylvania, New Jersey, and parts of the Midwest. In Indiana the rural schools of an entire township, sometimes as many as nine or more, were largely controlled by one elected trustee.[4]

In the South, rural teachers taught for the most part in county school districts that tended to be less democratic than those in the West and Midwest. Whether this was because Southerners were less accustomed to participating in local government than Northerners, or because Northerners who helped establish the Southern educational systems after the Civil War, but had become disenchanted with small districts, promoted the large-district system, is a matter of conjecture. Whatever the reason, most Southern states placed control of their country schools at the county level, and made most of their educational offices appointive rather than elective. (See Figure 4.1.)

Whether the school districts were more or less democratic, however, they still were controlled over many years by local officials, either at the county, township, or small-district level. The result was that nonprofessional people ran the schools and employed the teachers. As was the way in small communities, these nonprofessionals were likely to have been farmers. They might also have been friends, or even relatives, of the applicants for a teaching position. And they were, of course, the same people who provided the places where the teachers worked.

The schoolhouses in which rural teachers spent their days reflected the homes and degree of prosperity of the local people who built and maintained them. In every pioneer region, from colonial times forward, country teachers began teaching in log cabins in forested regions, and ''soddies'' on the sod-house frontier. Both were as primitive as the societies surrounding them. The log schoolhouse, for example, had a huge fireplace at one end of the building, and at the other a crude door supported

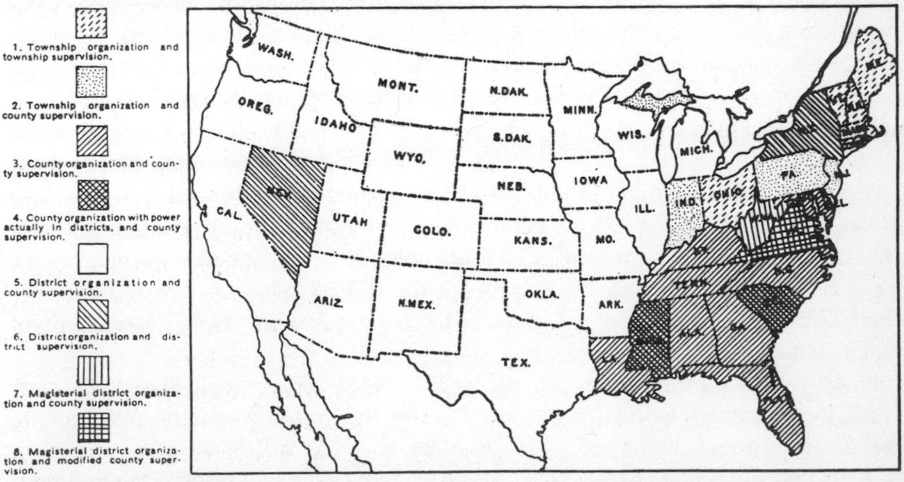

FIGURE 4.1 The System of Local School Organization and Supervision in the Several States.
Source: A. C. Monahan, *The Status of Rural Education in the United States*. U.S. Bureau of Education, Bulletin, 1913, No. 8 (Washington, D.C.: U.S. Government Printing Office, 1913), plate 13.

by leather hinges. Windows were slits cut from the logs; they were covered with paper in winter. Student desks were nonexistent. Children sat on homemade benches and wrote on tables attached to the walls, which forced them to face the wall as they wrote. Few schools, if any, had standardized textbooks, blackboards, or such helpful teaching devices as maps and charts.[5]

Such rude conditions continued in the South long after the Civil War—virtually, in fact, as long as there were one-room schoolhouses. Unaccustomed to constant involvement in school affairs and burdened by poverty and the segregation of the races, Southerners improved their teachers' workplaces slowly. Some notion of the quality and quantity of the schoolhouses in which Southern teachers taught may be seen by comparing them with those in the Midwest. In 1890, some 15 years after Reconstruction, the 16 former slaveholding states possessed 70,568 schoolhouses worth $28,481,750 in school property. This averaged approximately $1.45 per capita of the population. In the small democratic school systems of the 12 Midwestern states in the north central region, on the other hand, more than 97,000 schoolhouses with a total property value of $156,754,460, or slightly more than $7.00 per capita, dotted the landscape. Nearly all of this money was raised by local taxes.[6]

Included in the figures of Southern schoolhouses was a significant number of churches and abandoned buildings of one kind or another which were never intended to be schoolhouses. Even as late as World War I, the workplaces of hundreds of Southern teachers still were flimsy affairs. A survey made in 1913 in Orange County, Virginia, reported that all of the county's rural schools were "either of the one-room 'old-field' variety or old abandoned tenant houses, churches, or storerooms."[7] The vast majority had only one unsanitary privy, and some had none at all. Nor was the school furniture much better than the school that housed it. Of the 42 Orange County schools examined, 32 contained pineboard desks, presumably homemade, of the kind used before the Civil War. Only occasionally was a desk low enough for the small children's feet to reach the floor, and two schools had no desks whatsoever.[8]

Insofar as effective teaching was concerned, however, comfortable furniture was less a problem than the paucity of school apparatus—maps, globes, learning charts, dictionaries, and libraries. Once again, statistics suggest how little the Southern states were able or willing to pay for school apparatus. In 1890 the 16 Southern states spent only $2,179,791 for school sites, furniture, libraries, and apparatus for the 4,053,680 students enrolled in their schools. This was not even as much as the 11 sparsely settled Western states spent for the 515,673 students enrolled there. In the 1920s Southern teachers still spoke of having to take their own globes and maps to the schools in which they taught.[9]

Such conditions were deplorable enough for white rural schoolteachers, but they were incomparably worse for blacks. During Reconstruction it was difficult to build, or even rent, buildings for black students, a fact of life we might expect of that period. But a half century later, black teachers were still teaching in buildings unmatched anywhere else in the country for their variety and poverty. One study, published in 1916, noted that 61 percent of the black schools of Alabama, and 63 percent of those in Georgia, were not owned by public authorities, which meant that many black teachers taught in churches, lodge halls, tenant houses, barns, or whatever abandoned buildings were available. So indifferent, indeed, were the white school authorities to black education that black teachers not uncommonly had to provide the schoolhouses in which they taught. "The superintendent examines you," wrote one black teacher in Virginia in the 1880s; "the school board will tell you at what place they want you to teach, and many times you will have to look out for the schoolroom, benches, and everything else that is necessary."[10]

Moreover, the states did little to improve black schoolhouses in the succeeding years. In the 1890s the blacks had been systematically disenfranchised in part to improve, ironically, the education of poor white children. In the upheaval the blacks lost, of course, whatever small political leverage they had enjoyed to better their educational facilities through local and state taxes. In many instances they did not even receive back for their education that portion of taxes they had paid. Writing in 1914, Booker T. Washington gave an example of the disproportionate amount of public money spent on white versus black education in various school districts in three South Carolina counties. In one district $202.00 a year was spent on education for each white child and $3.12 for each black; in another district in another county the difference was $11.17 to 69 cents; and in still another, it was $7.45 to 48 cents.[11]

Left to their own devices, the blacks did what they could to provide school buildings, but this was little indeed. On his visits through the South, Washington saw a schoolroom without a stove, and children forced periodically to leave the schoolroom to warm themselves by an outdoor fire. A white educational authority confirmed Washington's assessment of the poverty of black rural schoolhouses: "I have seen," he wrote in 1909, "benches supported on brickbats, holes in floors and roofs, doors and windows sagging, and other such signs of neglect which could easily be remedied."[12]

True, in the years just before World War I, Julius Rosenwald, a partner in Sears, Roebuck and Company, had given money for the construction of model black rural schoolhouses, and many of these were constructed. But in comparison to the need the effort was pitifully small, and the majority of black teachers continued to teach in the most primitive schools under the most primitive conditions well into the period of World War II.[13]

Outside the South, however, rural teachers' workplaces improved following the Civil War as the farmers' economic conditions improved. Even before the Civil War the log cabin had given way to the little white frame schoolhouse of the kind the majority of country teachers taught in until after World War II.

The typical rural teachers' workplace for most of the nation was a rectangular building, often no larger than 23 feet long and 18 feet wide. At one end of the building stood a chimney and at the other, usually facing out upon a country road, the schoolhouse's one door. Three or four windows stretched across each of its longer sides to provide cross-ventilation, and a large stove, the building's central heating plant, stood either at the center of the room or at the rear. A long stovepipe ran from the stove along the ceiling until it connected at last with the chimney. At the end of the room opposite the door stood the teacher's desk, and behind that, fastened against the chimney wall, was a blackboard. An entryway for the children's wraps and lunchpails was located just inside the door, and somewhere, usually near the front of the room, stood a table with a water bucket on it.[14]

For years any number of these buildings were as barren of refinements as the grounds upon which they stood. They had neither shades nor curtains at the windows, no embellishments to alter their boxlike appearance, and no trees to shade the schoolroom. They had no wells, no playground equipment, and often only one privy—and sometimes none at all. They were, as Hamlin Garland described the one he attended in Iowa, "merely a square pine box painted a glaring white on the outside and a desolate drab within."[15]

Such descriptions of the rural teachers' workplace have become commonplace in both popular and scholarly literature, leaving the impression that all one-room schools were of this quality. "In particular, one-room schoolhouses received less of everything," ran a recent account describing the schools in 1890. "They were housed in older, makeshift facilities with insufficient books, supplies, and equipment. In ungraded schools, teachers with little formal education themselves coped with five-year-olds and young adults simultaneously."[16]

Surveys of country schools, so popular in the early decades of the twentieth century, tended to support this generalization. A study of South Dakota rural schools in 1918 declared that over half of the country schools had dirty walls, unsuitable seats for at least some of the children, and unsatisfactory lighting, heating, and ventilating systems. When comparisons were made, the study reported, the schools in the open country ranked behind the village and town schools in every category except dirty walls.[17]

Like most such surveys, this one, too, pointed out the obvious, but made no effort to compare the schools of 1918 with what they had been two decades before. Clearly the implication was that the farmers had made no improvements at all in their one-room schoolhouses in the post–Civil War years. This was simply untrue. The farmers had made such significant improvements in their schoolhouses across the years that for all their plainness many of them, perhaps even a majority in some sections, could no longer truthfully be called "makeshift affairs."

By the turn of the century certainly, if not before, farmers everywhere except in the South and perhaps in the far West (where rural schoolhouses were newer) were building, or had built their second and third schoolhouse or refurbished their old ones. They had dug wells on their school grounds, added patented desks where they had not had them, replaced the old water bucket with fountains, and built belfries and added bells. They had put jackets around their stoves to improve the circulation of air, erected new privies and screened the old, and planted trees on the schoolgrounds, and if their schoolhouses seemed makeshift affairs to some, they did not seem so to the children who attended them. "We have everything very convenient," a young Kansas girl wrote to the county superintendent in 1893. "We have a mirror, comb, towels, and a wash pan. Our schoolhouse will seat about thirty-eight persons."[18]

These were, of course, still schoolhouses of one room with the same basic structure that had prevailed for years. But in the years leading up to World War I, farmers everywhere, even in the South, were altering the architectural style of their buildings. Windows in the new schools were being placed on one side of the building only, clothes closets and storerooms were enlarged, roof lines were changed, front doors were moved to one side or the other, and in some cases the schoolhouses were enlarged by the addition of a basement, which provided a place for the furnace.[19]

More than that, in most schools across the Midwest and West, and in the Northeast as well, teachers in country schools now had available such teaching aids as dictionaries, maps, gloves, charts, standardized textbooks, and libraries of some hundred or so volumes. In many schools pianos or organs had been added, fences had been built around the schoolyards, and children were playing on new playground equipment.[20]

These improvements in the teachers' workplaces and in the school apparatus that made their teaching easier entailed financial sacrifices on the part of the farmers surpassing, perhaps, those being made by individual urbanites on behalf of education at the same time. Yet this development in rural education, like the advances made in country schoolteaching in the same period, has been largely overlooked in histories of education. Indeed, few professionals who wrote about country teachers found much to praise.

In the nation's pioneer regions, especially before the Civil War, country schoolteaching was, to be sure, a haphazard affair. Teachers without formal training "held school," as they said. They taught without the benefit of maps, charts, and even blackboards, and the only books available were those the children brought from home, which ranged from the Bible to well-used old blue-back spellers or one or another *McGuffey's Reader*. They had no established curriculum or any way of marking a student's progress. Children read through as many readers as they had, and if they were fortunate enough to complete the sixth reader they were through with school. Often, however, because no one kept a record of their progress, students began each school term reading in the same reader they had finished the year before, a practice that led to a saying that no one ever completed a country school.[21]

In the South such conditions, and worse, continued throughout the nineteenth and well into the twentieth century, especially in black schools and among black teachers. There, black rural teachers continued to be largely untrained, and remained virtually ignored and unsupervised by white county superintendents. "The negro schools of South Carolina," wrote one supervisor of white rural schools in 1912, "are for the most part without supervision of any kind. Frequently the county superintendent does not know where they are located, and sometimes the district board cannot tell where the Negro school is taught."[22]

Nor does it appear that black teachers followed a regular course of study or attempted to grade their students. The strong white prejudice against black children learning academic subjects was reflected in the efforts of both black and white educational leaders to promote vocational studies for blacks. Consequently, the material needed for the study of academic subjects—books, charts, maps—was woefully inadequate, so that it was not uncommon to see four or five children attempting to study from the same book. Under these circumstances, simply learning to read, write, and "figure" was a painfully slow process. In 1917, one researcher wrote:

> The Negro schoolhouses are miserable beyond all description. They are usually without comfort, equipment, proper lighting, or sanitation. Nearly all of the Negroes of school age in the district are crowded into these miserable structures during the short term which the school runs. Most of the teachers are absolutely untrained and have been given certificates by the county board, not because they have passed the examinations, but because it is necessary to have some kind of a Negro teacher. Among the rural schools which I have visited, I have found only one in which the highest class knew the multiplication table.[23]

With money contributed by Anna T. Jeanes, a wealthy Philadelphian, a major effort was made before and after World War I to provide successful black teachers to supervise the teachers in the black rural schools. Their purpose was not only to train the teachers but also to improve the environment in which they taught. Much favorable publicity greeted this work, but the supervisors had little impact upon the curriculum of black rural schools. Devoted, either through conviction or discretion, to vocational training, they made little attempt to promote an academic curriculum. In the end, then, in spite of this great effort, black teachers and black children continued to work in the worst educational environment in the land.[24]

Elsewhere throughout the country, however, by the late 1880s, and certainly by 1890, rural parents had come to expect their teachers to be much more than mere schoolkeepers. Because they taught children aged roughly five to 16 in one room, country teachers were expected to be surrogate parents for the younger children, and counsellors for the oldest. They were supposed to know the common branches of learning thoroughly, be able to stage effective programs for the benefit of parents, maintain school records, develop teaching schedules and lesson plans, and regulate play on the schoolground. Above all else they were expected to be disciplinarians, for it was a cardinal rule in rural America that the teacher who could not govern the school could not teach. Beyond all this, rural teachers were expected to be models for the children. They must be people of blameless character who, in addition to teaching, must be willing to participate in community affairs, teach a Sunday-school class perhaps, and quite possibly arrange a debate at the schoolhouse.[25]

These expectations resulted from the many important, but largely ignored, changes in country schoolteaching that had gradually taken place in the fading years of the nineteenth century. Many of these changes in the Northern states, and especially in the Midwest, are to be found within the little-used records, from hundreds of tiny one-room schools, that have been preserved in various archives. Contrary to the usual interpretation, they reveal that substantial advances had taken place in the management and teaching of those schools between the late 1870s and the turn of the century.

By 1900, rural teachers nearly everywhere were teaching a standardized curriculum, usually called a course of study, which had in most cases been prepared by state superintendents of public instruction. For the most part the course called for the teaching of the common branches of learning, which, besides the three R's, consisted of grammar, history, civics, orthoepy (pronunciation), geography, and hygiene (and, by the time of World War I, agriculture). As a prelude to dividing their schools into eight grades, most rural teachers were classifying their students into primary, intermediate, and grammar grades. Records were being kept of students' work and left for the succeeding teacher, so that all students could be properly placed at the beginning of every school term.[26]

To do all this successfully, country teachers had carefully drawn schedules that told them when and what, and even how, to teach each class throughout the day. Some of these schedules accompanied the course of study. Others were written into helpful record books that included, in addition to the course of study, pages for keeping a student's attendance and scholarly record, and instructions on how to classify the school. The most commonly used of these popular books, at least throughout the Midwest, was W. M. Welch's *Teachers' Classification Register with a Record of Each Pupil's Standing, and a course of Study for Common Schools*. So detailed were its instructions that even beginning, inexperienced teachers—of which there were many—could easily organize their schools without ever having taken a course in school management.[27]

These record books are among the best sources available for understanding exactly how teachers were teaching and students were learning in the country schools. They show how rural teachers brought order out of the apparent chaos of teaching so many children of different ages in one room, with a plan far more flexible than the "one best system" developing in the cities. Especially informative are those records containing notes on students that teachers left to their successors. Referring to their students by number, they would explain which student should be pushed ahead in one subject or another, and which should be kept back. The notes of one teacher in a Kansas school suggested that No. 1, who was 'way ahead of her mates, should be given every advantage; No. 3 should be encouraged but not pushed, and No. 20 was behind in all his subjects except history, "his forte."[28]

The ability of the rural teachers to alter their schedules to meet the students' needs was also apparent in the school records. When a Wisconsin teacher discovered that student No. 4 did not have enough to keep him busy in his reader, she put him in the next reading level and held a special recitation for him.

Country schoolteachers were not hampered in their teaching by an excess of supervision. If indeed the county superintendent visited them once a year, or even once a school term, it was surprising. Even in the 1920s, when superintendents were switching from buggies to automobiles, a Pennsylvania study showed that rural teachers there were supervised from only 15 minutes to eight hours in an entire year.[29] Apparently they preferred it this way. Only 4 percent of the suggestions for improving country schools made by Nebraska teachers in 1915 listed better supervision of teachers, a figure that must have frustrated the professionals who put great emphasis upon proper supervision of teachers. However that may be, because they were not closely supervised, rural teachers were free to work out their own teaching techniques, to try first this, then that, and over the years used a variety of techniques—most of which, in all probability, their own teachers had used.[30]

One universal teaching method that rural teachers used was (of course) the recitation, of which there might be as many as 30-plus every day. The purpose of the recitation was, as one country superintendent explained it "to develop the powers of the pupils," but in both country and urban schools it was used as much to discover what the students knew or did not know as it was to develop the students' abilities.[31] In the recitations students were required to repeat, sometimes almost verbatim, much of the material they had gleaned from the textbooks. Often this meant reciting from memory the multiplication tables, geographical place names, dates and events in history, and poems. It also meant, especially for the young children, reading aloud to the teacher, and much time spent on preparing for and practicing this.

But the recitation was only one of a number of techniques that rural teachers (in particular) used to instruct their students. Their methods were so varied, in fact, that their critics might have considered them progressive had they not been country teachers. This was especially true in the small schools, where much individual attention could be given students. Frequently students were sent to the blackboard to diagram sentences, work arithmetic problems, or draw maps of continents, nations, and states. If they were running behind in their recitation schedules, they might ask the older students to listen to the recitations of the younger ones, a technique interesting to both the student and the student teacher. If they had seatmates, as was often the case, and sometimes when they did not, they were allowed to study together during "slate time."

Nor were these teachers averse to using competitive methods to arouse student interest. Spell-downs and cipher-downs, in which the victorious student was rewarded with a "head-mark" (merit points awarded by the teacher), were at least weekly affairs that broke the monotony of recitations and slate work. Moreover, they prepared their students to participate in a variety of programs throughout the year: Arbor Day, the birthdays of Lincoln and Washington, Thanksgiving, and Christmas, to name only the most important program days.[32]

Country teachers relied as heavily on textbooks as did their urban counterparts. This was a practice widely criticized by educators who believed that forced memorization of so much textbook material that students did not completely understand was mere parroting, entailing a needless amount of drudgery and accomplishing little. But this was only one of the many criticisms that educators made of rural teachers' methods. In 1918, educational experts studied the teaching methods of rural teachers in 83 schools in both villages and the open country in South Dakota, and found almost *nothing* to their liking. Over and over, they complained of unnecessary reviews and hurried assignments.[33] Besides, this, they saw students unprepared for drills in arithmetic, teachers constantly wandering from the subject, inattentive students, and in some recitations students merely repeating verbatim what the textbooks said. Too, the teacher of one arithmetic class was criticized for failing to suggest the artistic effects that could be gained in properly laying matting in a room when the students were trying to discover whether it would cost more to lay the matting crosswise or lengthwise.[34]

Yet the study is as interesting for what it reveals about the work that the teachers were requiring in those small country schools as it is for the criticisms of the teachers. Students in the seventh grade, for example, were writing compositions about hogs, and second-grade students were attempting to multiply by two figures multiplicands running into the thousands. In geography, some students were learning the position, boundaries, and names of the New England states, and in civics older students were discussing the departments of government, the powers of Congress, and the plan of nominating the president and vice president. In one history lesson the teacher asked for a comparison between taxes raised in the Revolutionary War and those in the then-present war; and in a grammar class the teacher read a list of masculine nouns, the opposites of which students were required to write on the board. This elicited a discussion about the differences in the words, and even the critic seemed to think that this, and the teacher's division of one arithmetic class into two groups to compete in solving a set of multiplication problems on a chart, were good techniques.[35]

By the time this study was made, one-room schools nearly everywhere were being divided into eight grades, and the promotion of rural children from the eighth grade in countrywide ceremonies had become a popular and enthusiastically supported event in the lives of rural schoolchildren and their parents.[36] But graduation from these schools, at least in many sections of the nation, was neither automatic nor easy. The students' graduation normally depended upon the successful completion of county examinations, with a grade of 70 in the common branches of learning. Solving arithmetic problems involving fractions, decimals, and percentages; diagramming sentences and parsing words; elaborating upon the meaning of selected literary passages; spelling, defining, and diacritically marking words; explaining important historical events; and exhibiting a fair knowledge of the world's geography were among the many requirements for which rural teachers prepared their students.

These were examinations no illiterate student could pass—and of course not all students, literate or otherwise, did. Nevertheless, country teachers worked hard to prepare their students for them, for obviously a student's success or failure reflected upon them. The notes left by one Wisconsin teacher to her successor suggest not only the range of work being attempted in that one country school, but also the teacher's awareness that her students in "History A, Upper," would be facing the examinations in history at some time or another.[37]

To a large extent the rural teachers' methods were a reflection of what parents expected. Indeed, no schools in the nation were more closely attuned to the desires and expectations of their patrons. Nor were any parents, as a group, more concerned about the elementary education of their children than were those in rural areas, especially those in the Northern regions. They were the ones, after all, who demanded that their children know the basics, who desired to see their children perform in school exercises, and who wanted them to memorize poems and orations, win spelling matches, and solve difficult arithmetic problems. Teachers who varied far from the familiar methods of teaching these things did so at their peril.

Partly for this reason, rural teachers were less likely to be attracted by the educational changes brought about by the "new" education of the "progressive" years. A case in point was the effort to introduce nature study and agriculture in country schools. In the early 1900s, educators and rural reformers began pushing the study of nature and agriculture in the one-room schools. The reasons for doing so were various, but one of the most pertinent was the desire to relate education to life in accordance with the "progressive" educational theories then being developed. Theorists believed that the study of nature and agriculture, studies that country children would presumably be interested in, could be integrated with most other studies so that learning would be interesting and painless. Arithmetic, for example, could be related to farm problems, geography to the local topography, and history to the familiar community. An underlying assumption behind this program was the belief that it would help keep farm children on the farm, where presumably they belonged.[38]

For the most part, rural teachers did not welcome the additions to their already overcrowded curriculum. Only 4 percent of the Nebraska teachers surveyed in 1915, for example, indicated a preference for teaching nature or agriculture. For them it meant more studies to master to pass their examinations, and the task of trying to integrate the subjects they taught into either nature study or agriculture seemed impossible.[39] Here and there, however, teachers made efforts to include the study of nature and agriculture in one-room schools.

Too, attempts were made to introduce other progressive reforms aimed at replacing the old competitive, individualistic schools with student-centered, cooperative, democratic schools. For example, in 1912, Marie Turner Harvey, a teacher from the Normal school at Kirksville, Missouri, left her position there to teach in the little Porter school, District No. 3, Adair County, in order to demonstrate how progressive teaching could restore vitality to the school and even to the entire community.[40] Permitted by the county superintendent to forsake the county's course of study and proceed with whatever innovations she wished, she began by eliminating spelling books, copybooks, and even textbooks. She did away with report cards, prizes, quarterly examinations, and (as she wrote) ''every nerve-wracking, envy-creating artificial stimulus''—by which she presumably meant in particular the spell-downs and cipher-downs that had always been commonplace in country schools.[41] She even abolished the eight grades and the graduation ceremonies the people had become accustomed to, and returned to the classification system that was by that time outmoded. In the place of textbooks her students used farmers' bulletins and other source materials for their studies. She encouraged them to form agricultural clubs and to write essays on their clubs' activities for their grammar lessons, thus integrating the work of their hands with the work of their minds.[42]

Harvey's teaching drew national attention, but so strong was parents' opposition to the abolition of their children's chance to participate in the county eighth-grade graduation ceremonies, she was forced to have similar ceremonies at the Porter school. Nor was she fully able to integrate the various other studies into that of agriculture, eliminate school performances, or shun the use of memorization—which, after all, was necessary to learn the lessons she taught.[43]

Aside from such bold experiments as that at the Porter school, the teaching of agriculture never became as many educators had hoped: the focal subject around which peripheral subjects might be seen as related. Although added to the curriculum of many country schools, agriculture was taught in a perfunctory way, thus dashing the hopes of those who had seen in it a way to revolutionize country schoolteaching and the techniques of its teachers.[44]

It was often argued by educators (and even occasionally by farmers) that teachers in the country schools whose origins lay in towns and cities were to blame for the failure to make agriculture the centerpiece of the rural curriculum. Such teachers, they believed, tended to lure country children from the farm. Like modern assumptions that black and Hispanic teachers must teach black and Hispanic children because they best understand them, progressives believed that only teachers with rural roots should teach country children.[45] Contrary to the supposition about their roots, however, studies of rural teachers made in the period indicate that most of them *did* have rural backgrounds. The studies of Pennsylvania and Nebraska teachers made during the World War I era showed that 82 percent of those in Pennsylvania had been born and reared in the country, and that in Nebraska the vast majority had lived in country and town about equally.[46]

Obviously the failure to revolutionize the country school curriculum and country-school teaching through the study of agriculture could not be blamed on the urban origins of country schoolteachers. It could, however, be traced partly to teachers' unwillingness to alter their methods in order to integrate the study of agriculture into other subjects—but more especially to the persistence of local control of rural schools. The fact was that rural parents, who as we have seen controlled both the schools and the teachers, did not want the study of agriculture to dominate their school curriculum. Nor did they necessarily want their children to be farmers. Practical and conservative, they wanted to maintain the traditional curriculum, and they tended to look upon the attempt to foist the study of agriculture upon their schools as an effort of theorists to keep their children on the farm, restrict their children's opportunities to be whatever they wished to be, and deny them the same kind of education that urban children had.[47]

The confidence that progressive reformers had in their new theories was unbounded, but whatever hopes they might have had that rural teachers would accept the new techniques were most certainly unrealistic. When a majority of urban teachers were reluctant to adopt student-centered teaching devices, it was surely unlikely that unsupervised country teachers, still dominated by parents who expected their children to be taught traditional subjects in traditional ways, would accept such innovations. Moreover, the fact that most rural teachers taught for a very short time, that they rarely stayed in the same school for more than a year, and that by-and-large they were not career-oriented (as were most urban teachers) made their acceptance of revolutionary teaching techniques even less likely.

Through the years, state superintendents of public education had constantly complained about the rapid turnover of country teachers and their lack of professionalism. "Country teachers are, in most cases," ran the report of a Wisconsin committee on rural schools in 1900, "young, immature, half-trained, ineffective and lacking in professional ideals and ambition." These teachers, the report said, were divided "into two classes of unfit teachers: the callous apprentice class with no adequate concepts of the work they so lightly undertake, and the 'old-stagers' who remain year after year in the work because nothing else opens to them, as unfit in the end of their careers as in the opening."[48]

This harsh opinion of rural teachers was so often expressed by educational authorities as to become commonplace in the early 1900s. But it was not altogether fair. It was true, of course, that many of the country teachers lacked formal training.

In 1902, the state superintendent of education in Indiana noted that 2,231 of the more than 10,000 rural teachers had no training beyond the common schools, and 16 years later a Pennsylvania survey disclosed that 76 percent of all rural teachers there held provisional certificates indicating they had only the most minimal training.[49] Yet there was more to minimal training than might appear. To obtain even provisional certificates in most sections of the nation, rural teachers had to pass rigorous examinations in the common branches that contemporary university-trained elementary teachers would find difficult.[50]

Nor was it quite accurate to say that rural teachers had no interest in the profession. They studied at the county teachers' institutes in the summer, read papers at local teachers' association meetings, and spent a small portion of their salaries for professional purposes. The average teacher in Nebraska in 1915, for example, spent $14.28 for teachers' periodicals and institutes' expenses. Moreover, there was some validity to the argument that the young, inexperienced teachers, teaching but a short time, approached their tasks with more vigor and enthusiasm than did the highly trained professionals who had become bored or burned out with teaching.[51]

Still, statistics supported *some* of the Wisconsin superintendent's assertions about country schoolteachers. Certainly the rapid turnover in rural teachers suggested that those who taught must indeed be young, if not necessarily immature. By 1916, according to one account, out of a total teaching force of 365,000 some 92,000 left teaching each year, and various state studies revealed the brevity of the country teachers' careers. In the World War I period the average country teacher in Nebraska taught less than two years, and in Pennsylvania less than four. Their average age was 21 in Nebraska and 22 in Pennsylvania. So short-lived was the average country teacher's career, indeed, that throughout the nation shortly after World War I, nearly 30 percent of the rural teachers each year were new at the job. Only in the South did it appear that rural teachers remained longer in the profession—and there, some might well have fit the description of "old-stagers."[52]

Although studies showed that a significant number of rural teachers *expected* to continue teaching, their rapid exodus from the field raises the question of why they began teaching in the first place. What were their goals and aspirations?

Many of those who had gone from the East to teach in the West before the Civil War were reared in Christian homes, motivated by a missionary zeal to uplift the people in the pioneer regions. This was true, too, of Northern teachers who went South to teach the freedmen in the Reconstruction Era. To some extent this missionary purpose continued to inspire many rural teachers: Of 3,648 Alabama teachers polled in 1919, more than 11 percent asserted that they wished to help blot out illiteracy, and some 74 percent said they taught for the love of teaching.[53]

While teachers who asserted that they taught because they loved teaching were no doubt sincere, the fact that they left the profession after so short a time suggests that more mundane motives lured them into teaching—as perhaps they do today. From the very early days of the public school system, men teachers used the country school as a steppingstone to other careers. This practice remained common into the twentieth century: Of the 39 male teachers surveyed in the Nebraska survey of 1915, only 15 said they intended to remain in teaching, and only seven of those planned to continue teaching in country schools. So rapid in fact had men hurried from teaching that by 1910 only 21.4 percent of all the teachers in the common schools were male, and no doubt the percentage in the country schools was considerably less.[54]

Country-school teaching, then, was left largely to women, some of whom did consciously choose teaching careers. But when they did so, they generally aspired to teach in urban rather than rural schools. For the rest, teaching was not a career but the best of the choices they had before them while they waited for marriage, which was their real goal. Teaching was a noble and respectable occupation. It gave them a preferred status in the community and offered them a way to improve themselves. Moreover, it paid regularly, if not well. (Except for those with families to care for, the salary was less important than the job.) Like many contemporary teachers who depend in part upon their spouses' salaries for support, the salaries of young, unmarried female country teachers were supplemented by their parents, under whose roofs they sometimes lived while teaching or to whom they returned for vacations or when they had no employment.[55] Inspired thus by a variety of motives (usually as practical as they were), young rural women entered country-school teaching by the thousands in the late 1800s and early 1900s. Most taught for two or three years, then left the schoolhouse for marriage. Fortunately for us, a number of them left evidence of what it had been like to teach in a country school.

Well before the automobile era, one of the first problems that newly employed teachers had to confront was finding a suitable boarding place. In frontier regions, teachers often "boarded 'round," living first one place, then another. In those earliest years the homes they boarded in were likely to be log cabins very much like the schools in which they taught. Primitive and uncomfortable, heated by the one big fireplace, the cabins provided virtually no privacy or comfort.

Following the Civil War, the rural teachers' accommodations improved in most areas of the nation as farmers moved from log cabins and sod houses to the more commodious (often two-story) frame farmhouses. Even so, for as long as they were forced to live near the schools in which they taught, country teachers normally found less privacy in their boarding places than they might have preferred. Usually there were children in the home who could not be ignored, and not infrequently they were forced to share a bed with one of them. In such cases a place of quiet, where they might prepare the next day's lessons, was virtually nonexistent. But even when they had a private room it was likely to be too cold in the winter months to use for study. They had, of course, no indoor toilet, no bathtub, no running water—so that the mere matter of presenting a clean appearance at school was a problem. Moreover, when the teachers helped with the household chores, as they often did in partial payment for their board, their time for school preparation was further restricted.[56]

Even as late as 1915, more than 72 percent of the Nebraska teachers boarded in homes in which children were present, and more than 60 percent of them where they had no modern bathing facilities and no heat in their rooms (although 76 percent did have private rooms).[57] Some notion of what it was like to teach in a country school and board in a farm home can be glimpsed from a Nebraska teacher's protest against teaching agriculture. "Yes, indeed," she wrote, "I think most rural teachers are or would be satisfied [to teach agriculture] were it not that they are overburdened, having 30 or more recitations to hear a day, from seven to eight grades; the sweeping, dusting, firing to do; a great many papers to correct; the lessons to plan for too many grades; going to a boarding place tired and finding no comforts there, children hanging about you; supper at 8:30 to 9; poor light, a kerosene lamp, a chilly room, destitute of any comforts whatever.''[58]

Obviously the rural teachers' boarding place made teaching in a country school more difficult, but it must be remembered that the conditions most teachers found in their home away from home, while appalling to urbanites, were no different than those to which most of them were accustomed. Country-reared, for the most part, they were used to using outdoor privies, and taking baths in tin tubs sprinkled with what seemed no more than a thimbleful of water brought from the stove reservoir.

Most rural teachers, of course, tried to find a boarding place as close to their schoolhouse as possible, since, generally speaking, they had to walk to school, as did the children. Moreover, it was imperative that they arrive early, for they had more to do than teach. Dusting and sweeping, which went with the job, they could do after school; but lighting a fire in the stove and warming the room could be done only early in the morning. These were chores that country teachers disliked—but, strangely enough, only 4 percent of the suggestions for improving rural schools made by Nebraska teachers related to the janitorial service.[59]

Once school began, no time was left for chores, except to keep the fire going in the stove. From the opening of school to its close, the country teacher's life was filled with hearing recitations (as many as 26 a day in South Dakota in 1918, and virtually the same in Pennsylvania at about the same time).[60] There was a constant coming and going as children marched to and fro from the teacher's desk, the blackboards, the water pail, and the outside toilet, so that the little room hummed with activity enough to have satisfied those educators who believed that a noisy, bustling school was progressive. Only on those occasional moments when the teacher ordered the smaller children to lay their heads on their desks for a moment's rest did the usual noise level subside somewhat.

Few country teachers felt equally at home in all subjects as they hurried through their busy schedules. According to the Nebraska survey, they felt the least proficient in agriculture and the most adequate in arithmetic, followed by grammar, history, and reading. Not surprisingly, then, arithmetic was the only subject they most liked to teach. But possibly this was not only because they felt more confident teaching it, but because they encountered fewer disciplinary problems in the arithmetic classes than they experienced in others.[61]

In the pioneer era of every region, maintaining discipline was always a problem, as every reader of Edward Eggleston's *The Hoosier Schoolmaster* knows. Students often tried to ''run their teacher out'' (as they said), and sometimes they succeeded. Such episodes, however colorful, probably were somewhat exaggerated, but even as the pioneer period gave way to settled conditions and older boys of 17 and 18 stopped coming to school, nearly all rural teachers, like those in urban schools, had disciplinary problems of one kind or another.

In large schools of 40 or more pupils, skill and practice were needed for a teacher to prevent students from whispering, making faces, or showing funny sketches on a slate—to name but a few of the usual distractions—while she constantly engaged her students in recitations. Nor was it always easy for a teacher of age 20 or so to prevent fights on the playground, or to keep track of children who wandered from the schoolgrounds to hunt gophers or squirrels. And the privies were another problem. Squalid and graffiti-covered, they were a challenge to every country teacher who worried about sanitation or decorum.[62]

Many schools had written rules and regulations governing both the pupils' and the teacher's behavior, which served as guidelines for at least the teacher. According to the general rules, the teacher was expected to "at all times, exercise a firm and vigilant but prudent discipline, governing as far as possible by gentle means." But to follow the rules to the letter was almost impossible. It might be easy to "forbid the use of tobacco," or to send any pupil home who had "a contagious or infectious disease" or one who came to school "with offensive uncleanliness of person or clothes," although it might not be politic to do so. But the teacher was also expected to monitor every pupil's language. "Any pupil," ran the usual set of regulations, "who shall, in or around the school premises, write or otherwise use profane or unchaste language, or who shall draw or carve any obscene picture or representation, shall be liable to suspension or expulsion according to the nature of the case."[63]

Country-school teachers dealt with their disciplinary problems in a variety of ways handed down from teacher to teacher. They seated disruptive boys next to the girls, made the unruly stay after school, isolated them, made them stand in a corner, whipped them if necessary, and sometimes, if all else failed, expelled them as they were required to do if, as the rules stated, "the good order of the school" demanded it.[64]

The same rules and regulations by which the students and teachers were to be governed noted that "as visiting school tends to give life and animation, parents and guardians are requested to visit the school as often as possible, and District Board to visit them at least once a month." The district board rarely lived up to expectations in this respect, but parents and others often did visit the rural schools. Since there was no set time for such visitations, teachers simply learned to expect visitors at *any* time, and to make them welcome no matter how inconvenient their coming. The country school, after all, belonged to the parents, not the teacher, a fact of life most teachers sooner or later understood.[65]

Another visitor, infrequent but frequently dreaded, was the county superintendent. Often his appearance virtually paralyzed the young, inexperienced teachers, and so the superintendent would find them completely unable to conduct a recitation in his presence. More than one superintendent, in fact, found it advisable to write to the teachers before his coming, to allay their fears.[66]

Besides the county superintendent, country teachers worried about school programs, which were almost as much a part of the school curriculum in their schools as the three R's, and remained a vital part of rural education as long as the small schools existed. Not only were they an excellent teaching device, spurring the children's excitement and interest in learning. They also increased the parents' interest in the schools as they flocked to see their children spell, debate, recite, and/or orate.

In some ways, school programs gave parents more tangible evidence of their children's progress than did report cards, and rural teachers were judged in part by the quality of the programs they produced. If the children spoke their pieces well, if they recited the Gettysburg Address with feeling, or knew their lines in a play, parents were likely to be grateful. So the teachers, often under some strain, culled their teachers' periodicals and other sources for material suitable for programs for every occasion from Thanksgiving and Christmas to Arbor Day to the end of school, and used up some of their precious recitation time making certain that their students had learned whatever parts they were to play.[67]

Obviously it was not easy to teach in a country school. Little wonder, then, that those rural teachers who were career-oriented aspired to teach in urban schools, where living accommodations were better, janitorial service was not required, parents visited only on stated occasions, and teachers taught only one or two grades instead of eight. As the years passed, many of them did get their chance to teach elsewhere—if not exactly in an urban school, then in one or another of the consolidated rural schools that were modeled after the urban schools.

Between the two World Wars, the widespread use of the automobile and the improvement of country roads made it possible to bus ever more country children to new consolidated schools. Located most often in the small rural towns, and sometimes in the open country, the new schools were four-, sometimes six-, and sometimes eight-teacher schools. No longer did country teachers in those schools have to teach all grades, or worry much about a boarding place. Now they could live in a ''teacherage'' provided for them, or could drive their automobiles to school from wherever they wished to live. They were better-paid, too, and better trained. More and more of them went to the normal schools (or teachers' colleges, as they came to be called) in the 1930s, or took the ''normal course'' in high school. The schools became larger, too—and more cost-efficient, if not more caring—as local control gave way to the professionals.

But there was a price to be paid for it all. The small school and the opportunity for individualized instruction; the lack of supervision and freedom to experiment with teaching methods that worked; the intimate knowledge of the students and their backgrounds; the close ties between the people and the school; the appreciation and support of the parents—those characteristics of country-school teaching that made it rewarding—were largely lost, no doubt forever, for the sake of efficiency and the large school.

Notes

1. Richard Hofstadter, *The Age of Reform* (New York: Vintage Books, 1955), p. 23.
2. A. C. Monohan, ''The Status of Rural Education in the United States,'' in U.S. Bureau of Education, *Bulletin*, 1913, No. 8 (Washington, DC: Government Printing Office, 1913), p. 12a.
3. Ibid., pp. 60–67; for the operation of the district system see Wayne E. Fuller, *The Old Country School: The Story of Rural Education in the Midwest* (Chicago: University of Chicago Press, 1982), pp. 46–52.
4. State of Indiana, Department of Public Education, *Nineteenth Biennial Report of the State Superintendent, for the School Years Ending July 31, 1897, and*

July 31, 1898 (Indianapolis, 1898), pp. 447–448.

5. For good descriptions and photographs of the early log-cabin school see State of Indiana, Department of Public Education, *Twenty-Eighth Biennial Report of the State Superintendent, for the School Years Ending July 31, 1907, and July 31, 1908* (Indianapolis, 1909), pp. 201–205.
6. U.S. Bureau of Education, *Report of the Commissioner of Education for 1890* (Washington, DC: Government Printing Office, 1980), p. 18.
7. Ray S. Flanagan, "Sanitary Survey of the Schools of Orange County, Virginia," in U.S. Bureau of Education, *Bulletin,* 1914, No. 17 (Washington, DC: Government Printing Office, 1914), pp. 22 and 24.
8. Ibid., p. 23.
9. *Report of the Commissioner of Education in 1890,* pp. 7, 29, and 79; and Thad Sitton and Milan C. Rowold, *Ringing the Children In: Texas Country Schools* (College Station: Texas A&M University Press, 1987), pp. 78–79. For a summary of the differences between Northern and rural schools, see Louis R. Harlan, *Separate and Unequal: Public School Campaigns and Racism in the Southern Seaboard States 1901–1915* (New York: Antheneum, 1968), pp. 9–11.
10. Quoted in William Link, *A Hard and Lonely Place: Schooling, Society, and Reform in Rural Virginia, 1870–1920* (Chapel Hill: University of North Carolina Press, 1986), p. 42; and for the difficulties of finding schoolhouses for blacks during reconstruction, see William Preston Vaughn, *Schools for All: The Blacks and Public Education in the South, 1865–1873* (Lexington: University Press of Kentucky, 1974), pp. 25–27. For black schools in 1916, see Thomas J. Jones (ed.), *Negro Education: A Study of the Private and Higher Schools for Colored People in the United States* (New York: Arno Press, 1969), p. 33.
11. For the disenfranchisement of blacks, see Harlan, *Separate and Unequal,* pp. 37–44; for distinctions between black and white schools see Booker T. Washington, "Black and White in the South: Schools for Negroes," in *Outlook* 106 (March 1914), p. 591; and Horace Mann Bond, "Negro Education: Debate in the Alabama Constitutional Convention of 1901," in *Journal of Negro Education* 1 (April 1932), pp. 50–51.
12. U.S. Bureau of Education, *Report of the Commissioner of Education for 1909* (Washington, DC: Government Printing Office, 1909), p. 237; see also Harlen, *Separate and Unequal,* pp. 20–21, for a description of black schoolhouses in the seaboard states.
13. Louis R. Harlan, *Booker T. Washington: The Wizard of Tuskegee, 1901–1915* (New York: Oxford University Press, 1983), pp. 197–199, has an account of the Julius Rosenwald fund. See also Scott McCormick "The Julius Rosenwald Fund," in *Journal of Negro Education* 3 (October 1934), pp. 605–628.
14. An excellent description of one-room schools and their architecture may be found in Fred H. Shroeder, "The Little Red Schoolhouse," in Ray B. Browne and Marshall Fenwick (eds.), *Icons of America* (Bowling Green, Ohio: Popular Press [Bowling Green University], 1978), pp. 139–160.
15. Hamlin Garland, *A Son of the Middle Border* (Lincoln: Bison Books, University of Nebraska Press, 1979), p. 95.
16. Larry Cuban, *How Teachers Taught: Constancy and Change in American Classrooms, 1890–1980* (New York: Longman, 1984), pp. 18–19.
17. "The Educational System of South Dakota," in U.S. Bureau of Education, *Bulletin,* 1918, No. 31 (Washington, DC: Government Printing Office, 1918), p. 112.
18. *Educational Advance* (El Dorado, Kansas), December 1, 1983, p. 5. For improvements in the schoolhouses see Fuller, *The Old Country School,* pp. 74–78.
19. Fletcher B. Dresslar, "Rural Schoolhouses and Grounds," in U.S. Bureau of Education, *Bulletin,* 1914, No. 12 (Washington, DC: Government Printing Office, 1914).

20. *Sixty-First Annual Report of the Superintendent of Public Instruction of the State of Michigan with Accompanying Documents for the Year 1897* (Lansing, MI, 1898), pp. 18–28.
21. Carl F. Kaestle, *Pillars of the Republic: Common Schools and American Society, 1780–1860* (New York: Hill and Wang, 1983), Ch. 2.
22. "Negro Public Schools," in *Independent* 73 (July 25, 1912), p. 218; see also Harlan, *Separate and Unequal*, pp. 22–24.
23. "Summary of Educational Facilities," in Thomas J. Jones (ed.), *Negro Education: A Study of the Private and Higher Schools for Colored People in the United States* (New York: Arno Press, 1969), p. 15; see also Washington, "Black and White," p. 592. On the curriculum for black children in the 1920s, see Walter G. Daniels, "The Curriculum," in *Journal of Negro Education* 1 (July 1932), pp. 277–303.
24. See Lance George Edward Jones, *The Jeanes Teacher in the United States, 1908–1933: An Account of Twenty-Five Years' Experience in the Supervision of Negro Rural Schools* (Chapel Hill: University of North Carolina Press, 1937), for the complete story.
25. A summary of what rural people expected of their teachers can be found in Andrew Gulliford, *America's Country Schools* (Washington, DC: The Preservation Press, 1984), pp. 73–74.
26. School Records, 1876–1895, District No. 37, Osborne County, Kansas. (Topeka: State Historial Society); see also *Educational Advance*, March 1, 1893, p. 1.
27. School Records, District No. 37, Osborne County, Kansas.
28. "Remarks and Recommendations on Each Individual Pupil, School Term, Commencing October 3, 1892 and Ending March 31, 1893," in School Records, District No. 37, Osborne County, Kansas.
29. LeRoy Albert King, "Status of Rural Teachers in Pennsylvania," in U.S. Bureau of Education, *Bulletin*, 1921, No. 34 (Washington, DC: Government Printing Office, 1922), p. 80.
30. Committee from the Graduate School of Education, University of Nebraska, "The Rural Teacher in Nebraska," in U.S. Bureau of Education, *Bulletin*, 1919, No. 20 (Washington, DC: Government Printing Office, 1919), p. 63.
31. *Educational Advance*, April 1, 1893, p. 5.
32. See Sarah Gillespie Huftalen, *Journal*, November 16, 1906, in Sarah Gillespie Huftalen Papers, Iowa State Historical Society, Iowa City, IA, for a Thanksgiving program.
33. "The Educational System of South Dakota," in U.S. Bureau of Education, *Bulletin*, 1918, No. 31 (Washington, DC: Government Printing Office, 1918), p. 115.
34. Ibid., pp. 119 and 132–133.
35. Ibid., pp. 119–124.
36. *Twenty-First Biennial Report of the State Superintendent of Public Instruction to the Governor of the State of Nebraska, for the Biennium Beginning January 7, 1909 and Ending January 5, 1911* (n.p., n.d.), p. v; see also *Sixty-Second Report of the Public Schools of the State of Missouri, School Year Ending June 30, 1911* (Jefferson City, MO: n.d.), p. 34.
37. Wayne E. Fuller, *Old Country School*, pp. 213–215. See also School Records, Dane County, Wisconsin; State Historical Society of Wisconsin, Madison, WI.
38. Wayne E. Fuller, "Making Better Farmers: The Study of Agriculture in Midwestern Country Schools, 1900–1923," in *Agricultural History* 60 (Spring 1986), pp. 154–159.
39. "The Rural Teachers of Nebraska," p. 63.
40. Marie Turner Harvey, "Contributions of Teachers to the Development of Democracy: Rural Schools," in *Addresses and Proceedings*, National Education Association (Washington, DC: National Education Association, 1919), p. 101.
41. Marie Turner Harvey, "The Porter School: A New Vision of the Rural School in Country Life," *Addresses and Proceedings*, National Education Association (Washington, DC: National Ed-

ucation Association, 1924), pp. 676–677.

42. Marie Turner Harvey, "Is Progressive Education Procedure Practicable in the Small Rural School?" *Addresses and Proceedings,* National Education Association (Washington, DC: National Education Association, 1930), pp. 449–451.
43. Evelyn Dewey, *New Schools for Old: The Regeneration of the Porter School* (New York: E. P. Dutton, 1919), p. 237.
44. Fuller, "Making Better Farmers," pp. 164–167.
45. King, *"Status of Rural Teachers in Pennsylvania,"* p. 13.
46. Ibid., p. 79; "The Rural Teacher of Nebraska," p. 65.
47. Fuller, "Making Better Farmers," pp. 166–167.
48. "Report of the Committee of Six on Rural School," in *Biennial Report of the State Superintendent of Wisconsin for the Two Years Ending June 30, 1900* (Madison, 1901), p. 26.
49. State of Indiana, Department of Public Instruction, *Twenty-First Biennial Report of the State Superintendent of Public Instruction for the School Years Ending July 31, 1901 and July 31, 1902* (Indianapolis, 1903), p. 28; and King, "Status of Rural Teachers in Pennsylvania," p. 81.
50. For the kind of county examinations rural teachers were required to take, see *Sixty-First Annual Report,* Michigan, pp. 100–115.
51. "The Rural Teacher of Nebraska," p. 65.
52. Ibid., p. 65; King, "Status of Rural Teachers in Pennsylvania," p. 59; for the greater permanency of southern teachers, see "An Educational Study of Alabama," in U.S. Bureau of Education, *Bulletin,* 1919, No. 41 (Washington, DC: Government Printing Office, 1919), pp. 343–347.
53. For the missionary motive of women teachers, see Polly Welts Kaufman, *Women Teachers on the Frontier* (New Haven: Yale University Press, 1984), pp. 13–18; and "An Educational Study of Alabama," pp. 345–346.
54. "The Rural Teacher of Nebraska," p. 23; U.S. Bureau of Education, *Report of the Commissioner of Education for 1910,* p. 676; see also Vaughn, *Schools for All,* pp. 24–25.
55. Twenty-one percent of the teachers in the Nebraska study in 1915 lived at home when teaching, and paid no board: see "The Rural Teacher of Nebraska," p. 46. In Pennsylvania, 64 percent lived with parents or relatives, but nearly half of these paid a certain amount for board: see King, "Status of Teachers in Pennsylvania," p. 13.
56. "The Rural Teacher of Nebraska," p. 45.
57. Ibid., pp. 47 and 49.
58. Ibid., p. 57.
59. Ibid., p. 63.
60. *Educational System of South Dakota,* p. 114; King, "Status of Rural Teachers in Pennsylvania," pp. 20–21.
61. "The Rural Teacher of Nebraska," p. 33.
62. Sitton and Rowold, *Ringing in the Children,* pp. 111–135.
63. For rules and regulations see Teacher's Daily Register, School Records, District No. 3, Albion Township, Dane County, Wisconsin; State Historical Society of Wisconsin, Madison, WI.
64. Ibid.
65. Ibid.
66. Fuller, *The Old Country School,* p. 144.
67. See Indiana, *Twenty-First Biennial Report,* p. 218, for suggested Arbor Day Program.

5

Agents of Democracy

Urban Elementary-School Teachers and the Conditions of Teaching

James W. Fraser

Historians of education in general, and historians of teachers and teaching in specific, have failed to deal seriously with what English historian E. P. Thompson calls "the agency of working people"—that is, teachers themselves as active agents for change in schools where they taught.[1] In general, historians of education have paid surprisingly little attention to teachers, as opposed to theorists, administrators, and other leaders of the profession. And when teachers have been the center of attention, the story often has been more in terms of what was done *to* them by others—politicians, administrators, or union leaders—than in terms of their own role in the schools.

In the last few years, historians of education have begun to correct this problem. Richard A. Quantz has noted that "Until recently, historians have tended to treat teachers as nonpersons. Female teachers especially have been portrayed as objects rather than subjects, as either the unknowing tools of the social elite or as the exploited minority whose labor is bought cheaply. Rarely have they been treated as subjects in control of their own activities."[2] Ira Katznelson and Margaret Weir have also focused on the reality that "The most important group affecting working-class positions and activity regarding educational reform was the teachers."[3]

In examining the conditions of teaching in the elementary schools of the major urban centers of the United States, and in reviewing teachers' response to their own perceptions of their roles, and their reflections on their experience, many issues naturally emerge. As Katznelson and Weir have argued, "Teachers may assume multiple identities. . . . [T]hey may consider themselves professionals or workers. . . . [They] may view themselves as recipients of political patronage, bound to their benefactors by ethnic and political ties." In addition, Katznelson and Weir also note that the reality of school personnel policies meant that for the most part elementary teachers had yet another identity at the beginning of the twentieth century, "namely, teachers as women."[4] This chapter will explore all of these roles, examining the experience of urban elementary teachers as workers, professionals, recipients of patronage, and women.

There is, however, an additional theme which also needs to attention. At certain points in history or in certain locations it is a major theme; at other times it is a minority view. But again and again the issue emerges: What does it mean for teachers to assert for themselves the democratic rights which they were supposed to teach to the next generation? What does it mean, in Ella Flagg Young's words, for the school to function "as an intrinsic part of this democracy . . . where rights and duties will be inseparable; where the free movement of thought will develop great personalities."[5] As the nation's largest urban school systems began to take shape in the mid-nineteenth century, the role envisioned for teachers did not include such rights and duties, in terms of either the curriculum which they taught or the working conditions in the classrooms where they spent their time.

A number of historians have noted the problem that elementary-school teachers—nearly all women—faced. David Tyack cites an anonymous writer in *Harpers* in 1878 who wrote that "women teachers are often preferred by superintendents because they are more willing to comply with established regulations and less likely to ride headstrong hobbies."[6] Clearly, taking one's place in the hierarchy, not asserting one's rights—even in the sphere of one's own classroom—was the valued virtue. Nancy Hoffman has summarized the situation that most urban elementary teachers faced throughout the late nineteenth and early twentieth centuries: "The power the teacher exercised over the children 'beneath' her was more than matched by the power of professional school administrators over the teacher herself. In relation to the men above them, teachers might as well have been children."[7]

Not all teachers, however, accepted this definition of their work situations. As one of the leaders of Boston's women teachers insisted in 1917, "We Americans preach democracy but after all we are loath to practice it in many ways."[8] Leaders like Boston's Cora Bigelow and Chicago's Ella Flagg Young, and their counterparts across the country, found themselves asking what it would mean for teachers to become active agents for workplace democracy for themselves in terms of benefits, classroom working conditions, and the curriculum they were supposed to teach. It is a question which has dominated many of the issues facing teachers in urban schools throughout the last years of the nineteenth century and most of the twentieth.

It is generally agreed among historians that the "progressive" reforms of the late nineteenth and early twentieth centuries were imposed on teachers, and that in the process teachers lost power to newly emergent administrators bent on scientific, meritocratic management of the schools. Along the way, the teacher's role changed from that of being a recipient of political patronage to being a worker who was expected to follow orders. Teachers, for many good reasons, opposed these changes. But ultimately the changes, although designed to downgrade (or in Michael Apple's phrase "proletarianize") teachers, resulted in their being freed from the dependency of the patronage system. They were freed as workers to resist unfair demands made on them.[9] The teacher's role became that of activist worker free to organize for a much greater say in all aspects of school life. This organizing took many forms. Teachers struggled for basic benefits in terms of salary and pensions, but they also organized for a much greater voice in the structure of the classroom, the curriculum of the school, and the regulations of the systems in which they taught. In this new role, teachers were free, as their predecessors had not been, to be their own agents, and therefore agents of democracy for themselves and their successors.

The role of agent for a more democratic school was asserted in different ways at different times. Sometimes teachers were quite passive in accepting the definition of their rights and duties as given by others. But at other points, teachers were a very active, militant force, demanding a role in decisions affecting both what they taught and how they were rewarded. The struggle for the right to play an activist role in educational decision making is one which has taken place with some variations among many of the elementary-school teachers in most cities in the United States. It is a story which deserves more attention than it has received.

It is important to recognize, throughout our consideration of the period treated in this chapter (primarily 1880 to 1930), that urban teachers continued to be a minority of the nation's teaching force. The *Report of the Commissioner of Education* for 1890 indicates that 77 percent of children attended rural schools—that is, schools in districts of less than 4,000 people. The few large urban systems included a small minority of the nation's students and teachers. Still, they carried a disproportionate influence, partly from their sheer size—New York City had 683 schools, 36,000 teachers, and 1 million children in 1930—and partly from the access to the national media which has always characterized cities.[10] In addition, the graded elementary school, as opposed to the one-room common school, was an urban invention. In the 1880–1930 era the graded school was almost universally the workplace of urban elementary teachers, but not of their rural counterparts.

Issues Faced by Classroom Teachers

The Nineteenth-Century Experience

For the most part, nineteenth-century urban teachers were much less militant than their twentieth-century successors in asserting their rights, either in the classroom or in the profession at large. The elementary school as it is known today was an evolutionary development in the early decades of that century. Dame schools and various forms of reading schools had existed as adjuncts to the grammar schools from the earliest days of public schooling in the United States. But it was only in the nineteenth century that the system of public education was sufficiently regularized for there to be recognizable elementary schools with a teaching core of their own.

While the process was already well advanced before he arrived on the scene, no one has been more associated with reform of the organization of public schooling than Horace Mann, secretary of the Massachusetts Board of Education from 1837 to 1848. As publicist for the nation's emerging school system, Mann had a very clear understanding of the role of the schools: They were to teach democracy. Mann shared the concern of many of his day that "A republican form of government, without intelligence in the people, must be, on a vast scale, what a mad-house, without superintendent or keepers, would be, on a small one. . . ." But of course Mann also had the solution to his fears: "Without undervaluing any other human agency, it may be safely affirmed that the Common School . . . may become the most effective and benignant of all the forces of civilization."[11]

While Horace Mann and other early nineteenth-century reformers had urged growing urban school systems to develop more careful means of systematizing instruction to replace the ungraded one-room school house, the institution of the graded elementary-school building, divided into classrooms, was a Boston invention. In 1848 John Philbrick, later to be Boston's school superintendent, convinced the Boston school committee to build a new kind of school building. The new Quincy school was the first in the nation to be divided into graded classrooms. It was built with 12 classrooms, each with desks for 56 students. Students were to be divided according to grade level, and "all in the same class [should] attend to precisely the same branches of study. Let the Principal or Superintendent have the general supervision and control of the whole, and let him have one male assistant or sub-principal, and ten female assistants, one for each room."[12] As David Tyack has wryly noted, "Thus was stamped on mid-century America not only the graded school, but also the pedagogical harem."[13]

Once established in Boston, the graded school spread rapidly. By the 1860s most of the large cities had graded schools, and the U.S. Commissioner of Education's survey of educational practices in 45 cities in 1870 showed that the pattern of the eight-year graded elementary school had become the norm.[14] With the creation of the graded elementary school, with its supervising male principal and self-contained classrooms presided over by female classroom teachers, the structure of work for the nation's female elementary teachers was fairly well set.

The teacher's role in all of this was also clear. The teacher was not a role model for an activist democracy. It would be the turn of the century before teachers began to claim that role, and even then they did so in the face of significant opposition from most administrators and policymakers. Rather, the teacher, in Mann's and Philbrick's view, was the custodian and model of virtue, and it was the duty of school committees to be sure that he or she stayed that way. "In the contemplation of the law," Mann wrote in his *Fourth Report,* "the school committee are sentinels stationed at the door of every schoolhouse in the State, to see that no teacher ever crosses its threshold, who is not clothed, from the crown of his head to the sole of his foot, in garments of virtue. . . ."[15] The role of guardian and exemplar of virtue, albeit a passive kind of virtue, is one which would continue to be held up to teachers long after Mann had left the scene.

The Issue of Gender

The focus on the teacher as example of virtue also led fairly quickly to a growing trend to see teaching as "woman's true profession." As Nancy Hoffman has noted in her book of that title, many nineteenth-century educators believed that teaching, especially at the elementary level, "unlocked woman's instinct for mothering and prepared her for marriage. Women, they believed, took teaching jobs primarily because they loved children."[16] A generation of women quite consciously used this rhetoric to open up new opportunities for their sisters. Thus Catharine Beecher, one of the most effective recruiters of women to teaching, and publicist for their virtues in the profession, wrote of her commitment to "the cause of popular education, and as intimately connected with it, the elevation of my sex by the opening of a profession for them as educators of the young.''[17] For Beecher, the rhetoric of maternal virtue opened opportunities for women which had never before been available.

A few nineteenth-century women recognized the danger posed in Catharine Beecher's rhetoric. If teaching could be woman's true profession, it could also be a profession on the bottom of the social ladder. Thus Susan B. Anthony argued before the male delegates to a teacher's convention in 1853, who were worried about the status of their profession, that:

> It seems to me, gentlemen, that none of you quite comprehend the cause of the disrespect of which you complain. Do you not see that so long as society says a woman is incompetent to be a lawyer, minister, or doctor, but has ample ability to be a teacher, that every man of you who chooses that profession tacitly acknowledges that he has no more brains than a woman? . . . Would you exalt your profession, exalt those who labor with you?[18]

Anthony's was a minority voice, however. The lack of other opportunities made teaching an appealing profession for many women. As David Tyack and Elisabeth Hansot have argued, ''A far more common strategy for women educational leaders and one that conformed with their values and belief, was not openly to question the dominant ideology that woman's true vocation was to be wife and mother, but rather to seek to enlarge woman's sphere to encompass the entire education of children.''[19] As early as 1848, when John Philbrick announced his plan for the Quincy school, he did not feel the need to justify his decision that all but one of the ''assistants'' would be women.

The rhetoric of women's special virtue was strongly supported, in the minds of many school boards, by the fact that women teachers could be hired at much less cost than their male counterparts. Estimates of the earnings of men and women in city school systems indicated that in 1870 women earned approximately one-third of what men were paid in the same position, while by 1900 they still earned only one-half. More precise figures gathered for the NEA in a 1905 study of 467 city systems showed that the average salary for a woman elementary teacher was $650 per year, while men in the same position—where there *were* any—were paid $1,161. Women elementary-school principals were paid an average of $970, while their male counterparts received $1,542.[20] While the higher salaries for men were often justified in terms of the need to be sure that some males stayed in the teaching profession, the reality for most school boards was that the vast majority of teachers needed to be women if the budgets were to be balanced. As will be seen, changing this reality went to the heart of the concerns that early twentieth-century teachers had about the place they wanted to have in the schools of the nation.

The result of this combination of economic reality and the rhetoric that schools, especially elementary schools, were part of ''women's sphere,'' was a rapid turnover in the makeup of the teaching profession. Prior to the Civil War, the majority of teachers still were male, although in the teaching of younger children the percentage of women was growing. The war accelerated the change, and by 1870 the percentage of female teachers in the nation's schools was about 60, while by the 1930s it was 80, with the lower grades registering figures moving much closer to 100.[21]

While exact figures are hard to come by, any review of the reports and regulations of any of the large urban school systems indicates that nearly all, if not all, of the elementary classroom teachers were women. In 1905, an NEA study of 467 cities reported that only 2 percent of the teachers in elementary schools were men, while 38 percent of the principals were men. The figures for high schools were quite different: 38 percent of the teachers, and 94 percent of the principals, were men.[22] Given such statistics, when one talks of urban elementary-school teachers in the years between 1880 and 1930, one is essentially discussing women's experience.

Recipients of Patronage

In spite of the rhetoric of protected motherhood and virtue, reality for the mostly female teaching force was not so gentle. Especially in the nation's growing cities, nineteenth-century teachers were, in Katznelson and Weir's words, "recipients of patronage."[23] As Nancy Hoffman has argued, "In Boston, New York, Philadelphia, and smaller cities, the schools were the fiefdom of local ward politicians who gave out jobs as rewards to loyal voters and to 'buy' new ones."[24]

In the eyes of many contemporaries as well as historians, the ward politicians represented a more democratic approach to school governance than did the turn-of-the-century reformers who replaced them. Indeed, the battle between the older, ward-based system and its "progressive successors" has been viewed as "a war between democracy and efficiency."[25] As late as 1929, a retiring assistant superintendent in Boston remembered the personal contact of the old system, when the school committee members knew the teachers and "encouraged us and sustained our hands."[26] No one would say that of the new centralized school committees that appeared austere and remote.

At their best, these personal contacts were very important in protecting and supporting the teachers. Thus Julia Duff, a long-time Boston School Committee member who was swept out of office by the "progressive" reforms of 1905, had long advocated "Boston Schools for Boston Girls." Duff recognized clearly that the school system was a major employment opportunity for many of the city's young women, for she had been one of them. An 1878 graduate of the Boston Normal School, she taught for 14 years before her marriage and subsequent political career. As a school committee member, Duff worked hard to protect the normal school as a vehicle for local females to enter the teaching profession. She opposed expanding the student body to out-of-state students, insisting that her purpose to "to lift up young women [from Boston] to a point where they could secure modern advantages for advanced education that they might, as teachers, impart to the children the broadest possible knowledge." Allied with the committee's black member, Dr. Samuel E. Courtney, Duff fought to protect the normal school for Boston's girls, and Boston's teaching jobs for the normal-school graduates.

As Polly Kaufman has argued, "She did not see the schools as a vehicle to improve society by reforming other people's children." Rather, she wanted to be sure that her own children and those of her fellow Bostonians were treated with the respect that she felt to be their due, not only as students in school but as candidates for whatever financial benefits the schools might later be able to bestow on them as teachers. She defended the personal contacts that were allowed by a large school committee with many subcommittees, and she opposed "progressive" reforms at each step.[27]

At the same time, the patronage system was hardly empowering for teachers. Amelia Allison wrote of her experience with the patronage system in a series on "Confessions of Public School Teachers," published by the *Atlantic Monthly* in 1896. Having, with some difficulty, played the patronage system so as to secure a teaching job for herself, Allison came to be in danger because her father was not staying in line with his political organization. She described her experience:

> As our district was likely to have a close contest, it was suggested that my father be "whipped into line." The only lash that he could be made to feel, they thought, was a threat to remove me. They sent their candidate for school trustee to our home and he knocked timidly at the back door and made known his errand. In a very few minutes he walked rapidly away. His party was defeated—luckily for me, no doubt, for a local politician was asked how a teacher whose work was good could be dismissed without "charges." He replied, "We always have charges when we need them."[28]

If patronage could win jobs for a woman such as Allison, she was also forcefully reminded that patronage could also cost her a job. This was hardly a system designed to give its beneficiaries the self-respect for democratic citizens.

There has been a tendency among contemporary historians to romanticize the old pre-reform systems of school governance because what followed was so bad for teachers. It is not, however, a challenge to the view that turn-of-the-century education reform often resulted in the downgrading of the mostly female elementary teaching force, to say that the old patronage system also had its limitations. The reforms of these years did replace a school system in which teachers were treated with more respect than under the new plan of organization. At the same time, it is important for historians to avoid nostalgia for the old pre-reform system of school governance. Patronage, as scores of Amelia Allisons understood only too well, is hardly empowering to those who receive jobs and know that in return there are political debts to be paid.

Nancy Hoffman strikes the proper balance when she writes, "If previously the teacher feared a capricious and arbitrary politician who cared more for votes than education, now her destiny was in the hands of trained administrators hired by and in agreement with the school board."[29] The transition from capricious politician to hierarchical administrator did not, in its own right, significantly change the position of the elementary classroom teacher within the power structure of urban public education.

The Administrative Progressives and the Decline of Teacher Power

The low point for teacher influence in the schools came with the emergence of those whom David Tyack has called the "administrative progressives." If the politics of patronage had limited teachers' rights to assert a meaningful place for themselves, the campaigns to "take the schools out of politics" only made matters much worse. Tyack summarized the nature of these campaigns "to emulate the process of decision-making used by men on the board of directors of a modern business corporation." The reformers' goal was a school committee consisting of the community's most successful leaders. Teachers were not included in the emerging "progressive" power structure which came into being in most of the nation's cities in the years between 1880 and the close of World War I. On the contrary, the reformers were business and professional leaders and their university-based advisors. Once in power, they also hired a new breed of school administrators to manage the system they had taken over. As Tyack observed, "At the turn of the twentieth century, they planned a basic shift in the control of urban education which would vest political power in a small committee composed of 'successful men'."[30]

In city after city, the major outline was the same. These business-inspired reformers sought:

—A small school committee, preferably appointed (or, if elected, on a city-wide and not ward-based basis)
—A professional superintendent who would serve as the chief executive for the board
—The appointment of teachers through a merit-based system rather than the informal patronage arrangements which usually prevailed
—The application of "scientific management" to all phases of school life, linked to an end to "political influence" in the schools

Centralization began in New York City in 1896, followed by St. Louis and Atlanta in 1897, Baltimore in 1898, and Philadelphia and Boston in 1905. Chicago (1917) and San Francisco (1920) were late in joining the movement, though not for lack of trying on the part of the business elites of those cities.[31] A commission led by the University of Chicago's President, William Rainey Harper, had proposed major reforms of Chicago's school governance in 1899. The changes were presented again in 1901, 1903, 1905, and 1907, and defeated each time by an alliance of labor and women's organizations led by the Chicago Teachers Federation. It was only with the election of Republican mayor William "Big Bill" Thompson, and his appointment of the militantly antiunion Jack Loeb to the school committee, that the tide was turned in Chicago.[32]

That there was a clear class-base to these changes has been noted by a generation of historians following Samuel P. Hays, who wrote in an oft-quoted article that "The movement for reform in municipal government, therefore, constituted an attempt by upper-class, advanced professional, and large business groups to take formal political power from the previously dominant lower- and middle-class elements so that they might advance their own conceptions of desirable public policy."[33] A configuration of working-class, often immigrant, political leadership which had emerged in many of the nation's cities after the Civil War was swept aside, temporarily at least, by these reforms, and replaced by a political leadership with a decidedly different set of values and class-base.

A textbook example of these reforms was the reorganization of the Boston School Committee in 1905–1906. Prior to 1906, the city's school committee had included 24 members, divided into a variety of subcommittees and connected through the network of the city's neighborhoods to the teaching force. The old school committee was seen by reformers such as George A. O. Ernst as an "inherently vicious system," in which primary power resided with the subcommittees of the 24-member elected committee rather than being centralized in a professional superintendent. To a man like Ernst this rejection of "the cardinal principle of reliance upon experts" could only have been done for the most corrupt of reasons.[34]

The campaign to change Boston's school structure was led, as it was in many cities in the early years of the century, by a young generation of "good government reformers." In 1904 a Yankee banker, James Jackson Storrow, decided to seek basic changes in the structure of the school committee. He consulted with another well-known administrative progressive, Paul Hanus of the Division of Education at Harvard. The two men, following a national pattern of reform, decided that the crucial move was to abolish the large committee and replace it with a small centralized one of five members, elected at-large and likely to represent the city's business elite. They persuaded the state legislature to follow their plans, and the new committee was elected in December, 1905.[35]

By making such a shift, one of Storrow's allies insisted, "Political methods were changed for the best modern business standards."[36] "It was," David Tyack and Elisabeth Hansot have argued, "a conception of leadership designed to consolidate power in large and centralized organizations, whether steel mills, large department stores, or city school systems."[37] It was a form of leadership with which Storrow and his elite allies were quite comfortable. It also was a committee which would be characterized by a commitment to a kind of efficiency and top-down decision making which often took on a decidedly antiteacher tone.[38]

While New York, Chicago, and other Eastern and Midwestern cities followed a pattern very much like Boston's, recent historians have noted that in other parts of the nation the story was somewhat different.

Victor L. Shrader makes the case that in the San Francisco election of 1920, which brought reform to that city, the normal split of elite support for centralization and working-class opposition was dramatically altered. The old board, with its patronage base and its elected superintendent, was seen by many as dominated by the city's Catholics. As a result, San Francisco school politics were fought out on ethnic lines as the working class divided by religion. The Protestant working-class wards ultimately provided the margin of victory in support of the elite reforms.

Whatever its contribution to the history of school politics, Shrader's argument fails to answer the question of why the 800-member San Francisco Teacher Association supported the old system in such a unified way. Certainly not all these teachers were Catholic. For the Protestant teachers to move in this direction, against the ethnic ties of their own families, must have meant a fairly clear-cut understanding of the nature of the centralizing movement and the need to work against it.[39]

In Atlanta, on the other hand, a limited reform in which "the school board was reduced in size, and the administrative powers of the superintendent were increased" came about very early and very quickly.[40] A May 28, 1897 City Council meeting, ostensibly called to consider matters related to the waterworks, abolished the old school board and created a new one. As David N. Plank and Paul E. Peterson have argued, the case of reform in Atlanta was not so much a matter of a split between the elite and the working class as a division within the city's elite. Atlanta's politics were far too dominated by warring elites for the working class to have significant political influence, especially after 1890, when the half of the working class which was black was totally disenfranchised by the white primary. In the case of Atlanta, according to Plank and Peterson, the issues involved in reform were matters of economy and school discipline, and the jealousies among contending elites more than matters of patronage and control.[41]

In spite of this range of differences in different parts of the nation, however, one fact remains strong in all of the reform stories: Teachers opposed the reforms. Atlanta's teachers saw their salaries being cut and their powers reduced by the reformers, while San Francisco's teachers fought off reforms for two decades because of the "alliances among teachers and the board."[42] Why this unified opposition by teachers to moves to free them from political domination? The teachers saw all too clearly the antiteacher nature of the reformers.

Among the first actions of Boston's new reform committee was the selection of a new superintendent. The committee's choice, incumbent Superintendent Stratton Brooks, was certainly not a man known for valuing teachers. He answered the question of to what extent teachers should play a role in the development of school policy, "It seems clear to me that the answer is, not at all."[43] Brooks continued to implement his views for a well-organized, meritocratic school administration in which decision making emanated from the central authority of the committee and the superintendent who knew what was best for all involved in the system.

As he developed his politics, Superintendent Brooks seemed anxious to demonstrate a reality which Nancy Hoffman has described:

> The school reformers had no intention of granting teachers a voice. They were the laborers in the system. John Dewey was not the only one to point out the "obvious discrepancy" between the teacher's obligation to give lessons about democracy, and her obligation to take orders and remain silent at her workplace.[44]

It was, as will be seen, a discrepancy which the nation's teachers struggled to change, for they understood it very well even if many others chose to ignore it.

In some ways, however, the nature of the changes in the Progressive Era, as far as teachers were concerned, have been overstated. School bureaucracies had begun to grow in the middle of the nineteenth century, and the authority of school bureaucrats was frightening under both the old system and the new. Thus, Marian A. Dogherty described the tyranny of her Boston principal well before the reformers came to power. In her first year as a teacher, Dogherty had proudly watched one of her children read the assigned lesson, only to find that the principal was not happy with the performance:

> Our principal was a stickler for the proprieties, and the proper way to read in the public school in the year 1899 was to say, "Page 35, Chapter 4," and holding the book in the right hand, with the toes pointing at an angle of forty-five degrees, the head held straight and high, the eyes looking directly ahead, the pupil would lift up his voice and struggle in loud, unnatural tones. Now, I had attended to the position of the toes, the right arm, and the nose, but had failed to enforce the mentioning of page and chapter.

The result, of course, was that the principal was displeased with the new teacher's performance. "I had failed to perform my duty. . . . My heart sank."[45] Clearly, teachers like Dogherty were not in a strong position under either system. Many of them also meant to change the situation.

Writing in 1901, Ella Flagg Young responded to the situation as it existed in Chicago and elsewhere:

> The school cannot take up the question of the development of training for citizenship in a democracy while the teachers are still segregated in two classes, as are the citizens in an aristocracy. . . . In a short time the teachers must cease to occupy the position of initiators in the individual work of instruction and discipline, and must fall into a class of assistants, whose duty consists in carrying out instructions of a higher class which originates method for all.[46]

Often inspired by Young, her counterparts throughout the nation made the same arguments: The administrative progressives were taking power away from the teachers, deskilling them while giving authority (and often any money available for raises) to a new class of bureaucrat. The teachers fought back.

Along the way, teachers shifted their view of themselves. As recipients of patronage, teachers were always beholden to their patrons. But as workers, however much the transition initially meant a loss of power, teachers were also free to organize for their democratic rights, the same rights they were supposed to teach in the classroom. Perhaps more clearly than anyone else, Margaret Haley recognized this reality when she insisted that teachers had to work against the tendency toward making the teacher "a mere factory hand, whose duty it is to carry out mechanically and unquestioningly the ideas and orders of those clothed with authority of position."[47]

Teachers Respond to the Working Conditions in the Schools

Margaret Haley: Setting an Agenda for Activist Teachers

In 1904, Margaret Haley addressed the National Education Association. In this speech, to a less-than-friendly audience, Haley made quite clear her opposition to the centralization of school decision making in the hands of a small board and a professional superintendent. She preferred a broader democracy, for, she argued, "If the American people cannot be made to realize and meet their responsibility to the public school, no self-appointed custodians of the public intelligence and conscience can do it for them.'' And if the people were slow in asserting their democratic rights, the teachers would be in the forefront of the campaign as agents for democracy. ''The methods as well as the objects of teachers' organizations,'' Haley argued, ''must be in harmony with the fundamental object of the public school in a democracy, to preserve and develop the democratic ideal.''[48]

The appeal to democracy made for a good rhetorical flourish, but for Haley it was much more. At the beginning of the new century, Haley was making it quite clear to her audience that she, and many of her sisters in the profession, did not mean to accept working conditions in which they simply carried out the instructions of others. William Payne, a nineteenth-century expert on the school superintendency, described a view of school administration with which the majority of Haley's audience would have agreed: ''If there is to be a plan,'' Payne wrote, ''someone must devise it, while others must execute it. As the members of the human body execute the behests of the supreme intelligence, so in human society the many must follow the directions of the few.''[49] Haley had a very different conception of the organizational structure of the schools. Unless teachers could devise as well as execute what went on in their classrooms, the school would not model the democracy they were meant to serve, and the teachers would remain oppressed workers rather than professionals for whom the classroom was a place to model workplace democracy. The ''supreme intelligence'' of nonteaching administrators was something Haley and many of her colleagues rejected as both an assault on their working conditions as professionals and a contradiction of the democratic values they were to teach.

Describing the basis of Haley's ongoing battle with the male leadership of the NEA, Lawrence Cremin has written, ''Since its founding as the National Teachers' Association in 1857, the NEA had claimed to represent the aspirations of a single unified education profession . . . [T]he leaders of the organization as a whole took as a given that the task of building a profession representing the expertise required for the proper conduct of the nation's schools took precedence over matters of teacher salaries, academic freedom, and working conditions in the schools.'' Classroom teachers, particularly female elementary teachers in the nation's largest cities, began to realize, however, that this model of profession building kept them on the lowest rungs of the profession no matter what else happened. In some of the nation's largest cities, including Chicago, New York, Los Angeles, and Washington, D.C., elementary classroom teachers began to organize to create a very different set of working conditions for themselves:

> Predominantly women, they saw themselves as exploited by predominantly male administrators and boards of education, with no job security, no rights to academic freedom, and salary scales at approximately half of those for men of equivalent rank, training, and experience; and they made salaries, working conditions, and job security their primary concerns, believing that once salaries, working conditions, and job security improved, professional status would inevitably follow.[50]

The important point here is that these teachers did not just begin to work on a series of concerns related to their own self-interest. On the contrary, as advocated by leaders like Haley, they were making demands for a radical transformation of their profession, and for the conditions under which they labored in their daily work in the classroom.

Haley's speech to the NEA in 1904 outlined very clearly the agenda that would dominate the concerns of elementary teachers for the next 30 years. For Haley a commitment to a democratic classroom demanded a basic program for changing a situation in which she argued that teachers faced the following:

1. Greatly increased cost of living—and wholly inadequate teachers' salaries
2. Insecurity of tenure of office and lack of provision for old age
3. Overwork in overcrowded schoolrooms, exhausting both mind and body
4. Lack of recognition of the teacher as an educator in the school system, due to the increased tendency toward "factoryizing education"

It was a set of conditions which Haley, and many of her colleagues, set out to change in the first decades of the new century.[51] It also is a list which gives the historian a useful clue both to the daily experiences and concerns of classroom teachers working in the schools and to the campaigns which they would wage for change.

Pensions for Teachers

High on Haley's list was the issue of "provision for old age," and from the 1860s on, teachers had indicated their concern for some form of pension support once they could no longer teach. The issue of pensions for school teachers paralleled the development of pension programs for many other public employees, but in the case of teachers there was also a significant difference. In the earlier part of the nineteenth century, teaching was seen as a temporary vocation. Men might teach until another career (often the ministry) opened up. Women could teach until they married and began a family. But now teaching was becoming a profession. Women who entered the field stayed. Many, indeed, made quite deliberate choices to stay rather than give up the freedom and independence that the profession offered them. Pensions, like other benefits, became much more significant issues as the classroom became the workplace where many people saw themselves spending all of a professional career. And so, like other workers, they needed the benefits which a lifetime career had to provide.

At first this concern was addressed through self-help programs in which teachers organized for their mutual benefit and for the support of their older colleagues, "often by passing the hat."[52] For low-paid teachers, however, self-help quickly reached its limits. Thus teachers in New York and New Jersey began lobbying for publicly funded pensions. The first pension legislation was sponsored by the Brooklyn Teachers' Association in 1879 and eventually passed by the New York State legislature in 1895. New Jersey passed legislation a year later.[53]

From the beginning, pension reform was part of a larger strategy for Margaret Haley and her colleague Catherine Goggin in organizing teachers in Chicago. Katznelson and Weir have noted that "The pension issue, which first spurred teachers to organize, set the tone for future conflicts." The pension campaign also led to the formation of the Chicago Teachers' Federation, which "prohibited principals and other supervisors from joining, leaving an organization composed almost exclusively of women. The leadership of the CTF was drawn from grade school teachers."[54] In fact, Chicago's teachers won their pension legislation in 1895, two years before the powerful CTF was formally organized, but the Teachers' Federation was one of the most significant results of the campaign for a reasonable pension system.[55]

Later fights in Chicago and elsewhere would not be won so easily, but pension reform had many supporters. Thus, "Between 1911 and 1915, twenty-three states enacted legislation, so that by 1916 a total of thirty-three states had some system of retirement for public school teachers."[56] If the rest of Haley's agenda had been reached with equal ease, teachers would have had quite different experiences throughout the twentieth century.

Equal Pay for Equal Work

In the next issue around which teachers organized, the battle lines were much more clearly drawn. The women teachers were on one side. The vast majority of administrators, and indeed male teachers, were on the other. As school systems grew and were organized and bureaucratized throughout the nineteenth century, one of the results was a salary scale according to which teachers were paid. An individual rural teacher might bargain with the school committee before agreeing to teach in the town's only one-room schoolhouse. But in the cities, teachers were paid according to the salary scale. Indeed, an organized salary scale was one of the many forms which the bureaucratization of schooling took. And in nearly all of the nation's growing cities, the scale did not treat all teachers equally.

According to a 1905 survey by the National Education Association, the average female high-school teacher received 69 percent of her male counterpart's salary. For many elementary teachers, the situation was similar to that in New York City. In New York, from 1900 to 1912, women elementary teachers began at a salary of $600 per year and worked up to a maximum of $1,320. Their male counterparts began at $900 and could reach a maximum of $2,160. For high-school teachers the starting point for women was $1,100 to a maximum of $1,900, while for men the range was from $1,300 to $2,400. The fact that far more of the women teachers were clustered in the elementary grades only exacerbated the problem. This was the kind of blatant injustice against which many women teachers were prepared to fight. It was also the kind of privilege which others were quite prepared to defend.[57]

The issue of differentiated salaries for men and women in the teaching profession went to the heart of the conception of the elementary-school teacher. As has been seen, mid-nineteenth-century leaders like Catharine Beecher had sold school boards across the nation on the belief that the teaching profession was "women's true profession,'' as an extension of their mothering role. They had also convinced boards to hire women on the basis of teaching being a profession through which many young women would pass on the way to their real role as wife and mother. In such a situation, low pay was simply part of the reality of the apprenticeship.

Such a conception of women teachers did not die easily. At the height of the battle over equal pay for New York City's teachers, in 1907, *The New York Times* used this earlier rationale in an editorial opposing equal pay. Describing commencement at a normal college, the editors spoke of the ''crowd of sweet girl graduates with their golden hair'':

> As the male spectator contemplates this delightful show, his uppermost thought must be, What a shame such nice girls should have to teach school for a living; and his final and consolatory reflection that they will not be doing it long. How can anybody expect that they are going to take their provisional method of making a living as seriously as the male who takes it for life?

The *Times* did note that ''There may be detected occasional exceptions, who may seem destined for a life of celibacy and possibly school-teaching. But one does not legislate for exceptions.''[58] As long as teaching was a ''provisional method of making a living'' for most women, it was not a profession to be taken seriously. In the *Times*' view of things, equal pay would have been ''legislating for the exception.''

The myth that women taught only as a temporary measure was, in reality, becoming less and less true in the nation's cities. Nevertheless, it continued to fit well with the image of the teaching profession advocated by many of the leaders of the NEA, such as Lotus D. Coffman, who wrote in 1911, ''All of the graded school positions have been preempted by women; men still survive in public school work as 'managing' or executive officers.''[59] For men like Coffman, the division of the profession by sex, with the men as the managers, could be justified if the men were the only ones for whom education was a career.

It was precisely this distorted image of the profession (with female elementary teachers as the quasi-mindless operatives who carried out the plans of the male administrators) that a new generation of teachers meant to change. And the issue of salary was a key step in changing that image, as well as being an element of simple justice.

Initial skirmishes in the battle for equal pay for equal work began in the late nineteenth century. The first victories were in Western states, where there was a stronger pattern of women's rights and where the urban bureaucracies were less firmly entrenched. Thus a San Francisco teacher, Kate Kennedy, who also was active in both the suffrage movement and the Knights of Labor, organized other teachers to win legislation which in 1870 provided California teachers the right of equal pay for the same work.[60]

The issue was also raised farther east, but with much less success. Fanny Baker Ames, a well-known suffragist in Boston, won a seat on the Boston School Committee in 1895. One of her immediate demands was for equal pay for the women teachers in her city. Ames and her allies introduced a petition to the school committee to make "the compensation more equal by raising the salaries of women teachers." The *Women's Journal* supported Ames and the teachers, noting that the argument that men supported families was countered by the fact that 66 percent of the women teachers also had someone dependent on them. While Ames did succeed in achieving a raise for the women teachers, it did not bring them equity, and indeed it was only after World War II that Boston's teachers finally achieved equity in the salary scales.[61]

While the issue was being fought in many different cities, the campaign for equal pay for equal work was waged with greatest intensity in New York City. The Interborough Association of Women Teachers was organized in 1906 specifically to address the inequalities in salaries between men and women teachers. Grace Strachan, who had spent many years as a teacher in the city and was then a district superintendent, quickly emerged as the organization's leader and most effective spokesperson.[62]

At first, it seemed as if New York's women would have a very easy campaign. Both houses of the New York legislature passed a bill in 1907 phasing-in equality for the teachers of the state's largest city. The bill was vetoed, however—first by New York's Mayor George B. McClellan, Jr. (the state constitution from 1894 to 1938 gave the mayor a veto over legislation affecting city finances), and then by the governor, Charles Evans Hughes.[63] The battle, it turned out, would be longer, and much more intense, than originally anticipated.

With time to organize a response, the Association of Men Teachers and Principals did, indeed, fight back. Basically they opposed the equal-pay legislation for three reasons. First, they argued that salaries should be driven by market forces, and that "The wages paid to a [male] teacher must be sufficiently high to call him from other lines of work into teaching." Second, they argued that boys needed male role models, and that in the schools "The masculine traits' influence should be substituted for feminine." Finally, echoing the *Times,* they argued that it would not be good for women to be paid equally, since "If more money should be paid to them, it would tend to make them a celibate class" who ostensibly would have no need to marry.[64]

New York's women, however, were more than up to such arguments. One of them dismissed the "market" argument with the rejoinder that, under the current schedules, "You pay a third-class salary to a first-rate woman and a first-class salary to a third-rate man." Another added, "I'm sure if a man comes to sweep off the snow from your front step, you do not ask him if he is married and how many children he has, in order to fix the price of the work."[65]

An incisive debater herself, Strachan heaped scorn on her opponents. She told women teachers:

> I am sure that we all agree that men who are men will be welcome as teachers in our public schools to serve as models for our boys; but, I believe also, that you will agree with me that the man who believes that it would be unmanly to pay his sister the same salary as is paid to him when she does the same work is not the type of man we want in our public schools, is not the sort of man we want our sons and daughters to imitate."[66]

Indeed, she questioned the manhood of her opponents: ''It is a rather sad commentary on our profession,'' she wrote in 1910, ''that its men members are the only men who object to women members of the same profession getting the same pay for the same work. Who ever heard of a man lawyer fighting a woman lawyer in this way?''[67]

Strachan relied on much more than her quick tongue and pen, however. She and her sister teachers also built strong alliances in their campaign. Labor unions, civic organizations, and women's organizations lined up behind them. So did most of the city's newspapers—with the exception of the *Times*—and business groups.

The equal-pay legislation was introduced again in 1908, 1909, and 1911. It was stuck in committee in 1908, and vetoed in 1909. In 1911, however, the bill met a quite different fate. Having passed both houses of the legislature, it was quickly signed into law by a new mayor and a new governor, both of whom had been elected in part on a platform pledging them to this action. In six tumultuous years, New York's women teachers had won their campaign for equal pay for equal work. They had also provided for their colleagues throughout the nation a new model of what teacher militance could accomplish.[68]

Boston's teachers were among many to look to New York with admiration. In 1917, the *Boston Teachers News Letter* editorialized in favor of pending legislation:

> That subtle quality of soul and mind that makes a good teacher is not a matter of sex. It is manifestly unfair that under these conditions the man should be paid from $800 to $1200 a year more for doing absolutely the same work and not necessarily getting better results than the woman. New York, Chicago, St. Louis and other large cities have ceased to consider sex a basis in apportioning salaries. We hope to see Boston take its own place among these cities.[69]

It would be another 30 years before the campaign would succeed in Boston, but in most places results came more quickly. In 1904–1905, just prior to the beginning of the Interborough Association of Woman Teachers' campaign, only about 20 percent of women teachers received equal pay, according to a sample of 64 cities with populations of over 100,000. By 1924–1925, that percentage had jumped to almost 80.[70] Many factors in each locality went into the campaign, but New York's strong example was high on the list.

In addition to the successful example of the campaign of New York's teachers, of course, teachers in other cities across the nation were in a much stronger position to make demands for political change in the 1920s than they had been at the beginning of the century. With the passage of the nineteenth amendment in 1919, women (including women teachers) had won the right to vote and were in a position to bring much more direct political pressure on their elected leaders than they had found possible at the time of the New York campaign.

The campaign for equal pay for equal work was also one more factor in a larger battle for women teachers: that for the right to be in control of their professional lives as equals, not as second-class citizens. In winning equal pay they were undercutting the whole notion of a profession divided by sex role. In insisting that ''The subtle quality of soul and mind that makes a good teacher is not a matter of sex,'' these teachers were challenging a whole concept of the structure of work within the education profession.[71]

While historians have properly noted the differences between Strachan's single-issue push for equal pay and the much wider agenda proposed by Margaret Haley and her Chicago allies, it is possible to make too much of these differences. Certainly the women teachers in the two cities made different strategic choices. And in time there were also bitter personal differences between the leaders and their organizations, revolving primarily around the leadership of the National Education Association. But while those differences are of historical interest, they were of much less interest to contemporaries. If one reads through the writings of teachers and teacher leaders in the first two decades of the twentieth century, both Haley and Strachan are clearly seen as powerful role models. Female teachers freely took from the experience of each leader and each city as they crafted the agenda for achieving democratic equality for themselves in the nation's cities.[72]

Responding to ''Overwork in Overcrowded Schoolrooms''

While they campaigned for pensions and equal pay for their efforts, classroom teachers endured daily working conditions which were unhealthy, demeaning, and exhausting. Nancy Hoffman has described the basic conditions that turn-of-the-century urban elementary teachers faced as ''Eight hours a day in a dark, uncomfortable classroom with sixty or seventy children, some hungry and ill.''[73] No wonder Margaret Haley complained of ''overwork in overcrowded classrooms, exhausting both mind and body.'' Yet in fact very little has ever been written (at least by historians) about the realities and significance of those urban school health problems.

In Boston in 1895–1896, the local branch of the Association of Collegiate Alumnae (later the American Association of University Women) conducted a survey of the sanitary conditions of that city's schools.[74] As with so many educational studies in that era, the ACA turned to a university expert for advice. They also took a step which was quite unusual for those who were proposing reform in education: They surveyed every classroom teacher and every building master in every one of the 189 school buildings in the city of Boston. As a result of this unusually thorough study, the ACA concluded that many teachers were indeed working in unsafe and unsanitary conditions. The experts and the teachers agreed:

> Both condemned the use of certain entire buildings used for school purposes. Both explained the danger in case of fire on account of lack of fire escapes, inflammable material, narrow stairways, and doors opening inward; the almost general inadequacy of systems of heating, ventilation and plumbing.[75]

Clearly, teachers had reasons for their complaints.

The results of the survey was an appropriation of $300,000 to improve the sanitation and ventilation of many of the city's school buildings. The projected costs of improvements, and the question of who would control the expenditure of the money, became points of contention between the school committee, the city council, and the mayor's "Expert Committee on Sanitation and Ventilation of School Houses." In the end, the ACA became convinced of the "irresponsibility of the school committee," and the need for a major restructuring of the schools—including a greater role for teachers in setting school policy—before the issue of health and safety could be seriously addressed. In the meantime, however, the reality of the need was quite clear. School buildings in Boston, as in most big cities, were not healthy places for the teachers who worked there, or for their students.[76]

Classrooms were not only stuffy and unhealthy: often they were seriously overcrowded. Although class size was reduced significantly between 1890 and 1930, many teachers still faced classes which were truly staggering in the sheer numbers of students to be managed. In December 1903, *The World's Work* published Adele Marie Shaw's account of her visits to New York City school classrooms. Of one experience, Shaw wrote:

> In a Brooklyn school not far from the Bridge I visited a room where sixty-five very small children were packed into a space properly intended for twenty. A bright-faced young woman was steadying a sleeping baby upon his third-of-a-seat while she heard the remaining sixty-four recite.[77]

Similar scenes could be reported from almost every city in the nation.

Larry Cuban writes, in *How Teachers Taught,* that "While classes of 50 or more students were common around World War I, class size had been dropping since that time. In 1930, average class size in elementary schools hovered about 38 students." "Average class size" can be a misleading term, however, at any point in school history. Cuban also notes this reality:

> Special classes for "dull" students or handicapped ones were kept around 25 while other classes in the same building would be well over 45. To a teacher in the 1890s facing 75 students daily, the prospect of having only 40 in a class would have been a delight. By the 1930s, however, there was a public commitment and philosophy that expected teachers to provide individual attention to each child.

Given such numbers, however, anything resembling individual attention to a single child was very difficult to achieve.[78]

The strict discipline for which teachers were often criticized by progressive reformers is much less surprising in light of the sheer numbers of students that they faced each day. Some of the reformers did recognize this problem. Thus one critic of New York's schools noted that the rigid discipline was "the inseparable attendance of wholesale schooling. To manage successfully a hundred children, or even half that number, the teacher must reduce them as nearly as possible to a unit."[79]

Of course, this form of management, although anathema to some reformers, fit well with much of the nineteenth century's educational philosophy. Graded schools, with students carefully classified, instructed primarily on the basis of textbooks, and tested regularly, were the best guarantee of what David Tyack has called "the one best system." Boston Superintendent John Philbrick called the system simply "a good program"—one which he insisted was the same for schools everywhere:

"A good program for one city would be, in its substance . . . a good program for every other city."[80]

In the nature of this "good program," teachers had a clearly defined middle position. Whereas they exercised almost unlimited power over the children below them, there also was no limit to the power of the male administrators above them. Nancy Hoffman has been especially careful in describing this mediating role:

> If, in a characteristic vignette of the teacher outside her classroom, the ghetto poor clear the sidewalk before her, and men raise their caps as she passes, a characteristic vignette inside the classroom portrays the young female teacher trembling under the scrutiny of a supervisor or inspector.[81]

Many examples of the experience of the tyranny of supervisors were given in contemporary accounts of teachers who wrote about the supervisors who go about "from schoolroom to schoolroom, notebook and pencil in hand, sitting for a while in each room like malignant sphinxes, eyeing the frightened teacher, who in his terror does everything wrong, and then marking him in a doomsday book."[82]

There is a special irony for many teachers in this position. On the one hand, they were criticized for the rigid rules they followed. On the other, they were given no voice in the making of the rules. Thus Joseph Rice, perhaps the most famous of the school critics of the 1890s, described the recitation period in one classroom in which children were expected "to stand on the line, perfectly motionless, their bodies erect, their knees and feet together, the tips of their shoes touching the edge of a board in the floor." Rice wrote sarcastically of one teacher who asked, "How can you learn anything, with your knees and toes out order?"[83] Apparently it did not occur to Rice to ask who made the rules that led teachers to insist on such silliness.

When Maria Dogherty described her experience of being called to account because her children had not begun their reading with the statement of page and chapter, she was quite clear that such rigidity was not her choice. On the contrary, the rules of how to read that were in force in Boston in 1899, and which were of such importance to her supervisor, "seemed to me a cold douche on the interest of a story. . . ." Her flexibility was not shared, however:

> This grave omission at the very outset irritated the good man and he said in his most professional tone, "Perhaps, tomorrow, your teacher will tell you about Roman numerals." That was the first blow. I had failed to perform my duty and my superior officer had hinted as much with the additional suggestion that on the morrow I mend my ways.[84]

Perhaps much of the rigidity about which Rice and others complained was not as much the teacher's doing as the reformers assumed. In any case, in the structure of accountability in place at the turn of the century, authority to make a change did not rest with the teachers.

In addition to the rigid rules governing the system of instruction, urban elementary teachers also complained about the amount of paperwork that was expected of them. Mary Abigail Dodge, a former teacher who devoted her later career to improving education and advocating that women teachers should play a major role in the control of schools, published her own ironic view of the "Schoolteacher's Nightmare" in 1880:

> Twas Saturday night, and a teacher sat
> Alone, her task pursuing:
> She averaged this and she averaged that
> Of all her class was doing.[85]

The writings of other teachers portray similar Saturday evenings, although in less poetic form.

Almost 40 years later, the *Boston Teachers News Letter* praised Arthur H. Wilde for his statement that "In my judgment much clerical work is not only a weariness to the flesh of teachers but a positive handicap to their classroom efficiency."[86] A century after Dodge wrote her poem, many classroom teachers still could identify with the complaint, but in 1880 and even in 1917, there were very few limits on the amount of such work which supervisors and school systems could ask of their supposedly docile women workers.

The women, however, were not about to remain docile in the face of "overwork in overcrowded schoolrooms." Some of their most dramatic challenges took place soon after the turn of the century in the growing response by elementary teachers to the conditions they faced. And one vehicle which they adopted in those years—the teachers council—was especially well adapted to bringing many of the changes in the conditions of their work that they had long wanted.

Establishing Teachers Councils

When Margaret Haley proposed an agenda for teachers in their fight for democratic rights, she made it perfectly clear that one of the essential ingredients in the platform was addressing the deskilling (or, as she called it, "factoryizing") that was so much a part of the agenda of the administrative progressives. Teachers, she insisted, should bend their energies toward changing a situation in which they were expected, "to carry out mechanically and unquestioningly the ideas and orders of those clothed with the authority of position and who may or may not know the needs of the children or how to minister them."[87] Clearly Haley was outraged by the situation. She also knew, at least in part, how she believed teachers should go about changing it.

In the same speech, Haley also quoted John Dewey to the effect that "If there is a single public-school system in the United States where there is official and constitutional provision made for submitting questions of methods of discipline and teaching, and the questions of the curriculum, text-books, etc. to the discussion of those actually engaged in the work of teaching, that fact has escaped my notice." But Dewey and Haley both had the means at hand for changing the situation.[88]

Not everyone had accepted the second-class citizenship assigned to elementary classroom teachers by the organizers of the "one best system." In their unsuccessful attempt to reorganize the Boston schools in 1898, the Association of Collegiate Alumnae had proposed a system of school governance which would include a formal role for all teachers in the governance process. "The idea of a school faculty," the ACA reported, "is to bring into conference the superintendent, the supervisors, and a body of teachers representing every grade of instruction, thereby arousing the ambition of the teachers, and giving to them the power of initiative in considering courses of study and textbooks, as also in matters of discipline and sanitation."[89]

In her book *Isolation in the Schools* (1901), Ella Flagg Young developed more clearly than anyone before her what should be done to give teachers this "power of initiative." Young defined the councils which teachers in many school systems would try to establish when she proposed that "There should be organized, throughout every system, school councils whose membership in the aggregate should include every teacher and principal."[90] Haley called *Isolation in the Schools* "the Bible of the teachers of the United States on the question of academic freedom."[91] With *Isolation* in hand, Haley and her counterparts were ready to institute a new level of democracy in the schools of the nation's cities.

Teachers councils were much more than a means of school governance or a method of consulting with teachers. As supported by urban teachers, the councils were at the heart of their understanding of the role they wanted to play in the schools. Either teachers were to be cogs in a machine, and schools "a mere mill, grinding uniform grists," or teachers were to play a much more significant role, having "the power of initiative and execution."[92] Teachers councils in which elected representatives played a significant role in the development of educational policy were to make the difference.

When Ella Flagg Young wrote *Isolation in the Schools* she had already served as a teacher and administrator in the Chicago schools for many years. In fact, she was free to write in 1901 because in 1899 she had resigned from the system to protest the autocratic policies of the then superintendent, Edwin Cooley, who was closely allied with the Chicago business community and hostile to teachers' autonomy. Having done that, Young studied for her doctorate with John Dewey at the University of Chicago, and *Isolation* was her dissertation.[93]

Nine years later, Young was given the opportunity to put her theories into practice. Appointed in 1909 as superintendent of the Chicago schools Young, with Haley's support, immediately began to implement the idea of teachers councils. In *Isolation,* Young had warned that if something did not change, teachers would "fall into a class of assistants, whose duty consists of carrying out instructions of a higher class which originates methods for all." She did not want things to be that way. On the contrary, she insisted, "To secure this freedom of thought, there must be, within the various parts of the school, organizations for the consideration of questions of legislation."[94]

After 1909, Chicago *had* such organizations. By the time she was forced to leave office in 1915, *all* of Chicago's teachers were organized into councils which had a real say in the curriculum and the climate of the city's schools. Indeed, the councils survived Young for some time, until abolished by Superintendent William McAndrew in the 1920s.

The demand for a unified and elected teachers council was one of the most basic issues around which teachers in many other cities also rallied in those years. While the nation was celebrating the armistice ending World War I, Cora Bigelow, the militant president of the Boston teachers club, was reminding teachers that there were battles yet to be fought. "World democracy and school democracy should go hand in hand. . . . Autocracy wherever it occurs in school affairs must follow the trend of the times and give place to democracy."[95] And for Bigelow, one clear means of establishing more democratic schools was to establish teachers councils with authority not merely to consult regarding curricular matters but to give the teachers a unified voice in school matters. In time, Bigelow would be a very effective leader, as Boston's teachers used the council in a wide variety of ways.

One of the major points of disagreement between the teachers and Franklyn Dyer, who served as Boston superintendent from 1912 to 1918, had been over his reluctance to respond to their demand for a single teachers council which could speak with a united voice for all teachers before the school committee and the general public, as well as advising the superintendent. As early as 1916, Superintendent Dyer had established several small teachers councils to consult on the curriculum. He never seemed to understand the "spirit of cynicism" with which teachers greeted these councils.[96] The teachers, however, had something quite different in mind. Bigelow responded to Dyer's councils by reminding him that "At present the councils are called by the school authorities and therefore are not strictly representative of the teachers or the groups they represent. A more democratic way would be for the teachers also to appoint a certain number to each council."[97]

While a single teachers council eventually was established under Dyer, it was only under his successor, Frank Thompson, a former teacher who had "come up through the ranks," and who was very popular with the teachers, that the council took on the role that the teachers had envisioned. Perhaps unknowingly, the two superintendents summarized their differences. In his final report as superintendent, Dyer proudly reported, "In the past six years, as far as I am aware, scarcely a textbook has been adopted and no course of study written without consultation and advice from the teachers concerned."[98] A year later, Thompson described a very different kind of council which "had become a larger factor as a medium of expression of the attitude of the teaching force, both with regard to questions affecting the educational outlook and the economic welfare of the various ranks of teachers."[99] The focus on working conditions and "the economic welfare of the various ranks," as well as the curriculum and other "questions affecting the educational outlook," would indeed become a major part of the council's role in the years ahead.

John Dewey summarized the differences between the two views of the proper role for teachers in setting school policy:

> There isn't a sinister interest in the United States that isn't perfectly willing to leave in the hands of the teaching body the ultimate decision on points of that particular kind, which come to be known as "pedagogy" and "pedagogical methods." There is no certainty, there is no likelihood, however, that the views of the body of teachers, in most of the cities and towns of the United States, will at the present time have any real, positive, constructive influence in determining the basic educational policy of the schools of their communi-

> ties, so far as a more general aspect of education is concerned. As to things that in the long run affect the life of the community, that affect the relations of capital and labor and so on, the discussions and deliberations of these purely pedagogical bodies are, as we know, practically impotent.[100]

Such impotence Bigelow and her colleagues intended to end.

As in so many other things, the Boston teachers looked to Chicago for their model of how to proceed. They cited Young's superintendent's report in their own demand for councils: "We are now face to face with the fact that a democracy whose school system lacks confidence in the ability of the teachers to be active participants in planning its aims and methods is a logical contradiction of itself." They repeated Young's question, "Why talk about the public school as an indispensable requisite of democracy and then conduct it as a prop of an aristocracy?"[101] Here was an idea around which Boston's teachers could mobilize. When she left the presidency of the teachers' club in 1919, Bigelow listed the formation of the council as one of her major achievements.[102]

As Superintendent Thompson had suggested, the councils in the years after 1918 did focus on both working conditions and the curriculum. While both would prove important, in the years immediately after the end of World War I economic issues were in the forefront as teachers struggled to keep up with postwar inflation.

In one of the most dramatic events of Boston's educational history, the teachers council was the moving force in a campaign for a raise which brought Boston's teachers to the brink of a strike in 1919. As reported in the teachers' newsletter: "It was through the Advisory Council [that] all groups united in asking for a flat increase of $600 for all teachers of whatever ranks as well as for the school nurses."[103] When in November 1919 the school committee voted to hold its more modest schedule of raises, it was also the Advisory Council that took the lead in organizing the teachers to respond.

Indeed, the day after the school committee made its announcement, the teachers council voted to "pledge themselves to work for a flat increase of $600 to all the ranks of teachers."[104] The same day, the council also voted to appoint a publicity committee, which went to work immediately. They built a wide base of support so that "Parent–teachers associations, civic associations, church clubs, etc., to the number of 39, . . . scattered throughout Boston, passed resolutions definitely declaring for a flat increase of $600."[105]

While they were attempting to influence public opinion, the teachers also were continuing to negotiate with the school committee. The very fact that the school committee was willing not only to grant them an initial hearing, but to continue negotiations with the teachers council, is an indication both that the teachers had managed to elect some friends to the committee, and that the committee recognized that the teachers, organized through the council, were in a position to begin "a campaign to force the Committee to accept their views."[106]

The day after the school committee announced its refusal to change its position, the council called the mass meeting at which 2,500—out of about 3,000 teachers in the city—voted to take "whatever measures" their representatives called for, including a strike if necessary. The 2,500 teachers also resolved: "We are determined, and pledge ourselves to stand shoulder to shoulder, a unit, behind our chosen representatives in whatever measures they may deem wise.''[107] If there was to be a strike of Boston teachers, it would be the council which would call it.

It took the teachers slightly over a year to win their full $600 across-the-board raise. By 1920, however, the campaign was successful, and the demands voted through the teachers council had been met. This was, indeed, a long step toward meeting Dewey's concern that councils address issues affecting ''relations of capital and labor.''

While one of the most dramatic examples of the potential in teachers councils, the Boston campaign fit well with the goals of Haley and others in proposing the organization. At the same time, councils were never envisioned as addressing only issues of money and working conditions. They also were a vehicle for giving teachers a significant voice in the content of the curriculum. Indeed, they represented the exact opposite of the role of teachers in the curriculum envisioned by such earlier school leaders as John Philbrick and Franklyn Dyer.

In March 1920, Cora Bigelow, who had fought so hard against councils which were limited to curricular matters, and who had led the elementary teachers at the time of the 1919 campaign for a raise, also voiced the other role of the councils:

> It is generally recognized that the function of the council should be: to secure active and effective direction of the schools by affording the largest opportunities for initiative on the part of teachers in the formation of the courses of study and in the selection of textbooks; to encourage professional interests and to furnish a ready and effective means for the expression of sentiments and opinions with reference to questions of school policy.[108]

For Bigelow, councils needed to address both economic issues and curricular issues if they were to be successful.

The problem of American education was complex, Bigelow said. This militant teacher, who had led her Boston colleagues to the verge of a strike for a raise, also wrote: ''Higher salaries alone will not solve it.'' The whole issue of working conditions and control over the classroom, including the curriculum, also had to be addressed. ''No teacher could possibly succeed in her classroom if she reflected the psychological conditions under which some of them are forced to serve,'' Bigelow insisted.[109] The teachers council, in the hands of a leader like Bigelow, had become the means for transforming the whole hierarchical system of school administration in which powerless female operatives carried out the wishes of a small group of male administrators who did all of the thinking for the system.

Bigelow was far from alone in asserting this significant role for teachers councils. Mary Mellyn, a longtime assistant superintendent in Boston and a close friend of the teachers in many of their struggles, envisioned a similar role for teachers councils. For Mellyn, the whole purpose of teachers councils could be summed up in the word ''democratization.'' But there were two parallel parts to this democratization which Mellyn envisioned. First there had to be ''Democratization of Administration. . . . It is believed that there should be a larger share of teacher participation in the problems and policies of administration. . . . There should be a larger share of opportunity for discussion in Teachers Councils.'' At the same time, the goal of all of this discussion was democratization at every level of the school system, most of all in "democratized classroom procedure." In the minds of leaders like Mellyn, classrooms in which one would find "self-direction, opportunities for co-operative action, exercise of initiative, there we [would] have children in a democracy."[110]

In Mellyn's definition of the curricular goal of teachers councils the debate had come full circle. Teachers had been demanding councils because they felt that being asked to teach about democracy without being given democratic rights themselves was a contradiction. Now they were seeking to use the councils to achieve a highly democratized curriculum. A decade later, Assistant Superintendent Mellyn was still working with groups of teachers to develop curriculum materials on "Progressive Practice in Education."[111]

Challenging the National Education Association

When Margaret Haley outlined her convictions in "Why Teachers Should Organize," she did so as a speaker before the 1904 meeting of the National Education Association meeting in St. Louis. In doing this, she had not selected a friendly audience. Indeed, future Columbia University President Nicholas Murray Butler, one of the leaders of the old guard within the NEA, called Haley "a fiend in petticoats," and accused her and the other representatives of organized urban teachers of being Bolshevists. Haley returned the hostility.

For Haley the NEA, as she found it at the turn of the century, was "a conspiracy to make a despotism of our entire school system." It was not an organization with much respect for the actual daily experiences or urban teachers who worked in the nation's classrooms. She had a vision, however, of a day in which the organization could be the Chicago Teachers Federation writ large, an organization "within the control, and to be administered in the interest, of thousands of teachers who contribute to its income." In seeking this transformed role for the NEA, Haley was also seeking a transformed role for the classroom teacher as agent, rather than mere recipient, of change. She also recognized that such a transformation of the NEA would not be easy. "The aim of our opponents," she argued, "is to turn the association over in perpetuity to a small, self-perpetuating, independent, and self-governing organization. . . ." She was not going to let them do it.[112]

Haley began her attack on the NEA at its 1901 convention in Detroit. She did not begin modestly. On the contrary, she challenged the venerable former United States Commissioner of Education, William T. Harris. In his address to the convention, Harris was painting a portrait of education flourishing under capitalism. Haley, who had certainly had quite different experiences with big business in her years in Chicago, attacked the role of business in education, insisting that it tended to undercut teachers in terms of both autonomy and salary. As David Tyack and Elisabeth Hansot describe the scene:

> Harris, crochety, told the convention: "Pay no attention to what that teacher down there has said, for I take it she is a grade teacher, just out of her school room at the end of the school year, worn out, tired, and hysterical." . . .

"Nonsense," replied Haley, . . . "I know the facts. Mr. Harris, either you do not know or have not stated the facts."[113]

It was not an interchange designed to endear Haley to the old guard, but that was not her goal. She wanted to change the organization from one run by a group who saw themselves as self-appointed education leaders to one run by and for teachers. And she did not give up her campaign easily.

Two years later, in Boston, Haley challenged another of the NEA's venerable leaders, Harvard President Charles W. Eliot, because the program did not include any women among the hundreds of speakers at the general meetings. The rank and file, Haley insisted, wanted to discuss salaries, pensions, tenure, and class size, the immediate issues faced by the nation's teachers in their workplaces.[114] In the process of making the challenge, Haley was inspiring others to join her. Thus the Boston-based *Woman's Journal* responded that "It gives us an opportunity to show the women teachers, the grade teachers, that they have to wake up." The initial response of the old guard was to try to increase the centralization within the organization, giving the president the authority to appoint the committees rather than having them elected. Haley defeated the move, and in fact got herself a place on the agenda of the next year's meeting.[115]

It was in the following year that Haley used her opportunity to rally the nation's working teachers. She warned them that it was time for them to fight for their rights, not only for themselves but for the nation as a whole:

> Two ideals are struggling for supremacy in American life today; one the industrial ideal, dominating thru the supremacy of commercialism, which subordinates the worker to the product and the machine; the other, the ideal of democracy, the ideal of the educators, which places humanity above all machines, and demands that all activity shall be the expression of life.[116]

It was a call to arms for many of the classroom teachers.

The power of women teachers was also dramatically demonstrated on a national level at the 1910 meeting of the National Education Association in Boston. At that convention, Margaret Haley and Grace Strachan of New York City's Interborough Association of Women Teachers—although often at odds with each other over the details of teacher union policy—united in a campaign to elect Chicago Superintendent Ella Flagg Young as the president of the NEA. As had always happened previously, the NEA's nominating committee presented a man as the candidate for association president. But, as had never happened before, a minority report was also presented from the nominating committee.[117]

Katherine Blake, an associate of Strachan's in the IAWT, nominated Young, reminding the convention that "We have come here year after year, many of us, paid our money and listened, and it may seem to you surprising that we now ask to be heard." Strachan herself said, "I hope that the women who have formed so large a part of this Association for so many years, and have asked for nothing, will find that this time the Association will recognize their request for this high office, and that the election of Mrs. Young this morning will be unanimous."[118] The battle lines had been drawn too firmly for the election to be unanimous. During the several years before

1910, Haley and others had made it far too plain that the issues emerging in this election were not simply symbolic ones, but deeply held differences about the source of ideas and of power in the education of a democratic society. In the ensuing vote Young won—not unanimously, but by a decisive vote of 617 to 376.[119]

While Blake and Strachan spoke on the convention floor, Haley organized in the background. Nothing was left to chance in Young's election. Under the then existing NEA rules, any member who showed up was eligible to vote. Thus the location of the convention was very important in deciding which group of local teachers could have disproportionate impact on the outcome of a hard-fought decision.[120] The fact that the 1910 convention was in Boston gave its teachers an especially important role in Young's election fight. The Boston teachers remembered the 1910 convention fondly as a time of "solidarity" when they had helped to ensure Young's election.[121]

Unfortunately, the solidarity which made possible Young's election did not continue. When Grace Strachan herself ran for president in 1912, the Chicago teachers were concerned with other issues and did not support her. The alliance which led to Young's election was, unfortunately, short-lived, and Haley's dreams for the NEA were not to be realized for some time. Beginning in 1917, the NEA did adopt a policy of electing a woman as president every other year. However, such a symbolic move was far from the hopes which Strachan and Haley had for the NEA. It would be much later in the century before elementary teachers had a major voice in the organization.[122]

Marvin Lazerson is correct in writing that "Her struggle to make the NEA more democratic ousted the old guard of university presidents, but they were replaced by a new coalition of school administrators and professors of education, rather than by the elementary school teachers, as Haley had hoped."[123] Boston's Mary Mellyn clearly illustrated this sense of disappointment with the organization when she reported on a 1920 meeting:

> The program of the N.E.A. which pleaded for democratization in education was made up of college teachers of education and superintendents, with an occasional normal school teacher. No attempt was made to give evidence on that evening's program of teacher participation as far as the great teaching body was concerned.[124]

In terms of the NEA in Haley's lifetime, the victories were disappointing, although the opportunities that the struggles gave to mobilize teachers and inspire them with a vision of what might be was significant far beyond the NEA itself. And it was through these other alliances that teachers made their most significant gains in transforming the schools that were their workplaces.

Alliances Between Working Teachers and Other Centers of Power

Katznelson and Weir provide a useful definition of the reforms that were being imposed on the major urban school systems of the nation around the turn of the century. These were reforms in which "The corporation replaced the political party as the desirable form of organization. Professionalism, merit, and efficiency became the guiding values as an effort was made to reshape the schools into economically functional institutions and to insulate them from democratic politics."[125]

Reform of this sort came late to San Francisco. An alliance between teachers and the local political establishment postponed these developments there until 1920, when an alliance of Protestant nativists within the working class, and elite reformers, finally brought centralization and a professional manager to San Francisco's schools. The result was that for almost two decades longer than most cities, San Francisco's teachers were protected from the top-down disempowerment experienced by many teachers in other urban centers. The result, unfortunately for San Francisco's teachers, also was that although they escaped some of the harsh realities faced by their counterparts in Chicago, New York, and Boston, they did not have the first two decades of the century in which to view themselves as workers free from patronage and therefore able to organize along new lines to challenge conditions in their classrooms.[126]

In most other cities the experience was quite different. While it was painful, the loss of political influence through the patronage system also offered the teachers new freedom. In spite of the benefits that the old system did offer teachers, such an arrangement always held them in the role of beneficiaries of another's power. Once this was ended, teachers were free to assert their own power. And while it took time, the ultimate result was a reordering of the relationships among teachers, politicians, labor unions, and other women's organizations in which teachers were no longer beneficiaries but equal partners, free to enter into—and to refuse—alliances with their peers. This changing self-concept among women elementary teachers in some of the nation's largest cities opened up new ways for teachers to view themselves and to seek important changes in working conditions.

The new five-member school committee that took power in Boston in 1906 and quickly elected Stratton Brooks as the new professional manager for the city's schools was certainly in the mold of the reformers elsewhere. It was not a committee or a superintendent committed to empowering teachers. The older network of political connections through which teachers had access to decision making was closed off. In its place the committee set up a process of meritocracy and professional management.

Slowly the teachers began to rebuild their position. They did this, in large part, through a careful process of building alliances with others in labor and the women's movements, as well as with political leaders friendly to their position. In 1909 and 1910, in spite of a lack of enthusiasm on the part of both the superintendent and the committee, teachers—with support from Mayor John F. Fitzgerald (a politician long hostile to the progressive reformers)—had won both a raise and a pension system.[127]

In 1912, the School Voters' League—a women's voters organization in which teachers played a major role—began its campaign for a more sympathetic school committee. As one of its first moves, the league supported its secretary, Susan Walker FitzGerald, for the School Committee on a platform committed to teachers' rights and opposed to the superintendent. FitzGerald, a militant suffragist, was not supported by the leading educational reform organization, the Public School Association, which had nominated every successful candidate for the committee since it had helped create the smaller committee in 1905–1906. Because of this, a number of women broke with the PSA. FitzGerald was defeated; but the power of the PSA reformers had been weakened, and the lack of popular support for the superintendent had been demonstrated.[128]

Given these developments, it was no accident that the overwhelmingly female teaching force saw women's suffrage as a crucial issue for them. In an odd split, the Massachusetts state legislature, beginning in 1879, had given women the vote in school committee elections, but in spite of many attempts at change had never passed a wider suffrage for women. Thus Massachusetts women experienced a 41-year lag between their right to vote in school elections and the passage of the Nineteenth Amendment, which gave them full suffrage in 1920.[129]

The teachers used their limited suffrage effectively, especially through the work of the School Voters' League, in the years between 1912 and 1920. The *Boston Teachers News Letter* for February 1917 noted that the new officers for the School Voters' League included both such active supporters of the teachers' cause as Susan W. FitzGerald and Mary Morton Kehew, and such leaders of the organized teachers themselves as Cora E. Bigelow, Annie G. Scollard, Matilda A. Fraser, and Grace E. Lingham.[130] The fact that the upper-class women reformers such as FitzGerald and Kehew shared the offices of the organization with working teachers was an important symbol of teachers' new status.

As the campaign for the passage of the national suffrage amendment grew, Boston teachers also took an active role in that movement through their own suffrage organization, the "Teachers' Branch of the Boston Equal Suffrage Association."[131] The alliance with the larger suffrage movement also paid off for the teachers. At the height of the teachers' successful battle for a raise in 1919, the school committee recorded that "a communication was received from the Executive Board of the Boston League of Women Voters [the new name for the Woman Suffrage Association] under date of Oct. 11, 1919, stating that it had voted its hearty support to the efforts to secure a salary increase for the teachers of Boston." Suffrage for these teachers was not an upper-class women's interest but a practical necessity.[132]

In January of 1913 the Public School Association, which had nominated all of the successful candidates for school committee since the reforms of 1905, made a concession to women voters, if not to teachers, nominating Frances Curtis for the Boston School Committee. Curtis met the School Voters League's demand for a woman on the committee, but she was only a moderate suffragist and much more committed to the prerogatives of the superintendent than the needs of the teachers. More proteacher candidates challenged Curtis in the December 1918 election when two labor women—Mary Meehan, president of the Bindery Women's Union, and Mary Matthews, secretary of the Telephone Operators' Union—challenged her for reelection. Both union candidates were committed to equal pay for equal work, and to raises and better conditions for the teachers. Unfortunately from the teachers' perspective, Curtis was reelected to the committee, where she would continue to represent an increasingly minority PSA position until 1925. In the teachers' struggle for a raise in 1919, she kept reminding the teachers that they had to remember the taxpayers, too—not a position to endear her to her fellow women in the teaching force.[133]

From the teachers' perspective, more successful campaigns were to come, however. In December 1916, one of the PSA's successful nominees was an unusual candidate for that organization: Henry L. Abrahams, the Jewish leader of the cigar makers' union and secretary of the Central Labor Union, was militantly committed to the women teachers' demand of "equal pay for equal work."[134]

The following year, in one of the hardest-fought school committee elections in many years, the PSA slate was defeated by two Democrats, Michael Corcoran and R. J. Lane, the candidates supported by Mayor James Michael Curley. Curley was a consistently prounion mayor who struggled for many years to allow the fired police strikers of 1919 to reenter the force, and who could be expected to support the teachers as much as his predecessor Fitzgerald. Thus the teachers entered their successful salary negoations in 1918 and 1919 with three members of the committee—Abrahams, Corcoran, and Lane—strongly sympathetic to their position. It was a significant comeback from their position when the five-member "reform" committee took office in January 1906.[135]

Shortly after the 1917 election of the two proteacher candidates (Corcoran and Lane) to the school committee, Franklyn Dyer, Boston's second reform superintendent, announced that he would not be a candidate for reelection as superintendent in 1918. Whether he was reading the election returns or had already decided that six years in charge of Boston's schools was enough is unknown.[136] Whatever the case, the result was the election of Frank V. Thompson as his successor. Thompson, who had spent most of his career in Boston and was not part of the national network of educational reformers, was much more sympathetic to teachers' needs. He was, indeed, as close as Boston came to an Ella Flagg Young, and was much respected by the teachers during his brief tenure.[137]

Teachers in other cities made similar alliances to further their goals. In both New York and Chicago, strategic alliances with politicians moved forward the teachers' agenda at crucial moments. The Chicago Teachers Federation achieved some of its most significant victories right after the turn of the century when it helped to elect Judge Edward Dunne as mayor. Dunne appointed proteacher members to the board of education, and his board supported the development of teachers councils, abolished a secret teacher evaluation system, and eventually elected Ella Flagg Young as the city's superintendent.[138] While the teachers in the CTF could not vote themselves, they became a formidable political organization as they convinced fathers, brothers, and other male relatives and neighbors to support their position.

Similar political activism on the part of unenfranchised women teachers was essential for the success of the "Equal Pay for Equal Work" campaign in New York. As already indicated, the primary reasons the women in the Interborough Association of Women Teachers were defeated were the vetoes of the mayor and the governor. As Robert E. Doherty has argued, "Although equal pay for women was resisted by School Board officials, the Board of Estimate, the *New York Times,* men teachers, and some citizens, there were, in fact, only two major obstacles to the passage of the equal pay bill—the Mayor and the Governor." The solution was obvious: change the officeholders.

While there were many factors involved in the elections, teachers did finally win in 1911 when a new governor and a new mayor, John Alden Dix and William J. Gaynor respectively, came to power. Both had campaigned on a platform of support for equal pay, and both acted quickly on their promise when the opportunity was presented.[139]

The success of women's suffrage would greatly expand women teachers' opportunities to influence political leaders. However, the suport that teachers received from mayors Fitzgerald and Curley in Boston, Dunne in Chicago, and Gaynor in New York indicates the kind of organizing they were able to do even before they had the vote.

Of course, organized labor was a second base of support for teachers in all of their campaigns. Margaret Haley's strong alliance with the Chicago Federation of Labor was essential to her success. Throughout its campaigns to raise taxes for the support of schools and to secure teachers' rights, the CTF could count on their counterparts in the labor movement. Even when the CTF was forced, as a condition of rehiring 68 teachers dismissed by the school board, to disaffiliate from the CFL, John Fitzpatrick (the president of the labor federation) reminded the teachers that the two organizations were close enough to work together without formal ties.[140]

Labor in New York was also firmly on the side of the women teachers. The International Brotherhood of Locomotive Engineers was particularly clear in its insistence that "There is not a locomotive engineer, nor an electric motorman that would be willing to see a woman run an engine or motor for less than standard wage."[141] This argument had two sides to it. On the one hand, the engineers and their counterparts in organized labor were standing in solidarity with the teachers. On the other hand, they were making very sure that the nineteenth-century pattern in which women were hired as teachers at much lower wages than men, but eventually took over the profession, was not going to be repeated in their fields. Still, in building these alliances, the teachers were showing their own strength. Not only the engineers, but most New York City unions, stood solidly with the teachers.[142]

Finally the women teachers turned also to other women's groups. The fact that there was a "lively women's suffrage movement" in New York was certainly part of the political base on which the IAWT was able to build.[143] Ella Flagg Young in Chicago depended on her links with a much larger realm of women's organizations. Jane Addams and many others in a network of women's clubs supported Young and came to her defense. She, in turn was active in the organizations, and an advocate of suffrage and women's rights.[144]

It was a long road from the position of teachers in the late nineteenth century to that which they faced when suffrage became a reality in 1919. In spite of their successes, the first two decades of the twentieth century were difficult ones, and most victories could be turned into defeats all too quickly. Still, their position was quite different from what it had been in 1890. The teacher as recipient of patronage was always the junior partner in the arrangement. Haley in Chicago, Strachan in New York, Bigelow in Boston, and their counterparts in many other cities across the nation were junior partners to no one. When they dealt with politicians, labor leaders, and other women's organizations, they did so as equals, and the teachers who supported them were strengthened as a result. What it meant to teach in an urban elementary-school classroom was quite different—in terms of control over the curriculum, salary, and relationships to the administration—because of the alliances that teachers built during these decades.

Dare the School Build a New Social Order?

The 1920s were not good years for activist teachers. In city after city their accomplishments were undermined and their energies redirected. The clear victory of the reform faction in San Francisco meant that teachers and those parts of organized labor which remained loyal to them were without power in school matters. Mayor James Rolph created the image of openness by including a wide diversity of religious, labor, and business groups in his appointments to the school committee. But symbolic representation was quite different from actual power.[145] In Chicago, a political compromise in 1917 provided tenure for teachers on the condition that they end their formal affiliation with organized labor. While the CTF, with Haley as its leader, continued throughout the next decade, its power was severely limited. At the same time, Mayor Thompson combined the worst of both political corruption and anti-teacher biases in his administration of the city. When another campaign to "clean up the schools" was instituted in 1922, it was under business, not teacher, control.[146]

The constant accusation that teachers' unions were a first step toward Bolshevism, along with the clear hostility of the National Education Association toward teachers' unions in the years after 1920, divided the ranks of teachers. As late as 1919 many teachers, including especially those who were most active in seeking a greater voice for themselves and their colleagues, kept their membership in both the American Federation of Teachers and the NEA.[147] After 1920, however, the NEA shifted from neutrality to an active campaign against the AFT.[148] In 1920 the AFT had over 10,000 members nationally; just three years later that number had dropped to 3,000.[149] It was only with the Depression and World War II that the AFT would again become a powerful teachers' organization.

In addition to the divisions among their national organizations, teachers always faced an internal dilemma about what their role should be. The teacher as worker, actively seeking more democratic representation within the political power structure of education, was always at war with the image of the teacher as an apolitical professional. Marvin Lazerson has summed up the opinions of many historians regarding the decline in teacher militancy after 1920: "There was little to be gained by waging war with the heirarchy when one's goal was to join it. In the end, teachers gave up their rights of citizenship. They accepted the notion that education should be non-political and that as teachers they should refrain from agitating for the right to determine policy. In return, despite the ambiguities of their position they were pretty much left alone in their classrooms."[150]

While there are many cases in which Lazerson's generalization was certainly true, there also are many cases in which it was not true. Sometimes teachers were quite passive in accepting the definition of their rights as given by others. But at other points, teachers were a very active, militant force, demanding a role in decisions affecting both what they taught and how they were rewarded.

A little more than a decade after Boston's teachers had won a number of victories through their Teachers Council, George Counts called on teachers throughout the nation to dare to build a new social order. Speaking during the hardest days of the Depression, Counts asked teachers to "increase sufficiently their stock of courage, intelligence, and vision," so that they "might become a social force of some magnitude.'' Counts also had some very clear ideas about the direction in which this social force should move:

> Through powerful organizations they might at least reach the public conscience and come to exercise a larger measure of control over the schools than hitherto. . . . That the teachers should deliberately reach for power and then make the most of their conquest is my firm conviction.[151]

In these words Counts, whether he recognized it or not, was calling on teachers to continue a tradition which had been strong among them, to a greater or lesser degree, for the previous half-century.

It is, of course, true that the tradition to which Counts was appealing often was a minority one. There were many reasons why teachers were much more circumspect in many instances. Thus Richard A. Quantz, in describing the teachers of Hamilton, Ohio also sums up the experience of many teachers in Boston, Chicago, or any other of the largest cities when he writes: ''Teachers were expected to carry out orders, not initiate them. Teachers were people to be both respected and respectful, feared and fearful.''[152]

Too often the respectful (if not the fearful) side won, and teachers backed away from the power they might have had. But that is not the whole story, and to allow it to seem to be is to miss the point forcefully made by Michael Apple when he argues that ''There have been periods of exceptional militancy and clear political commitment.'' Of course, Apple also recognizes that ''Militancy and political commitment are but one set of ways in which control is contested. It is also fought for on the job itself in subtle and even 'unconscious' (one might say 'cultural') ways.''[153] The story is always complex, and often contradictory.

Nevertheless, any understanding of the roles and expectations of elementary-school teachers in the major metropolitan centers of the United States during the first half of the twentieth century would be incomplete without the stories of the Cora Bigelows as well as the Margaret Haleys, the Catherine Goggins, and the Grace Strachans. They were from a generation of women who planned and struggled to ensure that their vision of democracy might become a reality where they worked—in their classrooms and schools.

Notes

AUTHOR'S NOTE: The author is grateful to Professors Polly Kaufman and Thomas Brown for thoughtful criticism, and to the John W. McCormack Institute of Public Affairs, University of Massachusetts–Boston for research support.

1. E. P. Thompson, *The History of the English Working Class* (New York: Random House, 1963), p. 12.
2. Richard A. Quantz, ''The Complex Visions of Female Teachers and the Failure of Unionization in the 1930s: An Oral History,'' in *History of Education Quarterly* 25:4 (Winter 1985), pp. 439–458.
3. Ira Katznelson and Margaret Weir, *Schooling for All: Class, Race, and the Decline of the Democratic Ideal* (New York: Basic Books, 1985), p. 107; see also James W. Fraser, ''Who Were the Progressive Educators Anyway? A Case

Study of the Progressive Education Movement in Boston, 1905–1925,'' in *Educational Foundations* 2:1 (Spring 1988), pp. 4–30.

4. Katznelson and Weir, *Schooling for All,* p. 108.
5. Ella Flagg Young, *Isolation in the School* (Chicago: University of Chicago Press, 1901), p. 111.
6. David Tyack, *The One Best System: A History of American Urban Education* (Cambridge, MA: Harvard University Press, 1974), p. 60.
7. Nancy Hoffman, *Woman's ''True'' Profession: Voices from the History of Teaching* (Old Westburg, NY: The Feminist Press, 1981), pp. 202–203.
8. *Boston Teachers News Letter: Official Organ of the Boston Teachers Club* (February 1917), pp. 10–11 [hereafter cited as *BTNL*].
9. Michael W. Apple, *Teachers and Texts: A Political Economy of Class and Gender Relations in Education* (New York: Routledge & Kegan Paul, 1986), p. 33.
10. Larry Cuban, *How Teachers Taught: Constancy and Change in American Classrooms, 1890–1980* (New York: Longman, 1984), pp. 18 and 45.
11. Horace Mann, ''Twelfth Annual Report'' (1848), cited in Lawrence A. Cremin (ed.), *The Republic and The School: Horace Mann on the Education of Free Men* (New York: Teachers College Press, 1957), pp. 80 and 90.
12. John D. Philbrick, ''Report of the Superintendent'' (1856), p. 263, in Tyack, *One Best System,* p. 45.
13. Tyack, *One Best System,* p. 45.
14. Ibid.
15. Mann, ''Fourth Annual Report'' (1840), in Cremin (ed.), *The Republic and The School,* p. 52.
16. Hoffman, *Woman's ''True'' Profession,* p. xvii.
17. Catharine Beecher, *Educational Reminiscences and Suggestions* (New York: J. B. Ford & Co., 1874), p. 101; cited in Kathryn Kish Sklar, *Catharine Beecher: A Study in American Domesticity* (New York: W. W. Norton, 1973), p. 169.
18. David Tyack and Elisabeth Hansot, *Managers of Virtue: Public School Leadership in America, 1820–1980* (New York: Basic Books, 1982), pp. 64–65.
19. Tyack and Hansot, *Managers of Virtue,* p. 65.
20. *Report of the Committee on Salaries, Tenure, and Pensions of Public School Teachers in the United States to the National Council of Education,* July, 1905 (National Education Association, 1905), pp. 23, 54, and 74; cited in Tyack, *One Best System,* p. 62.
21. Robert E. Doherty, ''Tempest on the Hudson: The Struggle for 'Equal Pay for Equal Work' in the New York City Public Schools, 1907–1911,'' in *History of Education Quarterly* 19:4 (Winter 1979), pp. 413–434.
22. *Report of the Committee on Salaries, Tenure, and Pensions of Public School Teachers in the United States to the National Council of Education,* July, 1905 (National Education Association, 1905), p. 52; cited in Tyack, *One Best System,* p. 61.
23. Katznelson and Weir, *Schooling for All,* p. 108.
24. Hoffman, *Woman's ''True'' Profession,* p. 210.
25. Carl F. Kaestle, ''Foreword,'' in William J. Reese, *Power and the Promise of School Reform: Grass-Roots Movements During the Progressive Era* (Boston: Routledge & Kegan Paul, 1986), pp. xvi–xvii.
26. Boston Public Schools, Annual Report of the Superintendent, September 1929, School Document No. 7–1929 (Boston, 1929), p. 173.
27. For an excellent study of Julia Duff's role in Boston school history see Polly Welts Kaufman, ''Boston Women and City School Politics, 1872–1905: Nurturers and Protectors in Public Education,'' unpublished doctoral dissertation, Boston University School of Education, 1978, pp. 331–375.
28. Amelia Allison, ''Confessions of Public School Teachers,'' *Atlantic Monthly* (July 1896), reprinted in Hoffman, pp. 267–273.

29. Hoffman, *Woman's "True" Profession,* p. 211.
30. The phrase "administrative progressive" was coined by David Tyack in *The One Best System,* pp. 126–127. Tyack is probably the most insightful current observer of the problems of the "administrative progressives," both in *The One Best System* and in his more recent book with Elisabeth Hansot, *Managers of Virtue.* Still it remains true, as Tyack noted in the first book, that "We lack to this day any comprehensive account of the long history of dissent against the public school establishment" (p. 81). While Tyack and Hansot's examination of the stream of intellectual dissent that came to include John Dewey and many of his colleagues is very useful (*Managers of Virtue,* pp. 201–211), many more case studies will be needed before the full story can be told.
31. Hoffman, *Woman's "True" Profession,* pp. 200–217.
32. Katznelson and Weir, *Schooling for All,* pp. 114–115.
33. Samual P. Hays, "The Politics of Reform in Municipal Government in the Progressive Era," in *Pacific Northwest Quarterly* 55 (October 1964), pp. 157–169; reprinted in Blaine A. Brownell and Warren E. Stickle, *Bosses and Reformers: Urban Politics in America, 1880–1920* (Boston: Houghton Mifflin, 1973), pp. 137–161.
34. George A. O. Ernest, "The Movement for School Reform in Boston," in *Educational Review* 28 (December 1904), p. 433.
35. Henry Greenleaf Pearson, *Son of New England: James Jackson Storrow, 1864–1926* (Boston: Thomas Todd, 1932), p. 50; see also Michael B. Katz, *Class, Bureaucracy and Schools: The Illusion of Educational Change in America* (New York: Praeger, 1971), p. 115.
36. John F. Moors, quoted in Pearson, *Son of New England,* p. 68.
37. Tyack and Hansot, *Managers of Virtue,* p. 107.
38. For a detailed analysis of the 1905–1906 reforms, see Alice W. Karl, "Public School Politics in Boston, 1895–1920," doctoral dissertation, Harvard University, 1969; and James W. Fraser, "Mayor John F. Fitzgerald and Boston's Schools, 1905–1913," in *Historical Journal of Massachusetts* 12:2 (June 1984), pp. 117–130.
39. Victor L. Shrader, "Ethnicity, Religion, and Class: Progressive School Reform in San Francisco," in *History of Education Quarterly* 20:4 (Winter 1980), pp. 385–402.
40. David N. Plank and Paul E. Peterson, "Does Urban Reform Imply Class Conflict? The Case of Atlanta's Schools," in *History of Education Quarterly* 23:2 (Summer 1983), pp. 151–174.
41. Ibid.
42. Katznelson and Weir, *Schooling for All,* p. 113.
43. Stratton D. Brooks, "Dangers of School Reform," *Educational Review* 30 (March 1906), pp. 226–235.
44. Hoffman, *Woman's "True" Profession,* p. 212.
45. Marian A. Dogherty, *'Scusa Me Teacher* (Francestown, NH: Marshall Jones, 1943), p. 35.
46. Young, *Isolation in the School,* pp. 106–107.
47. Margaret Haley, "Why Teachers Should Organize," National Education Association Addresses and Proceedings (St. Louis, 1904); reprinted in Hoffman, *Woman's "True" Profession,* pp. 289–295.
48. Ibid.
49. William H. Payne, *Chapters on School Supervision: A Practical Treatise on Superintendence; Grading; Arranging Courses of Study; the Preparation and Use of Blanks, Records, and Reports; Examinations for Promotion, Etc.* (New York: American Book, 1903 [originally published in 1875]), pp. 13–17; cited in Tyack, *One Best System,* p. 59.
50. Lawrence A. Cremin, *American Education: The Metropolitan Experience, 1876–1980* (New York: Harper & Row, 1988), pp. 238–239.
51. Margaret Haley, "Why Teachers Should Organize," National Education

Association Addresses and Proceedings (St. Louis, 1904); reprinted in Hoffman, *Woman's "True" Profession,* pp. 289–295.

52. William Graebner, "Retirement in Education: The Economic and Social Functions of the Teachers' Pension," in *History of Education Quarterly* 18:4 (Winter 1978), pp. 397–418.
53. Graebner, "Retirement in Education," pp. 400–401.
54. Katznelson and Weir, *Schooling for All,* pp. 108–109.
55. Graebner, "Retirement in Education," p. 401.
56. Ibid.
57. Doherty, "Tempest on the Hudson," pp. 413–434.
58. New York *Times* (February 17, 1907), p. 1; cited in Doherty, "Tempest on the Hudson," p. 426.
59. Lotus Delta Coffman, "The Social Composition of the Teaching Population," in *Contributions to Education* 41 (New York: Teachers College, Columbia University, 1911), pp. 28 and 82; cited in Tyack, *One Best System,* p. 61.
60. Tyack, *One Best System,* p. 65.
61. Kaufman, "Boston Women and City School Politics," pp. 294–298.
62. Doherty, "Tempest on the Hudson," p. 417; The Interborough Association of Womens Teachers' history is also told briefly in Tyack, *One Best System,* pp. 267–268, and in more detail in Wayne J. Urban, *Why Teachers Organized* (Detroit: Wayne State University Press, 1982), pp. 89–99.
63. Doherty, "Tempest on the Hudson," p. 418.
64. Ibid, p. 419.
65. Ibid, p. 424.
66. Ibid, p. 425.
67. Grace C. Strachan, *Equal Pay for Equal Work* (New York: B. F. Buck, 1910), reprinted in Hoffman, *Woman's "True" Profession,* pp. 295–300.
68. Doherty, "Tempest on the Hudson," pp. 427–428.
69. *BTNL* (March 1917), p. 12.
70. Tyack, *One Best System,* p. 267.
71. *BTNL* (March 1917), p. 12
72. Edgar B. Wesley, *NEA: The First Hundred Years: The Building of the Teaching Profession* (New York: Harper & Bros., 1957), p. 327; Hoffman, *Woman's "True" Profession,* p. 296.
73. Hoffman, *Woman's "True" Profession,* p. 206.
74. Kaufman, "Boston Women and City School Politics," pp. 310–312.
75. Alice Upton Pearmain, "The Boston Schools: A Sanitary Investigation," in *Municipal Affairs* 2 (September 1898), pp. 497–501.
76. Ibid.
77. Adele Marie Shaw, "The True Character of the New York Public Schools," in *The World's Work* 7:2 (December 1903), pp. 4204–4221; cited in Hoffman, p. 221.
78. Cuban, *How Teachers Taught,* p. 50.
79. Tyack, *One Best System,* p. 54.
80. John D. Philbrick, "City School Systems in the United States," in U.S. Bureau of Education, *Circular of Information* No. 1 (Washington, DC: Government Printing Office, 1885), pp. 59 and 67; cited in Tyack, *One Best System,* p. 45.
81. Hoffman, *Woman's "True" Profession,* p. 208.
82. Charles B. Gilbert, *The School and Its Life* (New York: Silver Burdett, 1906), p. 85; cited in Hoffman, *Woman's "True" Profession,* p. 209.
83. Joseph M. Rice, *The Public School System of the United States* (New York: Century, 1893), p. 98; cited in Tyack, *One Best System,* pp. 55–56.
84. Marian A. Dogherty, *'Scusa Me Teacher,* p. 36.
85. Mary Abigail Dodge, "Schoolteacher's Nightmare," in *Our Common Schools* (Boston: Estes & Lauriat, 1880); cited in Hoffman, *Woman's "True" Profession,* p. 255.
86. *BTNL* (April 1917), p. 3.
87. Haley, "Why Teachers Should Organize," p. 291.
88. Ibid. p. 292.
89. Alice Upton Pearmain, "The Boston School: A Sanitary Investigation," in *Municipal Affairs* 2 (September 1898), p. 501.

90. Young, *Isolation in the School*, p. 108.
91. Tyack and Hansot, *Managers of Virtue*, p. 198.
92. Young, *Isolation in the School*, pp. 89 and 104.
93. Tyack and Hansot, *Managers of Virtue*, p. 197.; Katznelson and Weir, *Schooling for All*, p. 110.
94. Young, *Isolation in the School*, p. 107.
95. *BTNL* (December 1918), pp. 10–11.
96. Franklyn Dyer, "Official Recognition of Teachers' Councils," in *Educational Standards* (March 1916), pp. 21–22.
97. *BTNL* (February 1917), pp. 10–11.
98. Boston Public Schools, *Annual Report of the Superintendent*, School Document No. 23–1917 (November 1917), (Boston: City of Boston Printing Department, 1917), p. 13.
99. Boston Public Schools, *Annual Report of the Superintendent*, School Document No. 17–1919, pp. 4–5.
100. John Dewey, "Professional Organization of Teachers," in *Journal of Education* (October 30, 1919), p. 428.
101. *BTNL* (June 1918), p. 12.
102. *BTNL* (July 1919), p. 3.
103. *BTNL* (December 1919), p. 21.
104. *BTNL* (December 1919), p. 21.
105. *BTNL* (February 1920), p. 15.
106. *Annual Report of the School Committee, City of Boston, 1919–1920*, School Document No. 20–1919 (Boston: City of Boston Printing Department, 1919), pp. 7–8.
107. *BTNL* (December 1919), p. 23.
108. *BTNL* (March 1920), p. 8.
109. *BTNL* (April 1920), p. 13.
110. *BTNL* (April 1920), p. 5.
111. Urban, *Why Teachers Organized*, pp. 146–153.
112. Tyack and Hansot, *Managers of Virtue*, p. 186.
113. Ibid., pp. 186–187.
114. Kaufman, "Boston Women and City School Politics," pp. 386–387.
115. Ibid., pp. 387–388; and Tyack, *One Best System*, p. 266.
116. Haley, "Why Teachers Should Organize," p. 294.
117. Urban, *Why Teachers Organized*, pp. 111–133; and Tyack, *One Best System*, pp. 257–268.
118. National Education Association, *Journal of the Proceedings and Addresses of the Forty-Eighth Annual Meeting Held at Boston, Massachusetts, July 2–8, 1910* (Winona, MI: The National Education Association, 1910), pp. 33–34.
119. Ibid.
120. For a description of Haley's role in Young's election, see Urban, *Why Teachers Organized*, pp. 111–133; and Tyack, *One Best System*, pp. 257–268.
121. *BTNL* (March 1917), p. 8.
122. Wesley, *NEA: The First Hundred Years*, pp. 327–328.
123. Marvin Lazerson, "If All the World Were Chicago: American Education in the Twentieth Century," in *History of Education Quarterly* 24:2 (Summer 1984), pp. 165–179.
124. *BTNL* (April 1920), p. 6.
125. Katznelson and Weir, *Schooling for All*, p. 86.
126. Ibid., pp. 86–120; and Shrader, "Ethnicity, Religion, and Class," pp. 385–402.
127. I have explored these issues in more detail in "Mayor John F. Fitzgerald and Boston's School, 1905–1913, in *Historical Journal of Massachusetts* 7:2 (June 1984), pp. 117–130.
128. Kaufman, "Boston Women and City School Politics," pp. 390–391.
129. For an excellent analysis of the relationship of women teachers to the issue of women's right to vote, see both Karl and Kaufman. While Kaufman's excellent study focuses primarily on the pre–1905 era, many of her conclusions and some of her research are also applicable to the years under consideration in this study. In addition, for an interesting study of the impact of this split vote on Boston politics, see Lois Bannister Merk, "Boston's Historic Public School Crisis," in *New England Quarterly* 31 (June 1958), pp. 172–199.
130. *BTNL* (February 1917), p. 9.
131. *BTNL* (December 1917), p. 13.

132. *Proceedings of the School Committee, City of Boston,* October 15, 1917, p. 179; see also *BTNL* (April 1920), p. 15.

133. Kaufman, "Boston Women and City School Politics," pp. 393–396; see also "Elizabeth Burrage to Miss Harriot Curtis, September 23, 1957," a letter from the Administrative Librarian of the Boston School Committee to Frances Curtis' sister confirming the years Curtis served on the school committee; Curtis file, The Schlesinger Library, Radcliffe College; see also Mark A. DeWolfe Howe, "Boston Loses a Benefactor: Frances Greely Curtis Truly a First Citizen," *Boston Globe,* September 7, 1957.

134. Karl, "Public School Politics in Boston," pp. 364 and 380–381.

135. Ibid.; see also Francis Russell, *A City in Terror: 1919 The Boston Police Strike* (New York: Viking Press, 1975).

136. *Journal of Education* (January 10, 1918), p. 44.

137. "From Our New Superintendent," *BTNL* (October 1918), p. 3.

138. Tyack, *One Best System,* pp. 262–263.

139. Doherty, *'Scusa Me Teacher,* pp. 427–428.

140. Katznelson and Weir, *Schooling for All,* p. 117.

141. Doherty, *'Scusa Me Teacher,* pp. 427.

142. Ibid.

143. Ibid., p. 417.

144. Tyack and Hansot, *Managers of Virtue,* p. 197.

145. Katznelson and Weir, *Schooling for All,* p. 120.

146. Ibid., pp. 116–118.

147. See for example *BTNL* (July 1919), p. 10 (for support of NEA), and pp. 14 and 17–19 (for support of AFT).

148. *American Journal of Education* (November 1919), p. 96.

149. For the story of the drop in AFT membership nationally, see Urban, *Why Teachers Organized,* pp. 146–153.

150. Marvin Lazerson, "If All the World Were Chicago," p. 174.

151. George S. Count, *Dare the School Build a New Social Order?* (New York: John Day, 1932; republished with a Preface by Wayne J. Urban, Southern Illinois University Press, 1982), pp. 25–26.

152. Richard A. Quantz, "The Complex Visions of Female Teachers," pp. 439–458.

153. Apple, *Teachers and Text,* p. 48.

6

Career Ladders and the Early Public High-School Teacher

A Study of Inequality and Opportunity

David F. Labaree

In the 1980s, American schools once again came under heavy fire. This time it was the high school that became the primary target. A series of academic studies published during the decade argue that the high school of today is a far cry from the "people's college" on which early supporters placed the hopes of the young republic. To its contemporary critics, the high school appears to be little more than a "shopping mall," a temple of educational consumerism where students and teachers bargain away learning and promote credentialism.[1]

If high schools are seen to be part of an educational problem, perhaps today's teachers may be viewed as the key to an educational solution. Reformers talk about plans to transform the way in which we educate, certify, test, reward, and remove teachers, all aimed at improving the quality of education. One particularly prominent plan focuses on altering the arrangement of work incentives for the teacher through the introduction of career ladders. Both the Holmes Group and the Carnegie Forum on Education and the Economy suggest a form of career ladder that would eliminate the present undifferentiated structure of teaching and erect in its place a new structure with distinct tiers.

The Holmes Group calls for three different positions—instructor, professional teacher, and career professional; the Carnegie Forum calls for two—teacher and lead teacher. These different levels of occupational attainment would carry with them a corresponding set of differential rewards and responsibilities which the teacher could pursue without having to leave the classroom.[2]

How would these proposed career ladders help any response to the problems in contemporary schools, especially high schools? The aim is to give good teachers the incentive to stay in the profession instead of moving on to "more rewarding" jobs, and to provide all teachers with the impetus to work hard at improving their craft. The Holmes Group report puts it this way:

> Differentiating the teaching career . . . would make it possible for districts to go beyond limited financial incentives and to challenge and reward commitment. This is essential to encourage teachers to reinvest in their work, and earn rewards while remaining in their classrooms; it will also counterbalance the defection of talented, committed teachers into administration.[3]

The current interest in the problems of the high school, combined with the potential for reducing some of these problems by means of teacher career ladders, makes this an opportune time to examine the history of job mobility patterns among high-school teachers. My aim in this chapter is to explore the possibilities for career advancement that confronted the early public high-school teacher and to relate these to the present flat structure of the profession. I focus on the teachers in public high schools in the United States during the late nineteenth and early twentieth centuries, ending in the 1930s.

This is not a history of these teachers. It is a preliminary cross-sectional evaluation of the kinds of career ladders that were available to them during this period, and the various ways in which they did and did not succeed in achieving occupational mobility. The result should be read as a study in the historical sociology of teachers as workers.

What I find is that these early teachers were faced with a complex set of market incentives which encouraged them either to move out of teaching altogether or move up to a higher occupational level within the profession. These incentives presented no fewer than three different routes to advancement, three distinct career ladders, and the most successful practitioners tended to combine most or all of these routes.

First I will present the career histories of a few high-school teachers who pursued advancement in their profession during the late nineteenth and early twentieth centuries. Then I will sketch some of the distinguishing characteristics of each of the three mobility routes pursued by these teachers (along with the primary mechanisms that facilitated and retarded progress along these routes), and illustrate each with examples from the experiences of individual teachers. Finally, I will consider these historic career ladders in light of the opportunity structure of contemporary high-school teaching. There I will argue that the current Holmes and Carnegie proposals for teacher mobility are grounded in bureaucratic principles, in contrast with the market principles that formed the basis for the earlier career ladders.

Of course, the sources for this study are fragmented: The academic literature on the history of teaching is quite small, and the literature on high-school teaching is virtually nonexistent. At the same time, the primary sources on the latter subject are fraught with problems. For example, there is a considerable amount of information about high-school teachers in the records, reports, histories, and ceremonial publications of individual school districts and high schools. I draw on some of these sources here, but they are of only limited use in a discussion of career ladders because these ladders tended to run across (rather than within) these units. I also use the result of several surveys of high schools and their teachers, but these aggregate and cross-sectional accounts do not permit inferences about either the nature or available career choices of the development of careers over time. To study career ladders, one must examine a series of individual career histories and look for the patterns within them. The major sources I used to uncover these career histories of high-school teachers included their own published memoirs, correspondence, and diaries and biographical sketches provided by colleagues, children, and former students.

These kinds of sources pose some obvious difficulties. Their unsystematic nature means that any conclusions that I draw must be read as suggestive rather than authoritative. In addition, the sources strongly favor the most successful high-school teachers, since these are the ones who were most likely to publish their memoirs and to be remembered by others in print. For the most part, the subjects I found made education a career. Yet Thorndike found that the modal high-school teacher in 1907 had only three years of experience;[4] most people, especially the women, passed through the occupation quickly. The voice of these more typical short-timers is therefore missing from this study. However, for a study of career ladders, it is precisely the careerists who should be the objects of analysis, for we need to look at the ones who climbed the ladder, rather than those who stepped off after the first rung.

The fact that most high-school teachers did not attain upward mobility suggests that the career-ladder metaphor is a bit misleading, since it projects an image of accessibility that simply did not exist. A career pyramid is a more appropriate (if awkward) image for a process in which most teachers stayed at the lowest level and the numbers dropped off sharply at each succeeding level above. This pyramid model of career mobility is the same pattern found in large bureaucratic organizations, where only a small number of management employees ever reach the executive suite. By examining the careers of those high-school teachers who succeeded under such selective conditions, we can gain insight into the workings of this occupational mobility structure, the incentives and disincentives it offered to teachers in general, and the feasibility of reinstituting a form of such a mobility structure in contemporary schools.

The Setting: High-School Teachers in the 1890s

In 1894, at the same time that high-school enrollments began to soar throughout the country, U.S. Commissioner of Education William T. Harris published the results of the first relatively comprehensive survey of American high schools. The survey uncovered a total of 3,964 public high schools at that point, each with an average of 73 secondary students. But since these schools contained twice as many elementary students as they had high-school students, it appears that many of them were little more than extended elementary schools. A total of 12,120 teachers worked in the public high schools, for an average of 3.1 teachers per school, and these teachers were highly concentrated geographically: 48.2 percent taught in the North Central states and 32.2 percent in the Northeast, leaving only 14.8 percent in the South and 4.8 percent in the West. Overall, 52.7 percent of all public high-school teachers were women, but the sex ratio was relatively even in all areas of the country except the Northeast, where women accounted for 59.3 percent of the total.[5]

Four Career Histories

By looking at the career histories of four high-school teachers, we can see many of the central elements in the structure of occupational mobility that existed in the nineteenth and early twentieth centuries.

Mary Davison Bradford[6]

Born in Kenosha County, Wisconsin in 1859, Mary Davison entered Kenosha High School in 1870. In the spring of 1872 and 1873 she taught in a one-room country school at a pay of $25 a month, returning to her high-school studies each fall. She never graduated, however, because a smallpox quarantine imposed on her family prevented her from finishing her senior year. Instead, she taught in another rural school in the spring of 1874, and then picked up a year-long job teaching third grade in Kenosha. She spent the following year studying at Oshkosh Normal School, then went back in 1876 to teach at Kenosha High. The job was second assistant (at $400 a year) in a school where the rest of the faculty consisted of a female first assistant and a male principal.

After two years at this position she quit to get married and bear a son. Then, after an extended illness, her husband died in 1881. The following year she had no choice but to return to teaching, spending two years in the third grade and then regaining her second-assistant position in the high school at a salary of $500. In 1886 she moved up to the first-assistant spot, and in the next year won a raise to $600. At this point in her career she began to pursue a life teaching certificate, which required her to study in Madison every summer for the next half-dozen years. Her pay jumped to $1,000 in 1890, and in 1894 she finally received her life certificate.

That same year, Mary Bradford left the high school and took a teaching position at the Normal School in Stevens Point, Wisconsin, where she remained until 1906. Then from 1906 to 1909 she taught in the kindergarten training school at the Stout Institute in Menomonie, and spent the following year in the Normal School at Whitewater. Finally, in 1910 she returned to Kenosha as the superintendent of schools, a position she held until retirement.

Paul H. Hanus[7]

Paul Hanus was born in Prussia in 1855. Four years later, his family moved to Wisconsin. In 1871 he entered the preparatory department of the State Normal School at Platteville, and after a year was admitted into the school proper. However, in 1873 he left without graduating and took a job as a clerk for a New York City drug company. A year later he came back to Platteville and taught a fifth-grade class for a term before entering the University of Michigan in the scientific course. He received a B.S. in 1878 and took a job teaching science and mathematics at Denver High School, at a salary of $950, turning down an offer of a job teaching German at a rural Iowa high school for $780. A year later he became an instructor of mathematics (salary $1200) at the University of Colorado, then only a small college with a large preparatory department, both of which were housed in a single building. At the end of that year he quit when he was denied a promotion and a raise and, with the help of a partner, bought a drugstore in Denver. After only one year, Hanus sold his share in the store and returned to the University of Colorado in 1881 as a full professor of mathematics and with an increase in salary.

He remained at the university until 1886, when he accepted a position as principal of a new high school in Denver. When he arrived, this school (located on the upper floor of an elementary school) consisted of 35 students, two teachers, and the principal. By the time he left in 1890 it had grown to 150 students and four teachers, and had a full four-year course. In that year he became a professor of pedagogy at the brand-new Colorado State Normal School in Greeley, the only college graduate on the faculty. Then, in 1891, Charles W. Eliot recruited him to go to Harvard and head that school's new department of education at a salary of $2,000. He remained in this position long enough to preside over the founding of the Harvard Graduate School of Education in 1920, then retired one year later.

Margaret Fogelsong Ingram[8]

Margaret Fogelsong was born around 1885[9] in a small town in Missouri. After graduating from high school, she taught in a series of one-room rural schools (starting at $7 a week) on one-term contracts, while attending teachers' institutes during the summer. In pursuit of a life certificate, she enrolled in the State Normal School at Kirksville while continuing to teach part of the year in a one-room school and a graded elementary school. After graduation, she took a position as principal and sole teacher of a high school in a small town in Montana, at a salary of $80 a month—a big jump from the $40 she received at her previous job. The school had 54 students enrolled in a three-year program. After one year, the board decided to replace her with a man and offered her a combined second- and third-grade class instead, at $75. She accepted; but when the students revolted against the new principal, and the board asked her to take over her old job again, she angrily refused.

As a result of this experience, she resolved to seek a university education in order to insure her access to high-school teaching positions, and she began attending the University of Chicago during the summer. While continuing with her studies, she obtained a better job in a bigger town, teaching seventh and eighth grade in Bozeman (Montana). But there she found a superintendent who failed to support her efforts at restoring discipline. So, she moved on:

> Once again I packed my zinc-bound trunk and headed for Chicago, this time with no hint of a job for the next season. And I had expected such success once I had my life diploma from Kirksville. I was a hobo teacher! Anyway, I still had close connection with that resolution to get an education. The trouble seemed to be that education had a queer way of seeming to rise higher and move farther out of my reach, the more I struggled to attain to its lofty eminence.[10]

In desperation, she for a time considered a career in journalism, and even took a correspondence course in the subject. But she kept teaching. The next job was as supervisor of the fifth and sixth grade at the model school attached to a state normal school in Kentucky. Here she was dropped summarily in an economy move, and trundled once again back to Chicago, mulling over a decade of penury and gender discrimination in her chosen profession. In ten years of teaching she had earned an average of only $430 a year—which, with careful budgeting, was just enough to tide her over every summer.[11] However, "What rankled within my soul was the discrimination against me because of sex, upon the very threshold of my career." She summed up the situation this way:

> Too many good men left the profession. Too many weak superintendents leaned heavily upon their strong teachers, usually women, while they drew the lion's share of the pay, took the credit, and bossed, merely because they were men. Meantime, localities engaged in the expensive pastime of wrangling, the petty larceny of Nepotism, and the exacting of missionary devotion from their women teachers.[12]

Graduating from the University of Chicago in about 1912, she resolved to resist any situation that left her dependent on men, and to hold out for a minimum of $100 a month. Finding no such jobs available, she became a traveling agent for a textbook publisher for a time before finally landing a position as head of the English department at a high school in Marshall, Texas. (In a dozen years she had taught in four states—Missouri, Iowa, Montana, and Texas.) During her summers, she continued to study at Chicago, receiving a master's in education in 1914. In 1920 she left Marshall for Spearfish, South Dakota, to become head of the English department at the State Normal School. Four years later she enrolled at Columbia's Teachers College and earned a Ph.D., moving on to a position where she taught English to teacher candidates in the Jamaica Training School (part of the New York City public schools). Her account breaks off in the 1930s while she was still in this position.

Sadie Smith Trail[13]

Sadie Smith was born in 1873 in a sod house near the town of Western, Nebraska. Her mother died 14 months later, and Sadie was raised by foster parents. When she reached the appropriate age, her father sent her to high school in Crete, where she boarded with a family. She intended to become a teacher, but friends warned her that graduation from high school would make her overqualified for a teaching job in rural schools. She still completed high school, but hedged her bet by apprenticing herself to a local dressmaker.

In her senior year, Sadie taught as a substitute in a one-room school, and then, after graduation, attended a county teachers' institute and obtained a certificate. Subsequently, she taught for a two-month term (at $25 a month) at one rural school, and another term at a second school (at $30), but was not rehired at the latter when a local girl underbid her by $5. After this disappointment she worked in a Crete dressmaking shop for a while, then moved to Colorado Springs to join her father and stepmother. There, while she continued sewing, she studied for a third-grade teaching certificate. Upon receiving this, Sadie taught in yet another one-room school (now at $45 a month). Finding living conditions unpleasant, she passed another teachers' examination and took over a village school.

After two years in Colorado, Sadie Smith went back to Nebraska and attended Peru State Normal School, graduating a year later. She taught for a year in Dunbar, and attended the normal school in Lincoln that summer. Then, in the fall of 1896, she took a job as assistant teacher in a high school in North Bend, Nebraska. Her letters to her fiancé, Rollin Trail, provide a vivid picture of that experience.

Teaching duties were divided between the male principal and his new assistant, which meant that she was responsible for teaching no fewer than eight subjects during her first term alone: "Caesar, Latin Lessons, Algebra, General History, Literature, Botany, Physical Geography and Grammar." As she comments to Trail, "Perhaps I shall have plenty of spare time, but I can't see it now."[14] During her first year she was paid in scrip, not receiving the first cash payment until the following spring. But she was cheerful about attaining reelection for the next year at a raise of $5 per month. Meanwhile, she continued shuttling back to Lincoln every summer to pursue her studies, in the hope of finding a better (paying) job.

During Sadie's third year at North Bend, the principal assumed the title of superintendent, and announced that Sadie was now the principal. This elevation in title had little effect on either his or her work, however, and she was unimpressed, telling Trail, "If it amounted to anything I should feel elated, but it doesn't so I am no larger than before. . . ."[15] She still did the lion's share of the teaching. As her fiancé put it, "Your principal or superintendent Sherman must have learned how to draw pay with little work. Don't you grow weary of doing all the work? Does he get a good salary?"[16] "Yes," she responded, "his salary is a thousand a year. Somewhat larger than mine, you see," which at that point was $495 a year.[17]

Sadie Smith left North Bend in 1900 to become principal of the high school in Holdredge, Nebraska, where she stayed until her marriage to Trail in 1906. She then kept house for her civil-engineer husband in a variety of locations around the western United States, raising three children. When she became ill, they returned to Nebraska, where they lived until her husband died in 1916.

Widowhood propelled Sadie Trail back into teaching. Her daughter records that "She was principal of the high school in Waco, 1917–1919; superintendent of school at Carleton, 1919–1920; and high school principal at Castana, Iowa, 1920–1922."[18] At this point she returned to Lincoln, with family in tow, and taught in nearby Malcolm for a year, ending her career by teaching as a substitute in the Lincoln schools.

Alternative Routes to Advancement

All four of these high-school teachers reveal at least one trait in common, and that is ambition. Each in her or his own way was perpetually in pursuit of a better position. Unwilling to leave education for very long (although each of them did it for at least a short period), they aggressively sought to improve on their situation within the profession. They were generally aiming to attain two goals: better pay and better working conditions.

Not surprisingly, the discussion of money runs through all of the personal accounts of early high-school teachers. These teachers complain bitterly about the pay they received early in their careers, and make clear that the pursuit of higher salary was the most prominent reason motivating them to move from one job to another. And move they did. They shuttled from one position to another and from one place to another, in a zigzag pattern which made sense mostly in monetary terms.

But money was not the only factor. In addition, these teachers were seeking better conditions for living and working. These included a variety of factors: having a home of one's own instead of continuing to board out; living in a town that offered social and cultural amenities; working in a school that permitted the teacher to focus on a specialized subject area, instead of having diffuse responsibility for the whole curriculum; and finding a position that permitted a degree of autonomy and personal respect, free from arbitrary interference and sexist dependency.

Read as a group, these career histories suggest that there were at least three different routes to upward mobility for high-school teachers in the late nineteenth and early twentieth centuries. First, all four teachers sought to advance their careers by means of geographical mobility, particularly the movement from country to city. Second, they all climbed the school-level hierarchy from primary to secondary teaching, three of them ending up in higher education. Third, all of them also moved up the positional ladder from teacher to such positions as department head, principal, and superintendent. In addition, these histories suggest that there was a key factor that helped teachers climb these career ladders—namely education; for all of these teachers pursued advancement by means of acquiring additional education and certification. But they also point out factors that restricted this climb—most notably gender and (as we will see in later examples) race. Let us consider each of these issues in more detail.

Geographical Mobility: From Country to City

In their first century, the most striking characteristic of American common schools was the gross inequality of conditions that marked off the country from the city, and nowhere was this inequality more evident than in the high school. Large cities had both the population and the wealth to support large, free-standing high schools with a graded, four-year course taught by a well-educated and well-paid array of instructors responsible for only their area of specialization. By contrast, rural areas could at best support only small, ungraded schools located in a corner of the elementary-school building and taught by one or two poorly paid instructors whose limited education and experience were matched against a breathtaking range of subject-area responsibilities. The obvious result of this disparity was to induce career-minded high-school teachers to continually seek positions in progressively larger communities in order to improve both their pay and their working conditions.[19]

To a degree, this disparity still exists. Pay levels in large urban and suburban school districts today often are considerably higher than those in rural areas, a fact which provides continuing incentive for teacher migration. However, there are several factors that help undercut this incentive: State equalization formulas reduce the differences in local tax revenues and thus differences in teacher pay; tenure and pension concerns make teachers less willing to pursue opportunities in other districts and states; and the perception that urban districts offer poorer working conditions helps offset the attraction of higher salaries. As a result, compared with their contemporary counterparts, early elementary- and high-school teachers were faced with an occupational structure characterized by more geographical diversity and fewer constraints against capitalizing on it.

Lotus D. Coffman's 1910 national survey of American primary and secondary teachers suggests that teachers in general had a strong incentive to move from country to town to city.[20] Table 6.1 shows that the median education level, age, and experience of city teachers was markedly higher than that of rural teachers, presumably in part because the former were paid two or three times as much as the latter. Urban districts could afford to spend four times as much per student, and often keep school open twice as long as rural districts.[21]

Data on high-school teachers, however, are sketchy. Thorndike's 1907 study of this population did not distinguish between urban and rural settings, but it does show a wide range in pay. He found that for male high-school teachers, 5 percent earned less than $500, 51 percent earned between $500 and $1,000, 27 percent earned from $1,000 to $1,500, and 17 percent earned over $1,500. For women, he found that 22 percent earned less than $500, 59 percent earned from $500 to $1,000, and 19 percent earned more than $1,500.[22]

Other evidence suggests that a prime explanation for this highly differentiated pay structure is the gap between country and city. A national survey of teachers' salaries done in 1905 by the National Education Association showed that the pay of high-school teachers increased steadily with the size of the community supporting them (Table 6.2). The average pay for men ranged from $674 in communities of less than 8,000 to $1,886 in cities of more than a million, while women's pay ranged from $575 to $1,387.

Table 6.1 Median Characteristics of Primary and Secondary Teachers in Rural and Urban Areas, 1910

	Men			
	Experience in Years	*Years of Training Beyond Primary*	*Age*	*Salary*
Rural	2	3	22.8	$390
Town	12	4	32.7	613
Urban	12	6	34.6	919
	Women			
	Experience in Years	*Years of Training Beyond Primary*	*Age*	*Salary*
Rural	2	4	21.4	$366
Town	6	4	25.8	492
Urban	7	5	27.5	591

Source: Lotus D. Coffman, *The Social Composition of the Teaching Population* (New York: Teachers College Press, 1911), 25, 28, 33, and 39.

Table 6.2 Average Pay of High-School Teachers by Community Size, 1905

Population of Community	*Average Pay Males*	*Average Pay Females*	*Number of Communities*
1,000,000+	$1,886	$1,387	3
200,000–1,000,000	1,489	1,056	16
100,000–200,000	1,229	936	20
50,000–100,000	1,185	865	38
30,000–50,000	1,019	767	58
20,000–30,000	960	724	74
15,000–20,000	934	744	60
10,000–15,000	856	655	110
8,000–10,000	740	622	88
Less than 8,000	674	575	40

Source: National Education Association, *Report of the Committee on Salaries, Tenure and Pensions of Public School Teaqchers in the United States* (Winona, MN: National Educational Association, 1905), pp. 16 and 106–115.

Data from Indiana, compiled in 1903 by the state superintendent of public instruction, provides additional insight into the degree of differentiation among high-school work settings, according to location.[23] The key differentiating factor in Indiana at the turn of the century was whether or not a high school was "commissioned." A commissioned high school had to meet a variety of minimum state standards for curriculum and faculty (for example, it must have had at least two full-time teachers, one of whom had to be college-educated) which were closely related to the size of the community supporting the school. In 1903 there were approximately 1,003 high schools in the state; of these, 763 had two or more teachers, but only 185 of these were commissioned.[24]

As Table 6.3 shows, the average commissioned high school had nearly eight times as many students, and five times as many teachers, as the average noncommissioned school, and these teachers were paid 68 percent more.

Therefore, there was a powerful financial incentive for a teacher in a small rural high school to move on to one of the larger schools. The same superintendent's report provides data on conditions at each of the commissioned high schools. I selected a random sample of 20 schools from this group, and Table 6.4 shows the comparison in pay and teaching conditions between the five largest and five smallest schools in the sample. Even within this relatively elite group, the larger schools paid

Table 6.3 Characteristics of Commissioned and Noncommissioned High Schools in Indiana, 1903

	Number	*Average No. of Students*	*Average No. of Teachers*	*Average yearly pay*
Commissioned high schools	185	126	5.3	$726
Noncommissioned high schools	818	16	1.0	$432

Source: Fassett A. Cotton, *Education in Indiana: An Outline in the Growth of the Common School System* (Indianapolis: Superintendent of Public Instruction, 1904), p. 194.

Table 6.4 Characteristics of a Sample of Large and Small Commissioned High Schools in Indiana, 1903

	Number of Students	*Number of Students*	*Average Annual Pay of Teachers, Including Supt. and Principal*	*Average Number of Subjects Taught Per Teacher*
Median for five large* commissioned high schools	243	8	$820	1.1
Median for five small* commissioned high schools	40	3	$617	3.0
Median for twenty commissioned high schools (all sizes)	67	3	$682	2.2

* Size determined by number of students enrolled.

Source: Based on a random sample of 20 commissioned high schools drawn from Fasset A. Cotton, *Education in Indiana: An Outline in the Growth of the Common School System* (Indianapolis: Superintendent of Public Instruction, 1904), pp. 232–470.

their teachers 33 percent more than did the smaller schools.[25] But, in addition, the teachers in the larger schools were expected to teach only one subject area, while the teachers in the smaller schools had to teach three.

Yet the incentive was not entirely financial. In their personal accounts, high-school teachers complained frequently about being required to teach subjects in which they did not feel competent, and of thus being forced into the demeaning position of having to rely heavily on the text. Recall Sadie Trail's comment about being stuck with eight subjects in her first term. When Henry Johnson took a job at Lutheran High School (Albert Lea, Minnesota) in 1890, he had to teach thirteen classes covering seven subjects.[26] There was a serious difference in the workload facing teachers in rural and urban settings, and it provided a stimulus to seek positions in larger towns that was nearly as great as the desire for higher pay.

Notice one more thing about Table 6.4: Most schools in the sample were closer to the smallest high schools in terms of pay and specialization than they were to the largest schools, and this was within the category of commissioned high schools that constituted the most advanced 20 percent of the high schools in the state. Thus the proportion of high-school teachers in Indiana who were receiving more than $800 to teach only one subject was very small indeed. To the rest, the kinds of rewards and working conditions that existed in places like Laporte, Millersville, and Indianapolis (three places in the large-school sample) were both remote from their own teaching experience and thoroughly enticing.

If teaching in an urban high school was as attractive as I suggest, then teachers would have been likely to stay longer there than at a rural school, and they also would have been likely to stay in the profession longer had they landed a position in a city than if they were trapped in a rural school. The geographical mobility pattern, therefore, would have produced a situation in which urban high schools would collect teachers who had lengthy tenures in the school and extended professional experience.

Consider the experience factor first. Thorndike argues that years of experience provide the strongest explanation for the differences in pay among high-school teachers: For the first 22 years of teaching, women received $27 in additional pay for each year of experience; men received $28 for each of the first 12 years, and $8 for the years between 13 and 22.[27] Since the median number of years of experience was six for women and eight for men, most high-school teachers never climbed high enough on the experience ladder to cash in on it.[28] However, Thorndike does not include a variable measuring the urban–rural dimension, and as a result he overlooks the distinct possibility that the city was the crucial link between pay and experience, as high urban salaries attracted the most experienced high-school teachers.

School-level data on length of tenure at a given school provide more direct, if still fragmentary, support for the greater attractiveness of urban high schools. Princeton Township High School was founded in 1867 through the formation of a special high-school district around a county seat in a rural northwestern Illinois. In 1892, its supporters celebrated the school's twenty-fifth anniversary and published a memorial volume that contains the names of its faculty for each year.[29] Table 6.5 shows that, on average, these teachers remained at the school less than three years. In fact, 43 percent left after one year, and 66 percent were gone after two; only 16 percent stayed as long as five years. This was a substantial rural high school, with an enrollment of about 200 students, a faculty of six or seven, and enough backing to produce a memorial volume; it would have ranked among the largest of the

Table 6.5 Tenure of Teachers at Princeton Township (IL) High School, 1867–1892*

Number of Years at School	*Female Teachers (Percent)*	*Male Teachers (Percent)*	*Total Teachers (Percent)*
1	42.5	43.6	42.8
2	25.6	17.4	22.9
3	10.6	4.3	8.6
4	8.5	13.0	10.0
5	6.4	8.7	7.1
6 to 10	2.1	13.0	5.7
11 or more	4.3	0.0	2.9
	100.0%	100.0%	100.0%
N	47	23	70
Average tenure	2.91	2.96	2.93
Average tenure (without principals)	2.91	2.33	2.75

* Includes data on all teachers who were hired between 1867 and 1886, but reflects tenure through 1892.
Source: Richard Alston Metcalf, *A History of Princeton High School* (Princeton, IL: Princeton High School, 1892).

commissioned high schools in neighboring Indiana a quarter-century later. Even so, it experienced a very high faculty turnover. Its teachers either left teaching altogether, or moved on to a better opportunity in a larger town.

One step up the geographical mobility ladder from the township high school was a school such as the English High School in Worcester, Massachusetts. Founded in 1845, this was an older and larger school in a middle-sized Eastern city, which would suggest that teachers would have found it a more attractive place to seek a job, and would have been more likely to stay there. Table 6.6 shows data on the tenure of the women and men who taught there between 1845 and 1892, and these data provide some support for this view. In one way, the experience in Worcester was identical with the experience in Princeton, Illinois, for in both schools about 45 percent of the teachers left after the first year. But those teachers who remained at Worcester beyond this point showed a stronger tendency to stay for the longer term—especially the women. Compared with Princeton's, the average tenure for women there was about a year longer; and 24 percent of the female Worcester teachers taught there for six or more years, compared with only 6 percent of those in Princeton.

At the top end of the opportunity structure for high-school teachers were a small number of schools like Central High of Philadelphia. Founded in 1838 in the second largest city in the country, Central offered an extraordinarily attractive maximum salary ($1925 in 1880, for example), considerable prestige (its teachers, known as professors, were the leading educators in the city), subject specialization, and urban amenities; and, as a result, its faculty stuck with it for the long haul. The 16 men who taught there in 1880 ultimately stayed at the school for an average of no fewer than 30.3 years—more than ten times as long as teachers stayed in Princeton. In fact, the average tenure of all 120 men who taught at Central from 1838 to 1900 was

Table 6.6 Tenure of Teachers at Worcester (MA) English High School, 1845–1892*

Number of Years at School	*Female Teachers (Percent)*	*Male Teachers (Percent)*	*Total Teachers (Percent)*
1	39.8	46.2	42.6
2	7.9	15.4	11.3
3	11.1	19.2	14.8
4	11.1	0.0	6.1
5	6.3	3.8	5.2
6 to 10	15.9	9.6	13.0
11 or more	7.9	5.8	7.0
	100.0%	100.0%	100.0%
N	63	52	115
Average tenure	3.86	3.10	3.51
Average tenure (without principals)	3.86	2.77	3.44

* Includes data on all teachers who were hired between 1845 and 1885, but reflects tenure through 1892.

Source: *Dedication of the English High School, Worcester, MA, Monday, September 5, 1892*, pp. 72–76.

23.0 years.[30] What the evidence suggests, then, is that teachers were drawn to the larger urban high school by means of relatively high pay and good working conditions; and that once there, they stayed.

Survey data show that the relatively low position of the rural high-school teacher continued into the 1930s. In 1921, Emery N. Ferriss did a survey of rural high schools in New York State and found that the median teacher in these schools had 3.4 years of experience, and 49 percent were in their first year at their particular location.[31] In a national survey of rural high schools published in 1925, Ferriss reported that in schools with fewer than four teachers, 72.6 percent of the teachers were teaching three or more different subjects every day. Since the median school in this sample had 3.5 teachers, most rural high schools fit into this category.[32]

John Rufi's 1924 study of five small high schools in Pennsylvania showed that the average teacher was expected to cover between six and eight subjects.[33] Problems were even more severe in the South. A 1929 study of Alabama high-school teachers shows that the median rural teacher had 2.1 years of experience and 0.9 years at a particular job, compared with 4.8 and 2.5 respectively for the city teacher, and that the median rural salary was $1,066 vs. $1,411 in the city.[34] Combined, these studies show that the rural high school continued to act as a turnstyle for teachers, and that one reason for this was that these schools still offered difficult working conditions.

Given the heavy subject loads and low pay that characterized rural high-school teaching during the late nineteenth and early twentieth centuries, it is little wonder that the more ambitious and career-oriented minority of the high-school teaching population moved on as soon as it got the chance. Indeed, in his 1924 interviews with teachers at five small rural high schools, Rufi found that *all* of them wanted to leave for better jobs. The reasons they gave were understandable: unreasonable teaching schedule, lack of facilities, absence of social life, meager salaries, and poor living conditions.[35] Since the high schools in the larger towns and cities offered teachers a significant improvement in all of these conditions, it is hardly surprising that ambitious teachers migrated in that direction; nor is it surprising that, once lodged in these schools, they tended to remain.

School-Level Mobility: From Elementary to Secondary to Higher Education

In the late nineteenth and early twentieth centuries, public schoolteachers sought to gain career advancement by several methods in addition to geographical mobility. Prominent among these was to climb the ladder leading from one level of school to another. The main rungs of this ascent led from the primary to the secondary level and from there, for a number of individuals (especially in a success-biased sample drawn from memoir writers), into some form of higher education.

Yet, in an era when the grading of American schools was far from perfectly realized, there was a second form of school-level mobility, interstitial in character, which led from the ungraded to the graded form of schooling at each level. That is, ambitious teachers not only sought to rise to the next higher level of schooling, but they also tried to find positions within a given level, at schools that practiced the sharpest form of differentiation—both internally (by grading and subject specialization) and externally (by distinguishing itself clearly from the level of schooling below it).

At the elementary level, teachers sought to move as quickly as possible from the ungraded one-room school in the country to the graded multiteacher school found in towns and cities. Shifting then into an ungraded one- or two-teacher high school (often located in the elementary-school building) was an important form of career advancement, but the next step was to try for a position in a fully differentiated high school (with its own building and a specialized faculty).[36] Following this, the next logical move might be into a normal school, which (depending on time and place) had some of the characteristics of both a high school and a college. Finally, at that point a more clearly collegiate form of school, such as a teachers college or university, offered the best promise of career enhancement.

We saw evidence of this kind of upward mobility through the graded structure of schooling in the four career histories presented earlier. Mary Bradford started in a one-room country school, shifted to a graded elementary school, moved up to a high school, and then leveled off in a normal school. Paul Hanus taught briefly at a graded elementary school, then at a high school, a university preparatory department, high school again, a state normal school, and finally a university department of education. Margaret Ingram started in a one-room school, moved to a graded elementary, an ungraded high school, several graded elementaries, a graded high school, a state normal school, and then a university. Finally, Sadie Trail went from a series of country schools to several graded elementaries, then to an ungraded high school, and several other high schools that may or may not have been graded.

Let us examine, by considering evidence from their career histories, some of the routes that ten different teachers followed through the hierarchy of schools. Then we can explore how the incentives offered by this mobility structure spurred the pursuit of advancement. The summaries that follow (presented chronologically by birthdate) focus exclusively on the schools at which these teachers worked, leaving out other aspects of each person's career. School positions are as teachers unless otherwise noted.

Edward Hicks Magill[37]
- 1825 born in Solebury, PA
- 1841 one-room school
- 1844 graded elementary
- 1952 Providence High School (ungraded)
- 1859 Boston Latin School (partially graded)
- 1869 Swarthmore College (president)

John Swett[38]
- 1830 born in New Hampshire
- 1847 one-room schools in New England
- 1853 ungraded grammar school in San Francisco

1862 superintendent of public instruction (California)
1867 graded grammar school for girls (principal)
1869 deputy superintendent of schools, San Francisco
1873 graded grammar school for girls (principal)
1876 Girls High School (principal)
1890 superintendent of schools, San Francisco
1894 retired

Samuel Thurber[39]
1837 born in Providence, RI
1858 ungraded grammar school
1859 Providence High School (ungraded)
1867 Bangor High School (principal)
1869 high school in St. Louis (headmaster)
1870 high school in Hyde Park, MA (principal)
1872 Syracuse High School (principal)
1878 Worcester English High School (principal)
1880 Boston Girls High School
1883 Milton Academy (principal)
1887 Boston Girls High School
1909 retired

Julia Anne King[40]
1838 born in Milan, MI
1858 ungraded high school in St. Clair
Lansing High School (principal)
Kalamazoo College (head of ladies' dept.)
high school in Flint (9 years)
1876 high school in Charlotte (principal)
1881 State Normal School at Ypsilanti (preceptress, head of history dept.)
1915 retired

Lizette Woodworth Reese[41]
born in Baltimore, MD (birthdate unknown)
1873 one-room elementary parish school in Baltimore
1876 public elementary grammar school
1897 Colored High School
1901 Western High School
1921 retired

Henry Johnson[42]
1860 born in Sweden
1885 one-room school in Minnesota
1890 ungraded high school, Albert Lea
1891 superintendent of schools, Rushford
1894 ungraded high school, Northfield
1895 superintendent, Rushford
1895 State Normal School, Moorhead
1899 State Normal School, Charleston, IL

1906 Teachers College, Columbia
1936 retired

Emma Lott[43]
1867 born in Lansing, MI
1887 ninth grade in Portland (MI) High School
1891 second grade in Lansing
1893 Lansing High School (teacher, dean of girls, assistant principal)
1933 retired

Grace Annie Hill[44]
1874 born in Dedham, MA
1896 private schools
1900 Detroit Central High School
1917 Detroit Junior College (grew out of Central HS)
1923 College of the City of Detroit (grew out of Detroit JC)

Inez Taylor[45]
1877 born in Ohio
1894 one-room country school
1895 third–fourth grade in Hillsdale, MI
1903 left to raise children
1917 Hillsdale High School (graded)
1933 retired

Marie J. Rasey[46]
1891 born
1907 ungraded high school
1910 another ungraded high school
1913 graded high school in Illinois
1917 graded high school in Detroit
1919 Detroit Junior College

Overall, the careers of all ten of these teachers show signs of significant upward mobility—from lower- to higher-level schools, from ungraded to graded schools, or (most often) both. Only two of these ten teachers, Emma Lott and Marie Rasey, started their teaching careers in a high school; all the rest began at the elementary level. And, depending on how one counts state normal schools, either four or five of those teaching in them ended up in some form of higher education. One teacher (Grace Hill) actually rode up the school-level ladder as her school, Detroit's Central High School, transformed itself into a junior college (later becoming Wayne State University). Note also how frequently mobility across school levels overlapped with mobility from country to city. The strategy for getting ahead involved seeking a graded higher-level school, and these were most likely found in the more populous areas.

The incentives for pursuing a position at such a school were, once again, the superior pay and working conditions one could find there. For example, after teaching several years in various ungraded high schools and simultaneously acquiring two degrees, Marie Rasey found a job in the Detroit suburbs in 1917. However, "The stay here was short and unprofitable, largely because the great city beckoned to something more in keeping with her ambitions.'' When she suddenly attained a job in Detroit, she was exultant: ''Marie [Rasey] Garn was at last a high school teacher in Detroit, at a salary of $120 a month, and she did not question for a moment that with that princely salary she would soon be able to buy Cadillac Square.''[47]

But let us look at the effect of school level on teacher pay, apart from the effects of the rural–urban factor. Coffman estimates that the median pay for all male teachers in 1910 (the large majority of whom taught at the elementary level) was $489, while Thorndike fixes the pay of male high-school teachers (in 1907) at $900, 84 percent more. For all female teachers the median pay was $450, while female high-school teachers earned $650, 44 percent more.[48] The 1905 NEA salary survey showed that the average elementary teacher earned $661 while the average high-school teacher earned $1,046, a 58 percent advantage, and this advantage held for every size of community, ranging from those of less than 1,000 to those of more than 1 million in population.[49] Thus high-school teaching in general was substantially more lucrative than elementary-school teaching, and this fact alone was sufficient to explain why teachers aspired to gain what in effect was a promotion to the high school.

However, since high-school teachers were more highly concentrated in the better-paying urban districts, we need to examine pay differences within districts in order to isolate the effect of school level. Tables 6.7 and 6.8 show the distribution of teacher pay in Lansing (Michigan) and Philadelphia for two different years, 1894 and 1918. In 1894, Lansing male and female high-school teachers made between 41 percent and 79 percent more than the city's all female elementary teachers; and in 1918, male high-school teachers enjoyed a 60–220 percent advantage over the elementary teachers, while the female high-school teachers earned between 13 percent less and 150 percent more than women at the elementary level.

Philadelphia had a much more highly differentiated system of schools than Lansing, which led to a more complex structure of rewards. Yet, in the end, high schools there offered teachers the same sort of powerful financial incentive to seek

Table 6.7 Pay of Lansing (MI) Teachers by School Level, 1894 and 1918

Position	*1894 Pay*	*1918 Pay*
High School		
Principal	$1,200	$2,000
Assistant principal	700	1,350
Teachers	600–625	—
Male	—	1,200–1,600
Female	—	650–1,250
Elementary schools		
Principals	400–500	790–930
Teachers	350–425	500–750

Source: Frederick C. Aldinger, *History of the Lansing Public Schools, 1847–1944* (Lansing: Lansing School District, n.d.), pp. 71–72.

Table 6.8 Pay of Philadelphia Teachers by School Level, 1894 and 1918

Position	*1894 Pay*	*1918 Pay*
High Schools		
Male		
Central High School		
Principal	$4,000	$4,500
Professors	2,500	2,700
Manual training schools		
Principal	3,000	4,500
Teachers	2,000	2,700
Female		
Girls High School		
Principal	4,000	4,500
Teachers	1,150	1,750
Grammar schools		
Male		
Principals	1,865	3,100
Teachers	—	1,400
Female		
Principals	1,250	3,100
Teachers	—	1,100

Source: David F. Labaree, *The Making of an American High School: The Credentials Market and the Central High School of Philadelphia, 1838–1939* (New Haven: Yale University Press, 1988), Table 5.1.

a position at the secondary level. In the hierarchy of pay, there were three levels of high-school teaching in 1894, with men earning more than women, and teachers at Central earning more than those at other schools. In 1918, male high-school teachers there earned 93 percent more than men teaching grammar school, and female high-school teachers earned 59 percent more than their grammar-school counterparts.

The 1894 data for both cities reveal something else about the opportunity structure for teachers: Teachers received a bigger reward from being promoted to the high school than they did for being made principal. That is, school level provided a bigger incentive to teachers than did position in school. In Lansing, male and female high-school teachers earned from 20 percent to 56 percent more than did female elementary-school principals. In Philadelphia, male high-school teachers earned between 7 percent and 34 percent more than male grammar-school principals, while female high-school teachers earned 8 percent less than female lower-school principals. Thus, at least for men, the salary gap between high school and elementary school was wider than the gap between principal and teacher within a given level. As a result, ambitious teachers were forced to pursue a path of career advancement that took them into higher levels.

Positional Mobility: From Teaching to Administration

Not only did high-school teachers pursue career mobility by moving to the city and by aiming for higher-level schools, but they also sought advancement by aspiring to administrative positions at each school level. In particular this meant seeking to become principal or superintendent. For the contemporary American teacher, administration has become the primary remaining route for attaining occupational advancement, a route that the Holmes Group and others have complained about because it draws some of the most ambitious and (perhaps) most accomplished practitioners out of teaching and into full-time administration. However, two characteristics distinguish the form of positional mobility that was open to the early high-school teacher from the contemporary form: a blurring of the boundary between administration and teaching, and an extreme pattern of gender-differentiated access to administrative opportunities.

In the previous section we saw that an elementary-school principal frequently was paid less than a high-school teacher, which suggests that school-level mobility was a better way to get ahead than was promotion into administration within a given level. One reason for this was that, in a system marked by staggering attrition, high schools and high-school teachers were scarce and valuable commodities in relation to elementary schools and their principals. But another reason was that being a principal or superintendent in most school systems around the turn of the century did not mean very much. Most high schools were very small. As Harris reported in 1894, the average public high school had 3.1 teachers, and this estimate left out a large number of the smallest schools. In Indiana, the average in 1903 was only 1.8,[50] and by 1925, the median rural high school in the country still had a total faculty of only 3.5.[51]

All of these figures include the principal as part of the teaching force, for the simple practical reason that in schools this small, there was no room for a full-time administrator. These principals were in fact principal teachers. Sometimes they were the *only* teachers. More often they were the *lead* teachers in the school, who taught the more advanced students and did administration part-time. Ferriss found that among the rural high schools, the principal spent about 200 minutes a day teaching, 55 minutes doing clerical work, and 40 minutes supervising instruction.[52] Not a very glamourous or distinctive position for a teacher to aspire to.

In addition, about half of the time spent on instructional supervision was devoted to overseeing the workings of the elementary schools. For small districts, the high-school principal often was seen as the instructional leader of the system as a whole, acting as a quasi-superintendent. Some districts had no superintendent, and others had someone filling a clerical role under this title; in both cases, the high-school principal had to take charge. However, in a number of districts, it was the superintendent who acted as the instructional leader, frequently occupying an office in the high school and teaching classes there. The possibilities were rife for widespread confusion about the boundaries separating these positions. Often it was difficult to tell the difference between a high-school teacher and a principal, or between a principal and a superintendent, since frequently their functions were interchangeable.

One need only recall the situation that faced Sadie Trail in the high school at North Bend, Nebraska in 1896. She was hired to teach in a school where the only other teacher was the principal, who, in the absence of a superintendent, also supervised the lower schools. Yet in her third year, the principal suddenly took the title of superintendent, and she became principal—although there was no discernible change in the duties of either. Did this constitute positional mobility for either of them? She thought not. Later in her career, she was a principal in three different towns and a superintendent in one, but each time she left the position within two years. It is unclear whether any of these administrative posts consisted of much more than a teaching job with an impressive title. And this leads to the problem of gender.

The mobility of high-school teachers into administration was eased by the muddle over what distinguished an administrator from a teacher, but this led to a two-track system based on gender. Normally, women were offered jobs as high-school principals and superintendents only when no man wanted those positions. This generally meant that women ended up as administrators in the smallest districts, where the pay was too low to attract a man and where the job was basically a teaching job anyway.[53] Even under these circumstances, the appointment often was considered temporary until such time as a male candidate appeared. Remember how Margaret Ingram took a job as a small-town high-school principal, only to be summarily replaced after one year by a man who quickly turned out to be incompetent. Even when women succeeded in making it to the college level, they tended to do so as regular faculty instead of as chair, dean, or president.

For men, however, the picture was quite different. Blessed with the right of first refusal for administrative jobs in general, they could choose to pursue the most attractive possibilities, which meant the larger schools in the larger communities. Paul Hanus rose from high-school teacher in Denver to college professor, high-school principal, and finally university dean. John Swett found his way to San Francisco, where he went from grammar-school principal to state superintendent of public instruction to high school principal to city superintendent.[54] For these men, the promotional ladder seemed to reflect an opportunity structure that was more meritocratic than the one confronting the women. For example, Jesse Stuart started out in Kentucky in the 1920s teaching in a one-room rural elementary school, followed by a one-room high school. However, when his students won a state-wide academic achievement contest, he became principal of a city high school, and later the city and county superintendent. Another story of male merit rewarded that would have set Margaret Ingram to gnashing her teeth in frustration![55]

Promoting Mobility: Education

A key method by which high-school teachers moved up any or all of the three career ladders open to them was to pursue further education and acquire additional levels of certification. This is a familiar story, and a couple of examples will serve to flesh it out. Recall that Margaret Ingram graduated from high school, then taught while attending teachers' institutes in the summer. Later, she chose to seek a life certificate, attending the State Normal School while continuing to teach during the year. After some unpleasant experiences in small-town jobs, she began spending her summers going to classes at the University of Chicago, earning her B.A. in 1912. She still continued studying during the summer, gaining a master's in 1914, and then finally attaining a Ph.D. from Teachers College in the 1920s. All of her education after high school, with the possible exception of her doctorate, was obtained part-time while teaching. Each stage in her educational process in turn led to a higher-level position, and when each new position failed to satisfy her professional ambition, she went back to school.

Fern Persons[56] graduated from Olivet (Michigan) High School in 1913 and spent the following year at Eaton County Normal School. For the next ten years she taught at three different elementary schools, gradually working toward a life certificate—which she received in 1922 from Western Michigan College. She immediately began working on a bachelor's degree at Olivet College. In 1926 she moved up to teaching math at Olivet High School, and a year later received her B.A. and won the position of dean of women at the school. Continuing her education, she did graduate work at Northwestern and the University of Michigan, becoming principal at Olivet in 1931, the first woman to hold such a position in that part of the state. In 1939 she was awarded a master's from Michigan, then became acting superintendent while the male incumbent was absent during the war. Meanwhile, she continued piling up credits toward a doctorate.

This pattern runs through most of these teachers' personal accounts in one form or another. Educational enhancement provided a crucial catalyst for the ambitious high-school teacher seeking to get ahead. The education itself took on a variety of shapes—from teachers' institutes to city or county normal schools, state normal schools, teachers' college, liberal-arts colleges, and universities. It ranged from an informal study program in preparation for a certifying examination to a formal graduate degree. Education in all these various forms was then combined with one or all of the other mechanisms for occupational mobility, as degrees and certificates helped to support a teacher's upward progress toward a city school system, a higher-level school, and a higher position.

The most successful careerists among the early high-school teachers were the ones like Margaret Ingram, Fern Persons, Paul Hanus, and Mary Bradford, who used education to pursue all three routes to upward mobility at the same time. Here is where the analogy of the career ladder simply deconstructs, since it is rather awkward to picture them climbing all of these ladders simultaneously.[57]

Restricting Mobility: Gender and Race

There are two additional elements which, unlike education, have served to limit the possibilities for teacher mobility: gender and race. The impact of these two factors on the process of teacher advancement was to create largely separate mobility tracks leading up each of the three career ladders already identified. The routes to career success for men and whites were in this way parallel with those for women and blacks, yet the mechanisms for getting ahead worked more effectively for the former than for the latter.

We have seen a variety of statistics that show a significant difference in pay between men and women high-school teachers. Let us consider the evidence about whether or not these differences were the result of sexist pay practices or other factors. One plausible explanation would be that women were paid less because they left the profession earlier than men.[58] In apparent confirmation of this point, Thorndike, it should be recalled, found in 1907 that male and female high-school teachers earned a nearly identical pay increment ($28 and $27, respectively) for each additional year of experience during their first 12 years of teaching. Yet the median salary was $900 for men and $650 for women, while the median years of experience for each was eight years and six years respectively. Thus the extra two years of experience enjoyed by the men would only account for $50 of their $250 pay advantage. This suggests that the gender difference in pay arose not through differential pay increases or longer tenure but from the initial pay levels set when men and women were first hired to teach high school.

This interpretation receives some support from the data on pay differences between country and city. Thorndike's study drew on data from high-school teachers nationally, and, since the number of urban high-school teachers constituted a small fraction of this population, his median figures primarily reflect the condition of country and small-town teachers. There is another source from the previous decade that provides some insight into urban pay levels. In 1895, A. F. Nightingale, superintendent of the Chicago high schools, sent a questionnaire to superintendents in most of the largest school systems around the country, asking them about how they paid their male and female high-school teachers. He received salary data from 52 of them. By my rough calculation, the average male high-school teacher in the larger districts earned about $1,470 while his female counterparts earned $900.[59] This means that in urban high schools, male teachers earned 63 percent more than female teachers, while in small-town high schools (a decade later) the male advantage was 38 percent.[60] The respondents to Nightingale's survey explain this differential in terms of market pressures. One speaks for most of them when he says:

> Why do we pay men more than women? The market demands it. . . . The woman will stay at her work for years—the man, as soon as he becomes of value to the school, must be promoted, or he will leave to go where higher salaries are paid. It is a simple question of supply and demand, governing the price of work for the two sexes.[61]

Under these conditions, the city schools were in a better situation to compete for male teachers simply because they could afford to pay more than the country districts. Thus the gap between male and female teachers was greater in the city because the upper pay limit was less restrictive, allowing the high schools to attract and hold male teachers, while the absence of market alternatives prevented the female high-school teacher from capitalizing on these possibilities to the same extent. However, in the country high school, the limited local tax base put a lower ceiling on male salaries (even at the expense of driving men out of these jobs altogether), while the floor on female salaries could not be held at a level that was proportionately as far below the male level as was true in the city. After all, there was a certain annual pay below which even a country woman could not eke out a living.

This argument implies that city high schools had a higher proportion of male teachers than did country high schools, even though the evidence shows that cities had a smaller proportion of males in the teaching population as a whole. In fact, the NEA's 1905 survey shows that in cities with a population of more than 100,000, the males made up 41.0 percent of the high-school teaching force, while in towns of less than 15,000 the male proportion dropped to 25.1 percent.[62]

I would argue that this occurred for two reasons. First, as noted, cities could afford to pay what men demanded. Second, urban high-school teaching offered a degree of prestige and influence that made it attractive even in light of the other opportunities open to men. Given the small number of high schools that existed prior to this century, and the prominence of these institutions within their respective cities, high-school teachers—accorded the honorific title of professor—constituted the leading figures in the local educational community, and played a respected role in the public life of the noneducational community. In Philadelphia during the nineteenth century, for example, the professors (all men) from the only boys' high school were listed in back of the city directory along with the judges and political officeholders.

Two other factors contributed to the gender differences in pay among high-school teachers. The first was positional. Men were much more likely to hold the position of principal, and principals were paid more than other teachers. A prime reason for this situation was an ideological preference for having men in charge. One of Nightingale's superintendents put the case simply: "Why do we pay men more than women? The most important and responsible positions are filled by men. It is of quite rare occurrence for a woman to be considered successful either as a city superintendent or a high school principal."[63] The second factor was educational. Men at the turn of the century were more likely to be college graduates than women, especially at the start of their careers, and this gave them an advantage in competing for a high-school job, in demanding higher pay for such a job, and in making a claim for the principalship. By contrast, the career histories of even the most successful women high-school teachers show that they tended to acquire their education gradually over a lifetime, and that university training came (if at all) years after they entered the teaching profession.

In 1879, Myra Strober and Laura Best did a remarkable study of male–female pay differentials among San Francisco public-school teachers that pulls together many of these elements. They found that position and school level had a larger impact on these gender-based pay differentials than did experience and education. But when the effect of the other three variables was controlled, the most powerful factor influencing gender differences in pay was school level. The male high-school teacher enjoyed an advantage over his female counterpart which extended beyond education, experience, and position, and which simply came from *being in* a high school.[64]

When the expansion of high-school enrollment in the 1890s undercut the exclusiveness of high-school teaching, male teachers scrambled to hold on to the special position they had once occupied. For many, this meant returning to the university and seeking credentials that would take them into educational administration.[65] But the change propelled others into unionism, wherein male high-school teachers have continued to play a leadership role since the turn of century.[66]

If gender created a partially divergent and shortened career ladder for women in high-school teaching, race constructed a radically separated and truncated track for blacks. Whites could teach in black high schools (recall that Lizette Reese, a white woman, taught at the "Colored High School" in Baltimore,) but blacks could not teach in white schools. And the situation facing black teachers in black high schools was grim. One study found that as late as 1933 about half of the Southern black high schools in rural areas offered only one- or two-year programs, and about half had fewer than 40 students. Overall, 60 percent of all Southern black high schools had less than a four-year program, and these schools had on average less than one full-time teacher.

In effect, being a high-school teacher under these conditions was a part-time addition to one's grammar-school duties.[67] Too, pay levels for these teachers were commensurate with their abysmal working conditions. Average monthly pay levels for Southern public-school teachers in 1909–1910 were $60 for whites and $33 for blacks; in 1928–1929 the gap had narrowed only slightly, to $118 versus $73.[68]

Conclusion

This discussion has focused on the nature of the career ladders available to high-school teachers in the late nineteenth and early twentieth centuries. The opportunity structure within the profession offered three different routes to career advancement: moving from country to city, from lower- to higher-level schools, and from teaching into administration. A small number of the most ambitious early high-school teachers took advantage of all of these routes to achieve a substantial degree of career mobility.

The evidence for this mobility process that I have presented in this paper is not of the sort that leads to strong and confident conclusions about the nature of early high-school teaching as a form of work. One reason is that I have focused almost exclusively on the most successful cases, while in fact most high-school teachers never moved beyond the first rung or two on *any* of the three career ladders. Another is that my sources have largely consisted of rather idiosyncratic personal accounts, which are difficult to organize into a systematic understanding of the condition of high-school teachers more generally. Therefore, let me state again that the function of this discussion is not to analyze the typical high-school teacher but to examine the structure of incentives that shaped the possibilities for advancement by the exceptional teacher who stayed in the profession long enough to consider it a career.

With this limited goal in mind, I can venture two comments about general tendencies that appear in the preceding discussion. First, the opportunity structure within the profession was molded by two forces arising from the social context of schooling: a meritocratic ideology, and a structure of occupational opportunity stratified by gender and race. Second, the substantial changes that affected high-school teaching in the twentieth century had the effect of undercutting the importance of the first two routes to advancement (geographical and school-level mobility) and of ritualizing the positional route.

Meritocracy, Inequality, and Gender

The career ladders of high-school teachers modeled meritocratic ideology in two related ways.[69] First, the career histories of those teachers I found in print are framed in the style of the classic American success story. The full title of one of these accounts captures the spirit of this tradition: *Memoirs of Mary D. Bradford: Autobiography and Historical Reminiscence of Education in Wisconsin, through Progressive Service from Rural School to City Superintendent.* The genre is familiar, only instead of plotting the path from the log cabin to the White House, these authors display the triumphant steps leading from the rude one-room schoolhouse to the comfortable administrative offices of a major urban school system or university. It was a tough world, they grimly tell us, but true merit still ultimately gained its just reward.

Yet these stories do provide evidence that career advancement for the early high-school teacher was in fact partly structured along meritocratic lines. Given a form of school organization at the turn of the century that was, for the most part, prebureaucratic or only partially bureaucratic, career advancement was highly unstructured, and thus rewards tended to go to those teachers who were the most entrepreneurial.[70] These were ambitious women and men who carefully managed their careers, seeking out opportunities and promoting their interests. The open structure of American schooling during this period, in combination with the radical inequalities that existed within this structure, provided them with a set of rewarding ladders to climb. It is worth remembering that what made advancement possible was the abject poverty (financially *and* educationally) of American education at the bottom of these ladders. The poor conditions and low pay that existed in rural districts, in elementary schools, and in teaching generally compared with administration, and the low level of teacher training—all of these unpleasant facts about the early teaching experience for most teachers were themselves the source of great opportunity for the ambitious few. What made the incentives effective was that so few could take advantage of them. What made the career pyramid worth climbing was the extreme narrowing that occurred between bottom and top.

As we have seen, however, the meritocratic character of career mobility for high-school teachers was sharply undercut by the extreme differentiation of career opportunities by gender and race. Women and men, blacks and whites, had their own separate structures of inequality to climb, and these structures did not have the same shape. The pyramid of opportunity for women and blacks narrowed much more quickly as one moved upward. Women like Mary Bradford could move "from rural school to city superintendent," but the chances of making it were much smaller than for a man. During the course of this century, there has been a gradual but significant reduction in the differences in opportunity open to women and blacks in American secondary education. But ironically, one result of this change is that the range and flexibility of meritocratic career opportunities has at the same time declined for teachers of both sexes and both races.

Equality, Bureaucracy, and the Transformation of Teacher Incentives

During the course of the twentieth century, the opportunity structure for high-school teachers has undergone significant change. Two factors that helped bring about this change were the growing equalization of previous educational differences, and the relentless bureaucratization of school organization. Let us consider each of the major routes to advancement in light of these changes.

One important characteristic of American educational development in this century has been a gradual reduction in the extreme differences that marked off rural areas and small towns from cities. The migration of a large portion of the rural population to the city, the growth in the relative vitality of rural economies, and radical consolidation of rural school districts, all have helped reduce some of the old advantage enjoyed by urban schooling. And states have pushed the process even farther through their recent efforts to equalize per-capita support for schooling by means of redistributive funding formulas.

As I mentioned earlier, these changes have by no means ended differences in pay between urban and rural high schools. Teachers still move to urban and suburban districts in pursuit of a better salary; but the financial incentive is less now than it was, and it is even smaller if one takes into account cost of living. In addition, teachers frequently choose the less urbanized district because the teaching conditions there are seen as preferable, even if it means sacrificing a little in pay. Finally, tenure and pension rules make mobility generally less attractive.

There has also been a reduction in the incentive once offered by moving from one level of schooling to the next higher level. Bureaucratization has brought elementary and secondary schooling together under a common set of rules, and unionization has equalized the pay differences that were due to school level alone. Through its subject-matter specialization and departmental structure, the high school retains a different set of teaching conditions from the elementary school, but the old pay differential is gone. Also gone is the financial incentive to seek "promotion" from high school to university teaching. Now that unions have succeeded in raising pay scales for public schoolteachers, experienced teachers find that taking a college teaching position even after acquiring a Ph.D. requires a substantial cut in pay. When teachers do make this change, therefore, it tends to be in pursuit of different working conditions rather than more money. The pay incentive to change school levels—so powerful 50 years ago—simply has evaporated.

The ascendancy of bureaucratic organization has brought with it the emergence of position as the key incentive for upward mobility among ambitious high-school teachers. One reason for this is that bureaucratization led to a sharp differentiation of function between teachers and administrators, focusing the blurred boundaries and ill-defined responsibilities that characterized these positions in the early high school. Another reason is that, as the chances for advancement within teaching (by means of moving to the city or climbing to a higher school level) grew smaller over the course of the twentieth century, the prospects offered by the newly differentiated administrative positions looked increasingly attractive. "Getting ahead," which used to have multiple meanings, came to mean one thing: leaving the high-school classroom and entering administration. A variety of routes to career advancement finally converged on a single preferred path, which led to the principal's office and the superintendent's staff.

Even the way in which education leads to advancement has changed in character. Teachers' contracts and district policies have formalized the previously more entrepreneurial role of education in career enhancement by establishing a rigid connection between the accumulation of graduate credits and degrees, and the awarding of pay increases. But at the same time, education leads to less differentiation among contemporary high-school teachers than it did 50 or 100 years ago. The higher minimum for entering the profession (a B.A.), and the prevalence of state rules requiring graduate credits to maintain certification, have made it difficult for teachers to differentiate themselves from the pack by means of any sort of educational distinction short of a doctorate.

The gradual equalization of what was once a radically differentiated opportunity structure for high-school teachers, and the bureaucratization of what was once an open and improvised organization of schooling, produced momentous changes for those trying to make a career within public secondary education. The privileged teachers at the older high schools in large American cities experienced this change as a form of proletarianization through which they lost their former advantages of pay, prestige, and professional autonomy.[71] But for the more typical high-school teacher, working in a smaller school and a less populous area, these changes looked more like a thoroughly benevolent and desirable process of professionalization, one which was raising their status, improving their working conditions, and enhancing the quality of secondary education.

This general elevation of the entire occupational group led to the erosion of the old routes by which a select group of early high-school teachers once pursued career mobility. Yet for most teachers at American high schools, the loss of career ladders from which they were unlikely to benefit anyway was hardly cause for alarm. They lost a long shot at fulfilling the American dream of individual success, but they gained the ability to make a comfortable living in the high-school classroom.

The contemporary Holmes and Carnegie proposals for a multitiered teaching profession are an attempt to create a new form of career ladder to fit the new structure of the profession. The old career ladders were based on market incentives arising from the inequalities and disorganization of nineteenth-century schooling, characteristics that have been steadily declining during the current century. Instead of trying to recover the old system by striving to reinstate a declining set of market incentives, the current reform effort seeks to provide for teacher mobility by extending the trend toward the elaboration of bureaucratic structures within education. The old opportunity structure provided hierarchy everywhere except within teaching itself, which was (and still is) completely undifferentiated. In that earlier setting, the ambitious teacher was thrust into the role of an entrepreneur seeking to take advantage of the opportunities offered by the unregulated educational market. However, the proposed reform would provide a way for vertical differentiation to penetrate teaching itself, so that teachers could pursue upward mobility without having to leave their community, their school level, or even their classroom.

Although the old career ladders were based on market principles and the new are based on bureaucratic principles, both offer a hierarchy of rewards. Holmes and Carnegie in this sense, then, are proposing to fill the temporary vacuum of hierarchical incentives that occurred within teaching as a result of the demise of the old opportunity structure. The rationalization of schooling into "the one best system" reduced the inequalities that had stratified and segmented the profession—particularly geography, school level, race, and gender—and left teachers in a state of relative equality.

This condition has proven to be awkward, for reasons that are both ideological and organizational. From the perspective of meritocratic ideology, membership in an undifferentiated status group is tantamount to an admission of mediocrity, since merit is seen as rising to the top. Thus a profession with no top or bottom cannot be a profession at all, but must be some form of mass occupation. In addition, the flat structure of teaching is an anomaly within the bureaucratic structure of schooling. At present, schools are characterized by a hierarchy of positions within the administrative ranks, but by positional equality within the ranks of teachers. Thus educational bureaucracy has so far failed to extend into the group that has the primary responsibility for carrying out education.

The proposed stratification of teaching would provide a chance for teachers to be inducted simultaneously into both the meritocracy and the bureaucracy. The new career ladder would offer a top rung whose very exclusiveness would suggest excellence. At the same time, the incorporation of teaching into the larger school-system hierarchy would establish teachers as education's street-level bureaucrats. Thus these recent career-ladder proposals represent a continuation of the historical process that has progressively undermined one form of occupational inequality, based on an unregulated mix of achievement and ascription, and replaced it with another, based on a bureaucratically defined mix of certified merit and organizational position.

These reforms might prove effective as part of a "collective mobility project"[72] which raises the status of teachers under the mantle of merit, and they also might prove effective as a mechanism for extending bureaucratic control into classrooms. The more important question, however, is whether they will improve the quality of the teaching and learning that takes place in those classrooms.

Notes

AUTHOR'S NOTE: The author appreciates the comments and suggestions of William Reese, James Fraser, Donald Warren, Cleo Cherryholmes, Michael Sedlak, and Michael Apple.

1. Arthur G. Powell, Eleanor Farrar, and David K. Cohen, *The Shopping Mall High School: Winners and Losers in the Educational Marketplace* (Boston: Houghton Mifflin, 1985); Michael W. Sedlak, Christopher W. Wheeler, Diana C. Pullin, and Philip A. Cusick, *Selling Students Short: Classroom Bargains and Academic Reform in the American High School* (New York: Teachers Col-

lege Press, 1986); and Philip A. Cusick, *The Egalitarian Ideal and the American High School: Studies of Three Schools* (New York: Longman, 1983). See also Theodore R. Sizer, *Horace's Compromise: The Dilemma of the American High School* (Boston: Houghton Mifflin, 1984); and Ernest L. Boyer, *High School: A Report on Secondary Education in America* (New York: Harper & Row, 1983).

2. The Holmes Group, *Tomorrow's Teachers* (East Lansing, MI: The Holmes Group, 1986); and Carnegie Forum on Education and the Economy, *A Nation Prepared: Teachers for the Twenty-first Century* (Washington, DC: Carnegie Forum on Education and the Economy, 1986).
3. The Holmes Group, *Tomorrow's Teachers,* p. 36.
4. Edward L. Thorndike, "The Teaching Staff of Secondary Schools," in U.S. Bureau of Education *Bulletin* 4 (Washington, DC: Government Printing Office, 1909).
5. U.S. Bureau of Education, "Statistical Review of Secondary Education," in *Report of the Commissioner of Education,* 1893–1894 (Washington, DC: Government Printing Office, 1894), pp. 33–95; Tables 1 and 19.
6. Mary D. Bradford, *Memoirs of Mary D. Bradford: Autobiography and Historical Reminiscences of Education in Wisconsin, through Progressive Service from Rural School to City Superintendent* (Evansville, WI: Antes Press, 1932).
7. Paul H. Hanus, *Adventuring in Education* (Cambridge, MA: Harvard University Press, 1937).
8. Margaret Fogelsong Ingram, *Toward an Education* (New York: Comet Press, 1954).
9. This book is written as a memoir, not a historical record, and as a result there are very few dates in it. Some can be inferred, but for the most part the passage of time is recorded in a thoroughly impressionistic fashion.
10. Ingram, *Toward an Education,* p. 271.
11. Ibid., p. 284.
12. Ibid., p. 289.
13. Rosalie Trail Fuller (ed.), "A Nebraska High School Teacher in the 1890s: The Letters of Sadie B. Smith," in *Nebraska History* 58 (1977), pp. 447–474.
14. Ibid., p. 451.
15. Ibid., p. 463.
16. Ibid., p. 469.
17. Ibid., p. 470.
18. Ibid., p. 471.
19. One answer to this problem was for rural areas to create consolidated high schools. However, the issue of consolidation created conflict within rural communities over whether to build such a high school (which would be accredited and graded and blessed with a substantial faculty and an appropriate facility), or to keep the small, unaccredited high schools that were more accessible locally. Localism tended to win out because, in the absence of good transportation, the residents of the town where the consolidated school was located tended to benefit from it much more than did the surrounding farmers. See, for example, Frank A. Balyeat, "County High Schools in Oklahoma," in *Chronicles of Oklahoma* 37 (1959/60), pp. 196–210.
20. Lotus D. Coffman, *The Social Composition of the Teaching Population,* Columbia University Contributions to Education, No. 41 (New York: Teachers College Press, 1911).
21. The figures are for 1880. David B. Tyack and Myra H. Strober, "Jobs and Gender: A History of the Structuring of Educational Employment by Sex," in Patricia Schmuck, W. W. Charters, Jr., and Richard O. Carlson (eds.), *Educational Policy and Management: Sex Differentials* (New York: Academic Press, 1981), pp. 131–152.
22. Thorndike, "The Teaching Staff of Secondary Schools," pp. 13–14.
23. Fassett A. Cotton, *Education in Indiana: An Outline in the Growth of the Common School System* (Indianapolis: Superintendent of Public Instruction, 1904). This book was prepared for the Louisiana Purchase Exhibition held in St. Louis in 1904.
24. Given the ease with which a school

district could assign a grammar-school teacher part-time to teach a few "advanced" courses to a small number of students, and call this a high-school operation, data on the exact number of high schools were difficult to obtain, and varied according to the compiler's definition of what it took to be considered the equivalent of such a school.

25. Average salaries ranged from $520 to $1,100; the latter was at Indianapolis Shortridge High School, founded in 1853.
26. Henry Johnson, *The Other Side of Main Street: A History Teacher from Sauk Centre* (New York: Columbia University Press, 1943), p. 88.
27. Thorndike, "The Teaching Staff of Secondary Schools," p. 41.
28. Ibid., pp. 16–17.
29. Richard Alston Metcalf, *A History of Princeton High School* (Princeton, IL: Princeton High School, 1892).
30. Franklin S. Edmonds, *History of the Central High School of Philadelphia* (Philadelphia: Lippincott, 1902), pp. 319–349; David F. Labaree, "The People's College: A Sociological Analysis of the Central High School of Philadelphia, 1838–1920," doctoral dissertation, University of Pennsylvania, 1983, Table 2.2.
31. Emery N. Ferriss, *The Rural High School: Rural School Survey of New York State* (Philadelphia: William F. Fell, 1922), p. 105. (He also found that the median salary for teachers was only $1,222: ibid., p. 108.)
32. Emery N. Ferriss, "The Rural High School: Its Organization and Curriculum," in U.S. Bureau of Education *Bulletin* 10 (Washington, DC: Government Printing Office, 1925), pp. 2 and 13.
33. John Rufi, *The Small High School*, Columbia University Contributions to Education, No. 236 (New York: Teachers College Press, 1926), p. 63.
34. Henry C. Pannell, *The Preparation and Work of Alabama High School Teachers*, Columbia University Contributions to Education, No. 551 (New York: Teachers College Press, 1933), pp 33, 36, and 39.
35. Rufi, *The Small High School*, p. 50.
36. In 1890, only 9 out of 59 high schools in Connecticut were located in a separate building: in Illinois, only 38 out of 258 were thus differentiated. Theodore R. Sizer, *Secondary Schools at the Turn of the Century* (New Haven: Yale University Press, 1964), p. 39–40.
37. Edward Hicks Magill, *Sixty-five Years in the Life of a Teacher, 1841–1906* (Boston: Houghton Mifflin, 1907).
38. John Swett, *Public Education in California* (New York: Arno Press, 1969).
39. Charles Swain Thomas, *A Memorial of Samuel Thurber: Teacher and Scholar, 1837–1913* (Boston: New England Association of Teachers of English, 1914).
40. Mary A. Lord, "Julia Anne King," in *Michigan History Magazine* 38 (1954), pp. 306–312.
41. Lizette Woodworth Reese, *A Victorian Village* (New York: Farrar & Rinehart, 1929).
42. Johnson, *The Other Side of Main Street*.
43. Nellie Beaumont, "Emma Lott: 1867–1937," in *Michigan History Magazine* 41 (1957), pp. 335–363.
44. Anges Houghton Boss, "Grace Annie Hill (1874–1944)," in *Michigan History Magazine* 38 (1954), pp. 153–156.
45. Inez Taylor, "I am a Teacher," in *Michigan History Magazine* 45 (1961), p. 263–276.
46. Marie J. Rasey, *It Takes Time: An Autobiography of the Teaching Profession* (New York: Harper, 1953). Dates and locations are difficult to determine from this impressionistic account.
47. Rasey, *It Takes Time*, pp. 137 and 139.
48. Coffman, *The Social Composition of the Teaching Population*, pp. 38–39; and Thorndike, "The Teaching Staff of Secondary Schools," pp. 13–14.
49. National Education Association, *Report of the Committee on Salaries, Tenure, and Pensions of Public School Teachers in the United States* (Winona, MN: National Education Association, 1905), pp. 16 and 106–114. The average figures are for communities larger than 8,000.

50. Cotton, *Education in Indiana,* p. 194.
51. Ferriss, "The Rural High School," p. 2.
52. Ibid., pp. 16 and 18–19.
53. In a collection of biographical sketches of Michigan educators in 1900 one can find a sizeable number of female high-school principals listed, but they almost always worked in the smallest communities (Caro, Vassar, Blissfield, Allegan, Constantine, Norway, etc.) and retained major teaching responsibilities. *Educators of Michigan: Biographical* (Chicago: J. H. Beers, 1900).
54. Swett, *Public Education in California.*
55. Jesse Stuart, *The Thread That Runs So True* (New York: Scribners, 1949).
56. Mabel Gildart and Mary A. Lord, "A. Fern Persons," in *Michigan History Magazine* 41 (1957), pp. 471–476.
57. Coffman's analysis would seem to contradict the importance of education to occupational mobility. He argues that, for teachers in general in 1909, "There is no uniform tendency or relation existing between salary and education." But he notes that it is the first four years of school after the elementary level (the high-school years) that have little career impact. However, he found that the "correlation between salary and education becomes increasingly marked with each succeeding year after the fourth year." It is precisely this more advanced level of education that those teachers sought who aspired to positions in the high school and beyond. Coffman, *The Social Composition of the Teaching Population,* p. 45. Thorndike found a strong relationship between the education and pay of high-school teachers. Thorndike, "The Teaching Staff of Secondary Schools," p. 41.
58. John Rury has argued this point for teachers in general at the turn of the century, analyzing teachers listed in the 1900 census public-use sample. John L. Rury, "Gender, Salaries, and Career: American Teachers, 1900–1910," in *Issues in Education* 4 (1986), pp. 215–235.
59. A. P. Nightingale, "Ratio of Men to Women in the High Schools of the United States," in *School Review* 4 (1896), pp. 86–98. These averages are at best rough estimates. Some superintendents reported an average pay, but others simply reported two or three pay levels without indicating how many teachers earned each amount. In the latter case, I simply computed the average between the high and low figures, although this probably biases the result upward.
60. Strober and Langford found that in the largely urban school systems where schools were formalized (graded, with a longer school year and more credentials required for teaching), the proportion of female teachers was higher, and so was the pay differential between men and women. Myra H. Strober and Audrey Gordon Langford, "The Feminization of Public School Teaching: Cross-Sectional Analysis, 1850–1880," in *Signs* 11 (1986), pp. 212–235.
61. Nightingale, "Ratio of Men to Women," p. 92.
62. National Education Association, *Report of the Committee on Salaries,* pp. 16 and 106–114.
63. Ibid., pp. 89–90.
64. Myra H. Strober and Laura Best, "The Female/Male Salary Differential in Public Schools: Some Lessons from San Francisco, 1879," in *Economic Inquiry* 17 (1979), pp. 218–236.
65. Arthur G. Powell, "University Schools of Education in the Twentieth Century," in *Peabody Journal of Education* 54 (1976), pp. 3–20.
66. Wayne J. Urban, *Why Teachers Organized* (Detroit: Wayne State University, 1982).
67. Edward E. Redcay, *County Training Schools and Public Secondary Education for Negroes in the South* (Washington, DC: John F. Slater Fund, 1935), p. 57 and 63.
68. Henry A. Bullock, *A History of Negro Education in the South: From 1619 to the Present* (Cambridge: Harvard University Press, 1967), Table 4.
69. This discussion of meritocratic ideology and career advancement owes a considerable amount to David Tyack and Elis-

abeth Hansot, *Managers of Virtue: Public School Leadership in America, 1820–1980* (New York: Basic Books, 1982).

70. Especially for men in the mid-nineteenth century, this entrepreneurship frequently took the form of establishing proprietary schools. It was a common practice for men to gain experience and a following through teaching in the public schools, then cash in by going private. For example, Anson D. P. Van Buren, after teaching in a variety of public schools, took over the proprietary Battle Creek (MI) High School in 1849. Then, a year later, at the urging of local authorities, he merged his school into the public Battle Creek Union School and took over as head. But in 1851 he set up his own select high school in town. Anson D. P. Van Buren, "The Log Schoolhouse Era in Michigan," in Michigan Pioneer and Historical Society *Historical Collections* 14 (1889), pp. 283–403.

71. For an elaboration of this point in relation to one prominent example of such a school, the Central High School of Philadelphia, see David F. Labaree, *The Making of an American High School: The Credentials Market and the Central High School of Philadelphia, 1838–1939* (New Haven: Yale University Press, 1988), Ch. 4.

72. Magali S. Larson, *The Rise of Professionalism: A Sociological Analysis* (Berkeley: University of California, 1977).

7

Teacher Activism

Wayne J. Urban

This chapter looks at teacher activism, focusing mainly on historical studies over the past century. It begins, however, by showing that teachers were, for a variety of reasons, passive prior to the 1890s, and remained so in much of the country (particularly in small towns and rural areas) well after big-city teachers began to flirt with activism in that decade. Most of the teacher activism it describes has been channeled through one or another type of teacher organization—organizations which on occasion have cooperated with other organizations, or with other branches of the school establishment, such as the school administrators or school boards. More often, however, as we shall see, teacher organizations have gone their own way, believing that administrators and boards did not (or could not) speak for them. Before turning to accounts of teacher activism, however, it is appropriate to begin with a short discussion of the first three centuries of teacher activities, a period when teachers were not in a position to attempt actively to shape their occupational lives.

In the seventeenth and eighteenth centuries, and much of the nineteenth, the great bulk of the schools in which American teachers worked were an extension of, and complement to, existing social institutions such as family and church. In this context, teaching was an occupation with a fairly limited set of expectations and qualifications, and teachers tended to make their way in the world as individuals rather than as members of an organized or structured occupation. A teacher's major way to change any condition in the workplace was to move to another school, usually in another town or district. This is not to say that there were no long-lasting, established schools, or veteran teachers therein, but that teaching, by-and-large, was a transient occupation in which teachers were subject to the wishes—perhaps even the whims—of those who employed them.

One popular historical label characterizing this set of circumstances was the "district school."[1] This term refers specifically to the pattern of organization that characterized much of eighteenth- and nineteenth-century American schooling. To say that schools were organized by district is to describe a situation in which the neighborhood in city settings, or a small geographical area in rural settings, served as the unit of governance for the school. Teachers who taught in district schools faced their pupils and the pupils' parents unencumbered, as well as unprotected, by generally accepted work rules or conditions of employment that reflected teachers' expectations. Any influence a teacher possessed in this situation was earned on the job, not given by virtue of external indicators of occupational competence.

Nineteenth-century fiction yields two revealing portraits of the district schoolmaster. One, Washington Irving's Ichabod Crane, the antihero of *The Legend of*

Sleepy Hollow, shows a bumbling, ineffectual schoolmaster who is terrorized by bullies in his upstate New York community. The other, Edward Eggleston's *The Hoosier Schoolmaster,* is an intelligent young Midwestern schoolmaster who manages to outwit the area bullies, who were students in his classroom, and win over the citizens of the Flat Creek school district to the value of his educational ministrations.[2] Whether teachers were portrayed flatteringly by Eggleston or unflatteringly by Irving, the realities of district-school teaching were exposed in both novels.

The schoolmaster was in direct and intimate contact with his clientele—the students and their parents—and neighbors or townsfolk. While on occasion a hoosier schoolmaster like Eggleston's Ralph Hartsook might win over his clients, that victory was often short-lived, as the schoolmaster frequently left to see the greener pastures of a larger district or another occupation, or the town soured on its educator. In this situation, then, teaching was not a stable occupation, and, as often as not, teachers were transient individuals who moved from district to district or who taught school on the way to some other station in life.

The district-school environment, and the district-school ideology of strict community control over the schoolteacher, survived, though in somewhat altered circumstances, in the more rural and small-town areas of the United States until well into the twentieth century. Willard Waller's classic 1932 study, *The Sociology of Teaching,* describes in large part a schoolteacher who is subject to the strict moral scrutiny of the community, embodying the low status of a hired hand who must conform to a variety of community expectations in order to keep his job. Waller does not specifically address the rural or small-town setting which frames his work, but his experiences as professor of sociology at the University of Nebraska, as well as his own upbringing as the son of a school administrator in Illinois, provide the intellectual backdrop for the analysis in his work.[3]

As we shall see, the situation of urban schoolteachers, while different in some ways from that of their rural counterparts, also resembled in significant ways that of their country cousins.

Teacher Movements in the Mid–1800s

In the middle of the nineteenth century the common-school movement, started in Massachusetts and other Northeastern states, sought to alter the organizational structure of the district school. In terms of governance, and the working life of teachers, the key change offered by the common-school movement was the attempted centralization of school affairs, away from the district and toward the town, township, or even state level.

Concomitant with this centralization of governance, particularly at the state level, went the formalization of teacher training through the normal school. The establishment of normal schools meant that more women would be recruited into the teaching force to staff the growing enrollments in the common schools. The increasingly female teaching force meant that the leaders of teachers, mostly male, could use centralization at the local and state levels to develop an occupational hierarchy. The male leaders could use their high places in this developing hierarchy to speak in a voice distinct from, if not completely independent of, the wishes of their clients. Paul Mattingly's discussion of the "friends of education" who participated in the American Institute of Instruction demonstrates how, in the late nineteenth and early twentieth centuries, a male educational hierarchy developed within the teaching "profession," a term then used self-consciously by schoolmen to justify their own positions.[4]

Mattingly also uses the term "bureaucratic" to describe such developments within the teaching occupation. And Michael Katz painstakingly describes the bureaucratization of schooling at the local level that took place in Boston,[5] and also in other cities, at this time. One result of all of this activity was that, by the twentieth century, America's public schools, and particularly its urban public schools, had developed an occupational hierarchy with superintendents at the top, principals and other administrators on the next level, and high-school teachers (often stratified by sex, with males taking the higher-status positions) and elementary teachers at the lowest rung. The educational ideology underlying these arrangements has been described by David Tyack as the notion that there was a "one best system," which all urban public schools should strive to emulate.[6] It is in this context, of a centralizing and bureaucratizing school system, that teachers began to engage in the occupational struggles that have persisted since the late nineteenth century.

The rest of this chapter will look at some of those struggles. The reader should keep in mind that oftentimes these were between and/or among groups within the educational occupation which occupied different places in its hierarchy, as well as with outside forces and actors impinging on teachers.

Teachers and Reform at the Turn of the Century

Centralization of school governance at the local level was a reform movement that swept through many American cities in the late nineteenth and early twentieth centuries. David Tyack has studied this centralization movement in four cities, while Diane Ravitch has concentrated on it in New York.[7] Both of these scholars, as well as other students of the phenomenon, are cognizant of teacher opposition to centralization. They have also noted the community- or locally oriented ideology used by teacher opponents of that centralization.

A close look at that opposition shows also that teachers were more comfortable with the existing ward system of local governance of their cities' schools, because they had used it to develop regularities in occupational promotion. One cannot, and should not, say that teachers enjoyed occupational autonomy under the ward system. Rather, it seems clear that teachers were hired on the basis of whom they knew, as much as on what they knew about the schools, and they could be discharged if they violated community norms within their ward. It should also, however, be said that teachers could (and did) use the seniority system of promotion extant under the ward system to assess their own occupational situation and future prospects.

Teachers were hired at the lowest grade in the school, then moved up, grade by grade (or class by class within a grade), as vacancies occurred in grades above. Salary increases usually accompanied these "promotions." Administrative positions within the school (the principal and assistant principal posts) went to those teachers who had reached the highest-level teaching positions in the school. Principals who did not teach were an unknown phenomenon in most urban school-district elementary schools at this time. In fact, the accession of the full-time elementary principalship in many cities meant a decrease in the number of women principals and an increase in the number of men.[8]

The provision of full-time principals and other administrators was another outcome of the centralization and bureaucratization that occurred in the urban schools during the early twentieth century. Largely unsuccessful in opposing centralization, teachers turned to other possible innovations as a way to deal with the newly forming administrative hierarchy in the public schools. One of the devices sometimes favored by teachers was the teachers council. This body, which was a formal organizational vehicle through which the voice of the teaching force could advise the school administrators, was proposed as early as the 1890s.[9]

In that decade, councils were strongly advocated in Chicago by Ella Flagg Young, a district superintendent there, and teachers who had formed the Chicago Teachers Federation. When Young became Chicago's superintendent in 1909, she attempted to implement the councils in the city's schools, but with indifferent success. Attempts were also made to institute councils in a few other cities in the first 15 years of the twentieth century, and a veritable explosion of proposals for, and implementation of, councils took place in other cities after 1915. Superintendents and university professors of educational administration who proposed councils at this time were much more concerned with the creation of vehicles with which they might head off attempts of teachers to organize unions and other associations independent of the local administration, than they were with establishing legitimate channels to represent the teachers' voice.[10] The demise of the councils in the 1920s, after the first wave of union organizing by teachers had abated, is further indication that they were indeed unsuited to the task of representing teachers in the new world of centralized school bureaucracies.

Teachers' attempts to form their own associations, federations, and unions form the largest part of the story of their search for a way to be heard in the new educational bureaucracies of the twentieth century. One of the earliest, and most successful, attempts of teachers to form their own organization was the Chicago Teachers Federation (CTF), begun in 1897.[11]

The CTF was led for much of its first four decades by Margaret Haley. Studies of both Haley and her organization have emphasized the militance and courage with which this leader pursued the cause of her members. She took on the established businesses in the city, who were utilizing various strategies to avoid paying school taxes, and often pursued her goals in the state legislature when her local efforts were insufficient to achieve them. Haley also led her teachers to oppose the organizational reform efforts of various groups who sought centralization and other alterations in the administrative structure of the Chicago schools not unlike those going on in other cities. Largely unsuccessful in stopping these changes, she did however manage to uncover sources of additional revenue for city agencies through her campaigns against corporate tax evasion. She also was active in municipal tax-reform campaigns elsewhere in the country, often at the invitation of city teacher groups, as well as in the women's suffrage movement, which would come to successful fruition with ratification of the Nineteenth Amendment in 1920.[12]

As Haley pursued her goals for change in the Chicago schools, she brought her teacher group into a close alliance with the local federation of labor, which supported her in her tax battles as well as in other contests on behalf of the schools and their teachers. The Chicago Teachers Federation affiliated with the Chicago Federation of Labor in 1902, and this cooperation between teachers and local organized labor characterized teachers' efforts to improve their conditions in other cities in the country.

Efforts like these at the local level eventually led to the formation of a national teachers' union, the American Federation of Teachers (AFT), which was founded in 1912 and formally affiliated with the American Federation of Labor in 1916. The Chicago Teachers Federation was one of the founding locals in the AFT, as were other teacher groups from Chicago, and Gary, Indiana. Historians have chronicled the rapid early growth of the AFT in the immediate post–World War I years, but have also noted the abrupt halt in the increase of AFT membership in the early 1920s because of the growing strength of school administrators, and a generally conservative political climate nourished by postwar economic conditions.[13]

One explanation for the early success of the AFT stressed the economic plight of teachers confronted with the soaring costs and low salaries that plagued them at the end of World War I. Another pointed up teacher opposition to the new, centralized organizational arrangements, by then firmly entrenched in the city school systems of the country and spreading into the rural districts, in the form of a push for consolidation. Centralization also characterized school affairs at the state level, with increasing power being assumed by state boards of education and state superintendents of schools, neither of whom were particularly interested in the working conditions of teachers.

The decline of the AFT in the early 1920s has been attributed to the antiunion push, known variously as the open-shop movement or the American plan, that characterized industrial relations then. As industrialists moved to reclaim the gains that workers had made (often through unions) during the war years, they branded unions as dangerous, and even un-American. Teachers, who had never embraced organized labor wholeheartedly, were in a poor position to stem the antiunion tide. Thus the first wave of teacher unionism as a vehicle through which teachers might alleviate their economic situations and respond to the new administrative arrangements in the schools was to prove largely unable to maintain its momentum.[14]

Teachers were active elsewhere on the national scene in this period, however, again in pursuit of the twin goals of economic betterment and opposition to the new organizational arrangements that limited their traditional discretion in the schools. The National Education Association, by far the largest group of educators in the country, underwent a series of organizational battles in the years between 1895 and 1923, many of which involved the active participation of teachers. The goals that teachers pursued were diverse: They sought to do something about their salaries, to organize their local classroom-teacher associations into a national federation within the NEA, and to reorganize the NEA so that the teacher voice would be heard within it.[15]

Their achievements were limited, but real. They managed to alleviate the most obvious signs of male administrator dominance in the NEA by pushing through a scheme by which the association presidency would go to a female every other year. Thus, visible leadership of this association alternated between males and females, though the NEA was in fact run by its executive secretary, a male who had close ties to school administrators. Also, teachers participated in an organizational alteration of NEA affairs that took control away from a small, self-perpetuating clique of elite schoolmen and made election of NEA officers dependent on a floor vote at the national convention (a forum heavily influenced by the large number of local teachers who would turn out in whatever city the convention was held).

These efforts would not lead to the realization of an independent teacher voice, however, as teachers were defeated for control of the NEA in the early 1920s by a new group of school administrators who had helped them wrest control from the old guard. Administrators pushed through a representative format for conducting NEA business which channelled any teacher voice through state associations firmly controlled by school administrators.[16]

One of the problems with the existing historical literature on teacher's organizational efforts in the early twentieth century is that those efforts are chronicled most fully at the local and national levels. Organizations at the state level are relatively unstudied—though historians such as Jeffrey Mirel, and David Tyack and his collaborators, have paid *some* attention to state-level activities in the 1930s.[17] This lack of attention to these organizations may be due to the reluctance of professional historians to wrestle with the hagiography that often accompanies dissertation studies of state-level educational organizations. The potential gains to be made in studying state-level organizations, however, should override the dangers of engaging in narrow institutional study of little significance.

The next result of early teacher organizational efforts, then, proved to be largely a disappointment. Whether working through councils, the AFT, or NEA-affiliated groups, teachers were unable to head off the organizational changes that took place in the early twentieth century. By 1925, the schools were firmly controlled by their administrators, and teachers were incorporated into the developing school hierarchies at the lower-rung levels. Their attempts at independent advocacy of their economic interests also proved to be largely futile. Whatever progress that was to be made in teacher working conditions would be made under the patronage of school administrators.

From Disappointment to Depression: The Late 1920s and 1930s

Teachers and their organizations kept a low profile in the late 1920s, at least as measured by the attention given to those activities by historians. AFT and local teacher union membership plummeted in the 1920s, and the NEA retreated in terms of any outright advocacy of the cause of teachers. The advent of the Depression, however, brought teachers back into the limelight of educational affairs, and (since then) historians have taken considerable note of their activities. During the 1930s, teachers often labored in tandem with school administrators and school boards to attempt to mitigate the economic consequences of the Depression in the schools. Jeffrey Mirel has shown how the entire school organization in Detroit, for example, from teachers through administrators and to the board, attempted to head off the budget-cutting efforts of a business-driven movement to control school and other tax expenditures.[18]

In fact, cooperation between teachers and school board, to contain school-budget slashes existed in many cities. In others, however, as David Tyack and his colleagues have shown, teachers and other educators faced implacable opposition from school boards tied to large business interests. In Chicago—to cite an aggravated case—teachers were forced to take to the streets to protest their working conditions and the meager appropriations for the public schools. Their success was at best marginal, but their efforts indicated that teachers were unwilling to submit passively while powerful economic interests tried to control the schools and those who worked in them.[19]

One of the bitterest Depression-era battles involving teachers was waged not with the economically powerful, but with other unionists for control of the American Federation of Teachers. The ostensible issue in the AFT in the 1930s was the role of Communists in the teachers' unions, though there is considerable evidence that the underlying issue was the loss of jobs. By this time, the relatively small AFT membership was made up predominantly of teachers from the nation's largest cities (New York, Chicago, and Philadelphia being the most prominent).

Communists in the big-city locals were strongest in number among the ranks of the unemployed teachers. Critical of the loss of teacher jobs, they managed to obtain influential positions in the New York and Philadelphia locals. Those groups supported Communist-inspired attempts to radicalize the national teachers' union and turn it toward both domestic and international goals favored by the Communist party. Domestically, the plight of the unemployed teacher, an obvious target for those with radical ideas, engaged the attention of Communist unionists, while the union was split over the international issue of whether it would follow a Moscow-prescribed set of positions on political issues not related to the schools.[20]

Teachers themselves turned out to be pawns in this great ideological battle for control of the teachers' union. John Dewey and George Counts, famous intellectual leaders of American education, were pillars of the anti-Communist wing, along with Henry Linville and Abraham Lefkowitz, long-time leaders of the New York local. Their struggle with Communists for control of the union lasted more than five years, until the Communists were expelled.[21] It seemed to consume much of their energy, and almost totally diverted the attention of the union from the everyday problems of teachers that were deepening as the Depression wore on. By the time that the AFT had resolved the dispute, as we will see in the next section of this chapter, the organization was unprepared to respond to the new social and educational conditions created by World War II and its aftermath.

The tunnel vision of the educational intellectuals involved in the fight over communism deserves some comment, particularly since the views of the various ideological camps within teachers' organizations seem more attractive to historians than do the activities and perceptions of teachers. George Counts, whose presidency of the AFT in the late 1930s encompassed the period when the Communists were expelled from the union, is a case-in-point of an educational intellectual who seemed divorced from the concerns and understandings of teachers.

Counts's valuing of ideology over material reality was not confined to the fight over communism in the teachers' union. Perhaps his most famous work, *Dare the School Build a New Social Order?*, published in 1932, called on teachers to "deliberately reach for power" during the crisis of the Depression. Counts reasoned that the socioeconomic background (lower middle- and upper lower-class) of the majority of teachers, combined with the intellectual orientation of much of their work, made them prime candidates to lead the reconstruction of society necessitated by the Depression. Yet, had Counts studied closely the values that permeated much of the teaching force, the ideological predispositions of the very classes from which most teachers were drawn, and the conditions of control under which teachers were working, he would not have been as sanguine about the prospect of teachers leading a social and economic reconstruction.

It should be made clear that consideration of the social makeup of the teaching force and its implications for teacher activism was not lacking in Counts's time. During the same year in which *Dare the School* appeared, Willard Waller published a book which documented and explained the reasons behind the social and occupational conservatism of the teaching force.[22]

More recently, Richard Quantz has completed a set of oral-history interviews with Ohio teachers from one middle-size town which illustrates the ideological and structural obstacles that any meaningful teacher activism faced in the 1930s. From his interviews, Quantz has constructed metaphors which highlight gender, authority structure, the familial image that animated school organization, and the social–psychological perceptions of teachers. All of these predisposed teachers as a group to a passive and accepting stance, rather than one of radical activism.[23]

Although Quantz's analysis, like that of most oral historians, may be questioned on grounds of its generalizations (and perhaps his selective bias toward interview excerpts which support rather than question his metaphors), his work seems to indicate one avenue which historians need to pursue if they are to understand teachers in relation to other power groups in education, as well as many other aspects of teachers' lives. Quantz's work, along with oral histories of teachers by other scholars, promises to enrich the historical literature on teachers and teaching.[24]

Teacher Action in the 1940s and 1950s

The onslaught of World War II caused a marked decline in activism among teachers as many men left teaching to join the armed services, and the men and women who were left in the teaching force got caught up in the patriotism that accompanied the prosecution of the war effort. Almost immediately upon war's end, however, teachers in several cities took unprecedented action to try to mitigate their economic crisis.

Teachers, like most other Americans, were bowled over by the rampant inflation that accompanied the years immediately following the war, as prices that had been controlled by the government during the war soared. In Norwalk, Connecticut in 1946, and in Buffalo, New York and Minneapolis, Minnesota shortly after, teachers resorted to strikes to attempt to redress their grievances. For teachers of that time, strikes were an almost unprecedented weapon. To go on strike was to engage in (usually) illegal activity which graphically contradicted the image of teachers as public servants dedicated to their clients. Strikes also contrasted severely with the "professional" ideology of both of the national teacher organizations (strikes were simply unthinkable to the NEA, and were forbidden by AFT policy), and shocked many segments of the public—and of teachers—outside of the cities in which they took place.[25]

Detailed study of these three local strikes, and a number of other work stoppages that took place in the same period, is lacking. The historian who chooses to provide such study might safely start with the hypothesis that what distinguishes these three cities, and the other places where strikes took place, was their size and industrial character. They had strong labor movements which could be expected to sympathize with, if not provide outright support for, these attempts by teachers to strike to redress their economic grievances. This hypothesis, however, is not a substitute for the close study of these strikes. Such study should answer the question of how or why teachers came to undertake such radical action on their own behalf, 15 years after Counts exhorted them to take it on behalf of the entire society.

Teachers in the 1940s did not react only to war- and postwar-related events. One movement in the occupational arena by black teachers took place outside of both the mainstream teacher organizations and the local and state political arenas that most teacher activities had inhabited. Mark Tushnet's recent study of the NAACP's struggle against segregated education prior to the landmark *Brown* v. *Board* case of the 1950s highlights the legal battles that the civil rights group and its local affiliates waged against various aspects and consequences of school segregation, frequently with the cooperation of the segregated teacher organizations into which black teachers were forced. One of the major issues on which Tushnet focuses is the struggle, by black teachers for salaries equal to those of white teachers, that took place throughout the 1940s. The blacks' fight for equal pay, in the form of a single salary schedule for black and white teachers, involved court action, or the threat of such action, in many Southern cities and towns. Detailed case studies of some of these situations, while extant, are in unpublished dissertations.[26] Local case studies should supplement Tushnet's national and organizational focus, so that a more complete picture of the power struggles of black teachers can emerge.

Black teachers' fight for equal pay in the 1940s paralleled the early twentieth-century fight of women teachers, in New York city and elsewhere, for equal pay with men who did the same job as the women. Blacks' battle for equal pay also soon found its own echoes in the fight of women teachers in the late 1940s and 1950s for a single salary scale on which elementary teachers (overwhelmingly female) would be paid the same as secondary teachers (largely male).[27] This conflict within the education profession in the 1940s is another largely unstudied phenomenon, even by feminist historians who might be expected to pay attention to such a successful movement by women teachers. Close study of the achievement of a single salary scale by elementary teachers would enormously enrich our stock of knowledge of teachers as actors in policy disputes.

The gradual entrenchment of the single salary scale in the 1940s yielded a countertrend that many teachers found discomfiting: merit pay plans. These schemes had been tried in the schools as early as the 1910s, then seemingly in reaction to the recently enacted idea of teachers being paid on a salary scale. The renewed enthusiasm for merit pay in the 1940s and 1950s was directly related to the emergence of the single salary scale that brought the pay of women elementary teachers to the same level as that of their high-school (largely male) colleagues. Merit pay schemes in both the earlier period and at mid-century foundered because of their lack of precision, their potential for unfairness, and the long and protracted opposition of teachers and their organizations. The differentiated staffing plans of the 1960s were yet another attempt to introduce a merit pay scheme, and their indifferent success testifies both to the lack of precision and attention to fairness in their design and implementation, and to the implacable opposition of teacher groups.[28]

In the 1950s, teachers continued to experience the economic disadvantage of salaries that were not keeping pace with costs. They were not overcoming the gap between their pay and a decent standard of living, a situation their organizations had complained about since the immediate post–World War II years. Adoption of a single salary scale had not resolved the situation. It meant that all teachers would be paid on the same scale, not necessarily that the scale would equate with teachers' own ideas of a decent standard of living, or proper remuneration for their considerable efforts.

Teacher Organizing and Strikes in the 1960s and 1970s

The explosion of teacher strikes that plagued the public schools in the 1960s and 1970s continued, though in a substantially diminished fashion, into the 1980s. At its beginnings in the 1960s, the movement for teacher strikes was rooted in teachers' dissatisfaction with their salaries and other working conditions in the 1950s. In fact, the actual strike that is usually seen as the beginning of the modern era in educational labor relations, the New York strike of 1960, had intimate ties with the salary issues that had concerned teachers since World War II.

One cannot claim that the New York City teacher's strikes of the 1960s are understudied phenomena; in fact, that city's teachers and their organizations constitute one of the most comprehensively researched subjects in educational historiography. The problem with much of this work is that it has been written to address the ideological conflicts that plagued the New York local for most of its history, rather than the struggle of New York's teachers for occupational betterment.[29]

For the best insights into relations between the 1960s strikes in New York City and the conditions of the late 1940s which undergirded them, a sociologist, Stephen Cole, is the most fruitful source. Cole's study titled *The Unionization of Teachers* tied the militance of the United Federation of Teachers (UFT) the group which led the 1960 strike, to its mostly male and junior high-school teacher membership. These teachers were smarting from both the general economic conditions plaguing teachers, and the psychological slight of their being forced to be remunerated on the same scale as the women elementary teachers. Cole skillfully wove together the many strands of the early history of the UFT. He detailed its emergence as the one teacher voice in the city from the babble of voices of several teacher organizations representing different levels of teaching as well as different subject matters (a situation which dated back at least to the turn of the twentieth century). Cole showed how the UFT used the strike to cement itself in the minds of more and more teachers as the best choice for all teachers interested in ameliorating their economic conditions and standing up for themselves.[30]

Much of the success of the UFT, and other militant local unions, in waging and winning strikes during the 1960s should be attributed to the climate of the times. The relatively successful struggle of labor unions in the basic industries of the United States, such as steel and automobiles during the later 1950s and 1960s, surely spurred the teachers and their organizations. And the successful militance of black citizens in the civil rights movement was another prod to teacher militance. But the astute manipulation of situations and organizations by the teacher leaders of this period was another part of the reality that deserves attention.

Perhaps the most famous teacher leader to emerge from this period is Albert Shanker, activist and officer in the UFT during its first strikes. Shanker skillfully maneuvered through the strikes and the internal squabbles in the teachers' organization to become president of the UFT and, later, of its organizational parent, the American Federation of Teachers. (As of this printing he still held the national presidency.) Shanker himself has yet to produce a memoir of his early and subsequent union activities. Other unionists, however, have not been as silent.

David Selden, an early colleague of Shanker in UFT affairs who became the national AFT president in the early 1960s, has produced a rich memoir of early teacher organizing and subsequent infighting among the union leaders.[31] Selden and Shanker, after some years of teaching in the schools, worked together in early UFT organizing, but soon split over a variety of issues. From Selden's perspective, the dispute centered on his own ideological commitments to the larger social struggle, of which teacher unionism should be a part clashing with the pragmatic, opportunistic, and limited approach of his early colleague and later rival. Since Albert Shanker has yet to address himself to the issues raised by Selden, the student of teacher's activism in the 1960s and thereafter can only anticipate, and speculate about, this unionist's response to Selden's criticism.

In addition to the realities of teacher strikes and activism in the 1960s and after, students of that activism were also confronted with a theoretical rationale for it from an educational intellectual trained in the philosophy of education. Myron Lieberman produced two enormously influential books in the latter part of the 1950s. In *Education as a Profession* (1956) and *The Future of Public Education* (1960),

Lieberman provided both a manifesto and a program of action for emerging teacher organizations.

In the former volume, Lieberman methodically attacked those teachers and administrators who opposed teacher unions and teacher strikes as unprofessional. He rigorously analyzed the concept of professionalism, exposed the variety of ways in which teachers did not measure up to the label of professional, and skillfully argued that strong organizations were the major avenue that teachers could use to become more professional. In the latter volume, he continued his argument that teachers could become professional through strong organizations, and added to it the thesis that only by concentrating on the national arena and national educational policy could the reality of a truly professional teaching force come about.[32] He here took on the shibboleth of local control in American education, arguing that it was mindlessly invoked by teachers and teacher leaders. For Lieberman, however, local control really served as a vehicle for the economic penuriousness and educational narrowness that were hampering teacher attempts at professionalism, as well as any other educational improvements.

In both books Lieberman addressed himself specifically to the two national teachers' organizations, the National Education Association and the American Federation of Teachers. The first group he saw as a pseudo teacher organization, hampered in its advocacy of teachers and their causes because of its dominance by administrators. The second group, while more obviously reflecting teachers' economic interests, was criticized by Lieberman for the narrowness of its agenda. Concentrating on economic issues meant, for Lieberman, that the AFT did not address the seminal issues of teacher professionalization. Until the AFT confronted issues like teacher control over entry into the occupation, it would be able to provide only a very small part of the agenda that Lieberman considered important for the occupation.[33]

It is difficult to gauge the impact of the ideas of someone like Myron Lieberman on the development of teacher organizations. It might be said that he simply capitalized on what was already happening in the educational world, and attempted to build on that reality by providing a blueprint for the future. The outcome of his projections was mixed. His criticism of the NEA as administrator-dominated evidently was heard, as that group adopted a constitutional revision in the mid-1970s that left teachers clearly in command of the association. The subsequent departure of school superintendents, and elementary and secondary principals, was further testimony to the rise of teacher power within the NEA.

Lieberman also sought a merger between the NEA and the AFT, a marriage which appeared for a time in the 1970s to be in the offing as Albert Shanker's New York local and state unions also affiliated, briefly, with the NEA. Given the NEA's discard of administrator dominance, its increasing willingness to wear the label of teachers' union, and the brief period when the merger did occur in New York and a few other locations, it seemed that the obstacles to merger to these two groups were no longer ideological. Rather, the breakup of the merger in New York seemed to have been the result of the leaders of each group fearing loss of autonomy and reputation to the other, as well as of personal differences perhaps based on fear of loss of status and power.[34]

Ironically, Lieberman's own subsequent professional agenda included an abandonment of his commitment to teacher professionalization and teacher organizations at the same time that those organizations appeared to be responding to his recommendations. In a book published in 1986, he argued against collective bargaining and teacher unions, promoting in their place a free-market agenda in education which related hardly at all to his ideas about a professional teaching force.[35]

Confrontations and Accommodations: Notes on the Aftermath

The past quarter-century of teachers' strikes and other militant organizational activity has not passed without some interesting, and perhaps even unexpected, reactions. Most notably, the 1968 teachers' strike in New York City resulted in teachers being confronted by angry black parents who spearheaded a thrust for more community control in the city's schools. This movement threatened the job-security and other work-rule provisions that teachers had long fought for in citywide bargaining. The confrontation took on the name of the school district in which it took place, Ocean Hill–Brownsville. Impetus for the dispute came from a black community bereft of opportunities to implement the desegregation of schools promised in the *Brown* decision because of city schools that were becoming more and more minority enrolled, and a school bureaucracy choking on the size and complexity of its own organizational structure.

To deal with these problems, the city school board accepted the report of a Ford Foundation panel and decided to experiment with the decentralization of the public schools by creating three demonstration districts. Each experimental district was assigned a unit administrator and was to have a community board to advise that person. The district administrator and board in Ocean Hill–Brownsville soon came into conflict with the teachers' union, as well as with a group representing school principals. Ocean Hill–Brownsville district officials sought to transfer teachers and principals out of the district whom they deemed unacceptable to the community. The teacher and principal organizations saw these transfers as a repudiation of transfer procedures that had been negotiated with the board of education in collective-bargaining agreements. In accord with those provisions, they argued that no teacher could be transferred, except by the provisions of the contract that included presentation of charges against an individual, and the opportunity to have a hearing where the charges could be aired and answered.[36]

The issue of community officials' rights to participate in the meaningful education of their children versus teachers' rights to protection against unwarranted dismissal or transfer soon was complicated by racial overtones. The largely Jewish teaching force confronted an angry black community in many parts of the city, and ugly racial incidents in the demonstration district, and elsewhere in the city, proliferated. Extremists on both sides intensified the situation through a variety of provocative actions. Teachers struck on three separate occasions in the spring and fall of 1968 over the issue of involuntary transfers, the latter two strikes being citywide.[37]

The ultimate resolution of the dispute was initially harmful to the teachers' union. The UFT was convicted of an unlawful strike, and its leadership was fined. This confrontation between teacher rights and community prerogatives marked an alteration of the militant teacher's image in New York City. Up to this time, teacher organizations could claim to be on the side of the schools' clients, students and their parents, as teachers sought better benefits and working conditions. Improvement in teacher pay and working conditions, such as smaller class size, meant also a better school experience for students. The dispute over Ocean Hill, however, meant that white teachers, at least in New York City, could be (and were) perceived as part and parcel of the alien white world by black parents and students.[38]

A similar outcome, though one not related to racial issues, resulted from the statewide walkout of teachers in Florida in February of 1968. The 35,000 teachers who left their classrooms there claimed that their actions were motivated not by economic concerns, but by their desire to see their students get a better education. In a skilled propaganda campaign that split the majority of teachers who had walked out, the governor and local and state school officials were able to turn the teacher association's argument around: If teachers really were acting for the sake of their students, they had no business walking out of the schools in the first place.[39]

Though the results in both New York and Florida put teacher organization advocates on the defensive ideologically, they did not diminish the strength of those organizations in either locale. The United Federation of Teachers emerged from the Ocean Hill–Brownsville dispute in a healthy organizational state. It provided the impetus for a merger between the NEA and the AFT in the city and state of New York which, though short-lived, indicated the commitment of teachers throughout the state to the brand of activist protection of teacher rights characteristic of the New York City union and its leader, Albert Shanker. In Florida, the Florida Education Association suffered a severe defeat in the 1968 walkout, but within five years, union and association groups had merged. Florida's teacher organizations had rebuilt themselves in both the public schools and the state university system in that state, to the point where they were powerful and reasonably effective advocates of teacher causes.[40]

It is arguable whether the Florida and New York City outcomes were related to the decline in the number of teacher strikes that occurred in their aftermath. It is clear, however, that the incidence of teacher strikes has subsequently declined, though there still are some strikes every year (usually in the fall, as school commences). The decline in strikes, however, can be seen as a tactical move by teacher organizations, rather than as a sign that they no longer are vigorous advocates of their members. Their advocacy of the teachers' cause, particularly in the 1980s, has taken some precedented—and some unprecedented—turns.

Teachers Against the Tide in the 1980s

The dominance of national politics by a series of conservative presidential administrations since the end of Lyndon Johnson's term of office in 1968 has meant a gradual diminishing of federal attention to financial help for schools, and a definite lack of sympathy for the causes of teacher organizations on the part of the federal government. Teacher organizations have suffered the same decline in image and influence that has affected the larger labor movement in this period, despite the fact that both the NEA and the AFT have increased their influence in the formal circles of the Democratic party. While Jimmy Carter's fulfillment of a campaign promise to create a cabinet-level Department of Education endeared him to the NEA, which had sought that outcome since 1917, it has not meant significant new federal monies for schools or teachers.

The years of Ronald Reagan's two administrations, commencing in 1980, meant a marked decline in federal educational effort, at least as that effort could be measured in dollars and cents. Reagan administration personnel, however, were not silent on educational affairs. To many teachers and other educators, it seemed that Reagan officials were engaged in a war with the public schools, as part of their larger war with most public provisions in American society. However they were perceived by educators, Reaganites kept up a steady drumbeat of "educational excellence" rhetoric, beginning with publication of *A Nation at Risk* in 1983. This volume decried the level of learning in public schools and prescribed, as the solution for it, not increased funding but rather a renewed commitment to excellence in education.[41]

The federal thrust for excellence was echoed in the halls of many state governments. Governors such as Lamar Alexander of Tennessee, William Winter of Mississippi, Thomas Kean of New Jersey, and Joe Frank Harris of Georgia undertook as one of their prime challenges the improvement of schools. Taking declining Scholastic Aptitude Test scores, and scores on other standardized achievement tests, as prime indicators of educational malaise, these politicians sought, through a number of programs and policies, to produce results that would justify their efforts at educational change. Politically savvy superintendents, also, tended to make an increase in test scores a mark of achievement for their own administrations.[42] In the eyes of many teachers, however, it took little more than common sense to see that standardized test scores were a reflection of social, economic, and educational factors not likely to be subject to the quick fixes of politicians or ambitious superintendents. If such scores were to be increased quickly, these numbers almost surely reflected surface factors, and not any deep or long-lasting changes in educational quality.

One ramification of the reform efforts of the 1980s of relevance to this chapter was the attempt to introduce a career ladder, or other similar change, into teacher employment practices. In one way or another a career ladder seeks to divide the occupation of teacher into several ascending steps of increasing competence and responsibility, and to pay teachers differentially according to their place on the ladder. From the point of view of the organized teachers there seemed little doubt that the career ladder was a latter-day version of merit pay provisions that they, like teachers before them, had long fought against.

What was interesting in the discussion of various career-ladder plans, however, was the relative lack of unanimity of the teacher organizations in opposing this latest version of merit pay. The AFT showed itself more inclined to tolerate career-ladder plans than did the NEA, though neither group flatly opposed the notion. This lack of clear-cut opposition may have reflected a weakening in the organizational clout of teacher organizations, which realized that they could not stem the tide of attack on their members from politicians who reflected the general conservative tone of 1980s politics.[43]

Another plausible explanation for organized teacher actions, particularly when the stance on career ladders is combined with organized teacher participation in establishing a national standards board and national examination for teachers, is that the organizations were finally realizing, at least in part, the professional agenda set for them by Myron Lieberman in the 1960s. Teacher participation and cooperation in the setting of standards for entry through national examinations, and for promotion through a career ladder, is a long way from teacher control over the teaching occupation, however. Yet, perhaps a national system of employment standards and a state-regulated promotion scheme could eventually be controlled by teachers, after the politicians and other lay members of the reform coalitions lose interest in the schools.

College and university schools, departments, and colleges of education were, *in toto,* another kind of player in the new licensing-and-promotion game of the 1980s, however—a player who could be expected to stick it out with the teacher organizations long after the others have tired of the game. The ultimate resolution (if there is to be one) of the 1980s reforms in teacher employment and teacher education, and of the role of teacher organizations in this process, is sure to be of considerable interest to future historians.

Teachers and Historians

Some concluding comments about educational historians, the producers of most of the data on which this chapter has been based, seem to be in order. The first concerns the relative paucity of studies bearing directly on teachers and their attempts at occupational activism: Unlike many "topics" in educational history, teachers remain largely unstudied. Revisionist scholars, who since 1960 have enriched educational historiography, have been strangely silent on the topics of teachers, their activities, and their organizations. True, the impact of women's history on the history of education gives some promise that this situation will be remedied. And the work of Polly Kaufman, Geraldine Clifford, and Nancy Hoffman and her contributors has been particularly welcomed. Yet all of these authors have ignored teacher militance as a focus of their efforts.[44]

Looking at the work that has been done concerning teachers, the relatively nonanalytical character of it also deserves mention. Historians devoting their work to teachers and their activities, this writer included, have proved more adept at narrating teachers' struggles than at explaining them in ways that can be enlightening to nonhistorians and students of education policy. Perhaps the adoption of methodological and conceptual tools drawn from the social sciences could prove helpful to historians of teacher activism.

My own view, however, is not to turn to the social sciences for models of historical study. My preference is to look at studies of teachers and their organizations done in other countries—particularly in England, Canada, and Australia—as a source from which to draw ideas about our own work.

In England: Jenny Ozga and Martin Lawn have studied teachers in relation to issues of class and professionalism. Lawn also has been working on oral histories of teachers in England and Wales, has edited a book on teachers unions and political issues which contains essays on teachers in eight national settings, and has coedited a book on teacher work.[45] In Australia: Andrew Spaull has looked at federal (and several state) teacher organizations in his country; has compared Australian teachers, their organizations, and their policy roles, with their counterparts (and their related contributions) in Canada and the USA; and has coauthored a book on industrial relations in Australia's educational sector.[46] It is refreshing to view the efforts of scholars from other settings to study their own teaching force, and it is instructive to note the frank identification of these authors with the cause of the teachers they are studying. Such identification often is a problem for American historians overly leery of being seen as partisans or having their objectivity questioned.

Perhaps one of the major sources of both the strength of commitment of Lawn and Spaull to the teachers' cause, and the value of their studies of teachers, is their working within the confines of what, for lack of a better term, we might call a neo-Marxist tradition. Those of us in American educational history who are interested in teachers have avoided such ideas and frameworks. There no doubt are good reasons for this shyness, but it seems clear to at least this writer that the time has come to consider the categories of neo-Marxist historians such as Lawn and Spaull as guides for our own work. We should also note that nonhistorian, domestic neo-Marxists such as Michael Apple have written cogent analyses of the contemporary plight of teachers who are being systematically deskilled by various reform policies.[47] One does not have to embrace the entire agenda of neo-Marxism, or any other ideological movement, to profit from the insights that it can provide.

One other point that historians of teacher activism in the United States might take from foreign and domestic neo-Marxists is their commitment to the ideology of public schooling. Both the English and the Australians have had direct and intimate experience with the consequences of the privatization so greatly favored in the 1980s in Washington, DC. Perhaps the time has come for American educational historians to restate their *own* commitment to the ideal of public schooling. Surely the attempts of public school teachers to act on their own behalf in the twentieth century can be seen as a part of that ideal.

Notes

1. Robert L. Church and Michael W. Sedlak, *Education in the United States: An Interpretive History* (New York: Free Press, 1976), Ch. 1.
2. Washington Irving, *The Legend of Sleepy Hollow* (New York: The American Arts Union, 1849), and Edward Eggleston, *The Hoosier Schoolmaster: An Engaging Story of Life in a Backwoods Village of Indiana in the 1850's* (New York: Hart Publ. Co., 1976).
3. Willard Waller, *The Sociology of*

Teaching (New York: Science Editions, 1965; reprint of 1932 edition). On Waller's career, see William J. Goode, Frank F. Furstenberg, Jr., and Larry R. Mitchell, "Willard W. Waller—A Portrait," in Goode, Furstenberg, and Mitchell (eds.), *Willard W. Waller on the Family, Education, and War* (Chicago: University of Chicago Press, 1970), pp. 1–110. For the Nebraska locale and rural character of much of *The Sociology of Teaching*, see Goode, Furstenberg, and Mitchell, "Willard W. Waller—A Portrait," pp. 39–40.

4. Paul H. Mattingly, *The Classless Profession: American Schoolmen in the Nineteenth Century* (New York: New York Univerity Press, 1975).
5. Michael B. Katz, *Class, Bureaucracy, and Schools: The Illusion of Educational Change in America* (New York: Praeger, 1975), Ch. 2.
6. David B. Tyack, *The One Best System: A History of American Urban Education* (Cambridge: Harvard University Press, 1974).
7. Ibid.; and Diane Ravitch, *The Great School Wars* (New York: Basic Books, 1974). pp. 107–158.
8. Wayne J. Urban, *Why Teachers Organized* (Detroit: Wayne State University Press, 1982), pp. 29–32.
9. Ibid., p. 35–36..
10. Ibid., pp. 42–43; and Elmer John Ortman, *Teacher Councils: The Organized Means for Securing the Co-operation of All Workers in the School* (Montpelier, VT: Capital City Press, 1923), pp. 78–79.
11. The best account of the Chicago Teachers Federation is Robert L. Reid, "The Professionalization of Public School Teachers: The Chicago Experience, 1895–1920," doctoral dissertation, Northwestern University, 1963.
12. On Haley and the CTF, see Urban, *Why Teachers Organized*, Ch. 3; Reid, "Professionalization," *passim;* Robert L. Reid (ed.), *Battleground: The Autobiography of Margaret Haley* (Urbana: University of Illinois Press, 1982); and Marvin Lazerson, "Teachers Organize: What Margaret Haley Lost," in *History of Education Quarterly* 24 (1984), pp. 261–270.
13. Urban, *Why Teachers Organized*, Ch. 6; and William Edward Eaton, *The American Federation of Teachers, 1916–1961: A History of the Movement* (Carbondale: Southern Illinois University Press, 1975), Ch. 2.
14. Urban, *Why Teachers Organized*, Ch. 6; and Eaton, *The American Federation of Teachers*, Ch. 3.
15. Urban, *Why Teachers Organized*, Ch. 5.
16. Ibid.; and Frederick S. Buchanan, "Unpacking of the N.E.A.: The Role of Utah's Teachers at the 1920 Convention," in *Utah Historical Quarterly* 41 (1973), pp. 150–161.
17. Jeffrey Mirel, "The Politics of Educational Retrenchment in Detroit, 1929–1935," in *History of Education Quarterly* 24 (1984), pp. 323–358; and David Tyack, Robert Lowe, and Elisabeth Hansot, *Public Schools in Hard Times: The Great Depression and Recent Years* (Cambridge: Harvard University Press, 1984), pp. 85–91. On state educational activities, see also David Tyack, Thomas James, and Aaron Benavot, *Law and the Shaping of Public Education, 1785–1954* (Madison: University of Wisconsin Press, 1987), Ch. 4.
18. Mirel, "The Politics of Educational Retrenchment."
19. Tyack, Lowe, and Hansot, *Public Schools in Hard Times.*
20. Eaton, *The American Federation of Teachers*, Ch. 5; and Lana Muraskin, "The Teachers Union and the City of New York," doctoral dissertation, University of California at Berkeley, 1979.
21. Eaton, *The American Federation of Teachers*, Ch. 5; and Joseph W. Newman and Wayne J. Urban, "Communists in the American Federation of Teachers: A Too Often Told Story," in *History of Education Review* 14 (1985), pp. 15–24.
22. George S. Counts, *Dare the School Build a New Social Order?* (Carbondale: Southern Illinois University Press, 1978; reprint of 1932 edition); Eaton,

Ch. 4; and Tyack, Lowe, and Hansot, *Public Schools in Hard Times,* p. 27. Counts's *Dare the School* may be contrasted with Waller's *Sociology of Teaching,* published in the same year.

23. Richard A. Quantz, "The Complex Visions of Female Teachers and the Failure of Unionization in the 1930s: An Oral History," in *History of Education Quarterly* 25 (1985), pp. 439–458.

24. Ibid. Richard Altenbaugh of Northern Illinois University, and Rodman Webb and Patricia Ashton of the University of Florida also have done extensive, historically oriented interviewing of teachers.

25. Eaton, *The American Federation of Teachers,* pp. 143–151.

26. Mark Tushnet, *The NAACP Legal Strategy Against Segregated Education, 1925–1950* (Chapel Hill: University of North Carolina Press, 1987), Chs. 4, 5, and 6; Joseph W. Newman, "A History of the Atlanta Public School Teachers' Association, Local 89 of the American Federation of Teachers, 1919–1956," doctoral dissertation, Georgia State University, 1978; and Lawrence E. Block, "The History of the Public School Teachers Association of Baltimore City: A Study of the Internal Politics of Education," doctoral dissertation, John Hopkins University, 1972.

27. Grace Strachan, *Equal Pay for Equal Work* (New York: B. F. Buck, 1910); and Urban, *Why Teachers Organized,* pp. 91–99 and 177.

28. Wayne J. Urban, "Old Wine, New Bottles? Merit Pay and Organized Teachers," in Henry Johnson (ed.), *Merit, Money and Teachers' Careers: Studies on Merit Pay and Career Ladders for Teachers* (Lanham, MD; University Press of America, 1985), p. 25–38.

29. For highly ideologically charged accounts of the New York locals' history, compare Philip Taft, *United They Teach: The Story of the United Federation of Teachers* (Los Angeles: Nash Publishing, 1974), with Celia Lewis Zitron, *The New York City Teachers Union, 1916–1964: A Story of Educational and Social Commitment* (New York: Humanities Press, 1968).

30. Stephen Cole, *The Unionization of Teachers: A Case Study of the UFT* (New York: Praeger, 1969), Ch. 3.

31. David Selden, *The Teacher Rebellion* (Washington, DC: Howard University Press, 1985).

32. Myron Lieberman, *Education as a Profession* (Englewood Cliffs, NJ: Prentice-Hall, 1956); and Lieberman, *The Future of Public Education* (Chicago: University of Chicago Press, 1960).

33. Lieberman, *The Future of Public Education,* Ch. 9; and Lieberman, *Education as a Profession,* Chs. 9 and 10.

34. Marshall O. Donley, Jr., *Power to the Teacher: How America's Educators Became Militant* (Bloomington, IN: Indiana University Press, 1976), Ch. 11.

35. Myron Lieberman, *Beyond Public Education* (New York: Praeger, 1986).

36. Ravitch, *Great School Wars,* pp. 251–361.

37. Ibid., Ch. 33.

38. Ibid., Ch. 35.

39. Wayne J. Urban, "The Effects of Ideology and Power on a Teacher Walkout: Florida, 1968," in *Journal of Collective Negotiations in the Public Sector* 3 (1974), pp. 133–146.

40. Donley, *Power to the Teacher,* Ch. 11.

41. The National Commission on Excellence in Education, *A Nation at Risk* (Washington, DC: Government Printing Office, 1983).

42. Wayne J. Urban, "The Illusion of Educational Reform in Georgia," in *Journal of Thought* 22 (1987), pp. 31–36.

43. Urban, "Old Wine, New Bottles?"

44. Geraldine Jonçich Clifford, "Home and School in Nineteenth-Century America Some Personal History Reports from the United States," in *History of Educatio Quarterly* 18 (1978), pp. 3–34; Poll Welts Kaufman, *Women Teachers o the Frontier* (Hartford, CT: Yale Uni versity Press, 1984); and Nancy Hoff man (ed.), *Woman's "True" Pr*

fession: Voices from the History of Teaching (Old Westbury, NY: Feminist Press, 1981).

45. J. T. Ozga and M. A. Lawn, *Teachers, Professionalism and Class* (London: Falmer Press, 1981); Martin Lawn (ed.-), *The Politics of Teacher Unionism: International Perspectives* (Dover, NH: Croom Helm, 1985); and Martin Lawn and Gerald Grace (eds.), *Teachers: The Culture and Politics of Work* (Philadelphia: The Falmer Press, 1987).
46. Andrew Spaull et al., *Teacher Unionism in the 1980s: Four Perspectives* (Hawthorn, Victoria, Australia: Australian Council for Educational Research, 1986); A. D. Spaull (ed.), *Australian Teachers, from Colonial Schoolmasters to Militant Professionals* (Melbourne: Macmillan, 1976); and Andrew Spaull and Kevin Hince, *Industrial Relations and State Education in Australia* (Melbourne: AE Press, 1986).
47. Michael Apple, *Teachers and Texts: A Political Economy of Class and Gender Relations in Education* (New York: Routledge & Kegan Paul/Methuen, 1987).

SECTION

THREE

Teacher Education and Certification

Over the past two centuries, the reform of teacher preparation and certification has largely been a case of "more is better." Teacher-education institutions appeared early in the nineteenth century, gradually lengthening their programs from one to four or five years. During this period other changes occurred as well. Pre-service teacher preparation became primarily a function of public institutions, and it was elevated from essentially high-school to college-level work. A recent proposal calls for it to be raised to yet a higher level: the graduate course of study. The institutions that currently prepare most American teachers began as normal schools or teacher seminaries. Today they are regional state colleges and universities. In the late nineteenth century, research universities entered the teacher-education market, and while they have never dominated the field relative to the numbers of new teachers prepared, they have become the centers of educational research in the United States.

This institutional development is well known. Willard Elsbree had it in mind when he referred optimistically to the "evolution" of teacher professionalism. Even so, it contains several curious wrinkles. When this oft-noted success story becomes the focus of the history of teacher education, for example, one can miss the fact that most nineteenth-century teachers did not attend these institutions. Rather, they received formal on-the-job preparation through teacher institutes organized by state and local school authorities. Not until the twentieth century was pre-service teacher education common, and not until the 1950s did the majority of American teachers hold four-year college degrees. Muted as well in this evolutionary account are the status conflicts that have haunted teacher education from the outset: between institutions preparing secondary- and elementary-school teachers, within the education professorate, and between the education and the arts and sciences faculties. Finally, there is the special case of black teacher education and certification, which Elsbree ignored altogether.

The chapters in Section Three attempt to untangle these various threads. Jurgen Herbst focuses on teacher education in the past century, and William Johnson zeroes in on twentieth-century developments. Michael Sedlak traces the history of hiring practices and teacher certification since the late eighteenth century. Despite their specialized interests, the authors demonstrate why the history of teacher education and professionalization must be linked conceptually to the history of teachers. His reading of the latter leads Herbst to view as illusory the classification of teaching as a profession. He sees little hope that reforms of teacher education, however dramatic, can alone correct working conditions that have made teaching merely an occupation.

8

Teacher Preparation in the Nineteenth Century

Institutions and Purposes

Jurgen Herbst

A common theme runs through two major reports on teaching and teacher education issued in 1986. Both *Tomorrow's Teachers: A Report of the Holmes Group*, and *A Nation Prepared: Teachers for the Twenty-first Century*, the recommendations of the Carnegie Forum on Education and the Economy's Task Force on Teaching as a Profession, conclude that teaching in America's public schools will not improve and live up to the demands of the nation until classroom teachers see themselves, and come to be accepted by the public, as professionals.[1]

The Holmes Group asks that the education of teachers become more solid intellectually; that distinctions between beginners and more-competent teachers be recognized, entrance standards into the profession be raised, and the education of teachers be undertaken through active cooperation among universities and schools. Above all, in their schools and classrooms, teachers must exercise a greater degree of autonomy and professional leadership than they do now.[2]

The Carnegie Task Force seeks the same objectives through the creation of a National Board for Professional Teaching Standards, the restructuring of schools and the teaching profession, and the improvement of undergraduate education and graduate training of teachers. The report recommends that we provide incentives for minority members to enter teaching, and that teachers improve student performance. Teacher salaries and career opportunities, they urge, must become "competitive with those in other professions."[3]

The historian cannot but feel a sense of *déjà vu*. While the specific proposals of the two reports express contemporary views and solutions, the observer recognizes the persistence of the underlying theme. Ever since the 1830s, educational reformers have demanded that schoolteaching be elevated to the point of recognition as a profession. To Horace Mann, Henry Barnard, and their fellow crusaders, that meant the introduction of schools and programs of teacher education.

Teacher education has lain at the heart of all attempts at professionalization. The history of that movement throughout the nineteenth century in particular does not present an encouraging story. Indeed, the accomplishments of the movement then were severely limited, its failures many. As I shall try to point out, there was a persistent tendency to move away from what had been the initial—and never quite fulfilled—demand to prepare teachers for rural classrooms. Instead, students and others sought out normal schools and teachers colleges in search of post-elementary and, later, post-secondary general education. (One can easily imagine faculty members in the teacher-training institutions longing to offer more prestigious intellectual fare than instruction for elementary-school teachers.) The very ambivalence that hovers over the story helps to explain why in the 1980s, after 150 years of efforts to educate and train teachers for the public schools, we still hear the same demand that all our teachers finally become professionals.

Models for Massachusetts Normal Schools

The first endeavors in the United States to transform schoolkeeping into schoolteaching and to establish the latter as a profession through the opening of state normal schools date back to the public school revival of the 1830s. Mann and his supporters had drawn their inspiration partly from domestic and partly from foreign sources. A decade earlier, James C. Carter had urged that a state-supported and -directed institution be created for the training of common-school teachers. In such a school would be taught "the science of the development of the infant mind and . . . of communicating knowledge from one mind to another while in a different stage of maturity." The school's mission was to be the consolidation of the amateurish efforts of school supervision inherent in the decentralized district system. Only thus, wrote Carter, could Massachusetts "secure, at once, a uniform, intelligent, and independent tribunal for decisions on the qualifications of teachers."[4]

News of, and suggestions about, teacher education also came from across the ocean. In his book *Travels in the North of Germany,* Henry Edwin Dwight reported in 1829 that in Prussia only trained and certified teachers were permitted to teach. They were instructed in teacher seminars for two or three years in "the best methods of educating and of governing children as well as in the subjects they are to teach." Were such seminars to be established in the United States, Dwight suggested, one could expect that schoolteaching would "soon become a distinct profession."[5]

The same point was brought home in the June 1831 issue of the *American Annals of Education and Instruction.* The journal's editor, William Channing Woodbridge, a Congregational clergyman and ardent promoter of Pestalozzian pedagogy, published a translated report on teacher seminars in Prussia. In that country, he wrote, teaching was viewed as a profession:

> Teachers pursue the business for life and, like clergymen, are settled in particular places from which they rarely remove. The average of the time which they are usually able to devote to their professions [sic] is about *thirty-three* years; and they are generally about twenty-four years old when they engage as instructors.

In the seminars, instruction was offered "in the most practical manner; technical terms and subtle niceties, divisions and arrangements, are avoided as much as possible." Model schools attached to the seminars gave would-be teachers a chance to try their hands at actual classroom teaching.[6]

In these descriptions it was taken for granted that teachers were men. But that was not always the case. In August of 1831, Woodbridge opened his columns to the suggestion that young women might be professionally trained in teacher seminars. Sophia Frommichen, who for 39 years had taught in girls' schools in Germany and Russia, maintained that women teachers would surely improve the quality of schools. The employment of unmarried women or widows would not only lessen the financial burden of the taxpayers supporting the common schools but, by reducing poverty and dependence among single women, would also relieve demands on private charity and public welfare.

Teachers in the common schools, Frommichen wrote, need not be learned. Their job was "to render others dutiful, and to communicate instruction." That task required skills equally necessary for marriage and motherhood. To daughters of middle-class families Frommichen had this advice: "It is more honorable to be the independent teacher of a village school than to be the housekeeper in a nobleman's mansion, or the domestic or humble companion of an elevated, and often sickly, proud and peevish woman."[7] Frommichen considered too that teaching the children of the poor and degraded brought gratitude and honor to any woman who devoted her life to that task.

The most comprehensive and widely read account of teacher education abroad came from the pen of Victor Cousin, a professor of philosophy at the University of Paris. Cousin had been commissioned by France's minister of public instruction and ecclesiastical affairs to study the schools of Prussia and other German states. For nearly two weeks (in 1831) he traveled from Paris to Berlin via Frankfurt, Weimar, and Leipzig. On the way he briefly visited elementary and secondary schools, the teacher seminar in Weimar, and the University of Jena. Once in the Prussian capital, he stayed for four weeks. He was well received by Baron von Altenstein, the Prussian minister of ecclesiastical and educational affairs, and spent most of his time reading ordinances, reports, and correspondence in the Ministry, as well as visiting schools in Berlin and Potsdam. On his return he traveled through Halle, Bonn, Cologne, and Aachen.[8]

Cousin, like Woodbridge before him, reported at length on the preparation of teachers for the rural schools. Cousin agreed with Woodbridge's observations that the seminars did not exist to introduce students to academic instruction and city life. They recruited their charges from among poor, young country boys and prepared them to spend a lifetime as country teachers.

Cousin wrote glowingly of the paternally protective spirit that pervaded the administration of Prussia's teacher seminars, and of the requirements that schoolmasters be pious and discreet and unshakably loyal to the state. He praised the seminars, their supervision by the churches, and their deliberate location in towns of moderate size "to preserve the pupils from dissipation, allurements, and habits of a kind of life which does not accord with their future condition."[9] Future elementary teachers for the country schools evidently were not expected to come from well-to-do and middle-class homes. "Any man of mature age, of irreproachable morals and sincere piety," Cousin quoted a Prussian law of 1819, "who understands the duties of the office he aspires to fill, and gives satisfactory proofs that he does, is fit for the post of public teacher."[10]

It should not escape notice that Cousin's knowledge of the rural seminars and their students did not derive from extensive acquaintance with, and visits to, these institutions, but from his reading of office files in the Berlin ministry, and from his contacts with the top men in Prussia's administrative hierarchy. It seems strange also that, in reviewing the plans and curricula of the seminars, Cousin found relatively little to report on instruction in pedagogy proper. There are references to methods and didactics and the practice schools. Yet, over and again, he reverts to discipline and moral instruction as the heart of a sound pedagogy.

The first requirement for a candidate for a teaching position was a pure heart and an upright character. To be sure, Cousin found the discipline enforced in the smaller schools "somewhat monastic and military," but thought it appropriate and necessary for "young men taken from the lowest classes and not yet divested of a certain coarseness. . . ."[11] The small, rural seminar, substandard by anyone's definition of academic and institutional adequacy, but above all the competition in its moral and spiritual tone, was Cousin's prime exhibit for the superiority of the German system of teacher education.

Between Prussia and Massachusetts

In the 1830s Massachusetts, not unlike Prussia, was a small, rural state trying to cope with the strains of beginning industrialization, and to adjust its traditional decentralized administration to demands for greater economic productivity.[12] The Massachusetts school reformers noted that their European counterparts wrestled with problems which they recognized as their own. How to extend the reach of a centralized administration into the rural hinterlands? How to bring effective public schooling to a rural population? They perceived that the small seminars Cousin had described promised a solution to the lack of competent teachers in the rural common schools of Massachusetts. Cities like Boston might get along reasonably well with their more differentiated systems of primary-, grammar-, and high schools, and their distinctions among "masters" of grammar- and high schools and teachers of the primary schools. But the lack of qualified teachers for the state's rural common schools presented the most urgent problem.

The affinity of outlook between European educational aristocrats, administrators, and teacher educators on the one hand and American middle-class reformers on the other was not accidental. Men like Baron von Altenstein, Victor Cousin, and Horace Mann believed in progress and stability under responsible guidance. They shared a sense of moral elitism and nobility. In their respective societies they were men of rank and stature. They saw themselves as enlightened liberals in their social and political views, yet as staunch defenders of their respective political order. They expressed their convictions in the language of paternalistic *noblesse oblige*.

Their common ideological orientation—an Atlantic Whiggism, as I shall call it—explains to a large extent why American Whigs adopted Cousin's report so enthusiastically. They did not ask themselves whether Cousin wrote as a supporter of Louis Phillipe. They did not wince at his endorsement of the conservative trend of European restoration policies that saw in an alliance of throne and altar the best guarantee for social stability and political order.[13] They only heard the voice of the progressive reformer, the Pestalozzian, the philosopher whose lectures held out hope that a genuine people's system of elementary schools could be established, and who promised that the new normal schools and teacher seminars would turn schoolkeeping into a respectable profession. For the American Whigs that was promise enough.

Even so, there were striking differences between the schools and teachers of Prussia and Massachusetts. In both states, schoolmen had to hold in balance the desires for individual mobility and the demands for social stability. When Horace Mann and the New England reformers read Cousin's descriptions of the Prussian rural normal schools they applauded the paternalistic tone and intent, but they could not view the sons and daughters of rural Massachusetts as the children of illiterate, uneducated peasants. Massachusetts Whigs did not recognize a lower middle class. In Cousin's book they saw only a picture of efficiently trained teachers bringing educational progress to rural and urban schools alike.

The faith of American Whig reformers in the inevitability of the progress of republicanism made it difficult for them to perceive the geographic and social divisions that existed in Europe. They did not grasp the sharp division that existed in both Altenstein's Prussia and Cousin's France between the country and the city elementary schools. They did not realize that the gulf that yawned between seminar-trained elementary-school teachers and university-educated secondary-school teachers was deliberate and unbridgeable. They did not see the incongruities inherent in their attempt to develop a system of public schooling and teacher education for a democratic people from models and inspirations that reflected a bourgeois society deeply split among social classes and between country and city.

The First Massachusetts State Normal Schools

When, soon after New Year's Day in 1837, the Massachusetts Whigs began in earnest their campaign for state-supported normal schools, they received the support of the American Institute of Instruction. The institute complained that Massachusetts teachers were "exceedingly incompetent in *many* respects." Young men taught in order to support themselves during their college studies, or because they were waiting for more lucrative employment, or because they had failed in everything else. They experimented and learned on the job, disappointed their employers, and failed to be rehired for the next term. The only workable response to that situation, the institute asserted, was for the state to provide for the education of teachers.[14]

The members of the institute knew fully well that, under the conditions then prevailing, college- or academy-educated men were not to be had as teachers in the common schools. They had to find ways to improve the preparation of temporary teachers. The teacher they had in mind was a male who—accepting gladly (even proudly) his seasonal employment—had learned to make a virtue out of a necessity:

> As in the early history of Rome, the generous husbandman left his plow to fight the battles of the state, so, in Massachusetts, the free and intelligent citi-

> zen will, for a time, quit his business, his workshop, or his farm, to fight, for the sake of his children and the state, a more vital battle against immorality and ignorance.[15]

The institute suggested that state-supported normal schools should devote themselves to the training of citizen–teachers.

This proposal was not what Horace Mann had in mind. He had initially envisaged a corps of full-time, professional teachers on the German model as outlined by Cousin. He also knew that the likelihood of attracting a majority of males as teachers was slim. By 1837, women already accounted for more than 60 percent of common-school teachers in Massachusetts. Besides, women—unlike the only seasonably available men teachers—could teach in summer as well as in winter, and thus would increase in some measure the stability of the state's district schools.[16]

As it turned out, the Massachusetts legislature did not respond to the plea for the citizen–teacher, but instead proceeded in 1838 to establish four state normal schools. The first school opened in Lexington in July of 1839, under Cyrus Peirce as principal. It was for women only. Later it moved to West Newton, and then to Framingham. At Barre in central Massachusetts, instruction for both men and women began in September, with the Reverend Samuel P. Newman as principal. That school subsequently moved to Westfield. By 1840, Colonel Nicholas Tillinghast took command of students of both sexes at Bridgewater. Eventually a fourth school was opened, at Salem in 1854, with Richard Edwards as principal. Like that in Lexington, it accepted women only. Each of the schools also operated a model school to provide opportunities for practice teaching.[17]

The Massachusetts Board of Education had deliberately sought to place the normal schools in rural areas, where the need was greatest and they would serve towns and districts. The schools were to offer instruction in spelling, reading, writing, grammar, geography, arithmetic, and (if time allowed) rhetoric, logic, geometry, bookkeeping, navigation, surveying, history, physiology, mental and natural philosophy, and—always—"the principles of piety and morality common to all sects of Christians." As in Prussia, academic requirements were intentionally kept low. Graduates of the common schools were not expected to have fully absorbed the elementary curriculum. (The course of study was to extend over one year, yet at Barre and Bridgewater, students were admitted also for shorter periods of study, to enable them to earn their expenses by keeping school.)[18]

For young women in northeastern Massachusetts, the school in Lexington offered one of the few opportunities to advanced public education. Though they had to provide their own expenses for board, books, and incidentals, the women found the arrangement to be attractive financially, as it promised release from tuition fees for those who committed themselves to a period of teaching in the common schools.

When the Lexington school opened in 1839, the small number of applicants disappointed Mann and "Father Peirce," as the principal was called by his students. After their graduation from common school, most of the young women who applied to Lexington had spent from four to five years at home or at work. They needed a great deal of encouragement to pursue their studies. Peirce found their academic knowledge and skills discouragingly defective. "They have come to learn the Common Branches rather than to learn to *teach* them," he confided to his diary on June 22, 1840.[19] A review of the common-school curriculum and a first introduction to classroom teaching was all that could be accomplished in the time at hand.

Peirce's frustrations increased as time went on. He was particularly chagrined to find that some of his students did not even want to become teachers, and others did not have the necessary ability. He concluded that the normal-school students at Lexington were less talented than his high-school students at Nantucket had been: "What miserably clumsy work some of these girls make in Arithmetic, Grammar, Philosophy and Algebra! And they manifest very little Curiosity. . . ."[20]

When the second normal school began its work on September 4, 1839, at Barre in the central, rural part of the state, a dozen women and eight men enrolled. Many of them enrolled for only one term—a policy suggested by the seasonal nature of farm work. The men students, wanting to take advantage of the teaching opportunities open to them in the winter, enrolled primarily in the term beginning in August. Few were present at the normal school during the December term. The women students, on the other hand, signed up least frequently for the April term, which was when they preferred to teach in the common schools. Winter, by contrast, was a good time for them to be at the normal school.[21]

The students at Barre and Westfield were an older and more mature group than Peirce's young women at Framingham. They were, wrote James Greenough, assistant to Principal Dickinson from 1856 to 1871 and later president of the school, "diverse in age, in ability, and in acquisitions." They constituted a motley gathering, he added, whom many on the outside thought to be nondescript, queer and funny folk. Greenough himself felt that one could not but admire their devotion, and "even if they were somewhat narrow in their mental vision, one could see that it gained in intensity what it lost in breadth." They were "earnest men and women" who, through their intensity, transformed that earnestness into enthusiasm.[22] But neither at Framingham nor at Westfield did the "normalites" impress their observers as particularly gifted or capable. Their motivation was not scholarly learning but basic vocational preparation or improvement.

The most salient fact about the early Massachusetts normalites was that they were predominantly women. By 1849 the women's share among the Westfield students alone was larger than that among all Massachusetts teachers.[23] That bode ill for the dream, cherished by the members of the American Institute of Instruction, that many more male teachers would follow their call and assume the duties of citizen–teachers. But it did not displease Mann, who believed that women were by nature teachers *par excellence*. It was up to them to prove themselves worthy. To Mann, the preponderance of women among the normal-school students was an asset, not a liability.[24]

But Mann, too, was ultimately to be disappointed. His women teachers did not solve the rural-school crisis; those institutions did not reap the benefit of their training. An analysis of the Massachusetts normalites makes it evident that, far from providing professional teachers for the rural schools, the normal schools set their students on the road to upward social mobility. The rural schools could not but be aided in this process—but the help was incidental; one may well doubt that the schools were the ultimate gainers. The normalites were on the move both socially and geographically, and few stayed or returned to play the role of country schoolmaster or schoolmistress.

Criticism and the Response of the Westfield Principals

Ten years after the initial opening of the first normal school in Lexington, William B. Fowle, the editor of *The Common School Journal,* charged that the results of all the efforts to improve the standards of common-school teaching had been meager. The admission of too many immature and unqualified students had forced the normal schools to make up for the deficient common-school education of their pupils. It had prevented them from carrying out their real business, instruction in the art of teaching. How absurd, then, Mr. Fowle observed, to complain, as some did, that the normal schools did not offer Greek and Latin and other advanced studies.

The Common School Journal's editor also found fault with the model schools connected with the normal schools. The normalites disrupted the instruction of the model school's teacher, and, due to the brief period they spent in the model-school classroom, they also failed to benefit themselves from that experience. Teaching talent was best stimulated, the editor thought, on a monitorial plan according to which older students taught younger students, continually improving both their learning and their teaching skills.[25]

In the meantime, the state normal-school principals at the Barre and Westfield school—Messrs. Newman, Davis, Rowe, Wells, and Dickinson—also had become dissatisfied with the lack of progress of their school and students. But, unlike Cyrus Peirce at Lexington, they sought to remedy the situation by emphasizing advanced academic work rather than remedial elementary studies. They also began to stress what then came to be called educational science. They hoped that by raising the school's academic level, and by taking on the preparation of high-school teachers, they would attract better-prepared and -motivated students.

Difficulties with the Westfield town authorities led Principal Wells to close the model school in 1855 and to introduce in its place of a system of "mutual instruction." As the editor of *The Common School Journal* had suggested, normal-school students now taught in front of their own classmates, and were in turn evaluated by them for their performance. Wells took pride in the substitution of observation, experiment, and criticism for the traditional memorizing and book learning. He saw the change to be progress in professional work that demonstrated a growing acceptance of the theories of Johann Heinrich Pestalozzi.[26]

When in the 1870s Principal Dickinson introduced an advanced course with Latin, German, French, drawing, higher mathematics, chemistry, and natural history, the early period in the history of the Massachusetts state normal schools had come to an end. The Westfield principals had weathered their years of storm and stress. While they had been unable to find a solution to the problems of rural schools and their teachers, they had found a new challenge in the training of teachers for the high schools.

The High School as Normal School

The new Massachusetts high schools were to be found primarily in larger towns and cities. For the normal-school educators they came to offer a double function: as potential sites for the employment of normal-school graduates, and as suitable locations for normal-school instruction.[27] Thus when the first public city normal school was opened in Boston in 1852 as the Girls' High and Normal School, Nathan Bishop, the city's superintendent of schools, asked that it be used to train women teachers for the Boston grammar schools.[28]

Girls' High and Normal School Headmaster Dunton would subsequently demonstrate the success of this plan in Boston. By 1894, he could report, 1,018 (or 74 percent) of the 1,368 graduates of the Boston Normal School since 1873 had been appointed to Boston public schools, and 738 (or 54 percent) still were teaching.[29] This was a substantially higher rate than could be found in the state as a whole, where only 31 percent of all state normal-school graduates taught in the public schools.[30]

At the school's opening in 1852, students and their parents had shown little interest in normal-school training. Ever since the city, in its parsimony, had closed the Girls' High School in 1828 and supported only the English High School for Boys, Bostonians had pressed for a high school for their daughters. So when more and more women appeared as teachers in Boston's elementary and grammar schools, and the demand for their better preparation was raised, a call for a city normal school provided a perfect cover for what was really wanted—a high school. Larkin Dunton, subsequently to be Boston Normal's fourth headmaster, admitted that much when he reported that the normal school was asked for in Boston only because people were reluctant to revive the old high-school controversy.[31]

Once the institution was established as the Boston Normal School and its students were found to be insufficiently prepared for teacher training, a two-year high-school curriculum was introduced to precede the third-year normal-school work proper. By 1854, public pressure forced a change in name and curriculum, and the school became in name what it had already been in fact: the Boston Girls' High and Normal School. "But the normal features were soon quite overshadowed by the high school work," wrote Larkin Dunton.[32] Whether that occurred by necessity or by design is now a moot question. Suffice it to say that for 18 years the Boston Girls' High and Normal School functioned for all practical purposes as a high school.

The actual beginning of the school as a teacher-training institution then occurred in 1872. In that year, finding that "the normal element had again been crowded out by the high school work and that the school had almost lost its distinctively professional character," the Boston School Committee separated the two schools.[33] The Boston Normal School thereafter led an independent existence, until in 1924 it became the Teachers College of the City of Boston, and eventually the Boston State Teachers College and the Boston State College.

The Boston experience should prompt us to ask whether the same needs and responses existed (and should not have) all along at the other normal schools as well. Should we not ask whether the common-school teachers of Massachusetts had ever stood in need of normal-school training as long as their own common-school experience—not even to mention a nonexisting grammar- or high-school education—had been as deficient as that of the students of Cyrus Peirce? Was not the lesson that the early normal schools had taught "Before and above all else, teachers need an extended education in grammar- and high school, and a few years of growing and maturing"? In other words, a general—even a liberal—education had been missing in the careers of teachers. No vocational or professional training could ever replace or make up for that liability.

The Unfashionable Cause: Training the Elementary Teacher

Whether at Westfield or in Boston, by the last quarter of the century it became obvious that teacher educators began to ignore and forget the rural elementary-school teacher. The deficiencies in her prior education, combined with the unresponsiveness of the district system to professional improvements, still represented the most intractable problem of the school system. But now the growth of urban schools, the rise of the high schools, and the development of modern pedagogy opened new vistas for teacher educators. A new profession was aborning, and a new faith in a modern science of education tempted them to forget the unsolved problems of the past.

But not all normal-school proponents were ready to dispense with the education of elementary teachers. At Bridgewater, West Point graduate Principal Colonel Tillinghast reminded his students that the academic concern of normal schools was with the "foundation on which to build an education." He wanted a basic four-year training, and vigorously championed a less ambitious but far more thorough course. "A very few studies and long dwelling on them—this is my theory," he wrote in 1851.[34]

Tillinghast sought to remain faithful to the labors of Mann and Peirce. He knew that at the very time his Westfield colleagues attempted to make the study of pedagogy scientific, and to march in a collegiate direction (playing down the training of women teachers for the elementary school and introducing instruction for men in high-school subjects), nearly nine of ten Massachusetts teachers were women.[35] But at the same time, Tillinghast did not mean to reject the new trend altogether. At Bridgewater he wanted to combine the training of elementary-school teachers with the new departures in the science of education, school administration, and the training of high-school teachers. This proved a difficult task, and eventually the new dispensation of scientific pedagogy and training for high-school and administrative positions came to dominate the field.

The difficulties began to appear at the first annual convention in 1859 of what was to become the American Normal School Association. Here the Bridgewater approach competed successfully with the Westfield idea for the loyalties of the normal-school pedagogues. The convention resolved that "While the labors of the Normal School must be chiefly directed, for the present, to the right preparation of common school teachers, it ought not to omit from its plan the professional education of teachers of any grade. . . ."[36]

Eleven years later, at the 1870 convention of the National Education Association's

Department of Normal Schools in Cleveland, most of the normal-school educators present now seemed interested in the preparation of instructors for the high schools. Professor William Franklin Phelps, then of the Minnesota State Normal School at Winona, sought a compromise. He suggested a graded system which would establish and distinguish two separate kinds of normal schools—one to continue to prepare elementary teachers, the other to train "school officers and instructors in the higher departments."[37] Phelps himself favored the former type. The association, he said, should turn its attention to the area of greatest deficiency and need—the normal schools' training of elementary teachers. Their curriculum "should be selected less with reference to a preparation for the higher courses, if need be, than for the duties of life."[38]

Delegates from rural Midwestern states by-and-large supported Phelps's emphasis on training elementary teachers. For that purpose they suggested that county high schools add teacher-training departments, and that county normal or training schools should take over the education of elementary-school teachers.[39] The state normal schools could then devote their energies "to the work of educating school superintendents, teachers of high schools, [and] principals of training schools. . . ."[40]

The normal-school educators' final word in that debate came at their 1872 meeting in Boston. Their resolution proposed that there be a school or faculty of education at every university, and a professor of education at every college and high school. Every state should have at least one higher normal school (if possible two or more) for the training of teachers for high schools and for elementary normal schools, as well as for the preparation of city and county school superintendents. Then there should be elementary county normal schools for the training of teachers for primary and intermediate grades and for rural schools. Finally, every county should be encouraged to run a normal institute of from two to six weeks every year. Professor Phelps's great concern for the rural schools had been absorbed as only one item—and as such neither a very important nor an exciting one—in a grand shopping list in which everyone could find something of interest.[41] As far as the American Normal School Association was concerned, training teachers for the rural elementary schools had decidedly gone out of fashion.

The new vision was grandiose, indeed. Instead of being schools for teachers, the state normal schools would be transformed into teachers colleges for the education of the teachers of teachers. An all-inclusive system of scientific pedagogy was to be topped in each state by one central State Normal University. Its staff would be responsible for the training of professors of teaching for all educational institutions. These new pedagogical experts would hold the chairs of pedagogy in universities, colleges, and state normal schools, as also in the training schools, high schools, and academies. Once the system was in place, high-school teachers could again safely be educated in universities and colleges. The new professors of education trained at the state normal universities would see to it that scientific pedagogy would be taught there as well.[42]

Only a minority now stood up for the Horace Mann–Cyrus Peirce point of view of normal education as the preparation of teachers for the elementary schools. They pointed out that the reality of teacher education simply did not correspond to the blueprints of the professionals.[43] But theirs was a lost cause. By the 1890s even most of the Bridgewater graduates used their prolonged training as a platform from which to enter administrative positions and high-school classrooms, or to choose business, law, and other white-collar and professional careers. In very few, if any, cases did they regard elementary teaching as a career in itself. The new educational frontier lay in the cities, not in the country. The new professionals would make their careers in high schools, educational science, and school administration.

Teacher Education in the Midwest

Illinois

While normal-school educators debated their concerns at their national conventions, conditions in the rural Midwest prescribed a pattern of development which differed from that in the urbanized East. In the West the public school reformers had come to rely for the education of common-school teachers on private academies and colleges and on state universities. Besides, there was an insistent demand for agricultural and mechanical education that many thought was more suitable to the sons and daughters of Midwestern settlers than the traditional academic fare offered by the colleges. Teacher education, many thought, could well be offered in these institutions as well.

Partisans of state normal schools quickly perceived that in the nation's midsection the opinion of the people as represented in their legislatures mattered greatly. They listened carefully to what newspaper editorials and legislative committee reports had to say, and learned to play down their own preference for the state normal schools as specialized vocational schools. They noted that many settlers were willing to support normal schools only if they functioned as community colleges or people's universities and served the largest number of students with the greatest variety of academic and vocational subjects.

Different states, to be sure, followed different paths. Michigan, for example, kept the Eastern model. It opened its state normal school in Ypsilanti in the spring of 1853 as an institution separate from the state university at Ann Arbor and the state agricultural college that was to begin its work in East Lansing in 1855.[44] Illinois broke new ground with the establishment in 1857 of a full-fledged normal university which was to offer instruction in all vocational fields as well as in all the traditional academic areas. Wisconsin was ready to support teacher training in high schools, private academies, and colleges, and its state university entered the field only temporarily during the Civil War. After the war a number of state normal schools took over the task. In Kansas a tightfisted legislature restricted (in 1865) its state normal school at Emporia to the training of elementary teachers.

The most remarkable institution in the Midwest was Illinois Normal University at Normal, near Bloomington. Describing Eastern normal training as class-based education, its early historian, Charles A. Harper, argued that the new university was not, like the Eastern normal schools, "a plebeian thing, an upper class gesture of philanthropy to the poor and ignorant. . . .''[45] It was a people's university intended to respond to the growing demand for practical and utilitarian instruction in agricultural and industrial fields as much as to the need for common-school teachers.

In their desire to train schoolteachers, the educators at Normal remained faithful to the Bridgewater tradition and spoke up as defenders of the largely female elementary teachers and their needs. Like Nicholas Tillinghast, they were determined to preserve the unity of the teaching profession and to elevate teacher training until it would include the best and the latest of new pedagogical insight and wisdom. But, like their Massachusetts colleagues, they too found it difficult to persuade their students to pass through the school's full three-year course, let alone entice them to take advanced academic subjects.[46]

While the Bridgewater tradition remained potent at Normal into the 1890s, the school's popularity derived less from any particular pedagogical orientation than from its readiness to respond to the needs of its students and the surrounding communities. The model school, with its high-school department, not only offered opportunities for demonstration, practice, and experimentation in teaching the elementary and intermediate grades, but from 1860 to 1868 also served as the town of Normal's regular district school. When in 1862 a high-school department, and in 1864 a grammar-school department, were added, the school's usefulness increased dramatically.[47]

Throughout the 1860s, Illinois Normal University served a variety of ends: to continue to prepare the much-needed teachers for the state's rural elementary schools; to supply as well the teachers and administrators for the new high schools; to lead and direct the summer institutes for teachers already at work; to answer its neighborhood's calls for a high school; and to develop the new educational professionalism. It was fortuitous for the school's ambitious leaders that for ten years Normal was spared the competition of a state university, and thus dominated the field as the state's major public university. But the question that would not go away was whether an institution which (in the tradition of a community college or people's university) tried to answer every educational need of everyone who knocked at its doors, could hope to fulfill the demands for which it was created: to train the state's teachers of the common schools.

That question became even more pressing when the beginning of the 1890s ushered in a new era for Normal University. The new professionalism began to take command. The education of high-school teachers came to overshadow the training of teachers for the elementary schools, and the Herbartian interlude replaced the Bridgewater tradition. If Pestalozzianism and the idea of a normal school as an American version of a Prussian teacher seminar had constituted the first massive infusion of German pedagogy into the United States, then what became known during the 1890s as Herbartianism was the second. If Massachusetts had been the point of entry for the former, Illinois and Normal University in particular became gateways for the latter.

The distinctive contributions of the Herbartians gave to the training of elementary teachers a decided theoretical–systematic bent. American Herbartianism was more comprehensive than the ''object teaching'' doctrine that had found a home during the 1860s at Oswego State Normal School in New York. Its five-steps-of-instruction scheme provided a far more practical and easily understandable help to classroom teachers than William T. Harris's brand of pedagogical Hegelianism and G. Stanley Hall's child-study movement, two other then-current schools of thought in American pedagogy. The Herbartians introduced new concepts, such as apperception (that new knowledge was learned and understood best when it could be related to what was already known and familiar to the child) and the culture-epoch theory and the correlation of studies (that the subjects of the curriculum should be organized and integrated around historical periods). They placed great emphasis on the child's interest as a key factor to be considered in the learning process. Above all, they responded to the practical day-to-day questions of teachers in the classroom, and placed renewed importance on the model school as their laboratory.[48]

It was under the direction of David Felmley that in the early twentieth century Normal University became a center of pedagogical professionalism. Felmley introduced training for teachers of kindergartens, and of manual and household arts, agricultural and commercial subjects, and drama and music. He firmly asserted that "the normal school must make provision for the adequate training of teachers fitted to direct or to perform the work of every phase of the common school from the primary school to its culmination in the public high school."[49]

To Felmley, professionalism meant that only men could be professionals, and that therefore women, who would continue to teach in elementary schools, were excluded from the ranks of the profession. He argued that if the normal school succeeded in attracting men students, it would transform education into a profession, and teaching into an esteemed vocation. From this it followed that "to limit the activity of the normal schools of the Middle West to the preparation of elementary school teachers will cut off the attendance of men as completely as it has in New England." Men, wrote Felmley, "become village principals, principals of ward schools, county and city superintendents, teachers of agriculture, manual training, physics, biology, and other high school subjects." They added vigor to athletic, oratorical, musical, and dramatic contests.[50] The leadership of public education therefore had to be placed in the hands of male professionals, who would direct the female classroom teachers. Then, too, the problems of the rural classroom could be solved.

Wisconsin

In Wisconsin the spokesmen for private academies and colleges delayed the inauguration of normal training at the state university, and the creation of separate state normal schools, until after the outbreak of the Civil War. When in 1863 the university began to offer normal instruction to men and women, students enrolled primarily in preparatory and academic classes which gave them a general liberal education and prepared them for professional careers. The only institutions in which teachers were in fact trained were the colleges, academies, and high schools.

As the war came to an end, permanent state normal schools "whose sole business shall be the training of teachers'' were to be placed in different locations around the state.[51] The needs for common-school teaching were local, and not easily satisfied by one central institution. Taxpayers asked that these state normal schools offer a program of general secondary and postsecondary education in addition to teacher training. Thus, when the first state normal school was dedicated on October 9, 1866, in Platteville, the local newspaper stated that the importance of the school lay not in its expected contribution to the education of teachers for the common schools, but in its presence as an academic center for everyone's children regardless of their intended later occupations.[52]

The careers of the graduates demonstrate the fulfillment of this expectation. Few of the men and women stayed for any length of time as teachers in the classroom. Over the course of the first eight years after graduation between 1869 and 1877, the percentage of the 49 women who engaged in teaching dropped from 88 after two years to 29 after eight years. Of the 53 men, the corresponding drop occurred from 45 to 13 percent. Of those women still in the school after eight years, only one out of three was a classroom teacher, and one in 11 was in a position of professional leadership. By far the largest group had disappeared into marriage. Of another 12 percent we have no information.

The career pattern of the 53 men shows that eight years after graduation, 28 graduates, or 52 percent, were found in other professions or occupations. Lawyers lead the group with 11, followed by farmers and merchants with four each, physicians with two, and a smattering of other pursuits with one each. The next largest group consisted of professionals in education. Five of them were listed as high-school principals, four as principals, three as county superintendents, and one as a normal-school professor. This group of education professionals had shrunk from 21 two years after graduation to 13 after an additional six years. Even men in their elevated positions of professional leadership showed a notable lack of lifelong commitment to service in education.[53]

In its early years, Platteville Normal School, then, *had* furnished much-needed teachers and administrators for the public schools. But its graduates were not to *remain* in education. What the normal school accomplished far more impressively was to give a number of small-town and country boys a start as school teachers and administrators, and then send them on their way to professional and business careers. It did better with a few of its women graduates, who became teachers in normal schools or rose to administrative positions in the public schools, and stayed there. But the majority of the women graduates had left teaching when they married.

While the state normal schools thus pursued both elementary and remedial, as well as academic and preparatory, instruction, the legislature mandated in 1883 that the public high schools offer courses in the ''theory and art of teaching.''[54] In addition, summer teacher institutes for teachers already employed, and county training or normal schools, became the effective source of teachers for the rural district schools. The *Wisconsin Journal of Education* welcomed the appearance of the latter in the expectation that these schools would ''in due time . . . do the professional work now performed by the elementary course of the regular normals.''[55] The ''regulars'' could then devote themselves to more prestigious tasks.

Kansas

In Kansas, normal educators sought to create a state normal school on the Bridgewater–Illinois model, but legislators would not allow it. From the start they insisted that Emporia Normal School remain on the level of a training school and stick to the task for which it had been created: to prepare teachers for the elementary schools. Many legislators subscribed to the notion that elementary teachers in the rural schools were by definition temporary employees.

When the school opened its doors in February of 1865 its first principal, Lyman B. Kellog, insisted that "the primary object and purpose of the Normal School . . . [was] the instruction of both men and women in the art of teaching." The minds of male and female teachers were "to be improved by an enlarged and liberal course of study; but," he insisted, "it is all for the purpose of adding to their efficiency as teachers."[56] As at Normal, a three-year course was necessary to graduate, and students who received free tuition had to pledge that they would teach as many years in the state schools of Kansas as they had attended the normal school.

At the decade's end neither Kellog nor the state superintendent were entirely satisfied with the school's performance. Although it had shown an average annual attendance of 90 students in its normal department, only seven men and 13 women had graduated from the three-year course.[57] When Kellog sought to improve matters by introducing a high-school course, the legislature interfered, demanding that he stick to the original purpose of training elementary-school teachers.

Yet, by the early 1880s the attempt to broaden the school's base with a program of education for secondary teachers and administrators was revived by Albert R. Taylor, the new principal. Taylor placed a decided emphasis on adding professional training in such areas as kindergarten education, psychology, child study, school law, methods and management, and the philosophy and history of education. Enrollments climbed steadily, until by 1900 they had reached almost 1,800 students. The legislature took note and, as if to make amends for past injuries, reversed itself, in 1885 ordering the university at Lawrence to close its normal department.[58]

Applause was not universal. Criticism soon came from both within and outside the state. The school may have been praised by educational professionals, but laymen thought differently. While Emporia State Normal School had enjoyed a virtual monopoly of teacher training, they charged, the vast majority of Kansas rural elementary-school teachers had never seen its insides, nor that of any other normal school. In 1889 and 1899 over 60 percent of its nongraduates, the majority of whom were women, had taught on the average fewer than six years in the state's rural common schools.[59] As a critic would later point out, from the 1880s to the beginning of the 1920s, Kansas teachers "gave mediocre service which produced a mediocre product."[60]

President Taylor was little moved by such criticism. He wrote in his report of 1899 that the school's alumni accounted for most of the state's leaders in public education. Of the ill- or nonprepared elementary teachers he wrote that "in the natural order of things, most of them become home-keepers after a few years of service; and what fine mistresses of the manse does this education make of them!"[61] Such temporary teachers were unimportant and dispensable.

In Kansas as elsewhere, professionalization of teacher education meant that the normal schools deserted the field of classroom teacher training for the education of specialized and high-school teachers, administrators, and educational leaders. It meant a deliberate neglect of the state's overwhelmingly female ranks of teachers who were not expected to become, or to view themselves as, professionals. The future lay with the largely male leadership of public education. It involved a shift of focus away from the rural one-room school to the graded and high schools of the cities.

Teacher Education Between University and Community College

By the beginning of the twentieth century, teacher education was caught in a crossfire. The education professionals—state, city, and county superintendents; faculty members at normal schools and teachers colleges; editors of professional educational journals—wanted to upgrade their institutions to the college level with training for special fields, high-school teaching, educational administration, and educational research. In many states, legislators and taxpayers wanted the normal schools to become community colleges and offer courses in both liberal and vocational education. Training for elementary teachers was left to high schools and city and country training schools.

The normal schools' attempts to achieve collegiate status inevitably brought them on a collision course with the colleges and universities. These latter institutions were becoming increasingly interested in teacher training, especially in the education of teachers for the high schools. When in 1913 at Illinois President Felmley had stated that "high school teachers should be trained in the same environment as elementary teachers," he had, in fact, directly challenged the universities.[62] He accused them of ignoring methods and psychology courses. The "Brahminical pundits of the traditional college and the arrogance of the university" blocked the path of educational progress.[63]

Felmley's anger had been aroused when Edmund Janes James, president of the University of Illinois at Urbana, had said that he thought a great university should have a school of education which pursued both the training of teachers and the advanced study of education. When James then asked William Chandler Bagley of his faculty to oversee the university's growing involvement in education, Bagley urged the normal schools to pay their students in exchange for their five-year commitment as teachers in the elementary schools, just as West Point and Annapolis paid their committed military cadets.[64] Those of the normal-school "cadets" who wanted to continue teaching after their five-year stint could then avail themselves of further training at the university's school of education.

At Normal, President Felmley was bitterly resentful at this put-down of his school. By undercutting its work, he felt, the university made it very difficult for normal graduates to get high-school positions in the state. "Do you believe," he asked Urbana president James, "that the educational and intellectual interests of a state as large as Illinois are best served by such concentration? Does it not mean a sort of educational trust?"[65] The question remained unanswered.

The same conflicts were repeated, albeit with local variations, in Lawrence, Madison, and other university centers. In Kansas at about the same time as in Illinois, the university opened its school of education to train high-school and college teachers and administrators. Here, too, the university was not willing to let the state normal school move unchallenged into the training of secondary teachers and school administrators.[66] In Wisconsin, neither the university at Madison nor the state superintendent had initially seen any need for the university to concern itself with teacher education. But they came to view the university as the proper place to provide in-service and continuing professional education for school leaders, spokesmen, administrators, and high-school teachers.

As the century drew to its close and it became apparent that disputes would arise as to whether, without the addition of scholarly work in pedagogy, the normal schools could compete with the university in the preparation of high-school teachers and administrators, university faculty members suggested a division of labor. They preferred that they would train high-school teachers while the normal schools offered a two-year course for the training of rural and urban elementary teachers.[67] In 1918, Professor Michael Vincent O'Shea of the Madison faculty repeated the proposal for "educational economy" in which the county normal schools would train rural teachers, the state normal schools would provide primary-school teachers for graded and city schools, and the colleges and university would be responsible for the education of high-school teachers.[68]

The normal regents tried to circumvent the issue and announced that they would discontinue from the normal-school curriculum all subjects not primarily, definitely, and exclusively part of teacher education. As a trade-off for this retreat from general, academic, and vocational education they wanted legislative authorization for a full four-year program of professional education for high-school teachers and teachers of special subjects. It was their way to gain both degree-granting power and the status of a professional school.

This proposal, however, foundered on the shoals of popular opposition. For Wisconsin's taxpayers the dispute between the university and the normal schools was of little account; they saw it primarily as a battle over "turf." They cared, however, for the opportunities they desired for their children to receive both a general and a professional education close to their homes. Thus they resented the normal regents' decision to scuttle academic and vocational education in favor of a singleminded emphasis on teacher training. In May of 1925 they forced the legislature to reverse itself and permit the regents to change their normal schools into four-year teachers colleges which could award Bachelor of Education degrees to their graduates.

The Wisconsin state normal schools thus attained their long-hoped-for collegiate status. The regents were authorized to award one-year certificates for teachers in rural schools, on the same terms as such certificates had been awarded by the state superintendent to the graduates of county normal schools.[69] They also could offer general academic and vocational work. Yet they had to share with the university the prestigious tasks of training secondary-school teachers, special teachers, and administrators, and of providing in-service and continuing-education seminars and courses.

The Wisconsin case makes it clear that there were no winners in the battle of the normal schools with the university. Here as elsewhere the university had not succeeded in holding the normal schools strictly to the task of training classroom teachers and in preventing them from venturing into professional education. In Wisconsin the university would ultimately have to accept the former teachers colleges as equals in a statewide university system.

The historical significance of this development, however, lies in the fact that it was the normal schools, rather than the land-grant colleges, that really brought higher education to the people. If the latter permitted farmers and mechanics to send their sons and daughters to their centrally located state university or college, the former took public colleges and universities out to where they were most needed—into the hinterlands and small towns where the people lived and worked. With the normal schools, true democracy began in higher education.[70]

The Nineteenth-Century Record: Retreat from Teaching

By the end of the century, America's normal schools had failed to make themselves the reliable source of classroom teachers in the country's public elementary schools. They had not realized their original intent to give internal strength and staying power to the common-school movement by creating a professional corps of teachers. Horace Mann and his friends had not been able to challenge the power of local boards and county superintendents over the employment of teachers. Mann's successors in the East and the Midwest soon were persuaded to shift their attention to the more prestigious tasks of training education professionals.

The reasons for their failure were several. Unlike their models in Prussia, American teachers had not grown up in a class-based society. They did not accept a lifetime school-teaching position as a privilege or reward. Americans, and particularly Midwesterners, did not accept as given and fixed a system of inflexible social classes. They were forever on the move, geographically and socially, and they were to continue to view schoolteaching as a temporary occupation. For them, teaching was but a step on the ladder to either economic advance or matrimony.

New England's normal-school principals and instructors soon drew the consequences. They saw their students move to the better-paying city schools, or leave teaching altogether. They noted an older student group attend their institutions as steppingstones to further college and professional education or employment. Seeking to make the best of that situation and falling back on their own collegiate training, the New England schoolmen began to offer in their schools what their students sought in colleges, professional schools, and universities. They introduced a gospel of professional education which would join academic with a practical approach in the preparation of teachers for high school and special subjects. Eventually, they would add to it the professional training of school administrators and normal-school instructors.

The end result was that by 1900 the "treason" of the normal school became a dominant trend. Teachers for elementary classrooms were prepared in county or city training schools and in high schools, but increasingly less so in the state normal schools. These latter institutions began to pour their energies into the preparation of high-school teachers and administrators, into the continuing advanced training of experienced professionals, and into educational research. Whether, as in Wisconsin, they attempted to make themselves over into liberal-arts colleges, or whether, as in Illinois and Kansas, they saw themselves as professional schools, they wanted to shake their traditional status of precollegiate institutions and to take on the prestige and work of colleges and universities.

There were occasional protests. When requested by the governor of Missouri, the Carnegie Foundation for the Advancement of Teaching surveyed the state's institutions and programs for teacher education. It commissioned a select group of education professionals to investigate Missouri's state and city normal schools to determine "good practice in the largest field of professional training for public service in our country. . . ."[71]

The 1921 report, a massive volume of 400 pages of text and 50 of statistics, did not pull any punches. It severely criticized the Missouri normal schools for undermining the professional status of the state's elementary-school teachers. A curriculum which offered a hierarchically structured sequence leading from a first-year course of teachers of ungraded rural schools, to a fourth-year course "for the best positions, such as principals, assistants, professors, and county superintendents," the commission pointed out, was based on the incentive to climb "the educational ladder from the rural school to the graded town school, thence to the high school and superintendency, to be followed by 'institute' or normal school work." Many normal-school courses, the report stated, "were frankly makeshifts to help a teacher climb, say, from the seventh grade to a high school position."[72]

This deliberate encouragement of students to make elementary teaching a steppingstone toward high-school teaching, teaching and supervision of special subjects, and school administration, the commissioners emphasized, "constitutes the most serious charge against them [the normal schools.]" The commissioners drove home their point: "The thought of each kind of work as a goal in itself, worthy of extended and special preparation and of equal dignity with any other, does not occur. For the rural teacher the time when he shall become a 'principal, professor, or county superintendent' is the zenith of desire. . . ."[73]

Two years later, the Carnegie Survey in Missouri was echoed by the Zook Commission of the United States Bureau of Education, when it surveyed the institutions of higher education in Kansas. The commission charged that, without having accomplished their original goal, the Kansas normal schools had given in to pressures and temptations and had begun training high-school teachers and teachers of vocational schools. Legislative pressures and professional ambitions had diverted the attention of normal school educators "from their primary function, the training of elementary-school teachers." All the other activities influenced unfavorably "the superior quality of work otherwise possible in the preparation of elementary and rural school teachers. . . ." They added up, the commission thought, to a betrayal of a past obligation, and disregard for a present need.[74]

Hopes that the reports of the Zook and the Carnegie commissions might call back teacher educators to the task of educating and training elementary-school teachers were unrealistic. In the new century the hopes of the early school reformers to turn classroom teaching into a profession had changed into the ambitions of educational specialists and school administrators to see themselves as the true educational professionals. The new credo was well summed up in 1888 by James P. Wickersham, the former head of the first state normal school in Pennsylvania and superintendent of that state. Wickersham declared that the normal schools were able

> from the numbers that attend them, to instruct, train, and inspire with professional zeal a body of teachers who, when scattered over a State, will, as principals of high schools, as superintendents of schools, as writers in educational journals, as instructors at teachers' institutes, as leaders in educational reform, become a powerful agency in uplifting and making more efficient the whole work of education. . . . The normal schools can become the fountain of professional *esprit de corps* among the teachers of a State.[75]

As it was, by the beginning of the twentieth century, professionalism in education was to find its home in the graduate departments of educational administration and psychology, in the hierarchical establishments of state and city educational bureaucracies, and in the research-centered graduate schools of education and their programs for the continuing education of administrators and specialists. By contrast, the education of the country's largely female elementary-classroom teachers appeared to the overwhelmingly male ranks of professionals to be an unprestigious, albeit necessary and unavoidable, task not undertaken with much enthusiasm. The classroom teacher, after all, was the low woman on the professional totem pole.

Notes

AUTHOR'S NOTE: The theme of this chapter is developed at greater length in the author's forthcoming book, *And Sadly Teach: Teacher Education and Professionalization in American Culture* (Madison: University of Wisconsin Press).

1. The Holmes Group, *Tomorrow's Teachers: A Report of the Holmes Group* (East Lansing: Michigan State University, 1986); and Carnegie Forum on Education and the Economy, Task Force on Teaching as a Profession, *A Nation Prepared: Teachers for the Twenty-first Century* (New York: Carnegie Forum, 1986).
2. The Holmes Group, *Tomorrow's Teachers,* p. xx.
3. Carnegie Forum, *A Nation Prepared,* p. 3.
4. James G. Carter, "Outline of an Institution for the Education of Teachers," in *Boston Patriot* (February 1825). Reprinted in Arthur O. Norton (ed.), *The First State Normal School in America* (Cambridge, MA: Harvard University Press, 1926), p. 231.
5. Henry E. Dwight, *Travels in the North of Germany in the Years 1825 and 1826* (New York: G. & C. & H. Carvill 1829), pp. 244 and 253.
6. *American Annals of Education and Instruction* I, Part II (June 1831), p. 253–257 and 279.
7. "Seminary for Female Teachers," in *American Annals* I, Part II (August 1831), pp. 341–346.
8. Hermann Joseph Ody, *Victor Cousin: Ein Lebensbild im deutsch-französischen Kulturraum* (Saarbrücken: West-Ost Verlag, 1953), pp. 93–100.
9. Victor Cousin, *Report on the State of Public Instruction in Prussia* (New

York: Wiley & Long, 1835), pp. 62–64 and *passim*.
10. Ibid., p. 67
11. Ibid., pp. 205–206.
12. Oscar and Mary Handlin, *Commonwealth: Massachusetts, 1774–1861* (New York: New York University Press, 1947).
13. Cousin, *Report,* p. 293.
14. *American Journal of Education* 16 (March 1866), pp. 93–96.
15. Ibid., p. 96.
16. David A. Gould, "Policy and Pedagogues: School Reform and Teacher Professionalization in Massachusetts, 1840–1920," doctoral dissertation, Brandeis University, 1977, pp. 29–30.
17. Raymond B. Culver, *Horace Mann and Religion in the Massachusetts Public Schools* (New Haven: Yale University Press, 1929), pp. 111–126.
18. See Norton (ed.), *The First State Normal School,* p. xliii
19. Ibid., pp. 7 and 45.
20. Ibid., p. 68.
21. Massachusetts Board of Education, *Fourth Annual Report of the Secretary* (Boston: Dutton & Wentworth, 1841), p. 46.
22. James C. Greenough, "The State Normal School, Westfield," in Alfred M. Copeland (ed.), *A History of Hampden County Massachusetts,* Vol. I (Century Memorial Pub. Co., 1902), pp. 279–280.
23. "Typescript of Early Enrollments" and "Manuscript General Record Book, 1864–1876," Westfield State Normal School, Westfield, MA; and Gould, "Policy and Pedagogues," p. 29.
24. Massachusetts Board of Education, *Sixth Annual Report of the Secretary* (Boston, 1843), pp. 28 and 29.
25. *The Common School Journal* 12 (April 15, 1850), pp. 116–117.
26. Writers' Project, *The State Teachers College at Westfield* (Westfield, MA: State Teachers College, 1941), pp. 30–31.
27. Gould, "Policy and Pedagogues," p. 70.
28. Elizabeth Flynn, "What's Past Is Prologue," typescript history of Boston State College, Boston State College Archives, Boston, MA.
29. "Report of Dr. Larkin Dunton on the Boston Normal School," in *Fifteenth Annual Report of the Superintendent of Public Schools of the City of Boston, March 15, 1895* (Boston: Rockwell & Churchill, 1895), p. 332.
30. Gould, "Policy and Pedagogues," p. 85.
31. "Report of Dr. Larkin Dunton," p. 297.
32. Ibid.
33. Ibid., p. 298.
34. *American Journal of Education* 16 (September 1866), p. 451.
35. Gould, "Policy and Pedagogues," p. 29.
36. American Normal School Association, *Proceedings,* First Annual Convention, Trenton, NJ, 1859 (New York: A. S. Barnes & Burr, 1860), p. 106.
37. American Normal School and National Teachers' Association, *Addresses and Journal of Proceedings* (Washington, DC: James H. Holmes, 1871), pp. 12 and 13.
38. Ibid., p. 17.
39. Ibid., p. 25.
40. National Education Association, *Addresses and Journal of Proceedings* (Peoria, IL: N. C. Nason, 1873), pp. 183–184.
41. Ibid., p. 37.
42. Avery D. Mayo, "The Normal School in the United States," in *Education* 8 (December 1887), pp. 226, 231, and 232.
43. See, for example, George E. Gay, "Massachusetts Normal Schools," in *Education* 17 (May 1897), pp. 515–517.
44. Egbert R. Isbell, *A History of Eastern Michigan University, 1849–1965* (Ypsilanti: Eastern Michigan University, 1971), p. 1–29.
45. Charles A. Harper, *Development of the Teachers College in the United States with Special Reference to the Illinois State Normal University* (Bloomington

IL: McKnight & McKnight, 1935), pp. ii, 48–50, and 78.

46. Statistics in *Semi-Centennial History of the Illinois State Normal University, 1857–1907* (Normal, IL: Faculty Committee, 1907), pp. 40, 47, 50, and 52.
47. John A. H. Keith, "The Development of the Model School," in *Semi-Centennial History,* pp. 77–83; and Helen E. Marshall, *Grandest of Enterprises: Illinois State Normal University, 1857–1957* (Normal, IL: Illinois State Normal University, 1956), p. 93.
48. On American Herbartianism, see Harold B. Dunkel, *Herbart and Education* (New York: Random House, 1969), pp. 119–126; and Harold B. Dunkel, *Herbart and Herbartianism: An Educational Ghost Story* (Chicago: University of Chicago Press, 1970), pp. 241–283.
49. David Felmley, "The New Normal School Movement," in *Educational Review* 44 (April 1913), pp. 409–410.
50. Ibid., p. 414.
51. Albert Salisbury, *Historical Sketch of Normal Instruction in Wisconsin, 1846–1876* (Madison, 1876), pp. 23–25.
52. Jeff Wasserman, "Wisconsin Normal Schools and the Educational Hierarchy, 1860–1890," in *Journal of the Midwest History of Education Society* 7 (1979), p. 3; and *Report of the Board of Visitors of the State Normal School at Platteville* (Platteville [WI], 1867).
53. Based on the annual catalogues of the Wisconsin State Normal School at Platteville.
54. *Annual Report of the Board of Regents of Normal Schools of Wisconsin, 1880–81;* and *Annual Report of the Superintendent of Public Instruction, 1900* (WI), p. 92.
55. See various issues of *Wisconsin Journal of Education* 28 (February 1898), and 37 (March 1905), pp. 58–59; as well as *Annual Report of the Superintendent of Public Instruction* (1900), p. 26.
56. Lyman B. Kellog, "The Founding of the State Normal School," in *Collections of the Kansas State Historical Society* 12 (1911–1912), p. 96.
57. Numbers from *A History of the State Normal School of Kansas for the First Twenty-five Years* (Emporia, 1899), p. 144.
58. Albert R. Taylor, "History of Normal-School Work in Kansas," in *Kansas State Historical Society Quarterly* 6 (1900), pp. 117–118; and Clifford S. Griffin, *The University of Kansas: A History* (Lawrence: The University Press of Kansas, 1974), p. 132.
59. Based on *A History of the State Normal School of Kansas for the First Twenty-five Years* (Emporia, 1889), pp. 63–70. Numbers are taken from p. 144.
60. C. O. Wright, *100 Years in Kansas Education,* Vol. I (Topeka: The Kansas State Teachers Association, 1963), p. 78.
61. Taylor, "History of Normal-School Work," pp. 119–120.
62. Felmley, "The New Normal School Movement," p. 412.
63. Quoted in Marshall, *Grandest of Enterprises,* p. 249.
64. Henry C. Johnson Jr., and Erwin V. Johanningmeier, *Teachers for the Prairie: The University of Illinois and the Schools, 1868–1945* (Urbana, IL: University of Illinois Press, 1972), p. 160.
65. Marshall, *Grandest of Enterprises,* p. 252; and Johnson and Johanningmeier, *Teachers for the Prairie,* pp. 138–139 and 176–177.
66. Griffin, *The University of Kansas,* pp. 273–277.
67. Merle Curti and Vernon Carstensen, *The University of Wisconsin: A History,* Vol. II (Madison: The University of Wisconsin Press, 1949), pp. 255–257 and 262.
68. *Wisconsin Journal of Education* 47 (May 1918), pp. 126–131.
69. *General Laws of the State of Wisconsin, 1925,* Ch. 101.
70. Jurgen Herbst, "Nineteenth-Century Normal Schools in the United States: A Fresh Look," in *History of Education* 9 (1980), p. 227.
71. William S. Learned et al., *The Professional Preparation of Teachers for American Public Schools: A Study Based upon an Examination of Tax-Supported Normal Schools in the State*

of Missouri (New York: The Carnegie Foundation, 1920), p. xvi.

72. Learned et al., *The Professional Preparation*, pp. 82–83 and 91.
73. Ibid., pp. 83 and 170.
74. George F. Zook, *Report of a Survey of the State Institutions of Higher Learning in Kansas*, U.S. Bureau of Education *Bulletin* 40 (Washington, DC: Government Printing Office, 1923), p. 66, 68, and 72.
75. James P. Wickersham in "Proceedings," Department of Superintendence of the National Education Association, February 14–16, 1888, in U.S. Bureau of Education, *Circular of Information* 6 (Washington, DC: Government Printing Office, 1888), p. 73.

9

Teachers and Teacher Training in the Twentieth Century

William R. Johnson

In 1983 the American Educational Research Association (AERA) sponsored the publication of *Historical Inquiry in Education.*[1] Not one of the distinguished contributors focused on the history of either teachers or teacher education. Just these few years later, this present volume (also sponsored by AERA), is devoted exclusively to the history of teachers and teacher training. It seems hard to believe that only within the past decade or so have historians begun to pay much attention to schoolteachers and their preparation.[2]

Geraldine J. Clifford previously has pointed out the "virtual invisibility of teachers" in the history of education. She has argued that the more recent focus by historians on the bureaucratic characteristics of schools has served to reinforce the tendency to ignore teachers. Clifford's 1975 AERA Division F vice-presidential address, "Saints, Sinners, and People," can properly be viewed as the turning point in interest in teachers and teacher training; and her book *The Shape of American Education,* published in that same year, represented, in part, the first substantial attempt to view the teaching profession historically from a cultural perspective since Willard Elsbree's *The American Teacher,* which appeared in 1939. Two other works, Paul Mattingly's *The Classless Profession* and Paul Woodring's "The Development of Teacher Education," also were published in 1975.[3]

This chapter suggests that historians' lack of interest until recently in teachers and teacher training mirrored a cultural shift during the 1960s and 1970s in which the direct improvement of teachers was no longer the focal point of reform efforts. Instead, reformers centered their efforts on top-down strategies, such as "teacher-proof" curricula and accountability, which would force instructional change in the schools. Conversely, the recent revival of interest among historians in teachers and teacher training corresponds to a renewed respect for the importance of classroom teachers—a respect reflected, for example, in myriad plans to reward master teachers through merit pay and increased professional autonomy.

Though historians' interest in teachers and teacher training heightened after about 1975, there still are two major limitations to the secondary literature. First, most of the recent historical research has focused on the nineteenth century. Second, the institutions that have carried the greater burden of training teachers, like normal schools and (in the mid-twentieth century) state teachers colleges, have been virtually ignored. Therefore, it is difficult to generalize about the history of teachers and teacher training in the twentieth century. Much of what follows, then, must be viewed as suggestions for further research.

Where university schools of education are concerned, however, there is a secondary literature which permits some tentative conclusions. Unlike the fields of law and medicine, where the university professional-school model revolutionized training, and to some degree practice, in education, universities have not succeeded in defining a training paradigm that has transformed the education of teachers. The distinctive contribution that American universities made to public schooling was not in the training they offered practitioners, but in the way that university research supported and justified the emergence of centralized, bureaucratic school systems. Universities, in other words, appear to have had greater influence in shaping the *conditions* of professional practice, rather than the practice itself. Whether there were alternatives to this centralized university perspective remains unclear, though preliminary research in Maryland suggests there may have been attempts at the beginning of the twentieth century to create a horizontal, rather than a hierarchical, professional culture among teachers.

Teacher Preparation, 1950–1980: Outside Reformers and Top-down Reforms

Although teachers and teacher training were not subjects of historical examination during the 1960s, they underwent intense public scrutiny. Such scrutiny began in fact in the early 1950s, with the publication of *Quackery in the Public Schools* (1950), by Albert Lynd, and *Educational Wastelands* (1953) and *The Restoration of Learning* (1955), by Arthur Bestor.[4] These attacks on progressive education charged that educationists were anti-intellectual and -democratic. Such criticisms were later fueled by the 1957 launching of Sputnik, which generated books and articles devoted to explaining why Johnny couldn't read (or do math), whereas Ivan could.

The attack on educationists may have reached its apogee in 1963 with the publication of James D. Koerner's *The Miseducation of American Teachers*. Koerner argued that the "inferior intellectual quality of the Education faculty is *the* fundamental limitation of the field." "Educationists," who spoke the language of "Educanto," were a "sincere, humanitarian, well intentioned hard-working, poorly informed, badly educated and ineffectual group of men and women." He found education courses to be "puerile, repetitious, dull, and ambiguous," as well as "vague, insipid, time-wasting, adumbrations of the obvious."[5]

Despite some obvious thematic similarities, Koerner's work did not, however, fit squarely in the tradition of Lynd and Bestor. (Curiously, there is no reference to Lynd or Bestor in Koerner's book.) What is significant about *The Miseducation of American Teachers* is its treatment of classroom teachers: They are totally ignored, although by implication tarred with the same broad brush used to paint education professors and schools of education. Whereas in the books by Lynd and Bestor their existence had been treated with at least some measure of respect, classroom teachers became invisible in Koerner's work. Both Lynd and Bestor took pains to exclude teachers from the criticism they leveled at educationists. Indeed, both authors referred to letters they had received from teachers who agreed with their criticisms of progressive education; and Bestor, in *The Restoration of Learning*, devoted a chapter to the theme that many good teachers were thwarted by the curricular reforms of educationists. In fact, teachers became sort of lonely, underappreciated heroes in Bestor's later work. In *Restoration* he argued that the new curricula proposed by educationists completely "disregard the realities of teaching" and in their more extreme form conceal a "profound . . . contempt for the classroom teacher."[6] A decade later, in Koerner's *Miseducation*, the role of classroom teachers as potential allies for reformers never is considered. Teachers now were in danger of becoming invisible pawns.

Teachers came to be seen as less central to the improvement of the schools during the early 1960s because, beyond a consensus among lay critics that more intensive academic training was needed, there was no agreement on how to train teachers. This was not a matter of disagreement over which models of professional training ought to be supported. There were no models. Not even imperfect ones which might, through renovation and reform, hold promise for the future. This was a point noted by E. V. Johanningmeier in a review of Koerner published in the *Harvard Educational Review*. "One wishes," Johanningmeier wrote at the time, that Koerner "had used the famed Flexner report for a model. Flexner began his survey of medical schools with an idea, a defensible conception of what a medical school should be. Mr. Koerner had no such model."[7]

Koerner's conclusion in *Miseducation* that "there should be many paths, not one, to the teaching certificate,"[8] found support in James B. Conant's *The Education of American Teachers*, also published in 1963. Conant's work was critical of both academic and professional training offered by colleges and universities in their preparation of teachers. But whereas he was quite prescriptive in terms of the increased academic training that teachers needed, at both the high-school and the college level, when it came to the professional sequence of courses, Conant had little positive to recommend. One of his central recommendations was that all state-mandated requirements concerning the number of courses or credits in education be dropped.

Unable to point to a single model program for the training of teachers, Conant hoped that competition among the variety of programs then in existence might produce such a model. "Each college or university," he argued, "should be permitted to develop in detail whatever program of teacher education it considers most desirable." The competition that would result between teacher-training colleges and universities would "invigorate the institutions." Faculty would develop "more pride in the quality of their graduates," and superintendents and school boards would gradually recognize "that alumni of certain institutions tended to be better prepared than those of rival institutions."[9]

Conant set only two limits to the experimentation in teacher training that colleges and universities should be encouraged to embark upon. First, the president of each school had to be prepared to certify, on behalf of the faculty, that a candidate for a teaching position was "adequately prepared"; and, second, the institution must establish "in conjunction with a public school system a state-approved practice-teaching arrangement."[10] Conant's "model" for teacher education, then, prescribed academic subject matter (at both the high-school and college level), made no prescriptions whatever for professional courses, and invested great importance in an intensive period of practice teaching. (Indeed, he recommends that all professional education courses have a linked field component.) While this was not exactly an apprenticeship model of teacher preparation, it represented a movement in that direction.

Because both the Conant and the Koerner volumes concluded with a list of recommendations (27 from Conant and 13 from Koerner), they left the impression that a solid groundwork for the reform of teacher training had been laid. In retrospect, however, what is most interesting about the two books is how little firm direction they provide for the reform of teacher training beyond recommendations for more stringent academic preparation. When their recommendations touch upon the professional portion of the teacher-preparation sequence, they usually suggest elimination or reduction of (teacher colleges, undergraduate majors in education, specialized work at the master's level, etc.).

Moreover, both men rejected Master of Arts in Teaching (MAT) programs as a solution. Although Conant had been instrumental as president of Harvard in the establishment of the first MAT program in the 1930s, by the time *The Education of American Teachers* was published he no longer viewed them as central to the improvement of American education. Noting that the programs developed during the 1950s were expensive and heavily subsidized, Conant pointed out that they had trained only a very small percentage of teachers in the decade past. He concluded, and Koerner agreed, that such programs should continue to serve a limited role, but that fifth-year programs "will not and should not become the principal route to teaching careers."[11] Despite marked differences in the tone of their analysis, then, Conant and Koerner largely agreed that there were no obvious solutions, beyond more stringent academic training, to the reform of teacher education.

It is against this background that the popularity of teacher-proof curricula and later accountability can be better understood. Both were examples of top-down reform strategies designed to improve classroom instruction without necessarily improving teachers. The design of teacher-proof curricula dated from the mid-1950s, when the academic community, responding in part to critics like Bester but also to cold-war fears of Russian superiority in science and technology, began to participate in curriculum projects which focused on the ideas and methods of the academic disciplines. With private foundation support and federal funds channelled through the National Science Foundation, new curricula were developed and distributed in science, mathematics, and foreign languages. Later, in the 1960s curriculum development efforts were extended to areas in the humanities and socia sciences.[12]

Some of these curricula, like "Science—A Process Approach," attempted to se down the curriculum in minute detail. S—APA reduced content to "the smalles possible discrete steps so the learner is led in a systematic way to a predetermine end which is the sum of the steps taught." Here the teacher is no longer the centra figure in the instructional process. Prepackaged curriculum materials redefined th role of the teacher as a mechanical intermediary between subject and student. Nc all of the curricula developed, of course, were intended to be teacher-proof. Th Jerome Bruner–inspired "Man: A Course of Study" is a case-in-point. Th teacher's role here was potentially powerful, particularly as the curriculum focused on social and moral values. Whether teachers received sufficient training to play that role is another question; and in the absence of such training the burden of instructional improvement would be carried through the packaged texts, laboratory manuals, workbooks, and films.[13]

The accountability movement, which flowered in the 1970s, and which also reflected a mechanical view of the teacher's classroom role, had its beginnings in attempts during the 1960s to address the persistent inequalities in American society, particularly in urban centers and among minorities. Kenneth Clark, for example, argued that the various reasons advanced to explain why children of the ghetto failed, whether those explanations focused on intellectual inferiority or cultural deprivation, simply were alibis for educational neglect. Clark proposed to reward teachers for results, eventually proposing for the Washington, DC school system a plan that linked teachers' salaries to performance of students on standardized tests, and other measures of basic academic achievement.[14]

The notion of accountability received classic expression in 1970 when Leon Lessinger, then Associate Commissioner of Education, published *Every Kid a Winner: Accountability in Education.* The specific technique that Lessinger's book promoted was the performance contract. Outside firms of educational consultants and specialists would "contract" to teach specific skills to children, and would be paid only if students learned those skills as measured by outside evaluators. Designed to shake a lethargic, unresponsive educational bureaucracy, performance contracting was intended to force schools to "use a method management that uses engineering insights on which leading business firms rely—but which our schools have largely ignored."[15]

As state legislatures wrote accountability programs into law, the effect on the teacher-education programs was substantial. Nationwide, performance-based education (PBE) and Competency-Based Education (CBE) teacher-training programs were established which focused on the careful specification of objectives to be achieved, and the measurement of results that teachers obtained. Considerable time was devoted to the construction of precise behavioral objectives which could be subject to equally precise evaluation techniques. CBE/PBE teacher-training programs perhaps also deemphasized classroom instruction techniques, or at least relegated such training to student teaching, while defining the central professional task as the construction of behavioral objectives and curricular hierarchies. As in the case of the teacher-proof curricula, teachers were being introduced to devices that would control and channel their classroom behavior—though in this instance, as teachers constructed their daily or weekly instructional objectives, they were engaged in a process of externally-mandated self-control. Teacher-proof curricula thus, in a sense, became internalized.

Lessinger's contention that performance-based education simply represented successful management techniques "on which leading business firms rely" was wide of the mark. Performance-based education was *not* borrowed from successful business practice. It was borrowed instead from academic theorists in university business schools, men such as Robert McNamara, who believed that was the way that businesses ought to be run. McNamara was a graduate of the Harvard Business

School (where he had taught statistics for a time after graduation) and, according to David Halberstam, symbolized a new kind of executive in American business. He was among those men "who had not grown up in business, who were not part of the family, but who were modern, well-educated technicians who prided themselves that they were not tied to the past."[16]

A cursory inspection of journals like the *Harvard Business Review, Management Review,* and *California Management Review* from the mid-1970s finds them filled with minor McNamaras, professors in university schools of business and management, and schools of education, who extol the virtues of performance-based management. Those same articles reveal, however, that businessmen themselves apparently resisted performance-based management techniques, and the professors reluctantly concluded, in the words of one, that "as a technique for improving employee performance, performance appraisal has not lived up to expectations."[17]

Performance-based education, then, is best understood as an attempt by university professors of education to apply an *academic* perspective to the problems of a professional field. It was promulgated not because there was an abundance of hard evidence that it worked, but because it represented a scientific and technical viewpoint which promised control over American schools, much as it had promised (but never really delivered) control over American business. Most important, it fit the ethos of the twentieth-century university that has valued most highly scientific knowledge. And if the knowledge itself is not yet scientific (and few would argue that education is a hard science), at least the approach—systematic, rational, objective analysis—can be scientific. Like law professors who sought to establish academic careers at the turn of the century by promoting a science of law through the case method of instruction, university professors of education have attempted to establish their academic credentials by creating a science of education. Or at least a scientific approach to education.

The University Teacher Preparation Model: Research in Retrospect

There are a handful of institutional histories which can be used to examine the historical role played by American universities in shaping this professional ethos. Indeed, the histories of university schools of education represent the one significant exception to the earlier observation that historians generally ignored teachers and teacher training in the two decades after 1955. However, that historians have focused *only* on universities (and not on normal schools or four-year colleges) also suggests how dominant the university model of teacher training has become. As the preface to the history of Teachers College, Columbia University, proclaims, the history of that institution "is the history of American Teacher education writ small."[18]

On the surface, that is not an unreasonable claim. Teachers College, Columbia was the most influential teacher-training institution in the first half of the twentieth century. Not because of its undergraduate programs—after 1926 it had none—but because of the training it offered experienced teachers, administrators and, perhaps most of all, normal-school and teachers-college faculty through its myriad regular and summer-session courses. Its history represented the triumph of the university school of education, with its research emphasis. If not all universities prepared students exclusively at the graduate level, the Columbia model was one to which many aspired. Viewed in this way, the history of twentieth-century teacher training can be seen as a series of institutional displacements, with normal schools becoming state teachers colleges, then multipurpose liberal-arts colleges, and now, in many instances, regional state universities.

Even if achievement still falls short of aspiration, the university teacher-training model remains vigorous. Recent publications of the Holmes Group Report, representing the views of education deans at major research universities across the country, reassert the importance of educational research in defining professional knowledge and certifying professional competence. Moreover, the recent emphasis on articulating the "knowledge base" for teacher preparation, which pervades both professional journals and the halls of state departments of education, creates pressures on small colleges and universities to conform to the large research-university model of teacher training.[19]

Yet, as the histories of university schools of education make clear, the question is whether the university model of teacher training has been the best, or even an adequate, model. Three major themes emerge from an examination of those histories. First, university schools of education have tended to distance themselves from the training and concerns of classroom teachers. Second, and not unrelated to the first, the research agenda has not often produced knowledge useful to the practitioner, nor has it often gained respect among members of traditional academic disciplines. Third, university schools of education have produced no permanent, durable models of teacher training but rather a constant, almost generational, drift in search of, in Arthur G. Powell's apt phrase, "educational authority."[20]

Columbia was among the leaders in the deliberate movement toward graduate study when, in 1925, it eliminated its four-year undergraduate course in the School of Practical Arts. With the passing of the "so-called normal phase of the college," Columbia was free to concentrate on "the advanced professional training of educational leaders."[21] Harvard, too, moved exclusively to graduate-level training, though at least for a time—under Dean Henry W. Holmes in the 1930s—the training itself was focused on the preparation of practitioners. It is significant, however, that such a focus, according to Powell, was derided by professors like Chicago's Charles Judd, who "roundly attacked Harvard's continuing obsession with practitioner training and new obsession with school teachers."[22]

Although state universities were unable, for political reasons, to abandon the undergraduate preparation of teachers, they too emphasized graduate training and research, often at the expense of closer ties with teachers and schools. At the University of Illinois, Johnson and Johanningmeier concluded that if the criterion for the College of Education's development "is the relationship to schools and schooling, . . . the record is not a good one. The University, as the 'apex' of the state's school system, did (and cared to do) little to improve the 'base.' The schools were on the whole more used than aided, let alone led."[23]

Perhaps the central problem was the kind of research being produced in university schools of education. Holmes at Harvard believed that the university emphasis on research had driven a wedge between professors and practitioners by creating a hierarchy, reinforced by the scientific research values of the larger university community, which set education professors over teachers in the schools. Ironically, as education professors attempted to conform to academic standards in their research, the research they produced was often rejected by traditional academics. University of Illinois president David Kinley remarked in 1924 that ''when one reads the literature of this field [of education] he is tempted, as he is when he reads some of the literature of sociology and psychology, to wonder whether after all the so-called field of study did not emerge into public attention because its devotees invented a terminology and then thought they had a science.''[24] Complaints about the quality of research in education form a common theme in the histories of colleges of education; and that theme persists into the present, as analyzed in 1982 by Harry Judge in *American Graduate Schools of Education: A View from Abroad.*[25] There is a circular aspect to all this which is worth noting: As education professors attempted to establish academic credentials and forge academic careers, their research became more and more methodologically sophisticated, and thereby less and less accessible to practitioners.

The last of the three major themes suggested by the histories of university schools of education is that they have not provided permanent, clear-cut models for teacher training. One of the recurring motifs of the history of Teachers College, Columbia has been its role in introducing innovations which have been incorporated by other institutions. Such ''intellectual pioneering,'' however, also is likened to a ''nomadism in which the smoke of a neighbor on the horizon becomes the impetus to move on.''[26] This image of intellectual drift pervades Powell's history of the Harvard Graduate School of Education as well. In an epilogue titled ''Roots of Instability,'' he noted that at the beginning of the 1970s ''many puzzled or exhausted faculty members wondered if discontinuity and upheaval were inherent characteristics'' of the school. The history of Harvard's school of education, Powell concluded, has been characterized by ''drastic and wrenching change.''[27] The histories of university schools of education offer support, then, to the implicit conclusion reached by Conant and Koerner in 1963: No agreed-upon model of teacher training had yet been defined.

This intellectual diffuseness also was reflected in the curricula of twentieth-century schools of education. Again, Teachers College, Columbia, while not typical because of its size, exemplified the range of possibilities. According to Paul Woodring, Teachers College ''offered an enormous variety of courses in every conceivable education specialty,'' courses which represented ''a wide range of educational philosophies.''[28] Abraham Flexner, commenting on colleges of education in 1930, believed that such a vast array of courses led ''to all kinds of superficiality and immediacy, all kinds of 'rabbit paths'.''[29] It was not, of course, only at universities that courses proliferated. Earle U. Rugg, in a 1933 national survey of teachers, found 636 curricula distributed among 31 teachers colleges, or an average of slightly more than 20 curricula per institution.[30] Perhaps this absence of a unitary professional vision explains why education has been so subject to faddish thinking.

In law and medicine, research universities had led an intellectual revolution in professional training at the beginning of the twentieth century. The case method in law, and scientific discovery in medicine, provided a new, clearer, and to some degree narrower focus for the two professions. Indeed, one of the central problems facing both legal and medical educators in the twentieth century has been how to broaden what many have characterized as an excessively narrow and technical training. In education, universities did not lead an intellectual revolution which transformed the training of teachers. The experience in education is better described as a series of local uprisings, each decade or so, which have had little enduring impact except, perhaps, to clutter the curricular landscape with dead or wounded programs and theories. Nevertheless, it is still to the university school of education that many look today to improve the research base on which teacher training ought to rest.

The American Normal School: A "Practical" Alternative?

In order to understand why the university model of teacher training has triumphed, and what the triumph means, we need a better historical understanding of the normal-school model which it apparently replaced. Here the secondary literature is of little direct help. Historians have paid almost no attention to the normal schools—or to the state teachers colleges which many of the normals became. Although conventional wisdom characterizes these schools as offering intensely practical, nontheoretical, "nuts and bolts" kinds of training, we know little about what actually went on in these schools. It is time that the history of the normal schools, and of the teachers colleges that followed them, receive serious historical scrutiny.

Such scrutiny might alter our perceptions of the normal schools' so-called practical nature. Jurgen Herbst has pointed out that normal schools in the Midwest focused more on academic preparation than on professional training. Midwestern normal schools, he argued, "harbored ambitions to serve as academies and colleges for the general education of their students." Such schools, he further argued, "departed from the path of single-minded pedagogical professionalism as mapped out in the East" because of the desire of frontier communities to have post-elementary education widely available.[31] While Herbst is surely correct in his description of the academically oriented normal schools of the Midwest, there is evidence that, by 1890, normal schools in the East also had "departed from the path of single-minded professionalism." If the transformation of normal schools from pedagogical to academic institutions is more than a regional phenomenon, there is something more involved here than Midwestern populism.

Evidence that American normal schools had by 1890 become predominantly academic institutions, functioning much like state and regional high schools and academies, is found in a massive "History of Normal Schools in the United States," written around 1891 by M. E. Newell, former Maryland state superintendent of education and principal of the Maryland State Normal School, and published posthumously in 1900.[32] It is a source rich in information, most of it gleaned from the catalogues of normal schools throughout the United States but also containing Newell's personal observations about normal schools he had visited throughout his career.

The grand theme that emerges from Newell's study of normal schools is one of declension, from a course of study in the mid-nineteenth century that was largely professional to one that by 1890 was heavily academic. Newell compared, for example, the 1847 curriculum of the Westfield, Massachusetts normal school with its curriculum of 1889. With both a two-year and a four-year course in 1889, the latter curriculum contained less professional material than the 1847 curriculum. In 1889 all pedagogical training was crowded into the fourth term of the two-year course, under the title "Theory and Art of Teaching." The four-year course added only more academic branches. Of the 1889 Bridgewater, Massachusetts normal school, Newell noted a vast array of course offerings with the professional subjects relegated to a two-year course. "It goes without saying," he remarked, "that on some of these slices of bread the butter must be spread exceedingly thin."[33]

While the catalogs, as summarized by Newell, often do not report their curricula in ways in which the percentage of time devoted to professional subjects can be determined, those that do are suggestive. The two-year course of the state normal school of New Hampshire devoted 27 percent of its time to pedagogical subjects (36.5 percent if music and drawing are considered professional). The normal curriculum at Providence, Rhode Island stretched over three and one-half years, but less than 10 percent of the total time was spent on pedagogical training. By 1890, then, it would appear that concentration on academic training was the norm, not the exception, among American normal schools. Even Newell's Maryland State Normal School drifted rather quickly toward an academic emphasis. Established in 1866, by 1876 the catalog announced that the "main object" of the school continued to be the preparation of teachers, "but the general course is equally adapted to those who have no professional object in view, and wish merely to obtain a thorough and liberal education."[34]

Whether this drift toward a more traditional academic curriculum was a pattern followed by most normal schools is a question which deserves further historical investigation—particularly in the twentieth century, where the secondary literature is weakest. Moreover, that investigation must be prepared to be critical (though not dismissive) of the normal-school rhetoric, particularly claims that the academic subject matter taught in the normal school was in fact "professionalized."

Previous studies have tended to accept such assertions at face value.[35] For example, Charles Harper, in his history of Illinois State Normal University, asserts that the institution contributed to "the settling of that old time riddle of dualism between method and content—professional and academic. It emphasized repeatedly the identity of the two phases. Subject matter is professionalized if it is vital, meaningful, and worth teaching. All subject-matter courses must be in a sense method courses. On the other hand, all method courses must be subject-matter courses."[36] It is worth noting, however, that the 1933 national survey of teachers reported that a considerable portion of subject-matter instructors claimed some professionalization of their courses, but the visitation of classes in selected teachers colleges "did not result in the impression that there was a wide acceptance of the theory of professional treatment of subject matter," and an attempt to identify the "concrete ways" of professionalizing the academic courses was unsuccessful.[37]

Another area which deserves further historical investigation is the relationship between the normal school and the model school, in terms of both the curricula and the faculty of the two institutions. Newell again identifies the outlines of the problem:

> The proper adaptation and adjustment of the school of theory to the school of practice has long been felt to be the crucial task in the arrangement of the normal school curriculum. So difficult has been this problem that some schools have never attempted the solution; some have made the attempt and have abandoned it; some have accomplished the feat—on paper; some have established a school of practice without observation, and some a school of observation without practice; while some are conscientiously struggling with the experiment, and realizing that the "school of observation and practice" is like a loose tooth, more noticed for the pain it creates than for the services it renders.[38]

The history of the Maryland State Normal School (now Towson State University) provides an illustration of Newell's "loose tooth" metaphor from the students' perspective. There the model school had been reestablished in the late 1880s. During the 1890s, senior students were required to spend one week (whether both semesters is unclear) observing in the school. The students' reactions to this experience are recorded in the "Class Diary," a remarkably faithful day-by-day account of events in the normal school written by members of the senior class from 1895 through 1899.

In 1897 the first to observe are the gentlemen, who "begin a siege of four days—a period of time to which all students look forward with a little less than pleasure, a little more than pain." The following January, an entry in the diary notes the absence of a number of students from the opening exercises: "This was because an awful custom had begun again this year—Miss Richmond had some students go into the Model School to observe." In another place, the model-school observation is characterized as an "ordeal," and when, in 1898, assignments are again made to the model school, the entry reads: "I think when I have mentioned the model school I have said enough."[39]

The reasons for this distaste for observation in the model school never are made clear. At the least it suggests a tension between what students learned in the normal school (as well as how they learned—through memorization and rote recitation) and the practical activities of teaching in the model school. Whether normal-school students experienced pedagogical culture shock when they entered the model school is a hypothesis which research into the histories of other normal schools might confirm or disprove. Indeed, this is likely to be a fruitful focus for the further investigation of university schools of education as well. A study of the relationships between university faculty and model (or experimental) school faculty is likely to reveal a good deal about both philosophy and practice in the training of teachers. The more general question that needs to be addressed is why the Maryland State Normal School (and, if Newell's history is accurate, other normal schools as well) drifted toward a more academic and cultural emphasis in their course of study.

There are a number of reasons for that curricular shift. First, as Herbst has argued, there was community support for more widely available educational opportunity. Normal schools functioned as state high schools for many students, especially those from rural areas. Second, normal-school faculty justified the time spent on academic training as necessary to educate underprepared students about to embark on professional training. Third, it is likely that some normal-school faculty believed it was more prestigious to teach academic subjects. Finally, there is the intriguing suggestion by Arthur Powell, in a review of Paul Mattingly's *The Classless Profession,* that the nineteenth-century emphasis on moral character as the main source of professional identification "helped protect vulnerable educators from the charge that they possessed no technical expertise by downplaying the centrality of such expertise." The irony, according to Powell, was that so much effort was expended "in preserving the idea that character, and hence teaching skill, was personal and unique that relatively little incentive developed to accumulate a body of technical knowledge that could be passed on to succeeding generations of teachers."[40]

We should at least entertain the possibility, then, that one important reason for the normal-school emphasis on academic training was the absence of a core of theoretical knowledge which could guide professional practice. This is reinforced by a reading of the Maryland State Normal School faculty minutes recorded from 1905 to 1917. The topics discussed at the bimonthly meetings suggest both how central academic and cultural topics were to the normal-school faculty, and how a kind of professional aimlessness characterized their "pedagogical" discussions. In 1908, for example, the principal "urged that the faculty take up some line of pedagogical work." The faculty committee appointed to "consider plans for pedagogical meetings," however, apparently met with resistance from other faculty. In March of 1909 a resolution was passed which stated that "the heads of departments (including history) should not be excused from leading pedagogical discussions."[41]

Over the next eight years the struggle to impose a cohesive set of professional aims upon the Maryland State Normal School continued. What is interesting is the way in which the topics assigned for discussion gradually began to alternate between pedagogical presentations, usually by model-school faculty or outside guest speakers, and cultural presentations and discussions, led by the normal faculty. In the spring of 1913, for example, the following topics were discussed: the movement to establish vocational schools in Baltimore; the folly of floods and the movement of Congress to prevent them; criticism of the small amounts of money spent on education; normal schools; training high-school teachers in normal colleges; and the Dresden Art Congress. In May of that year, one Miss Davis reported on "courses of study in the elementary school"—but she was the principal of the elementary model school, not a member of the regular normal faculty.

When the regular faculty convened the following fall, the discussion again focused more on literary and cultural matters. They agreed that the first half of each meeting should focus on the "study of Pedagogy" (and decided to read together Gilbert's *What Children Study and Why*), and that the second half "be given to Story-telling, the stories to be told according to pedagogical principles, and to be criticized by the listeners." The subjects were to come from the grand operas, the great myths, and the great poems.[42]

At the next meeting that plan was followed. Yet the center would not hold. At the following meeting, on October 28, the topics discussed included a visit to an art exhibition in Philadelphia, and summaries of articles on "the Cubists, "Industrial Efficiency," "The International Congress in School Hygiene," "The High Cost of Living," and "The Development of the Radium Supply in Colorado." Over the following months, interspersed with a guest speaker on the Montessori method and continued discussion of a methods text (led by Miss Scarborough of the model school), the faculty told the stories of famous operas, and recounted tales by Sir Walter Scott and O. Henry.[43]

In 1914, while the discussions of the normal-school faculty continued, the Maryland state legislature authorized a study of the state's school system. The study team was headed by Abraham Flexner, famous for his 1910 study of medical education. Its report, released in 1916, concluded that the leadership of the Maryland State Normal School "has at times been distinctly inadequate." Further, "Lacking funds to employ trained and experienced teachers, the school has appointed to its staff its own recent graduates. Inbreeding has thus gone on with its usual bad effects."[44]

Even in the face of such criticism, the normal faculty were unable (or unwilling) to reorganize the school. Although the February 1916 faculty minutes note that "extracts from the School Survey were read," the following fall this entry appears: "Miss Bernhardt gave a report on 'How to Clean Silver.' The talk was followed by discussion." In January, 1917, the faculty heard talks on "Art in England," "Japanese and Chinese Lacquer Work," and the "open-air theatre."[45]

The emphasis that the Maryland State Normal School placed on academic training and cultural activities probes the traditional conception of normal schools as institutions where the academic offerings were meager "and confined largely to the methods and mechanics of the classroom."[46] Newell's 1900 history of American normal schools, and Jurgen Herbst's more recent work, support this interpretation. If it is true that normal schools did not embody a practical approach to teacher training, that would help explain why university schools of education, which deemphasized the practical in favor of the theoretical, became so influential so quickly.

As Powell has suggested, when university faculty "attempted at the end of the century to define educational expertise only through the quantitative and experimental procedures of emerging social science, there was little competitive tradition of systematic knowledge about education derived in other ways to offer as an alternative."[47] University schools of education became the dominant model because they entered a pedagogical and professional vacuum.

Professional Preparation in Law, Medicine, and Education: The Importance of Gender

The parallels to law and medicine we have observed are instructive. In both fields, university professors led the transformation of professional training with the introduction of the case method in law and the impact of scientific discovery in medicine. Yet in both law and medicine, powerful practitioners provided a balance to the academic perspective. This practitioner culture in some cases resisted, in others adapted, theoretical perspectives developed in the university. For example, prominent lawyers resisted the introduction of the case method of legal training and, while not entirely successful, they did succeed in curbing some of the method's excesses and in softening the professorial image of the lawyer as a scientist working in a legal laboratory of decided cases.[48] Similarly in medicine, where one would perhaps expect the least tension between theory and practice, physicians often placed clinical wisdom before theory. Charles L. Bosk, in *Forgive and Remember: Managing Medical Failure,* argues that there are two competing systems of legitimization for medical authority: clinical expertise and scientific evidence. But these systems are not of equal authority: "In the case of discrepant opinions, arguments based on clinical expertise override those based on scientific evidence." Scientific evidence, in other words, "takes its meaning in the light of the current clinical situation and past clinical experience."[49]

This is also the case in education. That student teachers shed or adjust theory learned in university classrooms when they come under the tutelage of an experienced classroom teacher is well documented. From the perspective of the classroom teacher the same norms apply as in medicine: Clinical knowledge is superior to theoretical knowledge; and student teachers, in the words of the Holmes Group Report, "relinquish the norms of professional colleges of education without a struggle."[50] In this context, however, that constitutes a criticism of teachers, not an acknowledgment of the value of clinical knowledge. The contrast here with law and medicine is striking. In those two professions it is taken for granted that clinical knowledge is important, and that it provides a kind of reality check on theory.

Why the low regard for clinical knowledge in education? Surely one reason is the gender of the majority of the nation's teaching force. It is clear that the nineteenth-century feminization of the teaching force, particularly at the elementary level, was one of the most profound transformations ever to affect American education. The reasons for this have been explored in detail elsewhere: Women were willing to work for less pay than men because they had fewer employment opportunities; women were said to be more nurturant than men, and thus were viewed as especially suitable for the elementary grades; and, less explicitly, females would be docile, dutiful, obedient workers in an increasingly bureaucratic school system presided over by male administrators.

The low prestige attached to the occupation of teaching in America has been linked to the numerical domination of female practitioners. One can argue that the historic tradition of male superiority did not give credence to female opinion, and thus what would be valued as clinical knowledge in other professions was simply written off as unimportant. But the problem of articulating clinical knowledge was compounded by nineteenth-century conventions of female reticence. George S. Grape, a professor at a private academy in Baltimore, Maryland, alluded to this in 1874 when he commented on the limited usefulness of teachers' institutes: "I have listened with the deepest sympathy to a lady in conversation, who for a half hour told, in a natural way, her trials and triumphs as a primary teacher. Yet our lady teachers, numbering three-fourths of our ranks, and confessedly our equals in the work of instruction, can rarely be induced to tell in public the very truths we meet to learn and teach."[51] If three-fourths of the teachers were rendered mute by conventions of silence and deference, that meant that a professional culture was neither widely shared (and thus shaped and honed) nor publicly visible. Without wishing to romanticize the "wisdom" these silent practitioners may have possessed, the fact that they were only listeners to the professional conversation meant, at the very least, that the research agenda would be fashioned without their participation—a problem as pertinent to the twentieth century as to the nineteenth.

Early in the twentieth century, then, universities faced little in the way of competing claims when they defined a scientific approach to education as the hallmark of the professional. The normal schools were becoming increasingly academic institutions, while the potential for a practitioner culture was undercut by its predominantly female membership.

Truncated Alternatives: Practitioner Culture and the Triumph of Top-down Reform

There were schools which demonstrated an alternate, more practical model of teacher training, but they did not develop systematic pedagogical theories, operating more along apprenticeship lines. These were the city training schools, which began to be established after about 1890. Newell identified three such schools: Boston Normal School, Cook County Normal, and the New York College for the Training of Teachers (now Teachers College, Columbia), and particularly its Horace Mann Practice School. Of the lattermost, Newell remarked that it "seems to have succeeded in solving the difficult problem" of adjusting theory to practice. "It has reversed the usual conditions, and in place of instruction with incidental training, it gives training with incidental instruction. In many normal schools . . . the students consider every hour not given to class recitations as so much time lost; but in a school like the New York College the time given to observation and practical teaching is felt to be all gain."[52]

What Newell describes here are large-scale, formalized apprenticeship arrangements in which theory, as well as academic instruction, was subordinated to practice. These city schools are worthy of further study. If they do in fact represent a tradition of teacher training which is more practical than the normal-school model, that alone would make them interesting. It would also be important to explain the apparent disappearance of that model. In law and medicine, apprenticeship training was first supplemented and then replaced by more theoretical university training. A recent study of the Frick Training School for Teachers in Pittsburgh, however, suggests that it was economics, not a revolution in pedagogical theory, which by the

1930s led to the closing of the city training schools.[53] Some assessment of the success of city training schools during the decades when they flourished, as well as comparison of those schools with normal schools and university demonstration or model schools, would be useful.

While the institutional histories of normal schools, city training schools, state teacher colleges, and universities and their model schools will be important in advancing our understanding of the history of teachers and teacher training, it is important that such institutional histories not be narrowly conceived. Indeed, the broader question that needs to be addressed concerns the strategies that people choose which would improve the quality of teachers. Preliminary research in Maryland suggests that experiments with professional journals, with system-wide school curricula, and with various supervisory models, represented other avenues for the improvement of teachers. What is interesting about these models, at least in the first decade of the twentieth century, is the extent to which they appear to reflect not a top-down attempt to impose reform upon teachers, but an effort to draw on the wisdom of teachers themselves.

The Atlantic Education Journal (published in Baltimore City from 1907 to 1912), for example, printed elaborate model lessons devised by individual city school teachers, offered for the use of other teachers. In neighboring Baltimore County, Maryland, teachers were involved in the construction of a system-wide elementary curriculum, one that eventually was published in 1915 and received national attention for a number of years. Also in Baltimore County, an official ''elementary substitute'' teacher was appointed whose assignment was to give a model lesson in a classroom, then to relieve that elementary-school teacher for a day so that the teacher might visit and observe a teacher in another school. This rather imaginative experiment suggests an early attempt to foster a horizontal professional culture which would enable teachers to share professional expertise and support each other in efforts to improve classroom instruction.

Within the space of two decades, however, professional journals were transformed into vehicles for reporting university research; and curriculum and supervision became a means to centralize control over large school districts. During the tenure (1900–1920) of School Superintendent Albert S. Cook in Baltimore County, the number of supervisors increased from one, appointed in 1905, to seven in 1915. Moreover, the superintendent's view of supervision subtly changed as well. In 1905, supervision was viewed as a means of encouraging strong teachers and assisting weak teachers. The supervisor herself was described as a ''cheerful, productive, helpful co-worker, who doesn't know all there is to know.'' By 1917, however, this collegial relationship had been replaced by a view which emphasized ''daily classroom visits . . . observing, teaching and testing the classes as occasion seemed to demand.''[54] The joint search for the best professional practice now became an opportunity for evaluation by superiors.

Curriculum design projects, too, eventually provided the opportunity to give teachers more detailed directives. The ''Suggestions on the Course of Study for the Baltimore County Schools'' (grades one through four) was issued in 1906 as a 107-page paper-bound booklet. The revised 1909 version, an ''Outline Course of Study for the Public Elementary Schools of Baltimore County'' (grades one through eight) was bound in buckram and 345 pages in length. By 1915 the "Course of Study" was a cloth-bound volume of 653 pages; and in its final edition, published in 1931, the tome was 846 pages long. The titles of the various versions are themselves revealing: What began as suggestions, then an outline, finally emerged as a detailed "Course" of study in 1915.[55]

Raymond E. Callahan, in his classic study of how business values shaped the administration of the public schools, noted the early and lasting importance of university professors of education in the educational efficiency movement. The writings of men like George Strayer, John Franklin Bobbitt, and Ellwood P. Cubberly helped justify and frame the move toward more-centralized control, not only in administration but, as the Baltimore County case suggests, in curriculum and supervision as well.[56] Superintendent Cook had studied at Teachers College, Columbia, and the thesis he wrote was titled "Education and Social Efficiency." Cook encouraged his teachers to attend Teachers College, and he frequently invited Teachers College faculty, in particular George Strayer, to visit the schools and address the teachers. Under the leadership of Cook and with the support of university-generated ideas, the Baltimore County schoolteacher gradually became part of a hierarchically organized, centrally controlled school system.[57]

The ultimate influence of the twentieth-century university school of education, then, has less to do with forging a distinctive role in the training of teachers than in the way that educational research helped to shape the conditions of professional practice. Universities did not revolutionize the initial training of practitioners, as happened in law and medicine; but they did play a substantial role in creating a teaching environment which was increasingly subject to centralized direction. The present irony is that recent reform proposals, even those advanced by deans of education at major research universities, call for more practitioner autonomy, not less. To create an environment in which autonomous professionals can flourish, however, means that the centralized system that the university helped create, and which university research continues to support, must in some significant measure be dismantled.

Notes

AUTHOR'S NOTE: Preparation of this chapter was assisted by support from the Spencer Foundation. The views expressed are solely the responsibility of the author.

1. John Hardin Best (ed.), *Historical Inquiry in Education: A Research Agenda* (Washington, D.C.: American Educational Research Association, 1983).
2. Research on teachers and teacher training came to a virtual halt with the publication of Lawrence A. Cremin et al., *A History of Teachers College, Columbia University* (New York: Columbia University Press, 1954), and Merle Borrowman, *The Liberal and Technical in Teacher Education* (New York: Bureau of Publications, Teachers College, Columbia University, 1956). The ten-year index to the *History of Education Quarterly* (1961–1970) has no references to normal schools, and only 4 references under "teachers," one of which cross-references Columbia University. The bibliography compiled by Jurgen Herbst, *The History of Amer-*

ican Education (Northbrook, IL: AHM Publishing Corp., 1973), lists 5 citations under general works on teachers and teaching, none published after 1956, cross-references 11 other works, only 2 of which were published after 1960 (both on the colonial period), and has an additional 45 citations to teacher training. Of those 45, only 6 are published after 1960, 4 in 1960 and 1961; and of the remaining 2, one was a book on the Conant report on teacher education, and the other Merle Borrowman's *Teacher Education in America: A Documentary History* (New York: Teachers College Press, 1965).

3. Geraldine J. Clifford, ''Saints, Sinners, and People: A Position Paper on the Historiography of American Education,'' in *History of Education Quarterly* 15:3 (Fall 1975), pp. 257–272. See also Clifford, *The Shape of American Education* (Englewood Cliffs, N.J.: Prentice–Hall, 1975); Willard S. Elsbree, *The American Teacher: Evolution of a Profession in a Democracy* (New York: American Book Co., 1939): Paul H. Mattingly, *The Classless Profession: American Schoolmen in the Nineteenth Century* (New York: New York University Press, 1975); and Paul Woodring, ''The Development of Teacher Education,'' in Kevin Ryan (ed.), *Teacher Education,* The Seventy-fourth Yearbook of the National Society for the Study of Education (Chicago: University of Chicago Press, 1975).
4. Albert Lynd, *Quackery in the Public Schools,* (Boston: Little, Brown, 1950); Arthur Bestor, *Educational Wastelands* (Urbana IL: University of Illinois Press, 1953); and Arthur Bestor, *The Restoration of Learning* (New York: Knopf, 1955).
5. James D. Koerner, *The Miseducation of American Teachers* (Boston: Houghton Mifflin, 1963), pp. 17, 37, 18, and 56.
6. Bestor, *Restoration,* p. 204. Chapter 14, ''Thwarting the Good Teacher,'' is relevant here.
7. E. V. Johanningmeier, ''Review of Koerner, *The Miseducation of American Teachers,*'' in *Harvard Educational Review* 34:1 (Winter 1964), p. 99.
8. Koerner, *Miseducation,* p. 61.
9. James B. Conant, *The Education of American Teachers* (New York: McGraw–Hill, 1963), pp. 60 and 63.
10. Ibid., p. 63.
11. Ibid., p. 205; and Koerner, *Miseducation,* p. 268.
12. See, generally, Joel Spring, *The Sorting Machine* (New York: McKay, 1976), especially pp. 92–139. A brief description of these curricula can be found in John I. Goodlad, *The Changing School Curriculum* (New York: The Fund for the Advancement of Education, 1966).
13. Robert M. McClure, ''The Reforms of the Fifties and Sixties: A Historical Look at the Near Past,'' in Robert M. McClure (ed.), *The Curriculum: Retrospect and Prospect* (Chicago: University of Chicago Press: The Seventieth Yearbook of the National Society for the Study of Education, Part I, 1971), pp. 45–75. The quote is on p. 67. See also: Bruce Joyce, ''Conceptions of Man and Their Implications for Teacher Education,'' in Ryan (ed.), *Teacher Education,* pp. 111–145.
14. Kenneth B. Clark, *Dark Ghetto: Dilemmas of Social Power* (New York: Harper & Row, 1965) especially Ch. 6, ''Ghetto Schools: Separate and Unequal.'' A briefer introduction to Clark's viewpoint can be found in ''Alternative Public School Systems,'' in *Harvard Educational Review* 38 (Winter 1968), pp. 100–113.
15. Leon Lessinger, *Every Kid a Winner: Accountability in Education* (New York: Simon & Schuster), p. 3.
16. David Halberstam, *The Best and the Brightest* (New York: Random House, 1969), pp. 18–23.
17. See, for example: Alan L. Patz, ''Performance Appraisal: Useful but Still Resisted,'' in *Harvard Business Review* (May–June 1975), pp. 74–80; Leif O. Olsen and Addison C. Bennett, ''Performance Appraisal: Management Technique or Social Process,'' in *Management Review* (December 1975), pp. 24–30; and Harold Koontz, ''Making MBO Effective,'' in *California Management Review* (Fall 1977), p.

5–13. The quote is from the Olsen and Bennett article. For a fuller discussion of these issues, see William R. Johnson, "Meeting Accountability or Evading Responsibility?" in *Theory into Practice* 17:5 (1979), p. 372–378.

18. Lawrence A. Cremin, David A. Shannon, and Mary Evelyn Townsend, *A History of Teachers College, Columbia University* (New York: Columbia University Press, 1954), p. v.

19. The Holmes Group, *Tomorrow's Teachers: A Report of the Holmes Group* (East Lansing, MI: The Holmes Group, 1986).

20. Arthur G. Powell, *The Uncertain Profession: Harvard and the Search for Educational Authority* (Cambridge MA: Harvard University Press, 1980).

21. Cremin et al., *A History of Teachers College*, pp. 79–80.

22. Powell, *The Uncertain Profession*, p. 160.

23. Henry C. Johnson, Jr. and Erwin V. Johanningmeier, *Teachers for the Prairie: The University of Illinois and the Schools, 1868–1945* (Urbana, IL: University of Illinois Press, 1972), p. 445.

24. Ibid., p. 230.

25. Harry Judge, *American Graduate Schools of Education: A View from Abroad* (New York: Ford Foundation, 1982).

26. Cremin et al., *A History of Teachers College*, p. 277.

27. Powell, *The Uncertain Profession*, p. 272.

28. Woodring, "The development of Teacher Education," p. 8.

29. Abraham Flexner, *Universities: American, English, German* (London/New York: Oxford University Press, 1930), p. 98.

30. Earle U. Rugg et al., *Teacher Education Curricula*, National Survey of the Education of Teachers, Vol. III, *Bulletin* 10 (Washington D.C: U.S. Office of Education, 1933), pp. 65–66.

31. Jurgen Herbst, "Nineteenth-century Normal Schools in the United States: A Fresh Look," in *History of Education* 9:3 (1980), pp. 220–224 and 226.

32. M. A. Newell, "Contributions to the History of Normal Schools in the United States," in *Report of the Commissioner of Education for the Year 1898–99*, Vol. 2 (Washington, DC: U. S. Government Printing Office, 1900), pp. 2263–2470. Newell who died in 1892, probably prepared the manuscript in 1890–91.

33. Ibid., pp. 2274 and 2277.

34. Ibid., pp. 2297, 2365, and 2363; and Maryland State Normal School *Catalog*, 1876, p. 2.

35. One exception to this is Walter S. Monroe, *Teaching–Learning Theory and Teacher Education, 1890 to 1950* (New York: Greenwood Press [Reprint], 1969; original published by University of Illinois Press, 1952). Monroe's work has not received the attention it deserves. Although awkwardly organized and repetitious, Monroe does attempt a critical analysis of pedagogical theories that often is illuminating and insightful.

36. Charles A. Harper, *The Development of the Teachers College in the United States, with Special Reference to the Illinois State Normal University* (Bloomington, IL: McKnight, 1935), pp. 355–356.

37. Monroe, *Teaching–Learning Theory*, p. 303. Monroe notes that in 1918 William C. Bagley, then engaged in a study of tax-supported normal schools in Missouri, made a plea for professionalized subject-matter courses. However, survey data collected over the next 15 years suggested a mixed attitude toward the recommendation, and "in practice there was little professionalization beyond what was accomplished in special-methods courses." *Ibid.*, p. 228.

38. Newell, "Contributions to the History of Normal Schools," p. 2463.

39. "Class Diary": October 26, 1897; January 27, 1898; October 17, 1898; and November 2, 1898 (Archives of Towson State University, Baltimore, MD). See also Herbert Andrews, "The Normal 'Nineties'," in *The Grub Street Wit* 2 (December 1976), pp. 8–13, for a discussion of the contents of this class diary.

40. Arthur G. Powell, "The Culture and

Politics of American Teachers,'' in *History of Education Quarterly* 18:2 (Summer 1978), pp. 191–192.

41. Faculty *Minutes,* February 1908; and March 1909 (Archives of Towson State University, Baltimore, MD).
42. Ibid., April 8, 1913; May 21, 1913; and October 1, 1913.
43. Ibid., October 14, 1913; October 28, 1913; November 25, 1913 (''Miss Campbell of Friends School gave a talk on the Montessori Method.''); January 13, 1914 (Miss McLeod gave ''very pleasingly'' the story of Verdi's Opera *Rigoletto.*); March 10, 1914; April 22, 1914; and May 12, 1914.
44. Abraham Flexner and Frank P. Bachman, *Public Education in Maryland* (New York: General Education Board, 1916), pp. 73, 79, and 71.
45. Faculty *Minutes,* February 7, 1916; October 24, 1916; and January 20 and 27, 1917.
46. Lawrence Cremin, *The Transformation of the Schools* (New York: Knopf, 1961), p. 169.
47. Powell, ''The Culture and Politics of American Teachers,'' pp. 191–192.
48. William R. Johnson, *Schooled Lawyers: A Study in the Clash of Professional Cultures* (New York: New York University Press, 1978), pp. 115–119 and 138–141.
49. Charles L. Bosk, *Forgive and Remember: Managing Medical Failure* (Chicago: University of Chicago Press, 1979), pp. 85–87.
50. The Holmes Group, *Tomorrow's Teachers,* p. 55.
51. *Maryland School Journal* 1:2 (October 1874), p. 56. For reflections on the professional price paid for the entry of ''fresh, inexpensive female recruits'' into teaching, see Donald Warren, ''Learning from Experience: History and Teacher Education,'' in *Educational Researcher* 14 (1985), p. 5–11. Warren is one of the few historians who have sought to bring the historical investigation of teachers into the twentieth century.
52. Newell, ''Contributions to the History of Normal Schools,'' pp. 2462, 2458, and 2463.
53. Richard J. Altenbaugh, ''Professional Socialization or Gender? The Case of the Frick (Pittsburgh) Training School for Teachers, 1912–1937,'' paper presented at the annual meeting of the American Educational Research Association, Washington, DC, April 1987.
54. Barbara Dennis Kelly, ''Progressive Educational Reform of the Baltimore County Public Schools, 1900–1920,'' (doctoral dissertation, University of Maryland, College Park, 1985), pp. 159–162.
55. Amy C. Crewe, *No Backward Step Was Taken: Highlights in the History of the Public Elementary Schools of Baltimore County* (Towson, MD: Teachers Association of Baltimore County, 1949), p. 146–148.
56. Raymond E. Callahan, *Education and the Cult of Efficiency* (Chicago: University of Chicago Press, 1962).
57. Kelly, ''Progressive Educational Reform,'' pp. 16 and 147–151.

10

"'Let Us Go and Buy a School Master''

Historical Perspectives on the Hiring of Teachers in the United States, 1750–1980

Michael W. Sedlak

After several generations of tranquility, the process of securing a teaching position surfaced once again in the 1980s to become a matter of mounting concern within the policy and higher educational communities. Governors, philanthropists, and business leaders had become discouraged enough with prevailing routes to practice, through professional education and state certification programs, to put their credibility and money behind alternative forms of entry—particularly through testing. Despite *pro forma* nods to comprehensive licensure approaches (involving academic education, clinical training, and formal performance evaluations), many of these alternatives became dedicated essentially to circumventing the professional educational and certification establishment by deregulating access to teaching positions.

By the 1980s as well, many leaders of the teacher education enterprise had become complacent after successfully struggling to have educational credentials replace examinations as the principal route to teaching positions. Although caught off guard by the deregulation movement, the professional educational community responded—in some cases predictably, and in other cases imaginatively—on a number of fronts, including efforts to strengthen the subject-matter learning of prospective teachers, plans to differentiate career responsibilities, and pledges to modify the clinical preparation of novices. In addition, they committed themselves publicly to reforming the process through which teachers are certified and hired, by moving the professional education of prospective teachers to the graduate level and by endorsing new forms of imaginative evaluation at the earliest stages of employment. These were changes promoted by (for example) the Holmes Group, a consortium of research universities (some of which had been only marginally engaged in teacher education), and advocated by the Carnegie Forum on Education and the Economy.[1]

The energy and resources committed to these movements reflects an increasing recognition of the importance of hiring to the improvement of learning in our schools. The public is coming to appreciate the central role that teaching plays in effective, efficient learning, and is once again focusing on the way in which teachers become entitled to practice professionally. Professional educators, civic leaders, parents—indeed, all citizens—are justifiably interested in protecting our children's opportunities to learn, particularly in compulsory, publicly supported institutions. As the latest waves of both promising and potentially destructive reform initiatives crest, it is timely to examine the ebb and flow of our traditions of recruiting teachers.

This chapter explores the hiring process in teaching since the early nineteenth century, and attempts to develop a tentative periodization of changing policy and practice. It focuses primarily on the means through which individuals have become entitled to teach, and the mechanisms that schools and communities have employed to recruit and hire teachers. In reconstructing recruitment and hiring patterns over time, this chapter considers the structure of the labor market in teaching, attending primarily to the question of whether licensing and hiring standards could be raised during periods of shortage. Since late in the 1980s precisely such a period apparently loomed ahead through the early 1990s, the matter of raising standards during a shortage became much more than merely academic. Teacher shortages have been commonplace since the mid-nineteenth century, and earlier efforts to respond to them reveal a great deal about persistent patterns of reform—particularly about the impact of powerful temptations to simply tinker with prevailing arrangements and assumptions rather than to consider the issue from a more comprehensive perspective, one based upon an accurate understanding of the relationship between labor-force dynamics and standards-raising proposals.

A number of organizations have ventured hesitatingly into the currents of reform on the eve of this latest predicted shortage of teachers because their leaders are acting on the appealing (albeit counterintuitive) assumption that their efforts will survive the actions of desperate communities determined to grant licenses to any warm body in order to fill all of their classrooms. An analysis of the historical relationship between shortages and standards would have powerful implications for their confidence in continuing down such a counterintuitive path.

This chapter argues that the history of hiring evolved in the following fashion: Up through the mid-nineteenth century, recruiting and hiring teachers was almost entirely a private, negotiated procedure which occurred between someone with authority to employ and pay a teacher, and someone willing to accept whatever instructional—and maintenance—responsibilities were wanted. Shortly after the mid-century, states increasingly began to centralize the certification process, initially by creating offices of inspectors and county superintendencies to administer examinations and bestow certificates, and later by allowing educational credentials to be substituted for examinations. This transitional period of limited centralization persisted through the early decades of the twentieth century as part of a general movement in expanding education for the professions.

By 1920, the vast majority of states had rejected examinations in favor of evidence of educational attainment for certification. The variety of institutions entitled to offer legitimate professional education gradually narrowed as collegiate-level programs eclipsed the two-year normal schools as the dominant preparatory model. During the severe teacher shortage of the 1920s, certification standards were raised at an unprecedented pace to an unheard-of level. By the early 1930s, as a consequence, virtually all states required four years of college for secondary certification, and a rapidly growing number required it for elementary teachers as well. By the end of the depression of the 1930s, hiring standards for teachers had basically reached contemporary levels: Certification for entering teachers was awarded on the basis of completing a four-year preparation experience.

Until the late 1980s, only relatively minor changes occurred—increasing the specialization of professional roles and certificates, or slightly expanding the number of professional courses, for example. Overall, the approach remained relatively consistent. The only substantive change occurred with the establishment of the National Teachers Examination during the 1940s, which, among other things, enabled attractive and desirable districts to select from among a surplus of applicants with appropriate educational credentials. The waves of initiatives that built during the 1980s began to challenge the traditional arrangements and patterns for the first time in half a century.

Negotiation in a Private Market

Through the first half of the nineteenth century, recruiting and hiring teachers was a local, private matter. Practices varied from region to region and community to community, but, essentially, teaching appointments were negotiated between a prospective teacher and someone or some group—usually a committee of elders, or ministers, or selectmen—with the authority to commit a district's or a school's funds for a relatively brief time.[2] Actual recruiting was accomplished through active solicitation, direct advertising, and the most flagrant forms of patronage and nepotism. In 1725, one observer recalled that adults needing teachers for their children, hearing of the impending arrival of a ship from Britain or Europe, would often say among themselves, "Let us go and buy a school master."[3] A half century later, at the time of the Revolution, the concept of procuring an immigrant teacher in this fashion remained common. For example, an advertisement in a Baltimore newspaper announced that a ship had just arrived with "various Irish products" for sale, "among which are school masters, beef, pork, and potatoes."[4]

Direct advertising for teachers and for teaching positions was common, particularly in the South: The *Virginia Gazette* of August 20, 1772 included the following advertisement:

> Wanted Immediately
>
> A Sober diligent Schoolmaster capable of teaching READING, WRITING, ARITHMETICK, and the *Latin* TONGUE. The School is quite new, has a convenient Lodging Room over it, is situated in a cheap Neighborhood, and its Income estimated at between sixty and eighty Pound a Year. Any Person qualified as above, and well recommended, will be put into immediate Possession of the School, on applying to the Minister of *Charles Parish, York* County.[5]

Prospective teachers occasionally advertised for positions, too. One young man published the following announcement in the *Georgia Gazette* for September 23 and October 7, 1767:

> A single man of good character who Teacheth the Principles of Latin, and French as accented in Paris, the right Spanish Castellans, and children to Read and Write English, would be glad of employment in a Latin School as an assistant, or in a private family in town or country. Any gentleman or ladies desirous to employ him in such capacity may hear of him by applying to the printer.[6]

Not all teachers who presented themselves for employment were as qualified as this young man appeared to be. During the colonial era, prevailing social policy often awarded teaching positions to individuals who were incapable of succeeding financially in the competitive economy. Public jobs like gravedigging, bellringing, and schoolteaching customarily were offered to social dependents: the handicapped, widows, alcoholics. But even this sort of private system of allocating opportunities in a community was commonly abused. Indeed, in many towns it tended to breed various forms of patronage customs.

Among others, Wayne Fuller and Marguerite Renner have written about the practice of educational authorities' awarding the most desirable teaching positions to their own relatives—especially their daughters, wives, and nieces—and to the relatives of political supporters. In districts where patronage was rampant, teaching positions rarely were advertised in newspapers or on handbills, and many times were not even announced by word-of-mouth. Instead, the school board members talked among themselves, then approached the individuals they wished to hire.[7]

Teaching positions were handed out in this fashion for a number of reasons. In Pittsburgh, the site of Renner's valuable study, members of the school committee, who were from prominent families, routinely hired their daughters and other relatives who requested the opportunity to earn an income while awaiting marriage. Indeed, one committee even dismissed one of the widows to whom it had earlier given a teaching position, so that family members could be placed on the public payroll. Members of one working-class committee actually refused to hire their own relatives in favor of giving teaching positions to young middle-class women who would enhance the social status of their school, an intriguing twist on typical patronage strategies.[8] Throughout the Midwest's rural communities, according to Fuller's delightful examples, nepotism and patronage systems were routinely viewed as ''protected industries'' for the children and relatives of school board members and other civic authorities who were hostile to outside efforts to usurp their traditional right to hire whomever they wanted, and to spend only as much of the public treasury on education as they deemed adequate.[9]

In addition to the obvious financial advantages of the patronage arrangements, this approach had other benefits. It could result, for example, in a passive, docile, compliant teaching force consisting of individuals both subject to the influence of family relations and unwilling to risk losing attractive positions they had attained not meritocratically but only through personal influence. Committees that allocated teaching opportunities through nepotism or personal influence possessed the power inherent in all patronage systems, an authority that left their curricular, management, and financial decisions unchallenged.[10]

Regardless of whether or not nepotism played a role in hiring decisions, during this era final appointments were customarily based on some sort of examination. Usually the individual or group that appointed or hired the teacher conducted the examination, but occasionally one person—ordinarily a minister—qualified one or more prospects, and the appointment committee then selected its teacher therefrom. Theoretically, candidates were questioned about subject-matter content, pedagogical knowledge, and the condition of their character and religious beliefs. Depending on local needs and the inclinations and abilities of the examiners, these assessments could be either demoralizingly rigorous or farcically simple rituals. Local district authorities ordinarily made up their own exams, and their concerns with order and discipline were all too apparent in their questions, particularly in rural districts. The examination of an applicant in a small New England town during the 1860s reveals these concerns:

Chairman: How old are you?
Candidate: I was eighteen years old the 27th day of last May.
Chairman: Where did you last attend school?
Candidate: At the Academy of S.
Chairman: Do you think you can make our big youngsters mind?
Candidate: Yes, I think I can.
Chairman: Well, I am satisfied. I guess you will do for our school. I will send over the certificate by the children tomorrow.[11]

Even when local authorities modeled their probes after examinations recommended by state educational officials, the thrust of the questions revealed everyone's concerns vividly, as reflected in the following items prepared for school committees in Maine during the 1840s:

How would you deal with a child who was (1) obstinately disobedient? (2) physically and mentally indolent? (3) addicted to falsehood? (4) impulsive?[12]

Assessments of academic knowledge often were not taken as seriously as evaluations of character, religious values, and physical strength. Committee members occasionally were unable to answer their own questions! In Indiana, for example, one candidate was asked, "What is the product of 25 cents by 25 cents?" After he responded that he did not know, "The examiner appeared a bit perplexed and said he thought the answer was six and one-fourth cents but he wasn't sure."[13] Another senior teacher recalled one of the most notorious examinations that he had ever experienced, held in 1860. The president of the local board of education prepared all of the questions. His geography questions, the applicant observed, were typical of all of the others:

1. Name all the rivers of the globe.
2. Name all the bays, gulfs, seas, lakes, and other bodies of water on the globe.
3. Name all the cities of the world.
4. Name all the countries of the world.
5. Bound each of the states in the United States.

The applicants had one hour to answer these questions. The senior teacher remembered that, at the end of the hour, some were at work on the first question, some on the second, and a few on the third. But what intrigued him most was that "When the report was made, we all stood exactly alike, 60 percent."[14]

Examinations were usually private events, attended only by the candidate and the examiners. This arrangement of allowing both standards and individual performances to remain discreet and flexible proved attractive to supporters of the patronage system of appointments. Because private examinations were so easily abused, however, some community leaders called for opening the events to the public. In addition to calming fears of favoritism, public examinations provided other benefits, some claimed. In an era of unprecedented community boosterism, when one local educational enterprise competed against another in efforts to improve neighborhood status and attract settlers, examining teachers and students in public could be attractive. One advocate of public examination in New Jersey in 1850 concluded with the following recommendation: "Indeed, why should there not be a county competition, to exhibit the best teachers, the best schools, and the best-educated scholars, with far more propriety than which county can produce the fattest hog or the largest turnip."[15]

Teaching certificates were bestowed on those who "passed" such examinations, whether they were rigorous academic exercises or the most perfunctory inquiries into one's physical or moral fitness. Certificates during the mid-nineteenth century, however, were valid usually for one year only, and generally only in the district that administered the examination. Applicants were examined annually, and district or state reciprocity did not exist. Some communities began to differentiate certificates according to the percentage of questions an applicant answered correctly. One Iowa county, for example, allowed candidates scoring 50 percent to teach for four months, those scoring 60 percent to teach for six months, and those scoring 90 percent or better to teach for an entire year. Other districts differentiated professional role responsibilities according to success on the examination, and granted different classes of certificates to principals and teachers.[16]

The private, decentralized market within which teaching appointments were secured worked rather well through the early nineteenth century. Schools themselves took so many forms, and communities were sufficiently independent in all else, that idiosyncratic hiring and examination practices bothered very few, and were jealously guarded prerogatives to many citizens. There were no institutions of professional education, or certification, to raise objections to negotiated arrangements. A general teacher shortage, combined with wildly fluctuating and inconsistent prerequisite qualifications, virtually assured any prospective teacher some sort of job, and secured someone for most communities needing a teacher. The structure accommodated reasonably well a society of enormous inequalities of wealth and aspiration.

Challenging the "Excess of Democracy"

Resistance to this privatized market began to build with the diffusion of the Common School Movement, particularly after the 1840s when it spread from New

England into the mid-Atlantic states and some portions of the Midwest. Individuals attempting to fashion teaching jobs into careers resented the assumptions of transiency and amateurism embedded in the prevailing arrangements. They grew frustrated by annual examinations, unpredictable standards, and temporary certificates. As teachers became more committed to effective education they also pressed for the depoliticization of hiring, since patronage systems appeared to undermine the meritocratic ethos that was building within the educational enterprise. This was the sense that, as schools would perform increasingly indispensable social functions (including resolving social problems and expanding economic opportunity), they should more visibly and explicitly reject all traditions and trappings of ascription.

Teachers were joined by a number of other constituencies concerned about the professional stature of education and especially troubled by the inadequacies of existing recruitment and hiring practices. The fledgling state boards of education were uniformly distressed by the flagrant abuse of local autonomy in hiring. Superintendents of public instruction pressed their legislatures to bring order and consistency to the licensure and appointment of teachers.

States responded in several ways to the quest for standardization and uniformity. Some created offices of county superintendencies and bestowed their incumbents with the responsibility for administering examinations and certifying teachers. Others attempted to subvert the localism of the district structure by organizing "townships" and appointing inspectors to assess community practices. One Michigan educator lent his voice to a movement arrogantly trying to challenge the "excess of democracy" symbolized by the jealously guarded hiring practices of local school authorities when he said:

> The only way I see to better the conditions of the schools is to take just as much of their control out of the hands of the people as possible. The people do not know the needs of the schools. They have been educated in these poor schools, and until the schools are better the people will be ignorant. . . . Centralization is what we need in school management.[17]

Over the course of the 1870s and 1880s, state after state improvised ways of strengthening control over important educational decisions. Fuller, among others, has portrayed the continuing struggle over the control of schooling that raged between farmers and residents of small towns and the increasingly professionalized state educational bureaucracies.[18] Some groups successfully restored the old arrangements and forced the dismantling of the township structure, or whittled away at the role and powers of the county superintendents until they were hardly more than gatherers of statistics. And of course many county superintendents abused their authority in much the same way that the local committees did. But although the appointment of standards-conscious officials beyond the district level proceeded inconsistently over the remainder of the nineteenth century, it ultimately raised the qualifications of the teaching force, and began to standardize the professional preparation and induction process of teachers in many parts of the United States.

Pennsylvania was one state that moved on a number of fronts during the early 1850s to undermine the power of the local committees. Turning over the functions of examining and certifying teachers to a county superintendent, and specifying prerequisite qualifications for all teachers, were two important strategies instituted.[19] As in many communities accustomed to autonomy in these matters, this action disturbed the local boards responsible for the Pittsburgh schools. The first superintendent of Allegheny County recalled the objections: ''The impression had gotten abroad (emanating doubtless from some rejected, disaffected applicants) that the object of the Superintendent was to embarrass and confuse the teachers, to reveal his ignorance, and to expose him to ridicule of the audience.''[20] By encouraging such a view, local district leaders undoubtedly tried to marshal the support of the teaching force to their posture of resistance.

Responding to such imagery, many teachers initially boycotted the examination, aided and abetted by district leaders who ignored the new certification requirement. Over the next few years, however, more and more teachers sat for the examination, as the two major professional organizations backed the new accountability mechanism and endorsed the regulations as beneficial for teachers.[21] Removing the examination and certification processes from the political arena and placing it in the educational enterprise itself helped to strengthen the commitment of the teaching force to the new arrangement. Under the jurisdiction of the county superintendents, the ''official examination provided a systematic method of identifying achievement and the certificate was the individual's proof of accomplishment,'' Renner has argued.[22] Opposition within the educational establishment evaporated rather quickly. Within one decade of its introduction in Pittsburgh, for example, virtually all teachers and administrators embraced the new system.

County commissioners in Michigan were plagued with other legacies of the local examination tradition. The commissioner from Huron County reported in 1895 that the recent regulations governing testing procedures had improved the licensing process substantially. Historically, the most unpleasant feature of the examinations in the area had been cheating, or, as he euphemistically commented, the ''tendency on the part of some teachers to assist each other in their work.'' With the adoption and ''prompt enforcement'' of the stringent regulations, he reported, ''We believe this evil has finally been stamped out.'' The revised testing procedures were ''in all respects credible to the teachers, and in conformity with the requirements of their high calling.'' Complaints now were voiced about the difficulty of the examinations, but he was ''not in sympathy with the grumblers.'' Another commissioner raised questions about the examination process in general, particularly with tests that assessed only knowledge in the school subjects:

> The difficult problem, how to license good teachers and reject the poor, is yet to be solved. The legislative acts regulating examinations are to be commended, but the examination is only a test of knowledge, sometimes hardly that, and does not indicate the power or skill a teacher may have. Some of the poorest teachers have been those who passed in excellent papers and obtained good standing. [W]ould it not be best to require some professional training, even though it be no more than the requirement to read one or more of the standard works on teaching? For many of our younger teachers come to their work with little or no idea of schoolroom work.[23]

Investing county superintendents with the power to assess the qualifications of prospective and practicing teachers led to a major conceptual shift in practice that may ultimately have dwarfed the impact of centralization itself. It was not uncommon for the newly appointed superintendents to move beyond examinations exclusively. Increasingly they encouraged attendance in professional educational programs. They began to recognize and reward normal-school training in addition to performance on subject-matter examinations. One of the toughest, most standards-conscious superintendents in Allegheny County, for example, announced that he would give preference to those "who had been diligently preparing themselves for their work by attending normal classes."[24]

Even though Pennsylvania had not yet passed legislation requiring professional education, its superintendent used his office's discretion to move the certification process away from relying only on examinations. These gatekeepers of certification, therefore, narrowed (and began the process of standardizing) access to teaching positions both by making the examinations more consistently rigorous and by favoring applicants who had participated in a recognized professional education program, particularly in district, county, or state normal schools. And in regions where normal schools were common, examinations included an increasing proportion of questions related to pedagogy and educational theory.[25] In this situation, the superintendents fundamentally altered the process of getting a teaching position in a public school.

Over the remainder of the nineteenth century the balance between examinations and professional education fluctuated as districts continued to exploit their remaining freedom to recruit and hire the teachers they believed were the most qualified or appropriate. But the trend toward expecting and rewarding professional educational credentials was clear in practice, even if it more slowly became evident in policy. California had been the first state to accept professional educational credentials in lieu of examinations in 1863. (Because teachers themselves had played a major role in the examination tradition dominant in California prior to the 1860s, this step represented a loss of power by teachers over the process of controlling entry into the profession.) The view held by California's leaders became increasingly prevalent, so that by 1900, 41 states recognized both normal-school diplomas and credentials from four-year colleges as acceptable for certification.[26]

The Triumph of Credentials

By 1900, therefore, both professional educational credentials and examinations were widely used as reasons to bestow teaching certificates. Whether through examination or education, certification was becoming centralized at the state level. The county superintendencies that had moved certification forward during the mid-nineteenth century were declining in power as states sought to tighten controls over the licensing of teachers, and because of a general movement toward centralization and standardization. This trend is evident in Table 10.1, which indicates a progressively rapid process of centralizing certification to the state level.[27]

Table 10.1 Jurisdiction over Teacher Certification

Jurisdictional Authority	*Number of States* 1894	1911	1919	1926
State systems (states issued all certificates)	3	15	26	36
State-controlled system (state prescribed rules and monitored examinations; counties issued some certificates)	1	2	7	4
Semi–state system (state regulations; county issued certificates)	17	18	10	5
State–county system (both issued certificates; county controlled examination for at least one certificate)	18	7	3	2
County system (county issued all certificates	4	1	0	0

Source: Katherine M. Cook, *State Laws and Regulations Governing Teachers' Certificates*, Bulletin No. 19, 1927 (Washington, DC: Bureau of Education, 1927), Table 2, p. 19.

Local certificates also were a victim of the effort to improve reciprocity that built during the late nineteenth century, especially in the North where groups of states made elaborate compacts to recognize one another's certificates.[28]

The next phase in the history of certifying and hiring teachers involved the accelerating dominance of the professional educational credential model, and the steady increase in the minimal duration of prerequisite study. Appointing individuals to teaching positions remained at the local level, of course, but states gradually defined through restrictions the pool of legal prospects. And states increasingly granted certificates on the basis of educational attainment rather than examination performance. By 1873, according to a leading analyst of this issue, policy deliberations were beginning to recognize credentials from normal schools as ''professional licenses,'' and several states were relying on them as the basis for certification. By 1897, 28 states accepted normal-school diplomas, and by 1921 all but one state ''recognized graduation from normal schools and universities as evidence of qualification for certification.''[29] By the World War I era, therefore, certification policies that bestowed licenses on the basis of credential acquisition had become the rule nationwide.

Despite the shift toward credentials in most regions, nevertheless, the examination tradition persisted in the South, where virtually every state continued to base certification on the basis of test performance as well as professional study. In other regions developments were mixed. In Indiana and Wisconsin, for example, centralization proceeded more slowly because of a reluctance to deploy the states' plenary power in education. Many states also continued to require examinations for high-school teaching certificates. But, as a reflection of the increasing impact of normal-school and university programs of study, many of these tests included questions drawn from professional education, including pedagogy, management, and educational history and philosophy.[30]

The expansion of the credential model grew dramatically as graduates of professional programs assumed leadership roles in state departments of education. Small-state departments were among the most highly professionalized sectors of the educational enterprise, and their staff members often owed their positions to their educational attainment, or were willing to respond to the lobbying of the professional education institutions. Many of those who owed their positions to their credentials distrusted examinations and pressed to reduce their impact on licensing. As one commentator observed: "The evil attendant upon the examination system that had been perfected to determine detailed knowledge of academic subject matter led to bitter opposition on the part of those trained in the newer professional school."[31]

The professionally trained educators objected to the view that it took only subject-matter knowledge in order to teach effectively. They were familiar with the tradition of abuse that continued to plague examinations, and were distressed with the gamesmanship and shallowness that contemporary testing practices tended to encourage and reward. Furthermore, during the late nineteenth and early twentieth centuries, other, more prestigious, occupations were abandoning informal idiosyncratic licensing practices for standardized educational credentials. Many believed that professionalization itself demanded advanced, formal professional education, sometimes as a substitute for examinations, sometimes in combination. Regardless of the reasons (some of which were sincere, while others were flagrantly self-protective), the movement of professionally educated leaders into positions of further leadership and influence led to the wider rejection of the tradition of testing aspiring professionals.[32]

Raising standards—by requiring professional education or by making the examinations more challenging and professionally relevant—undoubtedly resulted in much individual pain. Raised standards were assumed to limit access to teaching opportunities, particularly by closing off the mobility of youth from rural backgrounds. Shortly after World War I, for example, the Illinois superintendent for public instruction received a letter from an exasperated woman who was attempting to return to teaching at 46 after her husband died. She had been granted a temporary "Emergency Certificate" because of a spot shortage, but was unable to get "a certificate without 'Emergency' written on it," as she complained to—and pleaded with—the superintendent. The superintendent responded publicly to the letter in order to disclose the "strong appeals [that] can be made to the hearts of the certificating authorities and boards of education to relax or set aside the plain requirements of the law and to forget or subordinate the primal interests of the children who are to be taught." He raised the question of certification standards, arguing that, in teaching, traditions of licensing had too often been rooted in earlier days when it was common to select men who had some disability or handicap, "on the assumption that school teaching was an indoor occupation and required the minimum of physical health and completeness." The situation had changed, he commented, particularly since young middle-class women with strong academic qualifications began seeking and securing teaching positions:

> Most young women, looking forward to teaching school, try to prepare themselves in a very conscientious way for the work. There still remains, however, the old idea that in selecting a teacher certain charitable ends should be kept in view. Every attempt to lift the scholastic and professional requirements for

> teachers in Illinois has met with the statement that higher standards will keep the poor man's daughter from teaching, overlooking entirely the fact that there is much greater charity, much more of the milk of human kindness, much more of sound common sense in trying to secure for poor men's children the very best teacher that can be had rather than in trying to get for a poor man's daughter a job for which she is not qualified.[33]

The enterprise of licensing teachers changed in a variety of ways during the half-century prior to World War I. In addition to expanding the practice of bestowing certificates to candidates on the basis of professional education rather than examinations exclusively, the number of categories of certificates increased dramatically. Differentiation of professional roles in schools contributed fundamentally to this process. The growing public and professional fascination with precision, order, and "scientific" classification schemes of all kinds undoubtedly contributed to this explosion as well. The annual, temporary certificates common during the mid-nineteenth century were replaced in some places in the twentieth century by permanent or life certificates (usually when based on educational credentials).

The hierarchy of graded certificates mentioned above expanded to include an entire range of administrative—as well as teaching—opportunities for individuals with different combinations of credentials and experiences. High-school certificates were differentiated from elementary licenses. At the secondary level, subject-matter certificates began to become common, not just in the core academic fields, but also in the emerging areas of the practical arts, vocational fields, agriculture, the fine arts, and physical training. And teachers of very young children might have received their specialist credentials in kindergarten or primary teaching. By 1918 it was not uncommon for the differentiation process to have made available more than a score of different *levels* of certificates in many states, a number that expanded dramatically when certificates were awarded at the county and city levels as well.

Examples are revealing. Oklahoma recognized the following levels of *teaching* certificates (this does not include the specific fields associated with most levels): Life High-School State; 5-Year High-School State; 2-Year High-School State; Temporary High-School State; 5-Year Special High-School State; 1-Year Special High-School State; Life Elementary State; 5-Year Elementary State; 2-Year Elementary State; Temporary Elementary State; First-Grade County; Second-Grade County; Third-Grade County; Temporary County; and City. Even California, which tried to limit differentiation, had a dozen levels by the early 1920s.[34]

States began more seriously to differentiate between initial and continuing certification. Indeed, under the earlier pattern of temporary, annual certification, continuing or permanent licenses did not exist. During the late nineteenth century, state departments of education made increasingly fine distinctions among grades of continuing certificates, as is evident from the example of Oklahoma's policy. Graded continuing certificates were generally differentiated by amount of professional preparation, and often incorporated years of classroom experience. Permanent or life certificates were customarily reserved for those who had at least two years of normal schooling, and often required a bachelor's degree.

In addition to differentiating licenses, state certification agencies began to set ever-higher educational credential requirements. The standards that were legislated often were viewed as arbitrary. The way that Michigan's minimum requirements evolved, while not necessarily typical, reflects the intriguing and clumsy process of state involvement. The University of Michigan created one of the first permanent and separate chairs in education in any collegiate institution in the United States when it established a separate Department of the Theory and Art of Teaching (alternately called the Department of the Science and Art of Teaching) in 1879. A single faculty member taught all of the program's courses. The university established the degree requirement in teaching in the following manner:

> Since . . . the usual teaching load of a full professor in the university was then . . . ten semester hours, this was accepted as the recognized standard for the new incumbent [faculty member in the education department]—except that, out of sheer generosity of heart and from a sense of the practical desirability of the action—Dr. [William] Payne, the first individual to hold the newly established chair, added a one-hour course in practical talks on classroom management and teaching methods.[35]

Thus, as one historian concluded, "out of the exigencies of the time" emerged the "ideal of eleven semester hours of professional training as the standard for the high school teacher's certificate. No more could be demanded because no more could be taught." The "accidentally established" 11-hour standard quickly became "embodied in the laws of the State of Michigan as the minimum professional attainment required for a life certificate for high school teachers prepared in liberal arts colleges." This minimal standard was soon accepted in other states and by a variety of other certification and accreditation agencies across the nation—including the increasingly powerful North Central Association of Secondary Schools, which adopted it almost unanimously.[36]

In addition to changing the certification and licensure practices in many states, the educational community during the last half of the nineteenth century moved to standardize the working relationships among teachers, administrators, and local supervisors by expanding the use of formal written contracts. In contrast to the informal arrangements common earlier in the century, which were subject to revision at the whim of a selectman or school board member, the contracts that began to govern employee behavior in the late nineteenth century offered some sense of security to teachers. But whatever slight measure of security that was achieved through the utilization of written contracts carried a steep price. Although they differed tremendously from district to district, the contracts not only publicly specified an intimidating list of "professional" responsibilities (including building maintenance and related duties); but outlined in aggressive language the noninstructional behavioral and moral expectations that communities had for their teachers.

Young women, in particular, found dozens of proscriptions on their activities outside the classroom. Contracts typically forbade female teachers from socializing with men, and required that they be chaperoned by a relative whenever they ventured out in the evening.

Too, contracts specified a disheartening number of acts of insubordination.

Increasingly they prohibited new female teachers from marrying, and incorporated clauses for terminating the employment of women who married after they began teaching. These policies were grounded in both understandable economic assumptions and somewhat peverse beliefs. One exemplary economic assumption was the aforementioned colonial practice of distributing scarce public resources only to those who lacked other sources of support (such as a husband), despite the fact that many single women continued to live with their parents in more relative affluence than they would after they married. An example of a somewhat perverse belief might well be that of the inappropriateness of allowing sexually mature and experienced women to teach school. In order to teach, therefore, women were forced by contracts either to remain single (postponing or altogether forgoing marriage), or to hide their marriages as best they could. Some of the earliest historical evidence available regarding teacher "resistance" to managerial authority involved collusion by women teachers to keep marriages of colleagues secret in order to protect their careers.[37]

It is important to understand that employment contracts probably did not change conditions very much, since school boards and administrators could arbitrarily force teachers to do most any of the things that the contracts specified. The contracts did codify many conventional understandings, however, and requiring teachers to read and agree to them publicly undoubtedly was humiliating to many practitioners who had thought of pursuing "professional" careers.

Many of the onerous responsibilities and imposing personal restrictions were pruned away during the early twentieth century—in response to the differentiation of labor that accompanied consolidation of districts, the efforts of fledgling teacher organizations, and later the necessity to make teaching positions more attractive in order to combat shortages. In their place stood more predictably instructional and organizational maintenance requirements. Most states stipulated that all contracts demand that teachers keep school registers on student attendance, and report such data to the county and state superintendents. Many states held the year's final paycheck until the reports were submitted; Idaho required teachers to forfeit 10 percent of their salary if an acceptable register was not completed. Contracts obligated teachers to "enforce" the district's accepted curriculum, and to use only "adopted" texts.

Appeals procedures often were specified, as were political rights (at least off the school property, an important distinction included in contracts in Massachusetts in 1915). Contracts increasingly outlined other prerogatives for teachers, such as the opportunity to be excluded from jury duty while schools were in session (New Jersey). And, by the second decade of the twentieth century, contracts began to incorporate uniform pay scales: California eliminated salary differentials by gender in their contracts in 1915. The trend spread across the nation; standard contracts became more common over the next two decades. Experience had quickly demonstrated to teachers the real benefits and protections associated with formal contracts.[38]

By World War I, prevailing licensing and hiring practices had changed significantly. Although the labor market remained local, steady centralization reduced the prerogatives of civilian school committees. Certification moved consistently to the state level, and many policy changes were introduced, expanded, and enforced to curtail the arbitrariness of traditional teacher hiring practices. Examinations were standardized, and the assessment of prospective teachers was placed in the hands of county (and later state) authorities, an increasing proportion of whom were themselves professionally educated. They understandably began to substitute evidence of formal professional preparation for examinations as the basis of certification.

This centralization and standardization, and the increase in standards that it implied, occurred during a period of a tight labor market in teaching, perhaps something on the shortage side of equilibrium. The vast subsidy that young women teachers contributed to the educational enterprise made the process of school expansion relatively painless. But several other trends had begun to converge around the time of World War I, and these were to alter the recruitment and selection environment significantly.

Standards During a Shortage: Strengthening Credentials in the 1920s

The United States experienced a teacher shortage of unprecedented depth and breadth following World War I. One observer claimed that 10 percent of the nation's classrooms were at that time effectively teacherless. But since virtually all districts probably were able to round up *someone* to sit in each classroom (or, in the language of an earlier day, to "keep school"), the real magnitude of the shortage in 1919 was more evident in complaints about the qualifications of the teaching force. In addition to 50–60,000 unfillable teaching vacancies, another commentator added, there were roughly 120,000 new teachers without professional preparation, and 30,000 teachers with no schooling beyond the eighth grade. His estimates were corroborated by others. It was estimated that half of the nation's 600,000 teachers had no more than a high-school education: a similar proportion had no professional education whatsoever. One in five teachers was under 20 years of age, and half were under 26.[39]

The shortage occurred for several related reasons, including the military buildup which drew many male teachers into the armed forces. In this case the war merely aggravated a troubling trend which had been growing for decades as men abandoned teaching for work in better-paying occupations. Indeed, commentators argued that men already had begun to flee teaching as the process of feminization reached some imaginary tipping point during the late nineteenth century. The reality of low salaries added injury to the insult of a low-status job.[40] "On the walls of the Hall of the Board of Education of New York City are numerous United States Government advertisements for stenographers, typewriters, clerks, etc., with salaries ranging from $900 to $1,200 per year," noted one observer, whereas the typical teacher of that time earned less than $600 annually.[41] A sort of gallows humor surfaced to help teachers adapt to their straitened financial circumstances:

> Said the bank teller to a teacher who had presented her salary check to be cashed, "I am really very sorry to hand you these old, soiled bills. They are

> unhygienic and possibly dangerous." "Oh, never mind," replied the cheerful teacher, "Really and truly there is no danger. A microbe couldn't live on my salary."[42]

The prevalence of women in the classroom was driving the relative wages of teaching down, some maintained:

> Perhaps the principal reason why the effective salaries of teachers declined from 1896 to 1914, while the wealth of the country was increasing rapidly and standards of living were improving in nearly every other trade and profession, has been the unlimited supply of partly educated young women who act temporarily as teachers. They have no families to support and do not look on teaching as their life work.[43]

It was not only men who were defecting from teaching positions during the war era. Women, too, had found an increasing variety of employment opportunities opening to them during the emergency.[44] One observer told an audience at the National Education Association conference in 1918 that "Experienst [*sic*] teachers . . . throughout the country are resigning their positions for places in banks, in the government service, and in the various mercantile and industrial pursuits, where the responsibility is not so great and the remuneration is far greater." Enrollments in teacher-training institutions, particularly in normal schools, were declining.[45]

The shortage, which had become visible in some communities and at some levels in the school system as early as 1916, persisted through most of the 1920s. By 1926 an equilibrium between supply and demand was beginning to be reported from across the nation. Almost as quickly as the shortage had appeared during the war, spot surpluses began to appear by the end of the 1920s. By early 1933, reports of surpluses were widespread.[46]

What happened during the decade following the war to reverse the supply–demand relationship so dramatically? How did states, communities, schools, and other interested agencies respond to the shortage crisis? Did their actions have an impact on the labor market in teaching, or did the surplus appear for unrelated reasons?

The initial signs of shortage, on the eve of and during the war, were met logically by lowering certification standards and granting emergency licenses. After 1917 however, when educational and political leaders were able to gain some perspective on the roots and nature of the shortage, the practice of bestowing emergency certificates was roundly condemned, and other changes were advocated to restore equilibrium in the teaching force.

It was recommended first that teaching salaries be improved. To attract and retain teachers, districts did increase salaries—in fact, at an unprecedented pace during the 1920s. There is no doubt that improving teaching's extrinsic rewards did much to alleviate the crisis by attracting and holding thousands of individuals to the profession. And raising salaries did much to reverse the trend of feminization—or to halt the complete takeover of teaching by women—by drawing men back into teaching.[47]

In addition to increasing salaries, other benefits designed to make teaching mo appealing were strengthened. Tenure, for example, began to become widespread. Some districts began to eliminate codes prohibiting the employment of married women as classroom teachers. Uniform salary schedules began to reduce the whimsical and idiosyncratic reward systems that irritated teachers in many schools.[48]

Paralleling these improvements in ancillary benefits, a number of steps were taken to raise the status and prerogatives of teaching as an occupation. It occurred to many educational leaders that an occupation's standing and appeal reflected a variety of characteristics beyond the earning potential that it provided. Entrance and training standards, among other things, had an impact on the relative appeal of an occupation. They recognized that teaching had been caught in a historical bind: Providing instructors for the ever-expanding population of students had made it difficult to improve the educational qualifications of teachers much beyond the pace of the population in general. The educational level of the teaching force had increased, but really no faster than that of the nation's adult population. When the average American had attained an eighth-grade education, the typical teacher was a high-school graduate. As the average adult's educational attainment level approached 10 years, the average teacher's approached 14, equivalent roughly to a two-year normal course. The four-year (or one-level) ratio left the nation's elementary schools staffed with high-school graduates, and the high schools staffed with teachers holding bachelor's degrees.

This pattern and ratio disturbed many educational leaders who were convinced that it was essential to strengthen the professional status of teaching. They pressed states to respond to the shortage of the World War I era by raising certification standards for all teachers, but particularly for increasing the professional education of elementary teachers. In 1920, only ten states required four years of higher education for secondary certification. And, even in these states, teachers typically circumvented the standard. *No* states required elementary teachers to possess more than a normal-school education, 30 enforced *no* formal educational requirements, and a dozen prescribed *only* a high-school diploma.[49]

Anticipating the reaction to a demand for raising entry standards during a time of shortage, the most prominent scholar of the labor market in teaching during the World War I era argued in 1920 that "It may be contended that in light of the present teacher shortage this is not the time to do this, but it should be remembered that delay in raising standards will inevitably be followed by a reaction toward continuing the present low salary."[50] Salaries were likely to improve only when professional standards were strengthened, she noted:

> Experience in a number of states indicates that expected shortage does not usually follow the establishment of higher standards. Evidently the dignity and promise and opportunity offered are so improved by increased standards as to add to the attractiveness in the eyes of possible candidates.[51]

Enough state school officers were convinced by this reasoning to raise certification standards steadily throughout the shortage of the 1920s. Since the credential model had displaced the examination process during the century's early years, states approached the standards issue by increasing the required period of professional education. By 1930, the number of states that required bachelor's degrees for secondary certification more than doubled, from ten to 23. The timing of events in many states in the North, East, and West paralleled those in Michigan. Responding to pressure from the Michigan State Teachers Association, the state moved to adopt a normal-school graduation standard for elementary teachers during the early 1920s. At the secondary level, the North Central Association pressed the state to move beyond a simple baccalaureate requirement and endorse its proposal to redefine a "qualified" teacher as one who was certified to teach—and who taught—only in the subject(s) of his or her collegiate major or minor. The state gradually expanded the professional school requirements and standardized them, so that by 1925 they had begun to assume their current dimensions.[52]

Somewhat ahead of Michigan and other Northern states, California consistently set the pace for "progressive" licensure. In that state, the certification law of 1893 had established a minimum of graduation from an accredited university with at least 12 semester hours in pedagogical courses for a high-school teaching certificate. This ambitious requirement was increased even further in 1906, when the state board of education restricted secondary certificates to those with one year of graduate credits (with a few subject-field restrictions, all of which were removed in 1928).[53]

Southern states moved somewhat more slowly to raise standards of entry by centralizing the certification process and by abandoning the examination tradition for educational credentials. The region began to endorse normal-school preparation after the turn of the century, but apparently imposed a relatively nonaggressive policy of "advising" attendance. Some states, like North Carolina, which held on to its examination system until the 1920s, attempted to strengthen the professional education of teachers by requiring them to attend two-week county institutes, and promoted summer-school classes for teachers.[54] Teacher-training institutions were allowed to develop their own approaches to professional education with virtually no interference from the states. Over the course of the 1920s, standards in professional education throughout the South shifted, generally from summer-school and extension classes, brief institutes, and reading circles to formal pre-service educational programs.[55] Pressure for conformity came from the professional education establishment rather than from state governments.

In addition to strengthening the expectation of formal professional education, the standards-raising movement of the 1920s began to articulate and enforce regulations concerning the *content* of teacher-education programs. The package of courses in social and psychological foundations, generic and subject-matter pedagogy, and practice teaching began to assume the proportions that were recognizable in the 1980s.

Overall, certification standards increased significantly during the shortage of the 1920s. And raising standards had an immediate impact on the professional qualifications of the teaching force. A survey conducted early in 1925 revealed the extent to which states were approaching "the ideal of a trained teacher in every classroom." Between 1920 and 1925, for example, a number of states made substantial progress in raising the proportion of teachers with at least two years of normal schooling: North Carolina's "trained" teachers increased from 18 to 40 percent of the total force; Pennsylvania's grew from 50 to 78 percent; Oregon's jumped from 54 to 70 percent; and Wyoming's rose from 24 to 40 percent. The study's author attributed the improvement to "the influence of vigorous state policies" designed to raise certification and entry standards in teaching.[56]

Entry standards and the actual qualifications of teachers had been raised despite the shortage crisis of the decade. According to a massive federal report on licensure in teaching released in 1927, just as equilibrium in supply and demand was reached, during the preceding six years there had been "unusual and satisfactory progress in raising the standards of qualifications of prospective teachers, supervisors, and administrators through laws and regulations set up in each of the States for granting certificates." The report noted that the situation for standards-raising had been "favorable in many respects." It was a "strategic time to set up high standards" which resulted in a series of "unusually fruitful efforts."

In contrast to most prevailing opinion after the war, the federal study revealed that states found the method of raising standards by requiring additional professional education to be effective, and encountered no difficulties "because of shortness of teacher supply as qualifications are raised."[57] Higher standards improved the status of teaching, and in many cases indirectly led to salary increases. An editorial in the *Elementary School Journal* endorsed the federal report's conclusions that low standards produce low salaries, and that higher standards do not produce or materially aggravate shortages: "Where standards for teaching certificates are low, salaries are correspondingly low, and the percentage of unprepared teachers employed continues to be high. No state in which qualifications for certificates have been materially raised reports a shortage."[58] Other observers who commented on the relationship in the 1920s between standards-raising and the labor market agreed with that assessment.[59]

Standards During a Surplus: The Resurrection of Testing in the 1930s

The standards-raising movement of the 1920s accelerated during the 1930s, when a serious surplus of teachers made it much easier to enforce more elaborate requirements.[60] A number of trends rooted in demography, public policy, and the Depression contributed to the surplus of the 1930s. Teaching became more appealing because of measures enacted to alleviate the shortage of the 1920s, including salary increases, better job security through tenure, and other benefits mentioned above.[61] Normal schools were being converted into four-year teachers colleges, and universities increasingly established schools and colleges of education. Coupled with the expansion of public institutions during the 1920s and 1930s, particularly low-cost, convenient urban universities, these developments expanded access to professional education dramatically and resulted in a sharp increase in the number of teachers prepared in formal programs.

Gradually, more and more states were able to set certification standards at the bachelor's level. The number enforcing this requirement for high-school teachers increased from 23 to 40 between 1930 and 1940, and the ranks of those enforcing such a standard for elementary teachers grew from two to 11 during the decade of the 1930s.[62] Twenty states raised their "scholarship requirements" for certification in the two years between September 1, 1935 and September 1, 1937.[63]

Paralleling the movement to improve the qualifications of the teaching force by raising certification standards (the movement led primarily by the professional associations, the state departments, and the teacher-education institutions), other groups lobbied for reestablishing the examination tradition to best guarantee a competent teaching force. Initially, interest in examinations was rather inchoate and fragmented, and was roundly condemned in a series of scholarly studies during the 1930s.[64] The forces of credential-based certification had assumed that the examination tradition had been driven from legitimate dialogue. They generally agreed, according to the largest contemporary scholarly survey of the matter, that examinations, as they were customarily administered in the United States, too often permitted "the infiltration of poorly qualified teachers into the profession, instead of eliminating such teachers from consideration for employment."[65]

The Carnegie Foundation for the Advancement of Teaching took a strong stand against testing in 1932 when it recommended that all of the local and county certificates issued in California—those that had been bestowed on the basis of examination—be abolished.[66] Benjamin Frazier, who conducted the comprehensive review of licensure practices in teaching, recalled the conclusion of a speaker before the National Education Association in 1931: "The best interests of American childhood demand that certification of teachers be based on something more substantial than mere success in passing an examination."[67]

This criticism of the tradition of awarding initial professional certificates on the basis of performance on a single examination was not intended to dismiss the potential contribution of testing, and other forms of evaluation, to the appointment and promotion processes. Many critics of initial licensure testing agreed, for example, that examinations could help to discriminate among generally well-qualified applicants.[68] Indeed, during the surplus of the 1930s, pressure built for developing a respectable examination to help attractive districts to sift and sort among many applicants for few jobs. This need grew increasingly concentrated over the 1930s, and led to the creation of the National Teacher Examination (NTE), first administered in March 1940.

The most comprehensive interpretation of the history of the National Teacher Examination argues that its roots reside in the surplus of the 1930s, in the necessity of urban superintendents to select among certified teachers whose credentials were uneven, and in a generalized low evaluation of those drawn into teaching. This powerful market condition was complemented by continued fascination with science and efficiency that contributed to a "thriving intelligence and achievement testing movement" in schools.[69]

The National Teacher Examination was rooted directly in three testing projects of the late 1920s and early 1930s initiated by the Bureau of Public Personnel Association, the Teachers College Personnel Association, and the Carnegie Foundation for the Advancement of Teaching. The first project led to the development of an instrument to assess the professional and content knowledge of elementary teachers and was sold to personnel departments in larger school systems. The second effort, initiated by an affiliate of the American Council on Education and the American Association of Teachers Colleges, led to the preparation of an instrument designed to evaluate prospective teachers-college students and was sold to, and utilized in, 106 institutions during the 1930s.[70]

The third project, sponsored by the Carnegie Foundation in order to assess the quality of secondary and higher education in Pennsylvania, led to massive testing of adolescents and young adults—a number of whom indicated a preference for teaching careers—between 1928 and 1934.[71] The Carnegie effort, directed by William Learned and Ben Wood, who had done previous work on testing for the Carnegie Corporation, contributed to a series of "extensive nationwide college and graduate testing projects, one of which evolved into the Graduate Record Examination."[72] Learned and Wood's findings were publicized nationally and laid a foundation for alarm about the intellectual and academic abilities of prospective teachers, even those who were graduating from Pennsylvania's strongest institutions of higher education. The average score of the teachers was below that of everyone else who took the examinations except those seeking careers in business, art, agriculture, and the secretarial sciences.[73] Even worse, the prospective teachers in professional courses of study did poorly when compared with the *high-school* students who were tested.

Learned and Wood's comparison of scores led them to stinging conclusions about the "limited mental ability of the individuals who are specially prepared for teaching positions," whom they identified as "narrower people" with "uninformed and incompetent minds" and skills appropriate for elementary teaching perhaps, but unsuited for more-responsible positions in high schools.[74] Commentators generally avoided calling attention to the painful comparisons, although Lewis Terman classified some prospective teachers as "congenital ninth graders."[75]

Ben Wood, one of the senior researchers in the Carnegie project, was appointed as director of the Cooperative Testing Service of the American Council on Education in 1930. With extended support from the Rockefeller-sponsored General Education Board, the service was charged with preparing, publishing, and distributing subject-matter examinations.[76] In addition to cooperating with university testing bureaus across the nation, the service donated examinations to a variety of organizations, including the Carnegie project. Increasingly engaged in test construction and administration, school leaders in Providence, Rhode Island, requested a special edition of the service's examinations in 1932 "for use as one phase of their teacher selection procedure."[77] Other districts learned of the service's generosity, and within a few years districts in Philadelphia, Pittsburgh, and Cleveland were being supplied with tests. Since the General Education Board funding was to expire in 1940, the service announced that it could no longer continue to supply districts with the tests.

Disturbed by the service's threat, superintendents from several large districts met with the American Council on Education in 1939 and formed a National Committee on Teacher Examinations. The superintendents who were convened that year had become attracted to supplementary examinations for personnel decisions, and helped to secure funding from the Carnegie Corporation to construct, administer, and score teacher examinations through the Cooperative Testing Service, with Ben Wood remaining as director.[78] Work on the test began immediately, with a poll of superintendents and other administrators. The staff prepared a preliminary test consisting of five parts: English comprehension and expression, reasoning, general culture (history and social studies, current social problems, literature, fine arts, science, and mathematics), professional information, and contemporary affairs.[79]

Shortly after these preliminary discussions outlined the structure and substance of the proposed tests, Wood released an announcement of "a teacher examination service" which would help employers grapple with inconsistent certification and credential standards. The announcement stressed that the tests would be useful "as only one phase" of the teacher selection process, according to the subject's most thorough historian.[80] Wood had been attempting to gain support from members of the teacher-education community for his examination, and did what he could to assure them that the examination was not designed or intended to help superintendents circumvent the professional education sector. Wood's tendency to condemn the "horde of semi-literates who flaunt their diplomas before the credulous eyes of employer superintendents," or his observation that "education classes are as much if not more amply populated with morons than other departments," however, caused teacher educators to remain skeptical and distant from the entire enterprise.[81]

Upon hearing about the new testing venture, for example, the president of Shippensburg (Pennsylvania) State Teachers College challenged Wood in the pages of the *Harvard Educational Review*. He feared that the prestige and power of the American Council of Education could make the proposed examinations popular and influential enough to cause a great deal of inadvertent damage: "A note of warning should be sounded against a procedure which, under the guise of providing an improved teaching service to our schools, may actually destroy the gains of several decades of intelligent planning for a better teaching personnel."[82]

Through effective lobbying, the examination system of certification had been eliminated in Pennsylvania 20 years before, on the assumption that completing an accredited teacher-education program was better evidence of "the likelihood of teaching success" than were "the results of any examination." Over the 20 years since the state completed the shift toward licensure based upon credentials, "the improvement of the teaching service of the Pennsylvania schools has been phenomenal," he continued. The proportion of teachers with four years of professional education increased from 7.7 percent in 1920 to 44.5 percent in 1939. "Observation of classroom procedures and school programs" clearly indicated that practice had improved, he maintained.

> All this has occurred, not because the teacher candidates have studied textbooks in preparation for fixed examinations, but because they have lived in the atmosphere of institutions designed to provide over a period of years the associations, contacts, and experiences which will produce just such a result. The proposed imposition of a nation-wide examination service is likely to alter the character of these teacher-training institutions and reduce their prestige, and ultimately destroy them.[83]

Although the National Committee on Teacher Examinations conspicuously avoided making "extravagant claims" for the tests, the writer was convinced that if they became prestigious enough, "self-respecting school systems will demand that their teachers pass this battery of tests, and the meeting of this requirement will become so significant that all other considerations will shrink to insignificance in comparison."[84] Teacher-training institutions will inevitably be reduced to "tutoring schools for the passing of these tests."

Wood wanted continued support from the Carnegie Foundation to stabilize and extend the embryonic enterprise, but apparently the foundation "anticipated a furious reaction from many teachers and teachers colleges and was not eager to get involved."[85] Recognizing that his statements were offensive, and too often alienated constituencies that the testing movement would eventually need to regain a larger foothold in the licensure process, Wood accepted an invitation to address the American Association of Teachers Colleges on the eve of World War II. To this understandably hostile audience, Wood described and endorsed shared responsibility for preparing and certifying qualified teachers:

> In a world in which peoples squander billions on the gleam in some politician's eye, in which great nations revert to barbarism in worship of a maniacal super-salesman, in which American planes and bombs rain death on the innocent men, women and children of friendly nations, and in which we are confused by dozens of similar paradoxes, the only possible hope for our children lies in having them educated, so far as possible, by persons who are themselves educated. I believe that the wise and judicious use of examinations such as those provided by the National Committee on Teacher Examinations will help assure this boon for our school children.[86]

He tempered his remarks and enthusiasm for testing slightly, agreeing with critics that "objective examinations do not and cannot measure the total subtle complex which we call teaching ability." Members of the professional educational establishment had come to assume that their efforts to reshape the licensure process around academic credentials had essentially routed the examiners. This assumption would have caused them to view an aggressive national examination campaign with concern, particularly regarding claims about the tests' validity. Wood anticipated this hostility and reserve among teacher educators and tried—in his clumsy way—to calm his critics.

The Cooperative Test Service spent the latter months of 1939 and part of 1940 preparing the examinations. Despite efforts to engage a variety of people in developing the tests, argues Ann Jarvella Wilson, who has studied the issue most carefully, the organization, structure, and content of the examinations "bore a striking resemblance to those related tests which preceded them and had precipitated their creation," principally to the tests that Ben Wood had developed for the earlier Pennsylvania study.[87] In their final incarnation, the multiple-choice tests totaled 12 hours in length, including an eight-hour common examination on reasoning, comprehension, expression, contemporary affairs, social problems, subject-matter fields, and a series of segments on professional issues like education and social policy, child development, and methods.[88]

Most of the examination assessed prospective teachers' knowledge of basic college-course content and familiarity with current affairs, many questions being on military matters and New Deal politics. The "professional studies" component of the examination, totaling two hours out of 12, was intentionally kept relatively small, Wood claimed, to avoid giving the impression that the testing organization intended to exert "any undesirable influence on the teacher training curriculum." Professional knowledge items, consequently, were designed to assess familiarity with indisputable fundamentals: the awareness that John Dewey was the "chief contemporary exponent of the experimental method in philosophy," for example; or the recognition of various titles of "progressive" publications; or the knowledge that the best way to control adolescents was to exploit their obsession with "social approval." The superficial, definitive nature of such questions probably did little to calm the fears of the community of teacher educators. Once the examinations began to be administered during the 1940s, members of the teaching profession joined teacher educators in condemning the use of the National Teacher Examination (NTE) as a measure of "good teaching."[89]

As noted earlier, the first NTE was administered in March 1940. Nearly 4,000 candidates were examined in 23 centers. A disproportionate number of the centers were located in Pennsylvania, and roughly one-third of all of the examinees in the nation appeared at the Philadelphia center. This pattern was probably a legacy of the tradition of Pennsylvania's involvement with Ben Wood's testing ventures since the mid-1920s.[90] Because of their involvement with the Learned and Wood activities, district leaders in Pennsylvania were perhaps more accustomed to using standardized examinations in the selection process. The results of the earliest administrations of the NTE were analyzed extensively. "The most obvious finding from the administration of these examinations," wrote one analyst, "is that *candidates for teaching positions are not equally well qualified.*"[91]

The NTE's backers' ambitious effort to revitalize the examination tradition was virtually derailed by World War II, which drew off so many prospective teachers that the surplus disappeared almost instantly. The market for examinations collapsed just as quickly, since the NTE was potentially useful only as a supplementary sorting device to screen already licensed prospective teachers. The examination community had not yet really attempted to modify state certification procedures so as to reestablish testing as a prerequisite to licensure. The NTE was used only by superintendents and personnel departments in larger districts, to select teachers from a pool of already certified applicants.

Under new leadership, the Cooperative Test Service enacted a series of cost-cutting measures to keep the NTE project solvent. They stopped preparing new questions, but used one version for several years in succession, and reduced the number of items on the examination. To broaden the base of support for the examination, NTE began to involve representatives of the teacher-education community, to lower fees to encourage greater use, and to mount a successful campaign for several small grants from the Carnegie Corporation.[92]

The development that really kept the NTE afloat was South Carolina's decision to use the test in a new certification program for both continuing and prospective teachers. In 1940 the U.S. Supreme Court outlawed dual salary schedules based on race. They were customary throughout the South at the time. South Carolina responded with a certification plan that bestowed "graded" credentials on the basis of performance on the National Teacher Examination. Studies completed in 194 predicted that white teachers would score higher than black teachers: Under the new plan, "90 percent of the white teachers [but] only 27 percent of the black teachers would qualify for A or B certificates. . . . The remaining candidates—10 percent of the whites and 73 percent of the blacks—would receive C or D certificates."[93] Coupled with disproportionate state spending in favor of white children over black, South Carolina's use of the NTE effectively reestablished the dual salary schedule that the Court had prohibited. Indeed, South Carolina's widespread use of the NTE after 1945 proved to be a major source of income for the struggling project during the difficult postwar era.[94]

The American Council of Education, the NTE's parent sponsor, took another major step to protect the fledgling project when it merged its testing program with those of the College Entrance Examination Board and the Graduate Record Office to form the Educational Testing Service (ETS) in 1947. Production, administration, and evaluation of the NTE was transferred to ETS by 1951. Under the sponsorship of ETS the National Teacher Examination was pared down dramatically; during its initial administration under ETS, the exhaustive common component of the examination was shortened from 1,200 to 300 questions, and from eight to three hours. Wilson has observed that the components of the test still resembled those of its predecessor. But ETS continued to defend the NTE's role in selection, as a supplement to professional education. It was still justified on the basis of its ability to help administrators to make hiring decisions with "comparable measures for all teacher applicants without regard to the standards of the institutions which prepared them."[95]

The teacher surplus of the 1930s, therefore, provided the soil from which testing became reestablished as a legitimate supplement to the hiring process. The NTE was not widely used, however, because a rapid shift in the labor market—brought on by World War II—diminished the need for district administrators to make risky decisions about the potential of a number of teaching prospects competing for the same job.

Perennial Disequilibrium

World War II ushered in another serious teacher shortage in the United States. Initially the shortage was caused by the mobilization effort itself, which drew men and women into the military, and many women into higher-paying civilian jobs traditionally held by men. The labor market in teaching was on the verge of regaining stability when the children of the baby boom began to arrive in school during the early 1950s. Actually, the image of a general shortage during the 1950s masked important distinctions. There was a shortage of elementary teachers of crippling proportions (some estimated that the nation could attract only one-sixth as many qualified teachers as it needed at that level). With this shortage, however, there coexisted a substantial oversupply of high-school teachers, some analysts claiming that there were twice as many secondary teachers as were needed.[96] By 1960 this pattern would be reversed at the secondary level, as the oldest baby boomers began reaching the high schools.

The shortage was rooted in two cycles in the nation's birthrate pattern that aggravated one another. The pattern of family creation following the war contributed to the doubling of enrollment within a dozen years. But the low birth rate during the Depression and war years had left the college-age cohort—from which most teachers would be drawn—relatively small. This combination "exhausted the capacity of the system to prepare and place teachers," argued the leading analyst of labor-market fluctuations in teaching.[97]

As their counterparts had done during the shortage following World War I, political and educational leaders proposed a variety of policies to restore equilibrium. Some focused on improving salaries to prevent or minimize the defection of teachers attracted by the opportunities inherent in the booming economy of the 1950s and 1960s. Most strategies attempted to increase the number of teachers—by expanding access to publicly supported financial-aid and loan-forgiveness programs (National Defense Education Act of 1958); by granting deferments from the military draft; by establishing Master of Arts in Teaching programs to ease entrance into educational careers; and by creating a "teacher reserve plan" similar to that of the army reserve.[98]

And, just as had happened during the shortage of the 1920s, professional preparation standards were raised sharply during the shortage of the 1950s and 1960s. Following another brief flirtation with debased emergency certificates during the war, the earlier goal of requiring a bachelor's degree as a minimum standard for all teachers was reached. At the elementary level, 11 states enforced the bachelor's standard in 1940, 21 required it in 1950, and 46 relied on that standard in 1964. Since 40 states had enforced the bachelor's standard for secondary certification in 1940, the improvement was not as statistically vivid, but by 1960 every state held to that standard.[99]

Since certification had become almost entirely based upon professional educational credentials, attention became focused on the scope and substance of the preparation programs available to prospective teachers. Between 1940 and 1967 the minimal professional component expanded very slightly, to roughly 28 semester hours at the elementary level and 18 at the secondary level. Most institutions offered programs that required more than these minimums, however: A survey of accredited institutions in 1958 revealed that elementary programs more typically required 36 hours, and secondary programs 24.[100] Extended clinical experiences (as student teachers) became customary.

In contrast to what happened during the shortage period of the 1920s, the examination of teachers was revitalized slightly during the 1950s and 1960s. This occurred primarily in the South, where an increasing number of states followed South Carolina's lead in abandoning their illegal dual certification and salary schedules and relying upon allegedly meritocratic examinations that consistently perpetuated substantial racially based differentials in teaching income.[101]

Raising credential and certification standards did not aggravate the shortage. Indeed, by 1971 the nation was once again in the midst of another demoralizing teacher surplus. The surplus of the 1970s was caused in part once again by cyclical patterns in the birth rate which led to the unprecedented expansion of higher and professional education and the steady contraction of the elementary and secondary schools. And, once again, improvements in teaching's appeal and stature tempted many more college students to consider a career in education.

An oversupply of teachers in all regions and at every level, coupled with continued criticism of the unevenness of professional programs and evidence of troubled practice among highly credentialled teachers, encouraged many districts and some states to impose a variety of tests on those seeking teaching licenses. It even enticed a few states to experiment with examining tenured teachers, demanding regular tests for continued certification. This "first wave" of accountability reforms, imposed largely from above—from governors' offices and legislatures—gained momentum from the "excellence" campaigns of the mid–1980s.[102]

Before the first wave had even crested, a "second wave" of more comprehensive reforms emerged, symbolized by the publication of the Holmes Group Report, *Tomorrow's Teachers*; the Carnegie Forum on Education and the Economy's *Teachers for the Twenty-first Century*, and several other studies released in 1986. These organizations endorsed and engaged in tightening professional standards of practice in teaching through expanded programs of knowledge and performance assessment, improved professional education, and "empowering" teachers to make a more "professional" contribution to effective learning by restructuring the organization of work and authority relations in schools.[103]

Conclusion

This reconstruction of the hiring process in teaching in the United States since the late eighteenth century has attempted to develop a periodization that links change in policy and practice with shifts in the educational labor market. It has shown that responsibility for making hiring decisions became professionalized—that is, it became vested in the educational enterprise itself: state departments of education, county and district superintendents, local personnel departments. Taking the hiring decision out of the hands of civilians (either by limiting the "pool" of eligible, qualified applicants, or by giving school superintendents and personnel departments the right to employ teachers) led inexorably to a radical shift in criteria from idiosyncratic examinations to formal credentials representing the completion of professional education programs.

We have seen that credential standards were raised substantially during teacher shortages. When combined with other efforts to make teaching more attractive, strengthening requirements appears not to have aggravated shortages of crisis proportions. This interpretation does not suggest that raising standards is the most effective way of preventing a shortage, but it does suggest that making an occupation more exclusive by tightening its entry procedures somehow makes a field appealing to a larger group of individuals willing to invest more to gain access to that occupation.[104]

But it is also evident that any teacher shortage in the future will not be as easily addressed as shortages have been in the past—by drawing upon the hidden subsidy of thousands of women with few career opportunities. The expansion of employment opportunities for women during the 1970s and 1980s will inevitably shape the nation's ability to respond to teacher shortages in the future. Since little hiring has occurred after alternative careers in high status-occupations began to open to women in the late 1960s, communities will have to compete for talented women in an increasingly open labor market.[105]

This chapter also has shown that standards-raising in teaching proceeded without very much imagination until the late 1980s. Once the educational credential model became dominant it was merely extended; its substance was tinkered with slightly, but few probed seriously into the quality or impact of the experiences that the credentials presumably represented. Similarly, the examination tradition became more impartial (though some would challenge its claims to being more meritocratic or valid), but the tests changed little in their assumptions about essenttial professional skills, knowledge, and dispositions. Examinations commonly used in the 1980s encouraged virtually the same mechanical posture toward knowledge—and rewarded the same gamesmanship skills and superficial learning—that troubled critics a century ago.

The campaign of the late 1980s to shape the recruitment, preparation, induction, and retention of teachers indicates that many of its leaders have recognized the hollowness of many earlier reforms, the limitations that accompanied selective and isolated experimentation with a single component of the vast, interconnected educational enterprise. Proposals for comprehensive and integrated reform across a number of institutional fronts, particularly fundamental restructuring of the workplace itself, hold far more promise for actually improving the nature and distribution of school learning in America. Unless policymakers, foundation leaders, teacher educators, and school personnel develop a realistic perspective on the interaction of their enterprise's many components, creative and challenging responses to the problems of recruiting and retaining an effective teaching force will continue to be undermined.

Notes

AUTHOR'S NOTE: THE AUTHOR ACKNOWLEDGES THE CONTRIBUTION OF JOHN ZEULI OF MICHIGAN STATE UNIVERSITY.

1. The Holmes Group, *Tomorrow's Teachers* (East Lansing, MI: The Holmes Group, 1986); Carnegie Forum on Education and the Economy, *A Nation Prepared: Teachers for the Twenty-first Century* (New York: Carnegie Forum, 1986); Douglas E. Mitchell, Flora Ida Ortiz, and Tedi K. Mitchell, *Work Orientation and Job Performance: The Cultural Basis of Teaching Rewards and Incentives* (Albany, NY: State University of New York Press, 1987); and Linda Darling-Hammond and Barnett Berry, *The Evolution of Teacher Policy* (Santa Monica, CA: Rand Corporation, 1988). The historical scholarship on the issues examined in this chapter is thin and largely derivative. As a result, I have grounded my interpretation in a variety of relatively accessible primary sources. Because of this, my arguments are more subject than usual to reinterpretation based either upon a consideration of a broader base of primary evidence, or on alternative types of sources.
2. Willard S. Elsbree, *The American Teacher: Evolution of a Profession in a Democracy* (New York: American Book Co., 1939), p. 53.
3. Richard Hofstadter, *Anti-Intellectualism in American Life* (New York: Knopf, 1962), p. 313.
4. Hofstadter, *Anti-Intellectualism,* p. 313.
5. Elsbree, *American Teacher,* p. 56.

6. Ibid.
7. Wayne E. Fuller, *The Old Country School: The Story of Rural Education in the Middle West* (Chicago: University of Chicago Press, 1982); and Marguerite Renner, "Who Will Teach? Changing Job Opportunity and Roles for Women in the Evolution of the Pittsburgh Public Schools, 1830–1900" (Doctoral dissertation, University of Pittsburgh, 1981).
8. Renner, "Who Will Teach?" pp. 102 and 146.
9. Fuller, *Old Country School,* pp. 89–90 and 134.
10. Renner, "Who Will Teach?" pp. 145–149.
11. Elsbree, *American Teacher,* pp. 181–182.
12. *Maine School Report* (1848), p. 57, quoted in Elsbree, *American Teacher,* p. 180.
13. Elsbree, *American Teacher,* p. 183.
14. T. M. Stinnett, "Teacher Education, Certification, and Accreditation," in Edgar Fuller and Jim B. Pearson (eds.), *Education in the States: Nationwide Development Since 1900* (Washington, DC: National Education Association, 1969), p. 390; and Lucien B. Kinney, *Certification in Education* (Englewood Cliffs, NJ: Prentice–Hall, 1964), p. 48. Personal memorabilia corroborate the informal and private character of most examinations, and reveal a great deal about the nature of knowledge most desired by the examiners; see, for example, Lucia B. Downing, "Teaching in the Keeler 'Deestrict' School," in *Vermont Quarterly* 19 (October 1951), pp. 233–240. Ms. Downing's recollections of teaching in the 1880s, and those of other women during the nineteenth and twentieth centuries, have been reprinted in two valuable collections, one edited by Nancy Hoffman, *Woman's "True" Profession: Voices from the History of Teaching* (Old Westbury, NY: Feminist Press, 1981), the other by Polly Welts Kaufman, *Women Teachers on the Frontier* (New Haven, CT: Yale University Press, 1984).
15. *New Jersey School Report* (1850), p. 56, quoted in Elsbree, *American Teacher,* p. 184.
16. Elsbree, *American Teacher,* pp. 189–190.
17. Superintendent of Public Instruction of Michigan, *Annual Report* (1879), p. xxiii, quoted in Fuller, *Old Country School,* p. 113.
18. Fuller, *Old Country School,* pp. 116–119 and 133; and Ellwood P. Cubberley, *The Certification of Teachers,* National Society for the Scientific Study of Education, *Fifth Yearbook,* Part II (Chicago: University of Chicago Press, 1906). On the process of professionalization more generally, see Paul H. Mattingly, *The Classless Profession: American Schoolmen in the Nineteenth Century* (New York: New York University Press, 1975).
19. Renner, "Who Will Teach?" p. 168.
20. Ibid., p. 187.
21. Ibid.
22. Ibid., p. 189.
23. Superintendent of Public Instruction of Michigan, *Annual Report* (1895); and Cubberley, *Certification,* pp. 38–39.
24. Allegheny County, Pennsylvania, *Superintendent's Report* (1860), pp. 18–20, quoted in Renner, "Who Will Teach?" p. 191.
25. Elsbree, *American Teacher,* pp. 187–188.
26. Stinnett, "Teacher Education, Certification, and Accreditation," p. 391; and Elsbree, *American Teacher,* pp. 190ff.
27. Katherine M. Cook, *State Laws and Regulations Governing Teachers' Certificates,* in *Bulletin* No. 19, 1927 (Washington, DC: U.S. Bureau of Education, 1927); Katherine M. Cook, *State Laws and Regulations Governing Teachers' Certificates,* in *Bulletin* No. 22, 1921 (Washington, DC: U.S. Bureau of Education, 1921); Cubberley, *Certification;* and William R. Jackson, "The Present Status of the Certification of Teachers in the United States," in U.S. Bureau of Education, Commissioner of Education, *Biennial Report on Education in the United States* (Washington, DC: Government Printing Office, 1903), pp. 463–519.
28. Richard C. Barrett, "Reciprocity in Licensing Teachers," *Proceedings and*

Addresses (Washington, DC: National Education Association, 1902), pp. 299–305.

29. Cook, *State Laws* (1927), p. 3.
30. Cook, *State Laws* (1927), Table 4, Part 2, pp. 126–260; and Fuller, *Old Country School*, p. 138.
31. J. Cayce Morrison, "Certification for Improving Professional Leadership," in *American School Board Journal* 76 (1928), p. 49.
32. William S. Learned et al., *The Professional Preparation of Teachers for American Schools* (New York: Carnegie Foundation for the Advancement of Teaching, 1920).
33. "Sympathy and the Certification of Teachers," in *School and Society* 19 (June 28, 1924), p. 761; and Benjamin J. Burris, "The Problem of Certification in Relation to Teacher Training," in *Proceedings and Addresses* (Washington, DC: National Education Association, 1926), pp. 932–939.
34. Cook, *State Laws* (1927), pp. 103–104 and 48–49.
35. Calvin O. Davis, "The Training of Teachers in North Central Association Accredited High Schools," in *School and Society* 19 (April 5, 1924), p. 390.
36. Davis, "Training of Teachers," p. 390; and Barrett, "Reciprocity."
37. Michael Sedlak and Steven Schlossman, *Who Will Teach? Historical Perspectives on the Changing Appeal of Teaching as a Profession* (Santa Monica, CA: Rand Corporation, 1986). Reprinted in Ernst Z. Rothkopf (ed.), *Review of Research in Education* 14 (Washington, DC: American Educational Research Association, 1987), pp. 93–131.
38. William R. Hood (comp.), *Digest of State Laws Relating to Public Education*, in U.S. Bureau of Education *Bulletin* No. 47, 1915 (Washington, DC: Government Printing Office, 1916), pp. 436–444.
39. "Normal Schools and the Teacher Shortage," in *American School Board Journal* 60 (May 1920), pp. 58–59; Edward S. Evenden, "Fundamental Principles for Grading Teachers' Salaries," in *Teachers College Record* 22 (May 1921), p. 197; Sara Fahey, "Some Causes of the Present Decline of Teaching as a Profession," in *Proceedings and Addresses* (Washington, DC: National Education Association, 1919), pp. 383–387; Sara Fahey, "The Teacher's Salary as a Factor in Establishing Caste," in *Proceedings and Addresses* (Washington, DC: National Education Association, 1920), pp. 351–355; William C. Bagley, "Training of Teachers," in *Proceedings and Addresses* (Washington, DC: National Education Association, 1919), pp. 499–504; D. B. Waldo, "Adequate Compensation for Teaching Service in Public Schools," in *Proceedings and Addresses* (Washington, DC: National Education Association, 1919), pp. 494–499; F. W. Wright, "The Elementary Curriculum as Presented in Normal Schools," in *Proceedings and Addresses* (Washington, DC: National Education Association, 1922), pp. 1081; J. C. Brown, "State Normal Schools and the War," in *School and Society* 7 (June 15, 1918), pp. 694–699; and "The Scarcity of Teachers in New Jersey," in *School and Society* 10 (December 13, 1919), p. 706.
40. Timothy Weaver, *America's Teacher Quality Problem: Alternatives for Reform* (New York: Praeger, 1983); Timothy Weaver, "Solving the Problem of Teacher Quality, Part I," in *Phi Delta Kappan* 66 (October 1984), pp. 108–115; Timothy Weaver, "Solving the Problem of Teacher Quality, Part II," in *Phi Delta Kappan* 66 (November 1984), pp. 185–188; Benjamin W. Frazier, "Depression Tendencies vs. Long-Time Trends Affecting Teachers," in *American School Board Journal* 91 (September 1935), pp. 19–20; Sedlak and Schlossman, *Who Will Teach?*; W. Randolph Burgess, "Four Censuses of Teachers' Salaries," in *American School Board Journal* 61 (September 1920), pp. 27–28; "Teachers' Salaries and the Purchasing Power of the Dollar," in *School and Society* 13 (January 8, 1921), pp. 48–50; "The Exodus of Teachers," in *School and Society* 13 (May 14, 1921), pp. 581–582; and "Teachers' Salaries," in *School and*

Society 14 (August 27, 1921), pp. 97–99.

41. Isabel A. Ennis, "Causes of the Present Shortage of Teachers," in *Proceedings and Addresses* (Washington, DC: National Education Association, 1918), p. 388; "The Shortage of Teachers," in *School and Society* 8 (July 13, 1918), p. 53; and Leo Schussman, "The Teacher's Wage," in *American School Board Journal* 47 (November 1923), pp. 64, 66, and 68.
42. Waldo, "Adequate Compensation," p. 496.
43. "The Salaries of Teachers and the Cost of Living," in *School and Society* 7 (May 25, 1918), p. 624.
44. Ennis, "Present Shortage of Teachers"; Brown, "State Normal Schools"; and Bagley, "Training of Teachers."
45. Ennis, "Present Shortage of Teachers," p. 387; Brown, "State Normal Schools"; "Normal Schools and the Teacher Shortage," pp. 58–59.
46. R. H. Eliassen and Earl W. Anderson, "Teacher Supply and Demand," in *Review of Educational Research* 4 (June 1934), pp. 257–260; R. H. Eliassen and Earl W. Anderson, "Investigations of the Teacher Supply and Demand Reported in 1934," in *Educational Research Bulletin* 14 (1935), pp. 61–66; R. H. Eliassen and Earl W. Anderson, "Investigation of Teacher Supply and Demand Reported Since November, 1931," in *Educational Research Bulletin* 12 (1933), pp. 66–72; R. H. Eliassen and Earl W. Anderson, "Teacher Supply and Demand," in *Review of Educational Research* 7 (June 1937), pp. 239–241; John R. McCrory, "Elementary School Teacher Supply and Demand for 1924–25," in *School and Society* 20 (August 16, 1924), pp. 222–224; Caroline Bengston, "Teacher Supply," in *School and Society* 31 (May 30, 1930), p. 601; and "The Supply of Teachers and the Demand," in *Educational Research Bulletin* 9 (November 5, 1930), pp. 437–473.
47. Sedlak and Schlossman, *Who Will Teach?*
48. Sedlak and Schlossman, *Who Will Teach?*
49. Stinnett, "Teacher Education, Certification, and Accreditation," p. 393; Anthony C. LaBue, "Teacher Certification in the United States: A Brief History," in *Journal of Teacher Education* 11 (March 1960), pp. 147–172; Ralph W. McDonald, "The Professional-Standards Movement in Teaching—Its Origin, Purpose, and Future," in *Journal of Teacher Education* 2 (September 1951), pp. 163–171.
50. Katherine M. Cook, "Certification by Examination—the Open Door to the Teaching Profession," in *American School Board Journal* 61 (July 1920), p. 30.
51. Cook, "Certification by Examination," p. 30.
52. C. L. Goodrich, "The Annual Convention of the North Central Association," in *Michigan Educational Journal* 5 (May 1928), p. 548; Linda Forward and Briget Martin, "Teacher Preparation, Certification, and the Role of Accreditation in Michigan," unpublished seminar paper, Michigan State University, March 17, 1987; Davis, "The Training of Teachers"; and Stinnett, "Teacher Education, Certification, and Accreditation," p. 395.
53. Benjamin W. Frazier, *Development of State Programs for the Certification of Teachers,* in U.S. Office of Education, *Bulletin* No. 12, 1938 (Washington, DC: Government Printing Office, 1938), pp. 74–75.
54. Stinnett, "Teacher Education, Certification, and Accreditation," p. 398; and "Education of Teachers in Different States," in *School and Society* 15 (March 18, 1922), p. 304.
55. Stinnett, "Teacher Education, Certification, and Accreditation," p. 398.
56. William Bagley, "State Progress in Reducing the Proportion of Untrained Teachers," in *School and Society* 22 (July 25, 1925), pp. 113–114; Morrison, "Certification for Improving Professional Leadership," p. 49; Joseph Rosier, "Report of Committee on Standards, Requirements, and Credits of Teachers in Service," in *Proceedings and Addresses* (Washington, DC: National Educational Association, 1925),

pp. 237–241; and John J. Dynes, "How Certification Is Practiced in the Various States," in *Nation's Schools* 7 (April 1931), pp. 67–71.

57. Cook, *State Laws* (1927), pp. 1–2 and 10.
58. Ibid., p. 255.
59. Rosier, "Report of Committee on Standards"; and E. S. Evenden, *National Survey of the Education of Teachers,* Vol. 6, in U.S. Office of Education, *Bulletin* No. 10, 1933 (Washington, DC: Government Printing Office, 1933).
60. Stinnett, "Teacher Education, Certification, and Accreditation," p. 394ff.
61. Sedlak and Schlossman, *Who Will Teach?*
62. E. S. Evenden, "The Supply and Demand for Senior High School Teachers," in *School Life* 17 (January 1932), pp. 92–93; E. S. Evenden, "The Supply and Demand for Elementary Teachers," in *School Life* 17 (February 1932), pp. 112–114; E. S. Evenden, "The Demand and Supply of Junior High School Teachers," in *School Life* 17 (March 1932), pp. 132–133; Earl Anderson, "Teaching Opportunities in 1931," in *Educational Research Bulletin* 11 (1932), pp. 91–93; W. S. Deffenbaugh and William Zeigel, Jr., *Selection and Appointment of Teachers,* in U.S. Office of Education, *Bulletin* No. 17, 1932 (Washington, DC: Government Printing Office, 1933); "The Supply of Teachers and the Demand"; Michigan Education Association, *Certification and Training of Teachers in Michigan* (East Lansing: Michigan Education Association, 1937); National Education Association, *Teacher Supply and Demand,* Research Bulletin 9 (November 1931); Frazier, "Depression Tendencies"; and Theodore A. Siedle, "Trends in Teacher Preparation and Certification," in *Educational Administration and Supervision* 20 (March 1934), pp. 193–208.
63. Frazier, *Development of State Programs,* p. 2; and Frazier, "State Certification Requirements as a Basis for Promoting Professional Standards," in American Association of Teachers Colleges, *Fifteenth Yearbook* (1936), pp. 32–38.
64. Frazier, *Development of State Programs,* pp. 43ff.
65. Ibid.
66. Ibid., p. 45; and Carnegie Foundation for the Advancement of Teaching, *State Higher Education in California: Recommendations of the Committee of Seven* (Sacramento: California State Printing Office, 1932), pp. 55–56.
67. Frazier, *Development of State Programs,* p. 45.
68. Ibid., pp. 45–46.
69. Ann Jarvella Wilson, "Knowledge for Teachers: The Origin of the National Teacher Examination Program," paper presented at the annual meeting of the American Educational Research Association, 1985, pp. 2–3. My interpretation of the evolution of the National Teacher Examination is based heavily on Dr. Wilson's careful and valuable scholarship, and the following section is indebted to her several important studies of the subject.
70. Wilson, "Knowledge for Teachers," pp. 4–5.
71. Ibid., pp. 5–10.
72. Ibid., p. 8.
73. William Learned and Ben Wood, *The Student and His Knowledge: A Report to the Carnegie Foundation on the Results of High School and College Examinations of 1928, 1930, and 1932,* Bulletin No. 29 (New York: Carnegie Foundation for the Advancement of Teaching, 1938); Sedlak and Schlossman, *Who Will Teach?"*; and Donald Warren, "Learning from Experience: History and Teacher Education," in *Educational Researcher* 14 (December 1985), pp. 5–12.
74. Learned and Wood, *Student and His Knowledge,* pp. 351–353.
75. Lewis, Terman, "An Important Contribution," in *Journal of Higher Education* 10 (February 1939), p. 112.
76. Max McConn, "The Co-operative Test Service," in *Journal of Higher Education* 2 (May 1931), pp. 225–232.
77. Wilson, "Knowledge for Teachers," p. 11.

78. David Ryans, "The Professional Examination of Teaching Candidates: A Report of the First Annual Administration of the National Teacher Examinations," in *School and Society* 52 (October 5, 1940), p. 274; Wilson, "Knowledge for Teachers," p. 12.
79. Wilson, "Knowledge for Teachers," p. 12.
80. Ibid., p. 13; and Ryans, "Professional Examination of Teacher Candidates," pp. 273–284.
81. Ben Wood, "Teacher Selection: Tested Intelligence and Achievement of Teachers-in-Training," *Educational Record* 17 (July 1936), p. 381; and Ben Wood and F. S. Beers, "Knowledge Versus Thinking," in *Teachers College Record* 37 (March 1936), p. 498.
82. Albert Lindsay Rowland, "The Proposed Teacher Examination Service," in *Harvard Educational Review* 10 (May 1940), pp. 277–288.
83. Ibid.
84. Ibid.
85. Wilson, "Knowledge for Teachers," p. 15.
86. Ibid.
87. Ibid., pp. 17–18.
88. For best descriptions of examination content, see Ryans, "Professional Examination of Teacher Candidates," p. 275ff; and Wilson, "Knowledge for Teachers," pp. 18–23. See Wood and Beers, "Knowledge Versus Thinking," for a defense of the importance of factual knowledge.
89. Wilson, "Knowledge for Teachers"; and Ann Jarvella Wilson, "Historical Issues of Validity and Validation: The National Teacher Examinations," paper presented at the annual meeting of the American Educational Research Association, 1986, p. 6.
90. Ryans, "Professional Examination of Teacher Candidates," p. 276.
91. John C. Flannagan, "An Analysis of the Results from the First Annual Edition of the National Teacher Examinations," in *Journal of Experimental Education* 9 (March 1941), p. 239.
92. Wilson, "Historical Issues of Validity," pp. 7–9; and Howard H. Long, "Some Factors Influencing Objectivity in Teacher Selection," in *School and Society* 65 (March 8, 1947), pp. 179–182.
93. Ann Jarvella Wilson, "Historical Issues of Equity and Excellence: South Carolina's Adoption of the National Teacher Examinations," in *Urban Educator* 8 (Fall 1986), p. 81.
94. Wilson, "Historical Issues of Validity."
95. Ibid., pp. 10–11.
96. Weaver, *America's Teacher Quality Problem,* p. 17; and Benjamin Frazier, "Teacher Certification in Wartime," in U.S. Office of Education, Circular No. 23, 1942 (Washington, DC: Government Printing Office, 1942); and LaBue, "Teacher Certification in the United States," p. 162ff.
97. Weaver, *America's Teacher Quality Problem,* p. 18.
98. Ibid.
99. Ibid.; Stinnett, "Teacher Education, Certification, and Accreditation," p. 393; and LaBue, "Teacher Certification in the United States."
100. Stinnett, "Teacher Education, Certification, and Accreditation," pp. 418–420; and Earl Armstrong, "Tabular Summary of Teacher Certification Requirements in the United States," in U.S. Office of Education, Circular No. 233, July 1951 (Washington, DC: Government Printing Office, 1951).
101. Eugene E. Slaughter, "The Use of Examination for State Certification of Teachers," in *Journal of Teacher Education* 11 (1960), pp. 231–238.
102. Darling-Hammond and Berry, *Evolution of Teacher Policy;* Sherry A. Rubinstein, Matthew M. McDonough, and Richard G. Allen, "The Changing Nature of Teacher Certification Programs," in William Gorth and Michael Chernoff (eds.), *Testing for Teacher Certification* (Hillsdale, NJ: Lawrence Erlbaum Assoc., 1985), pp. 17–33; and Mitchell, Ortiz, and Mitchell, *Work Orientation and Job Performance.*
103. The Holmes Group, *Tomorrow's*

Teachers; Carnegie Forum, *A Nation Prepared;* Darling-Hammond and Berry, *Evolution of Teacher Policy;* Judith Lanier and Michael Sedlak, ''Teacher Efficacy and Quality Schooling,'' in Thomas J. Sergiovanni and John H. Moore (eds.), *Schooling for Tomorrow: Directing Reforms to Issues That Count* (Boston: Allyn & Bacon, 1989); and Mitchell, Ortiz, and Mitchell, *Work Orientation and Job Performance.*

104. Sedlak and Schlossman, *Who Will Teach?;* Lisa Hudson, ''The Size and Quality of Teacher Supply: When Bigger Is Better,'' paper presented at the annual meeting of the American Educational Research Association, 1987; and C. F. Manski, ''Academic Ability, Earnings, and the Decision to Become a Teacher: Evidence from the National Longitudinal Study of the High School Class of 1972,'' in D. A. Wise (ed.), *Public Sector Payrolls* (Chicago: University of Chicago Press, 1987), pp. 291–316.

105. Sedlak and Schlossman, *Who Will Teach?*

SECTION

FOUR

Issues and Questions

There is a ritual quality to educational reform in the United States. As if on schedule, sentiment for change coalesces every 20 years or so, typically around perceived deficiencies among students or schools. Following the familiar pattern, sooner or later attention focuses on strategies to improve the teaching force. The repetitiousness ought to make the history of teachers easier to reconstruct. But substantive advances and methodological innovations have disturbed what had become a relatively uninteresting field of study. After a period of intense activity earlier in the twentieth century, the history of teachers has again reached a formative stage. Historians can see more clearly work that needs doing. Like the research recently completed, the agenda bears on the interests of other scholars, teachers, and policy makers.

The chapters in Section Four explore these pending issues and questions. First, Geraldine Clifford examines the history of teachers through the lens of gender, looking specifically at policies, practices, and public meanings that can be traced to the transformation of teaching as "women's work." Next, Linda Perkins gleans historiographical and policy questions from the history of black teachers, emphasizing developments in the South. Then, treating the larger and more fundamental problem of persistence in school reform, Larry Cuban connects the pattern of repetitiousness to simple, hasty approaches in policy analysis and policy making.

The final two chapters turn specifically to historiographical problems that also are relevant to a broader audience. David Cohen proposes conceptual work and documentary research on the history of instruction, noting implications not only for the history of teachers but also for education policy and practice. Finally, the "we" in David Tyack's chapter title encompasses historians as well as other scholars, teachers, and policy makers. A good many people, he argues, need to know about the history of teachers—and stand to benefit from its findings.

FOUR

Issues and Questions

11

Man/Woman/Teacher

Gender, Family, and Career in American Educational History

Geraldine Jonçich Clifford

Oliver Johnson was about seven years old when he started going to school in frontier central Indiana in 1828. He recalled that "There was no such thing then as a woman teacher. It wasn't a woman's job, any more than milkin' a cow was a man's job."[1] Surprising as that may now seem, this situation was as it had always been with teachers—and, surely, as it was *meant* to be. Had not Saul of Tarsus,the Saint Paul of early Christianity, expressed only what everyone already knew to be wisdom when he proclaimed, "Let not a woman to teach, nor to usurp authority over the man, but to be in silence"? The Mishnah, the oral law of the Jews, admonished, "Nor may a woman be a teacher of children." As it was among the ancient Hebrews, Greeks, and Romans, so it was in old China: By tradition, teaching was "man's work."[2]

When Daniel Anthony sent his daughters to the district school near Battenville, New York around 1830, the schoolmaster refused to teach Susan long division; it was not, he thought, a skill needed by women. Anthony withdrew his children, opening a family school under the tutelage of young Mary Perkins. She would take more interest in the education of her own sex. And as Guelma, Susan, and Hannah Anthony reached age 15, each joined the growing movement of women into teaching.[3] Susan also became one of many women teachers to channel experiences of sex discrimination into a women's movement.

By 1860, women outnumbered men among teachers in the United States, and their preponderance has never been reversed. Teaching was well on its way to being "classic female work." A study of teachers in American novels published between 1900 and 1950 found women more than twice as numerous.[4] Private and parochial schools, which have educated around 10 percent of school children over the past century, had even higher female proportions than did public schools. The woman's path to the teacher's platform was so well worn that some began to urge women to set their aspirations higher:

> For many years the drift of advice has been on the side of "anything but teaching." The brilliant girls in colleges and high schools have been exhorted not to "waste themselves in teaching," and college committees have been organized and books published to enlighten the younger generation concerning the openings in business and in other less monotonous professions.[5]

This 1920 news story anticipates many present-day feminists who lament the decisions of women to become teachers, social workers, nurses, or librarians. They see these jobs as occupations without the scope, prestige, or potential to liberate and empower women. Feminists *and* conservatives alike have perceived "women's professions" as existing primarily to provide "an interlude between school and marriage," as affirmations of a rigid sexual division of labor.[6] The teaching profession has been called a "divided profession," its several divisions a root cause of its low relative status and limited power. "It is arguable that the greatest divide of all is sex, so much so that women and men have typically different career paths within the occupation," writes British sociologist Sandra Acker.[7]

Although the general outline of what is loosely called the "feminization" of teaching is known to most scholars, its meaning and intricacies, and its place in a larger analysis of the sociology of teaching, are only now beginning to be studied with fresh eyes. This chapter will build on that still rudimentary work, examining the history of teaching in the United States through the lens of gender. The path to understanding traversed here is littered with obstacles, since to assess the impact of gender on teachers and teaching is to confront a thicket of stereotypes and to do battle with established, arid, and ahistorical theories of professions. Such theories are part of a universal pattern of thought whereby the activities of men and women are evaluated asymmetrically, women's activities being ignored, subsumed, or measured by the standards of male experience.[8] Nonetheless, the influence of gender is now a lively topic for revisionism. It is described by Michael Apple as "the absent presence," by Nancy Hoffman as "that roar on the other side of silence." Gender is, writes David Tyack, an analytical variable as important to educational history and sociology as are social class, race, or ethnicity.[9]

In this chapter, domesticity and familism emerge as the principal dual theme in this analysis of gender and schoolteaching. A domestic ideology legitimated the initial hiring of women teachers, and family and career have continued to be linked, in both obvious and unexpected ways. After first reviewing and reexamining this and other causes of the well-known fact of women replacing men as the majority of teachers in the United States, we will consider teaching's images: Demeaning, gender-laden stereotypes plagued teachers even before the old-maid schoolma'am became a popular target. Finally, we will look beyond sociological concepts of career and professionalism to see teaching as stages in the lives of men as well as women.

Charting the Change: General Trends and Varying Practices

The "feminization" of education may be, as John Rury thinks, "the most unappreciated transformation of American schools in the nineteenth century."[10] From 1870 on, national and state statistics on the gender composition of the teaching profession are fairly complete. Nationally, that year, women constituted less than two-thirds of all teachers; in 1900 nearly three-quarters; and by 1920 an all-time high: 86 percent. From the mid-1920s, however, men began making small inroads into this by-now "woman's profession" largely because postwar teacher shortages drove up comparative salaries and increased the need for school administrators. Male preferment policies during the Depression further increased men's share of teaching jobs to nearly 25 percent by 1940. While that figure was halved in the next decade, repeated efforts were made to recruit men back into teaching following World War II.[11]

Several of the older teachers interviewed by Alice Rinehart commented on the contrast between their youth—when all the elementary schools' teachers and most of their principals were women—and the situation of the 1950s and 1960s: The husband of one teacher was the first male elementary teacher in her Pennsylvania town in her lifetime.[12] Despite these efforts, by the 1980s men had returned only to their 1870 proportion. Being one-third of all teachers nationally, their majority in the high schools (53.6 percent in 1973) shrank again to near parity with women.[13]

Historically, Massachusetts was the leader in employing women for the public schools. By 1850, men had dropped to under one-in-three teachers. While in any given year most nineteenth-century women were not employed outside the home, between the 1830s and 1880 enough such women taught at some time (or times) in their lives so that one-time teachers were a quarter of all native-born Massachusetts women.[14]

Elsewhere, teaching was not yet so closely identified with women's lives. In 1870, men were still half or more of all teachers in 20 of the reporting 45 states and territories. The male share among teachers ranged from 13 percent in Massachusetts to 92 percent in the New Mexico Territory—a difference of 79 points. Variations between nearby communities could be nearly as great: Contrast Washington, DC's 8 percent male with Virginia's 65 percent, or San Francisco's 2 percent male with California's 34 percent.[15] Cities led the nation in making the transition to a heavily female teaching force. In 1888, when men averaged one-third of the nation's teaching position nationally, they still amounted to under 10 percent of city teachers. Consequently, the more rural states and regions had consistently higher proportions of male instructors. The demographic trend was, however, toward urbanization, and this and other factors steadily reduced the interstate disparity. In 1934, for example, the range of male percentages was a mere 19 points—from 11 percent in Vermont to 30 percent in West Virginia.

One of the most serious attempts to study regional and state variation was published in 1937 by the University of Kentucky's Bureau of School Services. Its efforts to relate the proportion of men teachers in the various states to such indices as their educational rankings, population density, and taxpaying ability per enrolled student found statistically insignificant correlations or counterintuitive relationships. For example, there was a slight negative relationship between a state's taxable wealth per schoolchild and its percentage of male teachers. Given that women teachers were routinely paid less for the same work and should, therefore, have been preferred, the authors concluded that the explanation for the discrepancy probably lay in a general poverty that sent men into teaching as a result of a lack of alternative employments.[16]

Other factors contributing to diversity of practice in employing male teachers were race and ethnicity. In most states the proportion of men teachers in "colored" schools was somewhat higher, an interracial difference in the 1930s of two or three percentage points for the elementary schools, and still higher for high schools. Cities with greater-than-average proportions of male teachers in 1885 also were cities with sizeable German immigrant populations: Cincinnati, St. Louis, and Milwaukee. The relatively greater prestige of teaching in Germany, and its tradition of male teachers (even in primary schools), probably was a factor in teacher recruitment and hiring.

Knowing more about the ethnic composition of school boards would help to test this hypothesis. For example, an early expression of alarm at growing numbers of female teachers and principals came, in 1884, from Adolf Kraus, president of Chicago's board of education—another city with many German–Americans.[17] A writer in *Harper's* magazine informed Americans in 1878 that, in the view of the German government and the German public, women were unfit to be teachers: "They are accused of being too much under the influence of priests, of being too irritable, and having too little self-control, and it is thought that their influence tends to develop effeminacy in boys."[18]

The gender makeup of American teachers often was compared with that of other nations where, it turns out, men were also being replaced by women. In France, men's share decreased from half to one-third of elementary-school teachers between 1900 and 1936. Men were still 85 percent of teachers in German elementary schools in 1900, but the trend was in the same direction. From data gathered mostly in the 1930s, the median figure for 26 nations was 41.5 percent male. Among secondary-school teachers, however, men enjoyed numerical dominance worldwide; their median was 71.8 percent. Ireland (48 percent) and the United States (40 percent) were the only nations reported where men were less than half of secondary-school teachers.[19]

Men's twentieth-century share of American public high-school teaching positions has to date been far closer to parity: from a low of 46 percent in 1905 to a high of 54 percent in 1972. The imposing presence of women in American high-school faculties is, however, the more arresting fact internationally, since they were teaching primarily in coeducational schools while women secondary teachers abroad were typically concentrated in all-girls schools. American women also became prominant in secondary education earlier than elsewhere: By 1880, women were already 60 percent of high-school teachers—and a similar proportion of their students.

In the process of schooling girls, at that time, American public and parochial schools alike were preparing teachers. In speaking against curricular uniformity in the high school, for example, Boston's school superintendent, Edwin Seaver, pointed out in the 1888 *Annual Report of the Boston School Committee* that "nine-tenths of [male students] are sure to enter mercantile pursuits" while half of the girls "will enter the normal schools and become teachers."[20] By the late nineteenth century, many city high schools offered a "normal course," reserving teaching positions in the elementary schools for graduates. Under parental pressures, urban Catholic schools added high-school grades, to enable daughters to compete for teaching positions. And in 1890, a parishioner remarked that "thousands of Catholic girls . . . had graduated from being pupils of public schools into becoming teachers, and reflect credit alike on the race that produced them, the church to which they belong, and the country which afforded them and their Irish–Catholic parents the splendid opportunities which culminated in their education.''[21]

By the mid-nineteenth century, normal-school enrollments and participation in teachers' institutes also reflected a growing gender imbalance. At the war-depleted University of Wisconsin in 1865, there were 41 males and *no* females enrolled in traditional college courses; in the ''normal course'' there were *no* men and 66 women.[22] Bridgewater (Massachusetts) Normal School, reported to have the state's highest male enrollments, had male minorities ranging from 42 percent in the 1840s to 22 percent in the 1880s.[23]

The following quote concerning the ''lay convents'' of France fits the general lives of American ''normalites'' in the nineteenth and early twentieth centuries. Their schools were cloistered female enclaves, enlivened by a few males studying to perfect their teaching or to climb the ladder to better-rewarded positions in education.

> Descriptions of normal schools as ''lay convents'' abound in teachers' memoirs and contemporary reports. The label was appropriate not only because *normaliennes* had their mail censored, could not bring unapproved books into the school, and were kept apart from *normaliens* but also because normal school professors taught students that they were preparing for a special vocation, not just a job.[24]

While ''hopelessly in the minority, the men naturally did not feel unhappy'' at the gender imbalance, according to a member of the class of 1890 at the Milwaukee State Normal School.[25]

As normal schools became state teachers colleges, some cities established just such colleges *per se,* and universities opened departments of pedagogy, their student bodies continued to demonstrate that teaching had become ''women's work.'' Horace Mann became president of the new, coeducational Antioch College in 1853, he wrote, so that women might be made ''capable of filling the higher walks of instruction.''[26] While only about 5 percent of college graduates nationally had entered teaching in 1800, the profession attracted one-quarter of all graduates by 1900, more than any other field. The figure was even higher among collegiate women.[27] As dean of women at the University of California, Lucy Sprague discovered that 80 percent of women entering Berkeley in 1905 were there to earn a teacher's certificate. Such educators of women as President M. Carey Thomas of Bryn Mawr College clearly recognized that women were swelling college enrollments in joining the ranks of those studying to become teachers.

Historians on the ''Feminization'' of Schoolkeeping

The historian who looks will find that teacher gender has been a subject of discussion for most of the past two centuries. Even before Andrew Jackson's presidency, New England school boards debated whether they should hire women, and continued to argue the merits of male and female teachers whenever there was a choice to be made between them. From 1885 to World War I, national magazines and professional journals repeatedly published commentaries on the ''woman peril'' in teaching, as it appeared that women would drive the last man from the field. Women's predominance in teaching was a ''running sore'' in the circles of male school administrators and university professors of education, anxious that their own empires not be invaded by the female products of teachers colleges.[28] During the Depression and following World War II, strong efforts were made to recruit men back into teaching, in part to protect or restore the patriarchal position of men in the American family, as it was argued that exposure to strong male figures was needed in the socialization of adolescents, especially boys. The 1980s witnessed another concern, this time about the loss of able women to teaching as the ''male professions'' of law, medicine, and business promised women more rewards than did the ''social housekeeping'' jobs of teaching, nursing, and social work.

The small existing historiography has concentrated upon external events, giving little attention to the feelings or reactions of men and women teachers to women's encroachment on a historically male preserve, or to the eventual resistance this aroused. In 1908, *Educational Review* published an impressionistic article purporting to tap the psychological state that led most men to avoid teaching careers, and the rest to apologize for taking up teaching.[29] More systematic and sophisticated analyses must be applied in a widened investigation of the gender politics of teaching. Jacqueline Jones has recovered the reactions of women teachers to the male leadership of the missionary associations that sent them South to teach the freedmen following the Civil War, and Polly Kaufman has referred to the letters of Eastern women teaching in the West around 1850.[30] Persis Hunt examined the behavior of France's teachers around 1900, when sharp divisions occurred in teachers' organizations along gender lines. Laurence Block's political study of the Baltimore City Teachers Association documents a contest for organizational leadership in the early twentieth century that suggests a still-broader schism between the career- and family-linked interests of men and women teachers.[31] Robert Treacy looked at a long struggle in California around the University Elementary School (UES) at UCLA.[32] There, disaffected women administrators—losing status, power, and self-esteem as school administration became a male preserve—rallied around Corinne Seeds, her laboratory school, and the single women of the faculty. Their campaign, later led by the organized mothers of UES students, saved Seeds, her school, and her brand of progressive education, which remained influential in California's public schools even up through Sputnik.

Scholars' work to date offers a number of plausible, interacting factors to explain the transition of teaching from men to women in the United States during the nineteenth century, and the persistence of this pattern to the present. They relate to both demand and supply. These factors are presented below, without particular confidence that their categorizing and ordering will hold as analysis proceeds along new lines of research and theorizing—especially as gender is made a more explicit issue and we dig further into so-called ''grass roots history.''[33]

THE DRIVE FOR UNIVERSAL SCHOOLING

Sarah Josepha Hale, editor of *Godey's Ladies Book,* an influential magazine among the middle class, was one of the best-known women of the nineteenth century. In "Female Teachers for Common Schools" (1853), Hale proposed that Congress award land grants to support teacher-training institutions for women. Among the arguments she borrowed was Catharine Beecher's statements about the large numbers of children in the states and territories of the United States, some two million, "destitute, or nearly so, of proper means of education."[34] Given their other opportunities, sufficient men could not be induced to become teachers to meet this need, much less to staff existing classrooms; should women not be appointed, the dream of common schools "must be given up." Further, to make education universal, it must be "moderate in expense." Hale noted that women were able to teach at lower wages than men because they were not expected to support a family, to amass a fortune, or to pay taxes on their earnings.[35]

Proponents pointed out that the employment of more women would not only open classrooms where none existed, but would make possible longer school terms for the same investment. Even earlier in the century, when presented with the reality of a short summer term taught by a woman, and a two- or three-month winter term presided over by a man, school boards had yielded to those who argued "Let it be taught by a female, throughout the year . . . to supersede the necessity of closing the school at all, except for a vacation of three or four weeks."[36] Thus common schools would increase their effectiveness in creating and maintaining a unified population of moral, responsible, productive citizen–workers. As non-public schools became associated with Catholic immigrants in the second third of the nineteenth century, it seemed even more important to the Protestant establishment that common schools be enabled to rescue children from that "benighted" culture.[37]

Schoolmen also believed that improved public schools would attract a greater portion of the "most worthy and influential inhabitants"—many of whom still patronized private schools. Securing the patronage and the scrutiny of the middle class was considered necessary to the health and legitimacy of public education. And, as Schools Superintendent John W. Taylor assured San Franciscans in his 1880 *Annual Report:* "In replenishing the middle classes with young people of intelligence, the High Schools contribute largely to the prosperity of the whole country. It has been truly said that the prosperity of a republic is in the direct ratio of the replenishment of its middle classes."[38]

The proliferation of public high schools after 1890 was accelerated by the availability of women teachers.[39] High schools became part of a system of universal schooling at least a generation before this happened in the more advanced parts of Europe. Upwards of 10 percent of older adolescents were attending American high schools in 1910; Europe reached this level only after 1945. In 1930 the proportion of the age group attending general or academic high schools was five times higher in America than in Europe.[40] Thus, the lower wages of women teachers subsidized the education of the children of a would-be elite as much as they did that of the masses enrolled in the nation's elementary schools. The presence of women teachers in high schools undoubtedly also affected the enrollment of female students—the majority of high-school students to the present time; girls' presence reduced the cost to taxpayers of secondary schooling because of economies of scale.[41]

The schools' demands for teachers became insatiable, with the mass immigrations from southern and eastern Europe in the years between 1880 and 1925. Alarmed nativists called for intense efforts by schools to "Americanize" these foreigners' children.[42] This helps to explain why, in 1891, there were already 368,338 public-school classroom teachers employed nationally by local school districts. In contrast, the largest number of other public employees worked for the United States Post Office Department; they numbered 95,000, and two-thirds of this total were political appointees. The education of children had become a growth industry! Whether, under the demands for universal schooling, public school teaching had become a *new* profession, and hence not a matter of women competing with men for their work, is debatable. Clearly, however, teaching had become "woman's job" in fact as well as in rhetoric.

Sexual Asymmetry and Sex Role Learning

Anthropologist Michelle Rosaldo argues that *everywhere* sex stereotyping places emphasis upon woman's maternal roles. In so doing it creates "spheres": the "domestic" (female) and the "public" (male), promoting an implicit dichotomy between the "natural" (female, sexual, biological, and sometimes "disorderly") and the "cultural" (male, acquired, mastered, rational). In the final analysis, women's efforts to gain any prestige and wield authority are shaped by domestic values and imagery in order to be considered legitimate.[43] "Public" activities retain greater prestige, authority, and economic power, however.

The theory of the sexual division of labor holds that women's laboring will not only be somehow associated with domesticity but that when men and women work in the same occupation they will occupy different spheres, do different sorts of things, or have their work differentially valued. Thus, in education, men will, on average, teach more older than younger students, teach more boys than girls, and teach the "harder" subjects. Writing in the influential *Education Review* in 1906, a male educator opined that "women are nimble-witted in tact and moral virtues but their store of information is less deep and less thorough."[44] Historian Nancy Hoffman writes, "The structure of the school reinforced the notion that women were capable of teaching the ABCs and the virtues of cleanliness, obedience, and respect, while men taught about ideas, and organized the profession."[45] In Sandra Acker's words, men in schools get the administrative and curricular responsibilities women the "pastoral" ones and "the probabilities that the sexes will experience differential career lines and typical locations in school are striking enough to speak confidently of a sexual division of labour in teaching."[46]

The definition of gender roles changes, however. In 1929 economist Chase Going Woodhouse commented about a major factor promoting such change:

> For the first time in history, then, the average man is supporting his family in the economic sense. This has been true in the past only of a few in the more privileged class. For the mass of the people the wife with her garden, her poultry and her household production more than contributed her share to the economic support of the family, as she is still doing in the rural sections.[47]

Ironically, economic and organizational developments, already obvious in industrializing and urbans centers in the nineteenth century, may have made sexual stereotyping more rigid, emphasizing maternalism in the cultural definition of womanhood. The gradual movement of much of the productive economy, out of households and into shops and factories, deprived nineteenth-century women and girls of their former place in or near the economic mainstream. As women ceased to be involved in home industries (first in the manufacture of goods for sale or trade, and then in the production of consumer goods for the family itself), they were encouraged to focus their energies and identities upon their roles as the wives, mothers, and daughters of the putative or potential male wage-earner. Conversely, men were less able to monitor their children's upbringing as closely as they were formerly enjoined to do.

In the colonial era in British North America, motherhood did not either dominate women's roles or make her the lodestone of family life. Between the Puritan and the early Victorian family in America, however, there was a prescriptive transfer, to mothers, of many responsibilities once assigned to either fathers or both parents jointly. Historian Ruth Bloch notes that Puritan and Quaker clergy and physicians credited fathers with the active and even primary role in childhood education, "once the children became capable of rational thought and moral discrimination." This role for fathers gradually disappeared from the advice literature. As early as 1793, Rev. John Ogden noted, in his *The Female Guide,* that "business, and many cares call the father abroad, but home is the mother's province—here she reigns sole mistress the greatest part of her life."[48] According to the *Canadian Gem and Family Visitor* of 1849, their mother was the first "book" read by children.[49] Historian Lee Virginia Chambers-Schiller maintains that "The channeling of unmarried women into teaching paralleled the increasing responsibility borne by women for child rearing and socialization" at home.[50]

In those regions where many men still labored "at home," or where women retained much of their former productive activities as workers in domestic industries, one would expect to find the "education" of children still prominent in the definition of male sex roles. The American South and the rural frontier to the West were, indeed, places slower to assign local women the near-exclusive position of schoolteacher, especially for the "large scholars."[51] The lateness of the South in founding public school systems is explainable by many factors, but gender roles should not be ignored among them.

In the urban North, women were the majority of teachers decades before this happened in the South. The effects were undoubtedly the same, however: The process of "role modeling" ensured the continuation of women teachers' numbers. The woman teacher was one of the few models of the working woman with whom school girls had direct and protracted contact.

Economic necessity pushed Miriam Davis Colt into the labor force. Born around 1818, she was the twelfth of 17 children of a struggling farmer. In her autobiography she wrote:

> As I reviewed my father's circumstances, I knew that I must make my own way in life—go out and take care of myself; so the height of my aspirations were to attain to the position of school teacher, and I hoped that some day I should have a pair of scissors hanging at my side, fastened with a large scissor hook to my sink apron strings—have a green silk calash bonnet, and green ribbon to hold it over my face, and walk to and from school with a score or more of little urchins calling me school-ma'am; this would constitute my beau ideal of attainments and honor.[52]

She gained her objective at age 18 and continued teaching until her marriage at age 26—like many teachers, using some of her wages to further her own schooling at a local academy.

A one-time student in the New York City schools early in this century has written, "I have forgotten everything the schools ever taught me. But the glamour of the lady teachers, shining on the East Side world, I shall never forget."[53] The twentieth-century women teachers studied by Courtney Ann Vaughn-Roberson expressed the positive images of women teachers that animated many youngsters to enter the most prestigious occupation open to small-town and farm girls. Oklahoma's Mary Skelley had decided that the height of power was the schoolmistresses, seated on their elevated platforms at the front of the room and eating their lunchtime biscuits; she decided early to achieve their status. Jewell Peterson of Texas hoped from childhood to emulate the pretty, confident, privileged teachers who had taught her.[54] Conversely, the girls who became teachers—and the boys who did not!—may have been learning early that teaching was the wrong work for men. Noting how underworked and underpaid both she and a Mr. Peck were in their Greenville, Georgia school in 1861, Jennie Lines confined to her diary, "If I were a man I should rather do any thing than teach."[55]

Women teachers were not forced to show the cautious "reserve and dignity" toward female students expected of male teachers; this allowed their influence freer reign.[56] Around 1910, when Joseph Van Denburg was studying New York City high-school students, he included among the reasons for the greater persistence of girls in school, and their propensity to become teachers, the fact that "Most girls are very fond of their teachers and the impulse to emulate them is very strong indeed."[57] This is not to assert that boys cannot love and emulate their male teachers, but there were too many factors depleting the supply and restricting the opportunity for men to function as role models for boys. Occupational inheritance was progressively more likely among women teachers, with daughters following their mothers, sisters, or other female relatives into teaching.[58]

Demographic Change

From an economic point of view, the urban man's family was "an economic liability." Employment for school-age children grew scarce, given the loss of job for unskilled child workers with the advance of industrial technology, the extension and better enforcement of compulsory school attendance laws, and the coalition of reformers and organized labor seeking curbs on child labor. Wives might enter the labor force, but strong cultural pressures worked against this except among blacks and some immigrant groups. For daughters who had completed their schooling and were not yet ready to marry, however, there were encouragements to become employed. Teaching received a large proportion of such daughters, especially in the middle and aspiring parts of the working classes.[59] The very fact that young women were going to school longer suggests that they were looking to fill time freed by lessened responsibilities in their parents' homes.

"The single most important fact about women and the family in American history," writes historian Carl Degler, is the decline in family size. The falling birth rate in the United States is a secular trend, evident in the decennial censuses from the nation's start and interrupted only during the two decades after World War II. Records from eighteenth-century Massachusetts show a modal family size of eight live births; for cohorts born between 1800 and 1850 the rate declined to five children. It was under 2.1 in 1985. The span between first and last pregnancy of American Quaker women born before 1788 was 17.4 years; among American women born during the 1880s, childbearing lasted only 11.3 years.[60]

Daughters lost work as "mother's helpers" as their mothers experienced less pregnancy-related disability and there were fewer siblings to care for. It was less necessary to prohibit school homework for female students, as the Boston School Committee had done in the mid-nineteenth century. The virtual disappearance in the middle class of the once widespread practice of taking in boarders and lodgers also reduced girls' domestic responsibilities. In rural areas, farm machinery lessened the need to cook and launder for farm hands. Where school-age daughters had once routinely been brought home for domestic duties and child care, they were increasingly free to finish their schooling. This both strengthened their identification with that institution and increased their qualifications to teach in it.

Among females born around 1830, the cohort that made women the majority of Massachusetts' teachers, 71 percent of those aged 20 to 24 were single; among those at ages 30 to 34, 29 percent were still unmarried. The median age of first marriage was three to five years older among both men and women in 1880 than it was in 1870.[61] (Among men, the need to complete schooling or become established in nonfarming occupations delayed marriage.) Women's postponement of marriage, and the increasingly common decision to remain single, owed something to a growing countercultural distaste for domesticity and confinement, in an age when divorce was almost unheard of, birth control was a proscribed subject, and pregnancy caused women a prolonged seclusion.

Victorian notions of propriety prevented even use of the word "pregnant." In her diary, Jennie Lines wrote euphemistically of resigning her teaching position "on account of health & for some other reasons" and, later, of her impending confinement as her "hour of trial and anguish."[62] As women became better educated by women's-rights activists and novelists about the "costs" of financial dependence and the legal subjugation of married women, many acted to avoid or delay that state. The fear of childbirth, although largely confined to private discussion, was widespread: Diaries and correspondence between women, including mothers and daughters, acknowledged their anxiety about the traumas of childbirth and the specter of the kind of parturition death that before this present century agonizingly cut so many women's lives short.

Spinsterhood spread from New England, affecting other women born after 1840. Mary Livermore, a former teacher and founder of the suffrage paper *The Agitator*, lectured around the United States in the 1870s on the subject of the "superfluous woman." Given that single women numerically exceeded single men in 16 of the states on the Atlantic and Gulf coasts, a large body of the "most gifted, scholarly, and useful women" would remain unmarried, she argued; they required training that would lead them to independent and productive lives.[63] The values of economic independence and personal achievement began to be heard even among Southern women, after the Civil War. South Carolina teacher Elizabeth Grimball answered her parents' pleas to return home with "I will not be a dependent old maid at home with an allowance doled out to me when I could be made comfortable by my owr exertions."[64]

Numerical imbalances of the sexes also prompted some women teachers to mov west, where many quickly married the men who had gone before to farm, mine, o build the railroads. This vacated their positions to other women, some of whom tasting independence, decided against marriage. That schoolteaching was no reserved to women who had little chance to marry is shown by the behavior o women in Western states, where a surplus of men invited early marriage. Yet th young women who graduated from the Colorado State Normal School in its firs decade (1890–1900) behaved like their Eastern sisters; using teaching as a opportunity to deviate from the woman's "normal life course" of remaining home until marriage, and delaying or forgoing marriage in the process.[65]

Spinsterhood was an issue among women teachers themselves; their diaries ar letters make common reference to it. When Sarah Hale argued for women teaching, she was careful not to appear to be promoting celibacy: "This system wa not designed to make old maids of these ladies, but that they would be bett prepared for marriage after three or four years of teaching school."[66] Preside Raymond tried to position Vassar College between cultural taboos against th promotion of spinsterhood and its obligations to provide an education which wou outfit women with "the means of preparation for independent activity." preferred to speak of women who might not be able to marry despite th preferences for wifehood.[67] College-educated women were indeed found disp portionately among the unmarried, and many of these became teachers. Millic Shinn, the first woman to earn a doctorate in education (at the University California in 1898), reported that over 70 percent of a large sample of wom college graduates remained unmarried.[68] In the period 1890–1920, other stud reporting similar findings helped to intensify fears of "race suicide."

Class-based anxieties that the "better people" would not reproduce themsel were intensified by the ethnocentrism associated with sometimes hysterical reacti to large immigrations to the United States. In a period when 92 percent of all wom teachers were single, University of California President B. I. Wheeler told wom students in 1905, "You are not here with the ambition to be school teachers or maids, but you are here for the preparation for marriage and motherhood.''[69] Professor Julius Sachs of Teachers College, Columbia University, lamented that college girls pursued studies ''that will rear a race of teachers, not a race of women thoroughly equipped for home duties as well as for the general welfare of the community.'' In 1915 a male educator warned, ''The farmer that uses his land for golf-links and deer preserves instead of for corps has but one agricultural fate; the civilization that uses its women for stenographers, clerks and school-teachers instead of mothers has but one racial fate.''[70] ''The only clear probability of harm done by the present use of educational funds to hire women rather than men lies in the prevention of gifted and devoted women from having and rearing children of their own flesh and blood,'' wrote psychologist and eugenicist Edward L. Thorndike in a more measured analysis. ''It is likely the world loses more by the absence from motherhood of women teachers who might otherwise marry than by the absence from the teaching profession of the men who would have their places.''[71]

The broad and growing prejudice against the married woman teacher included the negative consequences shc had for the biological welfare of the white race. In 1931 *School Executives Magazine* published this candid assessment:

> My chief objection to married women teaching is the fact that it leads almost necessarily to childless homes or to the restriction of children in homes that really should produce more children. Every time you elect a married teacher, you tacitly endorse and encourage such practices which are the most reprehensible sins of the upper and middle classes.[72]

According to a 1934 study, in the midst of massive unemployment, those opposing married women teachers still worried that ''The married woman's fecundity is more or less restricted when she is engaged in regular out-of-home activities.[73]

The Opportunities of the Labor Market

In 1890 more than in 1980, there were ''men's jobs'' and ''women's jobs.'' Because so few occupations employed both men and women, it can be argued that teaching was both a ''good job'' for women in economic terms, as economists Carter and Prus show, and in other ''values.''[74] For example, although Susan B. Anthony earned one-third of what male teachers received for the same duties, she did not have to face the long hours, regimentation, and social stigma that women mill workers endured. As the mills employed more immigrants workers—men, women, and children—they lost whatever appeal they once had among Protestant families of native New England stock, even if mill operatives earned more than country teachers. The Curriers of rural New Hampshire were willing to allow their daughters to teach in the 1840s, but not to join some of their friends in the well known mills at Lowell, Massachusetts.[75]

Schoolkeeping was the most ''respectable'' of the occupations available to women. Teaching emerged as so genteel an occupation that Frances Donovan observed cynically that ''Ladies who did not teach developed a sentimental attitude towards the work, and recommended it as a fitting occupation for those indigent gentlewomen who loved babies and could play the piano.''[76] Iowa's Rosa Schreurs Jensen recalled that country girls of good family with aims of being independent had once been able to be the ''hired girl'' in some farmer's kitchen. That democratic tradition ended by the 1890s and she, like others of her sex, got a teacher's certificate instead. She hoped, at age 17, to teach the winter school of some man who was leaving for another career.[77]

Another Iowan, Louisa Conard, remembered that teaching, or clerking in a store, were the only occupations, aside from marriage, permitted to women when Conard left for Grinnel College in 1909.[78] It was not until the late nineteenth century that (apart from work in family-owned shops) retail sales positions and office jobs opened to women. Nursing, librarianship, and social work were options after 1900, but could not approach teaching in demand. Lucy Sprague was being unrealistic and snobbish, then, in criticizing the large numbers of women collegians preparing to teach. She had stated that ''A teacher's certificate is, in and of itself, a worthy aim in a university student if it does not crowd out other and better aims.''[79] There were few, if any, ''other and better aims.''

Barbara Welter contends that women's sometimes embattled and seemingly hard-won entry into any occupation may be less a victory for equal opportunity than ''a strategic retreat by the opposition.'' Teaching may represent one of those areas where woman gained ''not because of her efforts but because either society or the occupation had changed.''[80] Those advocating women teachers clearly knew that schoolkeeping could not attract sufficient men, nor keep many of those it had. In her 1819 appeal to the New York state legislature to support a female seminary to prepare teachers, Emma Willard contrasted female—''who have no higher pecuniary object to engage their attention''—with male teachers: ''Whenever able and enterprising men engage in this business, they consider it merely as a temporary employment.''[81] In 1835, Catharine Beecher argued that we cannot raise an army of teachers ''from the sex which finds it so much more honorable, easy and lucrative, to enter the many roads to wealth and honor open in this land.''[82]

When in 1912 psychologist Edward L. Thorndike surveyed the controversies about men and women in teaching, he concluded that the selection of women was done despite preferences, theories, and sentiments:

> With few exceptions, the choice of a woman rather than a man has meant, and still means, that the woman is so obviously able to do the work in question better, according to the standards of the time, that she is chosen in spite of sex prejudice. Superintendents and school boards are eager to get men to teach, but their sense of educational duty will not let them get the men who apply.[83]

Only in ''hard times'' and in stagnant locales was the supply of acceptable men likely to approach the schools' needs.[84] While downturns in the business cycle had to be waited out, American men were in the habit of abandoning their homes and moving to more promising areas. ''Western fever'' was how D. S. Doome explained leaving his Pennsylvania teacher's post after three years of firml disciplined teaching (he called teaching a branch of the War Department) in the la nineteenth century.[85] Land and gold rushes created geographical frontiers, but the modern corporation and its transportation and communications arms were other kinds of frontiers calling for men. For those with professional ambitions, there were seemingly endless opportunities in the reformed medical and legal fields, and in the expanding areas of journalism, engineering, and university teaching. The incentives offered to men were more money, greater career advancement, and, often, greater prestige—in part because of higher earnings.

Like women, black men did not profit much from the expansiveness of the economy. Many black male elementary-school teachers had a long tenure, and the mobility of black high-school teachers was primarily that of moving to better-paying school districts rather than into business or other professions (as was the case with many white males).[86] Hence, while male and white teachers outearned female and black teachers, the latter groups found teaching a more rewarding occupation than did the former. Black women were so disadvantaged in the labor market that the corps of teachers in Washington, DC included women with medical degrees.[87] They would have laughed bitterly at the words of a 1911 *Vassar College Bulletin:* that women drifted into teacher careers "for lack of knowledge of the opportunities in other fields."[88] Not until the agricultural depression of the 1920s and the general economic collapse of the 1930s did white men cash in their dreams of more profitable careers, turning back to teaching in large numbers.

The Consequences of War

This nation's wars had direct effects upon both sexes' roles in education. Each war took men into the military and into war-related industries, including agriculture, depriving the schools and colleges of male students and teachers. Women moved in to fill the vacuum. The War of Independence from England had the least visible effects of great significance for women. That long struggle permitted ordinary women to engage in many economic activities that expanded their urge to read, write, and calculate.[89] It also resulted in a new republic which convinced influential men of the need for more education and self-confidence among females so that they might better exercise their responsibilities as the "first teachers" of their sons, the enterprising "young republicans" who would protect this new experiment in representative government.[90] This ideology of the "republican mother" was, in turn, exploited by women. They used it to expand "woman's sphere" into schoolteaching and other public arenas, while the schooling they received qualified them for those roles.

Wars might be considered a mere subset of the general problem of male shortages if they did not also upset social relations, including gender expectations for oneself and the other sex. By the time of the Civil War a heightened consciousness of equality was clearly evident among American women. Since the majority of teachers in elementary schools already were women, these schools were less disrupted by war than was secondary and higher education. When male teachers returned to the home field and found women in their places, their problem was not that of dislodging the women, since a strong preference for men remained, especially in the upper grades. The issue was rather whether school boards and trustees would pay them salaries that were two or three times what women teachers had been earning. Very often they would not. Naturally, many younger men saw more promise in other careers. And the run of the well-connected older males became school administrators or college professors.

Although some schools employed women for the first time during the Civil War, the war's greatest effect on women was the pressures it placed upon the colleges. Those in the South had closed for the duration, and when they reopened most remained all-male schools (well into this century); this forced Southern women to find some semblance of higher education in female seminaries and women's colleges. In the Midwest, however, a number of institutions accepted women students rather than close, and when the war was over their female students could not be dislodged.

Once in place, coeducation spread, and by the turn of the century was the dominant pattern. Not only did their college educations outfit women technically for high-school teaching, but the experience of direct academic competition with male college students raised their sense of confidence and level of assertiveness. These were put to use in the early twentieth century when women teachers organized themselves, doing repeated battle with the male "establishment" of superintendents, college presidents, and the leadership of local and state professional organizations, around concerns specific to women teachers—for example, equal pay, the right to marry and still teach, maternity leaves, and pension equity for single women.

Although short-lived, American participation in World War I also affected teachers. Fifty thousand men left teaching and never returned to it. A number of college and normal-school women left school to take up teaching or other work.[91] A young man without a high-school education was able to get a rural Pennsylvania school to teach. (After two or three years he found a more suitable career as a rural mailman.)[92] When its Committee on the Economic and Legal Status of Women questioned members of the American Association of University Women in 1926, it found that "demand for services" was an important reason why married women took jobs; many had taught before the war and responded to wartime labor shortages, especially in the schools.[93]

The war ended with teacher shortages exacerbated by postwar growth, especially in the high schools. Between 1920 and 1930 the need for elementary-school teachers grew by 11 percent, and by 20 percent for high-school teachers. Wartime inflation reduced teachers' buying power. There were ominous declines in the numbers enrolled in teacher-training courses. Commentators were speaking of the effects of the war on teachers: "The war has quickened the social consciousness," and "New ambitions have been awakened in the breasts of many hitherto content with humble stations," wrote Prof. James Hosic of the Chicago Normal School.[9] The 1920 meeting of the Department of Superintendence of the National Education Association was filled with talk about restive teachers chafing at the undemocratic administration of schools: "They propose to take in their own hands the settlement of most professional and even some administrative problems," warned Prof. Michael O'Shea, and "to accomplish their aims, they propose to join hands with th

Federation of Labor. . . ."[95] Teaching's several crises made headlines in newspapers and general magazines by 1920. In response, salaries began to rise and administrative "snoopervision" to relax. Too, the appeal of teaching grew among men: By 1925 rising percentages of male teachers were evident.

World War II and its aftermath repeated this scenario, but there was a major addition—one that changed the demography of teaching more importantly than anything since women had first become the majority of teachers nearly a century before: Long-existing prohibitions against married women disappeared virtually everywhere during this emergency.[96] While many businesses and industries laid off women workers when the men began returning to civilian life in 1945 and 1946, this was not possible in teaching. For one thing, potential male teachers were diverted into colleges; five million men studied under the benefits of the "G. I. Bill." Moreover, the demands for additional teachers to instruct the children of the "baby boom" made it impossible to send married women home again. Nor was the supply of single women adequate to the task. The spinster teacher corp was aging and about to retire, and could not be replenished in the climate of the 1940s and 1950s, which encouraged early marriages and large families. In the pronatalist climate of the postwar decade, young women became part of the problem, not the solution, to unstaffed classrooms. Of necessity, men in school work had for the first time to deal massively with a new kind of woman: the employed, middle-class mother.[97]

The percentages of men in teaching grew from one in five in 1940 to one in three by 1968. But they returned, from the service or from college, to a changing world of teachers—one they helped to alter further. Married women, who were 18 percent of all women teachers in 1930 and 22 percent in 1940, outnumbered single women by 1953. By 1960, only 29 percent of women teachers were unmarried.[98] Unlike the situation of single women, most of whom supported themselves and sometimes also elderly parents, the immediate and long-term economic needs of the married woman teacher (with her "second income") and of the married man (supporting a large family) were perceived as sharply divergent.

By providing veterans with free education that enabled them to become teachers, the federal government's G. I. Bill continued the tradition of "eased entry" that began with the state normal schools of the 1830s.[99] Generous veteran preference policies of local districts smoothed their way into better positions and up the salary scale. Vast numbers of new schools opened, creating possibilities of principalships that were largely reserved for men. Nonetheless, the militancy of male teachers was not dampened. They led a movement that turned teachers' associations into unions and buried, probably forever, the then-reigning conception of teacher professionalism.

The Meanings of "Professionalism"

By modern standards the nineteenth-century drive for professional status made very modest demands on teachers. An eighth-grade education was sufficient to teach the rural common schools that the majority of Americans still attended. As late as 1910, under two-thirds of teachers had even a high-school education, and only 5 percent had more than that. Although some men with college degrees had taught when women were still denied a higher education, by the end of the nineteenth century, male teachers had less education on average than did women teachers. Since professionalism placed more emphasis upon formally acquired, technical qualifications than upon such ascribed characteristics as personality, strength, or family background, male gender became less important in the face of the new, external controls being placed upon lay school boards by county and state authorities. These had different effects on the two sexes. Extended formal education might occupy the time of the young woman until she was ready to marry, but it delayed the financial independence of the man to an age when he might earn more in another field. While a stint of teaching might buy a woman a trousseau, the same experience could not provide most young men with the means to marry and establish a household.

Because the standards of prior pedagogical preparation were so low for both sexes, state educational leaders imposed increasingly stringent requirements of what we now call inservice training. Teacher institutes grew from a two-day meeting in one's own county, or a few evenings in city districts, to annual meetings of several weeks' duration. Teachers had to transport and board themselves, as well as forgo any potential income. By the 1880s, summer institutes in Iowa lasted four weeks.[100] Also, the minimal age for public school teaching was being raised, and teacher certification was slowly moving from county to state authorization. At least as important was the lengthening school year, which was changing teaching from a seasonal employment to a commitment lasting most of the year. These were costly reforms—too costly for many men.

Studies of teaching reveal an inverse relationship between the standards imposed on the profession, and the percentage of male teachers.[101] As one after another of the above-named reforms were instituted, more men left teaching. In economic terms the "opportunity costs" of teaching became more than men were willing to pay, given the low pay and advancement possibilities relative to their other available occupations. Men had no more economic reason to remain in teaching than boys had to remain in high school. In 1890, the earnings of male teachers were half those earned by skilled blue-collar workers. In 1903, teaching salaries still were as low as six-tenths the average of other public employees.[102] The new requirements diminished the opportunity for older men to alternate teaching with farming, preaching, or selling, or for young men to read law or learn about machinery in their off-duty hours. In Rosa Jennings' Iowa of the 1890s, the new requirements for certification left the newly established state normal school largely to the young women; men, intending to use teaching as a steppingstone to something else, dropped out.

Conversely, professionalization was important in retaining the participation of female college graduates in schoolteaching. "The college woman is also proving herself the most efficient of all women," President Thomas of Bryn Mawr boasted in 1901. "She makes so successful a teacher that she is swiftly driving untrained women teachers out of the private and public schools. . . ; she is also driving men from the schools."[103] Among Carleton College graduates between 1904 and 1917 36 of 56 women questioned had taught. Grinnel alumnae between 1884 and 191 reported that 80 percent who had ever worked had been teachers. The same was true of over two thousand Vassar graduates polled in 1915. Among the surviving graduates of 38 classes at the University of Wisconsin, over half had supported themselves, 88 percent of these by teaching.[104] So, too, in our own times: In 1973, of all women college graduates in the labor force, 59 percent were working in education, chiefly as teachers. College educators sometimes spoke of opening other professions to women, work that called upon their drive for ''womanly service.''[105] Their women students asked, however, for pedagogy courses; teaching already had this favorable image among them.

Cultural Stereotypes of Teachers

Although a great deal of the rhetoric accompanying the movement of schoolteaching to the orbit of women's sphere resembles little more than rationalization for the objective conditions explored above, images possess power in their own right.[106] They may attract or repel the prospective teacher. They may justify the parent, school board member, or taxpayer in some action. They may affect teacher–student relationships. They certainly contribute to the morale and self-concept of teachers themselves.

Stereotypes are cultural constructions. Rooted, more or less firmly, in perceived reality, they also are public expressions of hopes and fears, prejudice, wishful thinking, the desire to appear large-minded while protecting one's narrowest interests. In these regards they are like the concept of gender: rooted, more or less firmly, in the biology of sex but so overlain with metaphysics, social and political symbolism, and historical experience as to defy unraveling. Socrates saw the teacher as midwife, Plato as a figure of authority; one evokes womanly and supportive imagery, the other patriarchal power. Seemingly contradictory qualities have contended in the image of teaching, including those of ''militants'' and ''mice'' in present-day accounts.[107]

Teacher images were suffused with expressions of gender even before women came to share the teacher's platform with men.[108] The suggestion of effeminacy lingered about teachers and students when schools were all-male institutions. Conversely, the threat of masculinization was a barrier thrown before women's advance—as students, teachers, or administrators. In what follows, however, we will look at the sex-specific images of men and women teachers, and also at their contradictions, before suggesting some of their bases in objective circumstances. (''Ichabods and Schoolmarms'' was a reference to teachers made at the National Education Association convention in 1920.)[109]

Ichabods: Men in Teaching

Something like the shamans of preliterate societies, who were both a priestly and a teaching class, the first schoolteachers in colonial America were ministers, usually conducting town schools as a ''sacred duty'' associated with their chief role. By the early nineteenth century, many laymen were also teaching. Qualities associated with the clergyman, however, long continued to define the teacher. The Reverend Thomas Gallaudet spoke in 1825 of "Christian sincerity" in urging men to enter the "domestic field of labor": teaching.[110] "Consecration" and "awakening" were familiar terms in the meetings of the more professional part of the teacher force and in the diaries and letters of individual teachers. The law implementing the Texas Constitution of 1869 held that the superintendent of instruction must possess good moral character, temperate habits, and belief in a Supreme Being.[111] The educational objective of "character formation" and the teacher's requisite of "Christian love" were not gender-specific, however, for they were expected in the mother as in the minister.

The ridiculous figure of the colonial schoolmaster, Ichabod Crane, in Washington Irving's *The Legend of Sleepy Hollow* must have struck a responsive chord, for something of the image has persisted. Teacher Labove in William Faulkner's *The Hamlet* is another figure of marginal acceptance in the world of men:

> They had accepted him, and although his designation of professor was a distinction, it was still a woman's distinction, functioning actually in a woman's world like the title of reverend. Although they would not have actually forbidden him the bottle, they would not have drunk with him, and though they were not quite as circumspect in what they said before him as they would have been with a true minister, if he had responded in kind he might have found himself out of a position when the next term began and he knew it.[112]

In 1938, Phi Delta Kappa published *Teaching as a Man's Job;* reprinted in 1939, 1945 and 1963, probably more than 100,000 copies were distributed to high-school boys.[113] Illustrated with photographs of men doing this "man-sized job," the sixty-page book sought to interest the "best young men" in "what some believe to be the greatest profession to which a man can devote his life." This men's honorary association in education acknowledged that the majority of teachers were now women, but claimed women's agreement with the principle that "American Education Needs Men."

But the fact that many did not expect or want teachers to "act like men" is clear at many points in history. In dynamic nineteenth-century America, the schoolroom undoubtedly represented to many men a refuge rather than a grappling with life, too often a place for the sickly and the feckless. Miriam Colt described her nephew as "still in poor health, but is doing what his health will permit, at teaching among the Indians up Lake Superior."[114] When Henry Seidel Canby was growing up in Wilmington, Delaware in the 1880s, he remembered that his friends and family imagined "that the teacher, even the college teacher, did his work in a childish world from which adult men and women had escaped by taking up the really important tasks of life."[115] A high-school principal described the teaching profession in 1896 as "a survival of the unfittest."[116] When the Baltimore City Teachers Association, then under male leadership, made its salary demands in 1955, Mayor D'Alesandro revealed something of his image of teachers: "When we have to take insults from the schoolteachers in print, when I have to take this from these schoolteachers here, I quit," he exploded.[117]

Historian Warren Button points to shifting nomenclature, with its contrasting images and reference groups: "schoolmaster," dominant in the colonial and early republican periods and associated with the classical curriculum of the academy. And "teacher," coming into prominence in the common schools and gradually preempting the language. He associates "teacher" with women: possessed of less education (hence not "masters" of subject matter) and cheaper to hire. Their students constituted the masses, and "The social status of the pupils tended to reduce the status of teachers, who themselves came most often from families of limited means."[118] In the very word "teacher," then, was there reason for men to avoid the profession or to feel uncomfortable and apologetic at being found among an army of women?[119] If there are negative associations to "teacher," do they derive primarily from "school," "children," "students"—or from "woman" and her concerns, regardless of setting?[120]

Schoolmarms: Women in Teaching

In 1825, when Gallaudet exhorted men to enroll in "a domestic field of labor," he probably had in mind that schoolteaching was historically rooted in the upbringing of the child in the family. Nonetheless, the connection between mother and teacher had already been made, and the schoolmistress was a significant presence in New England schoolhouses. The schooling of girls had been argued for on the grounds that women's education was preparation for marriage and motherhood. "I think female education is too much neglected," Elijah Fletcher wrote home in 1810, sending $100 to support the schooling of a sister in a female academy. "They are the ones who have the first education of children and ought to be qualified to instruct them correctly."[121] A latter-day expression is the aphorism "When you educate a man you educate an individual; when you educate a woman you educate a family."

The argument was extended to teaching by those whom historians call "domestic feminists"—men and women who favored women teachers—and by women who themselves wanted to teach. The Board of Education of the District of Columbia invoked Napoleon's words praising his mother's teaching, saying "Our experience fully carries out the opinion of that great man, in reference to women, not only as mothers but as teachers. . . ."[122] Women campaigned for the Boston School Committee on the grounds that the welfare of the schools demand a maternal understanding.[123] The essential conservatism of the position did not escape notice. As one Vassar student saw it in 1893, teaching represented for women the chief compromise between society's demand that women remain within the home, and woman's wish to work in society. Another student characterized teaching as "yielding to society and society's standards."[124] While teaching was the first public profession to be seen as "motherwork," the other "helping professions" more or less shared in this process of image-using. "Splitting my life into the two roles of social worker and mother raised problems of organization and energy, but no major emotional conflicts," Sophie Freud Loewenstein wrote in 1980.[125] A society that claimed to respect female selflessness and singularity certainly profited from cultivating that image of complementarity.[126]

Clearly, teaching and other emerging "women's professions" were not intended to create spinsters. Yet teaching often seemed to do that, and the image of the old maid teacher came to stand alongside that of the young woman teacher only waiting to marry. The dominant image of the nineteenth century, if popular culture is a reliable indicator, was that of the spinster: ''In the comic valentines of the nineties, the schoolma'am was depicted in hard crude color as a tall, thin, slab-sided female, her scraggly hair brushed straight back from a high and bulging forehead and fastened with a single pin in a skimpy wad at the back of her head.''[127]

Sadie Smith wrote from Holdrege, Nebraska, in 1903 about the household of teachers boarding with her. ''A pretty nice crowd,'' she thought. ''But we are school teachers, and hence genuine 'Old Maids,' not because of our dress or age, but simply because of occupation.''[128] Since romance played so large a part of the plot of novels about working women, many writers avoided teachers altogether.[129]

During the 1930s, intense competition for employment pitted sex against sex and single women against their married counterparts. Revealing characterizations of teachers, perhaps lurking there all along, rose into print. It was argued, for example, that ''mother understanding and mother love and mother experience'' were furnished by the married woman teacher; neither the spinster nor the male teacher could supply these. ''The important task of educating the young should be entrusted to women who lead a normal life,'' said one advocate of married teachers. ''The attractive woman who finds it easy to marry and establish a home is the kind of woman that schools need,'' said another. Those who defended the single woman as self-supporting while the married woman had a breadwinner were met with the retort that schools exist to benefit children, not as ''havens for spinsters.'' Implications of the single teacher's deviancy forced Dean Virginia Gildersleeve of Barnard College to protest ''the tendency of today to regard celibate teachers as 'frustrated'.''[130]

When Pauline Galvarro produced a dissertation in 1945 of over 100 pages of text and 500 pages of case records, ''A Study of Certain Emotional Problems of Women Teachers,'' everything that needed to be said on the respective merits of single and married women teachers had been said.[131] Very soon the debate would stop: The spinster teacher virtually disappeared from the contemporary imagery, if not from legend.

''I loathe children,'' says Meta Beggs, the village teacher in *Mountain Blood.* ''I'll grow old and die in pokey little schools, and wear prim calico dresses. . . .'' Rebellious and sensuous, Meta Beggs is the exception to the teacher stereotype. In her study of the images of single women in American novels, Dorothy Deegan found women teachers generally portrayed as both important in their function and unprepossessing in their persons.[132] The successful among them ended their careers by marriage and used their talents to advance their husband's career. Real-life women like Alice Freeman Palmer—one-time Michigan schoolteacher and president of Wellesley College—were praised when they gave up their careers for marriage. Meanwhile, those fictional teachers who persisted in their careers faced even more challenges than did male teachers: While men must gain respect to succeed, the novelists' women teachers must win their pupils' affection, and even their love.[133]

Gertrude, the mother in Johann Pestalozzi's *How Gertrude Teaches Her Children*

(1781), exemplified the ideal of the teacher in *avante garde* circles in nineteenth-century America: concerned, nurturing, and affectionate. Friedrich Froebel called the kindergarten teacher the highest form of motherhood. The qualities of self-discipline and theological sophistication that the Puritans considered so central to the education of even the young child, and that once made fathers and males model teachers, were giving way to a greater emphasis upon the sensitivity and empathy of the mother and father. Far from being a respectable occupation involving little drudgery, teaching was, Marion Harland argued, a natural expression of womanhood: ''It is the nature of being of the mother-sex to gather together into her care and brood over and instruct creatures younger and feebler than herself.''[134]

''That young women are the best teachers has been proved and acknowledged by those men who have made trial for the gentle sex in schools of the most difficult description,'' argued Sarah Hale, ''because of the superior tact and moral power natural to the female character.''[135] The good school was like the good home: feminine, innocent, affectionate, and religious. The outside society, from which the home and school were refuges, was, however, masculine: materialistic, irreligious, and hardhearted.[136] While some men teachers were celebrated for their piety, patience, and disavowal of physical punishment, the conventional widsom pictured women as the more intuitive masters of thc art of gentle persuasion. A Michigan superintendent was quoted in 1878 as saying, ''In visiting schools of small children taught by gentlemen I have been reminded of the condition of young children in the families of widowers.''[137] What was left for the man in education under this ideology? It was the job of ensuring the objective, rational structure surrounding or ''ordering'' the increasingly subjective organization of the ''family'' within the classroom. The male sphere was education policy making, school administration, and university teaching.

The domestic ideology was particularly important to the middle classes, where the Victorian family was also celebrated by the churches and press. Among the working classes and the payers of heavy taxes, however, the relatively low cost of women teachers probably carried more weight. For one thing, modern ideas of the naturally good child were far slower to penetrate the lower classes; more would have agreed, no doubt, with Plato had they known that he described the young child as an intractable wild creature possessed of an uncurbed reason.

Although it did not proscribe corporal punishment, the ''Rules and Regulations for the Government of the Public Free Schools'' of Texas, adopted in 1871, followed the best professional thinking of the time in stating that the greatest success in preserving order and discipline came ''through kindness and good counsel''; such teachers ''shall receive preference over all others in promotion.''[138] A writer in *Educational Review* in 1899 described what many had already seen: ''A weak woman with reasonable tact can now do the work which formerly required a bully.''[139] What today's radical critics of schooling call her, ''society's soft cop,'' was a model teacher a century ago.

There were costs in the domestication of schooling, however. The perceptions that teachers were ''mothering,'' or that women teachers were only marking time until marriage, had unfortunate effects for the image of professionalism that teaching was also trying to cultivate. For example, while some college women might complain about the lack of explicit preparation in pedagogy, a four-year college course was thought sufficient, since their careers were only preludes to marriage.[140] Family relationships divided teachers, undermining professional solidarity. As late as 1956, Baltimore's single women teachers voted against the men on the issue of integrating their pension system with Social Security; compared to their male colleagues, who also were better paid, spinster teachers had little to gain from the survivors' benefits available under the federal program.[141] With the rapidly increasing percentages of married women in teaching after 1960, they would become economic allies of the men newly recruited back into teaching, thus contributing to the growing militancy of organized teachers.

Factors Contributing to Teacher Image and Status

The imagery and power of teaching is affected by factors that apparently have little to do with the teacher's gender in any direct way. Professionals borrow the status of their clients—"gilt by association."[142] Work with young children is something parents have always done without special qualifications. Accordingly, it had low regard in ancient Greece and Rome. Pity the once mighty Dionysus, tyrant of Syracuse, spending his old age teaching children at Corinth, or Diotimus, "who sits on stones repeating Alpha and Beta to the children of Gargarus."[143] Teachers (all men) would have preferred not to open primary schools at all, but the difficulties of teaching older boys who had not been properly socialized to academic routines when young and pliable made the work of the *grammaticus* too difficult. The result was to accord him higher regard and pay than the primary teacher received for his necessary but tiresome and undistinguished labors. Not surprising, then, that women made their first appearances in eighteenth-century America as schoolteachers of young children and girls, both already low-status groups.[144] Only necessity, already described, gave them eventual access to older and male students.

Odes to home and child to the contrary notwithstanding, domestic activities confer small status or power to either sex. But woman could not be made separable from family. British writer Grant Allen characterized woman as "the sex sacrificed to reproductive necessities," her domain the home, nursery, and schoolroom; conversely, "all that is distinctively human is man—the field, the ship, the mine, the workshop."[145] He put crassly what public opinion largely left unquestioned. If stereotypically "domestic" qualities dominated the symbolization of schooling with the advent of women teachers, or even before, and if they are as socially devalued as "antithetical to the aggressive, instrumental roles needed in the world of men and work," as Sara Lightfoot and other students of gender contend, then schools and teachers can enjoy scant cultural power in society.[146]

The lower the social, occupational, and educational status of the viewer, the higher the apparent status of the teacher. Black teachers enjoyed high status in their community, and the career was very attractive to young men and women.[147] But these teachers were never able to bring their salaries to a commensurate level, being subject to white school boards and trustees determined to pay them even less than their white counterparts. When teachers visited in humble homes on the frontier, they usually were treated with extreme courtesy and given the best of what was available in bed and board; not so among their more privileged patrons.

It also seems probable that the questionable regard for teachers was a psychological necessity, given what taxpayers and patrons were willing to pay for the steadily rising costs of schooling. Despite the sacrifices that many communities made to support schools, Americans were more willing to hand over their children than their money, especially in ''cash poor'' rural areas.[148] The ''old field schools'' of the antebellum plantation South were neighborhood schools placed on old, unproductive tobacco lands—a fitting symbol of want in the midst of plenty. The ''little red schoolhouse'' of American legend was a testimony to the cheapness of red paint compared to white; in fact, many schools remained unpainted.

Another kind of pennypinching was the common attitude toward teacher qualifications. There was resistance to applying professional entry standards that would prevent local sons and daughters from gaining the teacher's position that gave some citizens the opportunity to recover their school taxes.[149] Sadie Smith was warned that her graduation from high school would limit her employability in Nebraska rural schools. She was not rehired at one school, underbid by a local girl with less education and no experience; Smith had been paid $30 per month; her replacement got $25. Taxpayers' organizations later reacted to teachers' attempts to acquire pensions, tenure, and sabbatical leaves as being unwarranted assaults on the public treasury.

Catharine Beecher might characterize teaching for women as being ''as honourable and as lucrative for her as legal, medical and theological professions are for men,'' but women teachers complained as bitterly about their salaries as did men, and many moved from school to school to improve their wages, as well as to secure more agreeable company. Horace Mann and other early exponents of women teachers argued that women could be hired for half or less the male price. Eventually, teacher leaders had to deny that women were happy to work for so little, and that they required less. Still, women's struggles for higher wages and for equal pay with male teachers antagonized schools boards and, perhaps, public opinion.[150] The magazine of the American Federation of Teachers in 1935 reprinted the words of the owner of a Cadillac, a prosperous physician, who responded to the complaint of a teacher that she was unable to pay for gas for the old flivver that took her to work because she had not received her pay for months: ''I said to her, 'What the hell right have you to have a car at all?' ''[151]

Teaching has been underpaid throughout history, regardless of the gender of the majority and the method of paying for teaching. The German teacher in the fifteenth century assisted at weddings and funerals to supplement his salary, as the Massachusetts schoolmaster dug graves and took the night watch, and the Dutch schoolmasters of New Amsterdam swept churches, assisted in baptisms, and shoveled snow. Hobby, who taught George Washington, also swept a church and served as sexton. The governor of South Carolina characterized the men teaching in the public schools in 1840 as demeaned by ''so miserable a pittance as the reward of their labors''; their acceptance of it was ''*prima-facie* evidence of [their] want of qualification.''[152]

The youthful character of the modal teacher was another factor affecting teacher wages, image, and occupational status. Indeed, in comparison with the maturity and community standing of the laymen who controlled local school boards, most teachers of either gender were disadvantaged. Even the best-educated teachers in America between 1620 and 1850 were young. These products of the classical colleges typically taught during their long winter vacations and immediately after graduation, often being in their mid-twenties when they were called to the ministry or other professions. Although the age for beginning teachers rose from about 15 in country schools in antebellum America to around 20 by 1910, the short teaching careers of many of both sexes meant that teachers could easily be perceived as callow youth, and rewarded accordingly. Those who still lived in parental homes, in the stage of "semidependency," were particularly at risk, regardless of age and gender.[153] But women had a special disadvantage, having so long been treated as children according to the law. Frances Donovan reports that as late as 1918 it was difficult for a single woman to get an apartment in Chicago, unless a near male relative cosigned her lease.

Although the public school has been called America's "secular church" due to the faith in the power of education demonstrated in its history, schooling has suffered wide swings in public regard. Stephen Sellers argues, for example, that the decline of the Puritan ministry in the eighteenth century coincided with the apparent decline in public education; the two institutions were closely linked and many teachers were clergymen.[154] The initial expansion of schooling in colonial Massachusetts was accompanied by a drop in the status of the families from which the new schoolmasters came, and subsequent growth may have repeated that process. The evidence consistently indicates that, compared to women teachers, teaching recruited more males from lower-status backgrounds, men using teaching as a vehicle of social mobility.[155] While this upward mobility also occurred among women, especially those of immigrant backgrounds, there were so few career options for women that teaching attracted many of middle and upper middle-class origins.

The statuses of schools and of teachers were dynamically related. When Yankee Salmon P. Chase was teaching school and reading law in Washington, DC in 1830, he noted that:

> Instructors here are not esteemed as they are at the North and no wonder for of all men assuming the duties of that relation I do not think a more miserable set could be selected than those who are located here. I do not associate with them and in fact tho I have been in the city for three years I am yet acquainted with but one teacher. How can a man expect to be pleased when his *profession* ranks him with a degraded *caste*?[156]

Did the Washington schools attract "inferior" men because education was little regarded there? Or did the quality of available teachers injure the repute of the schools? Clearly, once the association is made, the process becomes reinforcing until new factors enter and break the cycle. In many places in the nineteenth century, contemporary observers believed that hiring female teachers would launch an upward cycle of public regard.

When Walt Whitman was editor of the *Brooklyn Daily Eagle* he pleaded in 1847 for an end to masculine brutality in teaching:

> For teachers' own sakes—for the true height and majesty of their office, hardly second to the priesthood—they should one and all unite in precluding this petty and foolish punishment—this degrader and bringerdowner of their high standing. As things are, the word school-teacher is identified with a dozen unpleasant and ridiculous associations—a sour face, a whip, hard knuckles snapped on tender heads, no gentle, fatherly kindness, no inciting of young ambition in its noble phases, none of the beautifiers of authority, but all that is small, ludicrous, and in after life productive of indignation.[157]

It is doubtful that remembrance of the indignities imposed by teachers upon one's young self explains everything negative about teaching's image. George Gerbner thinks that the ambivalent image of the teacher reflects a cultural distrust "of the intellect on the loose." He writes: "All societies suspect what they need but cannot fully control." Moreover, in a society with so much of its hopes pinned on education, disappointment is inevitable: "It becomes only reasonable and realistic to show teachers full of goodness, but sapped of vitality and power."[158]

Trajectories of Teaching Careers

Despite the fact that high labor turnover has characterized this nation (except during severe economic depressions), teaching has been perceived as an exceptionally unstable occupation. It has been said that teaching is a "procession more than a profession." "I am not sorry that I have been a pedagogue," Salmon P. Chase wrote on his way to a career in law and politics. "It is a test—a criterion of strength—energy—power."[159] Harvard historian Albert Bushnell Hart lamented this transiency, however: "For more than a century teaching has been considered in this country, what it could hardly be in any other country, a makeshift for young men who expect to enter law or medicine," he wrote in 1893.[160] Among women teachers he thought the "epidemic of matrimony" was the cause. It was not, however, the sole root of turnover among women teachers, and it has probably been exaggerated as a problem. The Colorado teachers studied by Underwood resigned to take better positions more than they did for marriage.[161] "A large number will leave next year," Sadie Smith wrote of her fellow teachers in her Nebraska district in 1902. "Miss Gilchrist wishes to be nearer home; Miss Fraser is to go out of the profession, and Miss Nelson, larger salary, etc. . . ."[162]

The schoolmaster Epicurus "on coming across the works of Democritus turned eagerly to philosophy."[163] This long-lived impression of the retreat from teaching has haunted it. Witness the naming of famous former teachers—those who found it "a satisfactory stepping stone to other professions"—in a 1920 issue of *School and Society:* Frances Willard, Garfield, Taft, Foch, Clemenceau, McKinley, and Wilson.[164] Another belief is that loyalty to a particular school or district is typically short-lived, in part because there is so little opportunity for "promotion" through teaching "ranks" that geographic mobility must substitute.[165] Gwendolyn Jones's career displays both of these traits: moving west to California, moving from district to district, and then marrying a physician and leaving teaching altogether. Had she not moved, however, "It is unlikely that she would have obtained either so easily or so rapidly, professional or financial advancement," nor married a professional man (thereby assuring society of her success as a woman).[166] As it was with male teachers in the early nineteenth century, too long a tenure at a given school meant "not a praiseworthy stability but . . . a sinecure."[167] Moreover, the very movement of teachers of both sexes, caused their positions to be vacated and ready for new or mobile recruits to fill.

Additionally, teaching careers have been commonly interrupted during the adult life course. William A. Alcott stopped his ten-year teaching career, begun in 1816, to study medicine—to discipline his mind and to have "two strings to my bow."[168] After three years of practice, he returned to teaching and later authored *Confessions of a Schoolmaster*. Isabella D. Godding happily taught in Brooklyn's Girls High School from 1869 to 1902, before going home to Maine after her mother's death to care for her aged father.[169] Of the 38 long-time twentieth-century teachers interviewed by Alice Rinehart, 15 had interrupted their careers for from three to ten years: to start a family, to serve in the armed forces, to try another line of work. Black teachers were likely to stay in teaching longer, having less opportunity to use teaching as a stopgap or steppingstone.[170]

For women, far more than for men, family membership has determined or influenced entry to, persistence in, and departure from a teaching career. In the preprofessional years of Pittsburgh's public schools, for example, ward school boards hired middle-class widows, their daughters, or older single women to teach. School jobs were a form of welfare, a substitute for the support of a husband or father. Such teachers were replaced, beginning in 1847, by young women from socially important families who could simultaneously be hired for less and also confer prestige upon the public schools.[171] Subsequently, women were encouraged to think of themselves as professionals, and of teaching as a lifelong career, by actions like the enforcement of new credentialing laws, teachers' institutes, employing a city superintendent, opening a city normal school, creating a state teachers' association, and disseminating an ideology of noble service to children and the nation. These reforms created a colleague group providing both socialization to teaching and sociability among persons with shared interests. Similar processes worked everywhere—and, other things being equal, among men teachers as well.

To work in lieu of marriage was an unattractive option for the majority of women, although it was the career trajectory of a substantial number despite their initial preferences. The young women leaving the women's colleges, coeducational universities, and normal schools in the years after 1865 are on record as preferring to combine marriage with a career if that was possible, or to work only until marriage.[172] By the 1950s, the married woman teacher was an accepted fact and the college culture was telling women students that their lives would mean early marriage followed by resumption of career, usually teaching, when family duties were lighter.[173] Paradoxically, the lower age of first marriage for this generation meant their earlier return to the labor force. Thus women both acquired more of a "stake" in improving their work conditions, and presented their sons and daughters with a more compelling image of woman as "careerist."

Sociologists of occupation, almost all men themselves and operating through a paradigm that makes male experience the norm for all humans, considers such commitments to employment as "contingent," "partial," "undeveloped," "flawed." In its quest for universal laws of social behavior, ahistorical and context-free social science has had to treat the nexus of family and school in the teaching career as a pathology. Teaching, then, must be a "semiprofession" at best.[174]

The obligations of male teachers to family were different. The chief of these was to establish and support a family in a manner consistent with the man's advantages and education, and also with the norms for other men of his time and place. In the 1870s, for example, this creation of a new household was expected to occur between ages 25 and 30.[175] In a great many instances the breadwinner's role proscribed lifelong or full-time commitment to teaching, or (as was the case with the writing-school masters of colonial New England) delayed it until a man had established himself well enough at something else to be able to afford the luxury of teaching.[176] Later teachers sometimes followed this path. Earning $35 per month for half a year in 1910, one Pennsylvania teacher left his classrooms altogether to manage a family farm. He returned only in 1934, called back to manage an "ungovernable" rural school—and remained for 20 years. Another man, who taught from 1927 to 1968, adopted the locally common practice of mixing rural schoolteaching with academic study in order to qualify to teach in the secondary schools where the pay was greater. He commuted 200 miles by train every Saturday for four years, to attend New York University.[177] Yet another, whose teaching career began in 1908, sought promotion to teaching principal in another district in 1910; this move up added $4 to his monthly salary of $85. In the case of a great many men, if movement among schools and districts, or in and out of teaching, did not suffice, there still was a chance to try for the position of head teacher—and, after 1880 or so, for one or another of the proliferating administrative positions in an increasingly bureaucratized educational system.

We turn now to three patterns made by generations of teachers.

The Career Teacher

Nathan Tinsdale taught an early school in Lebanon, Connecticut for 30 years, attracting students even from abroad.[178] Colonial America's most famous teacher, however, was Ezekial Cheever, who taught for 50 years. (Despite his reputation and longevity, he had to petition the royal governor of Massachusetts for his back wages—not very different from the countless novice teachers trying to collect promised fees.) There were, then, men (and, later, women) teachers who rejected the social expectation that teaching was temporary work. But long-time teachers were the exception. When academies, subscription schools, "select schools," female seminaries, collegiate institutes, and other short-lived and undercapitalized schools dominated the "school business," many teaching careers were perforce brief. The prospects of longer teaching tenures brightened with the expansion and strengthening of public education. Men and women teachers became involved in collective efforts, especially after 1900, to obtain pension systems and tenure rights, both obvious signs of career aspirations.[179]

Those who contend that teaching with women is apt to be a temporary resort should look about them, advised a magazine author in 1878. "Almost any New Englander can count among his personal acquaintances women who have taught from fifteen to thirty years, and who will probably die in the harness."[180] Amy Morris Bradley was such a career teacher, beginning in a country school near her Maine home in 1840 and retiring as superintendent of schools in New Hanover County, North Carolina in 1891. During her youth she had the typical doubts about what her profession might mean for her life as a woman. Concerned with the opinion of men, she was rather torn between their interest in her as both a woman and a valued teacher. She was 26 and teaching in Charlestown, Massachusetts when, in 1849, she wrote:

> So sister mine you really wish I would get married, and not be a school-teacher any longer. . . . But you know I am not calculated to interest gentlemen much, and it does not matter either. I may do much more good in my present capacity than as a wife. Though I will not deny, that if I should get an opportunity—which *suited* me, I should do as others. . . . My plan is to remain here as long as I teach, then, I will come home and try to make myself useful in the families of my brothers and sisters. . . . I was reelected, as I have been informed, by a unanimous vote of the board—which is very pleasing, as it shows their approval [of me] as an instructress.[181]

Ignored examples of nineteenth-century women's long careers abound. Jennie White, a black teacher in Augusta, Georgia, taught for 36 years, so successfully that officials exempted her from the rule against employing married women in the public schools.[182] Across the continent a somewhat younger Carrie Williams graduated from San Jose State Normal School in 1896, beginning a 40-year career. She moved from elementary to secondary schools, even into "Boys Tech," crossing county lines with the same objectives of independence, choice, and deserved reward that animated mobile men teachers.[183]

Kate Taylor, of the 1910 class of Vassar College, bridled at those who took up teaching "until something else turns up"; she thought this turned the profession "into a mere substitute for the old-fashioned twiddling of one's thumbs and waiting for something to happen."[184] When teacher Henrietta Rodman and the Feminist Alliance rallied behind women teachers in New York City in 1914, existing regulations specified that married women could not be hired unless separated from their husbands for three years. Rodman's battle was successful, and even maternity leaves were allowed. Relatives of single women teachers sometimes had their own interests in career constancy. Frances Donovan characterized aged mothers as "veritable watch-dogs; they bark at all male intruders who threaten their economic security and resent any attempt to snatch away the beloved daughter around whom their whole life centers."[185]

Before the Depression, surveys reported that 60 percent of urban districts had regulations against employing or retaining married women teachers. Hard times only increased that number in what Walter Terpenning called, in 1932, a policy of "pure unadulterated asininity."[186] Growing up in the 1930s, one married career teacher recalled the conviction she acquired during her own school days, that she could never achieve her twin desires of teaching school and being a mother. All of her teachers were unmarried, under some contract or unwritten rule that assumed "that a woman had to be able to devote her whole self to the job." The unfairness of it later struck her: "A man could be a provider and a husband and everything else and run a profession, but a woman couldn't possibly handle it." Like vast numbers of women before her, one graduate of Slippery Rock State Teachers College left her position after four years of teaching. She had married and was required to quit, this in 1939. In South Bend, Indiana, in the same years, married women were allowed to teach as "substitutes," at much lower salaries.[187]

A return to teaching was a common historic pattern. After her junior year in high school, Luella Boelio took a six-week course to get her certificate to teach in a one-room school in Michigan. Using her savings, she entered Ypsilanti Normal College in 1901, over the objection of her grandfather that sending her to college wasted money since she was sure to marry (as she did in 1905). She returned to teaching as Mrs. Bower, a widow with five children, putting all through college and seeing three become teachers.[188] By traditional definitions, she would not be considered a career teacher, however, but a woman driven by unfortunate circumstances back into the labor market. Under current occupational theory her commitment to teaching would be described as "contingent."

Widowhood conferred certain career advantages on women teachers.[189] First, it exempted them from restrictions or prejudices against employing the married woman. Second, it gave them a perceived advantage over single women as having normal emotions and having led a "normal life." Finally, it gave them an acceptable economic reason to teach. This latter was especially important if they coveted administrative positions. Widowed Hannah Blackwell (1792–1870) used her Sunday-school teaching experience, her skills in household management, and the talents of three young daughters to open a successful private school. Her daughters subsequently taught in other schools, none happily, before two of them broke new trails by becoming physicians.[190] Sadie Smith had been a teacher and teaching principal before her marriage in 1906. Returning to education in 1916 as a widow with four dependents, she was thereafter teacher, high-school principal, and superintendent in various communities. Superintendents Ella Flagg Young of Chicago, a "sod" widow, and Susan Dorsey of Los Angeles, a "grass" widow, were better-known examples of the advantages to women of having once been married.

Contrasted with men's, the life-course curve for women's teaching careers has always shown something of a bimodal distribution. With the dropping of policies against the married woman teacher during World War II, this pattern grew to dominance. A common experience is that of the 60-year-old woman, with 15 years of teaching experience when interviewed in 1980, who explained that her decision to return during her children's adolescence was motivated by college expenses. The hours, and summer vacations, were an added inducement to her, and probably explain much about the fact that women teachers in 1960 were more likely to be married than were librarians and social workers.[191] Historically, however, this career trajectory in teaching—of stopping to have a family, returning to teaching if the need and opportunity arose—has long been more common than many believed. Local needs and personal reputation have allowed uncounted exceptions to the proposition that teaching was a position for the young and single.

In recent times, when the effects of the civil rights movement made teachers highly self-conscious of criticisms about their interest in all their students, the married woman teacher could again be censured, especially if she was a mother. A teacher in a Boston-area alternative school explained in 1980 that most of the teachers were single or divorced women: "I think that the commitment you have to make to this school is such that it's easier if you're not married." But this attitude was hard to sustain, given the new predominance of the middle-class teacher–mother. Another teacher in the same study said: "I just hated women who said, 'I'll be a teacher. Then I can be home when the kids get home.' I thought that was lousy motivation for teaching. And now I'm . . . saying that if that's part of your reason for job satisfaction you can still do a good job as a teacher, and there's nothing wrong with saying that you love the hours."[192]

THE "TEMPORARY" TEACHER

When schools still retained their close connections with established churches, the trajectories of male careers often led from teaching into the ministry. Of the 64 schoolmasters of Dedham, Massachusetts between 1644 and 1757, 31 eventually became ministers.[193] In more secular times, teaching remained a casual and convenient occupation for many men. Oliver Johnson remembered the single men teachers of antebellum Indiana as a "rovin class."[194] In 1846, *De Bow's Review* recounted the odyssey of the Erie Canal boatman who sought warmer work in the winter—teaching, as he explained it, "Everything almost that's going, reading, writing, geography, *Bells Letters,* and astronomy." Among Texas's itinerate teachers were a Mr. Cummins, who left with a company of volunteers to invade Mexico, and a Mr. Nash, who had come from Alabama in pursuit of someone who had swindled him. They existed alongside the more serious minister–teachers who founded the Texas Literary Institute and proposed plans for a public school system to the legislature.[195]

In "How to Get a Farm and Where to Find One" (1864), young men were urged to work as farmhands for seven or eight months a year and teach a winter school, in order to accumulate the savings to purchase a farm.[196] "Many of the one-room teachers were men because of the fact that they were also farmers," one teacher recalled of her own school days in the early twentieth century. "The most important part of their lives was their farming."[197] If these men saw teaching as a step to other goals, as an opportunity to become recognized as well as to earn money to invest in another occupation, so did many women. Teaching was a saleable skill which also put women into the orbit of marriageable men if their own communities lacked appropriate choices. Among the women teachers who went west around 1850, the fact of quick marriage, before completing one's contract, stirred debate among them and in their sponsoring organizations.

A school position was an instrumental choice in other ways. Nora and Kate Wiggin began teaching in the 1870s to "strengthen the doors against the voracious wolf whose howls had been persistently heard" since their father's death.[198] Sadie Smith wrote, in 1903, of her colleague, Miss Henderson, who wanted to give up schoolkeeping in Nebraska to teach music, "but a $500 debt hangs over her head and she feels compelled to endure the hardship of teaching."[199] Given the importance of the ideology of the self-made man, it should not surprise that women also were willing to travel the road that often led through numerous careers—even though males could dabble in careers and be called "enterprising," while such women were thought "flighty" or even deviant.[200]

It was important to most young teachers that they conform to at least gross societal expectations. To depart far from gender roles turned men or women into unsuitable marriage partners, for example. It was especially important that the young man not teach small children for long as their chief occupation. Salmon Chase wrote to a friend that he should complain frequently about the "forty noisy, dirty, ragged young idiots" that he had to teach, however much he enjoyed bringing them to submission, and to look forward loudly to his emancipation for some other, adult-like occupation. "You made a great mistake when you took so *long* a school. I counted the hours, minutes and even seconds with the utmost impatience. . . ." In fact, Chase taught for several more years. Not only did it provide the means for reading law, but he judged that "Upon our labours depend in a degree the happiness, the honour of our beloved country."[201]

In "Why Teaching Repels Men," C. W. Bardeen warned about the dangers of too much confinement in the classrooms:

> Teaching usually belittles a man. I do not say it ought to; I do not say it always does; I say it usually does. His daily dealing is with petty things, of interest only to his children and a few women assistants, and under regulations laid down by outside authority, so that large questions seldom come to him for consideration. His environment narrows him, he grows to have only one interest, and that limits him in public and in social life. . . . As a rule men teachers are uncouth, crude, ill at ease in company. . . . It is amazing what a difference it makes in a teacher's presence if he goes into business for a time and learns how to meet people.[202]

Mary Jane Mudge was 24 and in her seventh year of teaching in Lynn, Massachusetts, when she decided to put off her suitor. "I told B I had thought of his proposal, and have decided I had rather wait another year," she wrote in her diary in 1854. "I never was so prettily situated in school as I now am, and my salary never was so much."[203] Nonetheless, a woman should not teach so long, or put herself forward in her profession so as to make her one of those despised "strong-minded women," those "man-haters" so repulsive to "good company"—especially to the men who claimed to see the numbers of such women growing throughout the nineteenth century.[204] The young woman was repeatedly warned by physicians and moralists that delaying wedlock was "crucifying her gender by starving or sensualizing it''; that ''unused'' organs caused disease and decay.[205] Early marriage was required for the good of their constitutions, their future children, and the welfare of society.

Raised by a widow handyman in Norwich, Connecticut, Lydia Huntly Sigourney kept school until age 28, when she made what her friends considered a splendid match for an old maid of humble origin: an older hardware merchant with three difficult children, whose business was destined to go bad. She thereafter supported the family as a writer of virtuously sentimental verse. According to the conventional wisdom, young women in frontier schools usually married before three or four years of teaching. ''One who continued to teach for nine or ten years was commonly regarded as sunk and usually was!'' It is probable, however, that many believed to have left for marriage had actually taken other schools or other work. They might have a second chance in life, of course, for sorry widowers like Mr. Sigourney were not uncommon.[206]

In 1932 a writer in *American Teacher* studying press commentary and taxpayer's association publications concluded that:

> If reports are to be credited, our schools are only stepping stones wherein the ambitious teachers may serve their apprenticeship for the real jobs of affluence and honor. The bright woman teacher is only a matrimonial prospect and the intelligent man a potential leader of industry. All that remains after this skimming process is a ''soggy mass.''[207]

The image of short-lived teaching careers with the talent creamed off early has been an enduring one, along with the idea that entry to teaching has been ill-considered and quixotic in many cases. During the post-Sputnik involvement of university scholars in redesigning school curricula, to take it from the hands of those permissive teachers who had allowed Soviet Ivans to outrace American Johnnys, a professor of English condescendingly lamented the quality of those who became English teachers. Many, he said, are ''attractive and amiable young women who have become English majors in this roundabout way and have decided to teach English for a couple of years until a likely-looking man comes along whom they will try to marry.''[208]

Climbing the ''Career Ladder''

In 1888, when men were 33 percent of teachers, they were 96 percent of school managers and policy makers. Since the late years of the nineteenth century, the proliferation of positions in college and university teaching and school administration has been a major source of male withdrawal from classrooms. In the years between 1890 and 1930, schoolteaching overtook both the ministry and school administration as preparation for college teaching.[209] Pursuing either college teaching or the ''executive possibilities'' of the new ''science'' of school management was a way for men teachers to reestablish the difference between the two genders, and to escape the effeminacy generally associated with all schoolteaching since women had invaded and taken over the former male preserve of the high school. Thus, when Henry Parks Wright, one-time dean of Yale College, published *The Young Man and Teaching* (1920), he emphasized its two attractions for the college graduate: a more "immediate income" since "his studies in school and college and his experience as a student" furnish appropriate preparation for teaching; and, second, "the responsibilities of administration." The college-educated man, he stated quite explicitly, had ample opportunities to move quickly into leadership of a teaching force of normal-school-trained women.[210]

The general belief exists that the grading of schools explains the heavy majority that women early became among teachers in urban areas. This system permitted several women "assistants" to take the younger children, and a lone man to teach the oldest *and* preside over the school as the chief discipliner or "head teacher." Thus began the principle that "women teach and men manage." Yet the ability of women teachers to deal with the full range of school management problems was a key theme in the transition to women as teachers of the rural winter schools of New England before 1850. What Alonzo Potter wrote in 1842 was already an oft-heard litany: that "large and turbulent boys, whom it was quite difficult for men to govern by severe means, have been won into good behavior by the gentle treatment of a female teacher."[211] It is doubtful that the "large scholars" of the country schools were less of a challenge than the students in the city's upper grades in the period before 1950. It was obviously factors other than classroom management ability and the rewards of working with children that retained most women in classrooms with younger students.

What happened between Potter's expression of confidence in women's "governing" abilities and the 1890 convention of the National American Women Suffrage Association, when a speaker not only called woman "the teacher of the race; in virtue of her motherhood," but went on to reassure her listeners that "It is not part of woman's work to contend with man for supremacy"?[212] Was it in response to the first signs of a backlash against the "woman peril" in teaching, much of it charging that male students were being harmed by the excess of women teachers in the high schools?[213] Or did nothing "happen"? Did the denial of educational leadership to almost all women teachers rest instead upon economic competition, salaries increased as one moved upward in the grades? Or was it a sometimes-concealed but long-persisting aversion to the "school madam"—an energetic moralizer, of prim manners and Christian rectitude, already a subject of worldly ridicule by the early nineteenth century?[214] Perhaps the male leaders of the community preferred *bonhomie,* the quintessential Rotarian, in its school principals, and especially in the new role of the school superintendent? The story that David Tyack and Elisabeth Hansot tell of the collapse of women's hopes for school leadership, after the few victories in the early twentieth century, seems an inevitable repudiation of that largely male creation, the nineteenth-century female teacher stereotype, ready to be quashed for trying to step too far out of "Woman's Sphere."[215]

Another possible reason for an aversion to women administrators was the role model they set before the majority of teachers: other women. Since the early promoters of women teachers had, in effect, promised that they would be tractable and without personal ambition, Millicent Rutherford wonders if women in educational leadership "inspire restiveness in women teachers, making them less manageable than male educators preferred?"[216] Principal Elizabeth Smyth and her protégés played something of that role in wresting leadership from Baltimore's male teachers and running the Public School Teachers Association from 1924 to 1943.[217] There were, of course, other positions from which to challenge the limitations of gender. Mrs. Bridget Peixotto must have been such an influence even before becoming a principal in New York City in 1918; she had earlier brought successful action against school authorities for denying her maternity leave after 18 years of teaching.[218]

In a 1937 commentary on the preference for male administrators based on "a male prerogative" and "age-old hereditary rights," it was suggested that women redress the wrong, "not by angry protests and acidulous satire"—which evidently they were using—"but by fitting themselves to the extent of their capacity for the exercise of administrative responsibility, and by aquitting themselves in such positions as do fall to their lot not merely well enough but with outstanding success."[219] This was yet another example of the requirement set on the ambitious woman: that she had "better be better"![220]

Although college women led their own student organizations, and women officers presided over associations specific to women teachers, their sex was not expected to take leadership of mixed sex groups. As long as they did not try, the relations between the sexes were usually cordial, if distant.[221] The elementary school, being a world of women and children, gave many women the principalship before 1940. "We've never felt dominated or inferior in the elementary field," one woman teacher said of her teaching experiences, which began that year.[222] To ultraconservatives, however, the ability of the woman to gain economic independence through teaching was a fearsome challenge to patriarchy, best contained by recruiting more men teachers and by keeping all school management in their hands. The "lady teacher" who aspired to leave the classroom for the administrator's office or the presidency of a teachers' association was like the "rampant women" who worked in women's rights crusades: "unsexed women, unsexed in mind, all of them publicly propounding the doctrine that they should be allowed to step out of their appropriate sphere to the neglect of those duties which both human and divine law have assigned them."[223]

According to anthropologist Michelle Rosaldo, women's biological and cultural association with childrearing persistently denies them the "rituals of authority." "Only when she is old and free of the responsibility of children, when she is dissociated from childrearing and also from sexuality, can a woman build up the respect that comes with authority."[224] This attitude might explain why an activity might be managed by women until such time as it becomes important enough to be turned over to men. One of three sisters educated at Oberlin, all spinster teachers in the black schools of the District of Columbia, Mary Jane Patterson became principal in 1870 of the predecessor institution to now-famed Dunbar High School. After the school grew in numbers and reputation under her charge, the Board of Education assigned a male principal, and she returned to teaching.[225] The fact that she had no family responsibilities of her own was irrelevant; the important thing was that she was "woman."

Conclusion

Is the farmer—"small and slight, no longer young, who ran a farm, but had taught the winter term of school in his district year after year, because he had the gift of 'keeping order' "—a career teacher, a professional teacher?[226] If applied historically, conventional social science theory makes many men into noncareerists, since teaching has always been (as far as we can tell) an occupation that commonly has been episodic: an activity to which one returns given the need, the desire, the opportunity. Evaluating career or work commitment as "continuous upward movement through occupational stages" certainly does not work for women, argues sociologist Sari Biklen; women's career commitment has to be understood differently. It must reject as the sole definition for career and profession the expectations and experiences that have characterized most men's work lives, and reframe the issues by considering women workers' own perceptions.[227] The presence of what Jane Addams called "the family claim" requires not mere acknowledgment or apology, but reconceptualization in history and sociology.

"Teacher" is not a strictly "professional" role existing apart from family metaphors, try as the organizations of teachers and teacher–leaders did to create distance and distinction between the institutions of school and family. For uncounted centuries, institutions of education have operated *in loco parentis,* a principle recognized in both law and practice. Teachers function as surrogate parents in their relations to the pupil. A possible danger of the particular "maternalizing" of teaching associated with the campaign to attract women to teaching is its corollary expectation of identifying with one's pupils. Steedman asks if it is not often hard for some teachers "to make the prescribed act of identification and empathy with working-class children, children so very unlike themselves and those children they might possibly have one day?"[228]

School officials have themselves acted "parentally," seeking to protect, in a quasi-family way, the "innocence" and reputation of men and women teachers by all manners of rules governing their personal behavior (and by limiting their adulthood). But teaching is related to "family" in yet other senses. Whether public or private, schools represented an important local industry, and whatever restricted access to teaching jobs was strongly resisted. It might be higher professional standards that raised opportunity costs for local sons and daughters. This might be the married woman who wanted to continue teaching, thus depriving others of "their chance." Conversely, it might be official sentiment or policy pitted against married women teachers with well-connected local supporters. It might be the interests of one set of families against those of others. Polly Kaufman's study of the Boston School Committee records Irish protests at hiring the graduates of elite (Yankee) women's colleges instead of the Irish women who were, by 1900, about one-third of the products of the Boston Normal School. "Boston Schools for Boston Girls" was the rallying cry of the Irish faction.

For much of recorded history the prevailing image of the teacher was that of the stern, strict, authoritative "father"—although not all teachers ever functioned in that way, of course. Since the Enlightenment a powerful alternative image has been that of the loving, compassionate "mother." It is less a matter of one replacing the other than of their coexisting, creating a tension within teaching.[229] This fact may help explain some of the sharp swings over the past two centuries in the pendulum of public and expert opinion about pedagogy, curriculum, discipline, and the appropriate classroom atmosphere. In the last analysis these gendered roles may be a more important subject for the historian, sociologist, or epistemologist to unravel, than is the task of determining any effects of teachers' biological sex on the position of teachers and schools in society. "Feminization" or "masculinization" of the teaching profession is a woefully inadequate concept—either for purposes of historical analysis or for policy formation—if it means simply women's coming into numerical dominance in the teacher work force, or their losing something of that advantage to the male sex (as happened when men seized control of school administration, or increased their presence among teachers, after World War II).

Finally, as this chapter has sought to show, the inner, subjective meaning of family varies importantly according to the sex of the teacher. Teaching represented, for both sexes, "alienated work" in the sense of its chronic underpayment in income and prestige. It also was personally problematic in those cases where men were not able to differentiate their roles in education from those of women teachers and, therefore, experienced or feared effeminization. Nonetheless, the "career" did not alienate the man from his socially prescribed role as a man. The professional values of paid work, authority, objectivity, expertise, promotion, and deference from clients did function to enhance the male teacher's stature as independent adult, head of household, "man of the family." In most circumstances marriage was either irrelevant, or a perceived advantage, to the man. It justified, for example, more salary and power for him than the woman teacher, married *or* single, could assert; her claims rested on the grounds of civil rights, these *still* not yet fully granted in the court of public opinion.

In the case of women teachers, moreover, in society's eyes "career" and "professionalization" inevitably meant some degree of denial and alienation from prescribed devotion to the private world of home and family—which was, after all, the historical justification for the education of girls, and the employment of women as teachers. Because of family claims, the permanently single woman could not altogether escape the image of deviancy, dryness, unmet needs (no matter if, to schoolchildren and townspeople, she was the only independent woman they knew who owned a Model T or had been to Europe on a summer vacation). Because of family, and like other middle-class married women workers, the married teacher had to fight for the right to work, and then to defend herself from the twin charges of caring too little for her own family and neglecting her pupils. Woman's trained competence and personal ambition, valued in man, were suspect for being "unnatural," dysgenic, and ultimately antisocial.

Much about the effects of gender on teaching and schools remains unknown merely speculative at best. Important issues concerning schools' history appear to transcend teacher sex altogether—although gender may be seized upon to explain matters, like teacher prestige, that apparently have their root problems elsewhere Yet the cultural constructs of gender still have a manifestly tyrannical force. I writing about the semiprofessions, for example, Ida and Richard Simpson charac terize women as "relatively unambitious. . . . more interested in giving persona service to clients than in technical mastery of skills or in professional prerogatives to define how their skills will be put to use.''[230] Both sexes—and society—suffer from such thinking if, in the service profession of teaching, gender stereotypes make *her* attention to service ''unprofessional'' and *his* ''unmanly.''

Notes

AUTHOR'S NOTE: The author thanks Carol Page, her secretary, for help in preparing the manuscript.

1. Oliver Johnson, ''A Home in the Woods: Reminiscences of Early Marion County'' (As Related to Howard Johnson), *Indiana Historical Society Publications* 16:2 (1951), p. 175.
2. Clifton Landon Hall, ''Some Historical Considerations of the Status of the Teacher,'' doctoral dissertation, University of North Carolina, 1949.
3. Kathleen Lois Barry, ''Social Origins of the Nineteenth Century American Feminist Movement,'' doctoral dissertation, University of California at Berkeley, 1982, pp. 33 and 34. As Seminary and College, Mount Holyoke was a prolific producer of teachers like Mary Perkins. Until the 1980s, the largest number of its graduates who entered professions became teachers.
4. Arthur Foff, ''Scholars and Scapegoats,'' in *English Journal* 47 (1958), p. 120.
5. ''The Crisis in the New York City Schools,'' *New York Sun* (n.d.), reprinted in ''Quotations,'' in *School and Society* 11:267 (February 7, 1920), p. 175.
6. The quotation is from Adele Simmons, ''Education and Ideology in Nineteenth-Century America: The Response of Educational Institutions to the Changing Role of Women,'' in Berenice A. Carroll, *Liberating Women's History* (Urbana: University of Illinois Press, 1976), pp. 123–124. The standard view on the essentially ''conservative'' nature of the emerging women's professions is expressed in Jill K. Conway, ''Perspectives on the History of Women's Education in the United States,'' in *History of Education Quarterly* 14 (Spring 1974), pp. 1–12. The most important exception to feminist dismissals of teaching careers is Florence Howe. See her *Women and the Power to Change* (New York: McGraw–Hill, 1975). For a general review see Geraldine Jonçich Clifford, ''Women's Liberation and Women's Professions: Reconsidering the Past, Present, and Future,'' in John Mack Faragher and Florence Howe (eds.), *Women and Higher Education in American History* (New York: Norton, 1988).
7. Sandra Acker, ''Gender Divisions and Teachers' Careers,'' paper delivered at the Third International Interdisciplinary Congress on Women's Studies, Dublin, Ireland, July 1987.
8. Michelle Zimbalist Rosaldo, ''A Theoretical Overview,'' in Michelle Zimbalist Rosaldo and Louise Lamphere (eds.), *Woman, Culture, and Society* (Stanford, CA: Stanford University Press, 1974), especially pp. 19–23.
9. Michael Apple, ''Work, Gender, and Teaching,'' in *Teachers College Record* 84 (1983), pp. 611–628; and Nancy J. Hoffman, ''Feminist Scholarship and Women's Studies,'' in *Harvard Educational Review* 56 (1986), pp. 551–591. There is much for historians of gender to ponder in R. Laurence Moore, ''Insiders and Outsiders in American Historical Narrative and American History,'' in *American Historical Review* 87:2 (April 1982), pp. 390–412. In February 1982, with the assistance of Lana Muraskin of the National Institute of Education, David Tyack convened a Conference on Gender in the Historiography of Education at Stanford University; to add gender to the agenda of educational research and reduce the lag between it and women's studies and gender studies.

10. John Rury, "Education in the New Women's History," in *Educational Studies* 17:1 (Spring 1986), p. 8.

11. Men were 10 percent of elementary teachers in 1930 and 17 percent in 1980. Michael Sedlak and Steven Schlossman, *Who Will Teach? Historical Perspectives on the Changing Appeal of Teaching as a Profession* (Santa Monica: Rand Corporation, 1986); and Lois Scharf, *To Work and to Wed: Female Employment, Feminism, and the Great Depression* (Westport, CT: Greenwood Press, 1980). The best sources of national statistics are the decennial *Census[es]* of the United States and the *Biennial Surveys of Education in the United States* (Washington, DC: Government Printing Office) and the occasional publications of the National Education Association, such as *Status of the Teaching Profession,* Research Bullletin, Vol. 18 (Washington, DC: National Education Association, March 1940). There are discrepancies in the sources, however, and where these exist I have used those in Leo M. Chamberlain and Leonard E. Meece, "Men and Women in the Teaching Profession," in Bureau of School Service, College of Education, University of Kentucky, *Bulletin* 9, No. 3 (March 1937). See also John G. Richardson and Brenda Wooden Hatcher, "The Feminization of Public School Teaching, 1870–1920," in *Work and Occupations* 10:1 (February 1983), pp. 81–99.

12. Alice Duffy Rinehart, *Mortals in the Immortal Profession: An Oral History of Teaching* (New York: Irvington, 1983), p. 69.

13. Patricia A. Schmuck, "Women School Employees in the United States," in Patricia A. Schmuck (ed.), *Women Educators: Employees of Schools in Western Countries* (Albany: State University of New York Press, 1987), pp. 76–81.

14. Richard M. Bernard and Maris A. Vinovskis, "The Female School Teacher in Ante-Bellum Massachusetts," in *Journal of Social History* 10 (Spring 1977), pp. 332–345. Although its inadequacies are now clear, there is a great deal of useful information in Willard S. Elsbree, *The American Teacher: Evolution of a Profession in a Democracy* (New York: American Book Co., 1939).

15. David B. Tyack and Myra H. Strober, "Jobs and Gender: A History of the Structuring of Educational Employment by Sex," in Patricia A. Schmuck, W. W. Charters, Jr., and Richard O. Carlson (eds.), *Educational Policy and Management: Sex Differentials* (New York: Academic Press, 1981), p. 133.

16. Chamberlain and Meece, "Men and Women," p. 11.

17. The German immigrant populations of these cities in 1870 were Cincinnati (23 percent), St. Louis (19 percent), Milwaukee (30 percent), and Chicago (19 percent). In Leonard Dinnerstein and R. M. Reimers, *Ethnic Americans* (New York: Harper & Row, 1975), p. 29.

18. Anonymous, "The Schoolmistress," in *Harper's New Monthly Magazine* 57 (September 1878), p. 610.

19. The proportion of men teachers in foreign elementary schools in 1933 ranged from 92.5 percent in China to 10.2 percent in Uruguay. Among secondary-school teachers the range was from China's 92.7 percent to Ireland's 48.1 percent. In Chamberlain and Meece, "Men and Women," pp. 13–17. For comparisons between England and the United States see Michael Apple, "Teaching and 'Women's Work': A Comparative Historical and Ideological Analysis," in *Teachers College Record* 86:3 (Spring 1985), pp. 455–473.

20. Cited in John Rury, "Women at School: The Feminization of American High Schools, 1870–1900," paper delivered at History of Education Society, Columbia University, November 1987, p. 28.

21. Hasia R. Diner, *Erin's Daughters in America: Irish Immigrant Women in the Nineteenth Century* (Baltimore: Johns Hopkins University Press, 1983), p. 97

22. Catherine Clinton, *The Other Civil War American Women in the Nineteenth Century* (New York: Hill & Wang 1984), pp. 128–129.

23. Paul H. Mattingly, *The Classless Profession: American Schoolmen in the Nineteenth Century* (New York: New

York University Press, 1975), pp. 164–165 and 212; and Bernard and Vinovskis, "The Female School Teacher," pp. 334–335.

24. Linda L. Clark, *Schooling the Daughters of Marianne: Textbooks and the Socialization of Girls in Modern French Primary Schools* (Albany: State University of New York Press, 1984), p. 17.

25. William Harold Hermann, "The Rise of the Public Normal School System in Wisconsin," doctoral dissertation, University of Wisconsin, 1953, p. 373.

26. Mary Peabody Mann, *Life of Horace Mann* (Boston: Lee & Shepard, 1904), pp. 424–425.

27. Bailey B. Burritt, "Professional Distribution of College and University Graduates," in U.S. Bureau of Education, *Bulletin* No. 19 (Washington, DC: Government Printing Office, 1912), pp. 74–77.

28. For the general position toward females in these male bastions of the education profession see David Tyack and Elisabeth Hansot, *Managers of Virtue: Public School Leadership in America, 1820–1980* (New York: Basic Books, 1982), pp. 180–200; and Geraldine Jonçich Clifford and James W. Guthrie, *Ed School: A Brief for Professional Education* (Chicago: University of Chicago Press, 1988).

29. C. W. Bardeen, "Why Teaching Repels Men," in *Educational Review* 35 (April 1908), pp. 351–358. Direct mention of male discomfiture at being found in a "woman's profession" was not reported in this informal piece of "research."

30. Jacqueline Jones, *Soldiers of Light and Love: Northern Teachers and Georgia Blacks* (Chapel Hill: University of North Carolina Press, 1980); and Polly Welts Kaufman, *Women Teachers on the Frontier* (New Haven, CT: Yale University Press, 1984).

31. Persis Hunt, "The New Consciousness Among Teachers in France, 1881–1905," paper delivered at the American Historical Association, New Orleans, 19 December 1972; and Laurence Erwin Block, "The History of the Public School Teachers Association of Baltimore City: A Study of the Internal Politics of Education," doctoral dissertation, Johns Hopkins University, 1972.

32. Robert Emerson Treacy, "Progressivism and Corinne Seeds: UCLA and the University Elementary School," doctoral dissertation, University of Wisconsin, 1972. See also Clifford and Guthrie, *Ed School,* Ch. 7.

33. I am, for example, continuing to extract from a large body of nineteenth-century autobiographical writings on education those that deal with the experiences and consciousness of teachers. These materials, many of them the unpublished writings of ordinary Americans, will be the core of a book, *"Those Good Gertrudes": The Woman Teacher in America* (forthcoming).

34. Kathryn Kish Sklar, *Catharine Beecher: A Study in American Domesticity* (New Haven: Yale University Press, 1973).

35. Pamela Claire Hronek, "Women and Normal Schools: Tempe Normal, A Case Study, 1885–1925," doctoral dissertation, Arizona State University, 1985, pp. 53–55.

36. Alonzo Potter and George B. Emerson, *The School and the Schoolmaster, A Manual in Two Parts* (New York: Herper & Brothers, 1842), Part I, p. 204.

37. In France the wish of the Republic to laicize the girls schools taught by Catholic religious orders spurred the movement of secular women into primary-school teaching. This drive was evident by the 1870s and virtually complete by 1900, as women teachers became numerous in both girls and boys schools, in rural and urban areas. In the former year nuns (7,257) outnumbered lay *institutrices* (4,394) but not male teachers (36,437). In 1906 the numbers were 788 nuns, 56,948 *institutrices,* and 57,771 *instituteurs,* and by World War I, lay women outnumbered male colleagues and were teaching in all kinds of schools. Peter V. Meyers, "From Conflict to Cooperation: Men and Women Teachers in the Belle Epoque," in Donald N. Baker and Patrick J. Harrigan (eds.), *The Making of Frenchmen* (Waterloo, Ontario: Historical Reflections Press, 1980), pp. 494–495.

38. Department of Public Schools, City and County of San Francisco, *Twenty-Seventh Annual Report of the Superintendent of Public Schools for the School Year Ending June 30, 1880* (San Francisco: W. W. Hinton, 1880), p. 419.

39. For an good delienation of the social factors spurring high-school growth and change, see Robert L. Church and Michael W. Sedlak, *Education in the United States, An Interpretive History* (New York: Free Press, 1976), pp. 288–315.

40. Europe reached the point of having 30 percent of the age group in secondary schools only in the 1960s, 40 years after the United States. A. J. Heidenheimer, "The Politics of Public Education, Health and Welfare in the U.S.A. and Western Europe: How Growth and Reform Potentals Have Differed," in *British Journal of Political Science* 3 (1973), p. 320.

41. As John Rury points out, without female students it would have been impossible to maintain high schools in many places. In "Women at School," p. 42.

42. In the decade 1881–1890, over 5.2 million immigrants entered the United States, compared to 2.8 million in the previous decade. By 1930, 27.6 million "new" immigrants had arrived and were being "Americanized."

43. "Insofar as men, in their institutionalized relations of kinship, politics, and so on, define the public order, women are their opposite. Where men are classified in terms of ranked, institutional positions, women are simply women and their activities, interests, and differences receive only idiosyncratic note." In Rosaldo, "Theoretical Overview," p. 31.

44. William L. Felter, "The Education of Women," in *Educational Review* 31 (1906), pp. 354–355.

45. Nancy Hoffman, *Woman's "True" Profession: Voices from the History of Teaching* (New York: Feminist Press, 1981), pp. xxii.

46. Sandra Acker, "Women and Teaching: A Semi-Detached Sociology of a Semi-Profession," in Stephen Walker and Len Barton (eds.), *Gender, Class, and Education* (Sussex, England: Falmer Press, 1983), pp. 123–124.

47. Chase Going Woodhouse, "Married College Women in Business and the Professions," in *Annals of the American Academy of Political and Social Science* 143:232 (May 1929), p. 335.

48. Ruth H. Bloch, "American Feminine Ideals in Transition: The Rise of the Moral Mother, 1785–1815," in *Feminist Studies* 4:1 (February 1978), pp. 113–114. Only childbearing, breast-feeding, and the rudiments of the child's earliest training had been "uniquely maternal obligations" (p. 107).

49. Alison Prentice, "Education and the Metaphor of the Family: The Upper Canadian Example," in *History of Education Quarterly* 12:3 (Fall 1972), p. 287.

50. Lee Virginia Chambers-Schiller, *Liberty, A Better Husband: Single Women in America: The Generations of 1780–1840* (New Haven: Yale University Press, 1984), p. 32.

51. This point expands upon the conclusion that Southern women were less available to teach because of their greater involvement in domestic industries. See Myra H. Strober and Audri Gordon Lanford, "The Feminization of Public School Teaching: Cross-sectional Analysis, 1850–1880," in *Signs: Journal of Women in Culture and Society* 11:2 (1986), p. 217.

52. Miriam Davis Colt, *Went to Kansas, Being a Thrilling Account of an Ill-Fated Expedition* (Watertown, NY: L. Ingalls; Ann Arbor, MI: University Microfilms, 1966), p. 236.

53. Catherine Brody, "A New York Childhood," in *American Mercury* 14:53 (May 1928), p. 62.

54. Courtney Ann Vaughn-Roberson, "Sometimes Independent But No[t] Equal: Women Educators, 1900–1950 The Oklahoma Example," in *Pacifi[c] Historical Review* 53 (February 1984) p. 45.

55. Amelia Akehurst Lines, in Thomas Dye[r] (ed.), *"To Raise Myself a Little" The Diaries and Letters of Jennie, [a] Georgia Teacher, 1851–1886* (Athens

University of Georgia Press, 1982), p. 178.

56. "Men Teachers in Girls' Schools," in *Journal of Education* 74:20 (November 23, 1911), p. 546.

57. Joseph King Van Denburg, *Causes of the Elimination of Students in Public Secondary Schools of New York City* (New York: Teachers College, 1911), p. 56.

58. Among the teachers interviewed by Rinehart, over half reported teachers among their direct relations, in one case over four generations. Her reporting of the data does not permit comparisons between male and female teachers. In *Mortals in the Immortal Profession,* p. 20.

59. In speaking of the schoolroom as a locus of female power, along with the home, Tentler states that the female teacher "was usually too remote by virtue of her middle-class values and behavior to provide a role model for any but the daughters of upwardly-mobile working-class families." This may underestimate the influence of the many working-class teachers in American towns and cities even before 1900. Leslie Woodcock Tentler, *Wage-Earning Women: Industrial Work and Family Life in the United States, 1900–1930* (New York: Oxford University Press, 1979), pp. 81–82.

60. Carl Degler, *At Odds: Women and the Family in America, from the Revolution to the Present* (New York: Oxford University Press, 1980), p. 181. See also Rudy Ray Seward, *The American Family: A Demographic History* (Beverly Hills, CA: Sage Publications, 1987); Tamara K. Hareven and Maris A. Vinovskis (eds.), *Family and Population in Nineteenth-Century America* (Princeton, NJ: Princeton University Press, 1978); Robert V. Wells, "Demographic Change and the Life Cycle of American Families," in Theodore K. Rabb and Robert I. Rotberg, *Families in History* (New York: Harper & Row, 1973); Richard A. Easterlin, "Factors in the Decline of Farm Family Fertility in the United States: Some Preliminary Research Results," in *Journal of American History* 63:3 (December 1977), pp. 600–614; and Nancy Osterud and John Fulton, "Family Limitation and Age of Marriage in Sturbridge, Massachusetts, 1730–1850," in *Population Studies* 30:3 (November 1976), p. 483.

61. Peter R. Uhlenberg, "A Study of Cohort Life Cycles: Cohorts of Native Born Massachusetts Women, 1830–1920," in *Population Studies* 23:3 (November 1969), p. 409; and John Moddell, Frank Furstenburg, and Theodore Hershberg, "Social Change and the Transition to Adulthood in Historical Perspective," in *Journal of Family History* 1 (1976), pp. 7–32.

62. Lines, *"To Raise Myself a Little,"* pp. 184–185.

63. Mary Livermore, *The Story of My Life* (Hartford, CT: A. D. Worthington, 1897), p. 493.

64. Chambers-Schiller, *Liberty, a Better Husband,* p. 7.

65. Kathleen Underwood, "The Pace of Their Own Lives: Teacher Training and the Life Course of Western Women," in *Pacific Historical Review* 55:4 (November 1986), pp. 527 and 529.

66. Hronek, "Women and Normal Schools," p. 92.

67. Debra Herman, "College and After: The Vassar Experiment in Women's Education, 1861–1924," doctoral dissertation, Stanford University, 1979), pp. 28–29.

68. Ibid., p. 286.

69. Geraldine Jonçich Clifford, " 'Shaking Dangerous Questions from the Crease': Gender and American Higher Education," in *Feminist Issues* 3:2 (Fall 1983), p. 44.

70. Clinton, *The Other Civil War,* p. 131.

71. Edward L. Thorndike, *Education, A First Book* (New York: Macmillan, 1912), pp. 154 and 159–160. French fears of depopulation and its military consequences, given Germany's higher birth rate, caused textbooks to stress to boys and girls the virtues of large families, and schools emphasized domestic values and skills in girls' schooling. In Clark, *Schooling the Daughters of Marianne*, p. 106.

72. W. C. McGinnis, "The Married Woman Teacher," in *School Execu-*

tives Magazine 50 (June 1931), pp. 451–453.

73. David Wilbur Peters, *The Status of the Married Woman Teacher,* Teachers College, Columbia University Contributions to Education, No. 603 (New York: Teachers College, 1934), p. 52.

74. Susan B. Carter and Mark Prus, "The Labor Market and the American High School Girl, 1890–1928," in *Journal of Economic History* 62:1 (March 1982), pp. 163–171.

75. Allis Rosenberg Wolfe (ed.), "Letters of a Lowell Mill Girl and Friends, 1845–46," in *Labor History* 17:1 (Winter 1976), pp. 96–102.

76. Frances R. Donovan, *The Schoolma'am* (New York: Frederick A. Stokes, 1938), p. 7.

77. Rosa Schreurs Jennings, "The Country Teacher," in *Annals of Iowa* 31:1 (July 1951), p. 41.

78. Joan Grace Zimmerman, "College Culture in the Midwest, 1890–1930," doctoral dissertation, University of Virginia, 1978), p. 177.

79. Joyce Antler, *Lucy Sprague Mitchell: The Making of a Modern Woman* (New Haven, CT: Yale University Press, 1987).

80. Barbara Welter, "She Hath Done What She Could: Protestant Women's Missionary Careers in Nineteenth-Century America," in *American Quarterly* 30:5 (Winter 1978), p. 624.

81. Willystine Goodsell (ed.), *Pioneers of Women's Education in the United States: Emma Willard, Catharine Beecher and Mary Lyon* (New York: McGraw–Hill, 1931).

82. Catharine Beecher, *The Duty of American Women to Their Country* (New York: Harper & Bros., 1845), p. 63.

83. Thorndike, *Education. A First Book,* pp. 155–156.

84. A positive statistical relationship has been found between the level of women in teaching and the percent of the male labor force in nonagricultural work. In Richardson and Hatcher, "Feminization of Public School Teaching," p. 93.

85. George L. Farmakis, "The Role of the American Teacher: An Historical View Through Readings," doctoral dissertation, Wayne State University, 1971, pp. 324–325.

86. Leonard E. Meece, "Negro Education in Kentucky: A Comparative Study of White and Negro Education on the Elementary and Secondary School Levels," in Bureau of School Service, College of Education, University of Kentucky *Bulletin* 10, No. 3 (March 1938), p. 123.

87. Sharon Harley, "Beyond the Classroom: The Organizational Lives of Black Female Educators in the District of Columbia, 1890–1930," in *Journal of Negro Education* 51:3 (Summer 1982), pp. 254–265.

88. Herman, "College and After," p. 240.

89. In comparing the rising literacy rate among men of all social classes in colonial New England with the stagnant rates of women, Lockridge speculates that outright discrimination against the schooling of females may have been less important a factor than that only men were driven to use schools by a rising need for literacy due to commercial and urban pressures. Kenneth Lockridge, *Literacy in Colonial New England* (New York: W. W. Norton, 1974).

90. See Linda Kerber, *Women of the Republic: Intellect and Ideology in Revolutionary America* (Chapel Hill: University of North Carolina Press, 1980); Mary Beth Norton, *Liberty's Daughters'': The Revolutionary Experience of American Women, 1780–1800* (Boston: Little, Brown, 1980); and Clinton, *The Other Civil War.*

91. Herrmann, "Rise of the Public Normal School," p. 405.

92. Rinehart, *Mortals in the Immortal Profession,* p. 112.

93. Woodhouse, "Married College Women," p. 328.

94. James Fleming Hosic, "The Democratization of Supervision," in *School and Society* 11:273 (March 20, 1920), p. 332.

95. Michael V. O'Shea, "Dominant Educational Interests at the Cleveland Meeting," in *School and Society* 11:27 (March 27, 1920), p. 384.

96. The same thing happened in England. For the views of women teachers during wartime see Martin Lawn, "What Is the Teacher's Job? Work and Welfare in Elementary Teaching, 1940–1945," in Martin Lawn and Gerald Grace (eds.), *Teachers: The Culture and Politics of Work* (Sussex, England: Falmer Press, 1987), pp. 50–64.
97. With women outside of their proverbial place, "The female role was being stretched in a painful tug of war between behavior and attitudes." In Peter Gabriel Filene, *Him/Her/Self: Sex Roles in Modern America* (New York: Harcourt Brace Jovanovich, 1974), p. 188.
98. Farmakis, "Role of the American Teacher," p. 646; and Tyack and Strober, "Jobs and Gender," pp. 146–148.
99. "Eased entry" is the concept Lortie coined to describe the spread of free or low-cost, accessible, and nonselective teacher-education institutions in the United States. Such institutions represented partial compensation for the low wages and uncertain status of teaching. In Dan C. Lortie, *Schoolteacher: A Sociological Study* (Chicago: University of Chicago Press, 1975).
100. Thomas Morain, "The Departure of Males from the Teaching Profession in Nineteenth-Century Iowa," in *Civil War History* 26:2 (June 1980), pp. 161–170.
101. Teaching and librarianship were the same in this regard. John B. Parrish, "Women in Professional Teaching," in *Monthly Labor Review* 97 (May 1974), pp. 34–38.
102. Carter and Prus, "Labor Market," p. 165; and Heidenheimer, "Politics of Public Education," p. 321.
103. Sheila Rothman, *Woman's Proper Sphere: A History of Changing Ideals and Practices* (New York: Basic Books, 1978), p. 58.
104. Zimmerman, "College Culture," p. 199; Joan G. Zimmerman, "Daughters of Main Street: Culture and the Female Community at Grinnel, 1884–1917," in Mary Kelley (ed.), *Woman's Being, Woman's Place: Female Identity and Vocation in American History* (Boston: G. K. Hall, 1979), p. 157; Herman, "College and After," p. 234; and Helen Olin, *The Women of a State University* (New York: G. P. Putnam's Sons, 1909), p. 194.
105. Herman, "College and After," p. 249; and Cynthia Horsburgh Requardt, "Alternative Professions for Goucher College Graduates, 1892–1910," in *Maryland Historical Magazine* 74:3 (September 1979), pp. 274–281.
106. See, for example, Richard A. Quantz, "The Complex Visions of Female Teachers and the Failure of Unionization in the 1930s: An Oral History," in *History of Education Quarterly* 25:4 (Winter 1985), pp. 439–458.
107. Clyde Emerson DeBourg, "A Study of Roles for the Teacher From an Historical Perspective," doctoral dissertation, Michigan State University, 1980, p. 127; and Ronald G. Corwin, "The New Teaching Profession," in Kevin Ryan (ed.), *Teacher Education*, National Society for the Study of Education, 74th Yearbook, Part II (Chicago: University of Chicago Press, 1975), p. 230.
108. Clifford, "Shaking Dangerous Questions," pp. 40–54.
109. Price, "An Historical Analysis," p. 100.
110. Mattingly, *Classless Profession*, p. 21.
111. Anita Louise White, "The Teacher in Texas: 1836–1879," doctoral dissertation, Baylor University, 1972, pp. 95 and 153.
112. Foff, "Scholars and Scapegoats," p. 123.
113. Committee of Phi Delta Kappa, Edwin A. Lee, Chairman, *Teaching as a Man's Job* (Homewood, IL: Phi Delta Kappa, 1938). The 1963 version was published as *Teaching as a Career for a Man*. Publication figures are from Stanley Elam to William R. Riggle, August 13, 1980; letter courtesy of Dr. Riggle.
114. Colt, *Went to Kansas*, p. 274.
115. Henry Seidel Canby, *Alma Mater: The Gothic Age of the American College*

(New York: Farrar & Rinehart, 1936), p. 101.

116. Farmakis, "Role of the American Teacher," p. 354.

117. Block, "Public School Teachers Association," p. 186.

118. H. Warren Button and Eugene Provenzo, Jr., *History of Education and Culture in America* (Englewood Cliffs, NJ: Prentice–Hall, 1983), pp. 86–88.

119. E. E. Schwarztrauber, "The Teacher Orients Himself," in *The American Teacher* 16:3 (December 1931), pp. 18–19 and 30.

120. Anthropologist Sarah Lawrence Lightfoot argues that the cultural roles of both mothers and teachers have a "demeaning and negative caste." See "The Other Woman: Mothers and Teachers," in *Worlds Apart: Relationships Between Families and Schools* (New York: Basic Books, 1978), pp. 43–82.

121. Elijah Fletcher, *The Letters of Elijah Fletcher,* ed. Martha von Briesen (Charlottesville: University Press of Virginia, 1965), p. 16.

122. District of Columbia, Board of Education, *Annual Report of the Trustees of the Public Schools,* September 1, 1860, p. 8.

123. Polly Welts Kaufman, "Boston Women and City School Politics, 1872–1905: Nurturers and Protectors in Public Education," doctoral dissertation, Boston University, 1978.

124. Herman, "College and After," pp. 237 and 238. The consequences of domestic feminism are treated in Al Patrick, Robert L. Griswold, and Courtney Ann Vaughn Roberson, "Domestic Ideology and the Teaching Profession: A Case Study from Oklahoma, 1930–1983," in *Issues in Education* 3:2 (Fall 1985), pp. 139–157; and Barbara Finkelstein, "The Revolt Against Selfishness: Women and the Dilemmas of Professionalism in Early Childhood Education," in Bernard Spodek, Olivia N. Saracho, and Donald L. Peters (eds.), *Professionalism and the Early Childhood Practitioner* (New York: Teachers College Press, 1988).

125. Sophie Freud Lowenstein, "The Passion and Challenge of Teaching," in *Harvard Educational Review* 50:1 (February 1980), p. 4.

126. Chambers-Schiller, *Liberty, a Better Husband,* p. 163. For a critique of traditional social science in its analysis of teaching see Patti Lather, "The Absent Presence: Patriarchy, Capitalism, and the Nature of Teacher Work," in *Teacher Education Quarterly* 14:2 (Spring 1987), pp. 25–38. In France the coeducational nursery schools were named *écoles maternelles.*

127. Donovan, *The Schoolma'am,* p. 13.

128. Sadie B. Smith, "A Holdrege High School Teacher, 1900–1905: The Letters of Sadie B. Smith," in *Nebraska History* 60 (Fall 1979), p. 392.

129. Judith Nessman Taylor, "The Struggle for Work and Love: Working Women in American Novels, 1890–1925," doctoral dissertation, University of California at Berkeley, 1977, p. 13.

130. Scharf, *To Work or to Wed,* Ch. 4. It is important to keep in mind the different interest of single and married women teachers. The former were, for example, more likely to teach in the upper grades and high schools, where salaries were higher. See Peters, "Status of the Married Woman Teacher," p. 19.

131. Pauline Annin Galvarro, "A Study of Certain Emotional Problems of Women Teachers," doctoral dissertation, Northwestern University, 1945.

132. Dorothy Yost Deegan, *The Stereotype of the Single Woman in American Novels* (New York: Octagon Books, 1969), pp. 61, 93, and 138.

133. Foff, "Scholars and Scapegoats," p. 124.

134. Mary Virginia Terhune (Marion Harland pseud.), *Eve's Daughters* (1882), quoted in Rothman, *Woman's Proper Sphere,* p. 58.

135. Sarah Josepha Hale, "Editorial," in *Godey's Lady's Book* (January 1853), pp. 176–177.

136. James Wallace Milden, "The Sacred Sanctuary: Family Life in Nineteenth-Century America," doctoral disserta-

tion, University of Maryland, 1974), p. 207; and Prentice, "Education and Metaphor," pp. 281–303.

137. Harper, "The School-Mistress," p. 607.

138. White, "Teacher in Texas," pp. 136–137.

139. James C. Boykin, "Women in the Public Schools," in *Educational Review* 18 (1899), p. 138.

140. Herman, "College and After," p. 250.

141. Block, "Public School Teachers' Association of Baltimore," pp. 195–197.

142. Millicent Rutherford, "Feminism and the Secondary School Curriculum, 1890–1920," doctoral dissertation, Stanford University, p. 98.

143. William W. Brickman, "Power Conflicts and Crises in Teacher Education: Some Historical and International Perspectives," in Ayres Bagley (ed.), *Responding to the Power Crisis in Teacher Education* (Washington, DC: Society of Professors of Education, 1971), p. 5; and Hall, "Some Historical Considerations," pp. 103, 146, 150, and 151.

144. Stephen W. Sellers, "Family Backgrounds and Social Origins of Schoolmasters: Massachusetts, 1635–1800," paper presented at the annual meeting of the American Educational Research Association, Los Angeles, April 1981, pp. 13–14.

145. Grant Allen, "Woman's Place in Nature," in *Forum* 7 (June 1889), p. 263.

146. This concern is the evident explanation for such ill-tempered and overdrawn analyses as Redding S. Sugg, Jr., *Motherteacher: The Feminization of American Education* (Charlottesville: University Press of Virginia, 1978), and Patricia Cayo Sexton, *The Feminized Male: Classrooms, White Collars and the Decline of Manliness* (New York: Vintage Books, 1969).

147. Families often concentrated their resources on their daughters so that they might be teachers. See E. Wilbur Bock, "Farmer's Daughter Effect: The Case of the Negro Female Professionals," *Phylon* 30:1 (Spring 1969), pp. 17–26; and Ellen Tarry, *The Third Door: The Autobiography of an American Negro Woman* (New York: Ellen Tarry, 1955), pp. 75–76.

148. Black school patrons were persuaded by teachers to supplement tax revenue with contributions that enabled their schools in the rural South to remain open beyond their usual short terms. Cited in Victor H. Cary, "The Roles of Black Women in Education, 1865–1917, a paper presented at the Workshop on Gender in the History of Education, Stanford University, February 1982, p. 12.

149. That communities were commonly averse to hiring trained teachers is well documented in Wayne E. Fuller, *The Old Country School: The Story of Rural Education in the Middle West* (Chicago: University of Chicago Press, 1982).

150. Kay Kamin, "The Woman Peril in American Public Schools: How Perilous?"—paper presented at the Third Berkshire Conference on the History of Women, Bryn Mawr College, Bryn Mawr, PA, June 1976.

151. Warren C. Hawthorne, "Enemies of the Public Schools," in *American Teacher* 19:3 (January–February 1935), p. 13.

152. Farmakis, "Role of the American Teacher," pp. 23 and 104.

153. Sellers, "Family Background," p. 19; and John L. Rury, "Gender, Salaries, and Career: American Teachers, 1900–1910," in *Issues in Education* 4:3 (Winter 1986), pp. 215–235.

154. The Puritan decline is associated with factors like the increasing religious heterogeneity of New England's population and the assault on orthodoxy by the Great Awakening and the spread of evangelical influences. In Sellers, "Family Backgrounds," pp. 24–25.

155. See the survey of the research on the social origins of teachers in Sedlak and Schlossman, *Who Will Teach?*, pp. 29–35.

156. Arthur Meier Schlesinger, "Salmon Portland Chase, Undergraduate and Pedagogue" in *Ohio Archeological and Historical Society Publications* 28 (1919), p. 158.

157. Walt Whitman, *Brooklyn Evening Star,* October 22, 1845; and *Brooklyn Daily Eagle,* February 4, 1847. Quoted in Rebecca Ritchey Price, ''An Historical Analysis of the Concepts of Teacher in America Between the 1850s, 1930s and 1960s as Portrayed in the Writings of The Times,'' doctoral dissertation, Miami University, 1974, p. 31.
158. George Gerbner, ''Teacher Image and the Hidden Curriculum,'' in *The American Scholar* 42:1 (Winter 1972–1973), p. 91.
159. Schlesinger, ''Salmon Portland Chase,'' p. 155.
160. Albert Bushnell Hart, ''The Teacher as a Professional Expert,'' in *School Review* 1:1 (January 1893), p. 6.
161. Underwood, ''Their Own Lives,'' p. 528.
162. Smith, ''A Holdredge High School Teacher,'' p. 384.
163. The account is by Hermippus, in Hall, ''Some Historical Considerations,'' p. 152.
164. J. H. Kelley, ''Why High School Students of Ability Should Teach,'' in *School and Society* 11:276 (April 24, 1920), p. 505.
165. For a study of how contemporary Australian teachers exploit geographical mobility to enhance vertical mobility, and how family factors affect mobility decisions in both sexes, see Rupert D. I. Maclean, ''Career and Promotion Patterns of State School Teachers in Tasmania: A Sociological Analysis,'' doctoral dissertation, University of Tasmania, 1988, esp. pp. 365–366.
166. Donovan, *The Schoolma'am,* p. 198.
167. Mattingly, *The Classless Profession,* p. 106.
168. William A. Alcott, *Confessions of a Schoolmaster* (New York: Arno Press, 1969 [Rev. ed. of 1856]), p. 198.
169. Mount Holyoke College, Class of 1857, ''Report for 1905,'' typescript in College History Collection and Archives, Mount Holyoke College Library, South Hadley, MA.
170. Rinehart, *Mortals in the Immortal Profession,* p. 375; and Meece, ''Negro Education in Kentucky,'' pp. 100 and 123.
171. Academic qualifications were ignored, along with the efforts of state and county officials to impose new credential requirements. In Marguerite Renner, ''Who Will Teach? Changing Job Opportunity and Roles for Women in the Evolution of the Pittsburgh Public Schools, 1830–1900,'' doctoral dissertation, University of Pittsburgh, 1981, p. 146 *passim.*
172. This was true, at least, for Vassar women. In Herman, ''College and After,'' p. 274. I would contend it was widely the case, even in the years of the ''Cult of Single Blessedness.''
173. Paula S. Fass, ''The Female Paradox: Higher Education for Women, 1945–1963,'' in Paula S. Fass (ed.), *Outside In: Pluralism and the Transformation of American Education in the Twentieth Century* (New York: Oxford University Press, forthcoming).
174. The same criticism has been made of Ericksonian stages of ego development. See Erik Erickson, ''The Problem of Ego Identity,'' in *Psychological Issues* 1:1 (1959); pp. 101–164. Cf. J. B. Miller, *Toward a New Psychology of Women* (Boston: Beacon Press, 1976), and Neil J. Smelser and Erik Erickson (eds.), *Themes of Work and Love in Adulthood* (Cambridge, MA: Harvard University Press, 1980).
175. Milden, ''The Sacred Sanctuary,'' p. 65. Interviews with employed married women found that the foremost motivation for their working was to assist their husands in carrying the economic burden of raising family living standards. In Woodhouse, ''Married College Women,'' p. 328.
176. Sellers, ''Family Backgrounds,'' p 20.
177. Rinehart, *Mortals in the Immorta Profession,* pp. 21, 85, and 123.
178. Farmakis, ''Role of the America Teacher,'' pp. 24 and 30.
179. See, for example, William H. Issel ''Teachers and Educational Refor During the Progressive Era: A Cas Study of the Pittsburgh Teachers Ass

ciation," in *History of Education Quarterly* 7:2 (Summer 1967), pp. 223–224. It could be argued that this development reflects the greater presence in teaching of lower-status, working-class populations who viewed job security as paramount. There are more difficulties with this theory when considering women teachers.

180. Anonymous, "The School Mistress," p. 609.
181. Amy Morris Bradley to Mrs. Sarah Homans, March 25, 1849. Amy Morris Bradley Papers, Duke University Library, Durham, North Carolina. By permission.
182. Cary, "Roles of Black Women," p. 20. The deviation from rules in order to retain an individual was not uncommon. A single woman teacher told Galvarro in 1940 that she was due for promotion to a principalship because a successful woman principal had married; however, the Board decided to abandon its regulations against marriage in order to keep her. "Study of Emotional Problems," pp. 41–42.
183. In Rutherford, "Feminism and the Curriculum," pp. 17–18 and 102.
184. Herman, "College and After," p. 246.
185. Donovan, *The Schoolma'am*, p. 35.
186. Terpenning was professor of educational sociology at Kalamazoo State Teachers College. Quoted in Peters, "Status of the Married Woman Teacher," p. 33.
187. Sara Freedman, Jane Jackson, and Kathrine Boles, "The Effects of the Institutional Structure of Schools on Teachers" (Somerville, MA: Boston Women's Teachers' Group, September 1, 1982), p. 101; Rinehart, *Mortals in the Immortal Profession,* p. 178; and Galvarro, "Certain Emotional Problems," p. 526.
188. Luella Boelio Bower, in Delta Kappa Gamma of Michigan Collection (Box 2), Schlesinger Library, Radcliffe College, Cambridge, MA.
189. In 1900, married women were 4.5 percent of all women teachers, widows were 3 percent, and divorcees 0.5 percent. In 1930 there were 40,645 widows and divorced women among public school teachers. There were, in contrast, 660,754 single women teachers. In Rury, "Gender, Salaries and Career," p. 234, note 28, and Donovan, *The Schoolma'am,* pp. 33 and 73.
190. Margo Horn, " 'Sisters Worthy of Respect': Family Dynamics and Women's Roles in the Blackwell Family," in *Journal of Family History* 28 (Winter 1983), pp. 367–381.
191. Ida Harper Simpson and Richard L. Simpson, "Women and Bureaucracy in the Semi-Professions," in Amitai Etzioni (ed.), *The Semi-Professions and Their Organization* (New York: Free Press, 1969), p. 212; Freedman *et al.*, "Effects of Institutional Structure," p. 108. A study of women students in professional programs at Yale University in the 1960s found that 89 percent planned to work in their fields. Compared to the 91 percent of law and medical students, 35 percent of nursing and teaching students planned *not* to withdraw from their professions at some time during their careers. In Adeline Gordon Levine, "Marital and Occupational Plans of Women in Professional Schools: Law, Medicine, Nursing, Teaching," doctoral dissertation, Yale University, 1968, pp. 45, 52, and 62.
192. Freedman *et al.*, "Effects of Institutional Structure," pp. 107 and 108. A study of Dade County, Florida teachers in 1984 found that such "ancillary rewards" of teaching as a schedule allowing time for family and travel had increased in importance to teachers over a similar study 20 years before. In Robert B. Kottkamp, Eugene F. Provenzo, Jr., and Marilyn M. Cohn, "Stability and Change in a Profession: Two Decades of Teacher Attitudes, 1964–1984," in *Phi Delta Kappan* 67 (April 1986), p. 564.
193. Elsbree, *American Teacher,* p. 30.
194. Johnson, *A Home in the Woods,* p. 175.
195. *De Bows's Review* is cited in White, *The Teacher in Texas,* p. 96. See also pp. 80 and 164.
196. Quoted in Stanley Lebergott,

Manpower in Economic Growth: The American Record Since 1800 (New York: McGraw–Hill, 1964), p. 169.

197. Rinehart, *Mortals in the Immortal Profession,* p. 117.

198. Quoted in Carol Marie Roland, "The California Kindergarten Movement: A Study in Class and Social Feminism," doctoral dissertation, University of California, Riverside, 1980), p. 155.

199. Smith, "A Holdredge High School Teacher," p. 393.

200. See, for example, Anne Firor Scott, "Almira Lincoln Phelps: The Self-Made Woman in the Nineteenth Century," in *Maryland Historical Magazine* 73:3 (Fall 1980), pp. 203–216.

201. Schlesinger, "Salmon Portland Chase," pp. 124, 127, and 144.

202. Bardeen, "Why Teaching Repels Men," pp. 355 and 356.

203. In fact, she waited another two years to marry. Mary Jane Mudge, diary entry for October 11, 1854. Mudge Papers, Schlesinger Library, Radcliffe College, Cambridge, MA. By permission.

204. Milden, "The Sacred Sanctuary," p. 72; and Chambers-Schiller, *"Liberty, a Better Husband,"* p. 173.

205. Ibid., p. 66.

206. On Lydia Sigourney, see Emily Hahn, *Once Upon a Pedestal* (New York: Thomas Y. Crowell, 1974), pp. 145–146. See also Kaufman, *Women Teachers on the Frontier;* and Edward Everett Dale, "Teaching on the Prairie Plains, 1890–1900," in *Mississippi Valley Historical Review* 33:2 (September 1946), pp. 293–307.

207. J. M. Graybiel, "Tenure for Teachers a *Sine Qua Non* for the Welfare of the Public Schools," in *American Teacher* 16:6 (March 1932), p. 5.

208. Albert R. Kitzhaber, "Project English Curricululm Reform," in "The Project English Curriculum Studies: A Progress Report," in *Iowa English Year Book,* No. 9 (Fall 1964), p. 4.

209. Zimmerman, "College Culture," p. 220.

210. Henry Parks Wright, *The Young Man and Teaching* (New York: Macmillan, 1920), pp. 55–57.

211. Potter and Emerson, *The School and the Schoolmaster,* p. 208.

212. Susan B. Anthony and Ida Husted Harper (eds.), *The History of Woman Suffrage* 4 (Rochester, NY: Susan B. Anthony, 1902), p. 171.

213. See, for example, "Women as Teachers" (editorial) in *Educational Review* 2:4 (November 1891), pp. 358–363; A. F. Nightingale, "Ratio of Men to Women in the High Schools of the United States," *School Review* 4 (February 1896), pp. 86–98; Leonard P. Ayres, "What Educators Think About the Need for Employing Men Teachers in Our Public Schools," in *Journal of Educational Psychology* 2:1 (January 1911), pp. 89–93; F. E. Chadwick, "The Woman Peril in American Education," in *Educational Review* 47 (February 1914), pp. 109–119; and responses to Chadwick in subsequent issues.

214. When Isabella Graham, who had formed a girls' school to support her children, organized women volunteers to work in New York City to aid the unfortunate, she warned them, "You will experience much painful banter, you will be styled school madams. Let it pass. . . . Only be steadfast, draw not back and justify the prophecies of many." In Joanna B. Gillespie, "Clear Leadings of Providence: Pious Memoirs and the Problems of Self-Realization," in *Journal of the Early Republic* 5:2 (Summer 1985), p. 202.

215. "Pay no attention to what that teacher down there has said," William T. Harris replied dismissively when the male leadership of the National Education Association was challenged from the floor at its 1901 convention on the issue of teachers' salaries, "for I take it she is a grade teacher, just out of her school room at the end of school year, worn out, tired, and hysterical." The woman was Margaret Haley, head of the Chicago Teachers Union and teachers' first paid union organizer. Quoted in Tyack and Hansot, *Managers of Virtue,* p. 186.

216. Rutherford, "Feminism and the Curriculum," p. 63.
217. Block, "Public School Teachers Association," pp. 35–152.
218. In Erma Toomes Scarlette, "A Historical Study of Women in Public School Administration from 1900–1977," doctoral dissertation, University of North Carolina at Greensboro, 1979), p. 90; and Price, "The Married Woman Teacher," p. 39. Justice Seabury's reasoning was not, however, quite what some feminists might have wished: "The policy of our law favors marriage and the birth of children. . . ."
219. Chamberlain, "Men and Women," p. 33.
220. Women principals had, on average, three times more years of classroom teaching experience before becoming principals according to a 1968 study. For more on background factors, career lines, and assessments of job performance and style of male and female school administrators, see Neal Gross and Ann E. Trask, *The Sex Factor and the Management of Schools* (New York: Wiley, 1976). The rarity of men in infant and primary schools in England is the cause of their being quickly put forward for promotion. So, "Unlike women going into traditionally male professions, the men entering this traditionally female sector of education do not have to be twice as qualified, experienced, etc." In Jan Lee, "Pride and Prejudice: Teachers, Class and an Inner-City Infants School," in Martin Lawn and Gerald Grace (eds.), *Teachers: The Culture and Politics of Work* (Sussex, England: Falmer Press, 1987), p. 95.
221. For an account of rising tension between the sexes with rising numbers of women teachers in France, see Meyers, "From Conflict to Cooperation."
222. Rinehart, *Mortals in the Immortal Profession*, p. 322.
223. From a *New York Herald* editorial of 1853. Quoted in National American Woman Suffrage Association, *Victory, How Women Won It* (New York: H. W. Wilson Co., 1940), p. 35.
224. Rosaldo, "A Theoretical Overview," p. 28.
225. Ellen Henle [Lawson] and Marlene Merrill, "Antebellum Black Coeds at Oberlin College," in *Oberlin Alumni Magazine* (January–February 1980), p. 20.
226. Jennings, "The Country Teacher," p. 41.
227. Sari Knopp Biklen, "Can Elementary Schoolteaching Be a Career?: A Search for New Ways of Understanding Women's Work," in *Issues in Education* 3:3 (Winter 1985), pp. 215–231. See also the provocative Barbara Melosh, *The Physician's Hand: Work Culture and Conflict in American Nursing* (Philadelphia: Temple University Press, 1982).
228. Steedman, "Prisonhouses," p. 124.
229. Margaret Mead writes of the three images of the school in America: the Little Red School House, associated with the young woman teacher from the local community; the Academy, dominated by male presence, status, and values; and the City School, designed to wean immigrant children from foreign traditions. In *The School in American Culture* (Cambridge, MA: Harvard University Press, 1951).
230. Harper and Harper, "Women and Bureaucracy," p. 231; and Levin, "Marital and Occupational Plans," p. 73.

12

The History of Blacks in Teaching

Growth and Decline Within the Profession

Linda M. Perkins

The declining number of black teachers has become an increasing concern among education policy makers. It is a particularly troublesome development in light of the growing black student population in many urban school systems. Numerous articles have commented on causes and cures. Some argue that blacks are now shying away from the teaching profession, in part because of the difficulty many of them have in passing state examinations and in meeting other new certification standards. Others suggest that increased opportunities for blacks in more prestigious professions best explain the decline.[1]

Examination of the historical roles that teaching and teachers have played within the black community sheds considerable light on the issues raised in this debate. History is intricately interwoven with politics and the refusal of education for blacks in the South. The white South legally prohibited blacks from obtaining any type of education until Emancipation. Debate during the century following 1863 centered on whether blacks would be educated to challenge or to accommodate their oppressive educational, economic, and social conditions. James D. Anderson, an authority on the history of black education in the South, noted that by the early twentieth century the white South and Northern philanthropists were "interested in training an accommodationist black leadership that would encourage the masses to observe willingly the complicated system of Southern racial hierarchy."[2] This chapter will discuss how this political reality significantly influenced the preparation and selection of black teachers in the South over the better part of two centuries.

The chapter will also examine black response to the hostile racial climate in their communities as they sought to improve teacher preparation and working conditions. Current research suggests that blacks essentially lower teaching standards by opposing examinations and recertification efforts. Historically, however, blacks have been among the most vocal advocates of competent and well-trained teachers. Finally, the chapter will consider the impact of integration on the status of black teachers, and its implications for the future of blacks in teaching.

Antebellum Era

Black teachers have long held enormous influence and status within their communities. The widespread notion of black intellectual inferiority was one of the earlies justifications for slavery, so blacks placed a high priority on education in their attempt to dispel this belief. They also recognized education as the primary vehicle for race improvement.[3]

Although the North held most opportunities for black education prior to the Civil War, clandestine schools in the South opened during the 1830s in response to a ban on the education of slaves that sought to thwart the uprising of literate blacks. A study of black education prior to the Civil War by historian Carter G. Woodson found that "Clandestine schools were in operation in most of the large cities and towns of the South where such enlightenment of the Negroes was prohibited by law."[4] One school was conducted openly prior to 1819 by Julian Froumountaine, and then made secret after the 1830s. Another was operated by a Miss DeaVeaux for more than 25 years without the knowledge of whites.

Susan King Taylor, who served as a nurse and teacher for the Union army during the Civil War, wrote in her *Reminiscences* that she was educated in several of the "secret" schools of Savannah, Georgia. Similar schools were found in other areas. In Natchez, Mississippi, Milla Granson was taught by her master's children, and later made hundreds of slaves literate in classes she held after midnight. Throughout the slave-holding South, learning was placed at such a premium by blacks that many often risked their lives to obtain it. Most passed whatever amount of knowledge they gained to other slaves. Despite these efforts, however, it is estimated that by Emancipation, 95 percent of all blacks in the South were illiterate.

After the Civil War, many blacks became teachers to help eradicate the ignorance enforced on their people in the South. Teaching was viewed as a way to "uplift" or improve the race.[5] The 1871 *Report of the Commissioner of Education on the Improvement of Public Schools in the District of Columbia* underscored blacks' enthusiasm for education. It provided accounts of the history, from 1861 to 1868, of schools for blacks in the District of Columbia and in each of the (then) 35 states. The persistent theme was one of sacrifice and commitment by blacks to education, beginning with the successful effort "by three men who had been born and reared as slaves in Maryland and Virginia" to establish the first school built "expressively for the education of colored children."[6]

Many whites in the North established schools for blacks during the eighteenth and nineteenth centuries for religious and moral reasons, but blacks frequently were critical of these institutions and their teachers. Concerned not only with the pedagogy but also the politics of their education, free blacks of the antebellum era complained that many white teachers were educating blacks for subordinate roles in society. Such criticisms rested on bitter experience. In the 1820s the white trustees of the African Free School, established by the New York Manumission Society, discouraged higher education for blacks on the grounds that it was beyond their "sphere." Later in the decade, David Walker of Boston angrily recalled a white teacher's forbidding a black student to study grammar because the teacher viewed the subject as a privilege for white students only. Such incidents alerted black Northerners to the paramount importance of appointing black teachers to schools for their children.[7]

Although suspicious of white teachers, blacks especially wanted *competent* teachers for their schools. Well before the Civil War, *Freedom's Journal*, the first black newspaper in the nation, began protesting the small number of schools for blacks and the poor quality of teachers provided for them. It observed, in 1827, "We cannot believe that almost *anyone* is qualified to keep a school for our children." Blacks believed white teachers would not encourage the black students to "uplift" their race in any important manner. Expressing this point of view, a report of a black national convention in 1853 noted that "Their [white teachers'] whole tendency is to change him [the black student], not his condition—to educate him out of his sympathies, not to quicken and warm his sympathies, for all that is of worth to him is his elevation, and the elevation of his people."[8]

Such goals required qualified black teachers, but if they were to be found, they must first gain access to preparation programs. Blacks in the North were sporadically admitted to normal schools and colleges during the antebellum period. However, most acquired their advanced education at Oberlin College in Ohio, the only institution of higher education at the time to admit blacks and women on a regular basis. The writings of black women educated during this period reveal a missionary zeal in their desire to become teachers of their race.

One of these was Fanny Jackson Coppin. She graduated from Rhode Island Normal School in the 1850s and continued her education at Oberlin College, completing the "gentleman's course" in 1865. At the end of her life, Coppin wrote in her memoirs that since childhood her greatest desire was "to get an education and to teach [her] people." While at Oberlin, she established a night class for the freedmen who had poured into the abolitionist town during the Civil War. The school drew enormous attention in local and abolitionist papers. Of the school's success, Coppin remembered:

> It was deeply touching to me to see old men painfully following the simple words of spelling; so intensely eager to learn. I felt that for such people to have been kept in the darkness of ignorance was an unpardonable sin, and I rejoiced upon the course of life which I had long ago chosen.[9]

After graduating from Oberlin, Coppin went to the Institute for Colored Youth (ICY) in Philadelphia as a teacher, and later became principal. ICY, a well-known Quaker school, was transformed by Coppin into one of the nation's leading teacher-training institutions for blacks.

Reconstruction and Post–Civil War Years

As the Civil War came to a close, both private and public organizations assisted in the massive task of educating the newly freed blacks. The largest of these efforts were conducted by the American Missionary Association (AMA) of the Congregational Church and the Freedmen's Bureau of the federal government.

Many educated blacks in the North applied to teach through these and other agencies, while other blacks established their own schools independently or through black churches. Despite their qualifications, educated blacks saw their teaching appointment requests deferred or denied by missionary associations because of their race. Within the black community, teachers represented knowledge, culture, and intellectual and moral authority—all attributes that society had routinely denied blacks. Blacks ultimately considered for employment in the South by the AMA, the largest employer among the missionary associations, were regarded as an "experiment." Since blacks were perceived as morally degenerate and culturally backward, their applications were scrutinized closely.[10]

The issue of black teachers for black students became as heated in the South as it had in the North. Well-trained blacks believed their impact on black students would be infinitely greater than that of whites because of their kinship and desire to see blacks "elevated." Black teachers' letters of application stressed their sense of "duty" and "obligation" to their race, and their kinship with the newly freed blacks. Writing to the AMA, Mrs. E. Garrison Jackson of Rhode Island voiced commitment to this racial mission:

> Sir, I have a great desire to go and labor among the Freedmen of the South. I think it is our duty as a people to spend our lives in trying to elevate our own race. Who can feel for us if we do not feel for ourselves? And who can feel the sympathy that we can who are identified with them?[11]

Denied a teaching position by the Boston Educational Commission for racial reasons, John Oliver noted in his application to the AMA: "With my knowledge of both slavery and the slave and the condition in which the former has left the latter, I believe that I would be of great service to that people." Robert Harris, who had been taught privately as a slave when he lived in the South, wrote that he was a plasterer by trade and had also done railroad work, but was desirous of "assisting in the noble work of elevating and evangelizing our abused and oppressed race."[12]

Although some defenders of the missionary associations state that blacks were frequently overlooked because they lacked qualifications, records and testimonies of teachers do not confirm that judgment—particularly for the early years of the associations' work in the South. For example, the wealthy Charlotte Forten, of a famed black abolitionist family of Philadelphia, was trained at Salem State Normal School in Massachusetts and taught in Salem prior to her request to the Boston Educational Commission for a post in the South. When, like John Oliver, she was denied a position in spite of her qualifications, she accepted an appointment at Port Royal, South Carolina, through the Philadelphia Port Royal Relief Association.[13]

Many dismayed black teachers informed the AMA about the incompetent and racially insensitive white teachers they had encountered. In Virginia throughout the summer of 1864, AMA black teachers Sara G. Stanley and Edmonia Highgate reported to the AMA New York headquarters about white AMA teachers who made black social distinctions and continued to speak of black inferiority. Sallie Daffin and Clara Duncan, also black teachers, requested that the AMA dismiss the white matron of their mission house because she had "no interest in the cause." The black women's complaints were ignored, and the situation had worsened by the fall of 1864.

Sara Stanley continued to record "prejudice against complexion" found among some white teachers of the AMA. In addition to their racial biases, wrote Stanley to AMA Superintendent William Woodbury, some lacked "thorough" intellectual training. Stating what black parents throughout the country felt, Stanley warned the AMA that racially insensitive teachers brought great harm to the black community and undermined the association's educational goals. "My motive," she concluded, "is to utter a plea for those who have no voice to plea for themselves." Stanley said that blacks preferred black teachers because they knew who their true friends were, not through "*word* but *deed*."[14]

Jacqueline Jones's study of missionary educational activities in Georgia after Emancipation confirms Stanley's observation of black desire for black teachers. Blacks believed that racial sensitivity and respect were essential ingredients for the teachers of their youth. While some white teachers were committed and racially sensitive, many were not. Jones noted that blacks would frequently sacrifice to send their children to tuition schools with black teachers rather than to free schools with white teachers.[15]

It was a common practice of the AMA to send black teachers to the most undesirable locations, such as small rural schools, and assign them to teach only primary grades. By 1870, although 105 of the 533 employees commissioned by the AMA were black, most were student or assistant teachers and ministers. As the Southern public school system absorbed AMA's elementary schools after 1870, the organization began to focus upon normal and collegiate training. As with the elementary schools, however, well-trained blacks found difficulty getting teaching jobs in these new institutions. For example, Edmonia Highgate, a black AMA teacher from Syracuse, New York, wrote in 1870 of her desire to spend the rest of her life as a teacher at Tougaloo Normal School in Mississippi, which had been founded the previous year. Highgate confidently informed AMA officials of her qualifications, citing her previous teaching experience and her certificate of normal training from the Syracuse Board of Education. She stated that only caste prevented her from occupying a teaching position in that city. Caste, however, kept Highgate from obtaining an appointment at Tougaloo as well.

Even by 1895, of the 110 faculty members at the five AMA colleges for blacks, only four were black. And at the 17 AMA secondary schools of that time, only 12 of the 141 teachers were black. Clearly the issue was not the unavailability of competent black teachers. The issue with most AMA officials, as with white local school officials in the South, was whether blacks would remain deferential, accommodating, and subordinate to whites.[16]

In his study of blacks and the AMA in the South, Richardson found that the AMA often viewed blacks' desire for black teachers as "ingratitude, ludicrous ambition, or racial hostility." In theory, he noted, "The AMA favored black-operated and black-supported schools, but it rarely relinquished control of its own. In its view, blacks were not yet capable of assuming that responsibility. Some blacks began to wonder if the paternalistic AMA would ever perceive them as competent."[17] Richardson pointed out that of all the benevolent organizations, the AMA employed the largest number of Northern-trained black teachers (51) in 1868–1869. The impact of these relatively few teachers was considerable. Despite its paternalism and maternalism, the AMA was pivotal in the education of blacks in the South.

Recent research reveals that blacks preferred black teachers to whites not only because of the racism and indifference often apparent in the white teaching staff, but also because they recognized that black teachers were an inspiration to their children. One black parent stated in 1867 that a black teacher could inspire black students "such as no words could describe."[18] Indeed, black teachers engendered motivation and self-respect in their students.

Countering the view that very few competent blacks were available to fill teaching posts during this period, W. E. B. DuBois reported in 1900 that over 2,300 blacks had graduated from colleges and universities. Although most were from the newly founded black colleges in the South, which despite their name taught only at the secondary-school level, 400 were graduates of white institutions in the North. In addition, hundreds had attended college in both the North *and* the South. Nevertheless, Northern missionaries had a preference for those blacks born in the North, or those educated by Northern schools.[19] This preference would change dramatically after the white South and Northern philanthropists joined forces to acquire control over Southern black education.

Although the AMA was the largest employer of teachers in the South, many other benevolent organizations also employed them. Robert C. Morris's study of the education of blacks during Reconstruction reported that by the late 1860s, one-third of the teachers of blacks in the South were black. Some organizations had a substantial number of black teachers. For example, by 1868 blacks constituted 55 percent of the teaching staff of the Presbyterian Committee on Freedman. Many were educated blacks who had been employed in other occupations before teaching. Educated black ministers, businessmen, lawyers, editors, blacksmiths, and farmers rushed to fill the need for more teachers.[20]

While Southern blacks in the latter part of the nineteenth century fought for more and better schools, Northern blacks were fighting for integrated schools. School segregation varied from state to state and city to city outside the South. The main factor of determination was the number of blacks living in a particular area or city. School systems in the New England states were integrated, except for a few in Connecticut and Rhode Island cities. Integrated schools could be found in Michigan, Wisconsin, and Minnesota; northern sections of Illinois and Ohio; and rural areas of New York, Pennsylvania, and New Jersey. However, in large cities, with the greatest population of blacks in the North, segregated schools were maintained. Southern Illinois and Indiana exempted blacks from the school tax and excluded them from the public schools entirely. In 1869, Indiana provided segregated schools for blacks, and not until 1870 did Illinois provide education for all children. In certain instances, school boards integrated schools because of the financial burden of maintaining dual systems. But most often integration was the result of black community pressure in battles that frequently took years.[21]

The price that blacks paid for integrated schools was often the loss of black teaching jobs. Thus, it was not uncommon for blacks to argue for separate schools. *The Cleveland Gazette* in 1883 stated black sentiment on this issue: "We want absolute equality in the public schools—mixed scholars and mixed teachers—and if we can't have it, we want colored schools taught by colored teachers."[22] In advocating separate schools, black parents argued that their children were subjected to the insults of white teachers and students in mixed schools. A black magazine in 1876 reported that white teachers in black schools took no real interest in the pupils, but tolerated them "in order to . . . draw their money. . . . We are tired of white overseers."[23]

Concern over the elimination of black teachers in the North was paramount in the nineteenth century, and an issue that Southern blacks would also encounter in the next century. After New York City abolished compulsory segregation in 1873, no black teacher was hired for 22 years. Just a few black teachers existed in integrated schools in the North during this period. By the 1880s, Boston had two; Cambridge one; and Portland, Maine, one. By the 1890s Detroit had three; Cleveland seven; St. Paul and Chicago two each; Cincinnati, Dayton, and Columbus, Ohio, one each; and Worchester, Lynn, and Chelsea, Massachusetts, also one each. Black teachers appeared in Western states in the late nineteenth century, but not in great numbers.[24]

Although this chapter is concerned primarily with the training of black teachers and the politics of black education *in* the South, the effort to retain black teachers as Northern schools were integrated was a great challenge for blacks *outside* the South. Vincent P. Franklin's *The Education of Black Philadelphia* is an excellent case study of such efforts in the North during the first half of the twentieth century.[25]

Education for blacks in the South grew rapidly during the latter part of the nineteenth century: At the end of the Civil War, fewer than 100,000 blacks were enrolled in schools in the South; by the turn of the century, more than 1.5 million were. As this number increased the demand for teachers became extraordinary, and teachers from the North alone could not accommodate them. To meet the need, by 1867 the AMA offered normal training in Charleston, Nashville, Hampton, Talladega, and Atlanta; and by 1871 it operated 21 normal and secondary schools. In 1890, one-third of all black normal-school students in the South were trained by AMA institutions.[26] In this same year over 25,000 blacks were teachers in the South.[27]

During the brief period of Reconstruction, blacks in the South made enormous gains. Black men served in Congress, and scores of others were elected to state and local offices. Hundreds of educated blacks migrated from the North to assist in the "uplift" of their race and in the building of quality educational institutions. Black literacy increased to 65 percent by the 1890s. However, the white South continued to view education for blacks as undesirable and dangerous, and by the end of the century a white backlash emerged to limit black opportunities and aspirations. Those who attempted to establish institutions for Southern blacks based on Northern and New England models frequently were harassed. Many white Southerners feared that Northern white missionaries and educated blacks had unacceptably raised the political, economic, and social aspirations of local blacks.[28]

The Growth of the Black Public School "System"

The educational impoverishment of blacks in the South is a well-known story in the history of American education. Although the South could barely afford a single school system, the fear of race mixing, racial equality, and black progress resulted in the establishment of a dual system for blacks and whites. Abbreviated school years, starvation salaries, inadequate curricula, and inferior buildings and equipment were the norm for the black school teacher of the South. As education there developed into a "system" in the late nineteenth century, black teachers organized to express concern about educational inequalities, and to monitor educational progress.

The earliest documented organization of black teachers existed in Springfield, Ohio, in 1861. Twenty-three black teachers (13 women and eight men) met to discuss black student enrollment, teachers' salaries, student attendance records, and curricula. Similar organizations emerged in the South. The black Alabama State Teacher Association was established in 1882, the Negro Teachers Association of Virginia in 1888, and the Ida B. Wells Teachers Association in Oklahoma in 1893. By 1900, black teacher organizations existed in all Southern states, and in numerous states north of the Mason–Dixon line.[29]

Black education was enhanced in 1890 with the signing of the second Morrill Act. As a result of this legislation, 17 black land-grant colleges were established in the South. Black men headed each of these institutions, and by 1904 the presidents had organized the National Association of Land-Grant Colleges (NALGC). All of these institutions were of high-school grade, a situation which reflected the dearth of secondary schools available to prepare blacks for college in the early decades of the twentieth century. Howard University in Washington, DC was the only black college to enroll only college students. In that year it enrolled 1,053 college students, while all of the black land-grant colleges combined enrolled only 52 students of college level.[30]

As funds for white missionary support of Southern black education dwindled in the twentieth century, Northern white industrial philanthropy took on greater importance. Prominent among these efforts were the Southern Education Board, established in 1901 by Northern industrialists, and the General Education Board, founded in 1902 by John D. Rockefeller. Because the memberships of both boards were virtually identical, the General Education Board absorbed the Southern Education Board. In 1909 the General Education Board provided $53 million in grants to Southern education, and assumed "virtual monopolistic control of educational philanthropy for the South and the Negro."[31]

Funds to advance the cause of black education were established, including the Anna T. Jeanes Fund in 1908. The fund paid black supervisors to improve the quality of rural schools, where neglect was of great concern to black educators. By 1913, grants for the construction of black schools were provided by the Julius Rosenwald Fund. As a result of this fund, 5,000 schools for blacks had been built in 883 counties in 15 Southern and border states by 1932. These schools accounted for one-fifth of all schools for blacks in 12 Southern states.

These gifts, however, were not without strings attached. White philanthropists embraced the accommodationist philosophy of Booker T. Washington's Tuskegee–Hampton model for black higher education, and sought to replicate this in the institutions they funded. Washington assured the philanthropists that his conservative aproach to education would keep "the Negro humble, simple, and of service to the community."[32]

The "humble" manner advocated by Washington was often synonymous with servility. Pride and self-respect frequently were translated as arrogance and a desire by blacks to be white. In 1917, when Julius Rosenwald visited the AMA Fisk

University, a liberal-arts institution, he wrote to Abraham Flexner, secretary of the General Education Board, that "there seemed to be an air of superiority among them [Fisk students] and a desire to take on the spirit of the white university rather than the spirit which has always impressed me at Tuskegee."[33]

The view of classically trained blacks as pompous and arrogant seriously handicapped many of them in their search for employment as teachers. In 1911, DuBois and Dill found that the best-trained blacks from private liberal-arts colleges had the most difficulty obtaining teaching positions because white superintendents sought blacks primarily to train students in the manual trades. Noting these school authorities' emphasis on "technical teaching," DuBois and Dill warned that public schools for blacks in the South were so curtailed in curriculum that few prepared blacks for higher education. They concluded from their survey that most superintendents wanted only teachers of industrial and domestic sciences.

The politics of the situation were clear: Keep black aspirations low. As suggested by Rosenwald's comment, whites seemed afraid that liberally educated blacks thought of themselves as equal to whites. DuBois and Dill offered their assessment of the situation:

> Broadly trained Negro teachers are feared by many school authorities because they have "too much egotism" or "individuality" and because they can not be depended upon "to teach the Negro his place." The result is that many superintendents and trustees will, therefore, hire a half-trained graduate of an industrial school who can teach a few industries and then complain that the teacher lacks education and culture.[34]

The issues of curriculum, salary, and teacher preparation were paramount to those who taught black students at the public school and college levels. In an effort to coördinate the activities of black educators, in 1907 the black land-grant college presidents merged their organization, the NALGC, with the black state teacher associations to form the National Association of Teachers of Colored Schools (NATCS). As the name suggests, the organization in its early years was interracial.

The NATCS's growth paralleled that of the white National Education Association (NEA). Although blacks were not technically barred as members of the NEA, local and state chapters of the organization in the South prohibited black members. Consequently, few members of the NEA were black prior to the 1940s. Nevertheless, the NEA did discuss issues concerning black education at its conventions, and frequently had black educators address these gatherings. The themes concerning black education from 1884 to 1926 focused primarily on industrial education, education as a vehicle for moral uplift, and the "separate but equal" aspects of black education.[35]

While the NEA was not primarily concerned with equity for black education, members of NATCS were committed to raising institutional standards and improving the preparation of black teachers. The organization established departments to monitor improvement in college education; high-school, elementary, and rural school supervision; health education; agricultural education; and vocational education.

The NATCS regularly reported the status of black teachers and the progress of black schools. It faced many issues, including the major problem of poor teacher salaries. The organization reported that black teachers routinely earned one-half to two-thirds the salary of white teachers. The *Southern Workman,* an organ of Hampton Institute, recorded in 1911 that average salaries for black teachers had actually declined from $23.30 to $22.20 per month in South Carolina from 1885 to 1905. In North Carolina in 1906, black teachers in 30 counties earned less than $20 per month. During the first decade of the twentieth century, it was not uncommon in some areas for black teachers to earn less than day laborers, with salaries of only $10 per month.[36]

Teacher training was another issue of paramount concern to the black community (as it was to the country as a whole). With the spread and systemization of public schools, formal preparation became a necessary condition for entrance to the profession. By the turn of the century, chairs of pedagogy were established in colleges and universities in several states. Applicants for teaching positions in the nation's better elementary schools needed normal-school training, and those who sought high-school teaching posts needed college diplomas. The dramatic growth of high schools that offered normal training during this period also contributed to the education of teachers.[37]

Despite this rapid growth throughout the nation, few high schools existed for blacks, and the black curriculum debate hit full-force by 1910. The United States Commissioner of Education reported that only 141 public high schools for blacks existed in the nation, 123 of which were in the South.[38] Nearly half of the black public high schools were located in Missouri and Texas. W. T. B. Williams, president of the NATCS, argued:

> If Negroes are to have leaders of any considerable intelligence for the masses of their people, who are being pushed farther and farther out of contact with the white people every day, they too must have a considerable number of high schools maintained at public expense. . . . And the very presence of the elementary schools makes high schools a necessity, not only for the sake of preparing efficient teachers for the elementary schools but also to give a fitting outlet for the budding intelligence awakened in the lower schools.[39]

Although only a scant number of public high schools served Southern blacks in the early decades of the twentieth century, few normal schools existed to fill the gaps. Only one high school per state in the South provided normal training to black teachers. Virtually all black colleges—most of which were still essentially secondary schools—prepared their students for teaching.

The black teachers associations and their national organization, NATCS, made the need for normal training and teacher certification for blacks a recurring theme at annual conferences. However, as the need for competent black teachers outstripped the supply, many states waived teacher certification requirements for candidates. Black educators and their associations vigorously opposed such measures. In 1909, when the state of Virginia proposed lower examination standards for black teachers, their state associations met in protest and issued the following resolutions:

> That colored schools are at least as difficult to teach as any others, and accordingly as complete equipment should be required of the teachers of these schools as of those of any others.
>
> That the proposed action will tend to lower the grade of colored teachers in general because it will give the legalized approval of the state to poor preparation on the part of colored teachers; that it will not increase the number of good colored teachers in the state, but that it will perpetuate the poorer ones and increase the number of inadequately prepared teachers.
>
> That it will tend to stigmatize colored teachers in general as inferior, and thus rob them of the normal incentives for improvement, while it does not in any way take into consideration any of the reasons why the more capable young people are not led to offer themselves as teachers; that the action proposed would furnish additional excuse to the school boards for lowering further the already insufficient salaries paid to colored teachers, which, in no small measure, account for the quality of the teachers who take the examinations.[40]

Southern black communities were well aware that the white South's reaction to the need for more black teachers was to offer less training, resulting in lower scores on state teacher examinations. They could then pay even lower salaries than those normally given to black teachers. This strategy ensured that blacks would continue to get teachers with minimal training, and encouraged classically educated blacks to seek employment options other than teaching.

The credentials of black teachers in most rural areas were abysmal. The NATCS noted in 1910 that in one Mississippi county, only three out of the 27 black teachers employed had studied above the fifth grade.[41] And by 1915, the certification issue for black teachers in Virginia had not greatly improved. A report of black teachers for that year indicated that of 1,336 black teachers examined, only 36 percent were eligible for any type of certification, and only 28 qualified for a first-class certificate. A 1920 report concerning the teachers examination for blacks in Virginia revealed that more than two-thirds of those holding certificates possessed unsatisfactory qualifications, and only 3 percent held professional certificates.[42]

Although public education grew throughout the country, Southern black education depended on private institutions and funds from private sources. The black church and communities in rural areas significantly augmented teacher salaries, and churches frequently provided equipment and space for schools. Despite their impoverished economic position, however, black teachers came to be, along with ministers, among the most respected members of the community.[43]

Normal education for blacks was significantly helped in 1882 by a million-dollar fund from John F. Slater, a wealthy white New England merchant. The specific purpose was to train black teachers in the South. In the 1883 report of the fund, Slater reiterated the need for well-trained black teachers. He found that most elementary grades were taught by poorly trained black women and that the higher grades were taught, with rare exception, by Northern whites.[44]

The push for more and better institutions for black teacher training paralleled the well-known effort by Booker T. Washington to promote industrial education and character training. Simply put, Washington argued that blacks were primarily an infantile and rural people just emerging from slavery. The classical and liberal-arts courses taught by the institutions for blacks, established by Northern missionaries, were unsuited for the reality of black conditions in the South. According to Washington, classical education raised black aspirations unrealistically and educated them away from their surroundings. Many classically trained blacks agreed that students should have a balance between classical and industrial training. They objected, however, to Washington's reinforcement of the widespread belief that blacks were not prepared morally and intellectually to pursue the same fields as whites.

Washington served as president of the Alabama State Teachers Association from 1888 to 1892 and, according to Thelma Perry, many of the founders and leaders of the NATCS were Washington's disciples and former students.[45] He was also a prominent and frequent speaker at NEA conferences. The NEA was actually the first organization to provide Washington a national platform to discuss his views on black education. He addressed the NEA in 1884, 1896, 1904, and 1908. The responses tended to be positive. As Michael Schultz has observed, the NEA and most white educators accepted the Washington conservative philosophy of black vocational education because it conformed to dominant views of the time:

> The NEA reflected the basic, conservative philosophy that pervaded the nation during this era. Problems of the Negro were discussed at many of the conventions, but actually the organization did nothing. The problems were viewed in an impersonal, almost detached manner, and the NEA, like most of the nation, seemed willing to accept the fundamental beliefs of Booker T. Washington.[46]

Washington's message of industrial education was widespread by the 1900s. The *Southern Workman* frequently printed articles stressing the need for more industrial courses in the rural schools of the South. Carrie E. Bemus argued in 1902 for more industrial education in rural schools. She thought that Greek and Latin were a "waste of time" for black students, not because of limited student ability, but because "He [the black student] does not need Latin and Greek in dealing with the ignorant and dependent ones in his home community." Her view represented the widespread conviction that black teachers should have good training in "hand work." Because most black children of the rural South would receive no formal instruction beyond elementary school, they would need to be prepared to engage in some type of trade.[47]

Training in rural education was imperative for teachers of Southern black youth. More than 80 percent of blacks in 1900 lived in rural areas, and even by the 1930s over 50 percent were still outside the large cities. Rural blacks experienced the shortest school year (sometimes only eight to 12 weeks), the most poorly trained and least compensated teachers, and the worst facilities. Rural schools often lacked textbooks, desks, blackboards, and any teaching aids. Black churches provided financial aid to rural schools by supplementing the salaries of teachers—support which also enabled the school year to be extended.[48]

Fanny Jackson Coppin emphasized the preparation of teachers for rural black schools during her principalship at the Institute for Colored Youth in Philadelphia from 1865 to 1902. She prepared her normal classes for the realities of rural teaching. Three-quarters of the black teachers in Philadelphia and in Camden (New Jersey) were institute graduates, and went South to teach and head schools. All normal-school students at ICY were required to be so proficient in their subjects that they would not have to utilize textbooks. They were taught to draw and to make maps, since educational aids were rarely available. Coppin also employed a black physician to lecture to the normal classes on health, school hygiene, and preventative medicine. This was necessary, she informed the Quaker managers of the institution, because "It must be remembered that our normal classes will teach way down in Maryland, Virginia, etc., where they are often miles from a doctor."

Realizing that it would take a dedicated student of missionary zeal to forfeit a teaching position in the urban North to accept one in the rural South, where neither working conditions nor monetary rewards were appealing, Coppin lectured virtually each of her graduating classes:

> You can do much to alleviate the condition of our people. Do not be discouraged. The very places where you are needed most are those where you will get the least pay. Do not resign a position in the South which pays you $12 a month as a teacher for one in Pennsylvania which pays $50.[49]

Coppin painted a realistic picture of life as a black teacher in the rural South. However, Booker T. Washington, who was masterful at portraying the devastating condition of blacks in deceptively glowing terms, attempted to attract more competent black teachers to Southern rural areas by describing them as highly desirable locations:

> The teacher who goes into the country district has an opportunity that seldom comes to the teacher in the large city. There is more freedom in the country than in the city. There you have to work in harness and have a certain time for everything. Everyone has to sing at a certain time and in a certain way; has to do everything in the same manner and in the same way. In the country there is freedom. You are not bothered by superintendents in the South; you can do about as you please; teach any books you want, any subject, and in any manner. I advise all of you who are wide-awake to get as far into the country as you can, and after you have selected your place of work stay there year after year.[50]

Washington neglected to point out that teachers could use any book because usually no textbooks were provided. Also, the lack of supervision that Washington praised was perceived by leading black educators as a serious handicap in the weeding out of poorly trained and inept teachers.

In 1910, one year after Washington's upbeat description of the "freedom" of the rural black school teacher, the Alabama State Teacher's Association witnessed a dramatic increase in the number of black teachers at its annual conference. Prompted by the worsening condition of black schools, attendance jumped from 116 in 1908 to 788 in 1910. The need for improvement in rural black public schools was so critical that black teachers from all over the state journeyed to Birmingham to discuss ways to lengthen the school year, increase teacher salaries, establish secondary schools, and obtain better and more facilities for existing schools. One report of the conference stated "What one witnessed at the Birmingham meeting was the belated arrival, in the person of the country school teacher, of the representatives of the common, plodding masses on the farms and in the small towns." The writer continued:

> One of the best representatives of this class was a simple-minded, earnest black woman, who for seventeen years has been teaching a little country school in a village in Montgomery County. Nothing in this meeting was more interesting or more significant than the stories told by this woman and other teachers like her from the small towns or from the open country. These rural teachers described in simple, vivid language, the wretched conditions of the country schools and then went on to tell in detail how, from their own small earnings, colored communities had raised the money to rebuild or improve the schoolhouses and lengthen the school term.[51]

The situation did not improve quickly. A 1930 study by Fred McCuistion of the Julius Rosenwald Fund noted that 93 percent of black Southern schools were rural; 94 percent of black students were in elementary school but only 5 percent in high school; and fewer than 17 percent of the college-age group were in college. In addition, 60 percent of black elementary-school students were in the first three grades, while 85 percent dropped out prior to seventh grade. McCuistion also found that approximately 39 percent of all black teachers in the South had less than a high-school diploma; 58 percent had less than two years beyond high school, which was usually the minimum to teach elementary school at the time; and only 12 percent were college graduates. He stated that the typical Southern black schoolteacher was a female of rural heritage, 27 years old, and a high-school graduate with ten weeks of summer school. This teacher taught approximately 47 children in all six grades for six months.[52]

The issue of improved salaries to attract and retain well-trained teachers became the focus of black educators by the 1930s. McCuistion insisted: "A profession with an inadequately paid personnel cannot measure up to accepted standards of service. A profession expected to develop leaders must be composed of leaders."[53] Noting that the average annual salary for the Southern black teacher was $360 in 1930, he accurately observed that appeals such as those of Fanny Coppin to her pupils a generation earlier would no longer convince well-trained blacks to enter the teaching profession: "In past years a missionary spirit or religious loyalty inspired many leaders to devote their lives to teaching, but we can hardly expect this condition to continue."[54]

It was increasingly unrealistic to expect blacks to work within the teaching profession. While blacks continued to toil as teachers in rural areas because of personal dedication, many black women did so because other employment options simply were not available to them. When Alabama appropriated money for black public education in the 1880s, a black journalist in Birmingham expressed concern over the impact that low salaries would have on attracting competent teachers:

> I don't think the appropriations are enough to pay good, competent teachers in our schools, and some of our best young men and young ladies who have attended the schools, and have received their diplomas, have had to go away to other States to seek employment where salaries are better than they are in Alabama.[55]

As the trend to deny blacks appropriate teacher training and compensation continued, Horace Mann Bond noted that, by denying blacks appropriate teaching training, the South could continue to justify poverty-level salaries to black teachers. Job scarcity was so great by the 1930s that it was not uncommon for ten applicants to compete for one teaching position. Bond noted that white superintendents usually opted for the least qualified—and least expensive—applicant: "When one has ten applicants for a job paying $25 a month for five months, why pay $50 a month for the same job?"[56] Jacqueline Jones found that public officials in Georgia balked at hiring graduates of Atlanta University (a liberal-arts institution) well before the beginning of the twentieth century.[57]

Bond also found that politics frequently contributed to teacher appointments. In one parish in Louisiana, six members of the same black family had teaching appointments, although none of them had ever attended high school. On learning that these appointments resulted from political patronage that dated back to the Reconstruction Era, Bond observed: "The result [of these teaching appointments] was that sixty years after Reconstruction, the gratitude of one race to one family of another race resulted in foisting six immensely inadequate Negro teachers upon Negro school children."[58]

Whereas rural areas of the South attracted the least-prepared teachers, the opposite was true of urban areas. Major cities with black high schools attracted black educators with outstanding credentials from leading colleges and universities in the United States. Indeed, blacks with graduate degrees and experience abroad taught in such cities as Washington, Baltimore, Atlanta, New Orleans, and Kansas City.[59] As sociologist Charles S. Johnson concluded in 1938, "Teaching may be said to draw both the poorest and the best types of college graduates. Both types find their way into the teaching field because there are so few jobs in other fields for them."[60]

Measured in terms of teaching preparation only, educational opportunity for blacks varied widely in the South. A few students had access to distinguished faculties, but the great majority suffered the crippling effects of the separate and unequal schools to which they had been consigned.

The "New" Negro and Teaching

The decade of the 1920s witnessed increased black militancy and protest. After the end of World War I and the growth in civil rights organizations such as the NAACP and the National Urban League, blacks become increasingly outspoken in their demand to be included in the mainstream of American life, and to have equal treatment in all aspects of education and employment. This period also saw the growth of the black nationalist movement of Marcus Garvey; the black literacy movement of the Harlem Renaissance; expansion in black businesses and newspapers; and the dramatic increase in Southern migration to the urban North. In addition, the number of black college students multipled sixfold between 1917 and 1927—from 2,132 to 13,580. This new group of educated blacks was impatient with, and unsympathetic to, the missionary mentality characteristic of the first generation of educated blacks.

As new employment opportunities opened for blacks in the 1920s in business, social work, nursing, journalism, and civil service, many abandoned the field of teaching for financial reasons. DuBois and Dill had warned of the problem in 1911:

> The colored graduates of colleges and normal schc ls of high grade cannot afford to teach in most of the public schools of the South because of the wretched wages paid. Teachers from outside of the community often find it absolutely impossible to live on these wages. In many of the larger towns of the South the pay of Negro teachers is so small that many of the best teachers are being forced into other lines of work.[61]

Concern grew in Southern black communities over the defection of well-trained teachers. Educators at the annual NATCS conference in 1918 resolved "that colored teachers remain loyally at their posts and not allow themselves to be lured off by attractive wages into other fields."[62]

Black teacher resignations became so acute that by the 1920s black educators campaigned vigorously for increased and equitable salaries. An official of the NATCS noted in 1920 the critical shortage of black teachers and reiterated the now familiar theme:

> The causes leading to the general shortage of teachers have affected colored teachers especially. In the first place, there never has been an adequate supply of properly trained teachers of this race. And the salaries paid for their services have amounted to little more than half of the small salaries paid other teachers in the South. In order to meet their ordinary expenses in these days of the high cost of living colored teachers have been driven into other callings. Various forms of social work and the rapidly developing business enterprises among colored people have taken away from the schoolroom many of the more efficient instructors.[63]

By the 1930s black men and women were entering quite different professional occupations. The 1930 census reported that 45,672 black women were school teachers, compared with 8,767 black men. Charles S. Johnson's survey of black college graduates in 1938 confirmed the gender stratification of employment. Johnson surveyed 5,512 black college graduates (approximately 30 percent of the living black college graduates during the 1930s) and discovered that three-fourths of the graduates worked in the fields of education, medicine, law, business, religion, or social work. Women accounted for 2.1 percent of the medical profession among blacks; 1.9 percent of black lawyers; 8.6 percent of blacks in business; 83 percent of librarians and assistant librarians; 70 percent of black social workers; 71 percent of elementary-school teachers; and 63 percent of high-school teachers. Despite the predominance of women in public schoolteaching, few were represented in leadership positions. Johnson found that one in every 15 high-school principals, and one in every five elementary-school principals were women.[64]

Concern about blacks leaving the field of teaching collided with two related developments. Employment opportunities for all women began to widen, and a growing number of educated black feminists voiced their desire for greater employment opportunities. In the 1920s a national organization of black women graduates of liberal-arts institutions was established in Washington, DC. Named the National Association of College Women (NACW), the group was patterned in part after the white American Association of University Women. Headed by Lucy Diggs Slowe, the first black woman dean at Howard University, the group sought to encourage black women to pursue professions other than teaching.

In 1931, Slowe surveyed 153 first-year women at Howard University and discovered that 142 of them *wanted* to become teachers. Only one selected medicine, one law, five social work, two library science, and three business as professions. Slowe was concerned that 90 percent of the women at Howard, a liberal-arts institution, sought teaching as a career.[65] Not fully comprehending the political and racial reality of the South, she viewed this disproportion as a result of sexist, conservative institutions and family structures that counselled women to pursue a safe and traditional field. Support was needed, she thought, for the million blacks who were not students. Of these people she asked, "Who is to assume leadership of the underprivileged adults in our several communities?" Thus the NACW, with Slowe at its head, pushed to encourage black women college students to pursue the new fields that were becoming available to women: social work, civil service, and business.[66]

By the 1950s the career opportunities for educated black women had expanded still further. An important study of black women college graduates conducted in 1956 by Jeanne Noble found that while 56 percent were teachers, more than 70 percent in the 20–29 age group were pursuing other professions. Noble said that the younger group was exploring "new fields for Negroes." Of the decline in the number pursuing teaching careers, Noble commented: "This is indeed noteworthy and encouraging!"[67] This positive view of black women leaving the field of teaching would be repeated by other blacks throughout the ensuing decades.

One woman in Noble's study expressed a view that was becoming increasingly common among college-educated women:

> There are entirely too many fine Negro women in the teaching profession. There should be vocational guidance to encourage them into new fields. Around this part of the country middle-class women go into teaching because this is the highest type of position for them.[68]

This view that well-trained blacks were wasting their talents in the field of teaching has persisted.

The Impact of NAACP Activities on Black Teachers

The inequalities between black and white school systems were exacerbated to their widest divergence in a century by the Depression of the 1930s. Segregation prevailed throughout the North and South. In response to escalating discrimination against blacks nationwide, the membership of the NAACP grew nearly ninefold—from 50,556 in 1940 to nearly 450,000 in 1946. During this period blacks won some political gains. When black labor leader A. Phillip Randolph proposed a march on Washington in 1941 to protest job discrimination, the demonstration was averted by President Roosevelt with the establishment of the Fair Employment Practices Committee. And throughout the South, courts struck down prohibitions against black participation in primary elections. By the 1950s, nearly 1.25 million black voters were registered in the South. Even with these great strides in civil rights, however, W. E. B. DuBois was moved to comment in 1946 on the state of black education:

> The majority of Negro children in the United States, from 6 to 18, do not have the opportunity to learn to read and write. We know this is true in the country districts of Mississippi, Louisiana and a half dozen other southern states. But even in the towns and cities of the South, the Negro schools are so crowded and ill-equipped that no thorough teaching is possible.[69]

In 1936 the NAACP began a campaign to eradicate salary differences between black and white teachers in 15 Southern states. Lawsuits were instituted by individual teachers and black teachers' organizations. By the end of 1941 the NAACP had won half its lawsuits. The push for equal salaries continued in subsequent years. By 1948, 27 of 38 challenges had been resolved successfully.[70] Southern school boards, unable to block the courts' decisions, retaliated by intimidating, and in some cases firing, black teachers who sued their systems. The jobs of black teachers who were members of the NAACP were particularly vulnerable.

In addition, some school systems sought to eliminate black teachers by using test scores, training, and experience as criteria for salary. For decades, white school systems had cared little for the preparation and experience of black teachers. Now, faced with fair-treatment rulings, they seemed eager to adopt these standards. Most attempts to turn back the clock failed. Statistics from state and federal records reveal that of 12 of the Southern states reporting teachers' salaries in 1952, three reported blacks with higher salaries based on college preparation—North Carolina, Tennessee, and Virginia. Mississippi reported the lowest average for black teachers: 51 percent of the white salary.[71]

Despite the resolution of the salary issue, a larger battle remained—desegregation of the public schools. This final area of litigation by the NAACP would be critical to the fate of black teachers. As black Northerners learned a century earlier, the push for integrated schools often resulted in elimination of teaching positions for blacks.

In a landmark case of the early 1950s, black parents sued the Topeka, Kansas school system. The parents challenged the separate school facilities of the city in what would be known as *Brown* v. *Board of Education*. When the lower courts upheld the "separate but equal" doctrine, the case was appealed to the Supreme Court. In May of 1954, Chief Justice Earl Warren read the court's unanimous opinion.

> We conclude that in the field of public education the doctrine of "separate but equal" has no place. Separate educational facilities are inherently unequal. Therefore, we hold that the plaintiffs and others similarly situated for whom the actions have been brought are, by reason of the segregation complained of, deprived of the equal protection of the laws guaranteed by the Fourteenth Amendment.[72]

Notwithstanding the jubilation of the black community over the victory of *Brown*, the question of the fate of Southern black teachers immediately arose. The *Journal of Negro Education* had published an optimistic forecast the year before the ruling was announced. Surveying the 17 Southern states and the District of Columbia, the editor found that "The training of the Negro teachers is almost equal to that of the white teachers." He reported that 76 percent of white elementary teachers and 68 percent of black teachers had obtained 120 or more semester hours of training. In six of the states and the District of Columbia, the training of black teachers exceeded that of whites—83 percent compared to 78 percent. On statistical grounds alone, "It would be a very difficult task to replace any appreciable number of the 71,361 Negro teachers with white teachers." The editor also pointed out that the demand in many areas made it virtually impossible to eliminate black teachers. As evidence, he quoted a study of the National Commission on Teacher Education and Professional Standards of the National Education Association which reported a serious shortage of elementary-school teachers and anticipated that the shortage would continue for several years. He worried, however, that the white South might be prone to irrational fuming if the Court ruled against *de jure* school segregation.[73]

Within two years, the editor saw trends that seemed to confirm the black community's worst fears. He reported instances of black teachers losing their jobs across the Southern region. West Virginia had closed 19 black schools, and although some faculty were reassigned, 15 black teachers were not retained. Similar developments occurred in Kentucky. In Georgia, the State Board of Education tried to push forth a resolution to "revoke forever" the licenses of teachers who held membership in the NAACP or favored integration. The NAACP challenged the resolution, and the board in Georgia ultimately withdrew it. Nevertheless, black teachers got the message. The *Journal of Negro Education* offered this advice to black teachers: "Negro teachers in the South will have to select their activities in connection with integration in such a way that they will most effectively advance the cause and at the same time protect themselves from being personally vulnerable to the powers opposing integration." In the urban North, blacks were hired on a token basis, and in small cities and rural areas, blacks were informed that they would not be appointed.[74]

School systems in the deep South did not rush to integrate their schools. Even ten years after the historic *Brown* decision, only 2 percent of schools in 11 Southern states had integrated. The intimidation of black teachers continued.

The Current Dilemma

The Civil Rights Movement in the 1950s and 1960s, and the Civil Rights Act of 1964, expanded opportunities for blacks significantly. For college-trained blacks, professions that had been available only to a token few, or to none at all, gradually became accessible. The opening of previously closed doors to blacks was followed by new fields becoming available to women as a result of the "Women's Movement" of the 1970s. Both of these movements were of particular significance to black women, since (although overall slightly more educated than black men until the late 1960s and early 1970s) black women faced severely limited employment options.

Education was the field that provided the safest opportunity for employment and for making meaningful contributions to the community and race. But this no longer is the case. Today's black college students are educated primarily within predominantly white institutions. Their career choices mirror those of the larger society; they do not feel compelled to base them on the needs of their race.

This response has a historical precedent. Charles S. Johnson's study of black college graduates in 1938 demonstrated that students then were concerned to a large extent with professional and financial success. While it was more difficult to escape the proscription of race during that period, fully two-thirds of those polled indicated no affiliation with, or interest in, civil rights organizations.

Many black college students of today perceive of teaching as a career of a bygone era. A profession once reserved for black women, it represents a lack of career options. And it conjures up memories of the self-sacrificing, religious, well-loved and respected—but poorly paid—pillar of the black community.

Although many educators are lamenting the decline in teaching as a preferred career among college students generally, and among blacks in particular, some older blacks understand the decline. In a public television report on blacks and teaching, Dr. Yvonne Taylor, a black woman who is president of Wilberforce University, a historically black institution, viewed the lack of Education majors in a recent graduation class of her university as a sign of progress for blacks. She recalled that when she was a student, teaching and the ministry were the professions most accessible to blacks. Given a choice, she said, she would have chosen a different career. It appears that to many blacks, having the freedom not to choose teaching as a career has become a sign of liberation.

In the 1980s, blacks began in increasingly larger numbers to take advantage of the fact that professions other than teaching usually are more financially rewarding and prestigious. Black communities have always held educators in high esteem—but as communities have become more integrated, and teachers have moved their residences from the communities in which they teach, teacher status among blacks has dropped. As the number of black professionals grows in other fields, teachers lose significance. In addition, because society evaluates one's worth and status according to income, low salaries have contributed to the decline in teacher status within the black community as it assimilates the values of the larger society.

Despite the increased freedom that blacks now have to pursue other fields, this is period in history when black teachers are desperately needed. Blacks are far from obtaining educational equity and, ironically, the gains that they applauded in the 1960s and 1970s are slowly eroding. Many urban schools are basically segregated, with questionable quality of resources and limited facilities. Even well-integrated schools do not necessarily provide black students the role models important for their intellectual development; and mere integration has not ensured quality education. Unintentionally prophetic, perhaps, DuBois and Dill noted in 1911 that even though black students in the North "usually have the same facilities for schooling as other children have, they often lack encouragement and inspiration [from white teachers]."[75]

Throughout the first half of this century, blacks were found primarily in rural areas, requiring teachers with a special understanding of the needs of rural children. Today, black students are overwhelmingly located in urban schools. They need teachers attuned to urban environments, who can serve as role models while promoting academic achievement and cultural understanding. Yet the growing number of school-age blacks seems to be coinciding with the declining number of black teachers. In 1986, fewer than 7 percent of the nation's teachers were black—and this proportion is expected to decline further.[76]

Blacks have waged vigorous battles over the years to obtain educational equity. They understood that schools with competent, compassionate, and racially sensitive teachers were key ingredients for quality education for their children. The earliest black teachers of the nineteenth century fought to obtain positions within the mission schools of the South because they realized the impact their presence would have on black children who had only known white authority figures. Without a doubt, black teachers who devoted their lives to rural pupils made profound contributions. These teachers not only provided intellectual stimulation, but also motivated a generation of blacks to higher aspirations. The testimonies of black college students in the surveys of DuBois, Johnson, and Noble repeatedly mentioned black teachers who inspired, motivated, and supported them in their life's work.

The paucity of blacks entering the teaching profession in the 1980s was compounded by the sharp decline from earlier eras in the number of blacks attending college. Some believe that the lack of motivating black teachers is a contributing factor to the decline. The large percentages of blacks who enter the military and attend two-year colleges and noncollegiate post-secondary schools are also cited as factors in the decline in number of blacks obtaining baccalaureate degrees.[77]

Although it is of course possible for non-black teachers to have a positive impact on black students, the decreasing number of black teachers clearly influences the achievement level and percentage of blacks who pursue higher education. There is little indication that many future teachers will offer the "encouragement and inspiration" needed for blacks or other minority students. A 1987 study on studen enrollment in teacher-education programs noted a substantial increase in the applications of white females. Minority applications remained low. Ninety-one percent of the teacher-education candidates were white, compared to 4.3 percen black and 1.5 percent Hispanic. Females accounted for 76 percent of the white candidates. These candidates overwhelmingly stated no desire to teach in an inner-city school—where most minority students are found. Eighty-four percent o the candidates surveyed said they preferred to teach in either a suburban or rura school district.[78]

These data underscore the magnitude of the problems facing today's blac students. Many teacher-education students will not be able to teach in suburban o rural schools. Demographic data indicate that black and Hispanic students are the fastest-growing student populations, expected to constitute 33 to 40 percent of the nation's public school enrollments by the year 2000. Therefore, it is probable that a sizeable number of teacher-education students will teach in urban districts where black students and other minorities are concentrated. Obviously many who teach in the urban school systems will be doing so by default. It is not reasonable to assume that reluctant urban teachers will easily or gladly become the enthusiastic, motivating, inspirational, and encouraging teachers that minority students need.

The issue of teacher-competency testing has been raised as a possible deterrent to blacks entering teaching. As of 1989, 25 states require standardized tests for admission into teacher-education programs, and 34 require standardized certification tests for new teachers. While the pass rate for minority teachers has been substantially lower than that of white teachers, it is unclear whether this issue has contributed to the dramatic decline in black teacher-education students.[79]

Black educators have questioned teacher-competency testing and its effects on the number of blacks in teaching, but it does not appear that their voices are being heard. Their articles on this topic, such as those collected in a special issue of the *Journal of Negro Education,* are rarely cited in major documents on improvement of teacher education.[80]

While basic competency is an obvious goal for all teachers, the research of Linda Darling-Hammond and Arthur E. Wise has shown little relationship between scores on teacher-competency tests and measures of performance in the classroom.[81] In addition, important human qualities for teachers, such as compassion, warmth, and respect for diverse cultures, races, and ethnic groups cannot be measured by standardized tests.

Unlike the struggles of blacks in the nineteenth and early twentieth centuries to improve and increase the number of black teachers, current discussions on these issues tend not to include black participants. Blacks and other minorities have not been highly visible in The Holmes Group, for example. Although several minority-group members served as consultants and advisors to the group, none of these persons was from any of the historically black colleges and universities. Since these institutions produce nearly 50 percent of all black graduates in education, they have a significant stake in the plight of blacks in teacher education.

The future for blacks in the teaching profession is not bright. Impressive proposals to attract blacks back into teaching have been recommended by such organizations as the American Association of Colleges for Teacher Education. Among them are loan-forgiveness programs, precollegiate recruitment, and retention programs for blacks in teacher education.[82] None of these efforts is likely to increase the black teaching force significantly in the foreseeable future. Blacks are underrepresented not only in teaching but in virtually all of the professions.[83] To increase the number of black professionals in the next century, changes must be made in current black student schooling.

The nation's public school systems have not served blacks well throughout the nineteenth and twentieth centuries. As discussed in this chapter, private schooling has accounted for a substantial portion of black education. As working conditions within predominantly black schools continue to be poor, and achievement levels and attendance rates of black students remain low, it may be that blacks will need to return to private schools as an alternative to the unsuccessful efforts of the public schools. W. E. B. DuBois predicted the present crisis in black education almost three decades ago:

> If and when they [black students] are admitted to these [white] schools certain things will inevitably follow. Negro teachers will become rare and in many cases will disappear. Negro children will be instructed in the public schools and taught under unpleasant if not discouraging circumstances. Even more largely than today they will fall out of school, cease to enter high school, and fewer and fewer will go to college.[84]

DuBois called upon black communities and organizations to establish schools to "take on and carry the burden which they have hitherto left to the public schools."[85]

The above proposal is not to suggest that public school efforts to educate blacks and other minorities must be abandoned. This is where most minority students will continue to be educated. Apparently, however, if academic and professional achievement is to be advanced among the next generation, private black institutions must assume more prominent and agggressive roles in the education of black youth. Otherwise, blacks will remain largely absent from teaching—as well as from other professions.

Notes

1. On this issue see Patricia Albjerg Graham, "Black Teachers: A Drastically Scarce Resource," in *Phi Delta Kappan* 68:8 (April 1987), pp. 598–605.
2. James D. Anderson, "Northern Philanthropy and the Training of the Black Leadership: Fisk University, a Case Study, 1915–1930," in Vincent P. Franklin and James D. Anderson (eds.), *New Perspectives on Black Educational History* (Boston: G. K. Hall, 1978), p. 97.
3. See, e.g., the records of a black national political conference, *The Rights of All,* New York, September 18, 1829.
4. Carter G. Woodson, *The African Background Outlined: Or Handbook for the Study of the Negro* (New York: Negro Universities Press, 1968), p. 319.
5. Susan King Taylor, *Reminiscences of My Life in Camp* (New York: Arno Press, 1969); Henry Allen Bullock, *A History of Negro Education in the South from 1619 to the Present* (New York: Praeger, 1970), p. 25; and W. E. B. DuBois, *The Negro Common School* (Atlanta: Atlanta University Press, 1901), p. 21.
6. U.S. Congress, *Special Report of the Commissioner of Education on the Condition and Improvement of Public Schools in the District of Columbia* (Washington, DC: Government Printing Office, 1871), p. 195.
7. *David Walker's Appeal to the Coloured Citizens of the World* (New York: Hill & Wang, 1965 [1828]); and *The Rights of All.*
8. *Freedom's Journal,* June 1, 1827; and *Report of the Committee on Social Relations and Polity in the Proceedings of the Colored National Convention, held in Rochester, July 6th, 7th and 8th 1853* (Rochester, NY, 1853), p. 23.
9. Fanny Jackson Coppin, *Reminiscences of School Life and Hints on Teaching* (Philadelphia: AME Book Concern, 1913), p. 18.

10. On the issue of missionary selection of black teachers, see Linda M. Perkins, "The Black Female American Missionary Association Teacher in the South, 1860–70," in Jeffrey J. Crow and Flora J. Hatley (eds.), *Black Americans in North Carolina and the South* (Chapel Hill: University of North Carolina Press, 1984), pp. 123–136; Robert C. Morris, *Reading, 'Riting, and Reconstruction: The Education of Freedmen in the South, 1861–1870* (Chicago: University of Chicago Press, 1981), pp. 85–130; and Jacqueline Jones, *Soldiers of Light and Love: Northern Teachers and Georgia Blacks, 1865–1873* (Chapel Hill: University of North Carolina Press, 1980), pp. 49–84.

11. Mrs. E. Garrison Jackson, Newport, RI, to S. S. Jocelyn, June 13, 1864, in *American Missionary Association Papers*. American Missionary Association Archives, Amistad Research Center, New Orleans, LA.

12. Joe M. Richardson, *Christian Reconstruction: The American Missionary Association and Southern Blacks, 1861–1890* (Athens, GA: University of Georgia Press, 1986), p. 190.

3. For such arguments see James M. McPherson *The Abolitionist Legacy: From Reconstruction to the NAACP* (Princeton: Princeton University Press, 1975); Clara M. DeBoer "The Role of the Afro-Americans in the Origins and Work of the American Missionary Association, 1839–1877," doctoral dissertation, Rutgers University, 1973; and Ray Allen Billington (ed.), *The Journal of Charlotte L. Forten: A Free Negro in the Slave Era* (New York: Collier Books, 1967).

. Sara G. Stanley and Edmonia Highgate, Norfolk, VA, to William Woodbury, July 21, 1864; Sallie Daffin, Norfolk, VA, to William Woodbury, August 29, 1864; Clara Duncan, Norfolk, VA, to William Woodbury, August 29, 1864, in *American Missionary Association Papers*.

Jones, *Soldiers of Light and Love*, p. 70.

Edmonia Highgate, Cortland, NY, to the Reverend E. P. Smith, July 23, 1870, in *American Missionary Association Papers;* and McPherson, *Abolitionist Legacy*, p. 273.

17. Richardson, *Christian Reconstruction*, p. 249.

18. Ibid.

19. W. E. B. DuBois, *The College-Bred Negro American* (Atlanta: Atlanta University Press, 1900), p. 37; and Morris, *Reading, 'Riting, and Reconstruction*, p. 100.

20. Ibid., pp. 85, 92, and 108.

21. Leslie H. Fishel, Jr., and Benjamin Quarles, *The Negro American: A Documentary History* (Glenview, IL: William Morrow, 1967), pp. 262 and 293; and Leslie H. Fishel, Jr., "The North and the Negro, 1865–1900: A Study in Race Discrimination," doctoral dissertation, Harvard University, 1953, p. 202.

22. *The Cleveland Gazette*, August 25, 1883.

23. David Tyack, *The One Best System: A History of American Urban Education* (Cambridge, MA: Harvard University Press, 1974), p. 111.

24. Fishel, "The North and the Negro," p. 205.

25. Vincent P. Franklin, *The Education of Black Philadelphia: The Social and Educational History of a Minority Community, 1900–1950* (Philadelphia: University of Pennsylvania Press, 1979).

26. Fishel, "The North and the Negro," pp. 114 and 116.

27. W. E. B. DuBois, *The Negro Common School*, pp. 15 and 42.

28. For an extensive discussion of the politics of black education, see James D. Anderson, *The Education of Blacks in the South, 1860–1935* (Chapel Hill: University of North Carolina Press, 1988).

29. Thelma Perry, *The History of the American Teachers Association* (Washington, DC: National Education Association, 1975), p. 13.

30. Anderson, "Northern Philanthropy and the Training of the Black Leadership," p. 107.

31. Ibid., p. 100; and Louis R. Harlan, *Separate and Unequal: Public School Campaigns and Racism in the Southern Seaboard States 1901–1915* (Chapel Hill: University of North Carolina Press, 1958), pp. 86–87.
32. Harlan, *Separate and Unequal,* p. 259.
33. Ibid., p. 104.
34. W. E. B. DuBois and Augustus Granville Dill, *The Common School and the Negro American* (Atlanta: Atlanta University Press, 1911), pp. 104 and 106.
35. Michael John Schultz, Jr., *The National Education Association and the Black Teacher: The Integration of a Professional Organization* (Coral Gables, FL: University of Miami Press, 1970), p. 47.
36. Perry, *The History of the American Teachers Association.*
37. Jessie M. Pangburn, *The Evolution of the American Teachers College* (New York: Teachers College, Columbia University, 1932), pp. 85–87. Also see Geraldine Jonçich Clifford and James W. Guthrie, *Ed School: A Brief for Professional Education* (Chicago: University of Chicago Press, 1988), pp. 56–59.
38. See W. T. B. Williams, "The Outlook in Negro Education," in *Southern Workman* 40:11 (November 1911), p. 640.
39. *Idem.*
40. "Examinations for Colored Teachers in Virginia," in *Southern Workman* 38:4 (April 1909), p. 196.
41. Perry, *The History of the American Teachers Association.*
42. Arthur D. Wright, "Virginia's Negro Teachers," in *Southern Workman* 49:1 (January 1920), p. 37.
43. For an extensive discussion of the role of blacks in financially contributing to their own education, see James D. Anderson, *The Education of Blacks in the South, 1860–1935* (Chapel Hill: University of North Carolina Press, 1988).
44. Perry, *The History of the American Teachers Association,* p. 184.
45. Ibid., pp. 69–74.
46. Schultz, *The NEA and the Black Teacher,* p. 52.
47. Carrie E. Bemus, "The Kind of Normal School Needed for the Teachers of Rural Negroes," in *Southern Workman* 31:12 (December 1902), p. 648; and John H. Jinks, "The Training of Hand Work Teachers for Rural Schools," in *Southern Workman* 37:6 (June 1908), pp. 343–350.
48. Perry, *The History of the American Teachers Association.*
49. Linda M. Perkins, *Fanny Jackson Coppin and the Institute for Colored Youth, 1865–1902* (New York: Garland Publishing, 1987), p. 136.
50. Booker T. Washington, "Southern Negro Rural Schools and Teachers," in *Southern Workman* 38:8 (August 1909), p. 427.
51. Robert E. Park, "Alabama State Teachers' Association," in *Southern Workman* 30:5 (May 1910), p. 272.
52. Fred McCuistion, "The South's Negro Teaching Force," in *Journal of Negro Education* 1:1 (1932), p. 21.
53. Ibid.
54. Ibid.
55. Quoted in Vincent P. Franklin, *Blac Self-Determination* (Westport, CT Lawrence Hill & Co., 1984), p. 156
56. Horace Mann Bond, *The Education o the Negro in the American Social Orde* (New York: Octagon Books, 1966), p 267.
57. Jones, *Soldiers of Light and Love,* p 195.
58. Bond, *The Education of the Negro,* p 278.
59. Many highly trained blacks, includin Ph.D.'s, taught high school. For exam ple, Edward Bouchet, who was the fir black Ph.D. in the nation (physic Yale, 1876) taught high school for h entire professional career. Likewis Charles Turner, who earned a Ph.D. biology from the University of Chica in 1907, taught high school in St. Lo until his death in 1923. And, Anna Ju Cooper, who earned a Ph.D. from t University of Paris in 1925, also taug high school for her entire life. As result of the well-trained faculties o

number of outstanding black high schools in urban areas, many black scholars and professionals were produced by these institutions. For a discussion of the role of the black high school in producing black scholars and professionals, see Horace Mann Bond, *Black American Scholars: A Study of their Beginnings* (Detroit: Belamp, 1972). Also see Harry Washington Greene, *Holders of Doctorates Among American Negroes* (Boston: Meador, 1946).

60. Charles S. Johnson, *The Negro College Graduate* (New York: Negro Universities Press, 1969), p. 227.
61. DuBois and Dill, *The Common School and the Negro American,* p. 106.
62. "National Association of Teachers in Colored Schools," in *Southern Workman* 47:9 (September 1918), p. 420.
63. "Better Training for Negro Teachers," in *Southern Workman* 49:5 (May 1920), p. 203.
64. Johnson, *The Negro College Graduate,* p. 227.
65. Lucy Diggs Slowe, "The Education of Negro Women and Girls," speech delivered at Teachers College, Columbia University, March 11, 1931, in *Lucy Diggs Slowe Papers,* Moorland–Spingarn Collection, Howard University.
66. Ibid.
67. Jeanne L. Noble, *The Negro Woman's College Education* (New York: Teachers College, Columbia University, 1956), p. 87.
68. Ibid.
69. W. E. B. DuBois, "Education," in *Chicago Defender,* October 19, 1946.
70. Bullock, *A History of Negro Education,* p. 217.
71. Harry S. Ashmore, *The Negro and the Schools* (Chapel Hill: University of North Carolina Press, 1954), p. 159.
72. David Fellman (ed.), *The Supreme Court and Education,* 3d ed. (New York: Teachers College Press, Columbia University, 1976), pp. 138–139.
73. "The Negro Teacher and Desegregation of the Public Schools," in *Journal of Negro Education* 2:2 (Spring 1953), pp. 96–97.
74. *Journal of Negro Education* 24:4 (Fall 1955), pp. 405–408.
75. DuBois and Dill, *The Common School,* p. 7.
76. National Education Association, *Status of the American Public School Teacher, 1985–86* (Washington, DC: National Education Association, 1987).
77. American Council on Education, Office of Minority Concerns, *Minorities in Higher Education, Sixth Annual Report* (Washington, DC: American Council on Education, 1987), p. 15.
78. *Education Daily,* March 8, 1988, pp. 3–4.
79. J. G. Weiss, "Testing Teachers: Strategies for Damage Control," in National Education Association, *What Is the Appropriate Role of Testing in the Teaching Profession?* (Washington, DC: National Education Association, 1987).
80. See "Teacher Testing and Assessment," Special Issue Yearbook, in *Journal of Negro Education* 55:33 (Summer 1986).
81. Linda Darling-Hammond and Arthur E. Wise, "Teaching Standards or Standardized Teaching?" in *Educational Leadership* 41 (1983), pp. 66–69.
82. See "Minority Teacher Recruitment and Retention: A Call for Action," Policy Statement of the American Association of Colleges for Teacher Education (Washington, DC: American Association of Colleges for Teacher Education, September 1987).
83. The front page of the June 15, 1988, *Chronicle of Higher Education* highlighted the lack of black students in medical schools and in scientific and technical fields.
84. W. E. B. DuBois, "Whither Now and Why," in W. E. B. DuBois, *The Education of Black People: Ten Critiques 1906–1960,* ed. Herbert Aptheker (Amherst: University of Massachusetts Press, 1973), p. 151.
85. Ibid., p. 152.

13

The Persistence of Reform in American Schools

Larry Cuban

For every complicated problem there is a solution that is short, simple, and wrong.—*H. L. Mencken*

After decades of planned changes aimed at improving teaching, why do many of these same reforms appear repeatedly as solutions to classroom problems? And why do classrooms seem to be pretty much the same as they had been prior to and after the recurring changes? To informed observers of American schooling and thoughtful veteran practitioners alike, both questions are familiar—and point to the apparent contradiction of constancy amidst change.[1]

A few examples will help clarify the meaning of the two questions. The current passion among the states for a traditional education, one in which a core of academic subjects is mandated for study by every student, is one example of a durable solution dating back to before the turn of the century.

By the 1880s, many high schools had dozens of courses, taught for different lengths of time, spread across four or more curricula geared to students going into businesses and colleges directly after graduation. Colleges and universities found it difficult to measure the worth of so many different courses with varied titles on a student's record. Uniformity was absent.

In 1893 the report of the Committee of Ten on Secondary School studies (sponsored by the National Educational Association—the NEA) recommended for all high schools an academic core of four years of English, three years of history, three years of science, three years of mathematics, and a foreign language. Chaired by Harvard University President Charles Eliot, the committee urged that "Every subject which is taught at all in a secondary school should be taught in the same way and to the same extent to every pupil so long as he pursues it, no matter what the probable destination of the pupil may be, or at what point his education is to cease."[2]

The Committee of Ten's aim was to reduce the crazy quilt of courses and standardize the time allotted to a subject and how a subject was taught. By World War I, their recommendations had become mainstream practice. What was once good for those youth going on to college was now good for all.[3] During the same period, however, another generation of reformers sought to resurrect multiple courses of study tailored to the different futures of youth—the practice evident in earlier decades. Unlike Eliot and other reformers, progressives viewed such curricular variety as more in keeping with how they defined democracy and equality of education.

By 1918, another national report (also sponsored by the NEA), *The Cardina*

Principles of Secondary Education, set forth that generation's manifesto challenging the concept of a single best curriculum for all students. Progressives saw varied curricula designed for different futures as a way for secondary schools to concentrate attention on fulfilling individual students' potential while preparing them for their probable niches in society. Over the next three decades, this gospel of the secondary-school progressives created the comprehensive high school. Vocational education, college-preparatory courses, business classes, and other curricula expanded the old academic course of study that all past students had taken.[4]

By the early 1950s, however, the varied curricula became the target for yet another generation of reformers who saw anti-intellectual flabbiness and a diminished concern for excellence in nonacademic courses. Arthur Bestor's *Educational Wastelands: The Retreat from Learning in Our Public Schools* (1953), and Albert Lynd's *Quackery in the Public Schools* (1953), for example, blasted the low academic standards and the commensurate quality of teaching in high schools.[5]

With evidence of Russia's technological gains orbiting the earth in 1957, further barrages of criticism accelerated public concern for what critics labeled as "mindless" high-school courses. The result: New academic programs spilled over schools, poured on because of fears for national security, propelled with the backing of federal legislation (The National Education Defense Act, 1958), and made all the more urgent by James Bryant Conant's report on high schools (1959). The outcome—for a time, at least—proved seemingly beneficial. More and more high schools raised academic standards by increasing the number of courses in math, science, and foreign languages. Advanced-placement courses were established. Programs for gifted children flourished. Subsidized by foundations as well as federal funds, academics constructed new curricula based upon the nature of the disciplines and how scientists practiced biology, physics, math, and the social sciences.[6]

But by the mid–1960s and later, political and social movements aimed at freeing the individual from bureaucratic constraints and helping the poor, especially ethnic and racial minorities, swept across schools, affecting research, policy making, and school practices. If "desegregation," "compensatory education," and "magnet schools" became familiar phrases, so did "free schools," "open classrooms," and "flexible scheduling." By the early 1970s, many (but not all) of the previous decade's academic reforms receded, to be replaced by passionate efforts to again differentiate courses and schools, in order to accommodate low-income and minority children who had enjoyed little access to rigorous academic curricula and intellectually demanding teachers. Special programs, alternative schools, and new curricula dotted the urban and suburban school landscape in efforts to recapture students who had been either relegated to the margins of a high-school education or pushed out.[7]

By the late 1970s and early 1980s, however, a renewed call for a common core of academic content available to all students had again become evident. *A Nation at Risk* urged readers to demand of their schools higher academic standards and a common curriculum. State after state raised its graduation requirements—and once again more students took chemistry, geometry, and foreign languages.[8]

For almost a century this enduring debate over whether all students should take one curriculum or varied ones has shuttled back and forth among proponents of different versions of how an equal education should be defined in a democracy. Each time this argument has broken out, specialists have created new courses of study, teachers have written revised curriculum guides, and fresh texts have appeared. Yet, because there is no one correct definition of an equal education, and no one way to empirically prove the worth of one version of equal education over another, the controversy will occur again—and again.

During all these recurring changes when curriculum reforms have swept through schools and altered master schedules and handbooks of course offerings, teachers still have entered their classrooms, closed their doors, and taught in ways that have endured over decades with few significant alterations in practice. Those few researchers who have investigated how teachers have taught over the past century have documented a persistent continuity in the main elements of classroom instruction. (This has been especially the case in high schools; modest changes have more of a history of enduring in elementary schools).[9]

Definitions and Deeds: Change, Reforms, and Persistence

I now return to those two questions with which I began this chapter: Why do many reforms appear again and again as solutions to problems of teaching and teachers? And why do classrooms seem to be pretty much the same as they had been prior to and after the changes? The significance of such questions for policy makers, researchers, and practitioners determined to improve what occurs in schools and universities is self-evident: If planned changes appear and reappear but have had little impact in substantially altering what teachers do in their classrooms, then pressing for more reforms without examining why such repeated efforts have yielded so little is as promising as trying to convince an eight-year-old that studying Plato is more fun than eating an ice cream cone.

To answer these questions about reforms concerning teachers and teaching, I need to make clear what "change" is, what "reforms" are, what constitutes "persistence," and what "success" and "failure" mean when applied to the outcomes of these planned changes. I begin in this direct manner because these words come from the working vocabulary of improvement-minded researchers, policy makers, and practitioners. Yet these familiar words, often serving as a convenient shorthand among like-minded reformers, mask conflicting and complicated concepts that ultimately cause confusion among the most sincere, well-intentioned seekers of change.

Change

This characteristic American word that promises so much contains within it at least three assumptions that seldom get inspected.

First, most Americans view change as positive; it is growth, progress, and improvement wrapped in one package. Yet change may or may *not* be progress. The divorce that devastates one spouse finds the other relishing a newfound freedom. The bull-market crash wipes out millions of dollars for thousands of frightened investors who sell, yet lets other investors buy from panicked sellers, sit tight during the roller-coaster ride of stocks, and enjoy every dip and climb of a volatile market.

Or consider an example about schools. In the middle of the nineteenth century, tax-supported common schools took in boys and girls from cities and farms, migrants, and immigrants. Buildings went up. Teachers were hired. The school year lengthened. With more children attending classes, more students graduating, more children from different cultures sitting in classrooms than ever before, some observers saw these changes as improvements to schooling in a democracy. In the eyes of other observers, however, the "improvements" were viewed as calculated efforts by those with social and economic clout to design and impose a schooling that would shape children's beliefs and behavior to fit social needs as defined by those in power—in other words, as impositions of the powerful upon the weak. Determining progress, then, depends upon the goals and mental maps of the people making judgments about the change. Improvement is largely in the eye of the beholder; it is not necessarily synonymous with change.

Next, there is the assumption that change is divorced from stability, that it is a matter of either one or the other. Yet, change and stability coexist in the same person, group, organization, and culture. Psychologists often point to the durability of personality traits over time even as an individual grows from infant to child, from child to youth, and from youth to adult. Sociologists stress the persistent features that mark organizations as they evolve from infancy to maturity. Anthropologists record how both exotic and familiar cultures adapt ("change") traditions. Political scientists underscore the continuity of national impulses that persist through the centuries regardless of revolutionary changes in regimes. Constancy and change are entangled; it is no oxymoron to speak of stable forms of change, or continuity amidst change.[10]

Finally, there is the prevailing assumption that all changes are basically of the same type. They are not. Imagine a continuum of change with, at one end, planned efforts to alter what exists, and unplanned changes at the other. Planned changes are designs and blueprints that policy makers adopt, crossing their fingers when they delegate the implementation. (Many innovations, both the berated and the embraced, belong at the pole labeled "planned change.") In the middle of the continuum would be changes that result from bargaining and compromises struck between individuals and groups, such as changes that arise from negotiations among interest groups within and without organizations. These are changes resulting from the natural conflict that exists within organizations adjusting to their surroundings. At the other end of the continuum would be unplanned changes occurring from accidents and shifts in the environment of the organization.

Some examples to place along this continuum of change might help. When birthrates dip and school enrollments go down five years later, or when significant numbers of rural families move to the city, such demographic changes are both unplanned and difficult to predict, even though the *consequences* of such changes *can* be anticipated. Similarly, shifts in the national and world economies occur erratically, and appear to be well beyond the limited efforts of planners to control, much less direct. Social and political movements such as nuclear disarmament activities or civil rights actions arise, swell, and spill over countryside and cities in undetermined ways. The onset of a disease that infects millions (*e.g.*, AIDS) changes individual and community behavior. With such unplanned changes, private citizens and entire governments alike react, adapting to the altered conditions they face, trying to steer in the direction of the social or economic change but accommodating much as a hapless sailor hanging on to a tiller in a storm.

Unplanned social changes penetrate schools, too. Consider how economic changes expand and shrink the resources allocated to schooling; the civil rights movement's influence on student access to schools, hiring policies, and textbooks; the AIDS epidemic and its consequences for educating children about sexual relations in general and the specifics of the disease itself, much less the treatment of students with AIDS. In response to unplanned social and economic changes schools react, adapt, and compromise tirelessly to regain some level of stability.

Planned changes, however, are *designs*. The establishment of tax-supported public schools, for example, is an intentional effort by one generation to prepare the next to enter and sustain the society. Within the category of planned changes, there are at least two types: first- and second-order changes.[11] First-order changes are intentional efforts to enhance existing arrangements while correcting deficiencies in policies and practices. Those who propose first-order changes assume that the existing goals and structures of schooling are both adequate and desirable. First-order changes, then, try to make what exists more efficient and effective without disturbing the basic organizational features, and without substantially altering how adults and children perform their roles.

Examples of first-order changes include modifying certification standards for teachers and administrators, raising salaries, selecting smarter textbooks, adding (or deleting) courses to (or from) the curriculum, scheduling people and activities more efficiently, and introducing more effective forms of evaluation and training. The compensatory programs of the 1960s and since (both Title I of the Elementary and Secondary Act and its later consolidation into Chapter I) are instances of first-order reforms. The current school effectiveness movement and its swift spread into state-driven reforms of the 1980s, with their emphasis on higher expectations for students, more student time on academic tasks, strong instructional leadership at the school site, and tighter aligning of goals with curriculum, texts, and tests, is another instance of first-order reform.

Second-order changes seek to alter the fundamental ways in which organizations are put together because of major dissatisfaction with present arrangements. These changes introduce new goals, structures, and roles that transform familiar ways of performing duties into novel solutions to persistent problems. Often the original problem that produced the existing structures and roles is reframed and different structures and roles consistent with the reframed problem are introduced. Mid–nineteenth-century reformers sought to restructure one-room schools, and the role of the teacher, to fit a new vision of order, efficiency, and democracy. Moving from the one-room schoolhouse with one untrained, unsupervised teacher responsible for children ranging in age from 6 to 18 (where each child could get only a few minutes of the teacher's attention during the day), to a graded elementary school with a principal, a separate classroom for each teacher, children grouped by age, and a curriculum divided into grade-level chunks, was a second-order change.

An example of second-order changes in curriculum and instruction is when teachers and principals choose a pedagogy rooted in a vision of children as individuals who need to learn to make their own decisions, who need to connect what occurs in classrooms with activities outside the school, and who need to discover and create knowledge rather than only absorb it. Teachers and administrators who organize schools, classrooms, and lessons consistent with those beliefs produce very different schools and students from those educators who view children as small people who have to be filled with correct knowledge and trained to be big people.

Presently, there are a few reform proposals that have the capacity to become second-order changes. One is vouchers that would give parents a choice of where to send their children. Another is open enrollment districts—that is, the abolition of attendance boundaries and neighborhood schools. Designs that permit school staffs to make budgetary, personnel, and curricular decisions also are proposals for second-order changes. In each case, the intention is to alter a basic part of the fundamental design of schooling through enlarging choice and autonomy, or rearranging how schools are funded and operated.

Generally, since the beginning of the twentieth century, school reforms have been a series of first-order changes in graded schools and governance structures. Occasionally, certain second-order reforms such as student-centered instruction, nongraded schools, team teaching, and open-space architecture have been attempted in isolation, or uncoordinated with other efforts, with little enduring effects other than occasional adaptations by individual teachers and administrators. Finally, there have been curricular reforms aimed at second-order changes in teaching and learning (the "new math," "new biology") that have been transformed into first-order changes—ending up in classrooms as another set of textbooks.

In examining prevailing assumptions about planned change, I have inevitably slipped into describing reforms. I now need to elaborate the concept of reform, as applied to schools.

Reforms

A school reform is a planned solution to a perceived problem. Why a situation becomes defined as a problem, how the problem was defined previously (if at all), who did the defining and generated the alternative solutions, and how particular reforms or planned changes were selected and implemented, are appropriate questions to pursue in analyzing the origins and meaning of the reforms, prior to even assessing their consequences.

Every reform aimed at classrooms that I have studied carried within it a desire to end an unsatisfactory situation, as defined by those who designed the solution. An "unsatisfactory situation" means that particular goals determined by interested parties were blocked. It was a problem to that person or group. The reform was the solution picked to end the undesirable situation. Some illustrations might help in clarifying this definition of reform.

Consider the dissatisfaction of a small but vocal group of teachers within a newly remodeled elementary school containing open spaces called "pods" for teams of teachers to work with 100 or so children at one time. Although this small group of teachers enjoy the colorful walls, carpeting, and separate work spaces for each grade, they find the noise level among the 100 children in the open space disruptive to their teaching. What one class does distracts another, they claim; noise levels from students engaged in academic tasks interfere with the work of other teachers. The pod, according to these teachers, blocks achievement of their instructional goals. These teachers have defined a problem: how to alter the pod so as to end the distractions and noise that impede teaching and (they assert) learning?

If they are successful in recruiting the principal, other teachers, and parents to their definition of the problem, and secure agreement to the solutions they propose (movable bookcases and eight-foot high partitions to make classes self-contained for a few periods of the day), a teacher-initiated and -designed change to end an undesirable situation affecting their performance has occurred. Need I add that problem-defining and -solving are political processes?

School reforms, then, are time- and place-bound; they are political solutions to specific problems defined by groups and individuals inside (and/or outside) the schools who wish to remove perceived barriers to desirable performance. In groups and organizations, these problem definitions need to gain sufficient support to embrace particular solutions. Which solutions are chosen to be the reforms is contingent upon time, setting, resources, and people. In some instances, certain solutions appear, disappear, but then reappear over the decades (*e.g.*, curricular reforms aimed at stiffening academic standards). They persist.[12]

What, then, does "persistence in reforms" mean? At first glance the phrase appears to be a paradox, a play on the saying that the more something changes, the more it remains the same. I have already referred to the differing ways of viewing change, and the injudiciousness of divorcing constancy from change. Let me now discuss the word "persistence."

Persistence

I use the word in two senses. Both apply to regularities in behaviors rather than the erratic reappearance of isolated events. First, there is a durable impulse toward improvement that flows and ebbs throughout the history of schooling. A by-product of larger political, economic, and social changes in the culture, when the impulse runs strong it propels individuals and groups into sharp criticism of schools (what David Cohen calls the tradition of "school hating"), followed by ambitious efforts to alter what exists.[13] At other times it is weak, producing sporadic blasts of censure and occasional sniping before slipping away. This insistent drumbeat of sharp criticism harnessed to an urge to improve schools is, I will argue, basic to the larger culture in which Americans live; there is a marked durability of this drive on the part of Americans to be both dissatisfied with schools and anxious to reform them.

The second sense of the word is simply that particular solutions to problems within teaching, among teachers, and within teacher education keep resurfacing as preferred choices among an array of possibilities. Some examples may help.

In teacher education, over the past century and a half, new programs aimed at preparing recruits for the classroom have appeared and reappeared that either lean heavily on technical preparation (*e.g.*, how to prepare a lesson plan, handling questions in class, managing difficult students) or the liberal arts (*e.g.*, preparation in history, literature, science), or some combination of the two.[14] This durable debate over what constitutes a proper preparation for those entering classrooms merges with the larger recurring controversies over how well teachers are teaching, or the conditions of schooling. If reformers say that classroom teachers have a cold, then teacher-education institutions sneeze.

Within the past quarter-century, competency-based teacher education—a skills-based, technical curriculum in teacher education—has given way to many research universities' abolishing their undergraduate education courses and instituting fifth-year programs for liberal-arts graduates in which they take a few required courses in pedagogy and in content areas, and spend most of their time teaching under supervision of experienced teachers.[15]

Or note the familiar solution to the problem of teacher quality by increasing the quantity of formal schooling beyond grammar and high school of those entering classrooms. Periodic calls for increased salaries to attract higher-quality applicants is a similar solution to the same problem.[16] Therefore, the constant impulse to improve schools, and the durability of certain reforms (their periodic reappearance dressed in a new language or program) are what I mean by persistence of reform. But in using such words as "persistent" and "durable," how can one sort out "success" from "failure"?

Success and Failure of Reforms

In the literature describing a century of efforts to substantially alter teacher behavior, words like "success" and "failure" flourish: Progressive educational reforms succeeded in enlarging the school's role to include the physical and emotional as well as the moral and intellectual aspects of children. The curriculum reforms of the early 1960s failed; Title I (and now Chapter 1) programs for poor and/or minority children have either succeeded or failed, depending upon which studies are cited.[17] Yet amid these categorical judgments, few of which recognize degrees of success or failure, or the factors associated with each or the differing values that produce diverse conclusions, there are many implementation studies of programs that yield findings and speak a language that go well beyond such simple—and ultimately misleading—terms.[18]

Researchers stress that planned changes occurring in schools frequently get adapted as they are being implemented. Program adaptations are made by both policy makers and practitioners, in response to the specific setting, the times, the dominant beliefs of practitioners, and available dollars and people. The tailoring of a reform proceeds erratically but inexorably on its path into schools until what materializes in classrooms may be quite unlike the original design. Variations in programs and practices as a result of adaptations, then, blur the meaning of such terms as "success" and "failure."

What the unrelenting process of adaptation does in producing program variation is question the common, but implicit, criterion used to judge success of a reform: the fit between the original design and what was finally put into practice. Using as a standard the fidelity between intentions and practices is of course little more than the policy maker's wishes for a design untouched by others to be put into place as-is. Because designers of solutions for schools frequently are neither teachers nor principals, perceptions of what the problems are, and which solutions will work, often differ between adopters and implementers.

To those who design reforms, practitioners' modifications contaminate solutions. To practitioners, adaptations are essential for *any* solution to work in a school or classroom. To one, alterations in designs and variations in practice are evidence of decay and failure; to the other, the same variations are healthy signs of inventiveness, practicality, and (of course) success.

Policy makers' preoccupation with fidelity to the design and aversion to variation is linked to other criteria frequently used to judge success: Has the reform produced results yet? Did the reform solve the problem? Has the reform survived sufficiently to be still recognizable? These criteria, seldom invoked openly, nevertheless are commonly applied. The urgency for swift results leaves little time for seeing a reform implemented carefully or over a sustained period. Instead the frequent, unrelenting pressure for visible early gains drives policy makers and reformers to concentrate on keeping the plan as it is, and the implementers to concentrate on adapting it to the workplace.[19]

Does this mean that no judgment about success or failure can be made? No. A small number of researchers have explored how such judgments can be made. Matthew Miles and A. Michael Huberman, for example, have systematically charted how particular innovations aimed at school improvement achieved desired outcomes. They lay out the organizational factors at the district, school, and classroom levels associated with the successful starting of a program, its implementation, and gradual absorption into routine practices. In identifying factors related to those degrees of success and failure, their studies offer a map for judging planned changes. Miles and Huberman have helped to broaden our views of the complexities involved in assessing success and failure.[20]

Let me suggest another way of conceptualizing both outcomes. Imagine multiple continua. At one pole of each is success, at the other failure. Each continuum represents one dimension of a reform that may be judged significant—e.g., goals, predicted outcomes, fidelity, particular processes associated with success, incorporation into routines, and so on.[21] One example would be a continuum on whether a reform has succeeded in being installed into daily school or district routines. There have been, of course, many such successful reforms. The more obvious ones would be the graded elementary school with self-contained classrooms and segmented curriculum; the introduction of physical education;

extracurricular activities; testing for intelligence; the junior high school; vocational classes; counseling services; and sex education.[22]

At the other pole of the same continuum, failure is also clear: No sign of the reform either is currently visible or can be directly traced to its origins. There is no obvious residue. A number of researchers have documented these Edsels of reform, such as the introduction of radio to classrooms, the platoon system of alternating groups of children using the same facilities, and raising student achievement through contracting with private corporations. The failure of reforms targeted at one school have been thoroughly reported by Louis Smith in *Anatomy of An Innovation;* by Neal Gross and Joseph Giaquinta in *Implementing Organizational Innovations;* and in the various studies of what happened to the innovative social-studies curriculum of the late 1960s, ''Man as a Course of Study'' (MACOS).[23]

Where the difficulties arise with this or any other continuum is the middle, not the ends. What occurs in the middle range are solutions that get modified as they are put into practice in schools and classrooms. The evidence for success is ambiguous, open to conflicting interpretations. One can see traces, in current practices, of the original designs. In some classrooms where teachers make written contracts with students, the residue of the Dalton Plan introduced in the 1920s is evident. Elements of the ''new'' biology and physics curricula of the 1960s are now encased between the hard covers of textbooks. Buried within the framework of ''mastery learning'' (however defined) are the earlier efforts of Preston Search in Pueblo, Colorado in the 1880s, and Carleton Washburne's Winnetka Plan (from the 1920s) to create ways for teachers to tailor instruction to individual students.[24]

Depending upon *who* does the labeling, solutions cut to fit particular settings may be viewed as successes or failures. For those deeply invested in the adoption of a reform and nervous about the alterations made by others, the more changes made, the more likely it would be labeled ''failure.'' The fewer the alterations, they believe, the more likely the chance of its being labeled a moderate or partial success.

I offer a few examples. Increasing classroom use of, and student access to, microcomputers for instructional purposes became a popular solution in the 1980s to a cluster of ill-defined problems: teacher productivity, student motivation for learning, and the school's role in increasing the nation's economic competitiveness in global markets. Where on the continuum of success and failure would the following examples fall?

Five years after microcomputers were introduced in a high school to give each teacher in a 50-member faculty one classroom computer in addition to a laboratory filled with 30 desktop computers, 6 percent of the faculty used computers to prepare lessons for their students at least once a week, and 10 percent used them once a month for the same purpose. Another 6 percent used the computer to keep attendance, record homework, calculate grades, and produce interim progress reports every two weeks for each student. Finally, another 10 percent (different from the previous teachers) took their classes to the computer lab once a month, but did not use their classroom computers for instructional purposes. Is this reform a complete, moderate, or partial success?

Or if, after seven years, 5 percent of all university programs preparing teachers altered completely their programs in line with the majority of the Holmes Report's recommendations on teacher education, and another 20 percent partially did so, adapting some while rejecting others, where on the a continuum would it go?

I have inserted percentages into these examples to make clear that *most* of the intended changes were unfulfilled after five or more years. Anyone familiar with the history of organizational change in public schools and higher education might be impressed, even delighted, with such figures and would be reluctant to place them on the failure side of the continuum. But designers of these solutions, and the cadre of cheerleaders who worked hard for adoption, might be sorely disappointed in the slim harvest after so much time and money were invested. They might even agree with W. C. Fields: "If at first you don't succeed, try, try again. Then quit. There's no use being a damn fool about it."

In stressing the obvious subjectivity in judging reforms that accumulate adaptations on their journey to classrooms and are at neither end of the continuum, I make the self-evident point that one can make judgments about success and failure of reforms. But such judgments need shades of gray beyond the current black-or-white simplicities. A clearer grasp of historical trends and multiple criteria need to be invoked, and those making the judgments would need to reveal their criteria and make explicit how they reached such conclusions.[25]

I have devoted much attention to issues of success and failure because how each is defined and displayed among both professionals and lay audiences has a great deal to do with creating and sustaining a crisis mentality which seizes participants in those recurring moments of school reform. The optimism that accompanies a torrent of change often decays, leaving an odor of negative judgments with which the next generation of reformers must come to terms.

Applying the Terms: Improving Teacher Productivity

After defining change, reform, persistence, and success and failure, let me apply the definitions to a set of earlier reforms aimed at improving teacher and student productivity: getting teachers to use machines in their classrooms to improve student learning.

The dream of making teachers more efficient (that is, of getting students to learn more in less time with less effort and at less cost) has a checkered history extending back to medieval colleges and schools. This dream has endured from the invention of the lecture, centuries ago, to this century, when reformers first sought teaching efficiency and student productivity through film and radio (the 1920s through the 1940s) and, later, through instructional television (the early 1950s through the 1960s).

Thomas Edison expressed the fondest hopes of reformers in 1922 when he said:

> I believe that the motion picture is destined to revolutionize our educational system and that in a few years it will supplant largely, if not entirely, the use of textbooks. I should say that on the average we get about two percent efficiency out of schoolbooks as they are written today. The education of the fu-

ture, as I see it, will be conducted through the medium of the motion picture . . . where it should be possible to obtain one hundred percent efficiency.[26]

The dream resurfaced in the 1980s when educators, corporate executives, government officials, and parents united in urging teachers to use computers in their classrooms. William Norris, founder and chairman emeritus of Control Data Corporation, told an audience in 1987:

> One key to necessary reforms in education is the adoption of computer-based education (C.B.E.) as the primary mode of instruction in our schools. Under the direction of teachers certified not only in particular content areas but also in the use of advanced educational technologies, a C.B.E. program expanded from its current supplementary role would free teachers of inefficient traditional methods of instruction and recordkeeping. In turn, the money saved from improved efficiency could be used to raise teachers' salaries significantly.[27]

In the enduring search for increased classroom efficiency and productivity, the lecture, textbooks, film, radio, television, and the personal computer are blood relatives.

Both Edison and Norris, almost seven decades apart, said that familiar ways of teaching (teachers talking most of the time, whole-group instruction, the use of the chalkboard and textbook) are inefficient means of communicating knowledge and higher-level skills to children of varying abilities. To such well-intentioned reformers these machines were seen as fundamentally altering teaching practices and relationships with students. Stepping aside (along with the textbook) as the central source of knowledge, the teacher would become a guide to students in their quest for learning. No longer would teachers organize lessons based upon talking to the entire group, homework assignments, and motivating students. When these new machines were available and appropriately used, the usual array of teaching practices would give way to individualized instruction, work-stations for students, and using the teacher as a resource rather than the sole source of knowledge. In effect, these tools were intended by ardent reformers to be vehicles for second-order changes in teaching and learning.

Teachers adapted *some* of these intended second-order solutions, for either daily use or on a weekly basis (films, instructional television or videocassettes, and desktop computers in the classroom or in a school laboratory). Other teachers, by far the majority, used these tools monthly or even less often. Few of the following innovations, however, made it past the classroom door permanently: programmed learning, instructional television, talking typewriters, computer-assisted instruction, and language laboratories. In other words, what was intended as second-order reforms, for any number of reasons, became transformed into first-order changes by many teachers who wished to use these machines. But most teachers closed their doors on them.

In each successive wave of well-intentioned efforts by businessmen, administrators, and public officials to get teachers to use these supposedly powerful instructional tools, growing frustration among both educators and noneducators over limited use of machines in classrooms produced an easy but simplistic explanation for the infrequent use of these labor-saving, knowledge-sharing, and very expensive tools: teacher stubbornness anchored in inefficient, traditional classroom practices. Portraying teachers as dinosaurs, antiprogressives with Luddite chromosomes, became common fare among boosters of the new classroom technologies.[28]

To these advocates of electronic tools, *teachers* were the problem. Reforms intended to have revolutionary impact upon classrooms were largely termed failures only because most teachers used them infrequently. To informed observers of schools, however, aware of the organizational complexities and the impact of formal and informal structures on individual behavior, the same infrequently used tools had nonetheless expanded many teachers' repertoire of classroom practices. In short, adaptations in use of the machines had stuck for a substantial number of teachers, but not at the second-order level of use desired by designers and cheerleaders for the solution.

Informed observers would be unready to label such first-order changes as failures. Instead, a plausible conclusion to draw would be that such solutions have been *moderately* successful in expanding the range of tools available to teachers—provided, of course, that hard- and software were accessible. These observers may have appreciated, more than did the fervent reformers, the irony of technological improvements aimed at completely transforming teachers' classroom behavior becoming, over time, simply more tools added to the teacher's kit to carry out what had been occurring in classrooms for generations.

Irony aside, more and more promoters reluctantly have come to appreciate the complexity of getting teachers to use new technologies. Some scholars have reframed the problem of increasing use of technology in classrooms from teacher resistance and inertia to locating the problem in how organizational structures, cultural beliefs about knowledge, and learning shape attitudes and practices. Such reframing of the problem has begun to shift attention away from a rational, mechanistic perspective (i.e., improve the tools of learning and train teachers to use them) to one of getting teachers to believe in the tools, and for teachers to actively reshape them to the contours of the classroom.[29]

These and other efforts to reconsider how a problem initially defined one way can be viewed from another perspective, thereby generating different questions and evidence, again bring me back to the question I asked at the beginning of this chapter: Why do these efforts to improve the efficiency of teaching appear and reappear? And why do classrooms seem to be pretty much the same as they had been prior to the changes? Targeting the intransigence of teachers is insufficient and misleading, either to explain the limited use that most teachers have made of these machines, the hardy band of ardent users, or the constancy and change that mark schooling generally.

The final section of this chapter will move beyond the familiar, convenient, and simplistic explanation for what occurs in classrooms, to include other perspectives. Each explanation I offer is a way of seeing—a perspective on change and constancy in—the nature of schooling in a democracy, with suggested answers to the above questions. Moreover, each perspective has buried within it a definition of school problems, and embryonic solutions. Hence, I offer them now as a device to broaden the ways of defining what the problems are in reshaping teaching practices, and to expand the agenda of issues in the larger policy debate on reforming American schools.

School Reforms: Ways of Seeing

I will present each of the following perspectives as it might be set forth by an advocate, and then use it to explain why most teachers used machine technologies in their classrooms only minimally.

Political and Economic Cycles of Reform

The metaphor of the periodic cycle, the ebb and flow of events, explains why the same reforms seemingly appear and reappear over the history of schooling. A cycle contains within it a dialectic, a tugging back and forth between opposites, which produces a rough but evident rhythm to the occurrence of events: capitalism and democracy; private interest and public action; conservatism and liberalism. These cyclical movements are no simple pendulum swing between fixed points, yielding few changes; they are a rhythmic movement that seldom returns a situation to what it was earlier. In short, changes accumulate as cycles come and go.

A common rhythm to events is found in political cycles. In most democracies, economic factors (levels of employment, economic development, balance of trade, growth in gross national product, savings, etc.) determine to a great degree electoral changes. Electoral changes produce officials possessing ideas that can be labeled largely conservative or liberal. For example, in their eagerness to use public actions to solve social and economic problems, liberals pile up reform: The first two decades of this century belonged to the Progressive movement. In the wake of World War I, reform energies flagged, and while progressives still persisted, the 1920s became overtly conservative years wherein the "politics of public purpose gave way to the politics of private interest." Making money, becoming successful, pursuing what is best for each person, became prized outcomes admired both publicly and privately.[30]

Concern for individual interests of the 1920s evaporated in the Depression when liberals acted through the federal government to minimize the worst effects of the economic disaster. Concern for the poor, the aged, and the helpless was transformed into social programs. Reforms spilled over into the 1940s and the immediate postwar years. In the Eisenhower years, as in the 1920s, private interests surged forward, and public actions receded. The 1960s saw liberals seek out public ways of solving national ills in the New Frontier and the Great Society. By the early 1970s, Americans had experienced the trauma of Vietnam, race riots, the fall of a President, and campus violence. During the rest of the decade and into the 1980s, a return to cultivation of private interests and self-gratification reached its peak in the presidency of Ronald Reagan.

Schools react and adapt to the economic and political forces embedded in these cyclical turns. In the years when conservative values stressing private interests ran strong (i.e., in the 1920s, 1950s, and 1980s), schools were concerned with high academic standards, orderliness, efficiency, and productivity. Reforms were designed to deal with problems of inferior academic quality, lack of discipline in schools, and inefficiencies in operating schools. In years when liberal values dominated (i.e., in the early 1900s, 1930s, and 1960s), school reforms dealt with students who were outsiders, broadening what schools do in the community, and equal treatment.

Allowing for the inevitable lag time between cycles' working their ways into local school board actions, district efforts to introduce machine technologies (film, radio, instructional television, and microcomputers) to increase teacher efficiency and student productivity generally mesh with conservative years of the 1920s, 1950s, and 1980s. The dominance of private interests over public concerns in these decades translated to schools' concentrating on raising academic standards, promoting individual achievement, and seeking more efficient ways of teaching and learning—getting twice as much for half the cost, as it were. Although such innovations seldom were absent during other decades, their introduction and peaks of enthusiasm occurred during these conservative years.

Machine technologies, then, show up repeatedly in this century during those moments in the cycles when private interests dominate. But why do the classrooms seem to be pretty much the same as they had been before the changes? Because after reform energies slip and external pressures ease, most administrators and teachers fall back into familiar practices that frequently omit use of the machines. Only some become converts and include the technologies in their instructional repertoires. Thus, in the reform and reaction cycle, there are small, incremental changes that do occur—but to the unfamiliar eye, classrooms appear as totally unchanged places.[31]

School Reforms as Symbolic Solutions to National Crises

Public schooling came out of nineteenth-century efforts to eliminate grave social problems arising from demographic and economic changes which were altering the nation. To educate groups and individuals to know better what to do and how to behave (that is, to fit them more easily into the larger society) would reduce crime, poverty, and those seemingly intractable issues arising from the growth of factories, cities, and shifts in population. Schooling was viewed then (as now) as the major tool to help make individuals competent members of the nation.

Since individual choice is central to the economic and political belief systems of capitalism and democracy, schooling becomes crucial to the shaping of public and private values in understanding the rights and duties held by each individual. Thus, when there are national political, economic, or social problems that have been defined publicly as crises, schooling is viewed as a natural way of improving individual behavior which would then lead to a lessening or solution of national ills. Some examples might help:

Economic competition with Germany in the closing decades of the nineteenth century was part of the rationale for introducing vocational education to American schools.

Sputnik in the late 1950s fed the growing belief of Americans that the nation was losing its scientific edge to the Soviets, the reason being that high schools had failed in producing sufficient numbers of youth interested in math, science, and engineering.

In the 1980s, trade deficits with Japan, and the loss of American manufacturing to oversea locations, convinced many Americans that schools must be enlisted into the battle to regain our lost international edge in the economic struggle for primacy.

Adult and youth problems of chronic unemployment, intemperance, drug abuse, and deviant sexual activity frequently call for school programs that teach students how to get jobs and how to decrease harmful personal behavior.

Why schools get tagged with part of the responsibility for solving national ills is due to several factors. These include widespread institutional beliefs in schooling as essential for success to individuals in the broader society; the decentralized authority for operating the system; and the role played by various groups in defining crises and offering school reform as solutions.[32]

Consider the central fact of localism as the dominant feature in the governance of American schools. With no federal authority to direct schooling, responsibility is constitutionally fixed in the 50 states, which (in all but one case) delegate authority to local districts—over 15,000 in 1985. Within a local school district, different levels of policy making (school board) and administration (superintendent and principals) commonly are separated from practice (teaching students). Yet whenever there is a national problem (*e.g.*, recession, excessive drug abuse), a peculiar thing happens to the schools, local authority and different levels and such notwithstanding. Political, religious, economic, and other groups put forth definitions of what is wrong and what should be done. They frame the problem in terms that cause alarm. A crisis is constructed as shared citizen perceptions lead to calls for action. Since education is everybody's concern, schools once again become a ready solution to the crisis. It is in fact an organizationally decentralized national institution that integrates a society prizing individual action and choice!

Laws are passed. Directives are issued. Policies mandate new procedures and programs. Staffs are hired. Because of the decentralized organization, the federal, state, and local responses ripple unevenly through the systems, but nonetheless produce surprisingly similar responses at the local level (*e.g.*, competency testing, higher academic standards, computer literacy), due to the common beliefs shared about the importance of education. Whether changes actually occur in classrooms is of less importance: These reforms are largely symbolic, reaffirming the importance of beliefs in schooling.

Furthermore, notions of reform success and failure become blurred in the repeated construction of crises and the persistent reframing of national problems into school solutions. After all, how can one label any reform of schooling, especially those aimed at classrooms, a success if the same problems reappear?

Thus, a decentralized organization of education harnessed to popular beliefs in schooling as an instrument of individual improvement responds continually to perceived national economic, political, and social crises. Broad movements for school reform, and reactions to larger national problems, then, produce laws, policies, programs, and the like to improve schools—but leave ambiguous whether the results actually improve what occurs in classrooms.

Why, then, do technological solutions to improve teaching and learning recur? In a democratic and capitalistic society committed to competition and individual success through improved schooling, any tool available to make that success occur more swiftly and cheaply gets enlisted into solving the next national crisis. For example, with the computerization of the workplace during the past decade coming simultaneously with the declining competitiveness of American goods abroad, getting children to tap out commands on a desktop computer seemed to symbolize perfectly how America could regain its economic primacy. Schools that refused to respond to parental demands for classroom computers would risk a barrage of severe criticism and public action.

Will classrooms be largely the same after the introduction of these (and who knows what other) innovations? In the aftermath of the cheerleading for instructional television in the late 1950s and 1960s, the answer would be yes. Yet for microcomputers, it is too early to say. Clues have already appeared that machines often go unused, and that student use in schools remains largely marginal to the instructional program, occupying less than an hour or two a week. If this sort of reaction becomes the standard, such a result will again confirm the *symbolic* importance of reforms in reaffirming the *institutional* importance of education in reacting to national problems that get defined as crises.[33]

Organizational Complexities in the Implementation of Reform

The previous perspectives offer views that stress schools' reacting to societal and symbolic factors. In these perspectives, school reforms are adaptations to larger social, economic, and political issues within the nation. When the nation trips, schools take the fall. Certain aspects of schooling will, indeed, change in response to reforms (that is, new structures will appear, bureaucracy expand or shrink, different actors enter and exit, curricula change), but the practice of teaching will more than likely be altered only slightly.

The organizational perspective suggests that while the larger environment in which schools are nested generates impulses for school reforms, these reforms persist because each generation of reformers seldom comes to grips with the complexities of policy making, administration, and practice within schools. Reforms will occur in policies, rules, structures, and staff, but few lasting changes remain within classrooms. Failure to understand these organizational complexities dooms each generation of reformers to seeing their well-intentioned efforts drop with a thud at the teacher's door. Why?

Within school organizations there are three separate but interconnected worlds: policy makers, administrators, and practitioners. Within a federal, state, or local organization, each world has its own view of how schooling works, what (and who) is important and unimportant, what is a problem, and which rewards count.

Policy makers worry about the aims of education, securing adequate resources, and building structures to make the organization work. From competing constituencies, they try to finesse a consensus around purposes, allocation of funds, and policies to guide the organization. Managing conflict among competing claims from external and internal groups, policy makers seek least-common denominators in policies. Their rewards are political—that is, they get recognized, reappointed, reelected.

Administrators are the men and women sandwiched between policy makers and practitioners. They pursue the uneasy path between maintaining the organization and improving it. They make sure budgets are made, schedules are kept, reports are written, bids go for the lowest dollar, and performance is monitored. They advise policy makers and support practitioners. They decide whether to pursue, defer, adapt, or ignore what policy makers decide. They translate policy directives into understandable and doable rules for practitioners. Rewards to administrators flow from simply surviving and having practitioners they supervise feel reasonably good about what the organization is doing.

Practitioners are teachers. Their world is the classroom. Administrators are supposed to help them do their job well, not intervene or obstruct; policy makers are far-removed from collecting lunch money, marking papers, and questioning students on homework assignments. Yet while policy makers and administrators stand (as it were) outside the classroom, their influence on how teachers spend their time and use their space, and which children they will teach, is felt strongly amid classroom desks, chairs, and chalkboards. Still largely isolated from policy makers, administrators, and peers, teachers instruct, manage, and negotiate order with 30 or more students daily. Success ranges from completing a textbook in less than 30 weeks, to getting a nonreader to read, to having an especially noisy class pay attention to the lesson.

Efforts by administrators and policy makers to get teachers to alter their beliefs and practices in order to embrace different ones has had a history not calculated to give reformers much confidence. The reasons for stability in beliefs and practices seem to be connected to the classroom as a workplace. That is, organizational arrangements in the school support certain practices over others. In addition, there are in teaching popular and ancient beliefs about what teaching should be, how children should learn, and what knowledge is most worthwhile. In short, the world of the classroom is anchored in the particular history and culture of a society and its organizational imperatives, producing a setting in which traditional practices and beliefs change very slowly indeed. Constrained as teachers are, nonetheless they can (and do) enjoy a measure of freedom once the door is closed.[34]

These three separate but interdependent worlds contain not only inevitable conflict—personal and professional interests at each of the three levels frequently clash—but also (since their orbits overlap to some extent) turmoil. Policy makers respond to the turbulence in their world and convert impulses for changes in schools into broad, abstract policies called reforms. Invariably, the compromises they strike among competing coalitions in their world satisfy some and annoy others.

Administrators implement reform-minded policies by designing programs, regulations, and procedures that may approach the intent of the reforms but must fit existing specific situations. Commonly, policy makers find the new programs and regulations designed by administrators linked to the policies but still a few notches away from what the policy makers had in mind.

Faced now with new policies, programs, and regulations, practitioners seldom see the situation from the viewpoint of either the policy maker or the administrator. They see what is coming down to them as either helping or hindering their keeping a class's attention, covering material, and working with individual students. Teachers, in effect, bear the brunt of making choices about changes intended by the policy makers and translated by the administrators.

So the three worlds intersect, in a manner of speaking, and, in so merging, conflict. Ignorance of these three worlds by reformers, and of the inexorable conflict generated within and among them, may partially explain why each generation of fervent reformers comes anew upon the idea of introducing innovative technologies to classrooms to make teaching and learning more productive. It is of little surprise, then, that frequent efforts to introduce new technologies have had small success in penetrating classrooms permanently, or even pervasively.

The three perspectives presented here (i.e., political and economic cycles, reforms as symbolic solutions to national crises, and organizational complexities) expand the usual debates about planned change beyond the familiar one about rational change foiled by stubborn teachers. I have argued that in order to define public policy problems, multiple ways of seeing are necessary prior to determining which options (that is, which planned changes) should be adopted. While I have concentrated on the persistent impulse concerning innovative technologies and their impact upon classrooms, I believe that these perspectives apply just as well to other school reforms, and to the enduring issue of constancy amidst change in educational practice over the past century and a half.

The argument I have offered here is that whereas school reforms are, indeed, persistent over time, planned solutions intent upon altering teaching practices have had little enduring success. But *why* has there been this durability in reform impulses, and relative invulnerability of teaching practices to those innovations aimed at the classroom? I have no key to unlock this paradox. The above perspectives (and there are others) suggest possible explanations, each with a view of where reforms originate, how changes occur, and why classroom stability persists.[35]

But this is only a beginning (a crude and modest one, to be sure), made in hopes of widening the policy debates that currently exist, and those that will occur in future decades, beyond the common and narrow ones of the past. Were researchers, policy makers, and practitioners to be made more aware of the paradox of historical continuity in school reforms, and to expand their discussions about introducing planned changes into classrooms to include these and other points of view, the perceptions of repetitive failure in reform efforts, the consequences of disillusion, and a general unawareness of past school reforms would be less pronounced.

Perhaps we can learn from the ancient Chinese poets and painters who were entranced with the paradox of the waterfall: constant motion appearing as steadfast immobility. If so, history will have played a small but important part in the making of both better policy and a more sensitive understanding about the complexities of teaching.[36]

Notes

AUTHOR'S NOTE: I found the comments of Geraldine Clifford and Michael Sedlak helpful in revising this chapter.

1. Everyone comes to these questions in different ways. The continuity of schooling hit me between the eyes when I became a superintendent of schools in 1974 and visited over a thousand classrooms (some I went back to numerous times) in 35 schools in seven years. I recount that experience in *How Teachers Taught* (New York: Longman, 1984), p. 1. Seymour Sarason raised similar questions in *The Culture of the School and the Problem of Change* (Boston: Allyn & Bacon, 1971). John Goodlad and his associates also were puzzled by the constancy of certain processes in schooling when they completed *Looking Behind the Classroom Door* (Worthington, OH: Charles Jones, 1974). I offer these few sources as an unrepresentative sample of academics who have pursued such issues: Veteran practitioners write infrequently. But a quiet listener in faculty lounges, or over a beer with teachers or an administrator who has earned their trust, often will hear seasoned practitioners talk about how little things have changed since the 1970s (or 1960s—or, if these practitioners are *really* seasoned, the 1950s). In their own professional careers, the changes that have come and gone have left the basic processes of schooling pretty much the same.
2. Edward Krug (ed.), *Charles W. Eliot and Popular Education* (New York: Teachers College, Columbia University, 1961), p. 87.
3. For a solid treatment of the Committee of Ten, see Theodore Sizer, *Secondary Schools at the Turn of the Century* (New Haven: Yale University Press, 1964); and Edward Krug, *The Shaping of the American High School* (New York: Harper & Row, 1964), pp. 18–65.
4. Krug, *The Shaping of the American High School,* Chs. 14–17; Herbert Kliebard, *The Struggle for the American Curriculum, 1893–1958* (London: Routledge & Kegan Paul, 1986), Chs. 5 and 6; and Lawrence Cremin, *The Transformation of the School* (New York: Vintage, 1961), Chs. 6 and 7.
5. Arthur Bestor, *Educational Wastelands: The Retreat from Learning in Our Public Schools* (Urbana, IL: University of Illinois Press, 1953); and Albert Lynd, *Quackery in the Public Schools* (Boston: Little, Brown, 1953).
6. James B. Conant, *The American High School Today* (New York: McGraw–Hill, 1959).
7. Charles Silberman, *Crisis in the Classroom: The Remaking of American Education* (New York: Random House, 1970), Chs. 2–5.
8. National Commission on Excellence in Education, *A Nation at Risk* (Washington, DC: Government Printing Office, 1983).
9. David Tyack, Robert Lowe, and Elisabeth Hansot, *Public Schools in Hard Times* (Cambridge, MA: Harvard University Press, 1984); John Goodlad, *A Place Called School* (New York: McGraw–Hill, 1984); Judith A. Langer and Arthur N. Applebee, "The Uses of Writing in Academic Classrooms: A Study of Teaching and Learning" (Urbana, IL: National Council of Teachers of English, 1987); and Cuban, *How Teachers Taught.*
10. The distinction between progress and change is developed more fully in Rob-

ert Nisbet, *Social Change in History* (New York: Oxford University Press, 1969). For continuity and change, much has been written: See, for example, Nisbet, Ch. 7; Edward Shils, *Tradition* (Chicago: University of Chicago Press, 1981), Chs. 4–7; and James G. March, "Footnotes to Organizational Change," in *Administrative Science Quarterly* 26 (December, 1981), pp. 563–577. For further elaboration of the continuum of change, see Warren Bennis, Kenneth Benne, Robert Chin, and Kenneth Corey, *The Planning of Change,* 3d ed. (New York: Holt, Rinehart & Winston, 1976); Victor Baldridge and Terence Deal (eds.), *The Dynamics of Educational Change* (Berkeley, CA: McCutchan, 1983); Howard Aldrich, *Organizations and Environments* (Englewood Cliffs, NJ: Prentice–Hall, 1979); and Jeffrey Pfeffer and Gerald Salancik, *The External Control of Organizations: A Resource Dependence Perspective* (New York: Harper & Row, 1978).

11. The concepts of first- and second-order changes come from Paul Watzlawick, John Weakland, and Richard Fisch, *Change: Principles of Problem Formation and Problem Resolution* (New York: Norton, 1974).
12. For a further elaboration of how the organizational framing of problems is essentially a group and political process, see Douglas Yates, Jr., *The Politics of Management* (San Francisco: Jossey–Bass, 1985), Ch. 3.
13. David Cohen, "Teaching Practice: Plus Que Ça Change," in Philip W. Jackson (ed.), *Contributing to Educational Change* (Berkeley, CA: McCutchan, 1988), pp. 27–84.
14. Merle Borrowman, *The Liberal and Technical in Teacher Education* (New York: Teachers College, Columbia University, 1956).
15. *Tomorrow's Teachers: A Report of The Holmes Group* (East Lansing, MI: The Holmes Group, 1986)
16. Michael Sedlak and Stephen Schlossman, *Who Will Teach? Historical Perspectives on the Changing Appeal of Teaching as a Profession* (Santa Monica, CA: The Rand Corporation, 1986).
17. David Tyack, Michael Kirst, and Elisabeth Hansot, "Educational Reform: Retrospect and Prospect," in *Teachers College Record* 81 (1980), pp. 253–269; and Michael Kirst and Gail R. Meister, "Turbulence in American Secondary Schools: What Reforms Last?" in *Curriculum Inquiry* 15 (1985), pp. 169–186.
18. Michael Fullan, *The Meaning of Educational Change* (New York: Teachers College Press, Columbia University, 1982); Paul Berman, "Toward an Implementation Paradigm," in Rolf Lehming and M. Kane (eds.), *Improving Schools* (Beverly Hills, CA: Sage, 1981); Paul Berman and Milbrey McLaughlin, *Federal Programs Supporting Educational Change,* Vol. VIII, "Implementing and Sustaining Innovations" (Santa Monica, CA: The Rand Corporation, 1978); and A. Michael Huberman and Matthew Miles, *Innovation Up Close* (New York: Plenum Press, 1984). Keep in mind also that in some instances the innovation or design for change is so ill-timed, ill-considered, and lacking in resources that it *should* fail. Moreover, innovations forced upon a reluctant school or community with aims ill-matched to the goals and programs of the district are high risks to begin with.
19. Fullan, *Educational Change,* Chs. 4–6
20. Huberman and Miles, *Innovation Up Close,* Introduction and Chs. 3–8.
21. How long does a reform have to las before a judgment of success or failur can be made? What is the operationa definition of "success" in years? Wer the Lancasterian schools of the earl nineteenth century a failure because w have none today? Does the appearanc of classroom radio in the 1930s and it slide into obscurity by the 1950s mea that it failed? I raise these points becaus few writers consider the issue of longev ity as part of any assessment of succe and failure. In medicine, for example, there is no reappearance of a particul cancer in five years, the patient is said be cured. What is the expected life sp of a reform? Time, as a characteristic

the reform, could be another standard to determine success.

22. Kirst and Meister, in "Turbulence in American Secondary Schools," list reforms that "lasted."

23. Louis Smith and Pat Keith, *Anatomy of an Educational Innovation* (New York: Wiley, 1971; and Neal Gross and Joseph Giaquinta, *Implementing Organizational Innovations* (New York: Basic Books, 1971).

24. Cremin, *Transformation of the School*, pp. 295–298.

25. Donald Orlosky and B. Othanel Smith, "Educational Change: Its Origins and Characteristics," in *Phi Delta Kappan* (March 1972), pp. 412–414, wrestled with these categories of success and failure and subjectivity. They developed four categories: "[1] a change that has successfully been installed and has permeated the educational system; [2] a change that has successfully been installed and is sufficiently present that instances of the change are obvious; [3] a change that has not been accepted as a frequent characteristic of schools but has left a residue that influences educational practice; and [4] a change that has not been implemented in the schools and would be difficult to locate in any school system" (p. 412). The authors collapsed the first two categories and called them "successes," and did the same with the latter two, calling them "failures." On the issue of reliability in judging success and failure, the authors noted that they "independently classified the changes, then compared the results of their work." For the success–failure categories, they agreed on 68 percent of the calls (p. 412).

. Harry A. Wise, *Motion Pictures as an Aid in Teaching American History* (New Haven: Yale University Press, 1939), p. 1, for the Edison quote; also see Larry Cuban, *Teachers and Machines: The Classroom Use of Technology Since 1920* (New York: Teachers College Press, Columbia University, 1986).

. William C. Norris, "Computer-Based Education: A 'Key' to Reform," in *Education Week* (November 18, 1987), p. 28.

28. An example of a teacher-bashing quote would help. This one comes from an advocate of instructional television. "It has been found that teachers reject or at least resist change because of failure to recognize the need for improvement, fear of experimentation, unwillingness to give time, and disillusion or frustration with past experiences. In addition teachers traditionally tend to be conservative and usually will not be impressed by the results of investigations and research or new theories of education. "Javad Maftoon, " 'ITV'—Are Teachers Using IT?" in *T.H.E. Journal* (February 1982), p. 45.

29. For a provocative and insightful essay on why teachers use new technologies infrequently, see David Cohen, "Educational Technology, Policy, and Practice," in *Educational Evaluation and Policy Analysis* 9:2 (Summer 1987), pp. 153–170. Also, to examine further the growing complexity of explanations for teachers' general unresponsiveness to classroom innovations (especially in secondary schools), see Cuban, *How Teachers Taught* (Ch. 6), *Teachers and Machines* (Ch. 3), Carl Grant and Christine Sleeter, "Who Determines Teacher Work: The Teacher, the Organization, or Both?" in *Teaching and Teacher Education* 1 (1985), pp. 209–220; and A. Hargreaves, "The Significance of Classroom Coping Strategies," in Len Barton and Roland Meighan (eds.), *Sociological Interpretations of Schooling and Curriculum* (Driffield, England: Nafferton Books, 1978). Also of interest are the exceptions among teachers—that is, those who somehow ignore the prevailing constraints and adopt new technologies and other innovations to become serious users and different from their colleagues. I discuss a few such teachers in *How Teachers Taught*.

30. Arthur Schlesinger, Jr., *The Cycles of American History* (Boston: Houghton Mifflin, 1986), p. 32. Also, David Tyack and Thomas James, "Learning from Past Efforts to Reform High School," in *Phi Delta Kappan* (February 1983), develop this line of argument.

31. This perspective combines a number of

writers who argue from opposites or some dichotomy. Invariably, the metaphor used is the cycle or some variation of a natural rhythm. See, for example, Arthur M. Schlesinger, *Paths to the Present* (Boston: Houghton–Mifflin, 1964); Henry Adams, *History of the United States of America During the Administrations of Jefferson and Madison* (Englewood Cliffs, NJ: Prentice–Hall, 1963); and Albert O. Hirschman, *Shifting Involvements: Private Interests and Public Action* (Princeton, NJ: Princeton University Press, 1982). Variations on the cyclical argument can be made by linking reform and reactions to broad economic changes in the society, as a number of writers have. See Samuel Bowles and Herbert Gintis, *Schooling in Capitalist America: Educational Reform and the Contradictions of Economic Life* (New York: Basic Books, 1976); and Henry Levin and Martin Carnoy, *Schooling and Work in the Democratic State* (Stanford, CA: Stanford University Press, 1985).

32. For an analysis of why Americans turn continually to education as a solution for national problems, see Henry Perkinson, *The Imperfect Panacea: American Faith in Education, 1865–1965* (New York: Random House, 1968).

33. John Meyer and Brian Rowan, ''The Structure of Educational Organizations,'' in Marshall Meyer (ed.), *Environments and Organizations* (San Francisco: Jossey–Bass, 1978), pp. 78–109; John Meyer, ''The Politics of Educational Crises in the United States,'' in William Cummings *et al.*, *Educational Policies in Crisis: Japanese and American Perspectives* (New York: Praeger, 1986) pp. 144–158; and Thomas S. Popkewitz, ''Educational Reform as the Organization of Ritual: Stability as Change,'' in *Journal of Education* 164:1 (Winter 1982), pp. 5–29. An important variation within this perspective is Warren Susman's argument that reform is a permanent condition in American culture. He argues that the history of the nation is a history of reform that is anchored in traditional cultural beliefs in the perfectibility of Man and the moral rehabilitation of the nation by getting individuals to be more virtuous and less sinful. In making his argument, Susman answers puzzling questions about the persistence of reform: Why do the same crises that afflicted earlier generations of reformers recur? Why are both liberals and conservatives reformers? If reformers ''succeeded,'' why do the problems reappear? Are repeated ''successes'' really a basic ''failure''? Warren Susman, *Culture as History* (New York Pantheon, 1985), pp. 86–97.

34. Richard Elmore and Milbrey McLaughlin, ''Steady Work: Policy, Practice and the Reform of American Educa tion,'' unpublished paper, June, 1987 and David Cohen, ''Teaching Practice Plus Que Ça Change. . . .''

35. None of this, however, satisfactoril explains why (occasionally) certai teachers and administrators depart fro the stability and create sharp breaks wit traditions in their classrooms an schools. A convincing explanatio would have to account for the existenc of both such mavericks and stabilit

36. The reference to the image of the wate fall as a theme for artists in ancie China comes from Simon Leys, *Th Burning Forest: Essays on Chinese Cu ture and Politics* (New York: Ho 1986), p. 211.

14

Practice and Policy

Notes on the History of Instruction

David K. Cohen

From the beginning, instruction has been seen as a potent instrument of public policy in the United States. The Constitution was not yet ratified when several of the Founding Fathers broached educational schemes with a political point. In a spirit of hope and caution they proposed schools, universities, and other agencies of popular education: If Americans could be well-informed, this country's chancy experiment in representative government might endure.[1]

Within a few decades these ideas were picked up by state and local leaders, in whose minds hope and caution mixed increasingly with worry and fear. Irish immigrants, propertyless workers, and the gathering democracy of Jacksonian America led some to worry that the Great Experiment might falter on political ignorance or economic inequality. Others feared that the newcomers' crude manners or "barbaric" religion would corrupt society. Some of the common-school crusaders believed that education would protect against political tyranny that capitalized on voters' ignorance, or that arose from concentrated economic power, or both. Others hoped that the schools would resocialize morally degraded masses, teaching them obedience, respect for property, and the virtues of hard work. Some held both views at once. But all of the crusaders believed that teaching could solve deep and worrisome problems of both politics and morality.[2]

If the United States began with considerable faith in the potency of teaching, that faith has grown along with the country. By the end of the nineteenth century, instructing a great tide of poor European immigrants in The American Way had been added to the list of things teachers would do. In this case, as in earlier immigrations, it was thought that teachers would make up for moral and intellectual failures of instruction within families: What parents had not done or been able to do, teachers would. And the twentieth century barely had begun before economics began to displace politics and morality at the top of the list of things teaching would do for America. Progressive reformers argued for educational expansion on the grounds that schooling created human capital: Better-educated workers would be more productive, and would increase prosperity as well as social solidarity.[3] Educators echoed that schools should teach students what they needed to know for their jobs. Once again, academic instruction was seen as a compensation for teaching and learning that had been missed elsewhere. Progressives worried that young workers no longer were learning skilled trades from journeymen, as apprenticeship withered under the pressures of industrialism.[4] And they argued that few workers could still learn the old straighforward lessons about where their labor fit in, and how it would be useful, because the economic division of labor had grown so complex. Teachers would clear up these growing mysteries of everyday economic life.[5]

Since World War II, the good that teaching would do has grown astonishingly: technical mastery of the Soviets; social integration of racial, ethnic, and linguistic minorities; equal economic opportunity for the oppressed; safe driving; and, more recently, safe sex. In each of these cases and many more, teachers would make up for failures of instruction elsewhere in society, or in the past. Teachers would remedy what were held to be their own gross failings in math and science instruction, so that America could be strong. They would teach students the interracial tolerance and respect that so many parents, communities, and public institutions had not taught. They would attack economic inequalities in instruction, so that children from poor families no longer got the worst teaching, and might even get the best. And, most recently, teachers are to offer lessons in sexual sanity—to protect students from the mortal consequences of carnal carelessness.

How does this little recital bear on historical studies of teaching? First, in each o the instances noted, instruction was an object of both faith and doubt. Teaching wa seen as a potent solution for social problems, but more often than not, thos problems were thought to have arisen from some *instructional* failure. Faith ha been evident in persistent belief in the power of instruction to solve social problems and in the continuing expansion of instructional responsibilities. But doubt has bee no less apparent in persistent criticism of instructional performance, and i persistent worries about whether teaching can do the jobs it has been assigned. Thi old ambivalence seems to be everywhere in American ideas about education. Yet is largely absent from historical writing about teaching.

Second, while America has had great ambitions for the political and social goo that teachers would do, these ambitions almost always have been focused o conventional studies. Teachers were to liberate Americans, or protect democrac or increase productivity, by teaching some particular knowledge or skill: math an science to intending scientists, or reading and writing to future workers. In a sens this is no surprise, for teaching is always teaching something to someone. A David Hawkins wrote, teaching embraces "I, thou, and it."[6] Yet historical studi of teaching are nearly devoid of reference to teachers' encounters with studen over academic subjects. And they have hardly touched on the many possib connections between these academic encounters and America's larger ambitio for instruction.

Each of these themes opens up links between practice and policy. The tensi between faith and doubt has been as evident in national arguments about instructi and social reform as in teachers' worries about their efficacy in the classroo Teachers' struggles with the definition of academic work or problems of classroc discipline often have been seen as part of larger problems of political democracy social control. One distinctive feature of the American experience has been the la political and social significance with which we have invested the small worlds teaching and learning. Our appreciation of that past would be enhanced by explori the connections between the ordinary work of instruction and the larger problems social policy.

Faith and Doubt

America's ambivalence about schoolteaching certainly offers many opportunities for historical development: The veins of faith and doubt run richly through our national life. We might even begin at the beginning. After all, many early New England divines viewed themselves as teachers. For one thing, the role offered a formal encouragement: Congregational ministers often began as "teacher" to a congregation, before stepping up to a preaching position. For another, even after promotion these men viewed their assignment as an instructional one. They were Protestants, after all: Helping their flocks to learn God's word, and to understand His work were central to their ministry. And, as befitted their austere beliefs, the New England ministers envisioned instruction as a struggle for redemption. Faith and doubt about human chances for grace were central to their personal religious struggles, and central to their worries about the possible effects of instruction. Ambivalence about learning was generously mixed in their teaching, and in their writing about it. Some taught fiercely in spite of doubts that any human effort could affect divine determinations, while others were animated by a sense that they might help to tip the divine scales for parishioners.[7] In either case, teaching and learning were important locales for the religious struggles of old New England.

But New England's Calvinism was unusually ferocious, even in its time, and like many extreme sects it flourished only briefly. Perhaps Calvinistic ideas about instruction were just a relic of the Old World, a vision without much connection to our more recent and recognizable past. Some evidence seems to run in that direction. The old doctrines and practices did begin to fade, even in the late seventeenth century; they declined steadily through the next century, as the church became more catholic and worldly. By the early nineteenth century this fearful doctrine of redemption and reformation was mostly a memory; it had largely been supplanted by softer and more optimistic Protestant ideas and practices, as well as by secular doctrines of social progress through science and self-government. In both Protestant and Enlightenment streams of thought, learning and teaching were seen as natural, easy, yet powerful means of social and personal reformation. Most of what we now read about instruction in this period concerns the Common School Crusade, and it generally has been advertised as a remarkably optimistic movement.[8]

Instruction nonetheless remained an object of doubt. Despite high American hopes for learning and teaching—or perhaps because of the stakes that these hopes implied—boosters of teaching regularly doubted its success. So much hung in the balance: Class war, moral collapse, and a failed democracy headed the list of favorite concerns. These were alternatives awful to contemplate, but the school boosters contemplated them regularly. Horace Mann persistently fretted about the possible failures of instruction, and the dire political consequences that would follow. Catharine Beecher's great ambitions for an American instructional salvation were matched by her worries that teaching and learning would fail the country—or that the country might fail to try.[9]

But, however ambivalent, Beecher and Mann were hardly schoolteachers. Or they were teachers only in the sense that they sought to instruct a nation. Perhaps their hopes and fears were inflated by their grandiose vision: Would real teachers not have had more mundane concerns? In nineteenth-century America, though, schoolteachers also were ambitious reformers. They sought to bring literacy and culture to many communities that had little of either, and that often were ambivalent about whether they wanted any. Teachers also were often conscious of the great political hopes that rode on their work. Not surprisingly, when teachers wrote about their craft they sometimes cast the story in terms of personal struggles between faith in their meliorist mission and doubt about whether they and their charges could rise to the occasion.

The best extant example was published just a few decades after the Common School Crusade had begun in earnest: Edward Eggleston's little literary ethnography, *The Hoosier Schoolmaster.*[10] The story centers on a young teacher's ambitions to improve the youth of Flat Creek, Indiana, in the mid–nineteenth century, and his robust fear that the students, or the townspeople, or his own incapacity would defeat his efforts, leaving the community unimproved and himself a moral failure. Eggleston frankly portrayed teaching as a struggle between faith in the possibilities of human improvement, and doubt about teachers' and students' capacity to capitalize on those possibilities. America seemed to resonate to the story, for the book was a best seller. (Other published accounts by nineteenth-century teachers contain some evidence that they regarded their work in similar terms—as do some recently published fragments of correspondence and diaries.)[11]

While these scraps of evidence are suggestive, one still might wonder: Does a view with such plain religious roots make sense in our own more secular time? There are some signs that it does. At least a few teachers who chronicled thei twentieth-century work seemed to struggle with the same issue. Margaret Haley an George Dennison, among others, were full of hope that teaching might be a salvation for the country, but they sometimes doubted that America would permi it, or that they were up to the job.[12] And public argument about teaching and socia problem-solving during this century is littered with evidence of collisions betwee our distinctive faith in what teaching could do for America, and doubts abou whether teachers would deliver.

One early case in point is Joseph Meyer Rice's attacks on clumsy teaching, in th 1890s. Rice published a series of bitter reports on the failures of reading, writin and arithmetic instruction, mostly in American city schools. His was the first effo of its sort, and it created quite a stir.[13] He was, in fact, one of the earlie educational researchers, inventing and administering tests, interviewing teacher observing classes, drawing policy "implications" from his studies and dissemina ing them, and the like. He also was the first researcher to write for a nation audience about the failures of teachers and schools. In a sense, J. M. Rice was t first J. S. Coleman. Rice was of course much more of an amateur, but the two m played similar parts in the American conversation about teaching.

Yet for all of his sharp and often caustic criticism of teaching, Rice was optimist. His critique was larded with confidence that the damage could be repaire that teachers could do everything America wanted of them. The combination see odd: Why would a commentator who expressed such grave doubts about teachi also have such faith in its efficacy? The query is worth pursuing, for Rice was anomaly. In our century the severest critics of teaching also have been among its greatest boosters. James Coleman is one nice example, and Arthur Bestor is another. But many others could be added: George Counts's studies of secondary curriculum, social selection, and Chicago school wars qualify him as one of the most trenchant critics of American education. But *Dare the School Build a New Social Order?* proposes an agenda for instruction that reads as though it had been composed by someone who never had read, let alone written, Counts's earlier books.[14]

What explains the coexistence of faith and doubt in these great debates? One answer is familiar enough: Education has been a sort of civic religion for America. When things go wrong, believers ordinarily look for more of the same rather than abandoning their faith. Another answer is to consider the circumstances: Like Bestor and Coleman, Rice wrote from the midst of a great wave of educational expansion. Their critiques were framed by evidence of optimism in skyrocketing enrollments, ambitious institution-building, and an eruption of hopeful ideas for fundamental reform in teaching and learning. In Rice's time the leading advocates of reform included John Dewey, G. Stanley Hall, Edward L. Thorndike, Margaret Haley, and Franklin Bobbit. In Coleman's they included B. F. Skinner, Paul Goodman, John Holt, Martin Luther King, Jr., and the U.S. Supreme Court. There were plenty of bitter attacks on teaching at both times, but also plenty of evidence that education was growing despite the criticism, and that influential Americans saw no irreparable problems.

Still another answer is to consider the alternatives: If teaching did not put America on a new social, economic, or political footing, what would? The educational booms of the past hundred years also have been periods of worry about large social problems. When Rice wrote, the worries included urban decay, corruption in government and big business, and unchecked industrialism. Five or six decades later it was the Communist menace, growing racial inequality and perhaps race war, and persistent poverty. In times of crisis like these, concern over schools often have focused other, larger, less manageable puzzles of public life. And improved instruction often has stood in for alternative approaches to social problem solving, less favored in the United States: market regulation, redistribution of wealth, direct assistance to those in need, and the like. More than education has been at stake in American arguments about what teaching can do, even if few alternatives to educational reform have been extensively considered. In trying to understand why doubt and faith seem so solidly wedded in American discourse about instruction, there is room for more than one explanation.

However we may explain America's ambivalence about teaching, the condition is not restricted to people like Margaret Haley, John Dewey, and James Coleman, or to grand national arguments about schools and public policy. Many teachers still struggle with faith and doubt about their work. Recent social surveys and field research also reveal that teachers often continue to see themselves as social reformers on a small scale. But while regularly sustained by a faith that they can help students to improve, they also are regularly plagued by doubts about the evidence of improvement, about whether the observable improvements are substantial, and about whether they will last.[15] Teachers' faith and doubt no longer is expressed in religious terms, but in the languages of professionalism or social science. Like colleagues in the past, though, teachers are tugged by the competing pulls of conviction about the possibility of improving others, and doubt that the improvements will occur, or can be known.

I find this theme particularly appealing, for it connects teachers' enduring worries about a central problem in their classroom work with enduring American worries about the value of instruction. It would be easy to regard the history of teaching as small work on the small work of society, and to lump such scholarship with other efforts to learn more about the ordinary lives of ordinarily invisible people. But when such inquiries succeed, it is partly because they find great or troublesome themes in the ordinary and invisible.

Academic Encounters

My second proposed theme concerns teachers' encounters with students over academic work. Even though schoolteaching and learning typically center on academic subjects of some sort, historians have not considered teaching from this angle.[16] And they have not done so despite a long-standing professional interest in the history of academic work. We think of Edward Krug as the father of curriculum history, but by the time his book was published, several other historical studies had been in print for more than half a century.[17] Barry Franklin and Herbert Kliebard have more recently contributed to the history of school studies, but theirs are only the most visible of several such contributions.[18] Yet all of this work has only tangential bearing on the history of teaching. For curriculum historians attend only to David Hawkins's instructional "it," ignoring the "I and thou" who breathe life into academic material—or snuff it out. What teachers and students actually di with curriculum has not been included in historical studies of curriculum.[19] In thi respect, historians have followed the curious example of the curriculum reformer they study, who seem to have believed that words on paper (or pictures on screens could drive students' learning and teachers' work. Curriculum reformers produc the words and argue about them, and historians study the words and arguments What students and teachers did together remains virgin territory.

Or nearly so. At least one historian has considered the "I" and "thou" o teaching. Larry Cuban's book, *How Teachers Taught,* offers a careful scrutiny o teachers' and students' classroom relations since the turn of the twentieth centur It concludes that these relations have changed only marginally: With mode exceptions, teachers and students work together in mostly traditional ways.[20] Th book is part of Cuban's continuing effort to figure out why instruction seems to ha changed so little, despite so many efforts to reform it. I am a convinced admirer this work—but it does display a blindness of its own, complementary to that of t curriculum histories. For in exploring why relatively few teachings adopted t inquiry-oriented, open pedagogy that Dewey and other radicals proposed, Cub seems indifferent to the place of knowledge (Hawkins's "it") in teaching a learning.[21] Yet the conceptions of knowledge that dominated education at the ti were a profound barrier to innovative instruction.

For most of the period about which Cuban wrote, the reigning conceptions of academic knowledge were antithetical to the Deweyan ambitions for instruction whose fate he traced. University academics regarded knowledge as objective systems of fact and laws, not as human construction whose core ideas might be difficult or impossible to falsify. In the sciences and social sciences, knowledge was thought to be the result of patient discovery of social and physical reality, not the product of efforts to make sense of inherently ambigious evidence. In the dominant intellectual culture of the time, knowledge was thought to be an objective edifice built up cumulatively by dint of careful empirical investigation, rather than an imaginative construct that might never be entirely satisfactory, and almost surely would be subject to challenge and change. Humans were portrayed as discoverers and accumulators of knowledge, not as constructors and reconstructors. Even the reigning psychology of the time portrayed knowing as a relatively passive process, in which the mind learned from the habitual association of data impressed upon it by the external world. Children learned because man and nature taught them, not because they imaginatively and originally made sense of their surroundings. While schoolteachers accepted such ideas, theirs was not a perverse or unusual acceptance. The roots of this view of knowledge lay deep in modern thought; schoolteachers were no more unique in such beliefs than university academics and other intellectuals.[22]

There was little in these ideas that would have encouraged anyone to think of learning as a personal process of knowledge construction, or to view teaching as guidance for such construction. And there was much that supported a view of teaching as telling known and immutable truths, and of learning as absorbing such truths. After all, if knowledge was so solid, and if it was made by such patient extension of the existing stock, why should students not absorb what already was known, and learn thereby how the stock had grown, and how it would be expanded? School organization and classroom exigencies certainly help to explain why few teachers made fundamental changes in their practice, in response to innovative ideas about learning and teaching. But even if those organizational and logistical barriers magically had been swept away, teachers, along with nearly everyone else in America, held an inherited view of knowledge which was a formidable obstacle to adventurous teaching.[23] Even if their schools were perfectly organized, few teachers would have much changed their pedagogy after hearing or reading John Dewey.

Extant research on the history of teaching thus frames a paradox. Were a teacher-centered'' history[24] to exist, what teachers taught to whom seems one kely place to center it. But this central feature of teaching seems far from the center f research on the history of teaching. Historians know more about nearly erything else concerning teaching—teachers' schooling, their working conditions d contracts, the curriculum they presumably taught, how teachers were exploited d discriminated against, even the buildings in which they worked—than about achers' encounters with children over academic material. This central matter of aching is a large area of historical darkness.

Why did things turn out this way? Might they be corrected?

The most efficient explanation for historians' inattention also is the simplest: few materials extant. Recently published letters and diaries from nineteenth-century teachers give academic work passing attention.[25] They focus more on problems of discipline, on stoves that smoked and roofs that leaked, or on various personal trials and tribulations. If such material is at all representative, perhaps more digging would yield little gold.

But even if their archives were crammed with teachers' accounts of academic instruction, historians would have a problem. For teachers' conceptions of what they do often clash with their students' views of the same events. This is a common problem in many realms of historical inquiry, not to mention everyday life, but it would be particularly difficult in this case. For, lacking students' views of classrooms, a "teacher-centered history" easily could turn out to be a teacher-centric history. It might embody and advance the illusion that teachers are the only important people in classrooms. This possibility certainly seems plausible, given the habits of other academic students of instruction: Sociologists, psychologists, and economists pay much more attention to teachers' attributes and actions than to students'.

If students' perspectives were taken to be essential for the history of teaching, a teacher-centered history would therefore be even more remote. How many students kept diaries or wrote letters that focused on their schoolwork, much less on schoolwork for teachers who also wrote about the classes in which those students sat? If today's researchers—who have ready access to students who would readily offer their views of instruction—generally ignore students in favor of teachers, how could we reasonably expect historians to do any better? After all, they study students and teachers who no longer exist. It seems an impossible, or at least an unreasonable, requirement.

Do not the demands of such research explain why it has not been done? I think not. Much historical research is difficult, and some seems impossible even after i has been done well. Who would have imagined that Braudel's labors would hav turned out so brilliantly? I suspect that many materials for a history of instructio exist, undiscovered or unused only because we lack a sense of how they would b useful. It seems likely, for instance, that as more teachers' correspondence an diaries are published, we could learn more of their ideas about academic teachin and learning. It also seems likely that researchers could find more than just diarie and letters: Many teachers probably saved course and curriculum materials, an some may have saved students' work. Additionally, some schools and scho systems may have stored away old course materials and students' papers.[26]

Recent historical writing about teaching has not focused on such things, partl because issues of gender have been more compelling. Female teachers' accounts their efforts to carve out places for themselves in a man's world are beginning to g some attention, long overdue. But these women were teachers as well: Knowled was their stock-in-trade. How they understood and used it also is a crucial part their story, possibly even related to their search for a place in America.

This part of the teachers' story is significant in several ways. For one thin American teachers have been represented as the field agents in one of the world's m ambitious knowledge-diffusion experiments. They were charged with teaching e erything from rudimentary reading and writing to skilled trades and agriculture, a with doing so for an entire population. If schoolteachers were agents of popular enlightenment, purveyors of knowledge to a nation, then the knowledge they used and the ways they used it are central to their story. How did they construe the subject matter of instruction? What sort of arithmetic (or geography) did primary students and teachers work on, and how did they work? What views of the subjects seem to be represented? How did teachers respond to students' work—their errors of fact and interpretation, their good and bad guesses, and the like? How were knowledge and learning understood and presented in students' work, and in teachers' course doccuments? How did these two views compare? And how did the knowledge diffused through elementary and secondary schools compare with the knowledge that was discovered and synthesized in universities? Were they quite disparate a century ago, or were the contents of school and university education quite similar then? Have things changed since then? If so, how? And if not, why not?

From this angle, then, teachers' and students' confrontations with academic material are part of a larger social history of ideas. Some issues in that history concern the ways in which teachers and students have interpreted the knowledge on which they worked. For if teachers were field agents in this great experiment, their interpretations of knowledge, teaching, and learning can teach us something about the nature and effects of the enterprise. One large issue, for instance, is whether schools diffused specialized knowledge to an ignorant population, or purveyed to children knowledge that already was the common possession of adults. Or, better, how much did schools do of each, and how has it changed, if it has changed? Which way did the lines of diffusion run? From knowledge centers to a rough and ill-educated mass, or through the schools, from adults to children? Have schools been an agency for diffusing higher knowledge, or for recirculating ordinary knowledge?

These historical issues are linked to others. What connection or disconnections have there been between the knowledge produced and interpreted in universities and other authoritative centers of intellectual work, and the knowledge disseminated through popular institutions? Have schools been diffusion agencies for the knowledge producers? Or have they been a secluded social agency, producing and diffusing a curious concoction of their own—educators call it curriculum—that is not strongly related either to what universities produce or to what most adults know? Whatever the answers, have things changed in the past century?

These questions are considerable. But while they stand virtually untouched in academic inquiry, they do not stand alone. For teachers' and students' encounters with knowledge touch a large political problem in America, and absorb special significance from it. American teachers and students work together on academic matters in an enterprise that has been advertised as personally and politically liberating. Yet this liberating work has been mandated by the state. Common-school crusaders and their heirs portrayed teaching and learning as essential to students' liberation: Learning to read, write, and cipher would protect individual citizens from personal incapacity, economic slavery, and (thus) political domination. Such citizens would protect their society against economic inequality, or at least its effects in political tryanny. Yet the candidates for liberation seem to have had little choice about what to learn, or how, or when. The more that schooling for personal and political liberation succeeded and spread, the more students were drawn in for reasons that were unrelated to their desire to learn. In fact, many of the reasons for including more and more students seemed antithetical to personal liberation: legal compulsion, economic necessity, or social pressures. The claims for liberation are at least as old as public education, and if anything they are more evident today than a century ago. But the compulsions to learn also are more evident today, or at least more numerous: legislated requirements for study, state-mandated tests for graduation, and efforts to extend required schooling up and down the age range are only a few examples.

Public schools in the United States thus seem to embody a contradiction. Schools aim, or claim they aim, to set people free, and thus to ensure a free society. But this means of liberation has been compelled, and the compulsions have increased in number, and perhaps in force, as time has passed. Learning has been portrayed as the path to intellectual independence, and intellectual independence as the path to political autonomy and economic self-sufficiency. But students have been compelled to study, whether or not they have desired to learn. Can intellectual independence be mandated by state-required studies? Can students be forced to be free?

This large question should be rephrased, to make sense from the perspective of teachers and students: How was this tension or contradiction played out in classrooms? How did teachers and students cope with the problem of compulsory learning for the achievement of intellectual and political independence? If they embraced compulsion in their pedagogy, as some treatments seem to suggest,[27] what does that tell us about the claims for liberating education? If they tried to reject or moderate the claims of compulsion, and devise a liberating pedagogy, what did they do? And what did they think about their endeavors?

These questions do not treat of discipline alone, because discipline never occurs alone. Knowledge always is an element in the organization of classroom life, and my queries aim at how academic knowledge became embroiled in the classroom politics of education: How was classroom knowledge caught up in the competing claims of educational compulsion and liberation? We know that some teachers tried to use instruction to cultivate independence in students. How did they do it?

Bronson Alcott's journals offer an early and rather extraordinary version of this story.[28] And Horace Mann's report on Prussian education is an early commentary on how he imagined that nation's teachers managed the competing claims of compulsion and liberation.[29] But Alcott was not the only advocate of liberating instruction. Who were some others, and how did they try to cope with this problem? Additionally, it seems almost a sure bet that teachers tried to cope with this problem in many different ways. What were they? How did teachers interpret their efforts?

One reason that these questions seem plausible is that they connect with some things we already know. There are, for instance, some scraps of evidence that many Americans saw education, and perhaps even compulsory schooling, as a means of personal and political liberation. Leon Litwack has chronicled one particularly bitter and hopeful part of the story in his discussion of black liberation during Reconstruction,[30] but controversies over black education in the North contain similar material.[31] Some European immigrants offered personal testimonials about their classroom days, seeing only freedom and liberating opportunities where others saw an unfriendly and even hostile compulsory regime.[32]

But there is plenty of material on the other side. Many American writers, from James Fenimore Cooper to Paul Goodman, have portrayed school as a particularly nasty sort of oppression. All of these literary figures took education as a leading theme. Some were preoccupied with it; Twain and Thoreau immediately come to mind. They were great lovers of learning, but in the best American tradition were therefore also great haters of school. To the extent that this stream of literary work offers a picture of society, the picture is one in which teachers were mean, starchy, and narrow-minded oppressors of children. Schools were so awful that most important learning occurred outside them.[33] If we were to believe Twain and Thoreau, real learning could have occurred only outside of school.

Most American intellectuals have stood on one side or the other of this old argument about teaching. Many bullish boosters of school, like Horace Mann, saw nothing odd in advertising compulsory liberation. This was not because they were unaware of the issue. In his great flap with the Boston schoolmasters, Mann argued that soft compulsion, in which children were treated gently and as learners with minds and souls of their own, would succeed; but traditional, mindless, authoritarian compulsion would fail.[34] Others in the argument, like Mark Twain and Willard Waller, were bitter school-haters; they could see few opportunities for liberation within schoolhouse walls. They thought learning was liberating, but only when it arose from personal experience in chosen tasks beyond the dead grip of formal institutions.

This split in American educational ideas is old. And it has been so deep that even sophisticated observers seemed not to notice that teachers were caught in the middle.[35] But if few intellectuals saw this, many more ex-teachers did. In writing their memoirs, or handbooks for their less experienced colleagues, these nineteenth-century authors agonized over the problem of "classroom governance." Governance was important because that was where these teachers thought the competing claims of compulsion and liberation most forcefully collided. They wanted children to learn liberation in schools, but they did not believe that children would learn it in schools that treated them dictatorially. Still, they knew that school was compulsory, and that teachers were agents of the state.

Amos Kellog, one of the most articulate of these writers, saw this problem as a dilemma.[36] And he understood that it reached far beyond matters of discipline, to methods of study and conceptions of academic material. He noted that if academic material was construed as stuff for compulsory force-feeding, children would learn it poorly, or not at all, or would learn to hate it. But he thought that the dilemma could be successfully managed. Teachers could find ways to balance the claims of democracy and popular participation against the compulsion. Academic material could be constructed in ways that appealed to students' curiosity, and connected with their experience. If schoolwork were so constructed, children would eagerly learn. And they would learn independence along with cooperation—two essential democratic dispositions.

Kellog wrote about these problems as though they regularly came up in teaching and in discussions thereof. My perusal of other memoirs and handbooks leads me to think that his work is only one bit of a much larger body of material. It could be a rich resource for helping us to understand how teachers managed to teach, and how they thought about their work. There certainly is much to learn about how teachers coped with the dilemma of education for liberation within compulsory school agencies, and about how academic knowledge figured in the enterprise.

These are only scraps of evidence, of course, and they are only suggestive. One never knows if a historical theme makes sense until one wrestles with the evidence. But the many different scraps of this evidence reinforce my sense that this theme makes sense, and has promise. Additionally, it would permit us to connect teachers' and students' small confrontations over academic matters with larger political dramas of American education. Many Americans, intellectuals and not, have struggled with the problem of whether compulsory schooling also could make sense as an agency of political liberation and democratic learning. We still struggle with it.

Most Americans have come down on one side or another of the argument. But teachers, unlike the intellectuals who write about schools, and unlike the reformers who try to change them, rarely have had the luxury of picking a side and staying on it. They could not be consistent—either as sunny boosters or gloomy haters of school. Teachers had to find ways to handle both sides of this old American street.[37] They had to work the problem out on a daily and even hourly basis, and rework it many times in the course of a career. Historical inquiry could help to illuminate their struggles with this small version of a great political puzzle. That could immensely enrich our understanding of teaching—and of education in American politics.

Notes

AUTHOR'S NOTE: Thanks are due to David Tyack and Donald Warren, for inviting my contribution to this volume. This chapter has profited from several discussions with David Tyack, as well as from the comments of Magdalene Lampert and David Labaree.

1. Lawrence A. Cremin, *American Education: The National Experience, 1783–1876* (New York: Harper, 1980), pp. 1–13.
2. Carl Kaestle, *Pillars of the Republic* (New York: Hill & Wang, 1983), especially Chs. 5 and 6; David Tyack, "The Spread of Schooling in Victorian America," in *History of Education* 7:3 (1978), pp. 172–182; and David Cohen, "Loss as a Theme in Social Policy," in *Harvard Educational Review* 46:4 (November 1976), pp. 553–571.
3. These ideas have been alluded to in many places, but seem not to have been discussed in detail anywhere. For some helpful exposition and analysis, see Harvey Kantor, "Vocationalism in American Education: The Economic and Political Context, 1880–1930," and Joseph Kett, "The Adolescence of Vocational Education," both in Harvey Kantor and David Tyack, *Youth, Work and Schooling* (Stanford, CA: Stanford University Press, 1982). See also David Cohen and Barbara Neufeld, "The Failure of High School and the Progress of Education," in *Daedelus* 110:3 (Summer 1981), pp. 70–75.
4. These ideas were part of the common intellectual currency of the time. John Dewey made much of them, for example, in *The School and the Society* (Chicago: University of Chicago Press

1956), Combined Edition, especially in "The School and Social Progress," and "Waste in Education."

5. These ideas were not new at the turn of our century. Horace Mann and other reformers worried, in the mid-nineteenth century, about the social fragmentation that the division of labor would cause. And at the end of the eighteenth century, Adam Smith had written about the corrosive effects of the division of labor on workers' minds, and argued that it was an essential rationale for education.
6. David Hawkins, "I, Thou, and It," in his collection of essays, *The Informed Vision* (New York: Agathon, 1974), pp. 48–62.
7. There is, by this time, a large literature on old New England. Much of it contains material that bears on teaching and learning in Calvinistic theory and practice, but little deals explicitly with these matters. The best general treatments, for those interested in education, are Lawrence A. Cremin, *American Education: The Colonial Experience, 1607–1783* (New York: Harper, 1970), especially Part I, Ch. 2, and Part II, Ch. 5; and Perry Miller, *The New England Mind* (Cambridge: Harvard University Press, 1938–1953), 2 Vols. But neither of these remarkable works gives much direct discussion to ministerial practice as teaching, or to the ideas about pedagogy that circulated within the ministry—though their discussions of various related topics are fascinating and most helpful. Views of childrearing and education are discussed in Edmund S. Morgan, *The Puritan Family* (New York: Harper, 1966), and Philip J. Greven, *The Protestant Temperament* (New York: Knopf, 1977).
8. This characterization of the crusade seems to span interpretive gaps. Cubberley optimistically saw it as optimistic, while Cremin much more cautiously saw it as optimistic: Lawrence A. Cremin, *The Wonderful World of Ellwood Patterson Cubberley* (New York: Teachers College, 1965). The revisionist historians of the past several decades have debunked many of the earlier optimistic views of the crusaders' intentions. But these historians have questioned the crusaders' motives, not their optimism. Both David Tyack's and Carl Kaestle's judicious works (see note 3) also stress the reformers' optimism about education.
9. Kathryn Kish Sklar, *Catharine Beecher: A Study in American Domesticity* (New Haven: Yale University Press, 1973).
10. Edward E. Eggleston in (Vernon Loggins (ed.), *The Hoosier Schoolmaster* (New York: Hill & Wang, 1961). The book was first published in 1871.
11. See, for example: Edward H. Magill, *Sixty-Five Years in the Life of a Teacher* (Boston: Houghton Mifflin, 1907), pp. 18–26; and Hiram Orcutt, *Reminiscences of a School Life* (Cambridge, MA: 1898), pp. 50–53.
12. On Margaret Haley, who was the leading unionist organizer of teachers at the end of the last century and in the first few decades of our own, see her autobiography, *Battleground,* edited by Robert L. Reid (Urbana: University of Illinois Press, 1982). Haley was an indefatigable optimist and a fighter, yet in the closing chapter of her own story (pp. 270–276), she raises doubts about the success of public education that had troubled her for decades. Some of these were noticed early in her career, in her justly famous speech to the NEA, "Why Teachers Should Organize," in *Addresses and Proceedings,* National Education Association (Washington, DC: NEA, 1904), pp. 145–152. George Dennison's account of his efforts to start and operate a school for poor children outcast from the New York City schools is remarkable in many ways: George Dennison, *The Lives of Children* (New York: Vintage, 1969). Among these ways is the counterpoint between Dennison's determined helpfulness about teaching and learning, and the discussion near the book's end of the many difficulties of teaching humanely in the Deweyan tradition (pp. 246–282). Dennison notes, near the end, that he was leaving the school because "I've had my fill of children for a while" (p. 245).

13. Joseph M. Rice, *The Public School System of the United States* (New York: Century, 1893).
14. George Counts, *School and Society in Chicago* (Chicago: University of Chicago Press, 1925); Counts, *The Selective Character of Secondary Education* (Chicago: University of Chicago Press, 1922); and Counts, *The Senior High School Curriculum* (Chicago: University of Chicago Press, 1929). Counts's later book, *Dare the School Build a New Social Order?* (New York: John Day, 1932), has little of the critical insight of these earlier works; instead, it promotes teachers as the saviors of a nation on the verge of ruin. David Tyack, Robert Lowe, and Elisabeth Hansot, in *Public Schools in Hard Times* (Cambridge: Harvard University Press, 1984), say of this last book that Counts's ". . . exhortation to change the world through education, and his vision of a millennial future, were reminiscent of the nineteenth-century educational crusaders. . . ." (p. 19).
15. See, for example, Dan C. Lortie, *Schoolteacher* (Chicago: University of Chicago Press, 1975), especially Chs. 4–7. See also Gertrude McPherson, *Small Town Teacher* (Cambridge: Harvard University Press, 1972). McPherson discusses the problems of faith and doubt in a late twentieth-century social-science vocabulary, but the themes come booming through the sociology. It is a thoughtful, sensitive treatment. Her chapters on "Teachers' Self-Image" (pp. 29–49), "The Pupil and the Class" (especially pp. 83–89), and "Low Teacher Morale: Its Implications" (pp. 201–215), are particularly helpful. Magdalene Lampert, "How Do Teachers Manage to Teach?" in *Harvard Educational Review* 59:2 (May 1985), pp. 178–194, offers an account of dilemmas of teaching that bear on my discussion.
16. They are not alone in this: Lee Shulman, "Those Who Understand: Knowledge Growth in Teaching," in *Educational Researcher* (February 1986), pp. 4–14. Shulman notes that most educational inquirers have ignored subject matter, in their efforts to figure out what (generically) makes teaching tick.
17. Edward A. Krug, *The Shaping of the American High School* (New York: Harper, 1964); Richard B. Stout, *The Development of High School Curriculum in the North Central States from 1860 to 1918* (Chicago: University of Chicago Press, 1921); and George Van Dyke, "Trends in the Development of the High School Offering," in *School Review* 39, Part I (November 1931), pp. 657–664, and *School Review* 39, Part II (December 1931), pp. 737–747.
18. Herbert Kliebard, *The Struggle for the American Curriculum, 1893–1958* (Boston: Routledge & Kegan Paul, 1986); and Barry Franklin, *Building the American Community: The School Curriculum and the Search for Social Control* (Philadelphia: Falmer Press, 1986).
19. Barry Franklin, *Building the American Community,* deviates a bit from this pattern in the last chapter of his book, in which he explores the fate of efforts to implement new curriculum in one American city. For an instructive discussion of these two recent books, and of curriculum history, see David F. Labaree, "Politics, Markets, and the Compromised Curriculum," in *Harvard Educational Review* 57:4 (November 1987), pp. 483–494.
20. Larry Cuban, *How Teachers Taught* (New York: Longman, 1984).
21. The relevant pages in Cuban's analysis are 237–259.
22. For a somewhat more detailed discussion of these ideas see my essay, "Plus Que Ça Change . . ." in Philip W. Jackson (ed.), *Contributing to Educational Change: Perspectives on Research and Practice* (Berkeley, CA: McCutchan, 1988).
23. David Cohen, *op. cit.* There were, of course, contrary views about knowledge already in circulation at the turn of the century: Whitehead and Russell's *Principia Mathematica* is one example, and there are others. But while they loom large in retrospect, they were just the beginning of constructivist traditions in

science, and were little understood beyond a small academic group.

24. David Tyack discusses such a history in Chapter 15 in this volume.
25. See, for example, the collection in Polly Welts Kaufman, *Women Teachers on the Frontier* (New Haven: Yale University Press, 1984). Academic matters were not ignored in these letters and diaries, but then they were not at the front of teachers' attention.
26. With a little luck, we might even find materials that would permit us to explore how things changed—or not. Old school and classroom materials also could illuminate several related issues of a historical sort. Comparisons of older and recent tests—teacher-made or standardized—might shed some light on the debate about whether teaching standards are slipping or becoming more difficult. Administering some of the old standardized tests to similar contemporary populations could shed even more light on that question. There is, of course, much that we could not learn from such materials, including how teachers and students worked together in class.
27. Barbara Finkelstein, *Governing the Young: Teacher Behavior in Popular Primary Schools in Nineteenth Century United States* (Philadelphia: Falmer Press, 1989).
28. Alcott's teaching is discussed in Elizabeth Peabody, *Record of a School: Exemplifying the General Principles of Spiritual Culture* (Boston: Russell, Shattuck & Co., 1836).
29. Massachusetts Board of Education, *Seventh Annual Report of the Secretary to the Board,* Boston, 1844.
30. Leon Litwak, *Been in the Storm So Long* (New York: Knopf, 1979).
31. See, generally, Leon Litwak, *North of Slavery* (Chicago: University of Chicago Press, 1961), especially Ch. 4.
32. For instance, Mary Antin, in her hymn to America, *The Promised Land* (Boston: Houghton Mifflin, 1912), presents public school as free, open to all, without qualification. She does not even notice that they were compulsory (pp. 26–27 and 198–200).
33. I discuss these literary and popular traditions at slightly more length, and provide references, in "Plus Que Ça Change. . . ," and further in "Willard Waller: On Hating School and Loving Education," in Donald Willower and William Boyd, *Willard Waller on Education and the Schools* (Tempe, AZ: University Council for Educational Administration, 1988).
34. See the abridgment of the exchange in Michael Katz (ed.), *School Reform: Past and Present* (Boston: Little, Brown, 1971), pp. 113–125.
35. Few commentators on teaching have probed this point. Waller saw it, but mostly went on to ignore it. For the largest part, he wrote about teachers one-sidedly, as though they were a species of minor monster. For some notes on other school critics who also have ignored teachers' struggles with this issue, see my essay, "Willard Waller: On Hating School and Loving Education."
36. Amos Kellog, *School Management* (New York: 1887), especially Chs. 1 and 2.
37. Ann and Harold Berlak explore how British teachers manage dilemmas of practice (an analytic construct, not the teachers' idea), in *Dilemmas of Schooling* (New York: Methuen, 1981). Magdalene Lampert (in "How Do Teachers Manage to Teach?") writes about her own teaching from the perspective of the dilemmas that she sees in the work, and how she managed some of them. She does not take up the particular problem discussed here.

15

The Future of the Past

What Do We Need to Know About the History of Teaching?

David Tyack

Today Americans vigorously debate how to improve teaching. Differing views of history shape the forms of argument and different policy agendas. Policy makers do not have a choice about whether to use history. They do, willy-nilly. The question is, "How accurate is their historical map?" Present actions and future plans reflect beliefs—either implicit or explicit—about what went before. And people often want to know if the situation is getting better or worse.

During the past century, those who shaped policy about teachers mostly shared the view that the history of teachers was a tale of progress toward professionalism. Willard Elsbree's classic study published in 1939 said it all in its title: *The American Teacher: Evolution of a Profession in a Democracy*. In recent times that belief in a primitive past, and faith in a progressive future, has eroded. Some have substituted a contrary vision: a past golden age and a threatening future. The story lines differ. Conservatives may portray a past when confident teachers, scholarly and esteemed by the public, taught their students to master basic disciplines. Liberals may sketch an earlier era, when teachers were more autonomous and creative, free from present bureaucratic constraints.[1]

The chapters in this volume suggest how complex and nonlinear is the history of teachers and their work, and hence how complex must be an assessment of "progress." The concept of a golden age in the past is untenable. Throughout most of our history, teachers have been young and poorly paid. They came in and out of the occupation as though they were passing through a revolving door. Women bore the largest share of the work, but faced many kinds of discrimination. Teachers, minimally educated by present-day standards, enjoyed a respectable but hardly honorific social position. In rural communities and small towns, as Willard Waller showed, school patrons circumscribed the private as well as the professional lives of teachers, confining them within the narrow boundaries thought appropriate to the keepers of the "museum of virtue," the public school. In cities, teachers often had little voice in planning their work and were closely supervised to ensure that they, like their pupils, toed the line. There is little evidence that many teachers in the past were drawn from the higher echelons of academic talent. As Michael Sedlak observes in this volume, even in the 1930s, when there was a surplus of teachers, students in teacher education scored near the bottom of those taking a test of intellectual ability, falling below even the high-school pupils who took the examination. If one looks at the characteristics and daily lives of average teachers in the past, it is hard to discover any golden age.[2]

Both Elsbree's study and the recent research reported in this book do show certain kinds of improvement in the occupation of teaching. In the past half century in particular, the academic attainment, age, length of teaching experience, pay, and collective influence of teachers all have risen substantially. Tenure and less-restrictive community expectations have given them much more economic security and private autonomy than they once enjoyed. Some of the most egregious inequities in salary and status between men and women and between whites and blacks in the profession have been lessened as single salary schedules have been enacted and gross racial disparities corrected. The nineteenth-century dream of professionalization of educators—that all teachers should be specially trained and certified, and members of professional associations—has mostly been realized. After each new generation of educators has ratcheted its expectations upwards, such improvements have come to seem inadequate, and reformers have called for further requirements and higher standards. "Progress" always has fallen short of what teachers and the lay public have demanded, and hopes for the future often have colored views of the past.[3]

If current views of the history of teaching sometimes appear foreshortened and oversimplified, educational historians are partly to blame. Amidst a plethora of other topics that have seized their attention in recent decades, scholars have largely neglected teachers. (The last synthesis of the history of teachers—Elsbree's—appeared in 1939.) This neglect has begun to change, as this volume attests. Important new policy concerns and developments within social history (like women's history) are reshaping the ways in which historians are looking at teachers' lives and work. The craft of history is always "revisionist" in some sense, and the "past" is sure to be interpreted yet again differently in the future.[4]

This chapter explores two questions. First, how might history illuminate public policies concerning teachers? I suggest four ways: that history is a storehouse of experiments on dead people; that it can give a psychological distance that helps one distinguish highfalutin' talk from political interest; that it can reveal unintended consequences by taking a long time-frame for evaluation; and that it offers the possibility of "meta-analysis," by which I mean stepping back from a particular period or reform and asking about broad, underlying conditions which might have produced cycles of change or persistent forms of continuity (that is, what may appear to be erratic surges of reform may in fact display certain common features). I illustrate these policy uses with examples from the history of teachers and teacher education.[5]

The second question is: What might be the shape of new interpretive syntheses of the history of public school teachers and teaching? The two topics are not the same. Much of the new history, like the social sciences on which history draws, tells a great deal about *teachers* and the organizational context within which they work. But with a few exceptions, historians have not dealt much with *teaching,* by which I mean instruction in classrooms. As specialized knowledge accumulates, it is helpful to seek the broader patterns, of which discrete studies form a part. As historians go about filling gaps in knowledge and discovering new ways of seeing, it is also important to try to integrate this new knowledge into larger patterns of understanding. History can offer insight to policy makers by showing the connections between events as well as the genealogy of isolated issues.

I do not believe that historians will ever again achieve the coherence and simplicity of Elsbree's interpretation, nor would that be desirable. Pluralism of methods, outlooks, and evidence have enriched our understanding. But it is perhaps possible to discern from the chapters of this volume, and from related other research, some essential elements that might inform attempts to synthesize the history of teaching: a primary focus on the teachers themselves that seeks to explain their motivations and daily work; a combination of a broad demographic view of the teacher population with the cultural constructions of meaning provided by the life histories of the teachers themselves, including an exploration of how gender, ethnicity, and race shaped the occupation; an understanding of how schools as institutions changed over time and thus provided different workplaces and different organizational norms; and an attempt to illuminate the neglected center of the teaching process, instruction, probing both constancy and change in ways of teaching. Apart, each of these approaches probes an important area of the historical record; integrated, they might provide rich insight into historical change by linking broad social context, institutions, and individual experience.

Using History to Illuminate Education Policy

Among the pitfalls that beset historians who seek relevance to policy are the temptations to be cheerleaders for the latest fad, affirming the precedents for currently fashionable reforms; or to be wet blankets, arguing that those reforms were tried in the past and failed. Rarely is the story of reform so simple. History cannot provide policy makers with a list of prescriptions or prohibitions. It can, however, give insight into the trajectory of ideas and events over time.

First, history provides a storehouse of experiments on dead people. Most significant *problems* in education have a long history; diagnoses often sound alike in different periods (for example, of the causes of the high turnover of teachers or the low prestige of the occupation). *Solutions* tend to recycle as educational entrepreneurs with short memories reinvent old remedies. If some "new" idea has already been tried—and most have, in some form—it is valuable to analyze who introduced it, for what reasons, how well it worked, and what was its fate. Regarding history as a storehouse of natural experiments has two advantages: It is a cheap form of evaluation (no small matter when research funds are short), and it does not use live guinea pigs.[6]

Consider, for example, the present-day call for differentiating the roles and rewards of teachers as a means of attracting and retaining the most gifted instructors, creating meritocratic standards of performance and pay, and making schooling more efficient. Through legislation in many states this movement has taken the form of merit pay, career ladders, master or mentor teachers, and other ways to distinguish among teachers in their work and compensation. Both in the past and in the present teachers have resisted such reforms. They have not trusted administrators to assess who should receive merit pay. They have been reluctant to lose their autonomy in individual classrooms by adopting hierarchical models of team teaching and career ladders. For teachers, bureaucratization has been a two-edged sword: Although the consolidation and differentiation of schools have afforded them some buffering from the demands of lay people, bureaucratization has also brought new controls within the system that have threatened their freedom of action. Treating schools as though they were businesses in a market economy has made sense to some influential outsiders, but teachers have often questioned the underlying assumptions of the model, and ignored or sabotaged such reforms.[7]

Historians can explore this gap between reformers' proposals and unreformed teachers in a variety of ways. One approach would attend to the broader ideological and political climate: It appears, for example, that merit pay, career ladders, and hierarchical forms of team teaching have been especially popular with policy advocates during conservative times—the 1920s, 1950s and 1980s—when competitive market solutions have been in fashion. If one looks at the reforms from the point of view of the teachers themselves, alternative perspectives appear. Differentiating the roles and pay of teachers could have disrupted the tenuous autonomy that teachers enjoyed in the separate worlds of their classrooms, and the intrinsic satisfactions they gained from seeing their pupils make academic and social gains. Also David Labaree shows in his chapter that ambitious teachers had other ways to advance in the occupation: They could move to more desirable districts, step up to the next educational level, or enter administration.[8]

A second advantage of history in policy analysis is the perspective that time provides on the value conflicts that often have been, and still are, obscured by high-sounding justifications or angry polemics. All reforms have a political dimension; most, however, also are justified by arguments that seek to demonstrate that they serve the common good or embody high principle. Hence one needs to consider both the rhetoric of purpose and the political interests involved.

Teacher education provides a case in point. As Jurgen Herbst and William Johnson suggest in this volume, the history of teacher education, so replete with ideological arguments, is also a story of turf battles about markets. Departments within institutions competed for enrollments, and hence argued about which courses students should take. And institutions competed with each other for students, and argued about which type of school should prepare teachers for the different levels of the educational system. During the nineteenth century, only a very small fraction of elementary teachers attended normal schools or colleges at all, but by the second or third decade of the twentieth century, prospective teachers became a large part of the clientele of American higher education.[9]

Within higher education, people argued vigorously about which courses teachers should take. In part, the debate over such issues produced abstract disquisitions about liberal learning versus professionalism. But more was at stake than logic and scholarly virtue: Enrollments vitally affected the relative standing of different departments. In the 1950s, advocates of the liberal-arts disciplines like Arthur Bestor took off their gloves and pummeled "educationists." They argued that education courses—which they regarded as piffle—enjoyed a privileged status since state laws required them for certification. Whether philosophical or polemical, behind such ideological contests lay political questions that affected institutional interests: Would future teachers take courses in American history or methods of teaching, physics or philosophy of education, or a combination?[10]

But the battles were not only between departments in liberal arts and in education. They also erupted between different kinds of institutions that prepared teachers. Universities, normal schools, state colleges, and private colleges of many kinds competed especially about who was best suited to prepare high-school teachers. The story of how normal schools became four-year colleges is bound up with their ambition to train high-school teachers. The campaign to have a national agency accredit teacher-education institutions also represented a blend of professional aspiration and political maneuver, of institutional advantage and markets for services and graduates.[11]

Perhaps the clearest connection between teacher training and guaranteed markets for graduates can be found in a much-neglected but highly important segment of teacher education, the city normal training divisions of high schools. These flourished in the nineteenth and early twentieth centuries. Dozens of large cities had ''normal'' classes in high schools in order to prepare graduates (usually only women) to teach in the elementary grades of their districts; and, even in smaller cities, high-school graduates formed an important source of teachers for the graded schools. These normal training divisions of high schools were not simply specialized vocational agencies. They also were key tools for the bureaucratization of urban systems.

Advocates of high schools argued that a major purpose of secondary education was to prepare teachers for the lower grades. This prospect of guaranteed employment induced women to complete the high-school course of study. In these normal training classes, prospective teachers learned the standard operating procedures that administrators wanted them to follow in instructing pupils. But in the twentieth century, when educational leaders in normal schools and colleges sought to break into the urban markets for teachers, they often criticized the city normal high schools for creating inbreeding and mechanized instruction in city schools. Twentieth-century laws requiring teachers to pursue advanced education beyond the high school undermined the powerful—sometimes nearly monopolistic—market position of the city normal high schools.[12]

Contests about what kinds of institutions should prepare teachers at which level and stage of their careers have a long history, and continue today. It is a commonplace in politics that one should attend to the footwork as well as the rhetoric of a candidate, and such, of course, is the case for historians investigating the history of teacher education.

A third use of history in policy analysis takes advantage of the long time-frame possible in historical evaluations of policies to detect unintended results of reforms. One can study explicit policy directly by looking at the justifications, regulations, and laws. One can then, with more effort and ambiguous findings, attempt to evaluate implementation. But, frequently, deliberate change brings undeliberated side effects—both benign and unwelcome—that reveal themselves not in the short period normally allotted to evaluation but in the longer run of time. Time is the river historians fish in, and it sometimes brings surprises.

Consider, for example, Thomas Morain's account of the post–Civil War campaign in Iowa to make teaching a steadier and more professional occupation. Officials sought to do this in part by requiring teachers to attend summer institutes—perhaps the most common form of teacher education in the nineteenth century—and by lengthening the school term. These steps toward making teaching at least a semiprofession had an unintended result: They hastened the exodus of men from teaching. Many men had been willing to teach briefly in winter terms, when the job required no special training and allowed them to pursue warm-weather employment. The opportunity costs under such conditions were small. But when men had to abandon summer work to attend an institute, and when the school term was so long that it was becoming nearly a full-time job, men left teaching in droves. Reforms intended to elevate the status of teaching made it attractive to women but not to men, who had many more alternative occupations.[13]

Other policies intended to "professionalize" teaching—and to establish administration and curriculum design as specialized fields within education—sometimes had the result of diminishing teachers' sense of control over their own work, thereby undermining what most people would take to be an essential characteristic of professionals: a reasonable degree of autonomy to exercise their judgment. Supposedly the "science" of education was to give teachers the concepts and tools they needed to become experts (as in creating precise behavioral objectives). In practice, however, the application of "science" to instruction—with all its rhetoric of social efficiency—often meant that the planning of instruction was separated from its execution.

Curriculum experts and other administrators who busily prescribed their blueprints of instruction may have done more to deskill teaching than to professionalize it. Even the word "unprofessional" came to have a meaning that reflected the bureaucratic setting of teaching rather than the concept of the free-standing and competent professional. In everyday use, the term often designated a maverick who did not observe the proprieties of hierarchy (for example, not being "loyal" to a superior, or automatically taking the side of a fellow teacher over students, or wearing the "wrong" clothes).[14]

A fourth approach to the use of history in policy analysis also takes advantage of the historian's interest in change and constancy over long periods of time. This permits what might be called *meta-analysis*, or a stepping back from the particulars of reform in a single time and place to ask: What might be underlying conditions that produce regularities—cycles?—of change or that accentuate stability? Anthony Downs has observed that there is an "issue-attention cycle" in contemporary politics that has produced a common sequence of alarm, response, and then neglect.[15]

If one applies Down's idea to the history of efforts to "reform" teaching, one finds that teachers have been perceived as a "problem" in certain kinds of periods. By comparing periods when reformers discovered "the teacher problem," one might find some common patterns. These might include the rhetoric used to describe the situation, supply and demand of teachers, or enthusiasm for replacing the judgment and skill of the teacher by some form of teacher-proof instruction. It would be useful to investigate, for example, whether the recurrent waves of enthusiasm for technology in the classroom matched times of teacher-bashing and shortages of money or teachers (or both).[16]

Another subject that lends itself to meta-analysis is the question of why teachers, relatively quiescent over long periods, in certain times became militant—a subject discussed by Wayne Urban and James Fraser in this volume. In this case it is the teachers, not the public, who perceive the "teacher problem." The demographic characteristics of teachers (their youth and gender, for example), their high turnover, the insecurity of their jobs before tenure became common, their comparative isolation in the workplace, the restrictive stereotypes and social rules that communities used to constrain them, the top-down ideology of "professional" loyalty and tight supervision—these and other features of the occupation of teaching stymied organized protest. But on some occasions teachers did protest in organized ways to achieve their goals, and finding common elements in these situations could illuminate both quiescence and militance. In many such cases teachers seem to have begun with specific grievances, had leaders who were able to translate their discontents into policies that appealed to the rank and file, and won support from groups outside the schools, such as unions and community organizations. Understanding common elements and differences in organized protest movements of teachers might also illuminate the far more frequent phenomenon of individual resistance to, and sabotage of, unwelcome district office directives.[17]

Thus far I have been suggesting ways in which history might be useful in looking at conscious *policies* involving teachers. Policy talk will continue to attract the interest of historians, in part because it leaves written records and also because it offers a measuring rod by which to judge practice. The specific policy also focuses historical inquiry.

Focusing only on conscious policies, however, neglects all those major shifts in the history of teaching that took place quietly over long periods of time. The massive decline in the birth rate in the nineteenth century, and the rising participation of married women in the workforce in the middle of the twentieth century, for example, had great impact on the occupation of teaching. Silent changes often were quite as important as those that aroused attention. And focusing only on discrete policies neglects the connections among them, and may slight the larger turning points in the development of the occupation.

An emerging integrative history of teaching, then, must be far more than a study of individual conscious policies and their fate in the schools.

Notes Toward a New History of Teaching

Elsbree's *The American Teacher,* the last comprehensive book on the history of teachers, is now 50 years old yet still useful. Elsbree's story is largely a house history that shares much in common with the historiographical purposes and message of Ellwood P. Cubberley. Confidently, it tells a triumphant tale of battles won and an uncompleted agenda of professionalization to accomplish. He goes beyond the normative debates to tell also something about the institutional history of teaching. In common with most of his predecessors, however, Elsbree sees teaching more from the top down than from the inside out. Teachers are the objects of elite attention more than agents of their own destiny. Like other members of the educational elite who wrote about teachers, Elsbree tended to see improvement as the result of things that were *done to* teachers: better teacher education, certification, or supervision. He had little to say about the everyday lives of teachers or even about their work—instruction. Hence his book is not a history of teaching.[18]

As I have suggested, there will probably never again be a history of teachers that has the coherence of Elsbree's account. Its confident message and integration of parts arose from a set of values and a narrow frame of analysis that subsequent work in history has undermined. If historians, like bird watchers, can be categorized as *lumpers* and *splitters,* Elsbree can clearly be called a lumper (note his title speaks of THE teacher). Recent historians of education and of teaching have far more often been splitters. They have examined the differences between and among the experiences of men and women, blacks and whites, immigrants and native-born, urban and rural, North and South, and teachers of different class backgrounds. They have also used a multiplicity of new evidence and methods of analysis. And the concept of professionalization, which underlay Elsbree's dream of progress, has been attacked as an instrument of male and/or class domination, while other means of advancing the solidarity and power of teachers have been urged instead.

These changes in scholarship on teachers have not simply been additive, filling in gaps on particular subjects. At their best, as in some of the work in women's history, they have sought to provide a distinctly new way of seeing what had previously been taken for granted or glimpsed through inappropriate lenses. Gender, race, and class, for example, are not simply other variables to be added to conventional interpretations. Rather, they are fundamental analytic categories that may change the basic story line. The established scholarship, in this view, is not an "objective" account but simply one social reality constructed from the perspective of those who are dominant. Sandra Acker, for example, has analyzed how a male model of professionalization has inappropriately been applied to women teachers. In the process, scholars have blamed women for not behaving like male doctors and lawyers, and have failed to understand the logic of women's choices. Running through the sociological literature, she writes, is a conception of "women teachers as damaging, deficient, distracted, and sometimes even dim."[19]

The pioneer work of Geraldine Clifford shows that teaching occupied a quite different place in the life cycle of women and men. Men and women often saw teaching as a steppingstone job, but their destinations were quite different: for the man, another (perhaps more prestigious) position in the paid labor market; while for the woman, teaching often led to marriage and a forced or voluntary exit from paid work. Sari Biklen has shown that women teachers' sense of "career" may not match a model based on prestigious male occupations, but rationally reflects the set of responsibilities they face at home and at work—which typically are quite different from those of men. If women teachers took their chief satisfactions from their relations with their pupils, from seeing them develop academically and socially, rather than from "professional advancement" up the ladder, or if they valued teaching because it was congruent with family demands, such attitudes were sometimes seen not as assets but as lack of commitment. Teaching might be women's true profession, but women were not true professionals.[20]

Like gender, race constituted an important divide in the history of teaching. As

Linda Perkins's chapter indicates, teaching has historically been a socially valued and honorable occupation in the black community, and educators were often key leaders, along with ministers. Indeed, in the South, where a rigid caste system imposed a low job ceiling on both men and women, there were very few white-collar jobs of *any* kind outside of teaching available to blacks. Despite starvation-level salaries, the respectability of the occupation—especially for women in comparison with domestic service or field work—made it more attractive for blacks than for whites. In the North, blacks often were able to obtain valued teaching positions only in segregated schools—a trade-off with the white power structure. Whether in South or North, black public school teachers and principals typically were subordinated to white officials, and this added a further constraint on their freedom of action, however valued the job might be.[21]

As historians have sought to study the whole array of different kinds of people who taught, they have employed a wide range of units of analysis, sources, and methods. John Rury and a number of other colleagues have used census and district records to uncover demographic and economic data to give a *macro* portrait of the occupation. They have revealed much about the kinds of people who entered teaching—their age, sex, marital status, class, race and ethnicity, income, and the place of teaching in their life course.

Some historians have focused more on the *institutions* in which they taught. Wayne Fuller's chapter herein highlights, for example, the distinctiveness of rural schools. Throughout much of American history, country schools and city schools differed from urban schools in their relation to the surrounding community, in their organization and pedagogy, and in relative attractiveness to that small minority of teachers who chose teaching as a lifelong profession. Although urban schools often were regimented bureaucracies, many rural and small-town teachers migrated to the cities for greater pay and job security. The age and years of experience of urban teachers were substantially higher than was the case with those in the countryside.

Still other historians have focused more on the lives of *individual teachers*. They have uncovered documents—diaries, letters, biographies of teachers, and the like—and used oral history to discern how teachers themselves made sense of their lives.[22]

Although some historians claim special virtue for one kind of evidence or approach over the others, in fact they are all necessary and complementary, though sometimes in tension with one another. While specialists may call themselves "quantitative historians" or "oral historians," history itself is whole and requires *many* ways of knowing. Historical demography and quantitative methods tell much about the general characteristics of teachers but little about their culture or about how individuals gave meaning to their lives in classrooms. Understanding schools as institutions is essential to reconstructing teachers' workplaces and the opportunities and constraints they faced, but it is also necessary to relate teachers' lives in classrooms to the rest of their world. Diaries and oral histories provide rich portraits of how individuals construed their social reality in and out of school, but inevitably one is left with questions about how representative are the surviving samples, and how selective are the memories recorded. While life-history evidence gives a sense of immediacy, people living through events often do not—perhaps cannot—see the long-term trends visible to historians, who can look backward and have the advantage of knowing how things turned out.

Instead of thinking of the three levels of analysis—macro, institutional, and individual—as competing, one might regard them as analytic Chinese boxes, each nesting within the others. Likewise, different kinds of evidence—quantitative, that derived from institutional records, and life-history data—complement one another. Economic and demographic data, for example, provide a general portrait of who taught where and when, how much they earned in relation to people in other occupations, and how teaching might have fit into their life course. This evidence can of course be used for analytic as well as descriptive purposes; the face that most teachers were young women, for example, goes far toward explaining why they received low pay, and why community members and supervisors often thought it appropriate and necessary to subject them to close control.

The comparative demographics of teaching and of more prestigious professions like law and medicine also reveal much about why teachers remained low on the professional totem pole. Understanding the great variety in the institutional character of schools in the past (for example, the sharp contrasts between rural and urban schools) in turn helps to interpret the contrasting demographics of teachers in the two types of schools, and the reactions of individual teachers to their work. And looking at teaching from the perspective of the individual teacher shows that their motivations, satisfactions, and sense of career often were very different from the preconceptions of the institutional leaders who bossed them, or the scholars who studied them. Qualitative evidence from individuals often can illuminate the reasons for the patterns that demographic studies reveal.[23]

Thus far I have concentrated on new angles of vision provided by talking analytic categories like gender and race seriously, and on how to combine different units of analysis and diverse evidence and methodologies. One can discern in this new body of scholarship the beginnings of a new teacher-centered history of the occupation, as opposed to Elsbree's vision of a march toward a present agenda of professionalization. At present one can only speculate what might be the major turning points in the history of teachers and teaching.

Throughout most of the nineteenth century, teachers in the common schools of the countryside entered the occupation for a brief time in their early adulthood, were mostly untrained and minimally educated, were paid in rural areas about the same as farm and house workers, and used the occupation as a transition to marriage (for women) or as a steppingstone to other jobs (for men). For many teachers, however, a powerful Protestant–republican ideology of service gave resonant meaning to this everyday work. "As the Israelite awaits the readvent of the lost glory of his race, the Christian the dawn of the millennial day, and the millions the coming of that good time when the earth shall be greener and the skies brighter," said one educator, "so we believe in the golden age of schools and teachers. But for this inspiring hope, this vague but indistinguishable faith and longing for something worthier and better, who of us would not be at times ready to drop the oar and in hopelessness to drift any whither?" Teachers who shared this dream were more missionaries than professionals in aspiration.[24]

Only gradually was this evangelical frame of mind replaced by a contrasting ideology of teaching as a lifelong professional career that drew on science and expertise and took place in large bureaucratic institutions. The actual organizational forms of schooling remained disparate well into the twentieth century. The one-room black school of Dine Hollow, Alabama, was poles apart from the rich, progressive schools of Winnetka, Illinois. Middle-aged women teachers of immigrant background instructing 60 children in the sardine-packed classrooms of New York lived in quite a different world from that of a male high-school science teacher in Newton, Massachusetts. But over time the differences in the occupation began to narrow. Through the consolidation of rural schools to approximate a bureaucratic model, the impact of state laws standardizing requirements for teacher education and certification, the influence of mass educational organizations like the National Education Association, and the impact of committees and textbook publishers and elite pace-setters who nationalized standards and practices, both a new ideology of professionalization, and templates of proper bureaucratic structures, worked together over time to standardize teaching as an occupation.[25]

Such large-scale changes may have constituted the macro-context within which the occupation developed in different institutional settings. Within such turning points in the development of teaching, the differences of gender, race, ethnicity, class, and region continued to distinguish teachers, one from another. But a key question still remains: To what degree did the everyday work of teachers—instruction in classrooms—show elements of constancy *over* time and *between* different institutional settings and *among* teachers with different social characteristics?

On this key point—what and how teachers taught—there is comparatively little evidence. Demographic data provide dim illumination; institutional records such as school reports give few glimpses into classrooms; and even first-hand historical accounts by teachers, such as diaries, rarely contain thick descriptions of how and what they taught.

A puzzle emerges from what little scholarship does exist on the history of classroom instruction: It appears that while ideologies and structures of schooling changed, and teachers became older and considerably better-educated, their work displayed remarkable consistency. The British film ''Hope and Glory'' gives a revealing vignette of such constancy of standard practices: Schoolchildren leave their classroom to go to a bomb shelter, where they sit, equipped with gas masks, reciting to their teacher, who maintains the pedagogical order in that stark setting.

The most complete and useful study of the history of classroom instruction is Larry Cuban's *How Teachers Taught,* which exploits the scattered evidence of photographs, reports on classroom observations, surveys, and teachers' accounts of their work. He found that the instructional methods that public school teachers have used in the past century have varied relatively little over time and institutional context. While there have been some differences—elementary teachers, for example, used somewhat more ''progressive'' methods than did high-school teachers—the vast majority of teachers have employed traditional teacher-centered and textbook-centered forms of instruction, mostly recitation. Although the rhetoric of different pedagogical reform movements ruffled the surface of the educational sea, a fathom deep, in the classroom little changed. Despite the diversity of people who made up the teaching force, as workers they used similar procedures.[26]

There are, of course, many possible explanations for this constancy in classroom instruction. One is that teachers begin their socialization the day they walk into school as students: They observe and internalize the teacher-centered classroom as the way it *is* in schools. Willard Waller suggests another reason when he describes the public classroom as "a despotism in a perilous state of equilibrium," for the teacher is expected to *control* a group of children as well as to teach them desiccated, predetermined knowledge. Teacher-centered instruction is one way to maintain that authority *and* to monitor students' attention to tasks. Even teachers who want to introduce more student-centered methods find that they are subject to the structural constraints of the school itself and the expectations of principals, other teachers, parents, and students. Both the degree and the causes of constancy in teaching methods still are questions explored by only a few historians—yet this relative constancy has powerful policy implications: Many reforms aimed at altering teacher behavior assume that it can be easily changed by manipulating factors remote from the classroom.[27]

The history of instruction must become a central topic in the history of teachers, yet, as David Cohen has argued, what and how teachers have taught has been largely a black box. Cuban's work suggests that it would be a mistake to go too far in stressing differences among teachers—the "splitter" tendency of which I spoke earlier—if, in the performance of their work, teachers show a strong tendency to follow a common pattern. Historical study of continuities and constancy in instruction (the what as well as the how) might illuminate the deep structure of teaching and reveal why attempts to alter its fundamental character may be like writing on snow. Adding a time dimension to current ethnographies and other studies of classroom instruction could raise important issues neglected in current policy debates.[28]

These notes toward a new history of teaching end, as they began, with the observation that it would be mistaken to suppose that one could today again create an optimistic evolutionary synthesis like Elsbree's. Its coherence came from a unified but incomplete and problematic concept of professionalism. A multiplicity of voices are now heard where once a few spoke for the many. But it is not idle to hope that a new and complex history, focused on teachers and their work and their *own* needs and aspirations, could interpret their world, and inform policy.

It has been said that contemporary artists serve society as an early warning system of changes that impend in consciousness and experience. Perhaps historians, habitually backward-looking, will be able to help policy makers not only to *use* a sense of the past (which they do, consciously or unconsciously) but also to *make sense* of it.

Notes

AUTHOR'S NOTE: The author is grateful to Eric Bredo, David Cohen, Larry Cuban, Elisabeth Hansot, and Deborah Kerdeman for conversations and critical readings that informed this essay.

1. Willard S. Elsbree, *The American Teacher: Evolution of a Profession in a Democracy* (New York: American Book Co., 1939). A more recent study that focuses on the ideologies of male nineteenth-century school leaders is Paul H. Mattingly, *The Classless Profession: American Schoolmen in the Nineteenth Century* (New York: New York University Press, 1975).
2. Willard Waller, *The Sociology of Teaching* (New York: Russell & Russell, 1932); William J. Goode, Frank F. Furstenberg, Jr., and Larry R. Mitchell, *Willard Waller on the Family, Education, and War* (Chicago: University of Chicago Press, 1970); also see the forthcoming book on Waller, edited by Donald Willower and William Boyd, to be published by Jossey–Bass.
3. Michael Sedlak and Stephen Schlossman, *Who Will Teach? Historical Perspectives on the Changing Appeal of Teaching as a Profession* (Santa Monica, CA: Rand Corporation, 1986).
4. Geraldine Jonçich Clifford, "Saints, Sinners, and People: A Position Paper on the Historiography of American Education," in *History of Education Quarterly* 15 (Fall 1975); pp. 257–272; and Kathleen Weiler, "Women's History and the History of Women Teachers," paper delivered at AERA convention, New Orleans, April 1988.
5. Elisabeth Hansot and David Tyack, "A Usable Past: Using History in Educational Policy," in Ann Lieberman and Milbrey McLaughlin (eds.), *Policy Making in Education* (Chicago: University of Chicago Press, 1982), pp. 1–22.
6. David B. Tyack, Michael W. Kirst, and Elisabeth Hansot, "Educational Reform: Retrospect and Prospect," in *Teachers College Record* 81 (Spring 1980), pp. 253–269.
7. Linda Darling-Hammond and Barnett Berry, *The Evolution of Teacher Policy* (Washington, DC: Center for the Study of the Teaching Profession, 1988); and Milbrey Wallin McLaughlin and Sylvia Mei-Ling Yee, "School as a Place to Have a Career," in Ann Lieberman (ed.), *Building a Professional Culture in Schools* (New York: Teachers College Press, 1988), pp. 23–44.
8. McLaughlin and Yee note the gap between the *institutional* view of career that motivates current reform efforts and an *individually based* notion of career that looks at the actual motivations and goals of teachers. It is interesting to note that a 1984 replication of a 1964 questionnaire study by Dan C. Lortie showed that almost 87 percent of teachers gained the greatest intrinsic rewards from "reaching" their students—Robert B. Kottkamp, Eugene F. Provenzo, Jr., and Marilyn M. Cohn, "Stability and Change in a Profession: Two Decades of Teacher Attitudes, 1964–1984," in *Phi Delta Kappan* 67 (April 1986), pp. 559–567.
9. Charles A. Harper, *The Development of the Teachers College in the United States, with Special Reference to the Illinois State Normal University* (Bloomington, IL: McKnight, 1935).
10. Merle Borrowman, *The Liberal and Technical in Teacher Education* (New York: Bureau of Publications, Teachers College, Columbia University, 1956); and Arthur Bestor, *Educational Wastelands* (Urbana, IL: University of Illinois Press, 1953).
11. James D. Koerner, *The Miseducation of American Teachers* (Boston: Houghton Mifflin, 1963); and G. K. Hodenfield and T. M. Stinnett, *The Education of Teachers* (Englewood Cliffs, NJ: Prentice–Hall, 1961).
12. Nineteenth-century city school reports frequently discuss the functions and operations of these schools. For an overview, see Frank A. Manny, *City Training Schools for Teachers,* U.S. Bureau of Education, *Bulletin* No. 47, 1914 (Washington, DC: Government Printing Office, 1915).
13. Thomas Morain, "The Departure of Males from the Teaching Profession in Nineteenth Century Iowa," in *Civil War History* 26 (June 1980), pp. 161–170.
14. Raymond E. Callahan, *Education and the Cult of Efficiency* (Chicago: University of Chicago Press, 1962).
15. Anthony Downs, "Up and Down with

Ecology—The 'Issue–Attention Cycle,' " *Public Interest* 28 (Summer 1972), pp. 38–50.

16. Larry Cuban, *Teachers and Machines* (New York: Teachers College Press, 1986); and David Tyack and Elisabeth Hansot, "Futures That Never Happened: Technology and the Classroom," in *Education Week* (September 4, 1985), pp. 40 and 35.
17. Howard K. Beale, *Are American Teachers Free? An Analysis of Restraints upon the Freedom of Teaching in American Schools* (New York: Charles Scribners' Sons, 1936); and Kathleen C. Berkeley, " 'The Ladies Want to Bring about Reform in the Public Schools': Public Education and Women's Rights in the Post–Civil War South," in *History of Education Quarterly* 24 (Spring 1984), pp. 45–58.
18. Elsbree, *American Teacher;* and Ellwood P. Cubberley, *Public Education in the United States: A Study and Interpretation of American Educational History,* rev. ed. (Boston: Houghton Mifflin, 1934).
19. Sandra Acker, "Women and Teaching: A Semi-Detached Sociology of a Semi-Profession," in Stephen Walker and Len Barton (eds.), *Gender, Class, and Education* (Sussex, Eng.: Falmer Press, 1983), p. 124; and Sally Schwager, "Educating Women in America," in *Signs* 12 (Winter 1987), pp. 333–374.
20. Geraldine Jonçich Clifford, "History as Experience: The Uses of Personal-History Documents in the History of Education," in *History of Education Quarterly* 18 (Fall 1978), pp. 183–196; and Sari Knopp Biklen, "Can Elementary Schoolteaching Be a Career? A Search for New Ways of Understanding Women's Work," in *Issues in Education* 3 (Winter 1985), pp. 215–231; and Nancy Hoffman, *Woman's 'True' Profession: Voices from the History of Teaching* (Old Westbury, NY: Feminist Press, 1981).
21. Horace Mann Bond, *Education of the Negro in the American Social Order* (New York: Prentice–Hall, 1934); and James D. Anderson, *The Education of Blacks in the South, 1860–1935* (Chapel Hill: University of North Carolina Press, 1988).
22. A pioneer quantitative study of teachers was Richard Bernard and Maris A. Vinovskis, "The Female School Teacher in Ante-Bellum Massachusetts," in *Journal of Social History* 10 (Spring 1977); pp. 332–345. For a recent example of oral history, see Richard A. Quantz, "The Complex Visions of Female Teachers and the Failure of Unionization in the 1930s: An Oral History," in *History of Education Quarterly* 25 (Winter 1985), pp. 439–458.
23. A number of the studies cited by Clifford and Rury in this volume, exploring why teaching became a woman's occupation, have sought to combine broad statistical analysis with institutional and individual-level analysis.
24. David Tyack and Elisabeth Hansot, *Managers of Virtue: Public School Leadership in America, 1820–1980* (New York: Basic Books, 1982), p. 15.
25. On the importance of organizational setting for evaluating forms of "professionalism" I am indebted to a forthcoming study by Elisabeth Hansot; Milbrey Wallin McLaughlin, R. Scott Pfeifer, Deborah Swanson-Owens, and Sylvia Yee, "Why Teachers Won't Teach," in *Phi Delta Kappan* (February 1986), pp. 420–426; and McLaughlin and Yee, "School."
26. Larry Cuban, *How Teachers Taught* (New York: Longman, 1984).
27. Cuban, *Teachers;* Waller, *Teaching.*
28. In his chapter in this volume and in other publications cited there, David Cohen has made some fascinating forays into the history of instruction, this hole at the center of the history of teaching.

Bibliography

This list combines most references cited by the chapter authors. General works and specifically focused articles and papers have been omitted. References to reports of census and job market data havc not been repeated.

Readers should also consult individual chapters for primary sources, but they should note that these citations offer only a sample of the available supply. In states and cities across the country, one can find primary sources to the history of teachers lodged in historical societies, institutional libraries and archives, school records, and personal and family collections. Ingenuity and probably a travel budget are required to unearth them. Manuscript collections of the Library of Congress, the National Archives, and the Hoover Institution's Paul and Jean Hanna Collection on the Role of Education contain many relevant materials. Among the resources of the Hanna Collection is the Archives of the American Educational Research Association.

Reports of the old U.S. Bureau of Education, the state education agencies, and arious local school systems, especially those dated in the nineteenth and early wentieth centuries, offer much that can be used by scholars and policy makers nterested in teachers and their work. One of the best national collections of such ublished reports can be found in the research library of the U.S. Department of ducation in Washington, DC. Many state departments of education, however, ave maintained old records and reports that can prove to be invaluable. The overnment documents cited below illustrate the available sources, but the list is not xhaustive. Researchers should be particularly alert for the numerous educational tudies commissioned by Congress and state legislatures over the years.

Other secondary sources that offer promising leads include the educational eriodicals that enjoyed state or regional circulations and the ubiquitous state and cal school surveys that were once popular with educational leaders. Henry arnard's *American Journal of Education* remains a rich resource for understanding neteenth-century educational developments, including the emerging roles of achers.

OOKS, ARTICLES, CHAPTERS, AND REPORTS

BBOTT, EDITH. *Women in Industry*. New York: D. Appleton, 1909.

BERNETHY, JULIAN W. "The Passing of the Normal School." *Education* 23 (February 1903): 325–330.

ABERNETHY, THOMAS J. "Education in Westfield 1669–1969." In *Westfield Massachusetts 1669–1969: The First Three Hundred Years,* edited by Edward C. Janes and Roscoe S. Scott, Westfield, MA: Westfield Tri-Centennial Association, 1968.

ACKER, SANDRA. "Women and Teaching: A Semi Detached Sociology of a Semi-Profession." In *Gender, Class, and Education,* edited by Len Barton and Stephen Walker. Sussex, England: Falmer Press, 1983.

ALBELDA, RANDY. "Occupational Segregation by Race and Gender, 1958–1981." *Industrial and Labor Relations Review* 39 (1986): 404–411.

ALBREE, JOHN. *Charles Brooks and his Work for Normal Schools.* Medford, MA: J.C. Miller, 1907.

ALCOTT, WILLIAM. *Confessions of a Schoolmaster.* New York: Arno Press, 1969. (Originally published in Boston, 1839; revised, 1856.)

ALDINGER, FREDERICK C. *History of the Lansing Public Schools, 1847–1944.* Lansing, MI: Lansing School District, n.d.

ALDRICH, HOWARD. *Organizations and Environments.* Englewood Cliffs, NJ: Prentice–Hall, 1979.

ALLEN, ANN TAYLOR. " 'Let Us Live with Our Children': Kindergarten Movements in Germany and the United States, 1840–1914." *History of Education Quarterly* 28 (Spring 1988): 23–48.

———. "Spiritual Motherhood: German Feminists and the Kindergarten Movement, 1848–1911." *History of Education Quarterly* 22 (Fall 1982): 319–340.

ALLEN, GRANT. "Women's Place in Nature." *Forum* 7 (June 1889): 258–263.

AMERICAN ASSOCIATION OF COLLEGES FOR TEACHER EDUCATION. "Minority Teacher Recruitment and Retention: A Call for Action." Washington, DC: AACTE, 1987.

———. Teacher Education Policy in the States: 50-State Survey of Legislative and Administrative Actions. Washington, DC: AACTE, 1985.

AMERICAN COUNCIL ON EDUCATION, OFFICE OF MINORITY CONCERNS. *Minorities in Higher Education, Sixth Annual Report.* Washington, DC: ACE, 1987.

ANDERSON, EARL W. "Factors in Predicting Demand for Teachers." *Educational Research Bulletin* 11 (1932): 180–182.

———. "Teaching Opportunities in 1931." *Educational Research Bulletin* 11 (1932): 91–93.

ANDERSON, JAMES D. *The Education of Blacks in the South, 1860–1935.* Chapel Hill: University of North Carolina Press, 1988.

———. "Northern Philanthropy and the Training of the Black Leadership: Fisk University, a Case Study, 1915–1930." In *New Perspectives on Black Educational History,* edited by Vincent P. Franklin and James D. Anderson. Boston: G.K. Hall, 1978.

ANTHONY, SUSAN B., and IDA HUSTED HARPER, eds. *The History of Woman Suffrage.* New York: Susan B. Anthony, 1902.

ANTIN, MARY. *The Promised Land.* Boston: Houghton Mifflin, 1912.

ANTLER, JOYCE. *Lucy Sprague Mitchell: The Making of a Modern Woman.* New Haven, CT: Yale University Press, 1987.

APPLE, MICHAEL. *Teachers and Texts: A Political Economy of Class and Gender Relations in Education.* New York: Routledge and Kegan Paul, 1986.

———. "Teaching and 'Women's Work': A Comparative Historical and Ideological Analysis." *Teachers College Record* 86, no. 3 (Spring 1985): 445–473.

Ashmore, Harry S. *The Negro and the Schools*. Chapel Hill: University of North Carolina Press, 1954.

Atkinson, Fred Washington. *The Professional Preparation of Secondary Teachers in the United States*. Leipzig: Breitkopf and Haertel, 1893.

Axtell, James. *The School Upon a Hill: Education and Society in Colonial New England*. New Haven, CT: Yale University Press, 1974.

Ayres, Leonard P. "What Educators Think About the Need for Employing Men Teachers in Our Public Schools." *Journal of Educational Psychology* 2, no. 1 (January 1911): 89–93.

Bagley, William C. "Training of Teachers." *Proceedings and Addresses*, National Education Association. Washington, DC: NEA, 1919.

———. "State Progress in Reducing the Proportion of Untrained Teachers." *School and Society* 22 (May 1925): 113–114.

Bain, Winifred E. *An Analytical Study of Teaching in Nursery School, Kindergarten and First Grade*. New York: Bureau of Publications, Teachers College, Columbia University, 1928.

Balyeat, Frank A. "Country High Schools in Oklahoma." *Chronicles of Oklahoma* 37 (1959/60): 196–210.

Bardeen, C.W. "Why Teaching Repels Men." *Educational Review* 35 (April 1908): 351–358.

Barnard, Henry. *Normal Schools and Other Institutions, Agencies, and Means Designed for the Professional Education of Teachers*. Hartford, CT: Case, Tiffany, 1851.

———, ed. *Papers on Froebel's Kindergarten*. Hartford, CT: Office of Barnard's *American Journal of Education,* 1881.

Baron, Ava, and Susan E. Klepp. " 'If I Didn't Have My Sewing Machine . . .' Women and Sewing Machine Technology." In *A Needle, a Bobbin, A Strike: Women Needleworkers in America,* edited by Joan M. Jensen and Sue Davidson. Philadelphia: Temple University Press, 1984.

Barrett, Richard C. "Reciprocity in Licensing Teachers," *Proceedings and Addresses*, National Education Association, Washington, DC: NEA, 1902.

Baylor, Ruth M. *Elizabeth Palmer Peabody: Kindergarten Pioneer*. Philadelphia: University of Pennsylvania Press, 1965.

Beale, Howard K. *Are American Teachers Free? An Analysis of Restraints Upon the Freedom of Teaching in American Schools*. New York: Scribner's, 1936.

Beatty, Barbara. " 'The Kind of Knowledge of Most Worth to Young Women': Post-Secondary Vocational Training for Teaching and Motherhood at the Wheelock School, 1888–1914." *History of Higher Education Annual* 6 (1986): 29–50.

Beaumont, Nellie. "Emma Lott: 1867–1937." *Michigan History Magazine* 41 (1957): 335–336.

Beecher, Catharine. *The Duty of American Women to Their Country*. New York: Harper & Row, 1945.

———. Educational Reminiscences and Suggestions. New York: J.B. Ford, 1874.

Berkeley, Kathleen C. " 'The Ladies Want to Bring about Reform in the Public Schools': Public Education and Women's Rights in the Post-Civil War South." *History of Education Quarterly* 24 (Spring 1984): 45–58.

Berlak, Ann, and Harold Berlak. *Dilemmas of Schooling*. New York: Methuen, 1981.

BERN, ENID. "Memoirs of a Prairie School Teacher." *North Dakota History* 42, no. 3 (1975): 5–17.

BERNARD, RICHARD M., and MARIS A. VINOVSKIS. "The Female School Teacher in Ante Bellum Massachusetts." *Journal of Social History* 10 (Spring 1977): 332–345.

BEST, JOHN HARDIN, ed. *Historical Inquiry in Education: A Research Agenda*. Washington, DC: American Educational Research Association, 1983.

BESTOR, ARTHUR. *Educational Wastelands: The Retreat from Learning in Our Public Schools*. Urbana: University of Illinois Press, 1953.

BIGELOW, KARL W. "The Passing of the Teachers College, 1938–1956." *Teachers College Record* 58 (1957): 409–417.

BIKLEN, SARI KNOPP. "Can Elementary Schoolteaching be a Career?: A Search for New Ways of Understanding Women's Work."' *Issues in Education* 3, no. 3 (Winter 1985): 215–231.

BILLINGTON, ALLEN, ed. *The Journal of Charlotte L. Forten: A Free Negro in the Slave Era*. New York: Collier Books, 1967.

BLOCH, RUTH H. "American Feminine Ideals in Transition: The Rise of the Moral Mother, 1785–1815." *Feminist Studies* 4, no. 1 (February 1978): 101–126.

BLOW, SUSAN. *Educational Issues in the Kindergarten*. New York: D. Appleton, 1908.

———. *Symbolic Education: A Commentary on Froebel's "Mother Play."* New York: D. Appleton, 1894.

BOLGAR, R.R. "Victor Cousin and Nineteenth Century Education." *The Cambridge Journal* 2 (1949): 357–368.

BOND, HORACE MANN. *Black American Scholars: A Study of Their Beginnings*. Detroit: Belamp, 1972.

———. *The Education of the Negro in the American Social Order*. New York: Prentice-Hall, 1934. Reprint. New York: Octagon Books, 1966.

———. "Negro Education: Debate in the Alabama Constitutional Convention of 1901." *Journal of Negro Education* 1 (April 1932): 49–59.

BORROWMAN, MERLE L. *The Liberal and Technical In Teacher Education*. New York: Teachers College, Columbia University, 1956.

———, ed. *Teacher Education in America: A Documentary History*. New York: Teachers College Press, 1965.

BOSS, AGNES HOUGHTON. "Grace Annie Hill (1874–1944)." *Michigan History Magazine* 38 (1954): 153–156.

BOSTON LATIN SCHOOL ASSOCIATION. *Memorial of Francis Gardner LLD, Late Head Master of the Boston Latin School*. Boston: The Association, 1876.

BOWLES, FRANK, and FRANK A. DECOSTA. *Between Two Worlds: A Profile of Negro Higher Education*. New York: McGraw-Hill, 1971.

BOWLES, SAMUEL, and HERBERT GINTIS. *Schooling in Capitalist America: Educational Reform and the Contradictions of Economic Life*. New York: Basic Books, 1976.

BOYDEN, ALBERT G. *History and Alumni Record of the State Normal School at Bridgewater*. Boston, 1876.

BOYER, ERNEST L. *High School: A Report on Secondary Education in America*. New York: Harper & Row, 1983.

BOYKIN, JAMES C. "Women in the Public Schools." *Educational Review* 18 (September 1899): 138–143.

BOYLAN, ANNE M. "Evangelical Womenhood in the Nineteenth Century: The Role of Women in Sunday Schools." *Feminist Studies* 4, no. 3 (October 1978): 62–80.

BRADFORD, MARY D. *Memoirs of Mary D. Bradford: Autobiography and Historical Reminiscences of Education in Wisconsin, Through Progressive Service from Rural School to City Superintendent.* Evansville, WI: Antes Press, 1932.

BRAUN, SAMUEL, and ESTHER EDWARDS. *History and Theory of Early Childhood Education.* Worthington, OH: Charles A. Jones, 1972.

BRICKMAN, WILLIAM W. "Power Conflicts and Crises in Teacher Education: Some Historical and International Perspectives." In *Responding to the Power Crisis in Teacher Education,* edited by Ayres Bagley. Washington, DC: Society of Professors of Education, 1971.

BROCK, E. WILBUR. "Farmer's Daughter Effects: The Case of the Negro Female Professional." *Phylon* 30, no. 1 (Spring 1969): 17–26.

BRODY, CATHERINE. "A New York Childhood." *American Mercury* 14, no. 53 (May 1929): 57–66.

BROOKS, CHARLES. *Two Lectures.* Boston: John Wilson and Son, 1864.

BROOKS, STRATTON D. "Dangers of School Reform." *Educational Review* 30 (March 1906): 226–235.

BROWN, ELMER E. "The Development of Education as a University Subject." *Teachers College Record* 24 (1923): 190–196.

BROWN, J.C. "State Normal Schools and the War." *School and Society* 7 (June 1918): 694–699.

BRUBAKER, ELLEN A. "Miss Mary M. Martin, Teacher Extraordinary, 1847–1930." *Journal of Lancaster County (PA.) History* 68 (1964): 115–120.

BRUBACHER, JOHN S. *The Development of the Department of Education at Yale University, 1891–1958.* New Haven, CT: Yale University Press, 1960.

BUCHANAN, FREDERICK S. "Unpacking of the N.E.A.: The Role of Utah's Teachers at the 1920 Convention." *Utah Historical Quarterly* 41 (1973): 150–161.

BULLOCK, ALLEN. *A History of Negro Education in the South from 1619 to the Present.* New York: Praeger, 1970.

BULLOUGH, ROBERT V., JR. "Teachers and Teaching in the Nineteenth Century: St. George, Utah." *Journal of Curriculum Theorizing* 4 (1982): 199–206.

BURGESS, W. RANDOLPH. "Four Censuses of Teachers' Salaries." *American School Board Journal* 61 (September 1920): 27–28.

———. *Trends in School Costs.* New York: Russell Sage, 1920.

BURK, FREDERICK, and CAROLINE FREAR BURK. *A Study of the Kindergarten Problem.* San Francisco: Whitaker and Ray, 1899.

BURKE, AGNES, EDITH U. CONARD, ALICE DALGLIESH, CARLOTTE G. GARRISON, EDNA V. HUGHES, MARY E. RANKIN, and ALICE THORN. *A Conduct Curriculum for the Kindergarten and First Grade.* New York: Scribner's, 1924.

BURRIS, BENJAMIN J. "The Problem of Certification in Relation to Teacher Training." *Proceedings and Addresses,* National Education Association. Washington, DC: NEA, 1926.

BURRIS, VAL, and AMY WHARTON. "Sex Segregation in the U.S. Labor Force." *Review of Radical Political Economy* 14 (1982): 43–56.

BUTLER, LESLIE A. *The Michigan Schoolmaster's Club: A Story of the First Seven Decades.* Ann Arbor: University of Michigan, 1958.

CALIVER, AMBROSE. *Education of Negro Teachers*. Westport, CT: Greenwood Press, 1970. Originally published as Vol. 4 of the *National Survey of the Education of Teachers*, U.S. Office of Education, Bulletin 1933, no. 10. Washington, DC: Government Printing Office, 1933.

CALLAHAN, RAYMOND E. *Education and the Cult of Efficiency*. Chicago: University of Chicago Press, 1962.

CANBY, HENRY SEIDEL. *Alma Mater: The Gothic Age of the American College*. New York: Farrar and Rinehart, 1936.

CARLSON, RICHARD O. "Variation and Myth in the Social Status of Teachers." *Journal of Educational Sociology* 35 (November 1961): 104–118.

CARNEGIE FORUM ON EDUCATION AND THE ECONOMY. Task Force on Teaching as a Profession. *A Nation Prepared: Teachers for the 21st Century*. New York: Carnegie Forum on Education and the Economy, 1986.

CARROLL, BERENICE A. *Liberating Women's History*. Urbana: University of Illinois Press, 1976.

CARTER, JAMES C. *Essays on Popular Education*. Boston: Bowles and Dearborn, 1826.

CARTER, MICHAEL J., and SUSAN B. CARTER. "Women's Recent Progress in the Professions, or Women Get a Ticket to Ride After the Gravy Train Has Left the Station." *Feminist Studies* 7 (1981): 477–504.

CARTER, SUSAN B. "Occupational Segregation, Teacher Wages and American Economic Growth." *Journal of Economic History* 56, no. 2 (June 1986): 373–383.

———, and Mark Prus. "The Labor Market and the American High School Girl, 1890–1928." *Journal of Economic History* 62, no. 1 (March 1982): 163–171.

CARY, ALICE DUGGED. "Kindergarten for Negro Children." *Southern Workman* 29 (Augus 1900): 461–463.

CAVALLO, DOMINICK. "From Perfection to Habit: Moral Training in the America Kindergarten, 1860–1920." *History of Education Quarterly* 16 (Summer 1976): 147–161

———. "The Politics of Latency: Kindergarten Pedagogy, 1869–1930." In *Regulate Children/Liberated Children: Education in Psychological Perspective*, edited by Barbar Finkelstein. New York: Psychohistory Press, 1979.

CHADWICK, F.E. "The Woman Peril in American Education." *Educational Review* 4 (February 1914): 109–119.

CHAMBERLAIN, LEO M., and LEONARD E. MEECE. "Men and Women in the Teachin Profession." Bureau of School Service, College of Education, University of Kentucky *Bulletin* 9, no. 3 (March 1937).

CHAMBERS, WILL GRANT. "The Passing of the Normal School: A Reply." *Education* 2 (April 1903): 483–489.

CHAMBERS-SCHILLER, LEE VIRGINIA. *Liberty, a Better Husband: Single Women in Americ The Generations of 1780–1840*. New Haven, CT: Yale University Press, 1984.

CHURCH, ROBERT L., and MICHAEL W. SEDLAK. *Education in the United States: A Interpretive History*. New York: Free Press, 1976.

CLARK, KENNETH B. *Dark Ghetto: Dilemmas of Social Power*. New York: Harper & Ro 1965.

CLARK, LINDA L. *Schooling the Daughters of Marianne: Textbooks and the Socialization Girls in Modern French Primary Schools*. Albany: State University of New York Pres 1984.

CLIFFORD, GERALDINE JONÇICH. "Eve: Redeemed by Education and Teaching School." *History of Education Quarterly* 21 (Winter 1981): 479–492.

———. "Home and School in 19th Century America: Some Personal History Reports from the United States." *History of Education Quarterly* 18 (Spring 1978): 3–34.

———. " 'Marry, Stitch, Die, or Do Worse': Educating Women for Work." In *Youth, Work, and Schooling: Historical Perspectives on Vocationalism in American Education,* edited by Harvey Kantor and David B. Tyack. Stanford, CA: Stanford University Press, 1982.

———. "Saints, Sinners, and People: A Position Paper on the Historiography of American Education." *History of Education Quarterly* 15, no. 3 (Fall 1975): 257–272.

———. "Shaking Dangerous Questions from the Crease: Gender and American Higher Education." *Feminist Issues* 3, no. 2 (Fall 1983): 3–62.

———. "Those Good Gertrudes": The Woman Teacher in America. Forthcoming.

———. "Women's Liberation and Women's Professions: Reconsidering the Past, Present, and Future." In *Women and Higher Education in American History,* edited by John Mack Faragher and Florence Howe. New York: Norton, 1988.

———, and James W. Guthrie. *Ed School.* Chicago: University of Chicago Press, 1988.

CLINTON, CATHERINE. *The Other Civil War: American Women in the Nineteenth Century.* New York: Hill and Wang, 1984.

COFFMAN, LOTUS DELTA. *The Social Composition of the Teaching Population.* Contributions to Education, no. 41. New York: Teachers College, Columbia University, 1911.

COHEN, DAVID K. "Educational Technology, Policy, and Practice." *Educational Evaluation and Policy Analysis* 9, no. 2 (Summer 1987): 153–170.

———. "Loss As A Theme in Social Policy." *Harvard Educational Review* 46 (November 1976): 553–571.

———. "Teaching Practice, Plus Que Ça Change . . ." In *Contributing to Educational Change: Perspectives on Research and Practice,* edited by Philip Jackson. Chicago: National Society for the Study of Education [McCutchan], 1988.

———. "Willard Waller: On Hating School and Loving Education." In *Willard Waller on Education and the Schools,* edited by Donald Willower and William Boyd. Tempe, AZ: University Council for Educational Administration, 1988.

———, and Barbara Neufeld. "The Failures of School and the Progress of Education." *Daedelus* 110 (Summer 1981): 69–89.

COLE, STEPHEN. *The Unionization of Teachers: A Case Study of the UFT.* New York: Praeger, 1969.

COLT, MIRIAM DAVIS. *Went to Kansas, Being a Thrilling Account of an Ill-Fated Expedition.* New York: L. Ingalls, 1862 (Ann Arbor, MI: University Microfilms, 1966).

COMMITTEE OF PHI DELTA KAPPA (Edwin A. Lee, Chairman). *Teaching as a Man's Job.* Homewood, IL: Phi Delta Kappa, 1938.

CONANT, JAMES B. *The American High School Today.* New York: McGraw-Hill, 1959.

———. *The Education of American Teachers.* New York: McGraw-Hill, 1963.

CONWAY, JILL K. "Perspectives on the History of Women's Education in the United States." *History of Education Quarterly* 14 (Spring 1974): 1–12.

COOK, KATHERINE M. "Certification by Examination—the Open Door to the Teaching Profession." *American School Board Journal* 61 (July 1920): 29–30, 119.

COOKINGHAM, MARY E. "Bluestockings, Spinsters and Pedagogues: Women College Graduates, 1865–1910." *Population Studies* 38 (1984): 349–364.

COOPER, HERMAN. "The New Certification Regulations." *New York State Education* 22 (January 1935): 281–285.

COPPIN, FANNY JACKSON. *Reminiscences of School Life and Hints on Teaching*. Philadelphia: AME Book Concern, 1913.

COTTON, FASSET A. *Education in Indiana: An Outline in the Growth of the Common School System*. Indianapolis: Superintendent of Public Instruction, 1904.

COUNTS, GEORGE S. *Dare the School Build a New Social Order?*. New York: John Day, 1932. Reprint, with a Preface by Wayne J. Urban. Carbondale: Southern Illinois University Press, 1982.

———. *School and Society in Chicago*. Chicago: University of Chicago Press, 1925.

———. *The Selective Character of Secondary Education*. Chicago: University of Chicago Press, 1922.

———. *The Senior High School Curriculum*. Chicago: University of Chicago Press, 1929.

CORWIN, RONALD G. "The New Teaching Profession." In *Teacher Education*, edited by Kevin Ryan. National Society for the Study of Education, 74th Yearbook, part 2. Chicago: University of Chicago Press, 1975.

COUSIN, VICTOR. *Report on the State of Public Instruction in Prussia*. New York: Wiley & Long, 1835.

CREMIN, LAWRENCE A. *American Education: The Colonial Experience, 1607–1783*. New York: Harper & Row, 1970.

———. *American Education: The Metropolitan Experience, 1876–1980*. New York: Harper & Row, 1988.

———. *American Education: The National Experience, 1783–1876*. New York: Harper & Row, 1980.

———. *The Transformation of the School: Progressivism in American Education, 1876–1957*. New York: Knopf, 1961.

———, David A. Shannon, and Mary Evelyn Townsend, *A History of Teachers College, Columbia University*. New York: Columbia University Press, 1954.

Crewe, Amy C. *No Backward Step Was Taken: Highlights in the History of the Publi Elementary Schools of Baltimore County*. Towson, MD: Teachers Association of Baltimor County, 1949.

CUBAN, LARRY. *How Teachers Taught: Constancy and Change in American Classrooms 1890–1980*. New York: Longman, 1984.

———. *Teachers and Machines: The Classroom Use of Technology Since 1920*. New Yor Teachers College Press, 1986.

CUBBERLEY, ELLWOOD P. *The Certification of Teachers*. National Society for the Scientifi Study of Education, Fifth Yearbook. Chicago: University of Chicago Press, 1906.

———. *Public Education in the United States: A Study and Interpretation of America Educational History*. Rev. ed. Boston: Houghton Mifflin, 1934.

CUNNINGHAM, CHARLES E., and D. KEITH OSBORN, "A Historical Examination of Blac in Early Childhood Education." *Young Children* 34 (March 1979): 20–29.

CULVER, RAYMOND B. *Horace Mann and Religion in the Massachusetts Public School* New Haven, CT: Yale University Press, 1929.

CURTI, MERLE, and VERNON CARSTENSEN. *The University of Wisconsin: A History*. 2 vol Madison: University of Wisconsin Press, 1949.

CUSICK, PHILIP A. *The Egalitarian Ideal and the American High School: Studies of Thr Schools*. New York: Longman, 1983.

DALE, EDWARD EVERETT. "Teaching on the Prairie Plains, 1890–1900." *Mississippi Valley Historical Review* 33, no. 2 (September 1946): 293–307.

DANIELS, WALTER G. "The Curriculum." *Journal of Negro Education* 1 (July 1932): 277–303.

DARLING-HAMMOND, LINDA. *Beyond the Commission Reports: The Coming Crisis in Teaching*. Santa Monica, CA: Rand Corporation, 1984.

———, and Barnett Berry. *The Evolution of Teacher Policy*. Santa Monica, CA: Rand Corporation, 1988.

———, and Arthur E. Wise. "Teaching Standards or Standardized Teaching?" *Educational Leadership* 41 (1983): 66–69.

DAVID, CALVIN O. "The Training of Teachers in North Central Association Accredited High Schools." *School and Society* 19 (April 1924): 389–394.

DEEGAN, DOROTHY YOST. *The Stereotype of the Single Woman in American Novels*. New York: Octagon Books, 1969.

DEGLER, CARL. *At Odds: Women and the Family in America, from the Revolution to the Present*. New York: Oxford University Press, 1980.

DENNISON, GEORGE. *The Lives of Children*. New York: Vintage, 1969.

DEWEY, EVELYN. *New Schools for Old: The Regeneration of the Porter School*. New York: Dutton, 1919.

DEWEY, JOHN. *The School and Society*. Chicago: University of Chicago Press, 1956.

DEX, SHIRLEY. *The Sexual Division of Labor: Conceptual Revolutions in the Social Sciences*. New York: St. Martins, 1985.

DINER, HASIA. *Erin's Daughters in America: Irish Immigrant Women in the Nineteenth Century*. Baltimore: Johns Hopkins University Press, 1983.

INNERSTEIN, LEONARD, and R.M. REIMERS. *Ethnic Americans*. New York: Harper & Row, 1975.

OGHERTY, MARIAN A. *'Scusa Me Teacher*. Francestown, NH: Marshall Jones, 1943.

OHERTY, ROBERT E. "Tempest on the Hudson: The Struggle for 'Equal Pay for Equal Work' in the New York City Public Schools, 1907–1911." *History of Education Quarterly* 19, no. 4 (Winter 1979): 413–434.

ONLEY, MARSHALL O., JR. *Power to the Teacher: How America's Educators Became Militant*. Bloomington: Indiana University Press, 1976.

ONOVAN, FRANCES R. *The Schoolma'am*. New York: Frederick A. Stokes, 1938.

OUAI, ADOLF. *The Kindergarten: A Manual for the Introduction of Froebel's System of Primary Education into Public Schools*. New York: E. Steiger, 1871.

OWNING, LUCIA B. "Teaching in the Keeler 'Deestrict' School." *Vermont Quarterly* 19 (October 1951): 233–240.

UBLIN, THOMAS. "Women and Outwork in a Nineteenth-Century New England Town: Fitzwilliam, New Hampshire, 1830–1850." In *The Countryside in the Age of Capitalist Transformation*, edited by Steven Hahn and Jonathan Prude. Chapel Hill: University of North Carolina Press, 1985.

——. *Women at Work: The Transformation of Work and Community in Lowell, Massachusetts, 1826–1860*. New York: Columbia University Press 1979.

BOIS, W.E.B. *The College-Bred Negro American*. Atlanta: Atlanta University Press, 1900.

——. "Education." *Chicago Defender* 19 (October 1946).

———. *The Negro Common School.* Atlanta: Atlanta University Press, 1901.

———. "Whither Now and Why." *The Education of Black People: Ten Critiques 1906–1960,* edited by Herbert Aptheker. Amherst: University of Massachusetts Press, 1973.

———, and Augustus G. Dill. *The Common School and the Negro American.* Atlanta: Atlanta University Press, 1911.

DUNCKLEE, HELEN S. "The Kindergartner and Her Mothers' Meetings." *Kindergarten Review* 10, no. 1 (September 1899): 12–15.

DUNKEL, HAROLD B. *Herbart and Education.* New York: Random House, 1969.

———. *Herbart and Herbartianism: An Educational Ghost Story.* Chicago: University of Chicago Press, 1970.

DUNN, ESTHER. *Pursuit of Understanding: Autobiography of an Education.* New York: Macmillan, 1945.

DWIGHT, HENRY E. *Travels in the North of Germany in the Years 1825 and 1826.* New York: G. & C. & H. Carvill, 1829.

DWORKIN, ANTHONY. "The Changing Demography of Public School Teachers: Some Implications for Faculty Turnover in Urban Areas." *Sociology of Education* 53 (April 1980): 65–73.

DYER, FRANKLIN. "Official Recognition of Teachers' Councils." *Educational Standards* (March 1916): 21–22.

DYNES, JOHN J. "How Certification Is Practiced in the Various States." *Nation's Schools* 7 (April 1931): 67–71.

EASTERLIN, RICHARD A. "Factors in the Decline in Farm Family Fertility in the United States: Some Preliminary Research Results." *Journal of American History* 63, no. 3 (December 1977): 600–614.

EATON, WILLIAM EDWARD. *The American Federation of Teachers, 1916–1961: A History of the Movement.* Carbondale: Southern Illinois University Press, 1975.

EDMONDS, FRANKLIN S. *History of the Central High School of Philadelphia.* Philadelphia: Lippincott, 1902.

EDSON, A.W. "Legitimate Work of a State Normal School." *Education* 16 (January 1896): 274–277.

EDWARDS, RICHARD. "Normal Schools in the United States." *Proceedings,* National Teachers Association, 6th Annual Meeting, Harrisburg, 1865. Hartford, 1865.

EGGERTSEN, CLAUDE, ED. *Studies in the History of the School of Education, University of Michigan, 1868–1954.* Ann Arbor: University of Michigan Press, 1955.

EGGLESTON, EDWARD E. *The Hoosier Schoolmaster: An Engaging Story of Life in Backwoods Village of Indiana in the 1850's.* New York: Hart, 1976.

ELIASSEN, R.H., and EARL W. ANDERSON. "Investigation of Teacher Supply and Demand Reported Since November, 1931." *Educational Research Bulletin* 12 (1933): 66–72.

———. "Investigations of the Teacher Supply and Demand Reported in 1934." *Educational Research Bulletin* 14 (1935): 61–66.

———. "Teacher Supply and Demand." *Review of Educational Research* 4 (June 1934): 257–260, 326–328.

———. "Teacher Supply and Demand." *Review of Educational Research* 7 (June 193[illegible]): 239–241.

ELSBREE, WILLARD. *The American Teacher: Evolution of a Profession in a Democracy.* New York: American Book, 1939.

EMERSON, GEORGE B. *Reminiscences of an Old Teacher*. Boston: A. Mudge, 1878.

ENNIS, ISABEL A. "Causes of the Present Shortage of Teachers." *Proceedings and Addresses,* National Education Association. Washington, DC: NEA, 1918.

EPSTEIN, CYNTHIA FUCHS. *Women's Place: Options and Limits in Professional Careers.* Berkeley: University of California Press, 1970.

ERNST, GEORGE A.O. "The Movement for School Reform in Boston." *Educational Review* 28 (December 1904): 433–443.

EVENDEN, EDWARD S. "The Demand for and Supply of Junior High School Teachers." *School Life* 17 (March 1932) 132–133.

———. "Fundamental Principles for Grading Teachers' Salaries." *Teacher College Record* 22 (May 1921): 197–208.

———. "The Supply of and Demand for Elementary Teachers." *School Life* 17 (February 1932): 112–114.

———. "The Supply of and Demand for Senior School Teachers." *School Life* 17 (January 1932): 92–93.

FACULTY COMMITTEE. *Semi-Centennial History of the Illinois State Normal University, 1857–1907*. Normal, IL: Faculty Committee, 1907.

FAHEY, SARA H. "Some Causes of the Present Decline of Teaching as a Profession." *Proceedings and Addresses,* National Education Association. Washington, DC: NEA, 1919.

———. "The Teacher's Salary as a Factor in Establishing Caste." *Proceedings and Addresses,* National Education Association. Washington, DC: NEA, 1920.

FEINSTEIN, KAREN WOLK. "Kindergartens, Feminism, and the Professionalization of Motherhood." *International Journal of Women's Studies* 3, no. 1 (January-February 1980): 28–38.

FELLMAN, DAVID, ed. *The Supreme Court and Education*. 3d ed. New York: Teachers College Press, 1976.

FELMEY, DAVID. "The New Normal School Movement." *Educational Review* 44 (April 1913): 409–415.

FELTER, WILLIAM L. "The Education of Women." *Educational Review* 31 (April 1906): 351–363.

FERRIS, EMERY N. *The Rural High School: Rural School Survey of New York State*. Philadelphia: William F. Fell, 1922.

FILENE, PETER GABRIEL. *Him/Her/Self: Sex Roles in Modern America*. New York: Harcourt Brace Jovanovich, 1974.

FINKELSTEIN, BARBARA. *Governing the Young: Teacher Behavior in Popular Primary Schools in Nineteenth Century United States*. Philadelphia: Falmer Press, 1989.

———. "The Revolt Against Selfishness: Women and the Dilemmas of Professionalism in Early Childhood Education." In *Professionalism and the Early Childhood Practitioner,* edited by Bernard Spodek, Olivia N. Saracho, and Donald L. Peters. New York: Teachers College Press, 1988.

———. "Schooling and Schoolteachers: Selected Bibliography of Autobiographies in the Nineteenth Century." *History of Education Quarterly* 14, no. 2 (Summer 1974): 293–300.

FISHEL, LESLIE H., JR., and BENJAMIN QUARLES. *The Negro American: A Documentary History*. New York: Morrow, 1967.

FISHMAN, STERLING. "The Double-Vision of Education in the Nineteenth Century: The Romantic and the Grotesque." In *Regulated Children/Liberated Children,* edited by Barbara Finkelstein. New York: Psychohistory Press, 1980.

FLETCHER, ELIJAH. *The Letters of Elijah Fletcher,* edited by Martha von Briesen. Charlottesville: University Press of Virginia, 1965.

FLEXNER, ABRAHAM. *Universities: American, English, German.* New York: Oxford University Press, 1930.

———, and Frank P. Bachman. *Public Education in Maryland.* New York: General Education Board, 1916.

FOFF, ARTHUR. "Scholars and Scapegoats." *English Journal* 47 (1958): 118–126.

FOREST, ILSE. *Preschool Education: A Historical and Critical Study.* New York: Macmillan, 1927.

FRANKLIN, BARRY. *Building the American Community: The School Curriculum and the Search for Social Control.* Philadelphia: Falmer Press, 1986.

FRANKLIN, VINCENT P. *Black Self-Determination.* Westport, CT: Lawrence Hill, 1984.

———. *The Education of Black Philadelphia: The Social and Educational History of a Minority Community, 1900–1950.* Philadelphia: University of Pennsylvania Press, 1979.

FRASER, JAMES W. "Mayor John F. Fitzgerald and Boston's Schools, 1905–1913." *Historical Journal of Massachusetts* 12, no. 2 (June 1984): 117–130.

———. "Who Were the Progressive Educators Anyway? A Case Study of the Progressive Education Movement in Boston, 1905–1925." *Educational Foundations* 2, no. 1 (Spring 1988): 4–30.

FRAZIER, BENJAMIN W. "Depression Tendencies vs. Long-time Trends Affecting Teachers." *American School Board Journal* 91 (September 1935): 19–20.

———. "State Certification Requirements as a Basis for Promoting Professional Standards." American Association of Teachers Colleges, *Fifteenth Yearbook.* Washington, DC: National Education Association, 1936.

FREEDMAN, SARA, JANE JACKSON, and KATHERINE BOLES. "The Effects of the Institutional Structure of Schools on Teachers." Somerville, MA: Boston Women's Teachers' Group, September 1, 1982.

FREEMAN, RICHARD B. *Black Elite: The New Market for Highly Educated Black Americans* New York: McGraw-Hill, 1976.

FROEBEL, FRIEDRICH. *The Education of Man,* translated by William N. Hailmann. New York: D. Appleton, 1909.

———. *Pedagogics of the Kindergarten,* translated by Josephine Jarvis. New York: D. Appleton, 1895.

FULLAN, MICHAEL. *The Meaning of Educational Change.* New York: Teachers College Press, Columbia University, 1982.

FULLER, ROSALIE TRAIL, ed. "A Nebraska High School Teacher in the 1890s: The Letters of Sadie B. Smith." *Nebraska History* 58 (1977): 447–474.

FULLER, WAYNE E. "Making Better Farmers: The Study of Agriculture in Midwestern Country Schools, 1900–1923." *Agricultural History* 60 (Spring 1986): 154–168.

———. *The Old Country School: The Story of Rural Education in the Middle West.* Chicago: University of Chicago Press, 1982.

GARLAND, HAMLIN. *A Son of the Middle Border.* New York: Macmillan, 1941.

GAY, GEORGE E. "Massachusetts Normal Schools." *Education* 17 (May 1897): 513–51

GERBNER, GEORGE. "Teacher Image and the Hidden Curriculum." *The American Scholar* 41, no. 1 (Winter 1972–73): 66–92.

GERSMAN, ELINOR MONDALE. "A Selected Bibliography of Periodicals in Educational History." *History of Education Quarterly* 17, no. 3 (Fall 1977): 275–296.

GILBERT, CHARLES B. *The School and Its Life*. New York: Silver, Burdett, 1906.

GILDART, MABEL, and MARY A. LORD, "A. Fern Persons." *Michigan History Magazine* 41 (1957): 471–476.

GILLESPIE, JOANNA B. "Clear Leadings of Providence: Pious Memoirs and the Problems of Self-Realization." *Journal of the Early Republic* 5, no. 2 (Summer 1985): 197–221.

GOOD, HARRY G. *The Rise of the College of Education of the Ohio State University*. Columbus: College of Education, Ohio State University, 1960.

GOODLAD, JOHN I. *The Changing School Curriculum*. New York: The Fund for the Advancement of Education, 1966.

———. *A Place Called School*. New York: McGraw-Hill, 1984.

GOODSELL, WILLYSTINE, ed. *Pioneers of Women's Education in the United States: Emma Willard, Catharine Beecher, and Mary Lyon*. New York: McGraw-Hill, 1931.

GORDON, SARAH H. "Smith College Students: The First Ten Classes, 1879–1888." *History of Education Quarterly* 15, no. 2 (Summer 1975): 147–167.

GRAEBNER, WILLIAM. "Retirement in Education: The Economic and Social Functions of the Teachers' Pension." *History of Education Quarterly* 18, no. 4 (Winter 1978): 397–418.

GRAHAM, PATRICIA ALBJERG. "Black Teachers: A Drastically Scarce Resource." *Phi Delta Kappan* 68, no. 8 (1987): 598–605.

GRANT, CARL, and CHRISTINE E. SLEETER. "Who Determines Teacher Work: The Teacher, The Organization, or Both?" *Teaching and Teacher Education* 1 (1985): 209–220.

GRANT, DANIEL T. *When the Melon is Ripe: An Autobiography of a Georgia Negro High School Principal and Minister*. New York: Exposition, 1955.

GREEN, HARRY WASHINGTON. *Holders of Doctorates Among American Negroes*. Boston: Meador Publishing, 1946.

GREENOUGH, JAMES C. "The State Normal School, Westfield." In *A History of Hampden County Massachusetts*, Vol. 1, edited by Alfred M. Copeland. Century Memorial Publishing Company, 1902.

GRIFFIN, CLIFFORD S. *The University of Kansas: A History*. Lawrence: University Press of Kansas, 1974.

GRISCOM, JOHN. *Memoirs of John Griscom, LLD*. New York: Robert Carter, 1859.

GROSS, NEAL, and ANN E. TRASK. *The Sex Factor and the Management of Schools*. New York: Wiley, 1976.

GULLIFORD, ANDREW. *America's County Schools*. Washington, DC: The Preservation Press, 1984.

HAHN, EMILY. *Once Upon a Pedestal*. New York: Thomas Y. Crowell, 1974.

HAILMANN, WILLIAM N. *Kindergarten Culture in the Family and Kindergarten*. New York: Van Antwerp, Bragg, and Co., 1873.

HALE, RICHARD W., JR. *Tercentenary History of the Roxbury Latin School, 1645–1945*. Cambridge, MA: Riverside Press, 1946.

HALE, SARAH JOSEPHA. "Editorial." *Godey's Lady's Book* (January 1853): 176–177.

HALEY, MARGARET. "Why Teachers Should Organize." *Addresses and Proceedings*, National Education Association. Washington, DC: NEA, 1904.

HALL, G. STANLEY. *Aspects of Child Life and Education.* Boston: Ginn and Company, 1907.

HANLON, HELEN J., and DORA D. WISEMAN. "Lilly Lindquist Arndt." *Michigan History Magazine* 39 (1955): 495–497.

HANSOT, ELISABETH, and DAVID TYACK. "A Usable Past: Using History in Educational Policy." In *Policy Making in Education,* the Eighty-First Yearbook of the National Society for the Study of Education, Part 1, edited by Ann Lieberman and Milbrey W. McLaughlin. Chicago: University of Chicago Press, 1982.

HANUS, PAUL H. *Adventuring in Education.* Cambridge, MA: Harvard University Press, 1937.

HARLAN, LOUIS R. *Booker T. Washington: The Making of a Black Leader, 1856–1901.* New York: Oxford University Press, 1972.

———. *Booker T. Washington: The Wizard of Tuskegee, 1901–1915.* New York: Oxford University Press, 1983.

———. *Separate and Unequal: Public Schools and Racism in the Southern Seaboard States, 1901–1915.* New York: Atheneum, 1968.

HARLEY, SHARON. "Beyond the Classroom: The Organizational Lives of Black Female Educators in the District of Columbia, 1890–1930." *Journal of Negro Education* 51, no. 3 (Summer 1982): 254–265.

HAREVEN, TAMARA K., and MARIS A. VINOVSKIS, eds. *Family and Population in Nineteenth-Century America.* Princeton, NJ: Princeton University Press, 1978.

HARPER, CHARLES A. *A Century of Public Teacher Education: The Story of the State Teachers Colleges as They Evolved from Normal Schools.* Washington, DC: American Association of Teachers Colleges, 1939.

———. *The Development of the Teachers College in the United States, with Special Reference to the Illinois State Normal University.* Bloomington, IL: McKnight and McKnight, 1935.

HARRISON, ELIZABETH. "The Scope and Results of Mothers' Classes." *Addresses and Proceedings,* National Education Association. Washington, DC: NEA, 1903.

HART, ALBERT BUSHNELL. "The Teacher as a Professional Expert." *School Review* 1, no. 1 (1893): 4–14.

HART, IRVING H. *The First 75 Years.* Cedar Falls: Iowa State Teachers College, 1951.

HARVEY, MARIE TURNER. "Contributions of Teachers to the Development of Democracy: Rural Schools." *Addresses and Proceedings,* National Education Association. Washington, DC: NEA, 1919.

———. "Is Progressive Education Procedure Practicable in the Small Rural School?" *Addresses and Proceedings,* National Education Association. Washington, DC: NEA, 1930.

———. "The Porter School: A New Vision of the Rural School in Country Life." *Addresses and Proceedings,* National Education Association. Washington, DC: NEA, 1924.

HAWKINS, DAVID. "I, Thou, and It." In David Hawkins, *The Informed Vision.* New York: Agathon, 1974.

HAYS, SAMUEL P. "The Politics of Reform in Municipal Government in the Progressive Era." *Pacific Northwest Quarterly* 55 (October 1964): 157–169.

HAYTER, EARL W. *Education in Transition: The History of Northern Illinois University.* DeKalb: Northern Illinois University Press, 1974.

HEADLEY, NEITH. *The Kindergarten: Its Place in the Program of Education.* New York: The Center for Applied Research in Education, 1959.

HEIDENHEIMER, A.J. "The Politics of Public Education, Health, and Welfare in the USA and Western Europe: How Growth and Reform Potentials Have Differed." *British Journal of Political Science* 3 (1973): 315–340.

HENLE [LAWSON], ELLEN, and MARLENE MERRILL. "Antebellum Black Coeds at Oberlin College." *Oberline Alumni Magazine* (January-February 1980): 18–21.

HERBST, JURGEN. *The History of American Education.* Northbrook, IL: AHM Publishing, 1973.

———. "Nineteenth-Century Normal Schools in the United States: A Fresh Look," *History of Education* 9, no. 3 (1980): 219–227.

———. "Professionalization in Public Education, 1890–1920: The American High School Teacher." In *Industrielle Welt: Bildungsburgertum im 19. jahrhundert,* part I, edited by Werner Conze and Jurgen Kocka. Stuttgart: Klett–Cotta, 1985.

HIGGS, ROBERT. *The Transformation of American Society, 1870–1914.* Englewood Cliffs, NJ: Prentice-Hall, 1974.

HILL, PATTY SMITH. "The Free Kindergarten as the Basis for Education." Louisville Free Kindergarten Association, *Report for 1894–95.* Gutman Library, Harvard Graduate School of Education.

———. "The Free Kindergarten as an Educational Need of the South." Louisville Free Kindergarten Association, *Seventeenth Annual Report, 1904–05.* Gutman Library, Harvard Graduate School of Education.

———. "The Future of the Kindergarten." *Teachers College Record* 10 (November 1909): 29–58.

HIRSCHMAN, ALBERT O. *Shifting Involvements: Private Interests and Public Action.* Princeton, NJ: Princeton University Press, 1982.

A History of the State Normal School of Kansas for the First 25 Years. Emporia, 1889.

HODENFIELD, G.K., and T.M. STINNETT. *The Education of Teachers.* Englewood Cliffs, NJ: Prentice-Hall, 1961.

HODGSON, GODFREY. *America in Our Time: From World War II to Nixon.* New York: Vintage, 1976.

HOFFMAN, NANCY J. "Feminist Scholarship and Women's Studies." *Harvard Educational Review* 56, no. 4 (November 1986): 551–591.

———. *Woman's "True" Profession: Voices from the History of Teaching.* Old Westbury, NY: Feminist Press, 1981.

HOLMES GROUP. *Tomorrow's Teachers.* East Lansing, MI: The Holmes Group, 1986.

HORN, MARGO. "Sisters Worthy of Respect: Family Dynamics and Women's Roles in the Blackwell Family." *Journal of Family History* 68 (Winter 1983): 367–381.

HOSIC, JAMES FLEMING. "The Democratization of Supervision." *School and Society* 11, no. 273 (March 1920): 331–336.

HOWE, FLORENCE. *Women and the Power to Change.* New York: McGraw-Hill, 1975.

HUBERMAN, A. MICHAEL, and MATTHEW MILES. *Innovation Up Close.* New York: Plenum Press, 1984.

INGRAM, MARGARET FONGELSONG. *Toward an Education.* New York: Comet Press, 1954.

INTERNATIONAL KINDERGARTEN UNION. COMMITTEE OF NINETEEN. *The Kindergarten.* Boston: Houghton Mifflin, 1913.

———. *Pioneers of the Kindergarten Movement in America.* New York: Century Company, 1924.

IRVING, WASHINGTON. *The Legend of Sleepy Hollow*. New York: The American Arts Union, 1849.

ISBELL, EGBERT R. *A History of Eastern Michigan University, 1849–1965*. Ypsilanti: Eastern Michigan University, 1971.

ISSEL, WILLIAM H. "Teachers and Educational Reform During the Progressive Era: A Case Study of the Pittsburgh Teachers Association." *History of Education Quarterly* 7, no. 2 (Summer 1967): 220–233.

JACKSON, PHILIP. W. *Life in Classrooms*. New York: Holt, Rinehart and Winston, 1968.

JENNINGS, ROSA SCHREURS. "The Country Teacher." *Annals of Iowa* 31, no. 1 (July 1951): 41–62.

JENSEN, MERRIL, ed. *Regionalism in American History*. Madison: University of Wisconsin Press, 1951.

JOHANNINGMEIER, ERWIN V. Review of *The Miseducation of American Teacher*, by James D. Koerner. *Harvard Educational Review* 34, no. 1 (Winter 1964): 99.

JOHNSON, CHARLES S. *The Negro College Graduate*. Chapel Hill: University of North Carolina Press, 1938. Reprint. New York: Negro Universities Press, 1969.

JOHNSON, HARRIET. *Children in the Nursery School*. New York: Agathon, 1972.

JOHNSON, HENRY. *The Other Side of Main Street: A History Teacher from Sauk Centre*. New York: Columbia University Press, 1943.

JOHNSON, HENRY C., JR., and ERWIN V. JOHANNINGMEIER. *Teachers for the Prairie: The University of Illinois and the Schools, 1868–1945*. Urbana: University of Illinois Press, 1972.

JOHNSON, OLIVER. "A Home in the Woods: Reminiscences of Early Marion County (As Related to Howard Johnson)." *Indiana Historical Society Publications* 16, no. 2 (1951).

JOHNSON, WILLIAM R. "Empowering Practitioners: Holmes, Carnegie, and the Lessons of History." *History of Education Quarterly* 27, no. 2 (Summer 1987): 221–240.

———. "Meeting Accountability or Evading Responsibility?" *Theory Into Practice* 17, no. 5 (1979): 372–378.

———. *Schooled Lawyers: A Study in the Clash of Professional Cultures*. New York: New York University Press, 1978.

JONES, JACQUELINE. *Labor of Love, Labor of Sorrow: Black Women, Work, and the Family from Slavery to the Present*. New York: Basic Books, 1985.

———. *Soldiers of Light and Love: Northern Teachers and Georgia Blacks, 1865–1873*. Chapel Hill: University of North Carolina Press, 1980.

JONES, LANCE GEORGE EDWARD. *The Jeanes Teacher in the United States, 1908–1933: An Account of Twenty-Five Years Experience in the Supervision of Rural Negro Schools*. Chapel Hill: University of North Carolina Press, 1937.

JONES, THOMAS JESSE. *Negro Education: A Study of the Private and Higher Schools for Colored People in the United States*. New York: Arno Press, 1969.

JOYCE, BRUCE. "Conceptions of Man and Their Implications for Teacher Education." In *Teacher Education*, the Seventy-Fourth Yearbook of the National Society for the Study of Education, Part II, edited by Kevin Ryan. Chicago: University of Chicago Press, 1975.

JUDGE, HARRY. *American Graduate Schools of Education: A View from Abroad*. New York: Ford Foundation, 1982.

KAESTLE, CARL F. *The Evolution of an Urban School System: New York City, 1750–1850*. Cambridge, MA: Harvard University Press, 1970.

———. "Foreword." In William J. Reese, *Power and the Promise of School Reform:*

Grass-Roots Movements During the Progressive Era. Boston: Routledge & Kegan Paul, 1986.

———. *Pillars of the Republic: Common Schools and American Society, 1780–1860.* New York: Hill and Wang, 1983.

———, and Maris Vinovskis. *Education and Social Change in Nineteenth Century Massachusetts.* New York: Cambridge University Press, 1980.

KANTOR, HARVEY. "Vocationalism in American Education: The Economic and Political Context, 1880–1930." In *Youth, Work, and Schooling: Historical Perspectives on Vocationalism in American Education,* edited by Harvey Kantor and David Tyack. Stanford, CA: Stanford University Press, 1982.

KATZ, MICHAEL B. *Class, Bureaucracy, and Schools: The Illusion of Educational Change in America.* Expanded ed. New York: Praeger, 1975.

———, ed. *School Reform: Past and Present.* Boston: Little, Brown, 1971.

KATZNELSON, IRA, and MARGARET WEIR. *Schooling for All: Class, Race and the Decline of the Democratic Ideal.* New York: Basic Books, 1985.

KAUFMAN, POLLY WELTS. *Women Teachers on the Frontier.* New Haven, CT: Yale University Press, 1984.

KELLOG, AMOS. *School Management.* New York: 1887.

KELLOG, LYMAN B. "The Founding of the State Normal School." *Collections of the Kansas State Historical Society* 12 (1911–1912): 88–98.

———. "Normal Education in Kansas." *Proceedings and Lectures of the National Teachers' Association . . . 1866.* Albany: New York Teacher, 1867.

KERBER, LINDA. *Women of the Republic: Intellect and Ideology in Revolutionary America.* Chapel Hill: University of North Carolina Press, 1980.

KESSLER-HARRIS, ALICE. *Out to Work.* New York: Oxford University Press, 1982.

KETT, JOSEPH. "The Adolescence of Vocational Education." In *Youth, Work, and Schooling: Historical Perspectives on Vocationalism in American Education,* edited by Harvey Kantor and David Tyack. Stanford, CA: Stanford University Press, 1982.

KINNEY, LUCIEN B. *Certification in Education.* Englewood Cliffs, NJ: Prentice-Hall, 1964.

KIRST, MICHAEL, and GAIL R. MEISTER. "Turbulence in American Secondary Schools: What Reforms Last?" *Curriculum Inquiry* 15 (1985): 169–186.

KITZHABER, ALBERT R. "Project English Curriculum Reform." In *Iowa English Year Book* 9 (Fall 1964): 3–8.

KLIEBARD, HERBERT M. *The Struggle for the American Curriculum, 1893–1958.* Boston: Routledge and Kegan Paul, 1986.

KLUGER, RICHARD. *Simple Justice.* New York: Vintage, 1975.

KOERNER, JAMES D. *The Miseducation of American Teachers.* Boston: Houghton Mifflin, 1963.

KOTTCAMP, ROBERT B., EUGENE F. PROVENZO, JR., and MARILYN M. COHN. "Stability and Change in A Profession: Two Decades of Teacher Attitudes, 1964–1984." *Phi Delta Kappan* 67 (April 1986): 559–567.

KRAUS-BOELTE, MARIA, and JOHN KRAUS. *The Kindergarten.* New York: E. Steiger, 1877.

KRUG, EDWARD A., ed. *Charles W. Eliot and Popular Education.* New York: Teachers College, Columbia University, 1961.

———. *The Shaping of the American High School.* New York: Harper & Row, 1964.

LABAREE, DAVID F. *The Making of an American High School: The Credentials Market and the Central High School of Philadelphia, 1838–1939*. New Haven, CT: Yale University Press, 1988.

———. "Politics, Markets, and the Compromised Curriculum." *Harvard Educational Review* 57, no. 4 (November 1987): 483–494.

LaBue, Anthony C. "Teacher Certification in the United States: A Brief History." *Journal of Teacher Education* 11 (March 1960): 147–172.

Lampert, Magdalene. "How Do Teachers Manage to Teach." *Harvard Educational Review* 59, no. 2 (May 1985): 178–194.

Langdon, Grace. *Similarities and Differences in Teaching in Nursery School, Kindergarten, and First Grade*. New York: John Day, 1933.

Langer, Judith A., and Arthur N. Applebee. "The Uses of Writing in Academic Classrooms: A Study of Teaching and Learning." Urbana, IL: National Council of Teachers of English, 1987.

Lanier, Judith E. "Research on Teacher Education." In *Handbook of Research on Teaching,* edited by Merlin C. Witrock. New York: Macmillan, 1985.

———, and Michael Sedlak. "Teacher Efficacy and Quality Schooling." In *Schooling for Tomorrow: Directing Reforms to Issues that Count,* edited by Thomas J. Sergiovanni and John H. Moore. Boston: Allyn and Bacon, 1988.

Larson, Magali S. *The Rise of Professionalism: A Sociological Analysis*. Berkeley: University of California Press, 1977.

Lather, Patti. "The Absent Presence: Patriarchy, Capitalism, and the Nature of Teacher Work." *Teacher Education Quarterly* 14, no. 2 (Spring 1987): 25–38.

Lathrop, Delia A. "Training Schools: Their Place in Normal-School Work." In *Addresses and Journal of Proceedings,* National Education Association, annual meeting of 1873, Elmira, NY. Peoria, IL: N.C. Nason, 1873.

Lovapa, Anthony. *Prussian School Teachers: Profession and Office 1763–1848*. Chapel Hill: University of North Carolina Press, 1980.

Lawn, Martin, ed. *The Politics of Teacher Unionism: International Perspectives*. Dover, NH: Croom Helm, 1985.

Lawn, Martin. "What is the Teacher's Job? Work and Welfare in Elementary Teaching, 1940–1945." In *Teachers: The Culture and Politics of Work,* edited by Martin Lawn and Gerald Grace. London: Falmer Press, 1987.

Lawn, Martin, and Gerald Grace, eds. *Teachers: The Culture and Politics of Work* London: Falmer Press, 1987.

Lawson, Douglas E. "Corrective Note on the Early History of the American Kindergarten." *Educational Administration and Supervision* 25 (1939): 699–703.

Lazerson, Marvin. "If All the World Were Chicago: American Education in the Twentieth Century." *History of Education Quarterly* 24, no. 2 (Summer 1984): 165–179.

———. "Teachers Organize: What Margaret Haley Lost." *History of Education Quarterl* 24 (1984): 261–270.

———. "Urban Reform and the Schools: Kindergartens in Massachusetts, 1870–1915." *History of Education Quarterly* 11 (Summer 1971): 115–142.

Learned, William S. *The Oberlehrer: A Study of the Social and Professional Evolution the German Schoolmaster*. Cambridge, MA: Harvard University Press, 1914.

———, William C. Bagley et al. *The Professional Preparation of Teachers for Americ Public Schools: A Study Based Upon an Examination of Tax-Supported Normal Schools the State of Missouri*. New York: The Carnegie Foundation, 1920.

LEARNED, WILLIAM S., and BEN D. WOOD. *The Student and His Knowledge*. New York: Carnegie Foundation for the Advancement of Teaching, 1938.

LEBERGOTT, STANLEY. *Manpower in Economic Growth: The American Record Since 1800*. New York: McGraw-Hill, 1964.

LEE, JAN. "Price and Prejudice: Teachers, Class and an Inner-City Infants School." In *Teachers: The Culture and Politics of Work*, edited by Martin Lawn and Gerald Grace. London: Falmer Press, 1987.

LELAND BERNICE. "Ethel Winifred Bennett Chase." *Michigan History Magazine* 41 (1957): 439–442.

LENTZ, ELI G. *Seventy-Five Years in Retrospect: From Normal School to Teachers College to University: Southern Illinois University 1874–1949*. Carbondale, IL: University Editorial Board, 1955.

LESSINGER, LEON M. *Every Kid a Winner: Accountability in Education*. New York: Simon and Schuster, 1970.

LEVIN, HENRY, and MARTIN CARNOY. *Schooling and Work in the Democratic State*. Stanford, CA: Stanford University Press, 1985.

LIEBERMAN, MYRON. *Beyond Public Education*. New York: Praeger, 1986.

———. *Education as a Profession*. Englewood Cliffs, NJ: Prentice-Hall, 1956.

LIGHTFOOT, SARAH LAWRENCE. *Worlds Apart: Relationships Between Families and Schools*. New York: Basic Books, 1978.

LINES, AMELIA AKEHURST. *"To Raise Myself a Little": The Diaries and Letters of Jennie, a Georgia Teacher, 1851–1886*, edited by Thomas Dyer. Athens: University of Georgia Press, 1982.

LINK, WILLIAM. *A Hard and Lonely Place: Schooling, Society, and Reform in Rural Virginia, 1870–1920*. Chapel Hill: University of North Carolina Press, 1986.

LITWAK, LEON. *Been in the Storm So Long*. New York: Knopf, 1979.

———. *North of Slavery*. Chicago: University of Chicago Press, 1961.

LIVERMORE, MARY. *The Story of My Life*. Hartford, CT: A.D. Worthington, 1897.

LOCKRIDGE, KENNETH. *Literacy in Colonial New England*. New York: Norton, 1974.

LONG, HOWARD H. "Some Factors Influencing Objectivity in Teacher Selection." *School and Society* 65 (March 1947): 179–182.

LORD, MARY A. "Julia Anne King." *Michigan History Magazine* 38 (1954): 306–312.

LORTIE, DAN C. *Schoolteacher: A Sociological Study*. Chicago: University of Chicago Press, 1975.

LOWENSTEIN, SOPHIE FREUD. "The Passion and Challenge of Teaching." *Harvard Educational Review* 50, no. 1 (February 1980): 1–12.

LUCKEY, GEORGE W. A. *The Professional Training of Secondary School Teachers in the United States*. New York: Macmillan, 1903.

LYND, ALBERT. *Quackery in the Public Schools*. Boston: Little, Brown, 1953.

MCCLURE, ROBERT M. "The Reforms of the Fifties and Sixties: A Historical Look at the Near Past." In *The Curriculum: Retrospect and Prospect*, the Seventieth Yearbook of the National Society for the Study of Education, Part I, edited by Robert M. McClure. Chicago: University of Chicago Press, 1971.

MCCONN, MAX. "The Co-operative Test Service." *Journal of Higher Education* 2 (May 1931): 225–232.

McCormick, Scott. "This Julius Rosenwald Fund." *Journal of Negro Education* 3 (October 1934): 605–628.

McCrory, John R. "Elementary School Teacher Supply and Demand for 1924–25." *School and Society* 20 (August 1924): 222–224.

McCuistion, Fred. "The South's Negro Teaching Force." *Journal of Negro Education* 1, no. 1 (1932): 14–24.

McGinnis, W.C. "The Married Woman Teacher." *School Executives Magazine* 50 (June 1931): 451–453.

McGuire, Carson, and George D. White. "The Social Origins of Teachers—In Texas." In *The Teacher's Role in American Society,* edited by Lindley J. Stiles. New York: Harper & Bros., 1957.

McMillan, Margaret. *The Nursery School.* London: J.M. Dent and Sons, 1923.

McPherson, Gertrude. *Small Town Teacher.* Cambridge, MA: Harvard University Press, 1972.

McPherson, Jesse M. *The Abolitionist Legacy: From Reconstruction to the NAACP.* Princeton, NJ: Princeton University Press, 1975.

Magill, Edward Hicks. *Sixty-Five Years in the Life of a Teacher, 1841–1906.* Boston: Houghton Mifflin, 1907.

Main, Jackson Turner. *The Social Structure of Revolutionary America.* Princeton, NJ: Princeton University Press, 1965.

Male High School Teachers Association (NY). "Are There Too Many Women Teachers?" *Educational Review* 28 (1904): 98–105.

Mangun, Vernon Lamar. *The American Normal School: Its Rise and Development in Massachusetts.* Baltimore: Warwick & York, 1928.

Mann, Mary Peabody. *Life of Horace Mann.* Boston: Lee and Shepard, 1904.

Manski, C.F. "Academic Ability, Earnings, and the Decision to Become a Teacher: Evidence from the National Longitudinal Study of the High School Class of 1972." In *Public Sector Payrolls,* edited by David A. Wise. Chicago: University of Chicago Press, 1987.

March, James G. "Footnotes to Organizational Change." *Administrative Science Quarterly* 26 (December 1981): 563–577.

Margo, Robert. "Race, Educational Attainment, and the 1940 Census." *Journal of Economic History* 46 (1986): 189–198.

———. " 'Teacher Salaries in Black and White': The South in 1910." *Explorations in Economic History* 21 (1984): 306–326.

Marshall, Helen E. *Grandest of Enterprises: Illinois State Normal University, 1857–1957.* Normal: Illinois State Normal University, 1956.

Marson, Philip. *A Teacher Speaks.* New York: McKay, 1960.

Martin, Jane Rowland. "Excluding Women from the Educational Realm." *Harvard Educational Review* 52, no. 2 (May 1982): 133–148.

Matthaei, Julie A. *An Economic History of Women in America: Women's Work, the Sexual Division of Labor, and the Development of Capitalism.* New York: Schocken Books, 1982.

Mattingly, Paul H. *The Classless Profession: American Schoolmen of the Nineteenth Century.* New York: New York University Press, 1975.

May, Dean, and Maris Vinovskis. "A Ray of Millenial Light: Early Education and Social Reform in the Infant School Movement in Massachusetts, 1826–1840." In *Family and K in Urban Communities, 1700–1930,* edited by Tamara K. Hareven. New York: New Viewpoints, 1977.

MAYO, AVERY DWIGHT. "The Assault on the Normal Schools." *Lectures and Proceedings,* American Institute of Instruction, 48 (1877): 29–43.

———. "The New Teacher in America." *Addresses and Journal of Proceedings,* National Education Association, 1879. Salem, OH: Alan K. Tatem, 1879.

———. "The Normal School in the United States." *Education* 8 (December 1887): 223–234.

MEAD, MARGARET. *The School in American Culture.* Cambridge, MA: Harvard University Press, 1951.

MEECE, LEONARD E. "Negro Education in Kentucky: A Comparative Study of White and Negro Education on the Elementary and Secondary School Levels." Bureau of School Service, College of Education, University of Kentucky *Bulletin* 10, no. 3 (March 1938).

MELOSH, BARBARA. *The Physician's Hand: Work Culture and Conflict in American Nursing.* Philadelphia: Temple University Press, 1982.

MERK, LOIS BANNISTER. "Boston's Historic Public School Crisis." *New England Quarterly* 31 (June 1958): 172–199.

METCALF, RICHARD ALSTON. *A History of Princeton High School.* Princeton, IL: Princeton High School, 1892.

MEYER, JOHN. "The Politics of Educational Crises in the United States." In *Educational Policies in Crisis: Japanese and American Perspectives,* edited by William Cummings et al. New York: Praeger, 1986.

———, and Brian Rowan. "The Structure of Educational Organizations." In *Environments and Organizations,* edited by Marshall Meyer. San Francisco: Jossey-Bass, 1978.

MEYER, KARL W. "Post World-War II Conversion of the Teachers Colleges." *Journal of Teacher Education* 11 (1960): 335–339.

MEYERS, PETER V. "Professionalization and Societal Change: Rural Teachers in Nineteenth Century France." *Journal of Social History* 9 (1976): 542–558.

MEYN, MARGARET L. "Edith Hogue Kendall." *Michigan History Magazine* 41 (1957): 357–360.

MICHIGAN EDUCATION ASSOCIATION. *Certification and Training of Teachers in Michigan.* East Lansing: Michigan Education Association, 1937.

MILLER, J.B. *Toward a New Psychology of Women.* Boston: Beacon Press, 1976.

MIREL, JEFFREY. "The Politics of Educational Retrenchment in Detroit, 1929–1935." *History of Education Quarterly* 24, no. 3 (Fall 1984): 323–358.

MITCHELL, DOUGLAS E., FLORA IDA ORTIZ, and TEDI K. MITCHELL. *Work Orientation and Job Performance: The Cultural Basis of Teaching Rewards and Incentives.* Albany: State University of New York Press, 1987.

MODDELL, JOHN, FRANK FURSTENBURG, and THEODORE HERSHBERG. "Social Change and the Transition to Adulthood in Historical Perspective." *Journal of Family History* 1 (1976): 7–32.

MONROE, WALTER, S. *Teaching-Learning Theory and Teacher Education, 1890–1950.* Urbana: University of Illinois Press, 1952.

MOORE, R. LAURENCE. "Insiders and Outsiders in American Historical Narrative and American History." *American Historical Review* 81, no. 2 (April 1982): 390–412.

MORAIN, THOMAS. "The Departure of Males from the Teaching Profession in Nineteenth-Century Iowa." *Civil War History* 26, no. 2 (June 1980): 161–170.

MORRIS, ROBERT C. *Reading, 'Riting, and Reconstruction: The Education of Freedmen in the South, 1861–1870*. Chicago: University of Chicago Press, 1981.

MORRISON, J. CAYCE. "Certification for Improving Professional Leadership." *American School Board Journal* 76 (May 1928): 49–50, 169.

MURRAY, ANNA J. "A New Key to the Situation." *Southern Workman* 29 (September 1900): 503–507.

NATIONAL AMERICAN WOMAN SUFFRAGE ASSOCIATION. *Victory, How Women Won It*. New York: H.W. Wilson, 1940.

NATIONAL EDUCATION ASSOCIATION. *Report of the Committee on Salaries, Tenure, and Pensions of Public School Teachers of the United States*. Winnona, MN: NEA, 1905.

———. *Report of the Committee on Teachers' Salaries and the Cost of Living*. Ann Arbor, MI: NEA, 1913.

———. *Status of the American Public School Teacher, 1985–86*. Washington, DC: NEA, 1987.

———. *Status of the Teaching Profession*. Research Bulletin 18 (March 1940). Washington, DC: NEA, 1940.

"The Negro Teacher and Desegregation of the Public Schools." *Journal of Negro Education* 22, no. 2 (1953): 96–97.

NEWCOMER, MABLE. *A Century of Higher Education for American Women*. New York: Harper & Row, 1959.

NEWMAN, JOSEPH W., and WAYNE J. URBAN. "Communists in the American Federation of Teachers: A Too Often Told Story." *History of Education Review* 14 (1985): 15–24.

NIGHTINGALE, A.F. "Ratio of Men to Women in the High Schools of the United States." *School Review* 4 (February 1896): 86–98.

NOBLE, JEANNE L. *The Negro Woman's College Education*. New York: Teachers College, Columbia University, 1956.

"Normal Schools and the Teacher Shortage." *American School Board Journal* 60 (May 1920): 58–59.

NORTON, ARTHUR O., ed. *The First State Normal School in America; The Journals of Cyrus Pierce and Mary Swift*. Cambridge, MA: Harvard University Press, 1926.

NORTON, MARY BETH. *Liberty's Daughters: The Revolutionary Experience of American Women, 1780–1800*. Boston: Little, Brown, 1980.

ODY, HERMANN JOSEPH. *Victor Cousin: Ein Lebensbild im deutsch-franzosischen Kultur raum*. Saarbrucken: West-Ost Verlag, 1953.

OLIN, HELEN. *The Women of a State University*. New York: Putnam's, 1909.

OLSEN, LEIF O., and ADDISON C. BENNETT. "Performance Appraisal: Management Technique or Social Process." *Management Review* (December 1975): 24–30.

OLSON, JAMES M. "Social Views of Prussian Primary School Teachers." *Paedagogica Historica* 15 (1975): 73–89.

ORCUTT, HIRAM. *Reminiscences of a School Life*. Cambridge, MA: 1898.

ORLOSKY, DONALD, and B. OTHANEL SMITH. "Educational Change: Its Origins and Characteristics." *Phi Delta Kappan* (March 1972): 412–414.

ORTMAN, ELMER JOHN. *Teacher Councils: The Organized Means for Securing the Co-operation of All Workers in the School*. Montpelier, VT: Capital City Press, 1923.

OSTERUD, NANCY, and JOHN FULTON. "Family Limitation and Age of Marriage in Sturbridge, Massachusetts, 1730–1850." *Population Studies* 30, no. 3 (November 1976): 481–494.

OTTLEY, PASSIE FENTON. "Kindergartens for Coloured Children." *Southern Workman* 30 (February 1901): 103–104.

OZGA, J.T., and M.A. LAWN. *Teachers, Professionalism and Class.* London: Falmer Press, 1981.

PANGBURN, JESSIE M. *The Evolution of the American Teachers College.* New York: Teachers College, Columbia University, 1932.

PANNELL, HENRY C. *The Preparation and Work of Alabama High School Teachers.* Columbia University Contributions to Education, no. 551. New York: Teachers College Press, 1933.

PARK, ROBERT E. "Alabama State Teachers' Association." *Southern Workman* 39, no. 5 (1910): 272.

PARKER, SAMUEL CHESTER, and ALICE TEMPLE. *Unified Kindergarten and First Grade Teaching.* Boston: Ginn and Company, 1925.

PARRISH, JOHN B. "Women in Professional Training." *Monthly Labor Review* 97 (May 1974): 34–38.

PATRICK, AL, ROBERT L. GRISWOLD, and COURTNEY ANN VAUGHN ROBERSON. "Domestic Ideology and the Teaching Profession: A Case Study From Oklahoma, 1930–1983." *Issues in Education* 3, no. 2 (Fall 1985): 139–157.

PAVALKO, RONALD M. "Recruitment to Teaching: Patterns of Selection and Retention." *Sociology of Education* 43 (Summer 1970): 340–353.

PAYNE, WILLIAM H. *Chapters on School Supervision: A Practical Treatise on Superintendence; Grading; Arranging Courses of Study; the Preparation and Use of Blanks, Records, and Reports; Examinations for Promotion, etc.* New York: American Book, 1903.

PEABODY, ELIZABETH. *Guide to the Kindergarten and Intermediate Class.* New York: E. Stieger, 1877.

———. *Lectures in the Training School for Kindergartens.* Boston: D.C. Heath, 1886.

———. *Record of a School: Exemplifying the General Principles of Spiritual Culture.* Boston: Russell, Shattuck, 1836.

———, and MARY MANN. *Moral Culture of Infancy and Kindergarten Guide.* Boston: T.O.H.P. Burnham, 1863.

PEARMAIN, ALICE UPTON. "The Boston Schools: A Sanitary Investigation." *Municipal Affairs* 2 (September 1898): 497–501.

PEARSON, HENRY GREENLEAF. *Sons of New England: James Jackson Storrow, 1864–1926.* Boston: Thomas Todd, 1932.

PERKINS, LINDA M. "The Black Female American Missionary Association Teacher in the South, 1860–70." In *Black Americans in North Carolina and the South,* edited by Jeffrey J. Crow and Flora J. Hatley. Chapel Hill: University of North Carolina Press, 1984.

———. *Fanny Jackson Coppin and the Institute for Colored Youth, 1865–1902.* New York: Garland, 1987.

PERKINSON, HENRY. *The Imperfect Panacea: American Faith in Education, 1865–1965.* New York: Random House, 1968.

PERLOFF, HARVEY, EDGAR S. DUNN, JR., ERIK E. LAMPARD, and RICHARD F. MUTH. *Regions, Resources and Economic Growth.* Baltimore: Johns Hopkins University Press, 1960.

PERRY, THELMA. *The History of the American Teachers Association.* Washington, DC: National Education Association, 1975.

PETERS, DAVID WILBUR. *The Status of the Married Woman Teacher*. Teachers College Contributions to Education, No. 603. New York: Teachers College Press, 1934.

PFEFFER, JEFFREY, and GERALD SALANCIK. *The External Control of Organizations: A Resource Dependence Perspective*. New York: Harper & Row, 1978.

PHELPS, WILLIAM FRANKLIN. "Report on a Course of Study for Normal Schools." *Addresses and Journal of Proceedings*, American Normal School and the National Teachers' Association. Washington, DC: James L. Holmes, 1871.

PLANK, DAVID N., and PAUL E. PETERSON. "Does Urban Reform Imply Class Conflict? The Case of Atlanta's Schools." *History of Education Quarterly* 23, no. 2 (Summer 1983): 151–174.

POLLOCK, LOUISE. *National Kindergarten Manual*. Boston: DeWolfe, Fiske, 1889.

POPKEWITZ, THOMAS S. "Educational Reform as the Organization of Ritual: Stability as Change." *Journal of Education* 164, no. 1 (Winter 1982): 5–29.

POTTER, ALONZO, and GEORGE B. EMERSON. *The School and the Schoolmaster: A Manual in Two Parts*. New York: Harper and Brothers, 1842.

POWELL, ARTHUR G. "The Culture and Politics of American Teachers." *History of Education Quarterly* 18, no. 2 (Summer 1978): 187–191.

———. *The Uncertain Profession: Harvard and the Search for Educational Authority*. Cambridge, MA: Harvard University Press, 1980.

———. "University Schools of Education in the Twentieth Century." *Peabody Journal of Education* 54 (1976): 3–20.

———, ELENOR FARRAR, and DAVID K. COHEN. *The Shopping Mall High School: Winners and Losers in the Educational Marketplace*. Boston: Houghton Mifflin, 1985.

PRADT, J.B. "Essays on Normal Schools." *Wisconsin Journal on Education* 6 (August 1861): 343–346.

PRENTICE, ALLISON. "Education and the Metaphor of the Family: The Upper Canadian Example." *History of Education Quarterly* 12, no. 3 (Fall 1962): 281–303.

PRESSMAN, HARVEY, and ALAN GARTNER. "The New Racism in Education." *Social Policy* 17, no. 1 (September 1986): 11–15.

QUANTZ, RICHARD A. "The Complex Visions of Female Teachers and the Failure of Unionization in the 1930s: An Oral History." *History of Education Quarterly* 25, no. 4 (Winter 1985): 439–458.

RABINOWITZ, HOWARD N. "Half-A-Loaf: The Shift from White to Black Teachers in the Negro Schools in the Urban South, 1854–1980." *Journal of Southern History* 40 (1974): 565–594.

RANSOM, ROGER L., and RICHARD SUTCH. *One Kind of Freedom: The Economic Consequences of Emancipation*. New York: Cambridge University Press, 1977.

RASEY, MARIE J. *It Takes Time: An Autobiography of the Teaching Profession*. New York: Harper & Row, 1953.

RAVITCH, DIANE. *The Great School Wars*. New York: Basic Books, 1974.

REDCAY, EDWARD E. *County Training Schools and Public Secondary Education for Negroes in the South*. Washington, DC: John F. Slater Fund, 1935.

REESE, LIZETTE WOODWORTH. *A Victoria Village*. New York: Farrar and Rinehart, 1929

REESE, WILLIAM J. *Power and the Promise of School Reform: Grass-Roots Movements During the Progressive Era*. Boston: Routledge & Kegan Paul, 1986.

REID, ROBERT L., ed. *Battleground: The Autobiography of Margaret Haley*. Urbana: University of Illinois Press, 1982.

REQUARDT, CYNTHIA HORSBURGH. "Alternative Professions for Goucher College Graduates, 1892–1910." *Maryland Historical Magazine* 74, no. 3 (September 1979): 274–281.

RICE, JOSEPH M. *The Public School System of the United States*. New York: Century, 1893.

RICHARDSON, JOE M. *Christian Reconstruction: The American Missionary Association and Southern Blacks, 1861–1890*. Athens: University of Georgia Press, 1986.

RICHARDSON, JOHN G., and BRENDA WOODEN HATCHER. "The Feminization of Public School Teaching, 1870–1920." *Work and Occupations* 10, no. 1 (February 1983): 81–99.

RINEHART, ALICE DUFFY. *Mortals in the Immortal Profession: An Oral History of Teaching*. New York: Irvington, 1983.

ROBERSON, COURTNEY ANN VAUGHN. "Sometimes Independent But Not Equal: Women Educators, 1900–1950: The Oklahoma Example." *Pacific Historical Review* 53 (February 1984): 39–58.

ROGERS, DOROTHY. *Oswego: Fountainhead of Teacher Education: A Century in the Sheldon Tradition*. New York: D. Appleton, 1961.

ROSALDO, MICHELLE ZIMBALIST. "A Theoretical Overview." In *Women, Culture, and Society*, edited by Michelle Zimbalist Rosaldo and Louise Lamphers. Stanford, CA: Stanford University Press, 1974.

ROSIER, JOSEPH. "Report of Committee on Standards, Requirements, and Credits of Teachers in Service." *Proceedings and Addresses*, National Education Association. Washington, DC: NEA, 1925.

ROSS, ELIZABETH DALE. *The Kindergarten Crusade*. Athens: Ohio University Press, 1976.

ROTHMAN, SHEILA, *Woman's Proper Sphere: A History of Changing Ideals and Practices*. New York: Basic Books, 1978.

ROWLAND, ALBERT LINDSAY. "The Proposed Teacher Examination Service." *Harvard Educational Review* 10 (May 1940): 277–288.

RUBINSTEIN, SHERRY A., MATTHEW W. MCDONOUGH, and RICHARD G. ALLAN. "The Changing Nature of Teacher Certification Programs." In *Testing for Teacher Certification*, edited by William P. Gorth and Michael L. Chernoff. Hillsdale, NJ: Lawrence Erlbaum, 1985.

RUDY, WILLIS. "America's First Normal School: The Formative Years." *Journal of Teacher Education* 5 (December 1954): 263–270.

RUFI, JOHN. *The Small High School*. Columbia University Contributions to Education, no. 236. New York: Teachers College Press, 1926.

RUGG, HAROLD. *The Teacher of Teachers: Frontiers of Theory and Practice in Teacher Education, 1890–1950*. New York: Harper & Row, 1952.

RURY, JOHN L. "American School Enrollment in the Progressive Era: An Interpretive Inquiry." *History of Education* (UK) 13, no. 1 (March 1985): 49–67.

———. "Education in the New Women's History." *Educational Studies* 17, no. 1 (Spring 1986): 1–15.

———. "Gender, Salaries and Career: American Teachers, 1900–1910." *Issues in Education* 4, 3 (Winter 1986): 215–235.

———. "The New York African Free School, 1825–1835: Conflict Over Community Control." *Phylon* 45, no. 3 (September 1983): 187–198.

———. "Race and Common School Reform: The Strange Career of the MYSPECC, 1847–1860." *Urban Education* 20, no. 4 (January 1986): 473–492.

———. "The Variable School Year: Measuring American School Terms in 1900." *Journal of Research and Development in Education* 21, no. 3 (Spring 1988): 29–36.

RUSSELL, FRANCIS. *A City in Terror: 1919 The Boston Police Strike*. New York: Viking, 1975.

RUSSELL, JAMES E. *Founding Teachers College: Reminiscences of a Dean Emeritus*. New York: 1937.

RUSSELL, WILLIAM F. "A Century of Teacher Education." *Teachers College Record* 41 (1940): 481–492.

RYANS, DAVID G. "The Professional Examination of Teaching Candidates: A Report of the First Annual Administration of the National Teacher Examinations." *School and Society* 52 (October 1940): 273–284.

SALISBURY, ALBERT. *Historical Sketch of Normal Instruction in Wisconsin, 1846–1876*. Madison, WI: 1876.

SAMUEL, R.H., and R. HINTON THOMAS. *Education and Society in Modern Germany*. London: Routledge & Kegan Paul, 1949.

SANDERS, JAMES. *The Education of an Urban Minority: Catholics in Chicago, 1836–1965*. New York: Oxford University Press, 1977.

SARASON, SEYMOUR. *The Culture of the School and the Problem of Change*. Boston: Allyn and Bacon, 1971.

SCHARF, LOIS. *To Work and to Wed: Female Employment, Feminism, and the Great Depression*. Westport, CT: Greenwood Press, 1980.

SCHLEUNES, KARL A. "Enlightenment, Reform, Reaction: The Schooling Revolution in Prussia." *Central European History* 12 (December 1979): 315–342.

SCHMUCK, PATRICIA A. "Women School Employees in the United States." In *Women Educators: Employees of Schools in Western Countries,* edited by Patricia A. Schmuck. Albany: State University of New York Press, 1987.

SCHROEDER, FRED H. "The Little Red Schoolhouse." In *Icons of America,* edited by Ray B. Browne and Marshall Fenwick. Bowling Green, OH: Popular Press, Bowling Green University, 1978.

SCHULTZ, MICHAEL J., JR. *The National Education Association and the Black Teacher: The Integration of a Professional Organization*. Coral Gables, FL: University of Miami Press, 1970.

SCHULTZ, STANLEY K. *The Culture Factory: Public Schooling in Boston, 1790–1860*. New York: Oxford University Press, 1973.

SCHUSSMAN, LEO G. "The Teacher's Wage." *American School Board Journal* 47 (November 1923): 54, 66, 68.

SCHWAGER, SALLY. "Educating Women in America." *Signs* 12 (Winter 1987): 333–374.

SCOTT, ANNE FIROR. "Almira Lincoln Phelps: The Self-Made Woman in the Nineteenth Century." *Maryland Historical Magazine* 73, no. 3 (Fall 1980): 203–216.

SEDLAK, MICHAEL W., and STEPHEN SCHLOSSMAN. *Who Will Teach? Historical Perspectives on the Changing Appeal of Teaching as Profession*. Santa Monica, CA: Rand Corporation, 1986. Reprinted in *Review of Research in Education* 14 (1986), pp. 93–131.

SEDLAK, MICHAEL W., and TIMOTHY WALCH. *American Educational History: A Guide to Information Sources*. Detroit: Gale Research, 1981.

SEDLAK, MICHAEL W., CHRISTOPHER WHEELER, DIANA C. PULLIN, and PHILIP A. CUSICK. *Selling Students Short: Classroom Bargains and Academic Reform in the American High School*. New York: Teachers College Press, 1986.

SELDEN, DAVID. *The Teacher Rebellion*. Washington, DC: Howard University Press, 1985

SELLER, MAXINE. *Immigrant Women*. Philadelphia: Temple University Press, 1982.

SEWARD, RUDY RAY. *The American Family: A Demographic History*. Beverly Hills, CA: Sage Publications, 1987.

SEXTON, PATRICIA CAYO. *The Feminized Male: Classrooms, White Collars and Decline of Manliness*. New York: Vintage, 1969.

SHAPIRO, MICHAEL STEVEN. *Child's Garden: The Kindergarten Movement from Froebel to Dewey*. University Park: Pennsylvania's State University Press, 1983.

SHAW, ADELE MARIS. "The True Character of the New York Public Schools." *The World's Work* 7, no. 2 (December 1903): 4204–4221.

SHILS, EDWARD. *Tradition*. Chicago: University of Chicago Press, 1981.

SHRADER, VICTOR L. "Ethnicity, Religion, and Class: Progressive School Reform in San Francisco." *History of Education Quarterly* 20, no. 4 (Winter 1980): 385–402.

SHULMAN, LEE. "Those Who Understand: Knowledge Growth in Teaching." *Educational Researcher* (February 1986): 4–14.

SIEDLE, THEODORE A. "Trends in Teacher Preparation and Certification." *Educational Administration and Supervision* 20 (March 1934): 193–208.

SILBERMAN, CHARLES. *Crisis in the Classroom: The Remaking of American Education*. New York: Random House, 1970.

SIMMONS, ADELE. "Education and Ideology in Nineteenth-Century America: The Response of Educational Institutions to the Changing Role of Women." In *Liberating Women's History*, edited by Berenice A. Carroll. Urbana: University of Illinois Press, 1976.

SIMPSON, IDA HARPER, and RICHARD L. SIMPSON. "Women and Bureaucracy in the Semi-Professions." In *The Semi-Professions and Their Organization*, edited by Amitai Etzioni. New York: Free Press, 1969.

SITTON, THAD, and MILAM C. ROWOLD. *Ringing the Children In: Texas Country Schools*. College Station. Texas A & M University Press, 1987.

SIZER, THEODORE R. *Horace's Compromise: The Dilemma of the American High School*. Boston: Houghton Mifflin, 1984.

———. *Secondary Schools at the Turn of the Century*. New Haven, CT: Yale University Press, 1984.

SKLAR, KATHRYN KISH. *Catharine Beecher: A Study in American Domesticity*. New York: Norton, 1973.

SKOPP, DOUGLAS R. "The Elementary School Teachers in Revolt: Reform Proposals for Germany's Volksschulen in 1848 and 1849." *History of Education Quarterly* 22 (Fall 1982): 341–361.

SLAUGHTER, EUGENE E. "The Use of Examinations for State Certification of Teachers." *Journal of Teacher Education* 11 (June 1960): 211–238.

SMITH, LOUIS, and PAT KEITH. *Anatomy of an Educational Innovation*. New York: Wiley, 1971.

SMITH, SADIE B. "A Holdrege High School Teacher, 1900–1905: The Letters of Sadie Smith." *Nebraska History* 60 (Fall 1979): 372–400.

SOLOMON, BARBARA MILLER. *In the Company of Educated Women*. New Haven, CT: Yale University Press, 1985.

SPAULL, ANDREW D., ed. *Australian Teachers, From Colonial Schoolmasters to Militant Professionals*. Melbourne: Macmillan, 1976.

SPAULL, ANDREW D., and KEVIN HINCE. *Industrial Relations and State Education in Australia*. Melbourne: AE Press, 1986.

STIGLER, GEORGE. "Employment and Compensation in Education." National Bureau of

Economic Research, *Occasional Paper No. 33*. New York: National Bureau of Economic Research, 1950.

STILES, LINDLEY J., A.S. BARR, HARL R. DOUGLASS, and HUBERT H. MILLS. *Teacher Education in the United States*. New York: Ronald Press, 1960.

STILLMAN, LEWIS D. "Migration from Vermont (1776–1860)." *Proceedings of the Vermont Historical Society* New Series 5, no. 2 (1937).

STINNETT, T.M. "Teacher Education, Certification, and Accreditation." In *Education in the States: Nationwide Development Since 1900,* edited by Edgar Fuller and Jim B. Pearson. Washington, DC: National Education Association, 1969.

STONE, MASON S. "The First Normal School in America." *Teachers College Record* 24 (1923): 263–271.

STOUT, RICHARD B. *The Development of High School Curriculum in the North Central States from 1860 to 1918*. Chicago: University of Chicago Press, 1921.

STRACHAN, GRACE C. *Equal Pay for Equal Work*. New York: B.F. Buck, 1910.

STROBER, MYRA H., and LAURA BEST. "The Female/Male Salary Differential in Public Schools: Some Lessons from San Francisco, 1879." *Economic Inquiry* 17 (1979): 218–236.

STROBER, MYRA H., and DAVID B. TYACK. "Why do Women Teach and Men Manage? A Report of Research on Schools." *Signs: Journal of Women in Culture and Society* 5, no. 3 (Spring 1980): 494–503.

STUART, JESSE, *The Thread that Runs So True*. New York: Scribner's, 1949.

SUGG, REDDING S., JR. *Motherteacher: The Feminization of American Education*. Charlottesville: University of Virginia Press, 1978.

"The Supply of Teachers and the Demand." *Educational Research Bulletin* 9 (November 1930): 437–473.

SUSMAN, WARREN. *Culture as History*. New York: Pantheon Books, 1985.

SWETT, JOHN. *Public Education in California*. New York: Arno Press, 1969.

SYZMANSKI, ALBERT. *Class Structure: A Critical Perspective*. New York: Praeger, 1983.

TAFT, PHILIP. *United They Teach: The Story of the United Federation of Teachers*. Los Angeles: Nash, 1974.

TARRY, ELLEN. *The Third Door: The Autobiography of an American Negro Woman*. New York: Ellen Tarry, 1955.

TAYLOR, ALBERT R. "History of Normal-School Work in Kansas." *Kansas State Historical Society Quarterly* 6 (1900): 114–121.

TAYLOR, INEZ. "I am a Teacher." *Michigan History Magazine* 45 (1961): 263–276.

TAYLOR, SUSAN K. *Reminiscences of My Life in Camp*. New York: Arno Press, 1969. Reprint of 1902 edition.

"Teacher Demand and Supply." National Education Association *Research Bulletin* 9 (November 1931): 307–391.

TEMPLE, ALICE. *Survey of the Kindergarten of Richmond, Indiana*. Supplementary Educational Monographs, Vol. 1, No. 6. Chicago: University of Chicago Press, 1917.

TENTLER, LESLIE WOODCOCK. *Wage-Earning Women: Industrial Work and Family Life in the United States, 1900–1930*. New York: Oxford University Press, 1979.

TERHUNE, MARY VIRGINIA. [Marion Harland, pseud.] *Eve's Daughters*. New York: J.R. Anderson and H.S. Allen, 1882.

THOMAS, CHARLES SWAIN. *A Memorial of Samuel Thurber: Teacher and Scholar, 1837–1913*. Boston: New England Association of Teachers of English, 1914.

THOMPSON, E.P. *The History of the English Working Class*. New York: Random House, 1963.

THORNDIKE, EDWARD L. *Education, A First Book*. New York: Macmillan, 1912.

TROEN, SELWYN. *The Public and the Schools: Shaping the St. Louis System, 1838–1920*. Columbia: University of Missouri Press, 1975.

TUSHNET, MARK. *The NAACP Legal Strategy Against Segregated Education, 1925–1950*. Chapel Hill: University of North Carolina Press, 1987.

TYACK, DAVID B. "An American Tradition: The Changing Role of Schooling and Teaching." *Harvard Educational Review* 57, no. 2 (May 1987): 171–174.

———. *The One Best System: A History of American Urban Education*. Cambridge, MA: Harvard University Press, 1974.

———. "Pilgrim's Progress: Toward A Social History of the School Superintendency, 1860–1960." *History of Education Quarterly* 16, no. 3 (Fall 1976): 257–300.

———. "The Spread of Schooling in Victorian America." *History of Education* 7, no. 3 (1978): 172–182.

———, and ELISABETH HANSOT. "Futures that Never Happened: Technology and the Classroom." *Education Week* (September 1985): 35, 40.

———. *Managers of Virtue: Public School Leadership in America, 1820–1980*. New York: Basic Books, 1982.

TYACK, DAVID B., THOMAS JAMES, and AARON BENAVOT. *Law and the Shaping of Public Education, 1785–1954*. Madison: University of Wisconsin Press, 1987.

TYACK, DAVID B., MICHAEL KIRST, and ELISABETH HANSOT. "Educational Reform: Retrospect and Prospect." *Teachers College Record* 81 (1980): 253–269.

TYACK, DAVID B., ROBERT LOWE, and ELISABETH HANSOT. *Public Schools in Hard Times: The Great Depression and Recent Years*. Cambridge, MA: Harvard University Press, 1984.

TYACK, DAVID B., and MYRA STROBER. "Jobs and Gender: A History of the Structuring of Educational Employment by Sex." In *Educational Policy and Management: Sex Differentials*, edited by Patricia Schmuck, W.W. Charters, Jr., and Richard O. Carlson. New York: Academic Press, 1981.

TYLER, ALICE FELT. *Freedom's Ferment: Phases of American Social History from the Colonial Period to the Outbreak of the Civil War*. Minneapolis: University of Minnesota Press, 1944.

UHLENBERG, PETER R. "A Study of Cohort Life Cycles; Cohorts of Native Born Massachusetts Women, 1830–1920." *Population Studies* 23, no. 3 (November 1969): 407–420.

UNDERWOOD, KATHLEEN. "The Pace of Their Own Lives: Teacher Training and the Life Course of Western Women." *Pacific Historical Review* 55, no. 4 (November 1986): 513–530.

URBAN, WAYNE J. "The Effects of Ideology and Power on a Teacher Walkout: Florida, 1968.'" *Journal of Collective Negotiations in the Public Section* 3 (1974): 133–146.

———. "The Illusion of Educational Reform in Georgia." *Journal of Thought* 22 (1987): 31–36.

———. "Old Wine, New Bottles: Merit Pay and Organized Teachers." In *Merit, Money and Teachers' Careers: Studies on Merit Pay and Career Ladders for Teachers,* edited by Henry Johnson. Lanham, MD: University Press of America, 1985.

———. *Why Teachers Organized.* Detroit: Wayne State University Press, 1982.

VAN BUREN, ANSON D.P. "The Long Schoolhouse Era in Michigan." Michigan Pioneer and Historical Society, *Historical Collections* 14 (1889): 283–403.

VANDENBURG, JOSEPH KING. *Causes of the Elimination of Students in Public Secondary Schools of New York City.* New York: Teachers College Press, 1911.

VANDEWALKER, NINA C. *The Kindergarten in American Education.* New York; Macmillan, 1908.

———. "A Week in the Hampton Kindergarten." *Southern Workman* 36 (1907): 537–544.

VAN DYKE, GEORGE. "Trends in the Development of the High School Offering." *School Review* 39 (November 1931): 657–664 [Part I]; 39 (December 1931): 737–747 [Part II].

VAUGHN, WILLIAM PRESTON. *Schools for All: The Blacks and Public Education in the South, 1865–1873.* Lexington: University of Kentucky Press, 1974.

VOGEL, DANKWART. *Reformkonzeption der Lehrerbildung in den USA.* Weinheim: Beltz, 1981.

WALDO, D.B. "Adequate Compensation for Teaching Service in Public Schools." *Proceedings and Addresses,* National Education Association. Washington, DC: NEA, 1919.

WALKER, DAVID. *David Walker's Appeal to the Coloured Citizens of the World.* New York: Hill and Wang, 1965. Reprint of the 1828 edition.

WALLER, WILLARD. *The Sociology of Teaching.* New York: Russell and Russell, 1961.

WALSH, MARY ROTH. *"Doctors Wanted, No Women Need Apply": Sexual Barriers in the Medical Profession, 1835–1975.* New Haven, CT: Yale University Press, 1977.

WARREN, DONALD. "Learning from Experience: History and Teacher Education." *Educational Researcher* 14 (December 1985): 5–12.

———. "Messages from the Inside: Teachers as Clues in History and Policy." *International Journal of Educational Research.* 1989, in press.

WASSERMAN, JEFF. "Wisconsin Normal Schools and the Educational Hierarchy, 1860–1890." *Journal of the Midwest History of Education Society* 7 (1979), 1–9.

WATTENBERG, WILLIAM W., J. WILMER MENGE, ROLAND FAUNCE, JOHN C. SULLIVAN, RUTH E. ELLSWORTH, MILDRED PETERS, MARIE I. RASEY, and ELMER MCDAID. "Social Origins of Teachers—A Northern Industrial City." In *The Teachers Role in American Society,* edited by Lindley J. Stiles. New York: Harper & Row, 1957.

WEAVER, TIMOTHY. *America's Teacher Quality Problem: Alternatives for Reform.* New York: Praeger, 1983.

WEBER, EVELYN. *The Kindergarten: Its Encounter with Educational Thought in America.* New York: Teachers College Press, 1969.

WEDDLE, LORNA. "Cora Doolittle Jeffers." *Michigan History Magazine* 39 (1955): 338–342.

WEINER, LYNN Y. *From Working Girl to Working Mother: The Female Labor Force in the United States, 1820–1980.* Chapel Hill: University of North Carolina Press, 1985.

WELLS, ROBERT V. "Demographic Change and the Life Cycle of American Families." In *Families in History,* edited by Theodore K. Rabb and Robert I. Rotberg. New York: Harper & Row, 1973.

WELTER, BARBARA. "She Hath Done What She Could: Protestant Women's Missionary

Careers in Nineteenth-Century America." *American Quarterly* 30, no. 5 (Winter 1978): 624–638.

WESLEY, EDGAR B. *NEA: The First Hundred Years, The Building of the Teaching Profession.* New York: Harper & Row, 1957.

WHITE, SAMUEL W. "The Means of Providing the Mass of Teachers with Professional Instruction." *Addresses and Journal of Proceedings,* American Normal School and the National Teachers' Association. Washington, DC: James H. Holmes, 1871.

WHITE, WOODIE, JR. "The Decline of the Classroom and the Chicago Study of Education." *American Journal of Education* 90 (February 1982): 144–174.

WIEBE, EDWARD. *The Paradise of Childhood: A Practical Guide to the Kindergarten.* Quarter Century Edition. Springfield, MA: Milton Bradley, 1896.

WILLIAMSON, JEFFREY G., and PETER LINDERT. *American Inequality: A Macroeconomic History.* New York: Academic Press, 1980.

WILSON, ANN JARVELLA. "Historical Issues of Equity and Excellence: South Carolina's Adoption of the National Teacher Examinations." *Urban Educator* 8 (Fall 1986): 77–82.

WISE, HARRY A. *Motion Pictures as an Aid in Teaching American History.* New Haven, CT: Yale University Press, 1939.

WISHEY, BERNARD. *The Child and the Republic: The Dawn of Modern Child Nurture.* Philadelphia: University of Pennsylvania Press, 1968.

WOLFE, ALLIS ROSENBERG, ed. "Letters of a Lowell Mill Girl and Friends 1845–46." *Labor History* 17, no 1 (Winter 1976): 96–102.

"Women as Teachers" (editorial). *Educational Review* 2, no. 4 (November 1891): 358–363.

WOOD, BEN D., and F.S. BEERS. "Knowledge Versus Thinking?" *Teachers College Record* 37 (March 1936): 487–499.

WOODHOUSE, CHASE GOING. "Married College Women in Business and the Professions." *Annals of the American Academy of Political and Social Science* 143, no. 232 (May 1929): 325–338.

WOODRING, PAUL. "The Development of Teacher Education." In *Teacher Education,* the Seventy-fourth Yearbook of the National Society for the Study of Education, Part II, edited by Kevin Ryan. Chicago: University of Chicago Press, 1975.

WOODSON, CARTER G. *The African Background Outlined: Or Handbook for the Study of the Negro.* New York: Negro Universities Press, 1968. Reprint of 1936 edition.

WRIGHT, C.O. *100 Years in Kansas Education,* Vol. I. Topeka: Kansas State Teachers Association, 1963.

WRIGHT, F.W. "The Elementary School Curriculum as Presented in Normal Schools." *Proceedings and Addresses,* National Education Association. Washington, DC: NEA, 1922.

WRIGHT, HENRY PARKS. *The Young Man and Teaching.* New York: Macmillan, 1920.

WRITERS' PROJECT. *The State Teachers College at Westfield.* Westfield, MA: State Teachers College, 1941.

YATES, DOUGLAS. *The Politics of Management.* San Francisco: Jossey-Bass, 1985.

YATES, JOSEPHINE SILONE. "Education and Genetic Psychology." *Colored American Magazine* 10 (1906): 293–297.

———. "Kindergartens and Mothers' Clubs." *Colored American Magazine* 8 (1905): 304–311.

YOUNG, ELLA FLAGG. *Isolation in the School.* Chicago: University of Chicago Press, 1901.

ZAKOLSKI, F.C. "Social Psychology of the Nineteenth-Century Teacher." *Teacher Education Quarterly* 6 (Spring 1949): 158–167.

ZIMMERMAN, JOAN GRACE. "Daughters of Main Street: Culture and the Female Community at Grinnell, 1884–1917." In *Woman's Being, Woman's Place: Female Identity and Vocation in American History,* edited by Mary Kelley. Boston: G.K. Hall, 1979.

Zitron, Celia Lewis. *The New York City Teachers Union, 1916–1964: A Story of Educational and Social Commitment.* New York: Humanities Press, 1968.

GOVERNMENT DOCUMENTS

ABBOT, JULIA WADE. "The Child and the Kindergarten." United States Bureau of Education, *Kindergarten Circular,* No. 6 (February 1920). Washington, DC: Government Printing Office,* 1920.

ARMSTRONG, W. EARL. *Tabular Summary of Teacher Certification Requirements in the United States.* U.S. Office of Education, Circular No. 233. Washington, DC: GPO, 1951.

BOYKIN, JAMES C., and ROBERTA KING. "The Tangible Rewards of Teaching." United States Bureau of Education, Bulletin, No. 16. Washington, DC: GPO, 1914.

BURRITT, BAILEY B. "Professional Distribution of College and University Graduates." U.S. Bureau of Education, Bulletin, No. 19. Washington, DC: GPO, 1912.

COMMITTEE FOR THE GRADUATE SCHOOL OF EDUCATION, UNIVERSITY OF NEBRASKA. *The Rural Teacher of Nebraska.* U. S. Bureau of Education, Bulletin, 1919, No. 20. Washington, DC: GPO, 1919.

COOK, KATHERINE M. *State Laws and Regulations Governing Teachers' Certificates.* Office of Education, Bulletin, 1921, No. 22, Washington, DC: GPO, 1921.

———. *State Laws and Regulations Governing Teachers' Certificates.* Office of Education, Bulletin, 1927, No. 19. Washington, DC: GPO, 1927.

DEFFENBAUGH, W.S., and WILLIAM H. ZEIGEL. *Selection and Appointment of Teachers.* U.S. Office of Education, Bulletin, 1932, No. 17, Washington, DC: GPO, 1933.

DRESSLER, FLETCHER B. *Rural Schoolhouses and Grounds.* U. S. Bureau of Education Bulletin, 1914, No. 12. Washington, DC: GPO, 1914.

EVENDEN, EDWARD S. *Summary and Interpretation. National Survey of the Education of Teachers.* Vol. 6. U.S. Office of Education, Bulletin, 1933, No. 10. Washington, DC: GPO, 1933.

FERRISS, EMERY N. "The Rural High School: Its Organization and Curriculum." U.S. Bureau of Education, Bulletin, 1925, No. 10. Washington, DC: GPO, 1925.

FLANAGAN, RAY S. *Sanitary Survey of the Schools of Orange County, Virginia.* U.S. Bureau of Education, Bulletin, 1914, No. 17. Washington, DC: GPO, 1914.

FRAZIER, BENJAMIN W. *Development of State Programs for the Certification of Teachers.* U. S. Office of Education, Bulletin, 1938, No. 12. Washington, DC: GPO, 1938.

———. *Teacher Certification in Wartime.* U.S. Office of Education, Circular No. 213. Washington, DC: GPO, 1942.

GORDY, J.P. *Rise and Growth of the Normal School Idea in the United States.* U.S. Bureau of Education, Circular, No. 8. Washington, DC: 1891.

HILL, JOSEPH A. *Women in Gainful Occupations 1870 to 1920.* Census Monographs IX. Washington, DC: GPO, 1929.

* Hereafter cited as GPO.

Jackson, William R. "The Present Status of the Certification of Teachers in the United States." In U.S. Bureau of Education, Commissioner of Education, *Biennial Report on Education in the United States*. Washington, DC: GPO, 1903.

King, LeRoy Albert. *Status of Rural Teachers in Pennsylvania*. U.S. Bureau of Education, Bulletin, 1921, No. 34. Washington, DC: GPO, 1922.

Manny, A. *City Training School for Teachers*. U.S. Bureau of Education, Bulletin, 1914, No. 47. Washington, DC: GPO, 1915.

Monahan, A.C. *The Status of Rural Education in the United States*. U.S. Bureau of Education, Bulletin, 1913, No. 8. Washington, DC: GPO, 1913.

National Commission on Excellence in Education. *A Nation At Risk*. Washington, DC: GPO, 1983.

Newell, M.A. "Contributions to the History of Normal Schools in the United States." *Report of the Commissioner of Education for the Year 1898–99*, Vol. 2, pp. 2263–2470. Washington, DC: GPO, 1900.

Palmer, Luella A. "Adjustment Between Kindergarten and First Grade." United States Bureau of Education, Bulletin, 1915, No. 24. Washington, DC: GPO, 1915.

Philbrick, John D. *City School Systems in the United States*. U.S. Bureau of Education, Circular of Information No. 1, Washington, DC: GPO, 1885.

Thorndike, Edward L. "The Teaching Staff of Secondary Schools." U.S. Bureau of Education, Bulletin, 1909, No 4. Washington, DC: GPO, 1909.

United States Congress. *Special Report of the Commissioner of Education on the Condition and Improvement of Public Schools in the District of Columbia*. Washington, DC: GPO, 1871.

United States Department of the Interior, Bureau of Education. *An Educational Study of Alabama*. Bulletin, 1919, No. 4. Washington, DC: GPO, 1919.

———. *The Educational System of South Dakota*. Bulletin, 1918, No. 31. Washington, DC: GPO, 1918.

———. "The Kindergarten and Americanization." *Kindergarten Circular*, No. 3. Washington, DC: GPO, 1918.

———. "Kindergartens in the United States: Statistics and Present Problems." Bulletin, 1914, No. 6. Washington, DC: GPO, 1914.

Vandewalker, Nina C. "Kindergarten Training Schools." U.S. Bureau of Education, Bulletin, 1916, No. 5. Washington, DC: GPO, 1916.

———. "Kindergarten Progress from 1919–20 to 1921–22." U.S. Bureau of Education, *Kindergarten Circular*, No. 16. Washington, DC: GPO, 1924.

Waite, Mary G. "The Kindergarten in Certain City School Surveys." U.S. Bureau of Education, Bulletin, 1926, No. 13. Washington, DC: GPO, 1926.

Weber, S.E. "The Kindergarten as an Americanizer." U.S. Bureau of Education, *Kindergarten Circular*, No. 5. Washington, DC: GPO, 1919.

Winchester, Almira M. "Kindergarten Supervision in City Schools." U.S. Bureau of Education, Bulletin, 1918, No. 38. Washington, DC: GPO, 1919.

Zook, George F., Lotus D. Coffman, and A.R. Mann. *Report of a Survey of the State Institutions of Higher Learning in Kansas*. U.S. Bureau of Education, Bulletin, 1923, No. 40. Washington, DC: GPO, 1923.

Dissertations, Papers, and Manuscripts

Acker, Sandra. "Gender Divisions and Teachers' Careers." Paper presented at the Third International Interdisciplinary Congress on Women's Studies, Dublin, Ireland, July 1987.

Altenbaugh, Richard J. "Professional Socialization or Gender? The Case of the Frick (Pittsburgh) Training School for Teachers, 1912–1937." Paper presented at the annual meeting of the American Educational Research Association, Washington, DC, April 1987.

Barry, Kathleen Lois. "Social Origins of the Nineteenth-Century American Feminist Movement." Doctoral dissertation, University of California at Berkeley, 1982.

———. " 'A Vocation From on High': Preschool Teaching and Advocacy as a Career for Women in Nineteenth-Century Boston." Doctoral dissertation, Harvard University, 1981.

Block, Laurence Erwin. "The History of the Public School Teachers Association of Baltimore City: A Study of the Internal Politics of Education." Doctoral dissertation, Johns Hopkins University, 1972.

Bull, Barry L. "Professionalism and the Nature of Teacher Autonomy." Paper presented at the annual meeting of the American Educational Research Association, New Orleans, April 1988.

Byers, Libby Rhoda. "The Parent Cooperative Nursery School: An Experiment in Early Childhood Education as Led by Katherine Whiteside Taylor." Doctoral dissertation, University of California at Berkeley, 1973.

Cary, Victor H. "The Roles of Black Women in Education, 1865–1917." Paper presented at the Workshop on Gender in the History of Education, Stanford University, February 1982.

Colvin, Lloyd W. "A History of the School of Education at the University of Oregon." Doctoral dissertation, University of Oregon, 1964.

DeBoer, Clara. "The Role of the Afro-Americans in the Origins and Work of the American Missionary Association, 1839–1877." Doctoral dissertation, Rutgers University, 1973.

DeBough, Clyde Emerson. "A Study of Roles for the Teacher from an Historical Perspective." Doctoral dissertation, Michigan State University, 1980.

Farmakis, George L. "The Role of the American Teacher: An Historical View Through Readings." Doctoral dissertation, Wayne State University, 1971.

Fiorello, James Ralph. "General Education in the Preparation of Teachers at Westfield State College, 1839–1960." Doctoral dissertation, University of Connecticut, 1969.

Fishel, Leslie H., Jr. "The North and the Negro, 1865–1900: A Study in Race Discrimination." Doctoral dissertation, Harvard University, 1953.

Fisher, Hersha S. "The Education of Elizabeth Peabody." Doctoral dissertation, Harvard University, 1980.

Florell, David M. "Origin and History of the School of Education, University of California, Los Angeles." Doctoral dissertation, University of California at Berkeley, 1946.

Galvarro, Pauline Annin. "A Study of Certain Emotional Problems of Women Teachers." Doctoral dissertation, Northwestern University, 1945.

Gould, David A. "Policy and Pedagogues: School Reform and Teacher Professionalization in Massachusetts, 1840–1920." Doctoral dissertation, Brandeis University, 1977.

Hall, Clifton Landon. "Some Historical Considerations of the Status of the Teacher." Doctoral dissertation, University of North Carolina, 1949.

HERMAN, DEBRA. "College and After: The Vassar Experiment in Women's Education." Doctoral dissertation, Stanford University, 1979.

HERRMANN, WILLIAM HAROLD. "The Rise of the Public Normal School System in Wisconsin." Doctoral dissertation, University of Wisconsin, 1953.

HRONEK, PAMELA CLAIRE. "Women and Normal Schools: Tempe Normal, A Case Study, 1885–1925." Doctoral dissertation, Arizona State University, 1985.

HUDSON, LISA. "The Size and Quality of Teacher Supply: When Bigger is Better." Paper presented at the annual meeting of the American Educational Research Association, Washington, DC, 1987.

HUNT, PERSIS. "The New Consciousness Among Teachers in France, 1881–1905." Paper presented at the annual meeting of the American Historical Association, New Orleans, December 1972.

KAMIN, KAY. "The Women in Peril in American Public Schools: How Perilous?" Paper presented at the third Bershire Conference on the History of Women, Bryn Mawr College, Pennsylvania, June 1976.

KARL, ALICE W. "Public School Politics in Boston, 1895–1920." Doctoral dissertation, Harvard University, 1969.

KAUFMAN, POLLY WELTS. "Boston Women and City School Politics, 1872–1905: Nurturers and Protectors in Public Education." Doctoral dissertation, Boston University, 1978.

KELLY, BARBARA DENNIS. "Progressive Educational Reform of the Baltimore County Public Schools, 1900–1920." Doctoral dissertation, University of Maryland, College Park, 1985.

LABAREE, DAVID F. "The People's College: A Sociological Analysis of the Central High School of Philadelphia, 1838–1920." Doctoral dissertation, University of Pennsylvania, 1983.

LEVINE, ADELINE GORDON. "Marital and Occupational Plans of Women in Professional Schools: Law, Medicine, Nursing, Teaching." Doctoral dissertation, Yale University, 1968.

LEVITT, LEON. "A History to 1953 of the School of Education of the University of Southern California." Doctoral dissertation, University of Southern California, 1970.

MACLEAN, RUPERT D.I. "Career and Promotion Patterns of State School Teachers in Tasmania: A Sociological Study." Doctoral dissertation, University of Tasmania, 1988.

MICHAEL, SONYA. "Children's Interests/Mother's Rights: Women, Professionals, and the American Family, 1920–1945." Doctoral dissertation, Brown University, 1986.

MILDEN, JAMES WALLACE. "The Sacred Sanctuary: Family Life in 19th-Century America." Doctoral dissertation, University of Maryland, 1974.

NEWMAN, JOSEPH W. "A History of the Atlanta Public School Teachers' Association, Local 89 of the American Federation of Teachers, 1919–1956." Doctoral dissertation, Georgia State University, 1978.

PRESTON, JO ANNE. "Feminization of an Occupation: Teaching Becomes Women's Work in Nineteenth-Century New England." Doctoral dissertation, Brandeis University, 1982.

PRICE, REBECCA RITCHEY. "An Historical Analysis of the Concepts of Teacher in America Between the 1850s, 1930s, and 1960s as Portrayed in the Writings of the Times." Doctoral dissertation, Miami University, 1974.

REID, ROBERT L. "The Professionalization of Public School Teachers: The Chicago Experience, 1895–1920." Doctoral dissertation, Northwestern University, 1963.

RENNER, MARQUERITE. "Who Will Teach? Changing Job Opportunity and Roles for

Women in the Evolution of the Pittsburgh Public Schools, 1830–1900." Doctoral dissertation, University of Pittsburgh, 1981.

ROLAND, CAROL MARIE. "The California Kindergarten Movement: A Study in Class and Social Feminism." Doctoral dissertation, University of California, Riverside, 1980.

RURY, JOHN. "Women at School: The Feminization of American High Schools, 1870–1900." Paper delivered at the annual meeting of the History of Education Society, New York, November 1987.

RUTHERFORD, MILLICENT. "Feminism and the Secondary School Curriculum, 1890–1920." Doctoral dissertation, Stanford University, 1977.

SCARLETTE, ERMA TOOMES. "A Historical Study of Women in Public School Administration from 1900–1977." Doctoral dissertation, University of North Carolina at Greensboro, 1979.

SELLERS, STEPHEN W. "Family Backgrounds and Social Origins of Schoolmasters: Massachusetts, 1635–1800." Paper presented at the annual meeting of the American Educational Research Association, Los Angeles, April 1981.

TAYLOR, JUDITH NESSMAN. "The Struggle for Work and Love: Working Women in American Novels, 1890–1925." Doctoral dissertation, University of California at Berkeley, 1977.

TREACY, ROBERT EMERSON. "Progressivism and Corinne Seeds: UCLA and the University Elementary School." Doctoral dissertation, University of Wisconsin, 1972.

WEBSTER, PAUL REES. "History and Development of the Kansas Program for Training High School Teachers in Public Institutions." Typescript, Kansas State Historical Society, Topeka, 1932.

WEILER, KATHLEEN. "Women's History and the History of Women Teachers." Paper delivered at the American Educational Research Association, New Orleans, April 1988.

WHEELOCK, LUCY. "My Life Story." Unpublished autobiography. Lucy Wheelock Collection, Archives, Wheelock College.

WHITE, ANITA LOUISE. "The Teacher in Texas: 1836–1879." Doctoral dissertation, Baylor University, 1972.

WILSON, ANNE JARVELLA. "Historical Issues of Validity and Validation: The National Teacher Examination." Paper presented at the annual meeting of the American Educational Research Association, San Francisco, April 1986.

———. "Knowledge for Teachers: The Origin of the National Teacher Examinations Program." Paper presented at the annual meeting of the American Educational Research Association, Chicago, April 1985.

WOFFORD, KATE V. "A History of the Status and Training of Elementary School Teachers of the United States, 1860–1930." Doctoral dissertation, Teachers College, Columbia University, 1934.

ZEICHNER, KENNETH M. "The Role of the Teachers' Institute in Nineteenth Century Wisconsin." Paper presented at the annual meeting of the American Educational Research Association, Boston, April 1980.

ZIMMERMAN, JOAN GRACE. "College Culture in the Midwest, 1890–1930." Doctoral dissertation, University of Virginia, 1978.

Index

B

C

Y

Z